LONDON IN THE
NINETEENTH CENTURY

Jerry White has been writing about London for thirty years. His *London in the Twentieth Century: A City and Its People* won the Wolfson History Prize for 2001. His oral histories, *Rothschild Buildings: Life in an East End Tenement Block 1887–1920* (which won the Jewish Chronicle non-fiction book prize for 1980) and *Campbell Bunk: the Worst Street in North London Between the Wars*, were reprinted by Pimlico in 2003. He is Visiting Professor in London History at Birkbeck and in 2005 was awarded the honorary degree of Doctor of Literature by the University of London.

ALSO BY JERRY WHITE

London in the Twentieth Century:
A City and Its People

Rothschild Buildings: Life in an East End
Tenement Block 1887–1920

Campbell Bunk: the Worst Street in
North London Between the Wars

JERRY WHITE

London in the Nineteenth Century

A Human Awful Wonder of God

VINTAGE BOOKS
London

Published by Vintage 2008

2 4 6 8 10 9 7 5 3 1

Copyright © Jerry White 2007

Jerry White has asserted his right under the Copyright, Designs
and Patents Act 1988 to be identified as the author of this work

First published in Great Britain in 2007 by
Jonathan Cape
Random House, 20 Vauxhall Bridge Road,
London SW1V 2SA

www.vintage-books.co.uk

Addresses for companies within The Random House Group Limited can be
found at: www.randomhouse.co.uk/offices.htm

The Random House Group Limited Reg. No. 954009

A CIP catalogue record for this book
is available from the British Library

ISBN 9780712600309

The Random House Group Limited supports The Forest Stewardship
Council (FSC), the leading international forest certification organisation.
All our titles that are printed on Greenpeace approved FSC certified
paper carry the FSC logo. Our paper procurement policy can be
found at www.rbooks.co.uk/environment

 Mixed Sources
Product group from well-managed
forests and other controlled sources
www.fsc.org Cert no. TT-COC-2139
© 1996 Forest Stewardship Council

Printed and bound in Great Britain by
CPI Cox & Wyman, Reading RG1 8EX

For Sally Alexander

CONTENTS

ILLUSTRATIONS

LIST OF MAPS

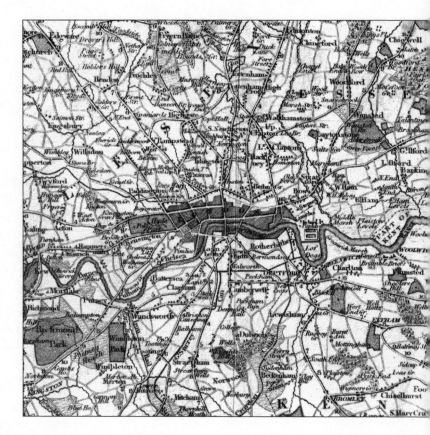

London in 1815

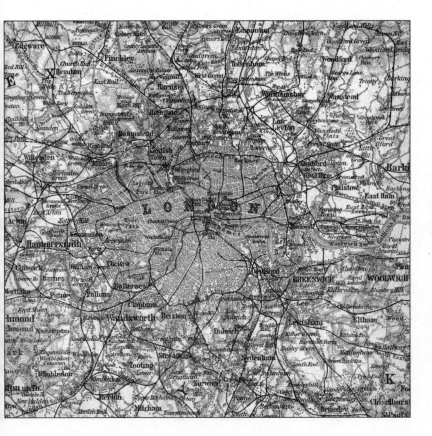

London in 1905

A NOTE ON MONEY

There is an official index on money values that relates today's prices to those in the nineteenth century. But in my view it understates the difference in buying power between then and now. I believe readers will not go far wrong if they think of a nineteenth-century pound as equivalent to £100 now. That holds broadly true for the century as a whole.

PRELUDE: TAMING THE LORD
OF MISRULE

EARLY in the morning of Friday 6 April 1810 the House of Commons resolved to confine Sir Francis Burdett, one of its number, in the Tower of London. He'd published a 'scandalous libel' on Parliament's arbitrary imprisonment of a radical for criticising the exclusion of strangers and press from a secret debate. There had been some shamefaced war business going on. Burdett was one of the richest men in London. Since 1802 he had been the leader of constitutional agitation for parliamentary reform. Member for Westminster, he could claim near-universal popularity among his middle-class voters and those without a vote, whom their enemies called 'the mob'. That same morning he barricaded himself inside his house at 78 Piccadilly and announced he would 'repel force by force'.

Huge numbers gathered in and around Piccadilly over the next four days. It was said at the time that the crowds were greater even than during the terrible Gordon Riots of thirty years before. All passers-by were made to shout, 'Burdett for ever!' and were pelted with stones and mud in default. The London homes of Burdett's main opponents were attacked at night and every accessible window stoned and broken. Police couldn't control the streets or protect property. So the military were called out. This was wartime and many soldiers in London were battle-hardened.

The display of force was extraordinary. Artillery was set up at the Tower and its moat flooded. Sixteen fieldpieces were stationed in St James's Park, a howitzer and a sixteen-pounder in Soho Square 'with matches lighted', there were cannons in Berkeley Square and 'all the troops within a hundred miles of London, both cavalry and infantry, were ordered to march to the Metropolis'. The Life Guards moved constantly to clear the streets, riding on the footway and driving 'the people before them pressing on them in such a way as to cause great terror, frequently doing some of them injury and compelling them to injure one another, striking those who could not get out of the way fast enough with the flat of their swords'. Cavalry charges were provoked by the crowd and met with crude barricades and brickbats. But some in the people's ranks were also armed. A guardsman was shot in the face, the troops responding with musket volleys. It is not known how many were killed or injured in the struggles round 78 Piccadilly. London looked like a city plunged into civil war.

Early on Monday 9 April Burdett eventually surrendered to arrest. He was conducted in an immense military column to the Tower along a route – through Hanover Square and Portland Road to the New Road, then City Road, Moorfields, Aldgate and the Minories – that took a great loop to avoid the crowded and dangerous parts of Westminster and the City. In front of Burdett's coach were four squadrons of Life Guards and Light Dragoons, and behind were more cavalry, supported by two battalions of the Foot Guards. The early start and suburban road took the people by surprise. But near the Tower great crowds met the escort with stones, bricks and mud. As the Tower gates closed behind Burdett a cannon sounded to announce his arrival. Word spread that the people had been fired upon by artillery and furious battles broke out with the returning troops around Trinity Square, Eastcheap and Fenchurch Street. There was gunfire from both sides. 'About twelve or fourteen persons were killed and wounded.' A City jury at the inquest of one victim brought in a verdict of murder against an unidentified guardsman but it was overturned in the courts. Long after, the Life Guards were taunted in the streets as 'Piccadilly Butchers'.[1]

At the beginning of the nineteenth century, penetrating every aspect of the city's collective life, London was to some extent at the mercy of a truculent, wilful populace, obstinately regardful of its rights and powers, sometimes reckless in its abuse of them. In large degree the contest between people and authority is the dominant story of London in these years. It's a story of the search for order, of how it was imposed on Londoners and accepted – sometimes welcomed – by them. It's a story of negotiation and compromise on both sides. And as people in the 1890s looked back with satisfaction on the rise of civility and the decline in misrule, they knew much remained to be done. Just how – and how far – Londoners were brought to heel must be a central strand in any history of London in the nineteenth century.

It's not, though, the whole story. Of all the centuries that London has lived through since its Roman beginnings the nineteenth must rank among the most remarkable. In one respect, at least, it might claim to be the greatest. That was in the brilliance and force and insatiable curiosity with which artists and writers captured the many-layered realities of this unique place. What did they see?

The sheer physical growth of London on the ground, and the huge accretion of people sucked into it, were probably the dominant facts in contemporaries' minds, at least from the 1830s on. In 1800 London's population was probably just larger than that of Paris, its close rival. By 1900 it was two and a half times greater and London was incomparably the largest city the world had ever seen. This was the century that redefined for ever the meaning of London on the ground, in world history and in the mind. This was the century, too, which haltingly put in place an infrastructure that still remained more or less intact into the twenty-first century: London's road network within twelve miles of Charing Cross and most of its rail links above and below ground; its embankments and sewers; its prisons and elementary schools, hospitals and theatres, libraries and museums, churches and colleges and halls and parks, even the most valued part of its domestic architecture.

And then this was the century which most firmly embedded London at the centre of the world economy. The world was bound to London through its manufactures, through its great publishing and printing and communications industry, which helped shape the world's values and opinions, and through its enormous port, at the heart of world shipping and even, for a time, world shipbuilding. But these ties were not as important as those less tangible ligaments which chained the world's finances to London through the organisation of interest rates, capital, credit, shares and bills of trade. For perhaps the entire century, certainly from 1815, London was the financial heart that kept money pumping the whole world over. It was this aspect of London, more than the trappings of court or state, which could claim for it the crown and title of 'Imperial City'.

On the other hand, London was a city of paradox. This metropolis of wealth and grandeur, culture and sophistication was also a hell of starving, degrading and heart-rending poverty. Economic orthodoxy demanded the lowest possible wage bill for the biggest possible profits. It kept London in thrall to a low-wage economy throughout the century. Most Londoners lived under the threat of poverty at some time in their lives; a large minority were at any time poor; and many faced hunger and cold almost every day and night of their lives.

The contrasts and inequalities of London life were perhaps no greater in these years than in the ages that had gone before, but it was in the nineteenth century that they became intolerable to a wide spectrum of Londoners. This was a century of class-consciousness: of discrimination between groups by minute divisions of fashion, taste, speech, smell, behaviour, spiritual belief and interests. It produced a caste system which rendered many untouchable and demanded separateness at home and play and work, even if separateness couldn't always be obtained. Yet there was consciousness, too, that these divisions offended against a prevailing Bible-based morality that preached equality in the eye of the Maker. The way out of this conundrum was to raise the moral condition of the people to the level of the middle-class moralists themselves. That required discipline, acquired from within if possible, imposed from without if not. And so, with class and religion in nineteenth-century London, we return inescapably to the question of order and how London strove to tame the Lord of Misrule.

In trying to make sense of this complex reality I've followed the structure of my earlier book *London in the Twentieth Century*, while making due allowance for shifts in themes and priorities. The nineteenth century has been so much more quarried by historians than the twentieth, and with such a multitude of preoccupations and interpretations, that any synthesis in a single volume is a daunting project. In attempting it I've returned most often to contemporary sources rather than reinterpreting the work of others. Even so, my first acknowledgement must be to the massed ranks of London historians who have so brilliantly illuminated the metropolitan past. Some homage to individuals is paid in the notes but I need to honour a generic debt here.

From the generic to the particular. Individuals and institutions have given me generous help. Sally Alexander has read, commented, supported for so long that I'm delighted to pay some recognition of it all on the dedication page. Andrew Williams trudged through every draft chapter and delved into the byways of Victorian fiction on my behalf. Bob Draper worked wonders with the maps and illustrations.

Lesley Levene was the copy editor of any author's dreams – respectable ones of course. And Will Sulkin and Jörg Hensgen at Jonathan Cape have been colleagues and editors combined. Over the years the staff at many libraries and archives have provided invaluable aid: at the London Library, without whom I could not go on (and on), so some blame attaches to them; at the British Library, British Library Newspapers, the British Library of Political and Economic Science at the London School of Economics, Warwick University Library, London Metropolitan Archives, the Family Records Centre, the London Borough of Tower Hamlets Local History Library, the local history collections of Islington and Lambeth public libraries, and Simon Blundell, librarian of the Reform Club. I would like to thank the London Topographical Society and Motco Enterprises Ltd for permission to reproduce several of the maps at the head of chapters; and I gratefully acknowledge the sources of illustrations listed on pages xi and xii. Finally my long-suffering family: Rosie Cooper, Catherine, Jennifer, Thomas and Duncan. They have all had far too much of London books: but I'm not sure the end is yet in sight.

Jerry White
Leamington Spa
September 2006

PART ONE

CITY

'I behold London, a Human awful wonder of God!'
William Blake, *Jerusalem*,
c. 1827

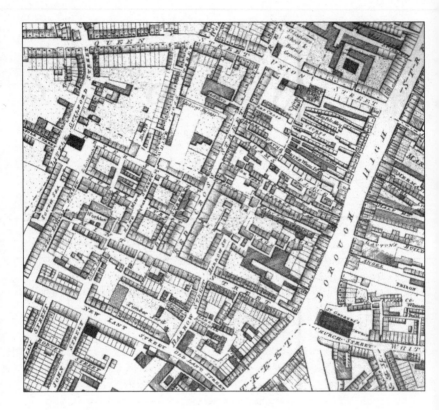

The Mint, 1813

I

THE MINT: OLD LONDON,
1800–1855

London, 1800

There is no spot like this in the neighbourhood of London, – no spot that looks so murderous, so melancholy, and so miserable. Many of these houses are very large, and very old; many of these courts stand just as they were when Cromwell sent out his spies to hunt up the Cavaliers . . . [Y]ears have gathered over this gloomy spot, blackening the steep roofs, and leaving them in all the decay and solitude of silence and neglect. Some of them have slumbered in Chancery, until the very moths have eaten away the names of the original possessors, – until the title-deeds can no longer be deciphered; for there is now no living being to be found, either to claim the titles, or pay the costs.[1]

THIS 'spot' was the 'Mint' or 'Old Mint', Southwark, just west of Borough High Street and a ten-minute stroll from London Bridge. It was a place of 'dilapidated-looking buildings', many 'uninhabited, unroofed, and in ruins', others 'shored up on all sides by huge timbers' stretching from 'blackened walls to the road' or across the narrow streets or even, like some vast wooden claw, up one side of a tottering house, over the roof and down the other. In the fifteenth and sixteenth centuries this ground had been partly covered by a noble mansion, Suffolk House. Henry VIII had chosen a wing of it in which to mint coin. But that was demolished in the early years of Elizabeth, leaving nothing but names – the Old Mint, Mint Street, Suffolk Place, Great Suffolk Street – to mark its gilded youth. Much of what replaced it was over 200 years old in 1800. Some 'fine old mansion' might survive, squatting 'like a drunken giant by the wayside'. One late-seventeenth-century 'manor house' – the Farm House in Harrow Street – carried on its business as a common lodging house for generations, and so did another called the Red House. In and around these great hulks, and behind the three-storey old-iron and sheep's-head shops on the main streets, their bulging leaded bay windows and dormers and great eaves overhanging the ground floors, were the narrow courts and alleys built up in the backlands, some houses still of timber, many with just two rooms, one on top of the other. Almost everything here was 'mouldering with age': when two houses in Lombard Street fell down in May 1814 they killed four of their occupants in the collapse.

This was no tiny enclave. It contained in 1820 some 3,000 families, 1,040 houses, a dozen streets and a maze of courts and alleys behind them. Here the land lay below the high-water mark of the Thames, less than half a mile away to the north. Any drainage was in ditches or 'open sewers' and cesspools. And so 'the sewage in many places bubbles up through the floors', 'oozing . . . through the pavement of the courts'. The houses were 'almost destitute of water', 'there was no boarding on the floors' and 'the inmates slept on the earth, on a few shavings generally'. Small wonder that when cholera first came to London, at the beginning of 1832, it chose the Mint as its earliest and most devastated district. Small wonder, too, that the Mint had traditionally been an alsatia for thieves, prostitutes, debtors, beggars and outlaws, a labyrinthine hidey-hole which bailiffs and police dared not penetrate except in force. In the Mint, 'We seem to have left civilisation behind us': 'every by-court and alley is choking with filth, vice, and crime'.[2]

Throughout the nineteenth century, with the Mint as one quintessential instance, old London was bad London. Old London epitomised decay, squalor, poverty, disease and disorder. It cluttered, threatened, stank, demoralised, infected, offended the eye. There were, for nineteenth-century Londoners, almost no saving graces in old London, and so virtually nothing worthwhile to be saved of it. Old London and its ways had to be overpowered and obliterated.

Yet what a task. For in 1800 there was so much of it, clustering round the cities of London and Westminster like some ulcerous growth.

We might take a tour, starting in the far south-west. Close to the river was the notorious slum near Westminster Abbey centred on the Almonry, Orchard Street, and Old and New Pye Streets. It lay next to Tothill Fields, on the very edge of London in 1800, and many knew it as the 'Devil's Acre'. Caxton had lived in the Almonry and houses there were thought to date back to his time. Further north were two old pockets of notoriety around St Martin-in-the-Fields at the west end of the Strand and Swallow Street at the east end of Piccadilly. To the west came St Giles, most notorious of all, a City suburb of the 1670s. By 1800 this was the 'Rookery', 'Little Dublin', 'Little Ireland' or the 'Holy Land' (an ironic comment on the faithfulness of its obstreperous Irish population to priestcraft). Perched at the eastern end of Oxford Street, even then a fashionable shopping centre for the west end of town, St Giles was an ever-present risk to the shopper, the wagoner or the parcel-carrier. Nearby lay Seven Dials and the streets off Drury Lane. Then the Clare Market area, from High Holborn to the Strand and even down to the river, a nest of seventeenth- and eighteenth-century streets, courts and alleys with an evil reputation: a popular legend claimed that an unlucky wayfarer had entered Portugal Street on his way to the Strand and had never emerged, his ghost still searching for a way back to civilisation.[3]

Still moving east, touching the north-west border of the City, lay the teeming thieves' quarter of Saffron Hill, Chick Lane and Field Lane, at the back of the stinking River Fleet: freshly washed silk handkerchiefs, loot from an army of pickpockets, would hang on poles and lines across Field Lane as thick as oak leaves in summer. Then the impenetrable nest of courts and alleys around Turnmill Street, Clerkenwell, which contained Jack Ketch's Warren. South of this came Smithfield, older than St Giles or Saffron Hill and hardly more respectable: scarcely, too, with its barbaric cattle market, less filthy. Then, moving east again, the old and very poor area between Barbican and Whitecross Street and Golden Lane, St Luke's.

Bishopsgate and Shoreditch, the ancient road to Cambridge at the eastern edge of the City, marked the beginnings of the 'east end of the town'. Along this old highway, from Shoreditch to the river, were a mass of overgrown villages grafted to London mainly in the seventeenth century, still with some housing predating the Great Fire of London of 1666. In the north lay the ragged 'Old Nichol', the Nichol Street district of Shoreditch and south-west Bethnal Green. South of that Spitalfields and the thieves' quarter around Flower and Dean Street, Wentworth Street and Rose Lane: here Petticoat Lane was the eastern distribution centre for stolen goods, as Field Lane was further west. South of that, Whitechapel, where scores of slaughterhouses added to the mayhem, and with a warren of lawless courts and alleys around Rosemary Lane and East Smithfield. Between that and the Thames was squeezed the poor river-plunderers' district of St Katharine's-by-the-Tower. And east from here, along the river to the marshes of the Isle of Dogs, stretched the sailors' towns that had edged out from London with the growth of the port from Elizabeth's time: Wapping on the foreshore, Ratcliffe to the north of that and Shadwell to the east.

South of the river, London was many times smaller than on the great north bank. In the east lay the wharfside district of Redriff or Rotherhithe, which, though straggling eastwards, clung tightly to the river. West of that were Horsleydown and Bermondsey, where an inlet of the river at St Saviour's Dock brought a tidal flow into ditches around Jacob's Island. Here ancient part-wooden houses had their back walls propped on stilts, their occupants drawing water in buckets from the filthy ooze below. West of Bermondsey came the old Borough, connected to London since Roman times by London Bridge. The district east of Borough High Street had been largely devastated by the Great Fire of Southwark in 1676, though it was quickly rebuilt (the Mint to the west had been spared, thanks to the prevailing wind). Flood, too, was an enemy. At high tides the Thames crept into the courts and alleys, filling basements and swamping ground floors to knee height and more, families having to be rescued by boat. Apart from the ancient fishermen's and watermen's district along Fore Street, Lambeth, old London on the Surrey side, virtually ended just west of the Mint.[4]

So this great ruinous ring of old London was extensive enough. Throughout the nineteenth century it would give all sorts of trouble. We shall have cause to be drawn back to these places time and again when writing of London in the century to come.

But it's also important to stress that in 1800 much of London was not old at all. Even in its historic heart, the City had largely been rebuilt in the 1670s and 1680s. And the streets built then had more often than not been touched up or rebuilt since as fresh fires or the pressing needs of trade required demolition and replacement. The houses in Cornhill, for instance, new-built after the Great Fire, 'are all in a more modern stile', the old houses destroyed by 'the many fires which have happened at different periods on both sides of the street'.[5] Fire would continue to be a potent force for reconstruction throughout the century to come. It was one reason why old London was in fact newer than the maps alone would indicate.

Even more important, since 1666 London had grown vigorously on all sides, most especially in the west. In this 'west end of the town' several great new towns had been added to the capital in a giant push westward as aristocratic family landholdings were exploited for development. Bloomsbury, on the Bedford Estate, was begun at the end of the seventeenth century and had been building northwards and westwards to Tottenham Court Road ever since. Soho, always more plebeian and cosmopolitan than its polite neighbour on the east, contained London's artists' quarter and was a centre of artisanal, bohemian and cultural life. It had been largely completed by 1720. To the west of Soho and some thirty years younger, Mayfair on the Grosvenor Estate had been developed by 1750 right up to Hyde Park (London's western boundary for the whole of the eighteenth century). So that huge district between Oxford Street and St James's and Pall Mall was generally not much more than a century old in 1800 and some of it no more than half that.

North of Oxford Street to the New Road (later renamed Marylebone, Euston and Pentonville roads) almost everything was less than fifty years old. From Tottenham Court Road to Edgware Road there were three new towns. West of Cleveland Street, hardly less wealthy suburbs than Mayfair had grown up on the Portland (Cavendish-Harley) and Portman estates in Marylebone; to the east, in what some called North Soho, was a more mixed and plebeian district, aspiring to greater things in Lord Southampton's estate, where the Adam Brothers were building Fitzroy Square, just south of the New Road. So north of Oxford Street much of the town was spanking new in 1800.

The New Road, connecting the villages of Paddington and Islington and laid down in 1756–7, was commonly accepted as London's northern boundary in 1800. Indeed, this was a boundary to which London had not yet filled out. Between the Foundling Hospital in Bloomsbury and the New Road were open fields, but beyond them – and so not yet joined to London – were new districts at Somers Town, Camden Town and Pentonville. Even City Road, the south-eastward continuation of the New Road, ran across open country in 1800. Hoxton, south Shoreditch and the western portions of Bethnal Green and Stepney marked London's edge in the east, although new docks still being built at the Isle of Dogs were drawing a thin line of development along the river through Limehouse to Poplar. Commercial Road, a new highway between the docks and London, was being built by a private company entirely over pasture and market gardens in 1800. These riverside districts were as new-built as Marylebone but for an artisan and labouring class rather than the merchants and professionals moving into the new houses in the west.

South of the river the two new bridges of mid-Georgian London had encouraged development in the suburbs at Lambeth (after Westminster Bridge was opened in 1750) and at St George's Fields, Southwark (after Blackfriars Bridge in 1769). These were mixed areas, with artisans, clerks and tradesmen jostling for house room with poorer labourers in freshly made 'back-slums'. So a good deal of south London in the west was less than fifty years old in 1800, with some fresh building still going on, as at London's edge in the north.

The great lines of communication within this city, despite so much of it being new, largely followed patterns laid down by the Romans seventeen centuries or so before. There was a radial system of eight ancient highways connecting London with all parts of Britain. Most important was the road north to Cambridge and south to the coast through Shoreditch, Bishopsgate, London Bridge, Borough High Street and Newington Causeway: it was London's backbone. For internal cross-city communications there were three great highways cutting through London west to east. Most northerly ran the ancient road from Oxford to Colchester – Oxford Street, struggling through or round St Giles to Holborn, Newgate, Cheapside, Cornhill, Leadenhall Street, Aldgate and Whitechapel. To the south was a more frac-tured line from Hyde Park Corner along Piccadilly, then through close streets (or taking in a diversion through Haymarket and Charing Cross) to the Strand and Fleet Street, and meeting Cheapside and the Colchester Road at St Paul's Churchyard. Each was subject to notorious bottlenecks and 'what is technically called a "lock", – that is, a line of carriages of every description inextricably massed and obstructing each other, as far as the eye could stretch . . .'[6] These were worst at the city's pinch-points, especially where the southern highway met the north at the junction of St Paul's Churchyard and Cheapside, at Temple Bar where Fleet Street met the Strand, and at the west or Charing Cross end of the Strand. Anywhere the chaos of traffic made life for pedestrians bewildering and dangerous: as in the Strand in 1803, when a broken-down hackney coach brought the traffic to a lock and two men and a woman, trying to cross the road, were trapped between two coal wagons and were crushed to death, 'notwithstanding their screams and shrieks'.[7] And in 1800 nearly all of London's enormous traffic was carried on roads of gravel poured on clay, which cloyed and hampered hoof and wheel and foot alike in wet weather.

The third highway was London's river. Some 3,000 boats and wherries plied for hire on the Thames in the early nineteenth century. Many were employed in cross-river traffic, the Thames a barrier to communications within London but still its greatest source of trade. For 1,700 years there had been just one permanent river crossing. In 1800 London Bridge was still Peter de Colechurch's near-immortal structure, finished in 1209. The massive piers of his bridge – eighteen after one was removed in 1758–60 – so held back the tidal flow that the difference in water level between one side of the bridge and the other was some five feet. Shooting the rapids at London Bridge was a thrill for even time-served watermen, and certainly their passengers. Every year people died doing it: four sailors drowned out of six when a cutter went down in August 1811, for instance. George Borrow, fresh from Norfolk, watched a small boat shoot the bridge, 'the boatman – a true boatman of Cockaigne that – elevating one of his skulls in triumph, the man hallooing, and the woman, a true Englishwoman that – of a certain type – waving her shawl'.[8] The restricted flow at London Bridge was the main reason for the river freezing, as it did spectacularly in early 1814, and one factor among others in the severe flooding of the Thames (1774, 1791, 1821, 1827) and the Fleet (1809), inundating mainly Lambeth, Southwark and Westminster.

The volume of bridge traffic was enormous even in the early years of the nineteenth century. On one day in July 1811 90,000 pedestrians, 5,500 vehicles and 764 horse-riders crossed London Bridge, which was just twenty-one feet wide. Blackfriars carried about two-thirds as much. George Borrow recalled his astonishment at first seeing that

Thousands of human beings were pouring over [London] bridge. But what chiefly struck my attention was a double row of carts and wagons, the generality drawn by horses as large as elephants, each row striving in a different direction, and not infrequently brought to a standstill. Oh the cracking of whips, the shouts and oaths of the carters, and the grating of wheels upon the enormous stones that formed the pavement![9]

There were thought to be over 30,000 vehicles in London in the pre-omnibus era around 1813, including 1,100 hackney coaches for hire and even 400 sedan chairs. Traffic staggered visitors to the city. In the West End the noise, for French-American traveller Louis Simond, was 'a universal hubbub; a sort of uniform grinding and shaking, like that experienced in a great mill with fifty pairs of stones . . .'[10]

The great avenues of communication east and west and north and south connected but did not unite the metropolis. There were, contemporaries explained, three Londons, divided by class and economic function.

The west end of town was home to court, Parliament and government. Here a wealthy leisured class enjoyed the relatively clean streets of Mayfair and Marylebone, living mainly on rents and investments which were cultivated and nurtured in the City. This was the second great London, based on money and commerce, with its own now ageing suburb in Bloomsbury. To the east of the City, in the 'east end of the town', was the manufacturing district and port, a workers' city, self-sufficient and isolated from the metropolis at the centre and in the west.[11]

These age-old divisions were, even by 1800, too unsophisticated to encapsulate London's diverse social topography. For plebeian London, as represented by manufacturing, penetrated every district, even the smart West End, where tailors and goldsmiths and carriage-builders brushed coat-skirts with gentlemen of private means. It was even denser in Soho and it overwhelmed the cluttered ring of old London round the edge of the City and Southwark. In fact, manufacturing in 1800 was strongest of all in the City itself, not yet – and not for a long time – turned over exclusively to the circulation of commodities and capital. The manipulation of money may have been the City function of most interest to the West End, but manufacturing was by far the greatest employer of City labour. The City remained a residential and industrial district beyond the first half of the nineteenth century, with artisans, clerks, warehousemen and shopmen living nearby or 'over the shop'. So workers skilled and unskilled – even casual labourers and beggars – could be found living almost anywhere in London. The popular polarity of 'St Giles and St James', used to describe the vast spectrum of poor and rich in London, disguised the fact that these irreconcilables were even closer to home. Westminster, even Mayfair, had its spots of poverty and squalor, sometimes infamously so.

With these complications in mind, the three Londons identified by contemporaries can be augmented by a fourth: old London's City fringe and Borough belt of poverty and wage labour that on the one hand threatened London with disorder and disease and on the other provided and sustained its very means of existence. And already in 1800, cross-cutting these four swathes of the metropolis, were some specialist neighbourhoods of long standing: law and letters near Temple Bar at the western edge of the City, bookselling and publishing at Paternoster Row by St Paul's, silk weaving in Spitalfields and Bethnal Green, leather curing in Bermondsey and half a dozen more that would be greatly multiplied as the new century matured.

Despite its complexity, and compared with what was to come, London was a small city in 1800. It was some five miles from Hyde Park Corner to Wapping and just over two from Sadler's Wells, Clerkenwell, to the obelisk in St George's Fields, Southwark. So this was a walkable city even though its sixty squares, 8,000 streets and uncountable courts and alleys were just too dense and occult for any one person to know intimately. 'London is a giant,' commented Louis Simond in 1817, 'strangers can only reach his feet.' For even at that time London was Europe's greatest city in extent and population. Its built-up area contained about 783,000 people, and there were a further 176,000 in the nearby villages and towns that would later merge in the County of London. The population of what would become Greater London brought the whole to just over 1.1 million in 1801.[12]

London's built-up area contained one in twelve of the people of England and Wales, a much smaller proportion than would be the case a century later. But even in 1800 there is no doubting the extraordinary power that London wielded over the minds and fortunes of the people of the British Isles. The young Thomas de Quincey was nearly fifteen when he journeyed from the West Country in the May of that year and 'first entered this mighty wilderness, the city – no! not the city, but the nation – of London'.

Often since then, at distances of two or three hundred miles or more from this colossal emporium of men, wealth, arts, and intellectual power, have I felt the sublime expression of her enormous magnitude in one simple form of ordinary occurrence – viz., in the vast droves of cattle, suppose upon the great north roads, all with their heads directed to London, and expounding the size of the attracting body, together with the force of its attractive power, by the never-ending succession of these droves, and the remoteness from the capital of all the lines upon which they are moving.[13]

Yet paying homage to this mighty metropolis by visiting it or moving there could be a difficult venture in 1800 and for forty years to come. A sea passage was the most convenient way to get to London from Cornwall, say, or from the far north. William Jerdan, a notable London journalist of the 1840s, was a Scot from Kelso. His first journey to London in 1801 involved coaching from Edinburgh to Berwick and then sailing in a smack to Wapping: it took him nine days. Paddle steamers would cut the journey time by the 1830s but even in 1842, when Alexander Bain left Aberdeen for London, he coached to Edinburgh and then was three days at sea; returning direct to Aberdeen by fast clipper took him five days, though it was a more comfortable passage for 'bad sailors'.[14]

Coaching from other parts of England was slow, uncomfortable and hazardous, especially when the coach neared London. Mrs Lynn Linton recalled that around 1830 a south-going coach ran twice a week through Eden, Cumberland, and the journey took three days and two nights. Dover was an eleven-hour trip around 1815 and express to Exeter took twenty-five hours. Even so, the volume of traffic was extensive. There were over 400 coaches from London, most leaving daily to all parts of the nation. As they returned, approaching London the numbers of passengers swamped the coaches available. 'It is not unusual,' it was reported in 1806, 'to see ten on the roof, three on the box (besides the driver), four behind, on what is called the "Gamon Board", and six on the dickey or chair; in all, often above thrice the number intended to be allowed.' When the Croydon coach overturned that year with sixteen outside passengers, two were killed and several injured.[15]

When visitors reached the metropolis they were generally amazed by what they saw. Its size stunned them and so did the grandeur and immensity of its great buildings. A first view of St Paul's 'overwhelmed us with awe; and I did not at that time imagine that the sense of magnitude could be more deeply impressed'. The city's street lighting by oil lamps 'had a most striking effect, particularly at a distance, and to strangers'. Even the primitive road surfaces and paving and litter-picking were considered exemplary compared with elsewhere, at least in the smarter parts of the town. And London's discomforts could impress as greatly as its 'Tumult and blaze', most notably its smoke and fog: the approach of London could be smelled and tasted on the wind for miles away, and the whiff of smoke 'could always distinguish a London letter . . . on putting it to the nose'.[16]

More impressive perhaps than all of these were Londoners themselves. Their sharpness, showiness, fashion-consciousness, arrogance and liveliness were admired or despised but could not be ignored. So Bob Tallyho, the country cousin of Tom Dashall in *Real Life in London* (1821) is made to say, 'If an acquaintance with London is to give a man these airs of superiority – this ascendancy – elegance of manners, and command of enjoyments – why, London for me . . .' William Jerdan thought 'a lad of sixteen or eighteen, educated in the country, knew less of other life, than a smart English child brought up in the capital . . . of only eight or ten years old'. And 'The superiority of metropolitan society cannot be disputed, and its more enlarged and liberal modes of thinking and acting,' wrote Cyrus Redding, a Cornishman who came to London aged twenty in 1805.[17]

London's place in the nation enlarged as the nation itself grew in population and extended its influence around the world. London would become – like Rome, its only true forebear in history, with which it was much compared at the time – the Imperial City. But before it could don the purple, the metropolis had to be made fit for the task.

Cyrus Redding, who wrote his compliment to metropolitan society in 1858, concluded, 'but neither then nor now, had I or have I, any affection for blackened brick walls, interminable streets, rattling vehicles, howling costermongers, wretchedness, poverty, and vice, made more deplorable and vicious by close contact with dissipation, wealth and luxury'. Many of Redding's criticisms would never be successfully resolved. But all, in some way, would be addressed in the nineteenth century. And in making London fit for its status as the greatest city the world had ever seen, efforts would begin first on the ground. There were three great driving forces that would tackle the job of transforming London's built environment. Though there was much overlap, they operated mainly in sequence. First, the crown – king and government together; second, private enterprise; last, London's local government.

'The ROME of Modern History', 1800–1830

From the end of the Napoleonic Wars to 1855 the crown led the attack on old London. But before 1815 the forces of change were more mixed. And first honours must go to the City Corporation for pushing forward schemes that had their origins in the early 1790s.

These were the City entrance improvements. Their originating genius had been Alderman William Pickett, a silversmith elected Lord Mayor in 1789–90, and a radical whose second claim on posterity's attention was his demand that Pitt's ministers remove the armed guard from the Bank of England as an 'unnecessary introduction of the military into the civil government of the nation'. In that he failed. But his first and more successful claim was to steer through the Corporation's creaking bureaucracy the improvement of two ancient ways into the City from Middlesex and Westminster. His success was won 'after many and great oppositions'. And it was a victory he never lived to see, the improvements taking shape some few years after his death in 1796.[18]

In the north-west of the City at the border with Holborn, Snow Hill had been 'for ages one of the most inconvenient and dangerous passages within the metropolis'. It was twisting, narrow and steep. Pickett proposed a new street to bypass Snow Hill in 'a gentle ascent' from Holborn Bridge to Newgate, taking down some 'decayed and wretched' houses in Old Bailey in the process. Demolition began about 1801 but the resumption of war in 1803 and consequent uncertainties delayed construction. In 1806 some grand houses by George Dance the Younger in the new Skinner Street – named after another improving alderman, lately defunct – were put up for disposal by lottery.[19]

Even more important were improvements at the 'court end' of the City, where the Strand joined Fleet Street at Temple Bar. The Bar itself – 'that leaden-headed old obstruction'[20] designed by Wren and forming a narrow gateway across the road, marking the boundary between Westminster and the City – had been under threat of demolition for a generation. But these improvements, which also began about 1801, left Temple Bar to be a curse to carters and cabbies for seven decades and more to come. They did, though, demolish Butcher Row around 1802, a narrow street on the north side of the Strand: 'a dirty place, composed of wretched fabrics and narrow passages ... The houses overhung their foundations, the receptacles of dirt and disease, and the bane of London.' The Strand was widened at this point and the side north of St Clement's Church was renamed Pickett Street. There were improvements beneath the surface too. The ancient leaky sewers here ran at cellar depth to the Thames and forced filth into houses, making them 'damp and noisome in the extreme'. So they were replaced by sound and deeper sewers which did a better job of dumping the city's excrement into the river. There were other improvements around the same time in Jewin Street, Aldersgate; and dozens of 'low buildings' which 'choked up' the approaches to the Houses of Parliament and Westminster Abbey were removed around 1804.[21]

Neither of the City entrance improvements would last long. Skinner Street was removed for Holborn Viaduct in the 1860s and Pickett Street for the Law Courts ten years later. This reminds us that London, even new London raised on the rubble of the old, was ever renewing itself. One reason for such short lives may have been the Corporation's inattention to taste, for 'certainly the useful was more sought after than the ornamental by the then city Vitruvius'. This was a complaint that would be heard again, in other parts of London, and for a long time to come. At the time, though, the City entrance works were a source of great astonishment and pride to Londoners. William Blake, returning to the city in September 1803 from a three-year stay in Sussex, noted his impressions of a place changing rapidly for the better: 'The shops in London improve; everything is elegant, clean and neat; the streets are widened where they were narrow; even Snow Hill is become almost level and is a very handsome street, and the narrow part of the Strand at St Clement's is widened and become very elegant.'[22]

Beyond the well-filled coffers of the City Corporation, the war years to 1815 were a difficult time for home investment, shaking confidence and damaging trade. Even so, a surprising number of projects involving risky but extensive private financing were begun. Some would have momentous significance for the shape of development in London for the century to come and beyond.

The London Docks, with their great warehouses and thief-proof wall that rambled for miles along the streets of the East End, required the demolition of 'straggling houses' and 'inferior streets' in Wapping and St George's in the East, south of Ratcliffe Highway in 1801–2. In St George's, 'twenty-four streets, thirty-three courts, yards, alleys, lanes, and rows' were cleared, 'a distinct gain to the sanitary conditions of the parish'.[23] City redevelopment for the Stock Exchange in Capel Court (1801–2), the Auction Mart (1808–9) and the Mincing Lane Sale Rooms (1811–12) expanded not only specialised exchanges at the expense of the coffee houses but removed cheap, decrepit old property as a consequence. And the formation of Great Dover Street from 1809 better connected London Bridge to the old road to Kent, bypassing the ruinous, narrow and dangerous Kent (later Tabard) Street and taking many old courts and alleys with it. The road was built by a private company relying on turnpikes and tolls to produce a 5 per cent dividend for the shareholders.

A different kind of private venture was the contemporary utilisation of coal gas for lighting by a Scot, William Murdock, in his Soho factory (1802) and by a German adopted-Londoner who anglicised his name to Frederick Albert Winsor. Winsor lit the gardens of Pall Mall and the Prince of Wales's Carlton House in the summer evenings of 1807 to demonstrate the utility and beauty of his invention. Investors were drawn to the flickering flames. Yet cash was scarce and things moved slowly. Five years later, with Winsor as founder, the Gas Light and Coke Company began the task of lighting London north of the Thames.

But gas lighting did not become generally used in London's streets until the early 1820s and was not universal till about 1842.[24]

Just as important as gas lighting, even more so for the future remoulding of London, were the three great bridge schemes brought forward before 1815. Each was the product of private investors buying shares in the bridge project and reaping dividends by way of tolls.

In 1800, as we saw, there were just three river crossings at London Bridge, Blackfriars and Westminster (the eighteenth-century wooden bridges at Battersea and Putney were too far out to be considered part of London at the time). Traffic volumes were so high they seemed to make any new bridge an attractive investment. Interest was sufficient to float as many as three new ventures, initiated by companies sanctioned by Acts of Parliament in 1809 and 1813. Vauxhall (first called the Regent Bridge) linked Pimlico to Vauxhall in Lambeth, at the southwest extremity of the town. Waterloo (at first called the Strand Bridge) connected the Strand and Covent Garden with Lambeth. And Southwark joined the City to Bankside. Vauxhall Bridge was the first of London's iron bridges. Designed by James Walker, it opened in 1816. Waterloo, by Scottish engineer John Rennie, was considered 'the finest bridge in Europe' of its day. It opened in 1817, on the second anniversary of the battle that renamed it. But it proved a white elephant to its backers, too close to the free bridge at Westminster for those who would not bear its halfpenny tolls for pedestrians, more for vehicles. Southwark Bridge, once again by the indispensable Rennie, also of iron and 'brilliantly lighted' with thirty gas lamps, was opened in 1819.[25]

Each bridge involved building new approach roads to bring traffic swiftly and safely to and from them. These connecting highways were essential components in making the bridges profitable. The greatest effects would be felt on the Surrey side, where Vauxhall and Waterloo bridges in particular stimulated vigorous house-building activity over marshy wilderness and market garden alike. It was these bridges in particular that transformed development prospects south of the Thames. John Britton, a notable London-watcher and antiquary, observed in 1826 how it was now right 'to have its ancient name of *South-wark* changed into the more appropriate one of *South London*, which is occasionally applied to it'.[26] There were consequences too for old London, as Southwark Bridge Road drove through the Tudor and Stuart remnants of Bankside, long known for its filth and disorder. But the proprietors of the new road fought shy of the difficulties of cutting through the Mint, swerving round it at its western edge.[27]

These three new bridges were giant projects. But they would seem as nothing to the vision and sweep of what was being planned and pegged out on the ground in the West End from 1811.

Pickett has been largely overlooked by history but John Nash, and of course his resplendent patron George IV, shine out still in the annals of London in modern times. George may have been gross, lascivious, quixotic, prodigal and spiteful, but he was the only monarch to combine energy, even passion, with all the resources of the crown for the greater glory of London. And Nash, his chosen vehicle for implementing and moulding his wide ambitions, may have been sycophantic, slapdash, pinchbeck, nepotistic, even venal, but he was a planner and designer of genius. What they achieved together between 1811 and 1830 was unprecedented in its day and is unmatched since.

It all began in the fields just north of the New Road. The Marybone or Mary-le-bone Park was crown land leased mainly for farming. To the south, since at least the 1760s, aristocratic landlords had made a fortune cutting up pasture into streets and squares for the wealthy. The leases of Mary-le-bone Park were to end in 1811. That provided an opportunity for the crown to share in the building speculations of its neighbours.

From the 1790s the stewards of crown property – the Commissioners of Woods and Forests and Land Revenues – had given thought to just how such a speculation might work on the ground. Their surveyor-general, John Fordyce – yet another talented London Scot – was the first to suggest a road which would link development land at Mary-le-bone Park with the Houses of Parliament at Westminster. In that way a gentleman in the new suburb could gain easy access to the business of state. It is Fordyce who must be credited with the skeleton of the plan which Nash so brilliantly and so pertinaciously followed through.

Nash could have done nothing, of course, had it not been for his relationship with the Regent, becoming close about the time the leases fell in. The Regent was an aggrandiser with a passion for building who saw in the 'beautification' of London glory to himself and his metropolis, and a stab at the pretensions of his enemy across the Channel. Nash's plan would 'quite eclipse Napoleon' in the contest of the nation's capitals. And George did not know, in either the bedroom or the counting house, the meaning of the word extravagance.

What of the plan itself? Mary-le-bone Park would become the

Regent's Park, combining pleasure ground and manicured landscape for rich men's country villas. It would be the beginning of a new town, complete with market and barracks for the Life Guards to protect life and property. Regent's Park would become an important component in the growth of new London from 1820.

But the New Street – finally to be called Regent Street – designed to connect the park with Westminster, carved a wide canyon through old London. In the north it extended Portland Place, a sequestered '"close" of great houses' built partly by Robert Adam on land leased from the Duke of Portland, with an elegant crescent facing the New Road and the entrance to the park. Nearly 200 years on, the six-storey stucco frontages of Park Crescent and its neighbours remain one of the architectural highlights of London. To the south, the new street joined Portland Place slightly to the east. The two were connected by Langham Place and All Souls' Church. A new circus at Oxford Street led into the main line of Regent Street south to Piccadilly.

We should pause here, because the precise choice of where the new street should run from Oxford Circus was very much Nash's own. In selecting it he had an explicit social purpose. In Fordyce's time a street further to the east, somewhere along the line of Great Portland Street through Golden Square, had been envisaged. But Nash exploited the obvious fact that Soho and the West End were vastly different social milieux and that the dividing line between the two was broadly along the line of Swallow Street, further to the west. If the eastward line were taken, then the new street would have decrepit seventeenth-century property on both sides. But if Swallow Street were followed, then Regent Street would clearly mark the great divide – no less than 120 feet wide and with palatial six-storey shops and residences on both sides – between aristocratic London in the west and plebeian London in the east. And if Swallow Street went, then so would its 'filthy labyrinthine environs' and 'dirty courts' filled with the poor. Years later it was recalled how 'thousands of poor were driven into the Strand, St Giles's, Lambeth, and other parts' by Nash's housebreakers.[28]

This social objective assumed determinative importance for Nash, as it did in the minds of the Regent, a parliamentary select committee and ministers. We know this because choosing Swallow Street as the route presented considerable architectural and practical difficulties in bringing the new street to the eastern end of Piccadilly. The solution, costly but brilliant, was to sweep the new street to the east in a quarter-circle or

Quadrant. This was difficult to achieve. The two curved terraces had to be built as single pieces rather than cut into separate building plots and sold to individual clients or speculators, as in the rest of Regent Street. It was so problematic that Nash himself had to take on the Quadrant as one job, rewarding his contractors with leases in the new terraces in lieu of cash. The Quadrant was given an unusually continental feel, with a colonnade on slim iron pillars, shielding pedestrians from the elements. The south-east end of the Quadrant dropped into a new circular space for many years called Regent, later Piccadilly, Circus.

From there it was intended that Lower Regent Street would lead directly south to George's town palace at Carlton House. But by 1825, with Regent Street built up, George had chosen Buckingham House on the borders of undeveloped Pimlico as his new palace. Carlton House was demolished and replaced with grand terraces either side of an open vista into a refurbished St James's Park. So the great scheme ended – entirely through happenstance – in parkland both north and south. It was the Regent's Park and Regent Street that James Elmes had most in mind when he called London 'the ROME of Modern History' in 1827.[29]

Who paid for this majestic vision? The crown had retained the freehold of much of west Soho as a result of earlier speculations and land exchanges. Regent Street was 1,700 yards long and 1,250 of those ran over crown property. But the rest had to be acquired by compulsory purchase involving parliamentary inquiries and an Act of Parliament. Nash had underestimated the value put on the property to be acquired, especially the 'goodwill' claimed by the shopkeepers, artisans and stablekeepers of Swallow Street. Nash's first forecast had been £385,000. The final cost to the public purse – borrowed mainly on mortgage from insurance companies – was £1,533,000. This would be remembered by all opponents of state extravagance in the years to come, even though the rising value of freehold property assuaged the debt many times over.[30]

There are three other points worth making here about this remarkable scheme. One was the continuing regard in which the overall plan was held by posterity, despite much criticism at the time. Not all contemporary opinion was against Nash by any means, and nor was it even a generation after the event. But his close ties with George, a much loathed monarch for many good reasons, brought opprobrium on him by association. And the evangelical conscience, which especially hated George's deplorable vices, identified in Nash's passion for stucco a

meretricious attitude to art and life that made Regent Street quite literally a whited sepulchre for many Victorians.

Second, and more down to earth, was the boost to Westminster's
sewerage that the new street provided. It added a third great new sewer
to the existing structures that channelled filth to the Thames, just as
Pickett Street had done for the west of the City.

Finally, there was the speed with which it was all done. The act permitting procurement was passed in 1813. The street was nearly all completed
by 1820. In nineteenth-century London that was astonishingly quick,
although some larger properties on the street were still being built until
1824. And the demolition of Carlton House and its replacement terraces
and gardens had to wait till about 1833 for completion.

By that time Nash had been moved to one side and George, who died
in 1830, removed entirely. But their grand plans lived on in the 'West
Strand Improvements'. These cleared an old conglomeration of 'vile
houses' from around St Martin-in-the-Fields,[31] and continued Pall Mall
into the new square forming in front of the National Gallery (1832–8).
Trafalgar Square itself took from 1829 to 1841 to lay out, and Nelson's
Column was not completed till 1849. These were the leisurely timescales
more usually associated with the development of old London, especially
after the death of George IV. But Nash's priceless vision eventually
resulted in London's greatest civic space. 'The year 1825 will ever be
memorable in the annals of London; for within that period more novel
improvements, changes, and events have occurred in the metropolis, than
during any other corresponding extent of time.'[32] The 1820s was the
most momentous decade of change in old London since the 1660s.

A number of other huge projects were getting off the ground as
Nash's great plan entered its final phase. Of these perhaps the most
influential was the City Corporation's demolition of London Bridge
and its replacement slightly upriver by a new Rennie-designed structure (1823–31). The new bridge brought about extensive demolitions
at the City approach, most notably for the new King William Street
running north-east almost to the Bank. But this was not all progress.
A Wren church, St Michael's Crooked Lane, was demolished. And some
smaller clearances on the Surrey side included the remains of an Anglo-
Norman priory. Very little of old London would be considered indispensable until much later in the century.

Also on the river, this time to the east of London Bridge, extensive
clearances of old and very poor clapboard-covered housing made way

for a new private venture, St Katharine's Dock (1824–8). Thomas Telford was the engineer on this project to build a dock closer to the centre of London than had ever been attempted before. In a poverty-stricken and lawless district, places with evocative names like Dark Entry, Cat's Hole, Pillory Lane and Rookery were wiped from the face of London. Some 1,250 houses were demolished and 11,300 people thrown onto the streets, probably more than twice as many as for Regent Street. These evictions were remarked upon less than the demolition of the ancient St Katharine's Hospital and the parish church of St Katharine's-by-the-Tower. Here some protests did occur, ending in a service for 'sixty poor children of the precinct', recipients of a local charity. 'They were the offspring of a neighbourhood of ill-fame, whence, by liberal hands, they had been plucked and preserved as brands from the burning fire.'[33]

Around the same time, further crown projects didn't involve Nash. The most far-reaching of these was the extension of the bureaucratic quarter in and around Whitehall. This involved the long-term redevelopment (from about 1796 to 1830) of Great, Middle and Little Scotland Yards, and rebuilding the Whitehall frontage north of Downing Street. Grand offices for the Privy Council and the Board of Trade were completed to a design of Sir John Soane in 1827. But this was a transformation with still a long way to go. There was a 'dirty public-house' on the corner of Downing Street and a 'row of third-rate lodging-houses between that and the Foreign Office' until 1839. And there were private residences in Whitehall for the rest of the century.[34]

More suggestive of the multi-layered social objectives of London improvements at this time is the story of the General Post Office. Since 1690 this had been in Lombard Street, the ancient centre of City banking. But it was too cramped for business and too decayed for official comfort and its removal had been mooted since 1789. The site chosen for the new GPO was in St Martin's-le-Grand and negotiations were under way in respect of it by 1813. Its selection was not merely commercial opportunity. The Office of Works – whose responsibility it was – had been guided to the site by the City Corporation, who offered to pay one-third of the purchase price of the land. The reason for the Corporation's largesse lay in the nature of the property there. It was the most notorious concentration of hovels and brothels in the City, 'infested with low women and strumpets of the worst description'. Round Court, New Rents, Mouldmaker's Rents (or Row), Dark Entry (again) and other places including 'a narrow passage, commonly, and not improperly, called *Little Hell*, leading into Bagnio Court' – most too small for even the mapmaker's art – occupied the whole of the east side of St Martin's-le-Grand. The new Post Office swept them all away. Purchase of the site, and possibly some demolitions, began in 1814, and around 1,200 people were evicted. But the new Post Office, after various financial problems, confusion and failures of nerve, did not finally open for business – to a design by Sir Robert Smirke – till 1828.[35]

Two years later, on 26 June 1830, George IV died. A reaction against the costliness and ostentation of his metropolitan improvements had already found loud voice. John Nash had been cross-examined by a parliamentary committee on the refurbishment of Buckingham Palace and found wanting. Eventually it would conclude that he had been 'chargeable with inexcusable irregularity and great negligence'.[36] The Duke of Wellington, then Prime Minister, blocked a baronetcy for Nash requested by George in 1829. But these were nothing to the backlash against luxury and improvidence that followed George's death. Every moral flaw that frail George had so openly flaunted during life seemed to swagger on in the dressy lavishness of his metropolitan improvements. Nash was dismissed as architect at Buckingham Palace and work there was suspended. And the reign of the retrencher and the tightwad – who had agitated from the wings for many years – began.

'Embellishment Subordinated', 1830–1855

Posterity never complains of extravagance in public works. But it almost always does of parsimony. Nash's plan for Regent's Park and the new street had been drawn up under three headings: 'Utility to the Public', 'Beauty of the Metropolis' and 'Practicability'. Henceforth, as the Select Committee on Metropolis Improvements put it in 1838, 'Embellishment' would be 'regarded as a matter of subordinate importance . . .'[37] The 'beauty of the metropolis' as an object of public policy died with George IV and would hardly be resurrected in the nineteenth century. Almost every metropolitan improvement begun after 1830 would suffer in some way from lack of care in design and appearance. Some suffered so badly that they would be objects of scorn for generations to come, opportunities disastrously squandered in the interests of short-term financial prudence, or penny-pinching.

Yet metropolitan improvements could not stop altogether – or, rather, they could not do so for long. At first the 1830s were as barren for the modernisation of London outside the City as the 1820s had been fruitful. But during the 1830s the pressures for change would build up and eventually overbear the forces of restraint. And the forward momentum was generated more than anything else by socio-political considerations rather than the commercial or communication needs of the capital.

Even up to 1830, the social objectives of redevelopment had often been explicit and important factors in metropolitan improvements. Butcher Row, Swallow Street, St Martin-in-the-Fields, St Katharine's-by-the-Tower, St Martin's-le-Grand, all had been shortlisted for clearance – even selected – on grounds of social expediency. Whatever the purpose for which replacement was sought, the removal of old London back-slums, and the ruthless dispersal of troublesome, dirty, pauper populations was a bonus that could clinch parliamentary support and statutory powers of purchase and demolition. After 1830, despite all the urgings of economy to do nothing, it was these social objectives that fashioned an irresistible imperative for change.

The first three years of the decade were greatly troubled. The revolutions of 1830 in France and Belgium warned of the power of a disgruntled people. There were London riots against the new king and Wellington when the latter declared against parliamentary reform at the end of the year. Pro-reform agitation made London's streets tense and occasionally violent until the Great Reform Act passed into law in June 1832. Even after that the ultra-radicals and organised workers kept the London authorities busy with political meetings, strikes, protests over the New Poor Law, the resurgence of London reform associations in 1836 and the birth of chartism a couple of years later.

Early in 1832, cholera had come to London for the first time. Its victims fell mainly in the worst districts of old London, especially south of the Thames. The rich were spared and many were blasé as a result. But for those in government, and in the ranks of a still-primitive civil service battling with a disease they didn't understand, the cholera epidemic was an enlightening moment. We can see, in the response of Charles Greville, Clerk to the Privy Council, the first stirrings of a social conscience that would find increasingly vociferous expression as the century grew older.

The awful thing is the vast extent of misery and distress which prevails, and the evidence of the rotten foundation on which the whole fabric of this gorgeous society rests, for I call that rotten which exhibits thousands upon thousands

of human beings reduced to the lowest stage of moral and physical degradation . . . I believe a general uncertainty pervades every class of society, from
the highest to the lowest; nobody looks upon any institution as secure, or any
interest as safe . . .[38]

What to do about the poor, how to reduce their cost to the nation,
how to prevent the crimes they committed and the diseases they spread,
how to suppress the political instability they provoked, these were the
most pressing questions of the 1830s. They pressed hardest in London
because there the poor seemed to pose the greatest danger to the wealthy
and to the very institutions of state. The poor threatened most acutely
when they congregated in large numbers in ill-drained, tight-clustered,
crumbling districts. Here they were impervious to police, to the civilising
influences of religion and education, even to the fresh air that might
disperse the stinking 'miasma' thought to be the agent of epidemic. Here
discontent was bred in the bone. And just such districts formed that
huge intractable girdle round the great cities of Westminster and London.

How were these districts to be improved? From the cholera onwards,
the local and religious authorities of the metropolis petitioned Parliament
for help in dealing with their troublesome enclaves. Parliament responded
by setting up a Select Committee on Metropolis Improvements in 1836.
Its second report (1838) dwelt on one solution. There was no better
way – indeed, no other way available at the time – than to drive new
streets through the worst parts of London.

There are some districts in this vast city through which no great thorough-
fares pass, and which being wholly occupied by a dense population, composed
of the lowest class of labourers, entirely secluded from the observation and
influence of wealthier and better educated neighbours, exhibit a state of moral
and physical degradation deeply to be deplored . . . The moral condition of
these poorer occupants must necessarily be improved by immediate communication with a more respectable inhabitancy; and the introduction at the same
time of improved habits and a freer circulation of air, will tend materially to
extirpate those prevalent diseases which are now not only so destructive among
themselves, but so dangerous to the neighbourhood around them.[39]

In choosing which areas to 'ventilate' first in this way, improved traffic
communications would be an important objective but not determinative. The dangers offered to London (and to better-off Londoners)
through crime and disease would prove most important of all. And in

effecting the improvements, cheapness would be a vital consideration. First, because the public purse, which had to borrow for purchase, demolition and street works – to be recouped over the years from building leases and improved ground rents – was more cash-strapped in the 1830s than at any other time in the nineteenth century.[40] Second, because the bungled cost control of the new Houses of Parliament, rebuilt after the fire of 1834 amid bitter wrangles over their design, focused parliamentary interest on value for money in public works at just this time.

If money was scarce, then priorities had to be chosen wisely. The top three troublesome districts where new streets were needed were identified by the select committee of 1838. First, the Rookery of St Giles, Holborn. Second, the Rose Lane and Essex Street area of Spitalfields and Whitechapel. Third, a new road to Pimlico through the Devil's Acre behind Westminster Abbey. Here were the lucky populations whose 'moral condition' would be improved by mass evictions and homelessness. Here were the people who made way for New Oxford Street, Commercial Street and Victoria Street.

It was really no surprise that the Rookery was chosen as the first bastion of the poor to fall. It was a very old concentration of misery and crime, home especially to a ragged Irish population since the eighteenth century. The Rookery was a small but dense district bounded by Great Russell Street, Charlotte Street, Broad Street and High Street: 'Within this space were George Street (once Dyott Street), Carrier Street, Maynard Street, and Church Street, which ran from north to south, and were intersected by Church Lane, Ivy Lane, Buckeridge Street, Bainbridge Street, and New Street. These, with an almost endless intricacy of courts and yards crossing each other, rendered the place like a rabbit-warren.' Buckeridge Street was full of thieves' and prostitutes' and cadgers' lodging houses at fourpence a night or threepence in the cellars. Jones Court was 'inhabited by coiners, utterers of base coin, and thieves', and its cellars connected with those in Buckeridge Street by short tunnels or holes just two feet high. Rat's Castle, Ivy Lane, 'was a large dirty building occupied by thieves and prostitutes, and boys who lived by plunder'. Some houses had 'no legitimate owner' for generations and fell down through neglect before they could be pulled down. The poverty and crowding here were astounding: 'I have found, in small houses of not more than ten feet square, forty people living, from the cellars up to the attics; I never met with such a scene of misery in my life . . .' And then the filth. There was 'scarcely a single sewer in any part of it'. Cesspools overflowed into the cellars and kennels in the road. 'In St Giles one feels asphyxiated by the stench: there is no air to breathe nor daylight to find one's way.'[41]

James Pennethorne, favourite pupil of John Nash, was appointed architect to the Commissioners of Woods and Forests and Land Revenues in 1839 to see through the select committee's chosen schemes, beginning in the Rookery. He proposed the clearance of the whole area, and not just the line of a new street, as the best means of safeguarding the investment value of the frontage sites. But financial difficulties led to pressure on costs of all the schemes proposed in 1838. The new streets were reduced in width and any larger ideas of redevelopment abandoned. Demolitions merely along the lines of Bainbridge and Buckeridge streets at the heart of the Rookery were completed by 1845 and New Oxford Street laid out by 1847. Its new shops, as Pennethorne had predicted, suffered from the remnants of the Rookery all around them, and no doubt from the street's narrowness compared to Oxford Street. Rents had to be lowered and its most ambitious shopping venture – the 'Royal Bazaar' – was bankrupt by 1854.[42]

Some 5,000 people were said to have been evicted from the Rookery and from the line of Endell Street, another improvement just to the south carried out at the same time. What happened to them? Many clearly didn't move far away. Church Lane became phenomenally overcrowded as displaced persons crammed into every square foot, two families occasionally sharing a room. In 1841 its population had been 655 in twenty-seven five-roomed houses. In 1847 it was 1,095, or eight persons to a room. Other streets nearby would have shared its fate. For those who couldn't find living space in the Rookery, most were absorbed into that great ring of old London. Some years later it was said that many had moved to Devil's Acre, Field Lane and Saffron Hill – to be moved on again in short order, as we shall see. Charles Dickens commented, 'Thus, we make our New Oxford Streets, and our other new streets, never heeding, never asking, where the wretches whom we clear out, crowd.'[43]

And the remnants of the Rookery? They changed a little with the times but not much. Even in 1874 George Street was a 'lane second to none in the Metropolis for squallor [*sic*] and dirt, and where the police find frequent active employment'. And in 1875 Church Lane was a 'little colony of Arabs as completely sequestered from London society as if it was part of Arabia Petraea . . . Its condition is a disgrace to the great city, and to the parish to which it belongs.' It was demolished in 1877 and replaced by warehouses.[44]

Besides being an explicit slum-clearance measure, New Oxford Street made a rational improvement to London's communications. It avoided narrow and roundabout Broad Street and connected Oxford Street direct to Holborn. And so with Cranbourn Street, another scheme carried out at the same time to join Piccadilly with Long Acre, likewise removing a western stricture. But this was more than could be said for Commercial Street, at the east end of the town, for some years at least.

The properties either side of the line of Essex Street, Rose Lane and Red Lion Street – the approximate route of the new street – were dreadful. Pennethorne thought them 'the very worst description of property in London', worse than the Rookery. 'There is no drainage of any sort or kind but the surface drainage', the privies and cesspools 'are scarcely ever emptied, but they flow over into the streets . . .' A dozen places listed by the medical officer to the Whitechapel poor law authorities in 1840 were all 'hot beds of fever'. Rose Lane was better than its neighbours. Even so, 'I have seen the place completely flooded with blood from the slaughter-house.'[45]

And the people! They 'are most intolerably filthy; they are the lowest description of Irish, many Germans, and many Jews, and they are, of all the people in the world, the most filthy'. 'I am told on good authority, by a man whose property overlooks the courts, that frequently, on a Sunday morning, he sees a dozen women perfectly naked, without the least dress at all, dancing to a fiddler.' According to the rector of Christ Church, Spitalfields, 'the whole route is inhabited by an exceedingly immoral population; women of the lowest character, receivers of stolen goods, thieves, and the most atrocious offenders, find in these obscure haunts concealment from the hands of justice . . .'[46]

Demolitions of some 250 houses proceeded in 1843–4 and building plots along the new carriageway were put up for auction at Christmas 1845. But many didn't sell and some sites remained empty until 1869. And – the result of more cost-cutting – the street itself was largely useless as a thoroughfare, ending as it did in a tangle of courts and alleys just past Spitalfields church. An extension north to Shoreditch High Street and the Eastern Counties Railway terminus was agreed in 1845 but not opened till 1858. That, though, was a 'matter of subordinate importance'. Commercial Street was before everything else a slum-clearance scheme.

Evicting the people was achievement enough.[47]

Finally Victoria Street. There seems nothing to choose in dirt, wretched-ness and crime between the Rookery or Rose Lane and the old secret nests behind the Abbey at Almonry, Duck Lane, Orchard Street and the Pye Streets. We read in a letter by Dickens to the philanthropist Angela Burdett-Coutts that the area is 'a maze of filth and squalor, so dense and deserted by all decency, that my apparition . . . brought out the people in a crowd'. We read in the *Illustrated London News* of 'those sinks of vice and iniquity', of '"Caxton's House"' and the Pest House, Tothill Fields or 'Five Chimneys', built in 1644 and now to be demolished. A police officer tells of tall old houses in New Way '"occupied by prostitutes and thieves . . . like rabbit warrens, from cellar to attic"'. And of the former grand mansions of the rich – Lord Dacre's, Admiral Kempenfelt's – long abandoned to the poor, with a family in every panelled room. From the worst of this old rookery perhaps some 200 houses and 2,500 people were removed. Some had only just arrived, '"vicious boys and girls, driven from their St Giles haunts . . ."' When driven on again, as usual they seem not to have gone very far. The census of 1851 contains a footnote ascribing part of the increase of population in the neighbouring parish of St John the Evangelist to the 'influx' from the clearances.[48]

Demolitions in the Devil's Acre began in 1847 and the new street opened in 1851. The east end was widened through to Broad Sanctuary, causing more evictions in 1853. But of all the speculative failures asso-ciated with metropolitan improvements this was about the worst. For sites didn't sell here either: 'It was at a standstill for some years and took slowly for building purposes, in fact it was only completely filled up in 1887.' And this despite the opening of Victoria Station in 1860. This was a wide street and a prestigious venture. But capitalists with money to invest in big sites and tall buildings were not easily attracted to a district, on the borders of Pimlico, which was always equivocal and fragile in its class appeal.[49]

We have now heard so much of demolitions and evictions and the attack on old London that it will probably come as a surprise to learn that the population grew in most of these inner areas between 1801 and 1851 and – even more surprising – that the number of houses often rose too.

Very few central districts showed population falls between 1801 and 1851. St Martin-in-the-Fields, the City Within the Walls, St Olave Southwark, and tiny places like the Precinct of the Savoy and Middle

Temple were the only districts to be less packed with people in mid-century than at the beginning. The rest showed an increase. And although numerous places – St Giles, St Margaret's Westminster, Spitalfields, north Whitechapel and others – saw a fall in the number of houses during the 1840s due to demolitions, even in central districts like these the number of houses had risen between 1801 and 1841. How did this happen?

We can tell from the maps. That of Spitalfields and Whitechapel in 1813 – to take one example – had shown gardens (or laystalls and rubbish tips) behind houses on Rose Lane and Essex Street. As pressure on house room increased, leaseholders built on these backlands to fill up every square foot. By 1838 all were filled with tiny courts and alleys. Pennethorne described how these courts were 'very small and very narrow, the access to them being only under gateways; in many cases they have been larger courts originally, and afterwards built in again with houses back to back, without any outlet behind, and only consisting of two rooms [one on top of the other] and almost a ladder for a staircase . . .' Some were built without privies at all or with 'only a few boards tacked together'. A few were just five feet wide between facing front walls, many ten feet or less. This property was the 'least [value] of any I have met with' – brick and timber shacks and shanties hardly lasting thirty years.[50] Even in the 1840s ready-made slums were run up wherever the opportunity arose, as at Newton's Rents, Stepney, built around 1845, a court with six houses on either side: each had one room, nine foot square – 'The conveniences [in 1851] are horrible. There is no water laid on. Ten houses inhabited, five of them have four and one five occupants; in one, two married men and two married women lived.'[51] Precisely similar processes had been going on at the same time in Clerkenwell, Saffron Hill, St Luke's, St Giles' Southwark – indeed, around the whole girdle of old London.

Thus had old London fought back against the forces of destruction. But those forces had gained a new ally which had already begun to make its presence felt. The railway.

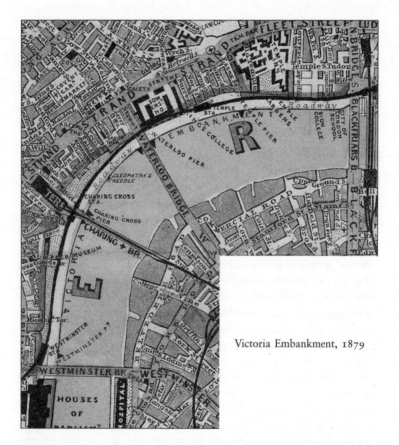

Victoria Embankment, 1879

II

VICTORIA EMBANKMENT: MODERN LONDON, 1855–1899

Railway Town: The City, 1855–1875

THE railway was the revolutionary invention of the age. For many it marked the true beginning of the nineteenth century. It recast conceptions of time and jettisoned old notions of speed. It did more to unify Great Britain than any political arrangement could have done. Its effects on the growth of new London, and London's place in the nation, we shall glimpse shortly. But the bullying power of the railway, the rapidity with which it devoured streets and houses to make way for its triumphant iron road and blistering steam, had a transformative effect on old London too, in more ways than one.

The first of the London railways opened close to the heart of the city on 14 December 1836. It ran from its terminus at the south end of London Bridge – the earliest of London's sixteen railway termini[1] – to Greenwich, less than four miles away. At eighteen miles an hour, sometimes over twenty, the journey time was cut from an hour by omnibus or steamboat to some twelve minutes. In its first fifteen months it carried 650,000 passengers, pleasure-seekers mainly for Greenwich's whitebait dinners and riverside pubs, its fine park and observatory, its uproarious fair.

The line ran on London's longest viaduct, a giant monument to the bricklayer's art, which lifted the rails over streets but demolished much poor house property in its way. The arches were let out as workshops and even a chapel and a pub. But untenanted arches had to be shut off to prevent their use for immoral purposes and for hiding the bodies of unwanted babies. The different meanings of railways for London – their speed, convenience, destructive power, their multi-layered impact on London's cultural life and social relationships – were all soon apparent from the very first runs on the London and Greenwich Railway around that Christmas of 1836.[2]

Much early railway development in London brought travellers merely to the edge of its built-up area, in the new suburbs of the nineteenth-century city. But a few of the early companies followed the example of the London and Greenwich by driving their lines as close to the centre as property prices and Parliament would allow. These two stumbling blocks went hand in hand. It was very difficult for railway companies to win parliamentary approval to bring lines and stations into wealthy districts, with all their disastrous consequences for property prices. So even the central lines stopped where cheaper property gave way to better.

Property was cheapest south of the river, hence the London Bridge terminus, and on the eastern edge of town, hence the Shoreditch or Bishopsgate terminus of the Eastern Counties (later Great Eastern) Railway, which was opened in July 1840 for trains at first just to Romford but later to East Anglia, and the London and Blackwall Railway to the new East India Docks on the Essex side of the Isle of Dogs. At first the City Corporation had opposed any intrenchment of its ancient boundaries on the grounds that railways would only make street congestion worse, but its position changed and in August 1841 the first permanent City terminus was opened at Fenchurch Street. Dock artisans stood in open 'stand-ups', managers and sightseers sat five-abreast in the 'superior' class. This line's arches, by the way, seem to have required the eviction of over 3,000 people through the East End, many from old squalid courts and alleys just north of Rosemary Lane (Royal Mint Street).[3]

Through the early 1840s and the 'Railway Mania' of 1845–7 companies were queueing up in Parliament for permission to build no fewer than nineteen lines in London, each with a new terminus in the City or Westminster. There were so many proposals, threatening to carve up the metropolis like some brick and iron cat's cradle, that a royal commission was established to consider how best the schemes might be adapted to some rational plan. One option favoured by many was a grand central station to which several companies might run their lines.

The Royal Commission on Metropolis Railway Termini reported in 1846. The intolerable burdens on property, on the people to be evicted and on those whose businesses would be affected were all spelled out. And so too were the insuperable barriers that viaducts would put in the way of street improvements and traffic flows. So it rejected seventeen of the nineteen planned termini, permitting just two railway extensions south of the river. It rejected, too, any notion of a great shared terminus in central London. On the contrary, it laid down for the north side of the Thames boundaries which railway companies would not be allowed to penetrate. In effect these were the limits of the built-up area as they had applied in 1800: Edgware Road and Park Lane on the west; the New Road, City Road and Finsbury Square on the north; Bishopsgate on the east. South of the river the district to be protected was everything within Borough High Street in the east, Vauxhall Bridge in the west and Kennington Lane in the south.

The royal commission of 1846 snuffed out the 1840s bout of railway mania in London. Relieved of potential competitors, the London and Blackwall Company at Fenchurch Street made the most of its uniquely valuable City asset. In 1849 it connected with the Eastern Counties line and allowed steam trains into the City, replacing the original stationary engines hauling coaches on an endless cable. London Bridge Station had already expanded by allowing new companies and new lines access in 1839, 1841 and again in 1845 and 1850. Also south of the river an important new terminus at Waterloo, on the edge of old London, opened in 1848, having secured permission before the royal commission had reported.[4]

Railways brought more sweeping changes to the City than blackened arches and smoking engines. Railway mania was a formative factor in the City's reinvention in the nineteenth century as a specialist financial and commercial district with no room for a resident population. New banks were as common as railway ventures, indeed were often conjoined. Growth in banking was mirrored in the multiplication of insurance companies, the equation between speed and risk representing a minor Victorian neurosis. Share-dealing flourished at almost unprecedented levels during the 1845–7 mania, facilitated by the development of the electric telegraph around the same time. It produced an unprecedented volume of work not just for brokers and jobbers but for printers, engravers, trade and other newspapers, all substantial City enterprises. And railway companies needed headquarters buildings. Prestige, investor confidence and financial networking required many of these to be in the City.

So from around 1840 to 1870 the transformation of the City of London moved at an ever faster pace. The new Royal Exchange (opened in 1844) greatly extended the site where it had burned down in 1838. An unsuccessful share-dealing centre, set up as an alternative to the Stock Exchange, opened as the Hall of Commerce in Threadneedle Street (1844). A new Coal Exchange was built by the City Corporation in Lower Thames Street (1849). The Stock Exchange, owned by a private consortium, was rebuilt and enlarged (1854). The first joint stock bank in the City – the London and Westminster Bank, Lothbury – opened in 1838. By 1847 it had been joined by the London Joint Stock, the Union Bank of London, the London and County, and the Commercial of London; in the 1850s, by the Bank of Australasia, City Bank and more. Both sides of Lombard Street, the old centre of London banking, were virtually rebuilt between 1857 and 1873. The same was true with insurance companies, thirty-two of which were established in London between 1845 and 1851 alone, and another ten set up in the City in the 1850s.

Alongside such specialist institutions as exchanges, banks, insurance companies and discount houses arose the general office block as a speculative venture. From the 1840s buildings entirely to let by the floor or part-floor became common. They were frequently called 'chambers', after their early forebears in the Inns of Court. The City Offices Company and the City of London Real Property Company, both especially active in the 1860s, were two among several niche providers of this sort of accommodation. And in and around the offices were anonymous new warehouses for a City that still dealt in real merchandise and not just the paper rights to transfer it from one merchant or banker to another.[5]

The new City that emerged from the old in these years was a storey or two higher than before and the buildings were more stout and grand, often taking the sites of several houses to make their presence felt. In the basements were strong rooms, the boilers, the clerks' gloomy lunch rooms; on the ground floor a grand reception area to show a glistering front; on the first a baronial boardroom and offices above; the third floor could be let out to tenants as office space to defray overheads; and a caretaker lived in the attics. Architectural styles were eclectic. Modernity was backward-looking: Italian Renaissance and Gothic were much in favour, with some classical neo-Georgian throwbacks. Ironically, genuinely old buildings were entirely dispensable in the rush to mock-medievalism. Ironically, too, for a pious age, City churches were complacently sacrificed in the name of Mammon. St Bartholomew Exchange and St Benet Fink went for the new Royal Exchange; St Benet Gracechurch, St Mary Somerset and All Hallows Staining went in the 1860s after the Union of Benefices Act 1860 made more churches redundant; thirteen in all by 1898, several by Sir Christopher Wren among them, most given over to the moneychangers.[6]

There were other changes too. The old coaching inns that had been such a feature of pre-railway London withered away. In the early years of the century there had been about twenty-five famous houses in the City alone, each with extensive stables and yards and many renowned for their accommodation for travellers. By 1899 all but one in London had gone – the Old Bull in Holborn. Some had been turned into hotels. Some had become carters' and carriers' yards. Some, pathetically bowing to the times, combined the business of public house with railway booking office. Most had been demolished for street improvements or for 'business premises'.[7]

And then the railway brought traffic. It did so directly, of course, by disgorging people into the City at Fenchurch Street or on its edge in the east at Bishopsgate, and London Bridge in the south. Fenchurch Street passenger traffic doubled to some 3.5 million in 1851 after trains started running there from Islington (via Bow!) the year before. Traffic into London Bridge Station rose from 5.6 million in 1850 to 10.8 million in 1854 and 13.5 million in 1859. An especially troublesome element of this railway traffic in the 1850s and after were through-passengers struggling across the City from London Bridge to, say, Euston, 'traversing with luggage a great portion of a crowded Metropolis'.[8]

Then the railways contributed indirectly as one important factor in enabling people to move away from the City as a residential area. The residential population of the City held up well until 1851. Then it was 128,000, just 400 fewer than in the highest census count in 1801 and 4,300 up on 1841. Indeed, the population density had never been higher: 8.8 persons per house, compared to 7.5 in 1801.[9]

But there was a dramatic falling away in the 1850s and even more in the 1860s. The population in 1861 was 113,000, a reduction of 12 per cent. By 1871 it dropped a third in a decade to 76,000. Crowding had reduced too to 8.1 persons per house. In the 1860s, though, this was an exodus less induced by the convenience of suburban travel than by sledgehammer and shovel.[10]

Those who left, or at least the men and boys among them, usually found themselves part of the army of workers and visitors who travelled daily into the City. Most came on foot – 400,000 every working day, it was said in 1854. A further 54,000 came in by rail, 30,000 by steamers, 88,000 by horse-bus, 52,000 by other vehicles, some 624,000 in all. That was more than if the combined populations of Liverpool and Birmingham had decamped to the square mile and home again each weekday. Every year from then notched up an increase on this already immense volume of people. The number of vehicles entering the City in a twelve-hour period rose by 57 per cent between 1850 and 1865, from 49,000 to 77,000. By 1866 not far short of three-quarters of a million (729,000) resorted to the City during twenty-four hours of a working day.[11]

Traffic in the City's narrow streets was both interminable and insufferable. 'Every one feels and deplores the evils of the congestion under which the olden portions of the metropolis – and more especially the City – that great heart and centre of all – suffer,' complained the *Illustrated London News* in 1854. It cited Chancery Lane, the main route between Fleet Street and Holborn, yet 'too narrow at one end to admit of the passage of two vehicles abreast, and where a vast amount of traffic is often brought to a stand-still by a costermonger's cart, or by a laundress's wheel-barrow'.[12]

The City Corporation had not been wholly unmindful of the growing sclerosis in its streets. But hardly any ambitious road scheme had been begun since that great improving decade of the 1820s, apart from Moorgate Street (about 1846) as a connection north from the earlier King William Street. The traffic crisis of the 1850s did, though, prompt some action. Cannon Street was widened from 1854 by the demolition and rebuilding of its south side. And Smithfield Metropolitan Cattle Market was closed in 1855, relocating to a green-field site in west Islington. It removed for ever from London one of its greatest traffic nuisances, vast droves of cattle making their own 'locks' every market day, and a unique 'panorama of cruelty and suffering', as Dickens called it, after decades of scandal and agitation.[13]

Most important of all were developments in the Fleet Valley, quite fortuitously a giant leap forward in modernising London. North of Holborn Hill the Fleet remained in parts an open sewer and along its reeking banks lay Field Lane, Saffron Hill, West Street (formerly and notoriously Chick Lane) and innumerable courts and alleys, a 'solid mass of misery, of low vice, of filth, fever, and crime'. There had been some piecemeal demolitions and culverting of Fleet Ditch at various times in the 1840s. But in 1855 there was still much pre-Fire property in places like Vine Street, Bear and Staff Yard and even Field Lane itself. The premises of the 'carrion butchers' – horse knackers or 'melters' – in Sharp's Alley were said to be home to some of the biggest and fiercest rats in London. A local trade in cats' skins revealed itself in 'writhing heaps of cats, literally skinned alive, and occasionally furnishing a living meal to the gaunt swine' which roamed the alleyways:

wonderful indeed it seems, that wealthy and populous London, with its splen-dour and resources, should tolerate so detestable a nook on the very confines of its spacious marts; that it should have never a besom to cleanse this foul and festering corner, a breeding place for fevers, cholera, and other more lingering, but equally fatal diseases, that congeal the vital fluids, under a continual access of slow poison.[14]

Improving this area by extending Farringdon Street northwards began to take shape in the late 1840s. By 1855 the new street, taking prop-erty just to the east of Field Lane, had reached Clerkenwell Green, sweeping away Sharp's Alley with it. From 1856 it inched forward again, reaching King's Cross Road in 1863. Long before then, the ground on either side of the carriageway had lain barren and unbuilt upon so long it was known as 'the Farringdon Street wastes'. But the object of the new street – at first called Victoria, later Farringdon, Road – had been as much slum clearance as metropolitan improve-ment. So rebuilding, as a critic of the City Corporation noted, was of little interest: the poor 'had been driven away, and what more could be wanted?'[15]

But the Farringdon Street wastes represented to others a historic opportunity. Since the 1830s the idea of building railways in London underground had been discussed by engineers and entrepreneurs. One impediment, though, had always been an obligation in law to buy any property on the line of a tunnel in case its foundations were under-mined. Yet here there was no property left along much of the route. The way had been cleared by the City Corporation.

This opportunity had been identified early on by Charles Pearson, City Corporation solicitor since 1839, and before that an influential radical common councilman. Pearson had been a visionary campaigner for working-class suburbs connected by rail to London as a cure for central overcrowding. He also kept alive the idea of a central London terminus to bring together in one place the lines of competing railway companies that would otherwise disarrange the centre. In 1851 Pearson proposed a 100-foot-wide road from King's Cross to Holborn Hill along the line of the Farringdon Street extension, with a tunnel beneath to accommodate eight sets of tracks. Road and tunnel would end, after running under a viaduct carrying Holborn Hill to Newgate, at a grand central station covering six acres on either side of Farringdon Street. It was a stunning vision, some of it twenty years ahead of its time. Pearson, though still a servant of the Corporation – these were libertarian times in matters of conflict of interest – established with some wealthy backers the City Terminus Company in 1852 to prosecute his scheme.

At around this time another company had also identified the potential of the Farringdon Street wastes. The Bayswater, Paddington and Holborn Bridge Railway proposed connecting through an underground railway those new western suburbs with the City at Farringdon Street. The western terminus would be at Paddington Station, first opened in 1838 but to be greatly extended in 1854. They planned to 'cut and cover' along the New Road to join Farringdon Road at King's Cross and then head south. Their surveyor, John Hargrave Stevens, was a colleague of Pearson's. He was surveyor of the City Corporation's western division.

This was the scheme which eventually prevailed. Its prime mover and first chairman was William Malins, who had foreseen that without underground railways London's traffic would render it '"almost insupportable for purposes of business, recreation and all ordinary transit from place to place"'.[16] Vitally, this underground railway offered the prospect of connecting travellers to London from the Midlands and the north directly with the City at Farringdon Street.

Powers were obtained in 1854 for what was now called the Metropolitan Railway. But the Crimean War constrained the availability of capital and in 1858, without a spade being dug, the company was close to winding up. Pearson came to the rescue. He agitated for the new project so successfully that the City Corporation subscribed for shares worth £200,000. Building began in 1859. It was hampered by technical difficulties even though it relied on cutting a deep trench rather than tunnelling – the foul Fleet burst through the workings in

1862, for example. But all obstacles were eventually overcome and, after four years' work, the first underground railway in the world opened between Paddington and Farringdon Street on 10 January 1863. That day 50,000 people turned up for a ticket but only half could be accommodated. Despite understandable public prejudice against travelling much of the way in a choking, stinking tunnel – trains were pulled by steam engines intended to be smokeless – it carried an average of 26,000 passengers a day in its first six months. The line was extended to Moorgate in December 1865.[17]

The Metropolitan Railway opened at a moment when London and the nation had already entered another railway mania. Through the 1850s new railway developments had stalled while capital was scarce and companies merged and restructured. Yet demand for rail travel continued to grow. New schemes burgeoned in the late 1850s. Victoria Station opened in October 1860, its lines entering from the south and crossing the river on the Grosvenor railway bridge to connect Pimlico with Brighton and Dover. By 1863 London was again the object of railway company attention. Some thirty-three railway and canal bills for new lines and a variety of suburban and central termini were now projected for the metropolis. If they were all sanctioned, a quarter of the City would be laid waste to make way for them. So almost a precise re-run of 1846 faced Parliament in 1863.

The conclusion of a parliamentary committee on Metropolitan Railway Communication was similar to the royal commission's seventeen years before. It too decided on an overground exclusion zone, but now for a larger London. This time it would extend from Barking in the east, Finsbury Park in the north, Willesden in the west, Brixton and Lewisham in the south. Within this new ring underground railways on the model of the Metropolitan Railway experiment were all that would be permitted.[18]

But by 1863, when the select committee reported, some schemes had already won parliamentary approval. The City especially was to be invaded more damagingly than ever before, and mainly from the south. Several companies were permitted to follow the Pimlico example and extend the southern network by building new railway bridges across the Thames, planting stations as bridgeheads on the north bank. Thus there was Charing Cross in Westminster, its line over a new Hungerford Bridge opened in January 1864; Ludgate Hill, its over a new and hideous railway bridge at Blackfriars opened in June 1865;

and lines from Waterloo and London Bridge were brought to within a few minutes' walk of the Bank at Cannon Street in September 1866, over another new bridge. Just one line entered the City from the north – the North London Railway's extension from Dalston to Broad Street in November 1865. It would soon become one of the most popular short-haul commuter lines in the country. All this involved frantic activity. London was reduced 'to the condition of a city in a state of siege. It has been invaded on every side by railway directors . . .' 'Railway invasion and compensation cases are the stock subject of the day,' it was reported in April 1866.[19] With these examples as precedents, the 1863 exclusion zone – and even the City at its very heart – would be penetrated again and again: for yet another GER terminus, at Liverpool Street (February 1874); for a station further into the City for the London, Chatham and Dover Railway (Holborn Viaduct, March 1874); and a third station for the same line at St Paul's (later Blackfriars Station, May 1886).

These were immensely destructive changes in the City, most of them impacting in the 1860s. They didn't operate alone. The Corporation of London was never more active than in these very years. It rebuilt Blackfriars Bridge at the same time that it was implementing its most ambitious and costly improvement scheme of the century. This was the construction from 1867 to 1869 of Holborn Viaduct – as Charles Pearson had recommended nearly twenty years before – to carry Holborn Hill to Newgate Street and Cheapside over the Fleet Valley (Farringdon Street). At the west end of the viaduct a traffic nexus was built at Holborn Circus (1872), with new streets to Ludgate Circus and Smithfield, where a modern wholesale meat market was completed in November 1868. The Queen opened both the new bridge and Holborn Viaduct on 6 November 1869, 'a great day in the annals of the City of London'.[20]

And approaching from the south-west was yet one more great street improvement. Cutting across New Bridge Street, just north of the new Blackfriars Bridge and heading to the Mansion House, was Queen Victoria Street. It was built as an extension to the new Victoria Embankment and opened in November 1871. It 'involved the destruction of much valuable property', costing over £2 million to purchase, one of the most expensive schemes of the century. Queen Victoria Street would install the final spoke in the City's hub. Seven streets now converged on the great forum fronted on the north by the Bank of

England, on the south by the Mansion House and on the east by the Royal Exchange.[21] The City had begun to assume the street pattern it would maintain for the next 100 years and more.

The 1860s were the most destructive and most creative decade in the City's history in the 200 years since the Great Fire. In 1851 there had been 14,580 inhabited houses in the City. In 1871 there were 9,415, a fall of 30 per cent in just ten years and most lost in those massive rail and road incursions. By 1901 there were only 3,934 inhabited houses in the City: 'The shopkeepers, clerks, and working men have all left the City. Only the caretakers remain, with a few residents in Banks and City Rectories.'[22]

The sheer chaos of the 1860s and 1870s, the 'havoc that has been made during this time by the railways which have entered and intersected the metropolis', was 'far greater than could have been imagined'. '"London has become a very city of hoardings"', houses destroyed, '"odd bits of streets snapped off . . . shapeless scraps of land, unneeded by the railway, and unavailable for other purposes . . . the abominable bridges . . . the viaducts that provide dry arches for the congregation and accommodation of street Arabs and gutter children . . . the colossal sheds of stations [that] mar the river's banks . . ."'[23]

And then there were the human consequences. We will never know how many people lost their homes during what must have seemed – even spread over ten or fifteen years – like some pitiless Armageddon. The City's critics claimed that 40,000 – maybe 50,000 – working-class occupiers were evicted from the line of Farringdon Street and Road.[24] That was an impossible exaggeration, but then the true figure is also impossible to get at. The best we can say is that perhaps 5,000 people were turned out and were forced to look for housing nearby, 'thrust into any hole and corner they could put their heads'. So we see crowding in St James Clerkenwell, adjacent to the Farringdon clearances, rise from 8.6 persons per house in 1841 to 9.6 in 1851, 9.9 in 1861 and 10.6 in 1871. Here 'respectable artisans . . . makers of little fancy articles and parts of watches, have been forced into the same dwellings with some of the worst class . . . driven from Field-lane and the "slums" near Sharp's-alley'. And even the Farringdon clearances were just a pebble on the beach. Over 56,000 people were probably displaced by London railway schemes alone between 1853 and 1884, and most of those must have been in and near the City between 1857 and 1874. Most, but not all, of those made homeless were the London poor.[25]

They would continue to suffer in this way throughout the remainder of the century. And from 22 December 1855 they had to contend with a new vector of modern London which addressed the problems of the old city with fresh vigour. This was the Metropolitan Board of Works.

'Stream of Death': The Thames, 1855–1875

Meantime, if your honour were in London, you would see a great embankment rising high and dry out of the Thames on the Middlesex shore, from Westminster Bridge to Blackfriars. A really fine work, and really getting on. Moreover, a great system of drainage. Another really fine work, and likewise really getting on. Lastly, a muddle of railways in all directions possible and impossible, with no general public scheme, no general public supervision, enormous waste of money, no fixable responsibility, no accountability . . .[26]

So Charles Dickens to a Swiss friend at the end of November 1865. It took much for Dickens – an outspoken critic of the ugliness and shabbiness of London when contrasted with the great cities of the Continent – to praise a contemporary London improvement, but he expressed what many agreed with at the time. The Victoria Embankment really was a 'magnificent roadway, one of the finest in Europe', and, as 'a piece of engineering skill . . . second to none of the great achievements that have marked the Victorian era'.[27]

It was not, though, a Victorian idea. Wren had thought of something similar in the 1660s, and John Gwynn, a century later, had advocated a 'quay' on both sides of the river along the whole length of the metropolis. In 1824 Sir Frederick Trench, a military man and an aide to George IV, the great improver, had promoted an embankment from Charing Cross to Blackfriars. He even brought in a bill to provide it. But he couldn't raise the capital, his bill provoked strong opposition from riverside interests and the scheme was dropped.[28]

In about 1834 the concept of 'Trench's Terrace' was revived in an imaginative way by the popular biblical and historical painter John Martin. He saw the embankment as not only a civic improvement of grandeur to tidy up London's shambling riverside of wharves, coal-stacks and boatyards but a means of protecting the Thames from pollution. He projected an embankment that carried an 'intercepting sewer' which would catch London's sewage before it entered the river, to carry it downstream beyond the built-up area. Martin's idea was warmly received but it too went nowhere.[29]

So did the City Corporation's plan designed by James Walker, adopted in January 1842, to build an embankment at its own expense even beyond the City's boundaries. The Corporation's ambitions fell foul of government rivalry. The First Commissioner of Woods and Forests and Land Revenues filed a suit in Chancery to force the City to show that it, rather than the crown, owned title to the river bed that it would reclaim for the roadway. The Corporation could later justly claim that this piece of Whitehall wrecking set back the Victoria Embankment by eighteen years at least. To make some amends, the government itself built an embankment from Millbank to Chelsea Hospital by 1854, but with no sewer.[30]

By then the need to do something drastic about the Thames and its banks had become of pressing concern. It was literally a matter of life and death. And the reason was sewage.

In 1855 the human waste of some 2.5 million Londoners was either left in the ground or put into the Thames. In the early part of the century house drainage was not to sewers but to cesspools or a 'bog-hole'. This was a pit under the privy into which waste dropped until it was full and was then dug out by hand. It was into one such that poor Mrs Wennels of Woolwich, her babe in arms, fell in 1829 when the rotten privy floor gave way: both were drowned in 'the abyss of filth beneath'. Many houses, even in the City, were built over their cesspools, 'perhaps merely boarded over – close beneath the feet of a family of human beings'. And 'the very best portions of the West End are literally honeycombed with cesspools. Many houses have from three to seven under them.' When not attended to, they overflowed into the saturated soil or over the courts and pavements. When dug out, or pumped out, as some were by the late 1840s, the excrement was carted through the streets to the country for spreading on the fields; or, until 1848, when the practice was suppressed, kept in giant heaps or laystalls in the night-soil men's yards to dry out before selling to farmers. A 'table mountain of manure' at Digby Street, Bethnal Green, sat beside 'extensive and deep lakes of putrefying *night soil* . . . dammed up with the more solid dung'.[31]

The stench of human excrement in London was so pervasive that it only became noticeable in its very worst manifestations. No part of London escaped. The drainage of Buckingham Palace was '"extremely defective"' at mid-century and '"its precincts are reeking with filth and pestilential odours"'. The drains were so bad there that the Queen needed her own rat-catcher, Jack Black, because '"Rats are everywhere about London"'. '"We are not any better off in Regent-street and Oxford-street,"' confessed Edwin Lankester, the eminent surgeon and scientist. '"I believe that one part of London is as bad as another as far as drainage goes."'[32]

Although cesspools were permitted even in new London houses until 1848 they had become gradually supplanted by sewers. At the beginning of the century it was in theory unlawful to put foul matter in sewers, these being reserved solely for surface water. But the tributaries of the Thames, such as the Fleet, Walbrook, Bayswater and Ranelagh, had been sewers for centuries and it had become custom and practice to drain into them directly or through pipes shared with other houses. With the slow-growing popularity in London of the water closet from about 1810, and especially after 1830, when 'its progress became rapid and remarkable', more and more human waste was put into the sewers. As the volume of water in them increased – by about one-third between 1810 and 1821, some specialists thought – they became more efficient at shooting shit into the Thames. Their very efficiency led to more and more new sewers being built, so that sewers in the City, for instance, had connected 11,200 houses out of some 16,200 by about 1852. And the very growth of London, where the number of houses increased from 136,000 in 1801 to 306,000 in 1851, meant an enormous growth in sewers too.[33] All these eventually opened into the river.

Fifty years of improved drainage had hardly made London a sweeter place. It was certainly not healthier. Asiatic cholera proved that. The first epidemic, which reached London in early 1832, killed 5,275, with Southwark worst hit, as we have seen. The next, in 1848–9, much more severe, killed 14,789 and again the southern districts were especially badly affected. Over half the deaths in 1849 occurred south of the river (7,137), a greater proportion even than in 1832.[34] Up to this point the means of contagion of this acute diarrhoeal fever, causing rapid death from dehydration in 48 per cent of cases, was not understood at all. The prevailing theory remained that of 'miasma', the poisons thought to be in air polluted with foul odours.

It was the next epidemic that proved at least to some of the scientific community that cholera was water-borne, as well as contagious between individuals. The cholera of 1853–4 killed 11,661 Londoners.

Again the southern districts contributed over half the deaths, proportionately two or three times as high as districts north of the Thames. But it was a particularly virulent local outbreak in Soho that led John Snow, a physician with a brilliant enquiring mind, to demonstrate that water contaminated by sewage was the true cause of epidemic cholera. 'Within two hundred and fifty yards,' he wrote, 'of the spot where Cambridge Street joins Broad Street, there were upwards of five hundred fatal attacks of cholera in ten days.' The pump at Broad Street, which many households used for their drinking supply, was extracting water from a well into which cesspools were leaking. The epidemic there ceased when the parochial authorities, informed by Snow, removed the handle from the pump.[35]

It was Snow too who went on to connect the large number of deaths in south London with the water supply. There were two main water companies involved – the Lambeth, and the Southwark and Vauxhall. It was the consumers of Southwark and Vauxhall water who suffered most in 1853–4. The reason was clear. The Lambeth company had recently switched its supply to new waterworks at Long Ditton. The Southwark and Vauxhall drew water straight from the Thames at Battersea and from there ran its lethal waters direct to people's homes.

The state of the Thames in the 1850s was horrible to contemplate. Contemplation, though, was unavoidable. It forced itself on Londoners' attention. It was indeed 'a stream of death, instead of a river of life and beauty'.[36] For London, over countless generations, had not so much turned its back on that unlovely river as its backside.

The Thames had never been entirely clean, of course, and even in the early years of the century the river had been black and stinking close to Blackfriars Bridge – not that far from the London Bridge waterworks, from whose wooden pipes the City drew its water until the late 1820s. Even so, it was clean enough for a seven-foot sturgeon weighing 160 pounds to be caught at Greenwich in 1802, and for some sort of fishing industry to be sustained at Lambeth until around 1830.[37]

But by the 1850s there were some sixty sewer outlets into the river. The Fleet, eighteen feet across, was the biggest. All vomited filth into the tideway. The sewage deposited 'black mud' on the river bed. At low water the 'fetid' mud at Millbank, for instance, stretched 140 yards from shore to water-line. In the hot summer of 1858, the 'Great Stink' drove MPs from their committee rooms facing the river and Dickens wrote to Lausanne that 'the Thames at London is most horrible', the stench having 'a most head-and-stomach distracting nature'.[38] That same summer Goldsworthy Gurney surveyed the Thames by boat.

I found that the principal stench came from the discoloured black water by the sides of the river, discoloured by sulphuretted hydrogen acting on organic matter; that no smell came from the water when we got into the middle, which was comparatively of a pure appearance . . . I found the colour and smell eased off, or ceased just below Blackwall; between Blackwall and Woolwich . . . the colour of the water changed there, and it became a clay-like water; there was a urinous smell with it for some distance . . . I traced it up the river, and I found that the black colour died off somewhere about Putney, or a little above Putney; then the yellow tint.[39]

So Thames water was black at the river's edge from 'insoluble sewage' for some eighteen miles, right through the built-up area and spilling out on either side. The Southwark and Vauxhall Water Company took its whole supply from this black water stretch and so, to a lesser extent, did other London water companies. Hence the spread of cholera, or a great deal of it. And hence something had to be done.

But, oh, the querulousness, the doubts, the vacillation, the personality clashes and party jealousies, the almost endless time-wasting before anything eventually *was* done. In looking back 150 years on the achievements of this mid-Victorian period from 1855 to 1875, we are apt to forget two things. That, in general, they took years too long to accomplish; and, in general, they were very equivocal achievements indeed. The first is true of the Victoria Embankment; and both are true of the Metropolitan Drainage Scheme, of which it was a vital part.

John Martin's innovative idea from the 1830s of intercepting sewers slumbered until 1845. It was then resurrected by Thomas Wicksteed, engineer to the East London Waterworks Company. In 1849 it became the policy of the new Metropolitan Commission of Sewers – an appointed body responsible for sewerage outside the City – that 'sewage should be kept out of the Thames altogether'. But the commission couldn't agree on a plan for doing so. It advertised for proposals, received 116, couldn't choose between them and resigned. In January 1851 came a breakthrough, of sorts. Frank Forster, the new commission's engineer, came forward with a plan for a series of intercepting sewers running east-west across London on either side of the river. Sewage in the low-level sewers nearest the Thames would be pumped up to the higher-level sewers, whence it would fall by gravity to outfalls at Galleon's Reach. In so far as this, with variations, was the scheme eventually built, Forster's plan was indeed a breakthrough. But it too was shelved for lack of money, and then became the subject of doubt and dispute when one of the commissioners put forward his own scheme. So it was one more opportunity squandered. Forster's 'health gave way under the anxieties of his position'. He resigned and died soon after.

He was replaced in 1852 by Joseph Bazalgette. Born at Enfield in 1819, Bazalgette had qualified as a civil engineer in 1838 and had at first worked on railway schemes. In 1849 he was Assistant Surveyor to the Commission of Sewers, until promoted on Forster's resignation. Bazalgette inherited Forster's plan. He worked on and improved it, and submitted it to the commission in 1854. But a new proposal by the General Board of Health to separate foul and surface water drainage in London once more paralysed the commission by giving it a choice of proposals to pursue.

Then in 1855 London local government was restructured. A London-wide Metropolitan Board of Works (MBW) was established that December. It now became the sewerage authority for the whole of London, including the City. And it wisely appointed Joseph Bazalgette as its engineer.

This really was a turning point, but it still took years to turn. Sir Benjamin Hall, architect of London government reform and First Commissioner of Works and Public Buildings in Palmerston's Liberal government, called in Bazalgette's scheme and declared it unlawful. Arrogant, controlling, meddling and bullying, Hall muddied already black water by having Bazalgette's scheme scrutinised by rival engineers. Professional jealousy, idiotic power games and bureaucratic obstruction frittered away another two and a half years. Eventually it fell to Benjamin Disraeli, the new Chancellor of the Exchequer in Lord Derby's Conservative government, to push through a change in the law and to find £3 million for the MBW and Bazalgette. That was the August of 1858, and the Great Stink was invigoratingly fresh in Parliament's nostrils.[40]

Work began straight away. By 1863 the sewage of the northern suburbs was already being intercepted and discharged into the river at Barking Creek. In 1864 the same arrangement was in place for the southern suburbs, draining to the outfall at Crossness. But two-thirds of London's sewage was still finding its way into the river. And this was because the low-level sewers could not be built until the Thames embankment was ready to receive them.

Here too there was a last-minute failure of nerve and confusion of roles. In 1860 a House of Commons select committee had recommended that at last an embankment be constructed on the northern shore and that the MBW design and build it. But a year later a royal commission proposed giving the job to 'a body of Special Commissioners', a recipe for chaos given that the MBW's sewer and the embankment had to be built together. The MBW managed to persuade government that this would indeed be a nonsense and an act giving it the necessary powers resulted in 1862. Buying the complex wharfage interests took two years. Works on the Victoria Embankment began in 1864 and took six years to complete.[41]

There was one final complicating factor. As we saw, the 1863 Select Committee on Metropolitan Railways had urged a new and wider exclusion zone for railway development. Within this area only underground lines would be permitted. In particular the select committee recommended the creation of an 'inner circuit' of underground railways which would connect the various London mainline termini, including those to be built on the north bank of the Thames as part of the extension of the southern railways.

It was the new Victoria Embankment that made this possible. Here, instead of cutting through some of the most expensive property in London, was a priceless opportunity to run the railway under what had formerly been the river bed. It would carry the southern portion of what eventually became the Circle (and District) Line. The Metropolitan District Railway Company obtained its powers in 1864 almost as the Victoria Embankment's first stone was laid. For the next six years the MBW would fume at the inability of the railway to move fast enough. At first there was the shortage of capital; then the need to amend the 1862 act to widen the embankment at the City end to accommodate the underground. During the delay that followed, the final cholera epidemic ever to hit London caused a further 5,596 deaths in the summer of 1866, with 70 per cent of them in the East End: the East London Waterworks Company had continued to take its water from the sewage-polluted River Lea.

Eventually, though, all was complete. The finest improvement of the Victorian age was opened by the Prince of Wales on 13 July 1870. The monarch whose name the great quay bore wished to do it herself but was indisposed. The Albert Embankment, on the south bank and mainly a flood prevention scheme, had begun in 1866 but – with no railway

– was finished much faster, opening in November 1869. The Chelsea Embankment, taking the Victoria Embankment and Millbank on to Battersea Bridge, was opened in May 1874. It was some time in 1875 that Bazalgette's great Metropolitan Drainage Scheme could be considered fully operational, seventeen years after it had begun.

Elsewhere things were 'likewise really getting on'. The Metropolitan Railway had cut a swathe through Bayswater to Gloucester Road and South Kensington by 1869. And the District moved east from South Kensington through Sloane Square, Victoria and Westminster. Trains ran from Paddington through South Kensington to Mansion House from July 1871. In the absence of investment in new railway projects, however, the 'Inner Circle' would not be completed until October 1884, when Mansion House and Moorgate Street were finally connected.[42]

It is worth noting two important ends left untied by Bazalgette's great scheme. First it was undersized for the volume of water coming into the system and was never designed to cope with unusually heavy storms. These caused raw sewage 'of a very offensive character' to be shot into the Thames when storm valves opened to relieve pressure on the sewers. And it was this that failed to solve the problem of flooding in heavy rain that affected parts of London into the late twentieth century. Second, the untreated sewage put straight into the Thames at Barking and Crossness caused stench and a build-up of black mud downriver from London in the 1860s and after. This would only be mitigated in the 1880s by new treatment works which sanitised the effluent before discharge into the river.

So even here, a mean-spirited reluctance ever to put enough capital into public works tarnished the very greatest of London's civic achievements of the nineteenth century after 1830. It would carry on doing so till the century's end.

Ancient and Modern, 1875–1899

From 1855, then, the building of modern London was led by the Metropolitan Board of Works – with help for a decade or two from the railway companies and their land-grabbing, trench-cutting ways. It had assistance too, especially until 1875, from that much maligned dinosaur of municipal administration, the City Corporation. But the MBW had so much more of old London to contend with. All that great ring of seventeenth- and eighteenth-century London round the City and south of the river was its domain. It stood defiantly in the way of modern London. To deal with it the MBW had one old weapon and one new.

The old weapon, in use for the whole century but especially since the late 1830s, was street improvements. They took place all over London, from Garrick Street (opened in 1861) onwards. The most important of these schemes for old London were Clerkenwell Road through Theobald's Road (finished in 1878) and the so-called Western Improvements, involving the construction of Shaftesbury Avenue and Charing Cross Road, and the widening of Coventry Street. These were sanctioned in 1877 but not completed until 1886–7. Costs and delays were extended by a new obligation on the MBW to build tenement flats to make good the accommodation destroyed. Pressures on the MBW to take as little land as possible and then to spend frugally on what replaced it contributed to the particular meanness of these important West End streets. They were shabby, narrow and undistinguished. Of all the missed opportunities to add to the grandeur of Nash's London this was the most abject. Indeed, the ineptitude with which Shaftesbury Avenue was allowed to join Piccadilly Circus ruined the symmetry of Nash's original and made a space which the language of geometry was inadequate to describe. Over 3,000 were evicted from some notorious places, including the whole of Monmouth Street, Seven Dials, celebrated as west London's old clothes' mart by Boz and others in the early years of the century.[43]

In all, between 1879 and 1897 over 12,000 were made homeless by the central street improvement schemes of the MBW and its successor from 1889, the London County Council (LCC). Over 10,000 were evicted in the 1880s alone. There were good traffic-relief reasons for all these ventures. But the apparent social gains of demolishing old housing – removing the causes of disease, scattering expensive paupers and breaking up districts where police found it hard to penetrate and crime could flourish – were of long-standing and equal importance. As Charles Booth said of Rosebery Avenue (opened in 1892), 'a double object was kept in view: to provide, in the first place, a good and direct thoroughfare leading from Islington . . . to the South-West; and secondly, to effect a clearance in some of the poorer streets and courts of Clerkenwell. Both objects have been realised . . .'[44]

This double object was apparent in other public projects of these years. It was most revealingly present when selecting the site for George Edmund Street's Gothic masterpiece, the Royal Courts of Justice, which opened in 1882. Lawyers had for years agitated for the co-location of the courts, spread over London from Guildhall to Westminster, in the old lawyers' rookery near Lincoln's Inn. When a royal commission reported in 1859 the site favoured was between St Clement Danes and Temple Bar, south of Carey Street on the north side of the Strand. Here lay some ancient pre-Fire places like Shire Lane (by then renamed Serle's Place), Hemlock Court, Boswell Court, Ship Yard – in all some 'thirty close, foul, and filthy courts, yards, lanes, and alleys'. The district was notorious for prostitution and low-life generally. In Serle's Place was 'Cadgers' Hall', a beggars' lodging house made of three interconnecting houses; and the 'Retreat', a thieves' lodging house, with secret passages 'into Crown Court, and so into the Strand'. Yet the presence of artisans and printers and law clerks, a quarter of the population not of the labouring class, reminds us how mixed even these 'very bad' areas were. Anyway, everything was swept away from 1866–8 for the Law Courts, although further muddle within government over whether they should go on the cleared site or on the new Victoria Embankment delayed the first stone being laid by six years. At last a monumental palace of law and order towered over the lawless courts and alleys that survived to the north around Clare Market. Many of the 4,200 evicted moved there.[45]

There was also one private-sector influence which was probably even more destructive than street improvements and great public projects. This was the intensification of commercial activity in the City which seeped more and more pervasively into its hinterland from the 1850s on. Between 1861 and 1891 the number of inhabited houses in the City and the northern ring around it (St Giles, Strand, Holborn, Shoreditch and Whitechapel) fell by nearly 20,000 or 30 per cent. The Royal Commission on the Housing of the Working Classes in 1884–5 received much evidence that 'the warehouses of the City of London are spreading over St Luke's and driving out the poor', and the same was said of Clerkenwell and south Shoreditch. The character of these inner areas altered radically from residential to commercial in the years between 1855 and 1885.[46]

Finally, the new element destroying old London was slum clearance. There had for a long time, of course, been a slum-clearance component to street improvements, but London had lagged behind other cities like Liverpool, Glasgow and Edinburgh in obtaining powers to clear those areas which were 'highly injurious to the moral and physical welfare of the inhabitants'.[47] In the debates in Parliament which led to the passing of the Artisans' and Labourers' Dwellings Improvement Act 1875, called the Cross Act after Sir Richard Cross, Disraeli's enlightened Home Secretary, this moral and physical duality was repeatedly stressed. The areas to be cleared would not only be unhealthy, they would be 'rookeries' where vice and crime flourished.[48]

Once these thieves' dens and brothels were cleared, new working-class flats – tenement blocks – would be built in their stead. But it was clear from the outset to all who knew anything about the matter that the people evicted from the slums would never find house-room in the new dwellings. First, because there was always a time-lag, sometimes a very lengthy one, between eviction and the new places becoming available; and people had to live somewhere in the meantime. Second, because the philanthropic tenement-block owners demanded regular rent payments, outlawed overcrowding and sought to apply rules of behaviour that were alien to the culture of the London poor.[49]

Twenty-five major slum-clearance schemes were carried out in London between 1876 and 1900 by the MBW and the LCC. They evicted over 39,000 people. But the evictions were not evenly spread across this last quarter-century. More than 17,500 were made homeless in the four years from 1878 to 1881, a time, too, of extensive street improvements in these very same areas.[50]

One of these schemes was in the Mint, substantially demolished surprisingly late on in the century by a combination of slum clearance and the new Marshalsea Road between 1881 and 1886. There was time, though, for the Mint to take a last bow. Its notoriety was revived in 1883 by a pamphlet called *The Bitter Cry of Outcast London* by a shady Congregational minister called the Rev. Andrew Mearns. It caused a sensation in the popular press by exposing life in the London slums as savage and incestuous. In the same year George R. Sims, a talented journalist and successful playwright, composed a number of articles with a similar theme for the *Pictorial World* and the *Daily News*, later reprinted as *How the Poor Live and Horrible London*. Both Mearns and Sims had visited the Mint in particular. They gave evidence about it to the royal commission of 1884–5, itself set up in the wake of the scandal they had provoked.[51]

The clearance of the Mint was small beer compared to later municipal ambitions. The greatest slum-clearance scheme of the century was carried out by the LCC in the 1890s. The Boundary Street scheme alone evicted 5,719 people from the Nichol Street area of south-west Bethnal Green and Holy Trinity Shoreditch. It had been a notoriously poor area for the whole century, its housing conditions in the 1860s 'a disgrace to civilisation'. Charles Booth thought that 'for brutality within the circle of family life, perhaps nothing in all London quite equalled the old Nichol Street neighbourhood'. Demolition and rebuilding here took many years. Even though there was some overlap between dwellings becoming available and evictions proceeding, just eleven persons from the old slums were housed in new dwellings on the site. The rest crowded as close as they could to their old homes. Just one in twenty residents subsequently traced had moved more than a mile away.[52]

On the Boundary Street site the LCC built a council estate of 1,069 dwellings, opened in March 1900 by the Prince of Wales. It was by far the biggest in London of its time. It would be a significant step forward in the making of modern London.

There had, though, been huge social and human costs in the assault on old London of which Boundary Street was a late and large example. The destruction of old London had involved across a century – most violently from about 1845 and with little or no abatement since – a class war of attrition, a social cleansing of inner London. At the core, creeping remorselessly, was the commercial expansion of the City into its hinterland in central London. Then, with increasing aggression from the beginning of Victoria's reign, the state – at first central and then local – worried and harried, from one street corner to the next, the troublesome London poor. So we see the abandoned slum children of St Giles, evicted in 1845 for New Oxford Street, moving into the Devil's Acre; cleared out again for Victoria Street around 1847, and perhaps again for its eastward extension in 1853; then, parents themselves by now, moved on by slum clearance from the Old Pye Street area nearby in 1880.

That this was a painful and alarming process the lawmakers knew well at the time. The Earl of Shaftesbury told the House of Lords so in the debates on Cross's Bill in May 1875.

It is vain to rely on the ample notice that is to be given to the inhabitants. They do not, and they really cannot, give heed to it. Occupied, as they are, day by day and hour by hour, they think only of the present; and they cannot afford time or loss of wage to run about in quest of other dwellings. And so when the moment arrives for the levelling of the domiciles in which they reside, they are like persons possessed – perplexity and dismay are everywhere; the district has all the air of a town taken by assault. Then they rush into every hole where they can be received . . . Every demand of health and decency is set aside . . .[53]

Ghastly though the housing was that they had left, the evictions caused living standards to fall through greater overcrowding in these central districts. We saw this in St Giles and Clerkenwell from the 1840s to the 1870s. By the 1890s, though, the expansion of London was able to provide more living space. This reduced some pressure on inner London housing. Even in a poor area like Clerkenwell, overcrowding diminished mainly because people were moving out for more and better accommodation in Islington and places nearby.[54]

At the end of the century old London still clung on in a hole and corner way behind the commercial façades of the wide streets cut through the slums, and a few steps away from the giant 'barracks' or tenement blocks towering over the neighbouring courts and alleys. In any of the notorious districts of 1800 hardly one had been obliterated in entirety. There was still a 'little district of ancient poverty' near Westminster Abbey; in Clerkenwell, 'Many old rookeries are gone, but others remain'; even in the remnants of the Mint in 1899, 'the palm for degradation was . . . still to be given to the group of old courts lying between Red Cross Street and the Borough High Street'.[55]

Remnants, though, they were. There was no longer the great impenetrable ring of narrow streets and lanes, not big enough for two carts to pass, or the stinking labyrinth of courts and alleys behind, that had seemed to go on for ever round the Cities of London and Westminster in 1800. And by 1899 London was a vastly different place in other ways too.

First, it was brighter. There were 30,000 gas-lit street lamps in London by 1850 and over 91,000 in an admittedly vastly bigger city by 1900. Supplementing these were the brilliantly lit windows and doorways of shops and gin palaces and public buildings. They were supplemented too – indeed, eased out – in the last fifteen years of the century by electric lighting. Experimental electric lighting had been demonstrated in London around 1858 but the idea lay dormant until the journalist and theatrical entrepreneur John Hollingshead brought apparatus from

Paris to London to light the outside of the Gaiety Theatre, Strand. His six arc lights, first lit in August 1878, cost him the enormous sum of £40 per week for nine months, 'until their novelty was a little worn off . . .' There were then installations on part of the Victoria Embankment, on Waterloo Bridge and at the British Museum around 1879. But once more a new venture proved slow to take. It was not until a privately run scheme to light the Grosvenor Art Gallery, New Bond Street, in 1885 that the true potential of the new lighting won popular approval. Surplus power from the gallery was sold to neighbouring shopkeepers and from there quickly became fashionable. From the early 1890s London local authorities began to produce electricity for street lighting in their own parochial generating stations. 'By the end of the century some 200 miles of [London's] streets and roads were lighted by electricity, and the light had become popular for factories, hotels, large warehouses, railway stations, trains and the houses of the rich.'[56]

Second, central London had become greener, although access to real countryside had become so much more difficult through the enormous expansion of the metropolis. The London parks were 'an ornament not elsewhere to be matched', according to Henry James, and they were added to in the new suburban London by protecting land from the builders (as, for instance, at Victoria Park in the east, opened in 1845, and Battersea Park in the south-west, opened in 1864). But of greater significance for London at the centre were a host of small local initiatives. Burials had ceased in City and central graveyards from the 1840s on, for urgent public-health reasons. Slowly the churchyards were reopened as public gardens, a movement especially strong in the 1880s and 1890s. Then some of the gardens of London squares were refreshed and opened to the public – as at Leicester Square in 1874, where the old 'Leicester Fields' had been for years a noxious dumping ground for rubbish and human waste. And public gardens were built into improvement schemes – as at Victoria, Albert and Chelsea embankments, and even in some slum-clearance schemes, like Wapping Recreation Ground in about 1886. Some ninety-five acres of green space were added to central London in this way, mainly in small pieces from 1880 on.[57]

Third, London was grander and airier. Many of the post-Nash street improvements may have disappointed by their stinginess in conception and implementation. But the grand scale of the embankment, of Victoria

Street and Queen Victoria Street were breathtaking for contemporaries. Even New Oxford Street and Charing Cross Road brought air and widened vistas to close-packed, stifling neighbourhoods. The same could be said for the scores of new and widened streets which transformed the feel and look of London on the ground.

Fourth, London was more mobile. There were two main reasons: the growth of London and functional change at the centre. As London grew, more and more Londoners lived further from the centre. And as the City and its fringes became entirely commercial, so jobs in central London increased in number. Therefore, in ever greater volume, people had to travel longer distances to work. In order to accommodate this growth – and the need to travel round London for work, pleasure and shopping – the volume of passenger traffic was enormous. In 1867, by local trains, the underground railway and the two principal omnibus companies, some 82 million journeys were made in London, 22.7 per head of population. In 1896, with horse trams adding to the available means of locomotion, the number of journeys was 682 million, 111.3 per head. Congestion on London's streets may not have been much eased, despite the number of new roads and the belated removal of obstructions like Middle Row Holborn (1867) and Temple Bar (1878). Even so, horse buses could average six miles an hour through central areas. And underground, and on the surface railways from the near suburbs, Londoners could average speeds of from fourteen to thirty miles an hour.[58]

Fifth, London was taller. Every new street of nineteenth-century London was lined with buildings which often towered over the structures behind by the equivalent of a storey or more. As the cycle of redevelopment affected the early street improvements – at New Oxford Street and Victoria Street, say – so the grand emporiums or hotels or offices or institutions or mansion blocks of the 1880s and 1890s added the equivalent of yet another storey by the century's end. The rising costs of inner London sites – it was said in the 1870s that a City man could recoup the cost of his new suburban home from the rent of one floor of his old central residence[59] – forced developers to build high. But prestige and bold self-advertisement demanded height too. The popularity of structural ironwork, another by-product of the railway age, made tall buildings more feasible and cheaper. The mid-century passion for Gothic drove turrets and spires high into the London air. And the slow acceptance in London of flats eventually helped push upwards the height of domestic architecture.

The first middle-class flats in London were built, six storeys high, at the Pimlico end of Victoria Street in 1853. But the mansion block did not at first catch on. For the workers, though, middle-class philanthropists and speculators increasingly built tenement blocks as the characteristically new form of London housing in the inner districts. They were given a further fillip in the 1870s from the Cross Act and the obligation to provide rehousing as part of street improvements. These great 'barrack' buildings, unpopular though they were among potential tenants, had become a common feature of the London skyline by 1890; at the end of the century charitable dwellings companies had built some 26,000 flats. They were joined in districts like Mayfair, Marylebone and Kensington by mansion blocks which obtained a belated popularity among middle-class tenants from the late 1880s on. Even the old houses of late-eighteenth century London grew in height. When ninety-nine-year leases fell in on the Portman Estate in Marylebone in 1888, Viscount Portman required an extra storey from leaseholders wishing to renew in the more desirable properties.[60]

Perhaps, though, the most striking instance of a taller London in working-class areas was the Board School. The School Board for London built some 400 permanent schools between 1870 and 1903. Many of these were great three-decker buildings on large plots. They loomed like fortresses over their 'catchment areas', beacon or penitentiary for the slum children in the courts and alleys far below.

Finally, London was up to date. Victorian architecture was famously varied in style, but one distinctive development marked out London buildings at the end of the century from those that had gone before. This was a radical shift in facing materials for almost all sorts of buildings, whether institutional or residential. Long gone of course, except in the suburbs, where it survived until the late 1860s, was Nash's 'plaster', that false-fronted stucco that so disgusted a more pious age. Gone, too, or just about, was the Italianate stonework of Charles Barry's Pall Mall and George Gilbert Scott's Whitehall; and the mock-medieval masonry of Barry's and Augustus Pugin's great Houses of Parliament and those scores of churches and public buildings got up in the Gothic style. In their place came something entirely different.

The new arrival was red brick and red (or sometimes yellow) terracotta. Well, not quite new, because red brick had been the popular building material of the late seventeenth and early eighteenth centuries in London. And in reviving these surfaces, which suffused late-nine-teenth-century London like the imperial colour on the map of the world, numerous 'old' styles were appropriately resurrected. Queen Anne, Dutch, French Renaissance, Romanesque, Byzantine, Gothic, Baroque, Scotch Baronial Gothic, Scotch Baronial Baroque: flights of fancy dressed in snatches of costume from the whole wardrobe of world architecture vied with one another in the same streetscape, quite often in the same structure.

Queen Anne style was the dominant voice, but speaking in conti-nental and early English dialects. Architectural historians date its birth to 1871 and a grand Bayswater house by J. J. Stevenson. But a better starting point is perhaps the house that William Makepeace Thackeray built for himself at 2 Palace Green, just behind Kensington Palace, between 1860 and 1862. This was 'the reddest house in all the town', according to Sir John Millais, the painter. And Thackeray's house was a loyal genuflexion to Queen Anne and her times from the man who had long coveted the role of historian to her reign and indeed the whole eighteenth century, picking up the story of English history where Thomas Babington Macaulay had left off.[61]

The fashion for red brick and terracotta decoration splashed out in every direction: in great public buildings, churches, theatres, offices, mansion blocks, even council estates and fire stations. The roll call of landmarks is extensive and distinguished: the Royal Albert Hall (Francis Fowke, 1871); the new St Pancras Railway Station and Hotel (Sir George Gilbert Scott, opened in 1874); Albert Hall Mansions (R. Norman Shaw, 1886); New Scotland Yard, Victoria Embankment (R. Norman Shaw, 1890); the Wigmore Hall (Sir Ernest George, 1890); the Weigh House Chapel, Mayfair (Alfred Waterhouse, 1891); the Boundary Street Estate (LCC architect's department, 1893–1900); the Prudential Assurance Company Offices, Holborn (Alfred and Paul Waterhouse, from 1899). There was much else, but greatest of all, perhaps, was John Francis Bentley's byzantine Westminster Cathedral (1895–1903). Even in many of those 400 Board Schools, the London School Board's architect E. R. Robson wove impressive variations on the Queen Anne theme.

As for the whole of the century, then, in moving forward even *fin-de-siècle* London looked nervously back. For some observers it was this characteristic that continued to give London a 'look as quaint, pictur-esque, and medieval as any old-world continental city', or so thought the young Arnold Bennett, a newcomer from the north, in 1897.[62]

But for old-timers it was the things lost and changed that struck home most. The London of Dickens 'is disappearing fast', wrote Justin McCarthy in 1891. 'There will soon have to be an edition of Dickens with copious explanatory notes on every page, or the younger readers will not know half the time what the author is talking about.' No one at the century's end could rely on anything from London's past surviving the house-breaker's pickaxe. St Mary-le-Strand was threatened with demolition in the 1890s. George Gissing visited Samuel Johnson's house at Gough Square, Fleet Street, in 1894 because it 'is shortly to be pulled down'. Percy Fitzgerald noted how – even in that age of red, and despite a nascent Georgian revival in parts of Westminster – 'the old Queen Anne bricks' were being every day brought down 'in showers of dust': 'These old buildings have few authorised friends or guardians beyond the amiable amateur.' In fact, St Mary-le-Strand and 17 Gough Square would be reprieved. But many others would go as the war on old London – which the nineteenth century began but could not finish – was waged into the early years of the new century.[63]

By that time, though, 'old London' encompassed a wider sweep. For in 1899 some of London which had not even been thought of in 1800, but which was newly built in the years of unparalleled growth that followed, was now tarnished and shabby and marked for destruction.

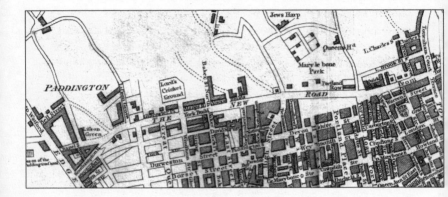

New Road, 1806

III

NEW ROAD: LONDON GROWING,
1800–1899

Cities of Palaces: Suburban London, 1800–1839

ON 3 February 1815 Leigh Hunt was freed from Horsemonger Lane
Gaol in the Borough after serving two years for a seditious libel on
the figure and morals of the Prince Regent. The ever-sensitive Hunt,
despite relatively luxurious treatment while in prison, had developed
agoraphobia.

> I am ashamed to say, that after stopping a little at the house of my friend
> Alsager [of *The Times*], I had not the courage to continue looking at the shoals
> of people passing to and fro, as the coach drove up the Strand. The whole
> business of life seemed a hideous impertinence. The first pleasant sensation I
> experienced was when the coach turned into the New Road, and I beheld the
> old hills of my affection standing where they used to do, and breathing me a
> welcome.[1]

They would not breathe so sweetly much longer. Hunt's coach had
already had to rattle over streets built up to – even across – the New
Road. The relentless march of London's edge would soon obscure the
northern heights in a dense carpet of slate and stucco, mortar and
macadam. By the end of the century those 'old hills' would merely exist
in the memories of men and women approaching the end of long lives.

    The enormous growth of London has been the central organising
fact of metropolitan history in the nineteenth century for most modern
commentators. So it was too for many contemporaries, at least from
1850 on. It was indeed astonishing, awesome, unprecedented in the

history of the world that a city should grow so big so fast. But London did not grow all of a piece, or all at one pace. There were three main periods, each with a particular character of its own.

The first, covering the four decades from 1800 to the end of the 1830s, was broadly bourgeois in tone, making its biggest push in the north and west, with its distinctive mode of communication the omnibus. The next four decades, a middle period of amazing hypergrowth, were broadly mixed and muddled in their class appeal, pushing in every direction at once in a frantic land-rush, with railways the engine of change. The last two decades, the 1880s and 1890s, saw still-vigorous expansion, this time most notably in the east, but with far greater maturity and precision in matching suburb to class, and once more with railways – aided by horse-trams – as its main iron-bound circulatory system. By then the appeal of the suburb had spread definitively to the lower-middle and artisan classes.

The outcome of all this was staggering. A built-up area some five miles across east–west and home to 960,000 people in 1801 had by the century's end swollen to the greatest city the world had ever seen. Now seventeen miles across. Now 6.58 million people, nearly seven times greater. This huge bulk would far exceed – in terms of the aggregation of humanity at least – anything that the next century would add to London.

London of course had never stood still. Even in 1800 it was on the move. And the city cast a forward shadow that darkened all around it. The edge of London was a stunted no man's land – 'neither of the town nor the country', Dickens called it – like necrotic tissue stealing remorselessly outwards from an unhealed wound. In 1800 the fields on which Bloomsbury would shortly be built 'lay waste and useless . . . the resort of degraded wretches, whose amusements consisted chiefly in fighting pitched battles, and other disorderly sports, especially on the sabbath day'. The same was true for the Five Fields, developed for Belgravia a few years later: 'rank grass and weeds in full luxuriance; bounded by mud-banks, and almost wholly given up to sheep and asses'. A shanty town of wooden hovels called Tomlin's New Town had desecrated Church lands in Paddington for forty years before Tyburnia was laid out in the 1830s. Squatters in vans and sheds camped out all over the urban edge: on the remnants of St George's Fields around 1800, for instance, at Bethnal Green or at Lock's Fields, Walworth. Here animal dealers lived in 'little huts, among dogs and fowls, rabbits, birds, and guinea-pigs; and surrounded with children, who all day long play in the dirt before the doors, and yet look as healthy and fresh in their filth as potatoes just turned out of the mould'. Brickfields, rubbish shoots and gravel pits were the commonest features of this 'blighted country'. At Battle Bridge, later King's Cross, great rubbish heaps – 'mountains of cinders and filth', 'hillocks of horse-dung', and piles of stinking 'waste grains and hop-husks' shot there by the London brewers – had accumulated over generations. The cinder mountains were said to have been sold to the Russians for brick-making to help rebuild Moscow after 1812.[2]

This transitory landscape pressed further and further out as the city grew. And Dickens's description of Holloway, a couple of miles from Battle Bridge and written fifty years on, can stand for the appearance of London's edge right across the century: 'a tract of suburban Sahara, where tiles and bricks were burnt, bones were boiled, carpets were beat, rubbish was shot, dogs were fought, and dust was heaped by contractors . . .'[3]

Land like this invited development. So London edged out slowly, adding street after street to its built-up area, even in the hungry years of the Napoleonic Wars, when money was short and investors' nerves frayed. This was less a suburbanising movement in areas like Clerkenwell, Stepney or Bermondsey than a snail-like creep forward of the urban fabric. More often than not these were new-built slums, brick and clapboard shanties with no drains and infrequent water supply and no better than the old London from which they oozed. As at Bethnal Green, where 'Stagnant foetid filth perpetually covers the bouldered footway . . . The privies are full, exposed, and overflowing, and the soil covers the front plots, in which heaps of filth are accu-mulated.' This was a haphazard process that left many gaps. So that when Sydney Waterlow, later a notable London philanthropist, was born a 'small weakling' at Finsbury in 1822 he was sent to live with his grandmother 'in the country' – at Mile End.[4]

London's suburbs grew in other ways. In south London, the roads driven into the country by the bridge companies at Southwark, Waterloo and Vauxhall encouraged first ribbon development along the highway and then speculation in the fields between, so that by the end of the 1830s north Lambeth, Kennington and Newington were largely built upon or cut up for building, and development had pushed south to Walworth New Town. Many of the streets behind the stately tall houses on either side of the main roads were of poor quality, run up for labourers, artisans and the cheapest sort of clerk. And much remained cheek-by-jowl with wasteland or marshy meadow that had not yet attracted the builders' notice.[5]

More important in the early period, though, was the engorgement of hamlets, villages and country towns just beyond London, especially in the north and west, and to a lesser extent south of the river. These were swollen by City men demanding country living away from the inconveniences of old London. This was well established by 1800, and it is clear that the search for a house in the country spanned a wide radius. When Mr L, 'an eminent stockbroker', shot himself over money troubles at his Cornhill counting house in April 1808, he had ridden 'to town that morning from his villa in the country, about fourteen miles distant'. Around 1815, Sir Richard Phillips noted 'that feature of modern manners which leads thousands of those who are engaged in the active business of the metropolis to sleep, and to keep their families, in neighbouring villages'. Before nine o'clock came the clerks; from nine to eleven shopkeepers, stockbrokers, lawyers and principals; from twelve 'saunters forth the man of wealth and ease'. The early ones walked, the later rode on horseback or in coaches, gigs and chaises. By the late 1820s, crime in the City was thought to have grown because shops and warehouses were deserted at night through 'the habits of the citizens, who live so much out of town', a practice that had 'increased wonderfully' in the past twenty years.[6]

This swelling out of places around London to make what from 1821 William Cobbett called 'The Wen' (or tumour) was apparent in every direction. It involved not just the accretion of new dwellings to old hamlets, but extensive ribbon development along the roads between them and to and from London. In Hackney, in the north-east, for instance, where Clapton, Dalston and Stamford Hill were popular among the merchant class. In Lower Holloway, in the north, where small villas for higher clerks started being built from the beginning of the century. In Gospel Oak and Kentish Town, in the north-west, for a middling class of solicitors, architects, manufacturers and the like. In the west, the 'Old Court Suburb' of Kensington and the villages of Knightsbridge and Brompton were favoured by 'nobility, gentry and clergy' seeking fresher air than Mayfair could now provide. And in the south, Camberwell and Clapham were popular rural retreats for the upper middle classes, the latter an earthly paradise for Anglican evangelicals.

As late as 1837 Champion Hill, Camberwell, was 'so retired, so tranquil'; and so was nearby Peckham Rye.[7]

When City men helped fill out these satellite villages they came to places with an already marked class structure of their own. So that Edgware in the 1820s, not too far out to be touched by the suburbanising urge, was home to 'Generally poor, labouring people; agricultural labourers principally'. And Chelsea – which Dickens could describe as 'in the country' in 1838 – contained every social grade from riverside driftwood finders to London's artistic (though hardly pecunious) elite. This hereditary mix would contribute to the complexities of class in London's suburbs as they grew beyond compare from the 1840s on.[8]

Last and most important, there was one further influence pushing at the boundaries of London in these early years. The creeping development at London's edge, and in the villages and places beyond its shadow, had been both opportunistic and piecemeal. But 1800–1840 also witnessed a revival of eighteenth-century ideas of town planning, focused on the exploitation of great estates adjoining London.

The foundation was laid in the very first year of the century by the fifth Duke of Bedford on his Bloomsbury estate.[9] The development of Bloomsbury north of Great Russell Street had begun in 1776. Its highest achievement in the last quarter of the eighteenth century was Bedford Square, the first great planned London square since the Covent Garden Piazza of the 1630s. But the true era of London squares was the early nineteenth century: 434 of London's 461 squares listed in 1928 were built between 1800 and 1850.[10]

The new era opened in 1800, when Tavistock Square was begun. So was Russell Square, on the site of the mid-seventeenth-century ducal mansion Bedford House and its enormous garden. The Bedford Estate office prescribed the character of the dwellings to be built and specified materials. It then made building agreements with contractors, who undertook to build as the office required. When completed, the estate offered the houses on ninety-nine-year leases to the contractors or their nominees (perhaps subcontractors or suppliers as a means of deferred payment). To ease cash flow, the estate loaned the builders money on mortgage, and the first few years' ground rents were set at a peppercorn. The largest builders in Bedford's Bloomsbury, and on the neighbouring Foundling Hospital Estate east of Southampton Row, were the energetic but wily James Burton in the first twenty years of the century, and the visionary Thomas Cubitt in the next twenty. Burton and Cubitt were generally responsible for the design of façades. But the layout of squares – Russell, Bloomsbury, Tavistock, Gordon, Woburn, Torrington, Brunswick, Mecklenburgh – and the streets connecting them, were all planned by the Bedford or Foundling Estate offices.

The ninety-nine-year leasehold system, largely peculiar to London, Wales and Cornwall and traditional on crown, aristocratic and Church lands, was blamed for the poor condition of much metropolitan housing towards the end of the century.[11] The leasehold system discouraged investment in houses with only fag-ends to run on the lease, or those houses built only to last the life of a short term. And it often failed to control sub-letting to 'house-knackers' or 'house-screwers', who maximised rent yield at the expense of dilapidated property. But on the Bedford, Grosvenor, Bishop of London and other estates it could also be used as a bulwark against social decline and physical deterioration, at least when supervised by an active estate surveyor or architect.

But no system could circumvent the swing of fortune in the business cycle. And Bloomsbury is a salutary example, from the very beginning, of how plans were frustrated and undermined by boom and bust in the nineteenth-century economy. So building raced ahead from 1800, reduced to a trickle from about 1806, boomed again from 1820 to an unprecedented peak in 1825, slumped the next year and was flat through the 1830s. It is for this reason that building on the Bedford Estate, starting in 1776, remember, did not finally end till 1860. It took some twenty-five years to finish Tavistock Square. Gordon Square's plans were devised in 1829 but the last brick wasn't laid until over thirty years later. To the north-west of the Bedford Estate, Fitzroy Square – begun around 1789 – seems to have remained unfinished until 1835. These were typical timescales until the 1840s, and frequently beyond. We should bear in mind, as one of those pervasive elements of metropolitan life like smoke and stench, that suburban London had an unfinished, transitory feel about it for generations at a time. You could live a lifetime in a London suburb and never see it finished.

This was one component in deterring potential tenants. But there were others. Bloomsbury, an aristocratic speculation designed with aristocrats in mind, never achieved the fashionable name it sought. By 1830 there was too much competition further west, and far away from the taint of shop that Bloomsbury had acquired. So the Bedford Estate never quite hit its mark. Thomas Trollope, elder brother of Anthony, was born in brand-new Keppel Street in 1810, his father a barrister. That was typical of early Bloomsbury, a big-wig lawyer's colony on the country side of the Inns of Court. But by 1820 houses there were being let out in rooms and around 1835 'all the district . . . became rather deteriorated in social estimation'. In *Vanity Fair* (1847–8) it is all little short of an embarrassment, a butt for snobs, where 'the Park Lane shoulder-knot aristocracy wondered more and more that such a thing [Amelia Sedley] could come out of Bloomsbury . . .'[12]

There was one more element in Bloomsbury's fall from grace. It was planned as a new town but smacked too much of the old town from which it emerged. It was just too urban and, because its planning was rooted in the 1770s, too old-fashioned. All this was quickly made plain. For at the time its building stalled, during the last ten years of the Napoleonic Wars, a truly suburban area was being planned and built that offered an entirely fresh alternative to metropolitan existence.

This was Regent's Park and the adjoining Eyre Estate at St John's Wood. The latter can reasonably be honoured – or despised – as the birthplace of English suburbia, at least in its familiar semi-detached form. That was the revolutionary design by an unknown hand set out for the Eyre Estate as early as 1794. Its imaginative layout was never adhered to when building tentatively began from 1808. But the semi-detached ideal, with its grander detached neighbours, survived to become the dominant building form in St John's Wood until development was largely complete, around 1830. James Burton was busy here too. And just like Bloomsbury, development was erratic. It stalled in 1812, when uncertainty over the line of the Regent's Canal from Paddington to Limehouse stopped house building at the northern end of the estate. It picked up briefly after the war, but didn't truly recover momentum until 1819. Demand for houses in 'the Wood' was never rampant among the nobility but the estate had strong appeal from the beginning among the new rich, especially men successful in the arts and professions, finance and trade. And it early bore a reputation for loose-laced easy virtue which it sustained till the century's end, as we shall see.[13]

It was ironic that the Regent's Canal project had caused St John's Wood to stumble, for the publication of John Nash's plan for the Regent's Park in 1812 seemed to guarantee commercial success. Here, in the fields just next door, the Regent proposed to build a suburban palace with space for his friends' country villas. This was the northern end of Nash's magnificent design which connected town and country along the noblest street in Europe.

But the plan changed over time. The idea of a palace was dropped and fewer grand villas (or small country mansions) were allowed into the park. Even so, the wonderful terraces at Park Crescent and Park Square, south and north of the New Road; York, Cornwall, Clarence and Hanover Terraces and Sussex Place along the south and west of the park's outer circle; and Chester Terrace and, the scheme's 'crowning glory', Cumberland Terrace on the east all combined to make a new town, even city, of 'dream palaces'.[14] It was a city, too, designed with an eighteenth-century conception of social cohesion. It had new barracks for cavalry – indispensable in those years before the New Police. It had a working-class quarter with its own market, to which a spur of the canal brought fresh produce from the market gardens of Middlesex and Berkshire. And it had, along the lines of St John's Wood, 'a miniature "garden suburb"' of individually designed villas in every available architectural style and none, for the modern-minded London bourgeoisie, at Park Village, East and West. The palaces and villas were dressed in stucco, the workers' colony in brown brick. But all sorts and conditions of men could take their leisure in the great park when it eventually opened in 1838. Never again would those with influence on London's suburbs aspire to construct a metropolitan microcosm on the city's edge.

With very different intent, the decision to remove the Regent's palace from Carlton House to Buckingham House helped two great aristocratic new towns to establish themselves on the unbuilt extremities of the West End.

The first of these was Belgravia, on land owned by Lord Grosvenor (the Duke of Westminster) where the Five Fields south of Knightsbridge virtually abutted the garden wall of the rebuilt Buckingham Palace. The speculative opportunities of this land south of Hyde Park had been talked about since the 1790s, but it needed George IV's choice of Buckingham House for his palace to guarantee the fashionability of a new town which would push out the London boundary to join Chelsea and Kensington. The Grosvenor Estate office, and its architects Thomas Cundy, father and son, and Thomas Cubitt, the greatest London builder of the nineteenth century, ensured that this was an area fit for princes by birth or by pocket.

The estate leased the whole of the Five Fields to Cubitt around 1824, although a year later he assigned the land for Belgrave Square to other speculators in order to lay off risk – Cubitt was active at the same time in almost every other expanding metropolitan district. Even so, he remained the main builder for the square, working to the designs of George Bashevi. Its first house was occupied in 1828 but the whole wasn't finished until 1840. Eaton Square was, like most of the rest of Belgravia, designed by Thomas Cubitt or his brother Lewis on a less grand scale than Bashevi's venture. It was begun in 1827 but not finally completed until 1853. So even here the half-finished feel of an area in transition dragged on for a couple of decades at least. It needed every complaisance of estate office and contractor to attract credit-worthy tenants to a 'new Settlement' where substandard lighting and unmade roads rendered them vulnerable to footpads and accidents.

At the end, though, the classical stucco palaces and mansions of Belgravia triumphantly captured the market they aimed for. The 'richest population in the world, Belgravia', it was said in 1851. Its residents could afford to pay highly for the privilege of living in the city's best-connected new town. A ninety-nine-year lease in Belgrave Square, for instance, could cost £12,460 in 1833, with the house only ready for occupation four years later. *Haut-ton* was secured by such high prices – as well as by eight bars and gates across the streets, keeping out unfashionables, among the last to be removed in London in the early 1890s. Here the post office directory read like an appendix to *Burke's Peerage*, and commoners had to make up in wealth anything they lacked in bloodline. So that between 1828 and 1859 the mansion at the south corner of Belgrave Square, number 24, was taken first by Thomas Kemp, the millionaire developer of Brighton's Kemp Town, then passed to Lady Drummond, then the Marquis of Tweeddale, then Lord Hill – the commander-in-chief of the army – after him Earl Ducie and finally Earl Brownlow. Perhaps nothing encapsulates Belgravia's cachet so much as the Duke of Bedford choosing as his town mansion 6 Belgrave Square rather than anywhere on his own estate.[15]

What happened in Belgravia from 1825 no doubt served to whet the appetites of other landowners at the western edge of London. Prominent among these was the Bishop of London. The Church lands in Paddington west of Edgware Road and north of the Uxbridge (later Bayswater) Road had long been ripe for speculation. Since the 1750s the Church seems, by trickery and political manoeuvring, to have secured to itself lands previously held in common from time out of

mind. St George's Row and Connaught Place – grand terraces facing
Hyde Park to the south – were in place to the designs of Samuel Pepys
Cockerell, the bishop's architect, by 1807. But west of St George's Row
the 500 or so 'miserable huts' of Tomlin's New Town were an impudent obstacle to expansion. And further development seemed unpro-
pitious until the building boom of the 1820s and the proven success
of Belgravia across the park.

So in 1827, the year of his death, Cockerell produced a plan which
not even Nash, let alone Cundy and Cubitt, could rival. This was
Tyburnia – named after the stinking brook and traditional London
gallows which had before 1783 been set up where Connaught Place
now stood. Unsurprisingly it was a name that didn't stick for long.[16]

Building only got under way in 1837. It began at Hyde Park Gardens
and moved north. By 1839 half of the estate between Uxbridge Road and
Grand Junction Road (later Sussex Gardens) had been laid out and part-
built. Like Belgravia, this ecclesiastical speculation attempted to entice
the aristocracy from eighteenth-century Mayfair and disappointing
Bloomsbury. But it merely succeeded in attracting the super-rich, the
newer the better. Thackeray, nervously tuned to the frequencies of class,
had cause in early 1843 to make a call in Tyburnia. He met

a kind handsome exceedingly vulgar woman who drops her h's over one of
the handsomest drawing rooms you ever saw: pillars, marble, stained glass,
hot and cold water all the way up the house and beauties innumerable. Squares
upon Squares are springing up in the old quarter, and little Albion Street now
lies shirking behind long rows of palaces, which have well nigh got to Bayswater.

A decade later and Thackeray could pinpoint Tyburnia – whose virtues
Dickens extolled as 'beyond question the healthiest part of London' – as
'the quarter of the city which the Indian world at present inhabits', where
nabob splendour found a fitting backdrop. The quality and grandeur of
its urban landscape would always ensure it maintained high caste.[17]

But how did these new suburbans get to town? By an entirely new
transport system. For the 1820s saw a new beginning in metropolitan
communications through the omnibus, a Parisian (and hence chic) innovation on London's streets from around Christmas 1828. The first
proper service was established by George Shillibeer, an enterprising
Bloomsbury mourning-coach builder with business connections in Paris,
on 4 July 1829. It ran from Paddington Green, a half-mile or so north

of Tyburnia, to the Bank. And the roads on which the omnibus ran were better than ever before. New suburban highways in west and north London (like Goldhawk Road, Camden Road and Seven Sisters Road) were built by the Metropolitan Roads Board from 1827, who also began to free the old roads from turnpikes and tolls.[18] The typical London two-horse omnibus carried twenty-two passengers, twelve or thirteen inside and the rest outside (on top). At first the 'busses' as they were called after a year or two, augmented the small army of short-stage or hackney coaches which formerly dominated public transport from the City and West End to the suburbs. The omnibus passenger was predominantly bourgeois or lower middle class – fares were high, usually 6d. And the profits to be made from omnibus routes stimulated rival companies, especially after the hackney coach monopoly was legislated against in January 1832. By the end of the 1830s every suburb was connected to central London by omnibus routes and by 1850 some 200,000 people were being carried daily.[19]

'These Outlandish Regions': Suburban London, 1840-1879

Tyburnia and the omnibus take us properly into the 1840s and another new era. Between 1801 and 1841 the number of occupied houses in what would later be the County of London grew from 136,000 to 263,000, or 32,000 on average every decade. Between 1841 and 1881 it grew by an average of 56,000 every ten years at an accelerating pace that peaked in the 1870s. If we include the land beyond the county to consider Greater London as a whole, the population doubled from 1,115,000 in 1801 to 2,235,000 in 1841; and more than doubled again to 4,767,000 in 1881.

If one element was more important than any other in attracting people to London and keeping them there, it was work. Apart from London's natural increase, disproportionately high because of the tendency to a younger population there than in the nation as a whole, London grew through immigration. Migrants came to London because the prospects for work were better there than anywhere else in the nation and even beyond. One great driver was the railway. It stimulated job creation directly and indirectly, as we saw in Chapter 2. Most railways led to London, and workers by brain and by hand followed in their wake. It is this holistic impact of the railways – rather than any simple read-off between railway lines and suburban growth – that marks the true measure of their dominance over London in these four decades. To this extent their influence on London's hypergrowth has been underrated by historians.

From July 1837, when the Birmingham Railway opened its first primitive terminus at Euston, London became rapidly connected with every part of the country. To Birmingham, Manchester and Liverpool by 1838. To the West Country from Paddington that same year. To most of East Anglia from Fenchurch Street and Shoreditch by 1844. To the south-west from Nine Elms by 1838 and Waterloo by 1848. To Brighton from London Bridge by 1841. To Paris as early as 1843 – there was a choice of eight different routes involving rail in that year. To Yorkshire, the North-East and Scotland from King's Cross by 1852. To the rest of the South-East and a fast route to the Continent from Victoria by 1860. To other parts of the Midlands and North from St Pancras by 1868. To Berkshire, Oxfordshire and the West Midlands from Marylebone by 1899. Even in 1850, before the Great Exhibition, *The Times* could claim, 'Thirty years ago not one countryman in one hundred had seen the metropolis. There is now scarcely one in the same number who has not spent the day there.'[20]

As we shall see, all this tripping would boost London's tourist industry from the 1840s on. And familiarity blew through some of the fog of mystique and apprehension deterring potential migrants to the city. There were other economic effects too. The increasing convenience of moving coal to London by train and goods like live meat, non-perishable foods, cottons, woollens and metals helped keep down the London cost of living, as well as the costs of London as a port and a manufacturing district for finished consumer goods. Some of these benefits were shared by London's hinterland. In Croydon, Thomas Frost noted 'social progress' and 'mental progress' brought by the railways in the 1840s and 1850s compared to twenty years before, partly due to an influx of new people and rapid access to entertainments and education in town.[21]

The direct suburbanising impact of the railways only began to have a major stimulating effect on London's growth in the 1860s, in combination with the last great railway boom. Until the early 1860s there was little evidence that the idea and practicability of suburban rail travel began to help pull people out of central London. Before then, London's growth in the 1840s and 1850s was more a quickening of the suburbanising urge that continued to rely on the omnibus. At this time its effectiveness was boosted by the formation of the London General Omnibus Company (LGOC) – at first a French venture but 'naturalised' in 1856. The 'General' colonised north London and left the south to Thomas Tilling and his rivals. Railway stations tended to follow the people moving out rather than new lines and stations planted in near-virgin territory drawing development to them.

By 1875, though, the symbiosis of suburb and railway was such that it was impossible to distinguish cause from effect. That year some 160 million journeys were made 'by people wishing to get from one part of the London area to another'. By the end of the century around 84 per cent of London's main-line termini traffic was suburban.[22]

What was the character of London's hypergrowth in these four decades? Outside the few remaining great estates, the London land-grab of 1840 to 1879 was a small speculator's dream, very often a nightmare. London building as a whole did not much pick up from the 1826 slump until 1842. A short rise then ended in 1846 but there was a strong recovery from 1848 to 1853, a slump again for the next four years and then from 1857 to 1868 an eleven-year boom of outstanding vigour.[23] The 1870s outpaced even this, adding over 68,000 houses in the county alone, 10,000 more than in the 1860s.

Speculation in London's suburban development took over from where railway speculation left off after 1846. It was a 'positive mania', with 'all classes entering the field'.[24] It was largely immune to changes in the price of money, which fluctuated considerably in these years. But the steady rise from the 1840s in bank and savings deposits, decade on decade, demonstrated an ever-growing capacity for investment in high-yield (though risky) building projects.[25] The more people having a flutter, the safer it seemed. And probably, over the long haul, most investors did well out of the process.

In all these four decades population grew faster than new housing supply in London county. But builders ran up houses although they knew they would be likely to stand empty for some time. Even empty houses provided, in theory at least, good security to borrow on mort-gage and build others in time for the market to pick up again. So 'over-building' was endemic in these years. And it would have an unfortunate effect on the social pretensions of London's suburbs, and indeed their physical condition, as we shall see in a moment.

The building process in the ring of meadow and farmland and market gardens outside the big estates was faithfully described to Henry Mayhew by a speculators' foreman or clerk of works in July 1850. For clarity he can't be improved upon.

'The party for whom I am foreman has just taken a large estate, and he contemplates making some thousands of pounds by means of the improved ground rents alone. There are several with him in the speculation, and this is the way in which such affairs are generally managed. A large plot of ground six or seven meadows, may be, somewhere in the suburbs is selected by the speculators as likely to be an eligible spot for building – that is to say, they think that a few squares, villas, and terraces about that part would be likely to let as soon as run up. Then the speculators [in the 1860s they would be called 'Field Rangers'] go to the freeholder or his solicitor, and offer to take the ground of him on a ninety-nine years' lease at a rent of about £50 a-year per acre, and may be they take as many as fifty acres at this rate. At the same time they make a proviso that the rent shall not commence until either so many houses are built, or perhaps before a twelvemonth has elapsed. If they didn't do this the enormous rent most likely would swallow them up before they had half got through their job. Well, may be, they erect half or two-thirds of the number of houses that they have stipulated to do before paying rent. These are what we term "call-birds", and are done to decoy others to build on the ground. For this purpose a street is frequently cut, the ground turned up on each side, just to show the plan, and the corner house, and three others, perhaps, are built just to let the public see the style of thing that it's going to be. Occasionally a church is begun, for this is found to be a great attraction in a new neighbourhood. Well, when things are sufficiently ripe this way, and the field has been well mapped out into plots, a board is stuck up, advertising "THIS GROUND TO BE LET, ON BUILDING LEASES." Several small builders then apply to take a portion of it, sufficient for two or three houses, may be, for which they agree to pay about five guineas a year (they generally make it *guineas* these gentlemen) for the ground-rent of each house. And when the parties who originally took the meadows on lease have got a sufficient number of these plots let off, and the small builders have run up a few of the carcases, they advertise that "a sale of well-secured rents will take place at the [Auction] Mart [at Bartholomew Lane until 1865, then rebuilt in Tokenhouse Yard, Lothbury] on such a day." Ground-rents, you must know, are considered to be one of the safest of all investments now-a-days; for if they are not paid, the ground landlord, you see, has the power of seizing the houses . . . there's a more ready sale for ground-rents than for anything else in the building line.'

In this way, and when fully built up and retained, a profit of £10,000 a year in ground rents could be made by the original speculators from an outlay of £2,500 a year. But, as here, it was more common for the original developers to capitalise on the potential of their speculation by selling out and moving on to the next rich pickings.[26]

Far from the orderly development of a suburb, this process bred chaos. In the 1870s, 80 per cent of London builders ran up fewer than six houses a year. They were among the most prone to bankruptcy of any group outside retail trade. Louis Bamberger, a prominent City timber merchant, found himself 'saddled' with built or half-built properties where builders could not afford to pay his bills. He found that to squeeze their own share of profit out of the speculation they had cut costs till their product was shoddy beyond belief. The floor joists in this cheap work during the 1870s were just 2½ inches by 6½ inches, 'all wane' – 'I don't suppose the newer generations have ever seen such a thing.' Notting Hill was the graveyard of so many ruined and absconding builders it was known as 'Rotten Hill'. Yet the taste of profit, and the sanctity of bricks and mortar, lured men from the trade they knew and into danger as a consequence. Like the draper who turned his hand to house building in Holloway and became one of the biggest developers there. But 'he came to grief, and the firm of solicitors who had been financing him lost the greater part of their fortune'. There was some silver lining, then, because solicitors were said, of any group, to have been those who screwed most out of the crazy system that built London's suburbs in these hectic years.[27]

In these areas there was no controlling hand, as in the landed-estate offices, to secure good-quality construction. Neither did things improve with the growth of building societies from the 1830s, or the freehold land societies from the 1840s and 1850s. These offered artisans and the lower middle classes the chance to combine small savings and buy an estate to cut into forty-shilling freehold plots and so gain the vote for parliamentary reform. But it all still relied on the small builder, as evanescent as London fog and just as pernicious. So houses might spring up on an estate at strange places and at odd times. And in this way a street might take twenty years to fill, a district forty years or more. These timescales were frequently met with in the earlier period. Now, though, the controlling aristocratic influence was absent. This was a free-for-all. And so the worst of these districts remained a half-lighted quagmire, stinking drains leeching into the subsoil, for the whole of the period until building was finished.

By far the greatest part of Victorian London that survived into the twenty-first century was the product of this speculative explosion from 1840 to 1879.

In the north, development spread from Regent's Park through Chalk Farm to Haverstock Hill. There was a solid mass of streets east from Chalk Farm linking Camden Town in the south to Kentish Town in the north. The semi-detached villas of Camden New Town at the south-west end of the Camden Road merged seamlessly into Lower and Upper Holloway in the west. Indeed Islington, with its great variety of districts, former hamlets each retaining their own subliminal character, was the north London phenomenon of these years. Even in 1841, with a long history as a suburban destination for City men and clerks, it was a substantial district of 8,500 houses and a population of 55,700. But by 1881 its housing stock had grown fourfold to 34,000 and its population was over five times larger at 283,000. If it had stood alone, Islington would have qualified as the sixth most populous town in England in 1881.

Further east, Hackney had gone the same way as Islington. Every available field had been built on, from De Beauvoir Town in the south-west to Victoria Park in the south-east. In the north development stopped more or less in a line from Stoke Newington Church Street to Clapton Station. Population growth here had also been remarkable, from 42,300 in 1841 to 186,500 in 1881. In the process, Hackney had become 'so essentially a London district' that it was now a 'comparatively unfashionable quarter'.[28]

In every case these north London suburbs were essentially mixed districts. There was a noticeable sifting and sorting by class but without any hermetic seals between them. The rich tended to live as far from old London as possible. The poor tended to live at the southern end, where the walk to work in central London was still manageable. But not all work was in the centre. From the beginning many of these great suburbs provided work of their own for artisans and labourers who lived nearby: slaughtermen at the Metropolitan Cattle Market in west Islington from 1855, for instance, and workers in the noxious trades of Belle Isle, just to the south; and the railway yards of Chalk Farm and the piano factories at Camden Town brought workers and their families to live nearby.

In east London, the real growth area was Poplar, especially the Isle of Dogs but also Bromley-by-Bow in the north. Poplar in 1841 contained

5,100 houses and 31,100 people. In 1881 it had grown fivefold to 156,500. This was predominantly a workers' suburb, attracted by the growth of docks and industrial sprawl along the rivershore. Even the dwellings were designed with the artisan in mind: of just two storeys, the main tenant living on the ground floor and letting out the two or three rooms above to lodgers, usually another family. Cubitt Town – named after William, its builder, Thomas's younger brother – was just such a district at the south-east tip of the Isle of Dogs. Over 80 per cent of its 1,000 or so houses were built between 1859 and 1867, with some further additions towards the end of the century.

It was in east London, too, that the earliest significant out-county development in London's history took place. This was at West Ham, whose population in 1841 was 12,700 but by 1881 had risen more than tenfold to 129,000. This was much more an industrial town than a London suburb, although some of its nuisance-causing industries were located here just because metropolitan by-laws banished them from London. So it contained an almost complete class mix (though without many super-rich), ranging from bourgeois and lower middle class (Forest Gate, Upton Park and the countryside round about) to artisan and labouring poor (Canning Town, Silvertown, Hallsville). Its main connections to London were the river and the railway, the latter certainly playing a large part in West Ham's growth from 1840: for a time Stratford was known as Hudson Town (after the 'railway king') when the Great Eastern Railway transferred its engine and carriage works there in 1847.[29]

Development south of the river in these years duplicates the picture in north London, though on a far smaller scale. In effect, this too was the urbanisation of what had been a mix of true suburban villages and ribbon development. The spatial pattern of the town – serried ranks of terraced houses or semi-detached villas, with little or no gaps between them – overwhelmed an originally rural environment which may have swollen over the years yet still retained much of its character until the 1840s. And it was assisted by suburban bridges that augmented London's traffic communications at Hammersmith (opened in 1827), Chelsea (1858), Lambeth (1862), Chelsea again (the Albert Bridge) and Wandsworth (both 1873). All except Chelsea Bridge were privately funded by share capital rewarded by tolls, until the bridges were bought by the Metropolitan Board of Works and made free of tolls, mostly in 1879.

In 1841 Camberwell had contained 6,800 houses and 39,900 people. But in 1881 its housing stock had risen fourfold to 27,300 and its population to 186,600. As in south London generally, the railway here seems to have had an important generative effect on development. 'Without a doubt the much-abused Chatham and Dover Metropolitan Extension Railway has done a great deal to bring about this result,' W. S. Clarke, the guide to London's suburbs, noted in 1881, 'but curiously enough no one seems to have anticipated it less than the company.'[30] The London, Chatham and Dover Railway would be a byword for the suburban traveller's nightmare for the rest of the century.[31]

Further west in south Lambeth, Brixton and Stockwell had gone the way of Camberwell and Peckham. Brixton was a suburb 'too regular in its architecture, too new in its associations, to suit the artist' but at least 'it is "genteel"'. Here too the railway was thought to have been a tremendous stimulus to the house builder: 'no station in London has a better service of trains' than Loughborough Junction, east Brixton, Clarke enthused.[32] Then Clapham had been built right up to the north side of the common, while retaining something of its suburban village feel. And Battersea had grown into a workers' colony around the railways at Clapham Junction and the London, Chatham and Dover Railway works near Queen's Road station. Development here really took off from the 1860s. And it incorporated a rare phenomenon, an estate of houses specially designed for the working man and his family – the teetotal working man in this case. The Shaftesbury Estate had its first stone laid by the evangelical peer of that name in 1872.[33] It would be the first experiment in workers' estates in suburban London and a model for many to come, mostly in the twentieth century. Then, out along the river, the Richmond and Windsor branch of the London and South-Western Railway did more to connect industrial Wandsworth and suburban Putney to London than the new bridges that crossed the river at those points. So development here had also to wait until the railways came in the 1860s.[34]

Crossing the river from Putney to Fulham, we enter the segment of London which in many ways displayed the most flamboyant expansion of all in these years – the west. These far-west districts at Fulham and Hammersmith, though, had merely begun to be grafted on to London. For the real growth points in the west were Kensington, Paddington and Westminster at Pimlico.

Pimlico had been prepared for building from the early 1820s. Thomas Cubitt spotted the potential of this land and began assembling a huge estate there. Its marshland was improved by importing soil from the excavations for St Katharine's Dock around 1828. Complicated infrastructural works of bridges over the Grosvenor Canal to link with Belgravia and of new sewers in the low-lying land delayed the first building until the mid-1830s. But the slump of that decade meant that development didn't really pick up until 1840 and after. It would continue, with stops and starts, for the next thirty years or so, well past Cubitt's death in 1855. 'Stuccoville' or 'Cubittopolis' to its detractors, 'South Belgravia' to its aspiring residents, plain Pimlico to the rest of London, this huge scheme was 'the largest single area of London developed by one man'. It would never attain the social status of its older and richer neighbour on the other side of the canal.[35]

The development of Paddington had properly begun with Tyburnia, but in 1841 its population was still compact at 25,200. Forty years on and it was over four times greater at 107,000. Here was a continuation of the great planned cities of palaces, as in Bayswater, with its spacious avenues at Westbourne Terrace and Gloucester Terrace, and in Maida Vale, its noble stucco mansions and detached houses, looking – with their Graeco-Roman columns and porticoes – for all the world like an imperial St John's Wood.

Kensington showed a similar, even sharper growth. In 1881 the population of the whole of Kensington was 166,300. In 1841 it had been 26,800. It had grown by more than six times and its housing stock by a factor of five. In North Kensington, Notting Hill Gate bordered Bayswater on the west, and west again was Notting Hill proper. Here were more great vistas along much of Ladbroke Grove, its spine, with Lansdowne and Stanley crescents forming a circus in the middle. But apart from the Ladbroke Estate, North Kensington lacked one overarching vision, and the district was let down – undermined – by the frequently poor quality of building. For a time it must have seemed like another Tyburnia in the making, but by 1881 Notting Hill had merged into Notting Dale and the Potteries district further west. And then into Shepherd's Bush in Hammersmith, where house property was on a less grand scale and similar to that being run up in Hackney, say, or Brixton. South of Notting Hill was the richest part of Kensington, around the 'Old Court Suburb' on either side of Kensington Church Street and west of Kensington Gardens and Palace;

and in Knightsbridge and Brompton south of Hyde Park. South Kensington in particular took off after the great museum district was put down on greenfield sites there with the proceeds of the Great Exhibition of 1851. Out of this came the South Kensington (later the Victoria and Albert) Museum, built in the grounds of Brompton House off Cromwell Road for the International Exhibition of 1862; the Royal Albert Hall, opened 1871; and the Natural History Museum, 1873–81. Surplus funds were spent on building stucco mansions nearby as the best investment for the future.[36] These were followed by the new-rich districts of Holland Park, Campden Hill and – most equivocal of all – Earl's Court.

From there Kensington merged with Chelsea, which had grown steadily from 1801 to 1871. Chelsea, because of its swollen-village origins, was a more mixed-class area than the plutocratic newcomer to the north. These southern districts of Kensington and parts of Chelsea would hold their attraction for London's super-rich and super-talented throughout the century, even if they were never generally so *haut-ton* as Mayfair and Belgravia. But the areas north of Bayswater Road and Notting Hill Gate proved much more dubious.

Before we consider why, it is worth pausing to look briefly at outer London at the end of the 1870s. For here, at all points of the compass (though much less so in the east), we can see in infancy a pattern repeating itself. Here the railway would be without doubt the main driver.[37] In the period from 1800 to 1840, Camberwell and Clapton and Holloway and Brompton had become suburbs while still retaining their rural and sequestered character for most newcomers. But from 1840 to 1880 they were urbanised, overrun, brought lock and stock into London. Now London was poised to march straight past them. In 1880 it was Acton and Ealing, Barnet and Finchley, Bromley and Bexley, Wimbledon and Kingston that made up the next generation of suburbs. By now they had begun to fill out. These in their turn would face – some more than others – incorporation into the insatiable city. That was a process which would take another sixty years to run its course.

Back to the troubled districts of Paddington and North Kensington. These areas displayed more graphically than anywhere else the folly of overbuilding in these years for a class that was never to move into the houses designed for it.[38] This was a problem everywhere within the great ring built up in these four decades. It was just more stark, more preposterous, in these north-west districts. One result of this over-building was that surprising feature, the brand-new suburban slum, where living conditions and the rough do-as-you-please behaviour of St Giles or Spitalfields or the Mint were transported, alive and kicking, to share London's suburban advantages with clerks and stockbrokers, curates and accountants. Often this was a single street or little area that had lost caste for some reason – stilted development over a number of years maybe, or bad building or miserly design. Such were the origins of places like Campbell Road, Holloway, 'the worst street in north London', or Sultan Street, Camberwell, or Litcham Street, Kentish Town.[39]

But sometimes whole districts went the same way. This was not just a phenomenon of these middle years of the century. The Lisson Grove area of Marylebone, just south-east of St John's Wood, had quickly turned into a slum almost as soon as it was built, after the Napoleonic Wars and in the 1820s. So did Portland Town, on the north-west of Regent's Park and again abutting St John's Wood, a rare example of an aristocratic estate where control over development slipped disas-trously from the very beginning. Both were described in 1828 as becoming 'filled with rogues and vagabonds', with Lisson Grove a 'second St Giles's'.[40]

The free-for-all period of London's suburban development threw up more of these districts, declassed ragged places from the start. The most notorious were in North Kensington, but Paddington also provided an extraordinary example south of the Grand Junction Canal. The Clarendon Street, Cirencester Street and Woodchester Street area contained grand houses 'built for a well-to-do class, and it is even now difficult to say why they have fallen so low', Charles Booth commented in the 1890s. 'Probably it has been mainly due to their being too tightly packed upon the ground.'[41] These streets appear to have gone wrong from the moment they were let. They would remain among the worst slums in London into the second half of the twentieth century.[42]

In North Kensington there were two large areas that had similarly never won the class of residents they had aimed at. Kensal New Town was developed in the 1860s and 1870s, its houses laid out in imposing though overlong vistas. One of the longest, Southam Street, was lined with tall stucco and brick houses, some with classical porticoes, and four or five storeys high. Yet from the outset, it seems, many of these were let by the floor or room to poor working-class lodgers. The few middle-class tenants comforted themselves by retitling the district Upper Westbourne Park – before moving on. To its detractors it was Soapsuds Island because of the numbers of women who took in washing there.[43]

Even worse, though, was Notting Dale, 'a perhaps unexampled concourse of the disreputable classes', a 'West-End Avernus' or hell on earth. This was a district intended once more for middle-class occupation. Bangor Street, one of its worst, had houses of ten rooms, and most of the rest were not much smaller. But it was doomed by its history. Potteries and brick kilns had long littered the ground in Notting Dale or nearby, and pig keepers had moved here from Tomlin's New Town when Tyburnia began to be built. The area was known as the Piggeries for this reason. It had a gypsy flavour, too, and George Borrow found one of the largest metropolitan 'gypsyries' here in 1864, just before redevelopment began. This rough population seems to have taken up lodgings in the new streets of Notting Dale, despite the best aspirations of its developer, as soon as the ground was built over in the late 1860s and 1870s. Soon no one else would live here. Its evil reputation blighted the Norland Estate to the south, the streets adjoining Notting Dale going the same way almost immediately; and so too the Bramley Road area to the north-west, in the heart of what had been known as the Potteries. In benighted Notting Dale, home to some 4,250 souls, thirty persons in a single house were commonly met with. Forty-three children out of every 100 born there would die before their first birthday as late as 1896.[44]

Notting Dale, Kensal New Town, the Clarendon Street area and other new-built slums of the 1860s and 1870s remind us of the great suburban contradiction that was especially acute in these years. The suburban ideal required both an improvement in living conditions and an escape from the insecurities of old London – stench, disease, the contact of poor people, crime. It promised cleaner air, a greener outlook, neighbours who shared one's values, respectability, privacy, security of property and person, and life à-la-mode. But this promise was sold short and became impossible to realise as the suburbs grew in area and density. Speculators sought to maximise profit by getting as many houses out of a plot as they could, while still maintaining the fiction of fashion and gentility and country living. The target class they pitched for just did not exist in the numbers necessary to sustain tone. So workers moved straight in or they filtered in as the early tenants left, taking a floor or room at a time, and applying punishing use to houses hardly built to withstand it. And the middle

classes, at least the middle and higher of them, would not stay long
where workers moved in.

Then virtually all the suburban building from 1840 was truly urban
in character. The houses may have been new – and that alone was a
major selling point because of the revulsion from old London. But they
seemed too much like town, packed as they usually were in long terraces
of tall houses with pocket-handkerchief gardens, sometimes just backyards. There was little of *rus in urbe* here, once the fashion for squares
had given way from 1850 to the passion for profit. And even when
there was 'country' to be had, it was often of that squalid edge-of-
town type represented by muddy lanes, pitch-black streets and blasted
fields. It was a lucky resident who did not have to live with these
inconveniences for a decade or more at a time: 'we reached a suburb
of new houses, intermingled with wretched patches of waste land, half
built over. Unfinished streets, unfinished crescents, unfinished squares,
unfinished shops, unfinished gardens surrounded us.'45

Worst of all, perhaps, the suburban ideal was undermined where it
hurt most – in the soul. Anti-suburban snobbery had a long tradition,
grounded in fears of new money – 'the mushroom aristocracy of trade'
– seizing for themselves the advantages of country living long claimed
by an aristocratic establishment.46 So the suburbs were satirised by
novelists like Thackeray as places 'whence you hear the sound of jingling
spinets and women singing'. Trollope captured in 1858 the horror with
which suburban living was regarded by the well-bred:

'Islington!' said the Honourable Mrs Val, nearly fainting.
'Is not Islington and St Giles' the same place?'47

All the charges that would later be thrown at suburbans were spelled
out by John Fisher Murray as early as 1844.

They are marvellously attached to gardening, and rejoice above all things in
a tree in a tub. They delight in a uniformity of ugliness, staring you out of
countenance with three windows in front, and a little green hall-door at one
side, giving to each house the appearance of having had a paralytic stroke;
they stand upon their dignity at a distance from the road, and are carefully
defended from intrusion by a body-guard of spikes bristling on a low wall.
They delight in outlandish and ridiculous names: a lot of tenements looking
out upon a dead wall in front, and a madhouse in the rear, club together, and
introduce themselves to your notice as OPTIC TERRACE . . . The natives of

these outlandish regions are less wealthy than genteel . . . they live here for
the benefit of their health – and fortune. When you visit them, they are eloquent
upon the merits of an atmosphere surcharged with dust, which they earnestly
recommend for your inhalation, under the attractive title of 'fresh air'.[48]

As the century played out, the intellectuals' rancour against the
suburbs and suburbans would only become more bitter. And by that
time there would be reason for an added dose of class hatred. For the
suburbans at the end of the century were very different from those at
the beginning.

The New Suburbans, 1880–1899

London grew more slowly in the last two decades of the century than
at any time since the 1830s. And population growth in the 1890s at
16.8 per cent for Greater London was the lowest recorded in the nineteenth century. Even so, the numbers involved were enormous. The
population of Greater London was 4,767,000 in 1881, 5,634,000 in
1891 and 6,581,000 in 1901. Over 60 per cent of all this growth took
place in outer London, beyond the county boundary.

The main direction of push in these years, so different from what
had gone before, was eastwards. That reflected a change in the class
mix of those moving out of central London in particular. For the new
suburbans were, more than at any time before, working people. That
is, working people broadly defined. We are dealing here with that great
social stratum of skilled manual workers (mechanical engineers, machine
builders, building craftsmen, train drivers, compositors, fine cabinet
makers and others) and the waged or salaried clerks, typists, telephonists, teachers, draughtsmen, petty officials and shop workers who
grew so largely in numbers during these two decades. And although
there may well have been class barriers neatly discriminating one component of this group from another, there was such great generational
fluidity between the London artisan whose sons and daughters grad-
uated to the post office as a counter clerk, or City bank as a 'type-
writist', or Oxford Street department store as a shop assistant, that
the connections were as strong as the distinctions. Between 'the upper-
grade artisan and lower-grade salaried classes . . . there is no longer
any marked social distinction', Charles Booth considered at the end of

the century.[49] It was this broad band that got on the move in the 1880s and 1890s. And mostly they moved east.

East London, of course, had always been workers' London. So the possibilities of the Essex countryside were always going to be explored first when the advantages of suburban living came to be considered by working-class Londoners. And it is important to remember that some of these suburbans would be first-time Londoners, moving direct to the outer belt from East Anglia or other districts. However the first residents got there, these would be suburbs designed for the working man and his family. Nothing here of the declassed districts in the north and west of London which had so often failed to hit their mark. Very little here, too, of the new-built suburban slum. These suburbs were socially and physically a reasonable fit. So the typical house in Leyton, Leytonstone, Walthamstow, outer West Ham, East Ham, Barking Town and as far out as Ilford was two-storey, terraced, usually of six rooms, with a small though highly prized garden. Street after street was built in this way, often in an unimaginative grid-pattern layout, for acre after acre.

The Cheap Trains Act 1883, which required special workmen's trains at low fares, was espoused most generously by the Great Eastern Railway, serving most of London-in-Essex. It helped grease the wheels of this eastward bulge. The whole of outer London grew by 119 per cent between 1881 and 1901. But in outer east London growth averaged 185 per cent. West Ham, East Ham, Leyton, Walthamstow, Ilford and Barking Town added between them over 400,000 people in these twenty years. The combined populations of these places qualified outer east London to be considered the nation's third largest city after London county and Liverpool.

This suburban movement of the upper working class and the lowest of the many middle classes was marked, too, in north and north-west London. The population of Tottenham nearly doubled in the 1880s, reaching 103,000 by 1901. Edmonton and Enfield, its smaller and more rural neighbours to the north, grew especially from an influx of engineers working at the Royal Small Arms Factory (home of the Lee Enfield rifle) and its associated explosives and other plant along the River Lea. War in South Africa gave a boost to employment, and accordingly local settlement, at the very end of the century. At Wood Green, the Noel Park Estate was a later version of the workers' garden village that had been inaugurated at Shaftesbury Park, Battersea, and at Queen's Park, not too far north of discredited Kensal New Town. All three were built by the Artizans', Labourers', and General Dwellings Company, neatly balancing the objectives of philanthropy and commercial solvency.

Queen's Park was in Willesden, and growth here in these two decades was truly phenomenal. Its population rose from 27,500 in 1881 to 114,800 in 1901. Much of this was again an upper-working-class and lower-middle-class mix, with a strong flavour of railway around the important nexus at Willesden Junction. Engineers were prominent, too, in Acton, further west, which also began to expand in these years. But nearby Kilburn managed to draw a more bourgeois tenantry, some of them no doubt pushed out from North Kensington, victims of its speculative disasters. Even so, 'Kilburn is becoming poorer, owing to increase of lodgers,' was Charles Booth's ominous judgement at the century's end.[50]

Kilburn was not the only middle-class suburb to grow in the north and west. Hornsey showed very marked growth, its population nearly doubling from 37,000 to 72,000 in these twenty years. There was development at Harringay and Finsbury Park in the south. And the northern heights at Crouch End were covered with generous three- and four-storey red-brick houses, running almost to the grounds of Alexandra Palace, which had been opened as the far north's main leisure attraction in 1873. The same was just beginning to happen in even more genteel Muswell Hill by the century's end.

Yet the worm in the suburban bud was apparent even in places like Crouch End. The sharp eye of George Gissing detected the 'smell of newness, of dampness' in a district where 'poverty tries to hide itself with venetian blinds': 'Whatever you touch is at once found to be sham.' Hope triumphed over experience most obviously at West End, Hampstead: 'In ten years the population at "West End" has increased twenty-fold,' wrote Booth. 'The place looks forlorn, and, the people seem still unaccustomed to their surroundings.'[51] Indeed, middle-class investment in a suburban home continued to be a risky venture in these years. Take North End, Fulham. Its smarter residents insisted on it being known as West Kensington. And if any name should have carried a cash premium, then Kensington was surely it. But here it proved pinchbeck. Compton Mackenzie's father, a successful theatrical manager with his own touring company, bought the ninety-nine-year lease of brand-new 54 Avonmore Road in 1886. He paid £1,000. It was built in up-to-the-minute red brick, 'four storeys high above a basement with stained glass in the front door'. The house was thought to be a good investment because a footbridge over the railway was mooted that would link the street with Cromwell Road. But the footbridge was never built. West Kensington proved to be of Fulham, Fulhamy. And Edward Compton could only sell the lease for £600 in 1901. He moved to Kensington proper.[52]

There was another transport mini-revolution in these years which aided working-class migration, supplementing the railways and their new workers' fares regime. This was the horse-tram, as proletarian as the omnibus was originally bourgeois. Trams first made a real mark on London in 1870. There had been some earlier experiments in 1861-2, with attempts to float tramway companies and obtain parliamentary sanction, but these had foundered. A large and successful scheme in Liverpool, approved in 1868, at last jolted London into action. Two lines were laid in south London and one in the east, north of the Thames.

The great advantage of trams was that the rails saved on horse power. Two horses could now pull up to fifty passengers, over twice the capacity of the omnibus. So fares could be pitched at a fraction of its rival's – most fares except the very longest or shortest were just 2d at the beginning, eventually driving down omnibus fares as a consequence. All this was designed to cater for a working-class demand that hitherto the omnibus and train had never properly addressed. In its first six months in 1870 the North Metropolitan Tramway carried over a million passengers on its Bow to Whitechapel route, so hugely popular was it among the new working-class suburbans of Poplar. The tram would remain a predominantly suburban mode of transport. The consent of street authorities was needed before tracks could be laid, and the vestries of St George's Hanover Square and St Marylebone, vehemently opposed to the vulgar new people-carriers, were able to keep trams out of the West End throughout the century. Even so, trams prospered so much that in five years they rivalled the great LGOC, carrying almost 49 million passengers a year by 1875.[53]

Trams went from strength to strength in the century's last two decades. They served some middle-class suburbs too, but their staple passenger was the new suburban. Average fares fell to just over 1d by 1896. That same year they carried 280 million passengers, just twenty million short of all the omnibus companies in London. The suburban tram network stretched from the edge of central London to Ponders End, Chingford, Dulwich and Wandsworth Town. But in the west? Not much at all. There was a lonely line from Harlesden Green and Kilburn Park to the social wilderness of Harrow Road near Paddington workhouse; and a small outer west London network from Richmond to Shepherd's Bush and Hammersmith. The western local authorities rejected the plebeian tram as a conveyance likely to import hobblede-hoys and devalue property values. Hostility to the tram was one reason – to be added to the failures of the 1860s and 1870s – for develop-ment lying uncharacteristically dormant in outer west London during these last twenty years of the century.

Improved communication networks were one symptom of the suburbs maturing and finding each a special place within the great metropolis. There were others. We have already noted that industry – and there-fore local jobs – had been present in some suburbs from the beginning and this was a tendency that strengthened markedly in these last twenty years. So people no longer had to travel into central London to work. Nor did they have to travel in to shop. Even the smartest could shop in Kensington High Street, 'one of the most fashionable and popular promenades in London' since the 1870s, 'popular' here meaning 'exclu-sive'.[54] Upper Street, Islington, was a shopping street to satisfy all bour-geois needs, a suburban Oxford Street with its own department store in Rackstraw's (opened in 1874). So too for theatres and music halls. There were suburban theatres at Deptford, Greenwich, Notting Hill, Fulham, Hammersmith, Chelsea, Battersea, Hampstead, Stratford (the Theatre Royal), Woolwich and no doubt elsewhere. Music hall was everywhere. In one cross-section of suburban south London, for instance, there was the Camberwell Empire and the Camberwell Palace of Varieties (both Denmark Hill), the famous Canterbury Music Hall and Gatti's Palace of Varieties (both Westminster Bridge Road), and the Empress Theatre of Varieties (Brixton). Crouch End even had its own opera house.[55]

The suburbs were also increasingly well provided with those 'lungs of London', the parks. In old London parks and gardens had been laid out on formerly built-up space, as we have seen. In suburban London the parks had to be rescued, plucked bodily from the developers' grasp. The heroes were various. There were plutocratic landlords who forfeited the profit they might have made, donating or selling land at low value to public authorities. There were committees of local worthies who agitated, raised funds and won a county or vestry contribution to buy up a country house garden and so save it from the builders. There were local authorities who mortgaged the rates to take over a threatened beauty spot. There was the City Corporation, which had no need to mortgage anything but used its wealth to buy 6,500 acres for the benefit of Londoners. And there was the enterprising Metropolitan Board of Works and its successor, which laid out great parks and preserved commons at Battersea, Blackheath, Bostall and Plumstead Heaths (Woolwich), Brockwell Park (Lambeth), Clapham Common, Finsbury Park, Hackney Marshes, Hampstead Heath and Parliament Hill, each over 100 acres in extent and some much more.

In all these ways – travel, work, shopping, amusements, open spaces – did the suburbs stand on their own feet and establish independence from the metropolitan maw. And the critical decades for doing so were these last two of the nineteenth century.

Yet despite these positive signs of maturity, the verdict of contemporaries on new London at the century's end was generally gloomy. This was less so for the very newest suburbs and the new suburbans – both of them bustling, energetic, optimistic, moving outwards and upwards. But it *was* so, and without relief, for that great stucco girdle laid round London layer by layer from around 1840 till the end of the 1870s.

Historians have made much of the nineteenth century's tendency towards 'the systematic sorting-out of London into single-purpose, homogeneous, specialised neighbourhoods'. 'However universal the tendency towards residential differentiation, Victorian London achieved it to an unprecedented degree. The new suburb was a highly efficient means both of functional and social segregation . . .'[56]

Now this is much overdrawn. Even at the very beginning of many new suburbs, we have seen how the developers' intent was frustrated by over-optimistic projections of a demand that didn't exist, and by the scale of development that rendered the suburbs urban before they were half-finished. Social segregation may have been aimed at but it was frequently missed. Even where it was achieved at the outset, it more often than not lasted but a moment in time. For by the end of the century, virtually all of new London inside the county boundary – with the important exceptions of parts of St John's Wood and Regent's Park, Belgravia, and the smartest districts of Kensington – were in a state of social flux that was both unanticipated and most unwelcome.

By the 1890s London's suburbs, most just twenty to forty years old, had begun to look their age and worse. Percy Fitzgerald remarked on that 'forlorn district beyond Islington [Barnsbury? Holloway? Kentish Town?] where there are rows upon rows of yellow villas, stuccoed, well smirched, stained, and decayed, with a spurious air of the country – villas that have seen better days . . .'[57] At the same time, 'Hackney is becoming poorer', wrote Charles Booth, our most reliable guide at the end of the century. 'The larger houses are turned into factories. The better-to-do residents are leaving, or have left.' Across that whole area of St Pancras, Islington, Stoke Newington and west Hackney, 'Those who come are poorer than those who go, and each district in turn grows poorer.' During the 1890s Islington's squares were being 'absorbed' by the lower middle class, who were 'dividing the houses and letting lodgings'. Camden Town had come down from 'a residential quarter of wealth and even fashion' around 1880 to 'largely a place of business' by 1896, with lodgers in every house. In 'the Wild West of Earl's Court' fashion was found to be retreating even from Kensington: 'There are guests who pay, or the drawing-room floor is let, or boarders are taken, or at length the fatal word "Apartments" appears in the fanlight over the door.' Even once-aristocratic Bayswater was caught in a continual 'see-saw movement' as poorer parts were rebuilt (and so moved up) while 'discarded houses' are 'divided by the landlord to suit a still poorer class of tenants'. And Cubitt's Pimlico was now 'an admixture of shabby gentility and vice, hardly less depressing than the low life of the old slums . . .' It showed 'the gradual decay and grimy dilapidation which is apt to overtake houses built for another class and altogether unsuited for their present occupants: short of paint, the plaster peeling and cracking; sordid and degraded dwellings, they remain a nightmare in the memory'.[58]

There were similar tales from south of the river.[59] We can see it in sharp detail by looking at the census enumerators' record books for any street between the very richest on the one hand and the very poorest on the other. Take Grove Lane, Camberwell, in 1891, used as a setting for George Gissing's *In the Year of Jubilee* (1894). Built between the 1840s and the 1860s, this long street was classed by Booth as mostly 'well-to-do' with some reduction to 'fairly comfortable' at the northern end. For Gissing it was 'a neighbourhood in decay, a bit of London which does not keep pace with the times'. The census shows it to have been surprisingly mixed, bearing out Gissing's observation. Out of some 334 residents whose occupations were noted, the largest group by far was 'clerks' (seventy-one or 21.3 per cent), followed by 'living on own

means' (one in eight). There was a smattering of professionals (solicitor, a couple of stockbrokers, doctors and so on); a large group in
retail (about 20 per cent in all, including fifteen commercial travellers)
and others in wholesale; and thirteen teachers, mostly women. But then
there was a working-class spectrum too, nine gardeners, seven boot
and shoe makers, a few in the building trades and in tailoring, even a
labourer and a sewer flusher.[60]

This incipient demoralisation of the suburbs had other effects by the
early 1890s. The acme of modernity in the 1860s and 1870s, a new
generation had grown up there which had become jaded with suburban
decline and saw a return to central London and a 'good address' as a
badge of material progress. This is the main theme of the Grossmith
brothers' *Diary of a Nobody* (1892), where the Pooters' impudent son,
Lupin, rejects his parents' Holloway idyll, long the sole object of their
social ambition. Lupin moves from Brickfield Terrace to Bayswater,
close to his fast friends Mr and Mrs Murray Posh: '"I am not going
to rot away my life in the suburbs."'[61]

One final demerit of suburban living might be mentioned here: the
discomfort of commuting at the end of the nineteenth century. Frank
Bullen, a clerk at the Meteorological Office in Victoria, moved from
Kilburn to Plashet, between West and East Ham, at the end of the
1880s. He had to spend nearly four hours a day travelling, had to
walk from Fenchurch Street to Victoria and back, and had to endure
the humiliation of affording only a workman's ticket and travelling in
'a close-packed, reeking compartment'.[62] The 'fuliginous' underground
was even worse. 'I had my first experience of Hades today,' reported
the American pressman R. D. Blumenfeld in his diary for 21 June 1887:

I got into the Underground railway at Baker Street ... It was very warm –
for London, at least. The compartment in which I sat was filled with passengers who were smoking pipes, as is the British habit, and as the smoke and
sulphur from the engine fill the tunnel, all the windows have to be closed.
The atmosphere was a mixture of sulphur, coal dust and foul fumes from the
oil lamp above; so that by the time we reached Moorgate Street I was near
dead of asphyxiation and heat.[63]

Compton Mackenzie recalled the third-class smokers' carriages on this
same line as particularly 'foul, the floors of all of them covered with
gobbets of stale saliva ...'[64]

The filthy Inner Circle was just one part of a transit system that by 1901 was moving at least 847 million passengers around London each year, over three times more than in 1881.[65] This was a vastly different London from that walkable city of 1800. Now it seemed to go on for ever, in every direction. Straggling outposts of London town could be discerned as far west as Hanwell High Street and as far east as Romford; as far north as Potters Bar, as far south as Beckenham and Mitcham. True, it was not all a single built-up area between these furthest limits. But urban London now broadly covered over ten miles in every direction, from Hammersmith to Upton Park, and Wood Green to Crystal Palace. This was no longer a walkable city. And it had not been so for half a century at least.

Even more than London's physical presence on the ground, it was the size of its population that most staggered contemporaries. Greater London, at 6.58 million people, was home to one in five of the population of England and Wales. Londoners had never before made up such a huge proportion of the nation's people. No city in Great Britain or the world could come close to it. There were more Londoners than the residents of Edinburgh, Glasgow, Dublin, Belfast, Cardiff, Birmingham, Manchester, Liverpool, Newcastle, Bradford, Bristol, Leicester, Nottingham, Sheffield, Leeds, Salford, Oldham and Bolton put together. London's people outnumbered the Parisians, Berliners and Viennese combined. London contained 2.85 million people more than New York, the world's second-largest city. Its population was much larger than that of several European nations, equivalent to the sum total of Greece, Denmark and Bosnia-Herzegovina. And so on. The modern world had never seen such a city. To bring so many people together was an unequalled social experiment. Just who were these Londoners? And what did they make of each other?

PART TWO

PEOPLE

'In the Exchanges of London every Nation walk'd
And London walk'd in every Nation, mutual in love and harmony.'
William Blake, *Jerusalem*,
c. 1827

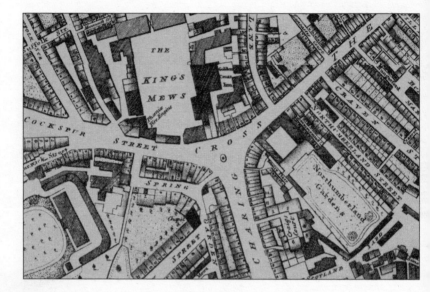

Charing Cross, 1813

IV

CHARING CROSS: THE LONDON WHIRLPOOL

'The Mighty Magnet'

LONDON was a whirlpool and Charing Cross the 'roaring vortex' at its heart. Even in the eighteenth century, according to Dr Johnson, 'the full tide of human existence is at Charing Cross'. And in the nineteenth the ancient triangular junction of Whitehall, the Strand and Cockspur Street only gained in significance. From 1831 the statue of Charles I at Charing Cross became the official centre of London, the point on which all cab fares were based and distances from the metropolis were measured, 'the "Hub" of the Empire'. From 1864, Charing Cross railway station provided one of London's great meeting places: 'under the clock at Charing Cross' was the starting point of myriad encounters. It was an endpoint too. The Golden Cross Hotel was a famous coaching terminus for stages from 'nearly every large town in the United Kingdom'. For the early decades of the century the Golden Cross and the inns nearby were filled with newcomers and visitors just arrived or just about to depart. When provincial Londoners wished to meet their countrymen it was often at the taverns of Charing Cross that they arranged to do so. At the Admiral Duncan, for instance, in March 1824, 'the men of Cumberland and Westmorland in the metropolis met together, and resolved to found the Annual North Country Wrestling Matches', held later and most famously at Islington's Royal Agricultural Hall.[1]

The proportion of people living in the county of London but born outside it tended to fall away as the century grew older. Sixty per cent of Londoners were London-born in 1841, the first time birthplace was noted in the census, but 66.5 per cent in 1901. The *numbers* of provincials, though, actually rose, with over 1.3 million Londoners in 1901 born in Scotland, Wales and England outside London, compared to 750,000 fifty years before. By the century's end a very substantial provincial element had also settled in outer London. In the peak decade of the 1870s almost half a million people migrated to the County of London alone, and for the last sixty years of the century immigration seems to have averaged from 30,000 to 50,000 each year.[2]

Moving to London was one of the great social facts in the life of the nation. In 1888 'Coming up from the country to London' was a subject

of universal interest. There is hardly a household in the land that is not more or less concerned with it. There is no parish, however remote or obscure, from the Hebrides to Cornwall, from which young men do not find their way to London. There is, perhaps, none who has not a relative or friend who has made his journey to the great city and fought his battle there . . . [The] mighty magnet exerts its mysterious fascination, and the number of young men and women who come to London every year is steadily on the increase.[3]

It is hard to know whether the lure of London, 'its mysterious fascination', was any less strong at the beginning of the century than here at its end. But probably not. What Charles Booth called the 'dazzle and glitter' of London had always worked on the imagination of provincials wherever in the kingdom they lived. Robert Plumer Ward noted in 1825 how 'All would be Statesmen, Philosophers, or people of fashion. All, too, run to London.' London uniquely offered that 'contagion of numbers, the sense of something going on', the 'gigantic lottery of chances' for the audacious, so that 'if you blow a penny whistle at the Hebrides, to ends of fame or fortune, you must try your luck with it in London town'. London's pleasures – theatre the very symbol 'of metropolitanism as opposed to provincialism' – and 'its amusements for the body, mind and soul', could stimulate and satisfy every appetite. Most of all, London seemed to offer greater rewards than those obtainable elsewhere for the same amount of effort: fame, even riches, for the artist, writer and preacher; higher wages for the craftsman and labourer; an inexhaustible supply of master and mistress for the domestic servant; opportunities without limit for the chancer and the thief; and hope against hope for the beggar and the drifter. London's lure had probably always displayed these attractions. To that extent it was timeless.[4]

There were, though, some new elements during the century that helped London's light burn even brighter. First, the railways made travel easier for the middle classes from the late 1830s and for the working classes from the late 1880s and 1890s. They meant that London could be sampled, metropolitan awe tasted and savoured. Second, the Great Exhibition at the Crystal Palace, Hyde Park, in 1851 attracted six million visitors to the capital. Nothing like its draw for country people had ever been seen in London. Silver watches were pawned 'by the bushel' to book places on Thomas Cook's excursion trains from Bradford and Leeds; in one giant outing 800 Surrey and Sussex agricultural labourers were brought in their smocks by their local clergy; and exhibitors of machinery and other manufactures sent their workpeople to share in their firms' pride of endeavour. Never had London played host to so many potential Londoners as in those six hectic months from May to October. It would not do so again for a hundred years to come.[5]

Third, of more subtle impact but probably just as momentous, was the influence on the provincial mind of the London writer in the nineteenth century. The 1820s were powerfully productive of texts that sought to glamorise London and all it had to offer a youngster in search of adventure. Most notable was Pierce Egan's *Life in London* (1821), where Jerry Hawthorn was conducted round all the sights of the metropolis, both raffish and respectable, in the company of Corinthian Tom and Bob Logic the Oxonian. The book, with its plates by Isaac and George Cruikshank, was staggeringly popular, and so was W. T. Moncrieff's stage adaptation at the Adelphi that same year. Egan's example was followed, bettered in many ways, by the anonymous *Real Life in London* (1821–2). And the London explorings of the American writer Washington Irving in *The Sketch Book of Geoffrey Crayon, Gent.* (also 1821) were markedly influential on the young Charles Dickens and a whole generation of readers. But it was Dickens himself, of course, who most of all fired the imagination of provincials and who spiced their appetite for the fascinating metropolis. From 1833 with *Sketches by Boz*, sensationally from 1836 with *Pickwick Papers*, and for the next thirty years and more in the most memorable, engaging and complex realisation of London and the Londoner ever to get into print, Dickens endowed his contemporaries and their successors with an insatiable passion for exploring his London. Justin McCarthy recalled the 'sort of London mania which was very contagious in those days [the 1860s and 1870s] among boys who had never been in London, and it got its chief impulse from Dickens'.[6]

However they were seduced there, where were these newcomers from? And who were they?

Like any magnet, London drew most from those who were closest to it. Of 1,173,000 provincial-born Londoners in 1881, 734,000 or almost 63 per cent came from the South-East, south Midlands and East Anglia.[7] Most were women. Women always made up the majority of Londoners in the nineteenth century and they especially dominated migration from the countryside around London. Among eastern counties-born Londoners in 1881 there were 1,312 women for every 1,000 men. An unknown but probably very high proportion of these were recruited into the many varied forms of domestic service that London had to offer. This accounted, in areas like Paddington, Hampstead and Kensington, for both the high volume of provincial-born and the large majorities of women. Inevitably, too, migrants to London tended to be single workers or childless couples rather than families with children. So London had a significantly greater proportion of its population in the twenty to fifty age range than England and Wales as a whole (44 per cent against 39 per cent in 1881, for instance).[8]

Every corner of the nation sent a host of aspirants to make their way to the giant city, to win or lose, to stay or move on. The most talented people in the nation had London in their sights. Painters like the brilliant David Wilkie, not yet twenty, who sailed in a Leith packet from Edinburgh to London in 1805: 'Try your fortune in London,' he urged his brother a year later, 'for here you could learn a great number of things you can never learn anywhere else . . .' Writers like Eliza Lynn (Mrs Lynn Linton), who came to London aged eighteen from Cumberland in 1845 to try her hand at fiction and leader-writing for the *Morning Chronicle*. She visited frequently at a bohemian ménage at Bayswater where London-born George Henry Lewes, 'audacious', 'extreme', with 'neither shame nor reticence', was a regular. He would exert an insuperable fascination on another provincial writer, Marian Evans (George Eliot), who left Coventry for a berth in London's Grub Street in 1851 at the age of thirty-one: she eloped with the married Lewes three years later, eventually to live as man and wife in wicked St John's Wood.[9] And among these newcomers were some of the great 'Londonists' (the term is the journalist Marcus Fall's, from around 1880) who helped define the meaning of London in the nineteenth-century mind's eye.

There were Charles Dickens (born in Portsmouth in 1812, moved to London in 1822), Walter Besant (born in Portsea in 1836, moved to London in 1854), Charles Booth (born in Liverpool in 1840, moved to London in 1875), George Gissing (born in Wakefield in 1857, moved to London in 1877), Arthur Machen (born in Gwent in 1863, moved to London in 1880).

There were Christian zealots and entrepreneurs of the Cross who saw London as the only arena in which to fight lions or court a bishopric. Mrs Linton recalled a Birmingham evangelical, a 'great provincial light' around 1850, desperate to 'get to London': '"I am an oak in a flower-pot here."' Somerset-born George Williams left Bridgwater for Ludgate Hill in 1841, aged twenty, to spread the Gospel among his fellow drapers' assistants: he would form the Young Men's Christian Association just three years later, holding all his life to the view 'that the first twenty-four hours of a young man's life in London usually settled his eternity in heaven or hell'. William Booth came to London from Nottingham in 1849, a Methodist by conversion and more interested in saving souls than pawnbroking, which he pursued for a time at Walworth. He would go on to found the Salvation Army in London in 1878. 'In the notes made for his autobiography he set down under the title of "London" the one word "Loneliness!"'[10]

Country craftsmen were lured to London by higher wages and by the advantage their apprenticeships gave them over London men, who were not usually 'time-served' and who specialised in just one aspect of their craft. Newcomers would often be preferred as foremen in the printing or building trades because they were 'all-round men'. So we see John Brown, a shoemaker, walking to London from Cambridge around 1814 to seek the fortune his home town denied him: 'London was to me the great centre of attraction, whereof I had heard much and read more . . .' Cheltenham-born William Adams, aged twenty-two and a compositor, tramped to London in 1855 from the Lake District in search of regular employment. He had visited the Great Exhibition and the promise of work in the giant city did not disappoint him. At Henry Vizetelly's *Illustrated Times* he was 'in clover'. Adams was luckier than Robert Blatchford, a runaway apprentice brushmaker. In 1871, about twenty, he walked 124 miles from his Yarmouth workshop but found London 'coldly hostile and forbidding'. 'London did not want me: had no use for me . . . London had not noticed that another ant had crept amongst its eager, bustling swarms.'[11]

Then there were the town and country labourers for whom London seemed to offer so much more choice than could ever come their way at home. But, as with the craftsmen, not everything would work out. Elizabeth Jones, thirty-eight, came perhaps too late in life from Bath to London to find a domestic situation. In February 1830 she 'perished for want of the common necessaries of life', having had nothing for three days but 1½d worth of coffee, sleeping for five weeks on the winter streets in a 'thin cotton gown . . . and nothing whatever under it'. On the other hand, Susan Bartrup or Barltrop, an agricultural labourer's daughter, walked forty miles from Broxted in Essex in 1837 to find a 'situation'. She did so, married, brought up an influential son, the worker intellectual Frederick Rogers, and died in east London seventy years later. Lucy Luck and her husband, Will, were evicted by a spiteful employer from their tied cottage near Luton around 1874, so they tried their fortune in London. Will, a ploughman, could adapt his country skills to become a horse keeper for a railway carrier; Lucy was a straw plaiter for the hat shops in Westbourne Grove, Paddington, earning more for her skills than Luton employers had ever paid her.[12]

Finally there were the beggars. John Burn ('The Beggar Boy'), brought up in Dumfries, had a professional beggar for a stepfather, a discharged soldier who was a good man but a better drinker. He brought the family to London in 1810 so that he might 'pass the Board at Chelsea [Military Hospital], in order to become an out-pensioner'. They walked all the way, lodging in Church Lane, St Giles. 'The very atmosphere of London, or else its gin, very soon produced an exhilarating effect upon my mentor.' So the family was brought lower than in Scotland, now 'among strangers, many of whom were brutalized into heartless grinning savages by drunkenness'. The application was unsuccessful and the family returned north about a month later.[13] At the other end of the century we have Sam Shaw, born 1884 in Birmingham, his home 'the last word in poverty', his father battling with periodic bouts of insanity. Around 1894 the family, seven strong, went on the tramp to London 'where everybody would buy our matches and Dad's newspapers'. They lodged in one room in Bangor Street, Notting Dale, a neat indication of how the geography of London beggary had changed across the century. Soon Sam would be arrested for 'wandering', committed to Feltham Industrial School until he was sixteen.[14]

For those provincial newcomers who settled in London, their place of origin often influenced where they chose to make their home. In general the radial leylines of London tended to deposit migrants along the old highways from their counties of origin: men and women from East Anglia were to be found especially in east London, and from Kent in the south-eastern districts like Deptford and Greenwich, and so on. The great railway termini reinforced this effect. The Welsh were considered clannish and there was some clustering of the 18,000 or so London Welsh by mid-century in the servant-keeping areas of west London, close to their rail link at Paddington. They made up a large proportion of London dairymen and milkmaids, were famous among London drapers and laid down a rich seam of London gold smelters – 'handsome, portly and jovial', as Charles Dickens saw them in the early 1850s. Similarly, Harold Bellman, 'the Cornish Cockney' and building society entrepreneur, was born in Paddington in 1886. His father had been a carriage builder in Cornwall who moved to London around 1880: 'true to the tradition of those days', he settled close to the station that 'formed a link with the West Country'.[15]

The London Scots too were said around 1840 to cluster and network. Bread Street, in the City, was largely occupied by people from Paisley and Scotch bakers were notably common in London. In 1867 Clyde-trained iron-shipbuilders were so common on the Isle of Dogs at Millwall that 'the Scottish dialect and Christian names' were prevalent, pubs had signs like the Burns and Highland Mary, and other spirits were accommodated at 'the kirk'. But otherwise the 50,000 or so Scots living in the County of London in 1881 seem to have been pretty evenly spread. There was, though, contact between them. The London Scots were great institution builders: the Scottish Hospital off Fleet Street dated from the seventeenth century; the Caledonian Asylum for orphans of Scottish soldiers, sailors and marines was established in Hatton Garden, Holborn, in 1815; and the Caledonian Society provided wider relief to the London Scottish poor from 1820. By the end of the century they also had their highland games, annual dinner, Scottish dancing gala and a London Scottish golf club.[16]

Wherever provincial Londoners set out from, there was one generally apparent feature of where they settled. Outside the servant-keeping areas of the West End, where the bourgeois or aristocrat from anywhere might feel at home, it was not in central London that newcomers took root. Provincial-born Londoners seemed most comfortable at the edge of London, that great new belt of the Victorian metropolis emerging from 1840 to 1880. The old troubled central area, inherited from the eighteenth century, was left to the cockney. Increasingly so as the century wore on.

Cockneys

I am the great-grandson of a Thames waterman, and the River Thames runs through all my boyish recollections and through the stories of my early life that have been told me by my father and others. All my forebears worked on the river and were mostly engaged in carrying goods used in the building and timber trades.[17]

That was Harry Gosling, born in York Street, Lambeth, in 1861. Now by rights – or by prejudice – Gosling should have been a weakling or a fool. 'There is a strong conviction in the minds of many, incapable however of strict verification, that Londoners tend to die out after the second or at least the third generation', their stock vitiated and exhausted by inter-breeding in the smoky city. Charles Booth, apparently sympathetic to the vitiation theory, noted how 'we may listen in vain for the accent of the Cockney among the leaders of the working men'. But in fact Gosling was a trade union leader on the waterfront at the very time Booth was writing (1893), a president of the Transport and General Workers' Union, a member of the first Labour cabinet and overall a great achiever. So was Thomas Okey, born 1852 at Quaker Street, Spitalfields, in his grand-father's basket-making home and workshop. Okey's father was also a basket maker and young Thomas too was put to the trade. But an ear for languages set him on a career which ended as Professor of Italian at Cambridge University. And we can use G. K. Chesterton's experience to remind ourselves that the vitiation theory never extended to the bour-geois London-bred. His father was 'the head of a hereditary business of house-agents and surveyors, which had already [in 1874] been established for some three generations in Kensington . . .'[18]

It is possible that the cockney bloodline in all these cases was 'nour-ished', to cite Booth again, 'by the absorption every year of large numbers of persons of stronger physique, who leaven the whole mass . . .' Booth meant men but, given the preponderance of marriageable migrant women, the union of a London-born man and a country-born woman was extremely common. Arthur Harding – none more cockney than he, the 'terror' of Bethnal Green in the first years of the twentieth century – was born in the Old Nichol Street area in 1886. His mother had come to London from Norfolk some thirty years before, moving to Hoxton as a rag picker around 1875. His father was a Londoner well enough, born in Pearl Street, Spitalfields – but of Cornish stock, his family migrating probably at mid-century or just before.[19]

This pattern was typical. The London-born had generally one or both parents born elsewhere. Londoners could indeed rarely boast two full sets of London-born grandparents, not because such a combination would be genetically bankrupt but because metropolitan demography, right through the nineteenth century, made it inherently improbable.

Where were the London-born most commonly to be found? Gaps in the census records leave the best available comparison between 1851 and 1881, but even this is incomplete.[20] In the first of these years the proportion of London-born was 61.7 per cent and in the second 63.3 per cent. At both a single district stands out as utterly unique. That was Bethnal Green. In 1851 82.2 per cent of its residents were London-born and in 1881 83.5 per cent. It seems a strange accident of history that turned this overspill district of Huguenot Spitalfields, full of French silk weavers in the early eighteenth century, into an almost exclusively native-born colony – far more London than the rest of the capital – during the nineteenth. The explanation resides in silk weaving itself. The industry slowly declined but never moved away. Its requirements for wide-lighted lofts led to a characteristic housing form, special to the area, which helped root silk weaving there. By 1800 this was a township dominated by one industry and the traditions of its inventive workforce. The silk weavers' institutions – their educational societies, allotments and gardens and pigeon lofts – all clung on to Bethnal Green. And the weavers' sons and daughters, even when working in other trades, clung on too. French surnames persisted in Bethnal Green in 1851 but by then their bearers had been speaking with a cockney accent for almost a century and a half.

Bethnal Green was entirely exceptional. The other clusters of the London-born were more evenly matched. The densest were in the inner East End, close to Bethnal Green – Mile End Old Town and Shoreditch. Stepney and St George's in the East both had over 70 per cent London-born in 1881, though Jewish immigration would transform the make-up of both in the next twenty years. At the 'Orchard House' area of Bow Creek (Poplar), 'Many of the families have been here four or five generations'. In the Carr Street area of Limehouse, 'Families have been resident on the same spot for a long period, and ... act as though the place belonged to them.'[21] Clerkenwell and St Luke's (Finsbury) made another London-born enclave: 'There are costermongers in Whitecross-street [it was said in 1873] who can trace their descent to the time when Golden-lane was lined with hedge-rows' and blind Milton might be met there.[22] West of Gray's Inn Road the London-born fell to normal proportions or something far below them, and for the completion of the inner arc of cockney London we need to cross Waterloo Bridge and move east. Part of north Lambeth, Bankside, the Borough, Walworth, Bermondsey and Rotherhithe were substantially London-born areas by 1881 (around 70–73 per cent), more markedly so than in 1851. The City, by the way, despite its centrality, was no haven at all of the London-born, just 59.2 per cent in 1851. Here the leavening of country-bred drapers' apprentices and domestic servants kept cockneys in constant jostle with provincials.

The central cockney districts had two other notable features. The first was high fertility. Charles Booth analysed the birth rates of fifty London districts over the period 1891–5. The average birth rate in London in 1895 was 30.5 per 1,000 population. Booth found the top five most fertile districts to be Whitechapel and Spitalfields (43.3 per 1,000, but now much affected by Jewish immigration); Old Street and south Shoreditch (39.9); Waterloo and St Saviour's (39.4); Bethnal Green (38.9); and north Lambeth (38.3). In these enclaves of the London-born, the age at marriage or cohabitation tended to be younger than elsewhere in London. Early marriage was one – usually not very successful – attempted escape from poverty. And poverty was the other defining feature of cockney London.[23] Charles Booth estimated in 1889 that 30.7 per cent of all Londoners lived in poverty. Again, it was cockney London that provided the very poorest districts in London: Waterloo and St Saviour's (52 per cent poverty); Bermondsey (50.3 per cent); Old Street and south Shoreditch (47.7 per cent); Bethnal Green (47 per cent); Gray's Inn and Clerkenwell (45 per cent). In London 'poverty and distress is home-made, and not imported from outside'.[24]

We can demonstrate this connection between the London-born and the London poor operating in the new suburban slums built between 1840 and 1880. At Campbell Road, Islington, for instance, which by 1881 had become one of the most infamous and poorest streets in London, 51.4 per cent of adults were born in London. That compared to 35 per cent in next-door (and respectable) Palmerston Road. And the astonishing comparison here was the proportion of Islington-born – 20.9 per cent in Campbell Road, just 7.5 per cent in Palmerston Road.

It was the local poor who gravitated to Campbell Road rather than the poor of London more generally.[25]

These dense clusterings of the London-born, their attachment to the inner arc on the north and east of the City and along the south bank of the Thames, their high fertility and propensity to become the very poorest of the London poor do not by any means account for the whole spectrum of native Londoners. After all, most born Londoners were the children of one or two provincials moving in. Most of these were scattered widely over suburban London and across all classes. There were 2.4 million London-born living in the county in 1881: some 800,000, almost exactly one-third, lived in this dense inner arc; the rest ranged over the remainder of north, south and east London, most sparsely in the west and south-west.[26]

Wherever they lived, were native-born Londoners distinguishable from their provincial-born neighbours? Contemporaries certainly thought so. The distinctiveness of 'The Cockney' as portrayed in the public prints or on the music-hall stage changed greatly over time during the nineteenth century, a creation of art not nature.[27] But beyond these plastic representations were there some core characteristics which rendered the native Londoner more readily discernible than not?

There's no doubt that many Londoners were marked out by their language. Telling first on the ear was the dialect itself. When Samuel Bamford, a radical handloom weaver from Lancashire, was imprisoned at Coldbath Fields House of Correction, Clerkenwell, on a treason charge in 1817, he found two of his ward-mates to be 'an old coal meter and his son' whose 'conversation and manners . . . were of the most perfect Cockney cast. They started back and stood wide agape when I opened upon them in broad Lancashire; the old man put on his spectacles and peered at me as if I were uttering barbarous Russ, or a Lappish incantation. On the other hand they confounded me with their v's and w's . . .'[28] This transposition of *v* for *w* – 'vife' and 'wictuals', 'wery' and 'vhich' – was for many generations the most characteristic element of London speech. It was faithfully transcribed by Egan, Dickens, Thackeray and others. It seems largely to have disappeared from common parlance some time between 1850 and 1870, although *w* for *v* (not the other way round) was still detectable in the 1890s. Other elements – the absent (sometimes wrongly placed) aspirate, the glottal stop (which cut consonants from the middle and end of words), the replacement of *e* for *a* in words like 'catch', *v* for *th* in words like

'they' or 'there' and *ff* for *th* in most others, double negatives ('I don't
know nuffing'), double superlatives ('more better', 'more quicker'), the
substitution of 'learn' for 'teach', 'dawg' for 'dog', 'wuss' for 'worse',
'axed' for 'asked', a redundant *r* in 'jawrache' or 'Mariar Ann', 'gite'
for 'gate', 'Victawia' for 'Victoria' and so on – seem all to have been
well established by 1880, many in place for generations before that.
This was the London dialect as learned in the street and as resolutely
resistant to correction in the National, British, Ragged, Sunday and
Board Schools of nineteenth-century London.[29]

But it was definitely not the language of the London-born bourgeoisie. Pronunciation was one of the very clearest markers of class in
London. No one born into (or aspiring to) a class above the lower
middle could tolerate speech tainted by the common tongue of London.
G. K. Chesterton recalled 'the enormous importance' attached to
'speaking correctly' in bourgeois Kensington in the 1870s:

There was a whole world in which nobody was any more likely to drop an
h than to pick up a title . . . I am told . . . that about the age of three or four,
I screamed for a hat hanging on a peg, and at last in convulsions of fury
uttered the awful words, 'If you don't give it me, I'll say 'at.' I felt sure that
would lay all my relations prostrate for miles around.[30]

An equally strong component of the Londoner's language was its
distinctive slang. This was much more fluid than changes in pronunciation or dialect. Bamford, reflecting on his cockney fellow inmates,

soon discovered that one half of their nouns were of no known language, or
even dialect; but were mere slang terms, used by classes (workmen, thieves,
or prostitutes, as the case might be) and arbitrary in the localities where they
had obtained currency. The speech of a born and resident Cockney, is probably never two years the same. New incidents and objects are continually
giving rise to new ideas and expressions; every genius, and there are some
droll ones, carries his lexicon at his tongue's end; and if he be assured and
flippant, as he probably will be, he will certainly obtain utterers for his coinage;
and the more grotesque and un-English it is, the better will be its acceptance.[31]

The most un-English of all was costermongers' and thieves' and
flower sellers' back-slang, where words were more or less reversed:
spoken rapidly, it sounded (and sounds) like a foreign language. It was
the argot of those few whose communications required absolute secrecy

from third parties. But for the common run of Londoners, slang words and expressions occupied not just the same class territory as the London dialect. Slang went wider. It selectively penetrated the speech of the young bourgeois and aristocrat. Thackeray noted 'that darling London jargon, so dear and indispensable to London people, so little understood by persons out of the world'.[32]

So if London pronunciation was kept in tight class bounds, London slang was not. The great seven-volume dictionary of *Slang and Its Analogues* by John Farmer and W. E. Henley (1890–1904) is most of all the living record of London speech in the nineteenth century in all its arcane and ribald twists and turns. Here London itself, its social geography laden with meaning, provides inspiration to irony and imagery and the ever popular rhyming slang. So a 'Camden Town' was a halfpenny or 'brown'; a 'Field Lane duck' was (not rhyming this) a baked sheep's head; a 'Spitalfields breakfast' was no breakfast at all; a 'Fulham virgin' was a fast woman; a 'Whitechapel brougham' was a hand-barrow; a 'Hampstead donkey' was a body louse; and so on.[33]

London slang, as Bamford pointed out, was a quick-change artiste. The slang recounted by, say, Pierce Egan in the 1820s, Dickens at mid-century and Kipling in the 1890s may have some overlap but in general each has a very different vocabulary and feel to it. This accelerated obsolescence was neatly observed by the journalist Charles Mackay. He recalled from his own experience of the early 1820s and the period from 1832 to 1852 the London slang catchwords and phrases used in the streets to deflate pomposity and tickle a crowd. One followed another in quick succession as the fashionable put-down of the day. 'Quoz!' 'What a shocking bad hat!' 'Walker-r-r!' 'There he goes with his eye out!' 'Has your mother sold her mangle?' 'Flare up!' 'Does your mother know you're out?' 'Who are *you*?' And no doubt there were others, each quickly used up and overtaken by the next, some to be revived by later generations.[34]

The liveliness, inventiveness and up-to-dateness of London slang were all features found in the Londoners who used it, or so contemporaries discerned. But the reverse side of these virtues – shallowness, flippancy and an ill-merited superiority complex – were just as evident. Perhaps the influence of the streets was definitive. The children of the London poor grew up in them; the children of the London lower middle classes played in them and passed through them to school and shop. The streets offered theatre, real-life drama, excitement, an infinite variety of events and personalities, the bustle of commerce, ceaseless stimulation for the mind. Frederick Rogers from Whitechapel, a sandwich-board carrier when ten years old around 1856, thought 'the busy City life brought a touch of idealism into our boyish lives, and showed us the possibility of escape in the future from the work we were doing then'. This moral example of the streets, whichever way it led, involved minute observation, sharpness (especially in dealings over money or barter), quick-wittedness, alertness and humour. These were the elements of cleverness – superficial at one level but vital skills in an essentially commercial environment – that endowed the cockneys with their much remarked upon self-confidence. 'Jarman was Young London personified,' Jerome K. Jerome wrote of a 'young fellow in the commercial line' around 1880: 'blatant, yet kind-hearted; aggressively self-assertive, generous to a fault; cunning, yet at the same time frank; shrewd, cheery, and full of pluck. "Never say die" was his motto, and anything less dead it would be difficult to imagine.' And Hazlitt summed up the essential democratic spirit of characters like this: '*Your true Cockney is your only true leveller*. Let him be as low as he will, he fancies he is as good as any body else.'[35]

The variety of street life offered high-pressure vicarious experience: agonising death in an accident, violent altercation, language colourful and ripe, the secrets of sex revealed in some alley or yard. For the children of the poor, all this knowingness was combined with premature responsibility. No one was too young to bear a burden or turn a penny. And anyone who turned a penny claimed worth, status and value. William Makepeace Thackeray, born in Calcutta in 1811 but a scholar at Charterhouse, Smithfield, from 1822 – was a fine observer of London life and his reflections on the intellectual property of the London poor compared with that of other classes rings entirely true.

A pauper child in London at seven years old knows how to go to market, to fetch the beer, to pawn father's coat, to choose the largest fried fish or the nicest ham-bone, to nurse Mary Jane of three – to conduct a hundred operations of trade or housekeeping, which a little Belgravian does not perhaps acquire in all the days of her life. Poverty and necessity force this precociousness on the poor little brat. There are children who are accomplished shop-lifters and liars almost as soon as they can toddle and speak.[36]

These skills were valuable. They meant money. And this materialistic seam in the Londoner's soul struck many outsiders as a defining characteristic of the breed, one that spread well beyond the ranks of the poor. It was plainly discerned by George Wilson, a surgeon with a passion for chemistry, born in Edinburgh but drawn to London in 1840 by its dominance in science under Michael Faraday and others. He found that 'the professional business spirit of the London schools is alien to the true study of their subjects . . . The London students are notoriously the most unscientific students on the face of the earth.'[37] This materialism and anti-idealism of the London milieu was one factor in the isolation of life in London that so many experienced – and lamented or celebrated according to taste. It was a pillar of that indifference which was perhaps the defining feature of London life. And it was one element, too, in the restlessness and incompleteness of life in London, that lack of attachment to 'home', the turbulence that seemed to keep Londoners almost permanently on the move.

'A City in Motion'

Once moved into London, like a provincial newcomer, and even once rooted like a seasoned cockney, moving around was one of the great facts of London life. All classes were affected. In *The Whirlpool* (1897) George Gissing makes his hero remark that '"if one lives in London, it's in the nature of things to change houses once a year or so"'. Charles Booth called south-west London in the 1890s 'a city in motion', and that could have stood for all London across every decade of the century. In middle-class west Fulham, he said, 'Families shift to another and fresher house, with as little hesitation as rooms are changed at an hotel. A new house is thought no more of than a new suit of clothes.' And Arthur Machen noted this feature when, in 1880 aged seventeen, he became 'a dweller in the tents of London. Tents, I say advisedly, for, with the rarest exceptions, Londoners have no homes.'[38]

All sorts of pressures and temptations kept London on the move. We have already seen how demolitions moved tens of thousands around, especially between 1840 and 1880 in the central districts. Many moves were nearby, as we also saw. But from the 1870s in particular the connection between inner clearances and the new suburban slums became stronger. So the shabby Langford Road area of Fulham was said to have 'received many of those turned out of the demolished courts round Drury Lane' in the late 1890s. A 'whole colony of very rough people', moved from Somers Town by railway extensions, settled in 'badly built streets near Junction Road', Archway. The poorest of those evicted to make way for Marylebone Station before 1899 moved to Kensal New Town. And so on.[39]

The opportunities and temptations of the seasons also kept large numbers of Londoners on the move. 'The London Season' itself, running from the beginning of May till the end of July, brought thousands of bourgeois and upper-middle-class families to the boarding-house regions of London for these three hectic and expensive months. 'In every eligible street throughout the whole metropolis' – we are talking here mainly of the West End – 'are to be found private lodgings that are not equalled, for cleanliness and other comforts, by those of any other city of Europe,' boasted a guide of 1818. The favourite streets then for the best-class lodgings were those running north and south from Piccadilly. Here 'Ready-furnished lodgings, by the week or month', were available from two to six guineas a week for a first floor. The expansion of London and the railways brought about more choice for those county families, adventurers from home and abroad, and the nouveaux riches with social foothills to scale, who from the middle of the century all found attendance in London for the season indispensable. By 1889 West End prices for private apartments were £2 to £15 a week. And Bayswater, Tyburnia, Pimlico and Bloomsbury had all been added to the London boarding-house districts since the first two decades of the century.[40]

Seasonal movements among the upper crust were more than matched by those in society's lower depths. Many thousands of the labouring poor kept only winter quarters in London, spending the summer as farm labourers haymaking and fruit picking, brickmaking for London's new suburbs, navvying on canals and railways, travelling round the country with fairs and shows, or on the tramp for odd jobs or a handout. Men and women so engaged came back to London in October and November, filling the tramps' lodging houses of the Dust-'Ole at Woolwich, or the Mint, Mill Lane (Deptford), Bangor Street, Flower's Mews (Archway) and a dozen or so other places which changed across the century but which all half-emptied in the summer.[41]

It is possible to obtain some glimpses into these peripatetic lives from workhouse admission records, in this case from Islington in 1889–90. Edward Martin, twenty-two, single, with no settled home since about the age of ten: 'I go down in the Country Hopping &c', overwintering in various Holloway lodging houses. An eighty-year old man – 'I have not a soul in the world belonging to me' – went into the workhouse in December and said he was 'Going when warm weather comes'. A travelling hawker, born in Swindon, was admitted from the tramps' lodging houses at Highgate: 'I make Gordon Place my home when I am over this way.' And 'I go away every summer,' said Charles Hodges, thirty-one, a labourer who came back to various Islington addresses around October time.[42]

There were many other pressures on the poor that caused them to move 'like fish in a river', as a Bethnal Green school board visitor put it around 1889. The commonest was indebtedness to the land-lord (for rent or breakages or theft) and to local shopkeepers, them-selves so poor they had to give credit to win custom. This moonlight flitting – shooting or bolting the moon – was a common device among the poor and one reason for short stays at several addresses. But many moves were nearby, and these were likely to have been motivated by a search for better or more convenient or cheaper housing: for a lower rent, for more space, a room free from damp or in better repair or with easier access to water or a lavatory. Other moves were prompted by a desire to be close to kin or workmates or friends who might help out in emergencies. And there may have been difficulties that put them under pressure from neighbours to move on quickly – domestic dishar-mony, filthy habits, aggressiveness in drink, cruelty to children.[43]

Whatever the reason, high mobility among the poor – at least from house to house in a circumscribed neighbourhood rather than from district to district – was more usual than not. And sometimes it could reach an extreme degree of restlessness. Take the case of Thomas Neal, 'the Islington murderer', who killed his 24-year-old wife, Theresa, at 81 St Peter's Street in 1890. They were married seven years before in Bethnal Green. Their children were eight, seven, five, four, two and a half and five months, the eight-year-old having a different mother, who died soon after childbirth in Shoreditch workhouse. The family had been at many addresses in south Islington and Finsbury. They had lived at 81 St Peter's Street one week; before that they had lodged at Parkfield Street (three weeks); Seckford Street (two months); Quinn Buildings (two weeks); Britannia Row (five months); 125 Pentonville Road (three weeks); Charlton Crescent (six months); Dalston (one month); Harrison Street, Gray's Inn Road (four months); 229 Pentonville Road (four months); Charlton Crescent (over twelve months as main tenant and ratepayer); 229 Pentonville Road (six months); Henry Street, Pentonville (three months); Richard Street (four months) and Parkfield Street for two years, renting the whole house for £34 a year plus rates. Neal was hanged at Newgate in March 1890. A public subscription was launched to help support his orphaned children.[44]

We don't know what brought down Thomas Neal from the nominally secure status of a whole-house tenant. But even among lower-middle-class suburbans mobility was common enough, and for similar reasons to those which pushed and pulled the poor around the metropolis. Dickens recalled Lant Street, Borough, in the 1820s, a mixed district of skilled workers, some clerks and those devoted to 'the healthful and invigorating pursuit of mangling': 'The population is migratory, usually disappearing on the verge of quarter-day, and generally by night. His Majesty's revenues are seldom collected in this happy valley; the rents are dubious; and the water communication is very frequently cut off.' Alfred Barrett (a novelist and journalist who wrote extensively under the pseudonym R. Andom) was a true suburban. Born in Brixton in 1869, by the late 1890s he had addresses in Leytonstone, Woodford and South Woodford. In his comic novel *Martha and I: Being Scenes from Our Suburban Life* (1898), his chosen suburb 'was known to landlords and tax and bill collectors as "Sloper's Island"' because of the number of 'moonshooters' around quarter-day, when rents and rates fell due. 'So bad did the thing become at last, that the landlords syndicated and hired a man to loaf about the neighbourhood, as quarter-day drew on, to watch their interests.' Barrett's suburbans were clerks and officials, but the 'Artisan's Village near Loughborough Junction', Brixton, was also called 'Sloper's Island' from around 1870. And we know of the aristocratic moonshooters, flitting from London to Boulogne or Paris or Brussels and back again, who fill the novels of Thackeray in the 1840s and 1850s and who had their real-life models in Lady Blessington and her companion Count D'Orsay, with numberless others besides.[45]

For all classes, bigger and dearer living space, if possible in a better neighbourhood, might follow an improvement in circumstances, and a smaller and shabbier a fall from financial grace. And relocation could follow a hundred other alterations in family prospects. Benjamin Farjeon, a popular novelist whose library of 8,000 books had to be accommodated with each move, had four children through the 1880s and 1890s. 'Before a baby was born, they always moved', generally around the Swiss Cottage area (which Farjeon called South Hampstead) and Notting Hill. And the Admiralty civil servant and fine novelist

William Hale White (Mark Rutherford) moved out of Marylebone to one damp suburban villa after another. Despairing of finding anything satisfactory for rent, he eventually built his own place on land he bought at Carshalton in 1868.[46]

White's six- or seven-year search for a suburban idyll was one tiny mark in a pattern that asserted itself ever more strongly as the century grew older. Among the countless moves of families within London two motifs stand out. One is the opportunistic and frequent movement around a small townscape, maybe within a district of a mile or two's diameter, where local resources – street markets, schools, pawnshops, kinship networks, church-based or other charities, a local labour market (perhaps most important of all) – could always be relied on. This pattern remained an important fact of life for working-class Londoners across the century.

The other motif was the suburbanising urge. As we have seen, this affected the middle classes ever more powerfully from the 1840s and 1850s and by the 1880s and 1890s had spread to almost all, including, in the case of suburban slums, the very poor. The movement out broadly followed the same radial lines as the movement in. By the 1890s the effects were social, even political. Ernest Benn was a worker for the Liberal Party and lived in Cable Street, Stepney, during 1891–3.

As I watched the development of St George's-in-the-East and Wapping . . . I was able to see the rush to the new unplanned paradise on the immediate outskirts of London. Within a single year we lost all the officials of the local Liberal and Radical Association. The bearded, patriarchal, pawnbroker Jacobs, who was our Treasurer . . . was one of the first to go; he and his wife embodied between them, to my personal knowledge, the best of what we call the Christian virtues. Freeman, the tobacconist, our Honorary Secretary, and Sly, the tent and sail-maker, our Chairman, deserted us about the same time, going off to become good Conservatives in the fashionable new suburbs, and leaving the cause of Liberalism in less responsible hands. The dock officials swarmed out of the neighbourhood to enjoy the new delights.[47]

And the same could have been written at this period of Finsbury (with its printers and engineers), Southwark (with its hatters and printers) and Holborn (with its engineers and scientific instrument makers).

The fashionable movement out swept up many who were excited by the notion of country living but who quickly became disillusioned and pined for the London they had left behind. This too affected a minority of all classes across the century. James Hain Friswell, another popular writer, moved for health reasons in 1870 from Bloomsbury to Bexley Heath, where his daughter found life 'very dull indeed. To us young people it was social banishment.' Thomas Okey, newly married, lamented his move to Kent around 1895, 'for, like most cockneys, we had an over-weighted estimate of the joys of country life . . .' A man who had been evicted from a Clerkenwell slum in the early 1880s ended up in a 'comfortable cottage and garden' somewhere in Buckinghamshire. He 'did not like it at all; it was very dull, and he wished he was back in Red Lion Market'. And when Charles Lamb retired from the family's home near the Angel, Islington, to Enfield for his sister Mary's health in 1827 (Mary had murdered their mother and suffered recurrent bouts of mental illness) he had many regrets: 'I *hate* the country.' All these missed the bustle, excitement and conveniences of London life, and its cheek-by-jowl companionship in streets, courts and alleys. But it was by no means everyone who found London congenial or neighbourly. By no means at all.[48]

'Neighbours of Ours'[49]

'The next-door neighbour of a man in London is generally as great a stranger to him as if he lived at the distance of York.' So wrote Pierce Egan in 1821, thirty years or so before the period of London's hyper-growth began and when (we might think) the sheer weight of numbers had not yet had its alienating impact. William Hazlitt agreed in 1826 that in London 'a man does not know his next-door neighbour'. Perhaps this was a phenomenon that told most on the provincial for whom – back home – neighbours were real enough: '"I hev lived in London without knowing how the people in the floor above, or below me, got a living; although the same roof has sheltered us for weeks."' There is plenty of evidence that this feeling about London life had certainly not diminished, and if anything had strengthened, by the century's end. When Mrs Emma Vowles gave evidence at the trial of the Lambeth poisoner Thomas Neill Cream in 1892, she had lived at 27 Lambeth Road for nearly three years.'The neighbour in the next house on my left is named Payne: I only know her to say "Good morning." The person on the right I did not know to speak to.'[50]

To a large extent this commonly expressed feeling was one result of the rapid mobility of London's shifting population, across all classes.

People moved on after only a short time. Many stole away secretly in the middle of the night. There was little incentive here to do otherwise than keep one's business to one's self.

Partly too this exclusiveness was an extension into private space of that public indifference which the stranger was quick to notice as the main characteristic of people in the London streets. It was marked by a blank gaze, preoccupation with self at the expense of others and aggression. Max Schlesinger, a German visitor to London around 1850, noted how 'A Londoner . . . will run against you, and make you revolve on your own axis, without so much as looking round to see how you feel after the shock . . .' Some of this may have been deliberate. In 1821 'the unoffending passengers of either sex are frequently obstructed on, or absolutely pushed off the pavement by a trio of arm-in-arm puppies', a complaint that rang loudly right through the century. But mostly it was the result of ignorance on the newcomer's side. *The Picture of London* for 1818 advised visitors of the rule of the London pavement: 'Much unpleasant jostling will be saved, by attending to the established custom of taking the wall when it is on the right hand, and of giving it when it is on the left.' And W. E. Adams, the Cheltenham compositor, recalled his days at Kennington in the 1850s when he would read the *Morning Star* for the whole hour it took him to walk to Fleet Street 'by keeping to the right'. 'The feat . . . was only possible when people kept in line. All I found it necessary to do, where the traffic was thickest, was to walk immediately behind someone else.' But those who did not observe the rule 'had as bad a time of it as a dog at a fair' and 'were so buffeted about' that eventually they too were forced into line.[51]

But if a bruising could be avoided by adopting local customs, loneliness could not, at least at first. For Thomas de Quincey 'No loneliness can be like that' among 'faces never-ending' in London's streets 'as yet unknown'. This seems to have been an almost universally experienced element of London-shock, that bundle of feelings involving awe and damaged self-esteem that struck so many first-comers to the metropolis in the nineteenth century. 'There is no lonelier city in the world,' affirmed Benjamin Farjeon, surely then one of its most popular citizens, in 1884. Walter Besant recalled his student days at King's College, London, in the 1850s, when he shared a room with his brother at Featherstone Buildings, Holborn. Walter's brother worked in the City, had many friends 'and was out nearly every evening'. But Walter's silent study hours distracted him beyond endurance: 'To this day [*c.* 1899] I cannot think of those lonely evenings in my London lodging without a touch of the old terror.'⁵²

For some, this lasted all their London days. Charles Dickens remarked, 'There is a numerous class of people in this great metropolis who seem not to possess a single friend, and whom nobody appears to care for.' And fifty years on George Gissing, perhaps an isolated man by nature, confided to his diary, 'I have lived in London ten years, and now, on a day like this when I am very lonely and depressed, there is not one single house in which I should be welcome if I presented myself, not one family – nay, not one person – who would certainly receive me with good will.'⁵³

Isolation could be compounded by the infinite subdivisions by which metropolitan society tried to keep itself to itself. There was 'diversity' enough in Victorian London but its motive power was class and its object was separate development. This was an ideal more aimed at than attained, as we saw in London's suburbs from 1840 to 1880. But the resulting social compromises, at least in part, could be put out of mind, soap-sponged from consciousness. '"No, I don't know a single person here to speak to; I don't associate with my neighbours; I keep myself to myself and don't speak to anybody,"' one 'respectable' person in a mixed area told Nellie Benson in the late 1880s.⁵⁴

We have already noted that there were separate modes of transport for the classes and the masses, and different modes of speech. There were separate shops, even types of shop utterly unknown from one class to another, separate ways of dressing that rendered the class of the wearer instantly recognisable. There were – with important exceptions that altered over time – separate amusements, and for ever and a day there were separate schools. Then there were separate neighbourhoods long before the period of suburban hypergrowth added new opportunities for grading Londoners into their appropriate spatial compartments. When John Fisher Murray wittily subdivided London's 'private neighbourhoods' in 1844 it was old London he had mainly in mind. There were exclusive neighbourhoods (like Park Lane), ultra-fashionable (Portman Square), fashionable (Lower Mount Street), quasi-fashionable (east side of Arlington Street), mixed (Piccadilly – live at any house numbered under fifty 'and you are ruined for life'), East Indian (Portland Place), high genteel (Baker Street), low genteel (suburbs of the New Road etc.) and equivocal (those where industry or commerce rubbed shoulders with residential). And we can add shabby genteel (which Dickens thought unique to London), artisan and low, with many exquisite subgradations in between. All of these were the geographical expression of forces – economic, social, psychological – which attempted to separate Londoners one from another and which could only have made worse the isolation of those who felt it difficult to belong in London at all. They also kept many Londoners in complete ignorance of their fellow citizens just a short distance away.[55]

Now all these factors were real enough in repelling many provincial newcomers from the city which had tempted them to try their fortune. For some they were short-lived and curable; for others a permanent condition that would sooner or later expel them. But none of these was the whole reality. Each had within it the germ of an opposite and entirely positive experience that was unique to living in London.

Take the indifference of the London crowd. Its sheer energy, its encyclopedic representation of humanity in all its forms, its living demonstration of the interconnectedness of human experience were for many nothing short of an inspiration. Hazlitt expressed this well: 'In London there is a *public*; and each man is part of it.' But it was Mary Ward, philanthropist and novelist, who perhaps put it best when she recounted an ecstatic moment from 1885. She had been in London four years.

I can recall one summer afternoon, in particular, when as I was in a hansom driving idly westward towards Hyde Park Gate, thinking of a hundred things at once, this consciousness of *intensification*, of a heightened meaning in everything – the broad street, the crowd of moving figures and carriages, the houses looking down upon it – seized upon me with a rush. "Yes, it is good – the mere living!" Joy in the infinite variety of the great city as compared with the "cloistered virtue" of Oxford; the sheer pleasure of novelty, of the kind new faces, and the social discoveries one felt opening on many sides; the delight of new perceptions, new powers in oneself; – all this seemed to flower for me in those few minutes of reverie – if one can apply such a word to an experience so vivid.[56]

Or take loneliness. The anonymity of London was for many a delight. '"There one can live as one chooses,"' says troubled Jude Fawley in Thomas Hardy's novel *Jude the Obscure* (1895). Margaret Nevinson, a vicar's daughter from Leicester who became a London schoolteacher around 1880, 'was very happy in London; I liked the freedom, especially when I got a latch-key, the symbol of bachelor independence'.

'Eccentricity of any kind is not, *cannot* be tolerated in a country place . . .' wrote John Fisher Murray. 'In London, on the contrary, there is no eccentricity too eccentric . . . and, whether a man chooses to stand on his head or his heels . . . makes not the smallest difference to any human being save himself.' Booth characterised London as 'the city which asks no questions'. And Harry Snell, a Nottinghamshire man who cycled to Woolwich for a clerk's job when twenty-five in 1890, recalled his 'refreshing sense of relief', his 'feeling of liberation', on exchanging 'the old environment' for 'the busier life of the metropolis.' That would be typical of great numbers of new Londoners right across the century.[57]

And then neighbourliness. 'Londoners have no neighbours' cannot stand as sufficient description of the relationships between those thrown together by chance in London. Once the surface of that universal indifference of the Londoner-in-public was penetrated, many new arrivals remarked on the friendliness of the Londoner-in-private, a warmth sometimes not encountered anywhere else. David Wilkie compared London favourably to his native Edinburgh in 1806: 'I like it a great deal better; for the people are much more affable and free.' And Alexander Somerville, another Scot, came to London in 1834, a soldier courtmartialled for his radical politics. In a coffee shop in Finsbury Square he fell into conversation with a cabinet maker who, much taken by his new acquaintance, invited Somerville to Sunday dinner. The cabinet maker's wife, 'a Londoner born, told me much that I did not know; and displayed that vivacity, intelligence, and generous hospitality – the hospitality not of the table alone, but of manners and conversation, which leave no doubt upon the visitor's mind, that he is welcome – a hospitality peculiarly characteristic of the genuine native of London'.[58]

These qualities also showed themselves among neighbours. It would have been extraordinary if the almost universal taste for 'At Homes' among the London middle and upper classes did not involve entertaining neighbours as well as the congenial coterie of like-minded friends and acquaintances at their core. And similarly the lavish children's parties, most especially at Christmas, which were such a feature of middle-class London life in the second half of the century. Certainly lower-middle-class Robert Hyde, later founder of the Industrial Society, recalled a children's party at a 'neighbouring house' in Forest Gate around 1889 because he had to hide his disreputable shoes beneath him whenever he sat on the floor for round games. Molly Hughes's experience of Canonbury from 1870 to 1885 – 'During our fifteen years in the one house we never had the slightest acquaintance with our "semi-detached"' – was probably by no means uncommon. But hers was a suburban stockbroker's family whose financial ups-and-downs gave cause for secrecy and it was very different for John Grosch, his father in trade in Kentish Town in the 1890s, who could name all the shopkeepers in the terrace, enumerate their peculiarities and praise their 'neighbourliness'. Eliza Lynn knew all the business and every foible and eccentricity of her fellow boarders at Montague Place within months of her first coming to London in 1845. And Benjamin Farjeon – typical of no one, it is true to say – befriended 'All the poor people' in Adelaide Road, Swiss Cottage, where he lived at 196 from around 1886. 'They knew and loved him, he did much more than give them pence, he left behind him fun and a moment of warmth.'[59]

No doubt there was more cause and opportunity for neighbouring in working-class districts and among the poor. In respectable model dwellings, around 1889, 'a Lady Resident' noted in her diary how the women 'call upon one another' in the afternoons; how a neighbour, knowing of our diarist's unlikely partiality to sprats, 'sends me in a plateful by her most careful child'; and how it was impossible for people to be 'overlooked altogether, or flagrantly neglected by relatives in illness or old age'. In places like this, in streets where the turnover of lodgers was not too frantic – and most, even the roughest, had settled families, often related, who might move around within the street but rarely outside it – and in the courts and alleys of the poor, certain support networks could be expected to operate more often than not.[60]

So in a family crisis – incapacitating illness, childbirth, a fire, death – children might be taken in and cared for in the short term, nursing and midwifery might be forthcoming from experienced mothers. Sometimes these services might call for a small payment. Then a street collection might be made to replace goods or help defray the costs of a respectable funeral, and the poorest might beg – not always success-fully – food and (earlier in the century) a jug of water. Borrowing necessaries like coal and food, pots and pans, might also be negoti-ated. At 8 St Stephen Street, Tottenham Court Road, in the early 1880s, ninety-seven people shared two WCs and the water supply was irreg-ular. The next-door neighbour 'often obliges the women with water, and allows the most respectable of the people to come into her place to wash'. Neighbours gave information about charities, say, or the opportunity of a job, neighbour sometimes speaking up for neighbour. In 'Our Court', where Thomas Wright found poor-quality house room after eviction for railway clearances in the1860s, neighbours conspired to give early warning of the approaching tallyman – a door-to-door salesman leaving goods on credit – so that people who owed him money could hide away; and all joined in to barricade the court against evictions by the landlord. Support like this made the clearance of courts and alleys for new roads, railways or model dwellings doubly painful. A Clerkenwell vicar explained why people who were evicted tried to live locally if they could: 'They are clannish and kind to one another, and helpful to one another. They are very good people socially in that matter; they keep to their surroundings; they do not want to be driven away.' All over cockney London, 'The old inhabitants love the place; nothing would induce them to move elsewhere.'[61]

Sometimes neighbouring could transcend mutual self-interest (you scratch my back, I'll scratch yours) or a value system which incorporated kindliness and a duty to assist if one could. Frederick Rogers, a neglected hero of the battle for old age pensions, recalled the surgery of Dr John Watkins at Falcon Square, City, around 1867. Watkins, in his seventies at the time, treated his poorest patients free, specialising in spinal and ophthalmic problems. Rogers attended the surgery at five in the morning for a spinal weakness. By then Watkins would have seen other patients. He noted regulars who epitomised 'the loving self-sacrifice that manifested itself among the sick poor'. 'A lame sailor – an alien and a foreigner – was brought each day by a bright-faced ragged lad' from Poplar: the sailor, 'a crippled derelict', was penniless and could have given the boy nothing. And 'a helpless cripple', about fourteen years old, was carried on the back of his friend, a couple of years older, 'for something over a mile each morning, waited while the doctor "dressed" him, and then carried him back again'.[62]

Such 'loving self-sacrifice' could extend to strangers. William Andrews, a night watchman guarding some houses marked for demolition in Flower and Dean Street, Spitalfields, noticed early on Boxing Day morning 1891 a man in rags on some trestles in the bitter cold. '"Arn't [sic] you cold, old man, sitting here all night?" and he replied, "Yes, sir, I am. I suppose you have not a halfpenny you could give me to get a cup of coffee with."' Andrews, who was lame, had just threepence for his railway fare home. '"No, I have only three pennies, but you can have one of them, and I'll walk part of my journey."' But the penny came too late and the man, his name unknown, collapsed and died half an hour later, of starvation and exposure.[63]

Of course, not all was 'loving self-sacrifice' between neighbours. There were rows, scraps, feuds, vendettas. In 1866, when a woman in Southwark protested about noise from singing in the street disturbing her sick children 'a volley of stones' broke ten out of twelve windowpanes in her room: she was too poor to mend them. In May 1872 two south London women were given penal servitude for life for grievous bodily harm on Susan Snellgrove. They had knocked out her eye, deliberately intending to blind her. Snellgrove had been summonsed as an identification witness against a notorious street robber, Daniel Harris, and was attacked on her way to court by the two women and their 'companions'. And for lower-middle-class Jerome K. Jerome, growing up in working-class Poplar in the 1860s and 1870s and bullied by street children, 'Terror lived in every street, hid, waiting for me, round each corner.' Looking back on Kentish Town in the 1890s, John Grosch noted how 'People were brutal and pugnacious', compared to London in the 1940s.[64]

Rows would erupt over almost anything – falling below the street's standards of cleanliness or childcare; criticism considered unjust; telling off a neighbour's child; a drunken misunderstanding; refusal to share; failure to return something borrowed; name-calling (the incessant taunt of 'Four Eyes!' levelled at Tommy Jackson in 1880s Clerkenwell imported 'a streak of sourness into my disposition' that lasted all his life); taking liberties with property or person; suspected theft. Rows like these might be another cause to move on, to get out of the way of a stronger and more aggressive neighbour. And rows which came to blows might easily lead to charges brought before the magistrates. The low streets and courts and alleys of cockney London were fiercely litigious places, schooled in court procedure, polished in the best way of getting across a point of view. But all of this was the very opposite of indifference and helps give the lie, just as much as good neighbouring does, to 'Londoners have no neighbours' as some universal truth.[65]

So tension within neighbourhoods, even those with a strong communal feeling, was a fact of daily life. But how did Londoners fare when neighbourhoods received an 'influx' of 'foreigners', of people who were far more 'strange' than the English provincials and the Welsh and Scots? The Irish, say, or blacks or lascars or Chinese or East European Jews? And how did these strangers become Londoners in their turn?

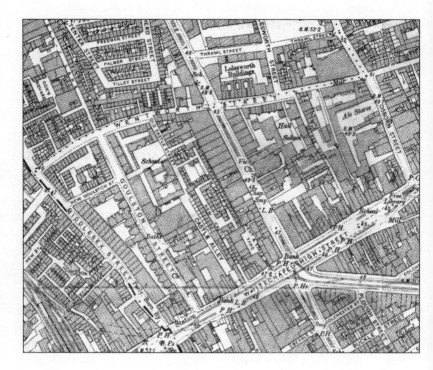

Wentworth Street, 1894

V

WENTWORTH STREET:
THE LONDON MEDLEY

Wentworth Street, Spitalfields

Leaving Christ Church behind us, we cross the road for the Jewish quarter.
In less than two minutes the almost unspeakable scene is before us. We seem
to be in a world of dissolving views. We suddenly find ourselves in a foreign
land. The street we enter might be a street in Warsaw or Cracow. We have
taken leave of everything English, and entered an alien world. Wentworth
Street – that is its name – is even a greater Sunday-market than the better-
known thoroughfare of which it is a branch – Middlesex Street ('Petticoat
Lane'). It is the market of the thickly-herded, poorer immigrant Jews – the
Ashkenazi Jews from Poland, Russia, Germany, and Holland . . . In the heart
of London, it is yet like a foreign town, with its own liberties of trade, its
own segregated peoples, religions, customs, and industries.[1]

WENTWORTH Street was the 'Jews' Market' to outsiders, 'The Lane' to
its stallholders and customers. In 1896, when Henry Walker, a Christian
propagandist, registered his shock and outrage at first seeing it, the
market was of recent origin. In this full-blown state it was less than
fifteen years old. And it was indeed an utterly alien import, developed
by the East European Jews whose coming changed this part of London
beyond recognition for three-quarters of a century to come.

Wentworth Street might reasonably stand as symbol for a London
that became palpably more 'foreign' as the nineteenth century grew
older. Before the 1880s, Wentworth Street and its neighbourhood had
a very different notoriety as a thieves' hideaway, a place of street robbers
and coiners and cheap prostitutes. Its population was English, with
just a smattering of Irish and some Jews at the City end. Before

Commercial Street cut it in two in the 1840s it was as ill-favoured a place as any in London. But in the 1890s the western half was the great 'ghetto' mart and at the eastern end immigrant Jews were fast displacing the old-established outcast population.

Other parts of London had gone the same way as Wentworth Street, even if to less dramatic effect. London in the 1890s could justly claim to be the most cosmopolitan city in Europe. In 1841 its foreign-born population – we'll exclude the Irish from this definition – was probably just 13,000, less than 1 per cent of the population. By 1901 there were 135,000, 3 per cent of Londoners, who were foreigners by birth. Nineteen out of twenty were Europeans, for London had been the main Old World beneficiary of people displaced by a turbulent century. Opening in 1800 at a moment of global conflict, for the next 100 years continental Europe lurched from revolution to war and back again, expelling refugees like chaff in a threshing room. Agrarian reform and industrialisation moved far greater numbers of economic migrants from the countryside to the cities. And with the help of another revolution, this time in transport and communications, the cities now could be anywhere. By the century's end London's cosmopolitan character was itself a gravitational force drawing strangers from abroad. For they knew they would find their countrymen among the tens of thousands who had already braved the journey and ground out some sort of livelihood there.

This exotic mix of Londoners from abroad gave a distinctive flavour to London life by the 1890s. It helped change Londoners' eating habits, a host of French, Italian, German and other restaurants tickling retarded English palates: there was a even a City chain of Australian restaurants by 1880 which 'revolutionised London catering' and was noted for its 'attractive young women behind the counters'. It opened the home-grown imagination to new styles, fads, tastes, ideas and values, so that 'London society' – meaning high fashion – 'is the most cosmopolitan of any in existence'. Most of all, foreign migration diversified the feel and look of London. It was not only the Jewish East End that shocked and repelled on the one hand, while evoking fascination and wonder on the other.[2]

Although London in 1800 couldn't compete in this regard with London in 1899, all the seeds of that later multicultural coexistence were present in the earlier period. Long traditions of worldwide settlement in London survived generation after generation. But one element strongly felt in the first half of the century found itself eclipsed in the second. This was the Irish migrant.

'Little Ireland'

In the beginning were the Irish. For centuries before the Act of Union of 1801 there had been an Irish presence in London. At the time of union they represented by far the largest group of strangers in the metropolis. They were not all as 'foreign' as the Irish poor. Ireland exported some of its most talented sons to London to work in the law and in Grub Street and, after 1801, in politics. Irish aristocrats and plutocrats merged more or less invisibly with London society, migrating for the season or moving permanently to town as absentee landlords.[3] In 1841, the first time a tally was taken, there were 73,000 Irish-born in London, around 4 per cent of the population. It seems reasonable to assume that a similar proportion – so some 37,000 – would have been found there at the beginning of the century.

The patterns already laid down by 1800 for economic migration from Ireland to London were complex. There was a great deal of seasonal migration, just as we saw among the English poor. So the great market gardens around London brought in thousands during the summer months: Irish potato pullers in Poplar and West Ham, hop and fruit pickers in Kentish London, vegetable and flower cultivators from Acton to Barking and Mortlake to Woolwich. They shipped to Bristol or London in the spring, tramped to the fields, made do in crude huts or under canvas, sent money back to their families and returned to Ireland in October. This was a movement mainly of men, with some women and children among them. Most were agricultural labourers from County Cork in the south and rural Leinster in the west. They carried with them some native rivalries: in Poplar in August 1804 an 'alarming riot' of several hundred armed with 'bludgeons' fought to determine whether Munster or Connaught bred the better men.[4]

It was out of this seasonal ebb and flow that many, like jetsam on a beach, found their way to London proper. Overwintering in London, rather than the voyage home with its costs and discomforts, must have appealed to single men and women, and to those husbands and fathers anxious to cut adrift from domestic liabilities. Those migrants who came as a family needed all-year-round work and that required city living. And the prospect of setting up in the giant metropolis was not as daunting as it might otherwise have been for a rural people because since the seventeenth century the Irish had made some London districts peculiarly their own.

The oldest, biggest, densest, most notorious of these was Little Ireland, the Rookery of St Giles. The Irish first appear in the parish records here in 1640. At the end of the Napoleonic Wars there were said to be 6,000 Irish poor living there; probably there were others not labelled poor, artisans and shopkeepers for instance, who might have been added to the total. But St Giles was far from alone. There were Irish 'colonies' all over London: in the Saffron Hill area, home to about 5,000 at the same period; in Whitechapel and near the docks – 14,000 Irish Catholics were said to live in six riverside parishes in 1816; in the Westminster slums near Great Peter Street, where a fierce riot among the Irish turned against the police in May 1822; in the Gray's Inn Lane area around filthy Baldwin's Gardens; in the Borough west of the Mint; in Leyton and West Ham, at 'Paddy's Island' in Plaistow and at Putney, where Irish labourers staked out their own suburban arcadias; and then in odd out-of-the-way places where a few Irish tenants gained a foothold and others came to join them. Like Calmel Buildings, off Orchard Street, Marylebone, just round the corner from plutocratic Portman Square. In 1815 some 700 poor Irish and a 100 pigs lived there, 'often three or four families in one room', their rubbish and filth filling up the narrow court between twenty-four small houses. A Calmel Society of Marylebone worthies was established to remove the nuisance, reform the Irish and relieve the poor rates, apparently with little success.[5]

It was not, in fact, the poorest part of the Irish agricultural population that made its way to London. Some means, at least in pre-famine years, had to be found to pay for the crossing. Only the fittest and most ambitious would muster the resources. But there was a wide gap between rural Irish and metropolitan living standards. Once in the capital, these newcomers were among the very poorest of London's many poor. And the slow pace of a rural upbringing did no favours in a city where quick wits, application and perseverance paid a dividend; and where employers increasingly looked for regularity and sobriety in their workforce.

Accordingly, many Irish migrants eked a living at the outer edges of the London economy. They featured visibly among the ranks of the London beggars, as probably they always had. In 1823, of 1,493 beggars 'registered' in London by the Mendicity Society 434 (nearly one in three) were Irish-born. Begging too was mostly seasonal, tiding over those who would return to the fields in the spring. Sometimes it was a full-time endeavour. Like Mrs Keefe, who kept her two 'little' children out of St Giles Roman Catholic free school: '"God bless you, Sir, these children can earn eight shillings a day for me!"' And that was no small sum in 1815.[6]

Close to the beggars in self-sufficiency and the ability to choose when and how to work came the street sellers. Henry Mayhew thought there were some 10,000 Irish street sellers in London in the early 1850s, many of them taking over the nut and orange trade from the Jews. Then there were casual labouring opportunities involving that hard graft in which it was sometimes difficult to interest the cockney: coal and ballast heaving and 'lumping' (unloading) timber in the docks; railroad building (navvying); paviours', plasterers' and bricklayers' labourers; all kinds of lifting and carrying jobs. By 1850 nine out of ten ticketed porters at Covent Garden market were Irishmen, and Irishwomen found much casual portering work there too. Then there were Irishmen among the poorest sort of artisans, like tailors and especially shoemakers. Irish shoemakers formed the largest single occupational group noted by the census enumerators in Field Lane in 1841, for instance. And Irish workers displaced the English from 'translating' or renovating old boots and shoes, the main livelihood of the cellar dwellers in Monmouth Street, Seven Dials. Irishwomen found a place at the cheapest end of domestic labour as charwomen and laundresses. There was a prejudice against them in more genteel homes: '"Irish, did ye say? Och! sure now, and isn't it Cornwall I am?"' replies hot-tempered Norah Connor to her mistress's objection to an Irish servant in *The Greatest Plague of Life* by the Brothers Mayhew (1847).[7]

The Great Famine of 1846–9 altered the character of London's Irish population in at least three ways. First, it pushed more families (as distinct from single workers) out of the Irish countryside so that the numbers of Irish-born children and dependent elderly in London rose as never before. Second, the Irish landlord class, desperate to relieve themselves of a pauper population starving on the rates, subsidised the passage to England. The new arrivals now were among the very poorest that Ireland's rural population had to offer. And third, this new migration was more markedly permanent than previously, for the famine dispossessed a generation from the prospect of return to an Irish 'home'.[8]

London received the largest single share of those migrants who chose England over America as a destination. The 1851 census counted 109,000 Irish-born in London, up a third on the decade before and the highest number of the whole century. But the Irish-born proportion of Londoners – one in twenty-two or so – was far lower than in Liverpool, say, or Glasgow.[9] Yet despite its dilution among a host of Londoners, the famine migration was a genuine crisis for the Irish in London that resonated long into the 1850s. Its components were homelessness, overcrowding and destitution.

The Asylum for the Houseless Poor at Playhouse Yard, Whitecross Street, City, admitted some 1,200 Irish people a year in the early 1840s. They were taken off the streets for three days to give them food and shelter and the opportunity to find somewhere to live. But in 1846–7 the numbers rose to 7,576 and in 1847–8 to 10,756. Even in 1848–9, when the worst of the famine was passing, 5,068 were helped in this way.[10]

These homeless people and their compatriots came to a city that was crowded at the best of times. But there could hardly have been a worse time than the late 1840s to find somewhere to live in the Irish districts of London. We remember the demolitions in St Giles for New Oxford Street and the overcrowding in Church Lane; and the clearances for Victoria Street, Farringdon Road and Commercial Street, districts with large numbers of Irish too. A St Giles clergyman noted around 1852 how '"*the Irishman*, HOWEVER POOR, *never wants hospitality* . . . The landlord of this room has let two of the other corners, keeping the third and fourth for himself; and *then, when these poor 'creatures' are shivering in the cold outside, it is not in his heart not to let them occupy the fourth corner, for one night, rent free.*"' To show how bad things could get, Thomas Beames investigated a court in the Saffron Hill area around 1849. In a five-roomed house he found one room occupied by a husband and wife, probably the tenant of the whole property. But in the other four rooms were eighty-six people. The most crowded was home to twenty-eight. The occupiers were chiefly Irish and recent migrants. No other group of Londoners at any time in the nineteenth century had to put up with such living conditions. By the late 1850s reports like these faded away. The crisis subsided and newcomers were able to find more and slightly better living space.[11]

The poverty of the famine migrants haunted them longer than the housing crisis. Many were starving poor. If they sought help from the workhouse they were at risk of being 'passed back' to the famine-stricken country they'd escaped. So usually they bore their privations without help, living on what they could get from begging and the poorest sort of wage labour. A family at the Asylum for the Houseless Poor, spotted by Henry Mayhew in the bitter cold January of 1850, had come originally from Cork. Even after three years in the world's richest city their plight was pitiful. The mother's toes poked through her shoes. She was 'half-clad' in a cloak and gown and nothing underneath. Her eleven-year-old daughter wore just a cloak and a petticoat under it; a pair of women's shoes were tied to her feet with string. 'The youngest boy was almost a dwarf. He was three years old but so stunted that he seemed scarce half that age . . .' In the winter the family begged; in the summer the husband went into the country and took the family with him.[12]

What charity there was came from the Roman Catholic Church, the greatest Irish institution in London. Prosperous Catholics chose priests as the 'medium' to distribute alms and 'there is no doubt' that priests gave from their own pockets too. Attendance at mass may have been irregular enough – 70 to 75 per cent of London Catholics abstained throughout the century – and a call for the last sacrament was often the only time a priest knew of the existence of large numbers of his London flock. But most Irish migrants called themselves Catholic, had some concept of their religious obligations, loved (sometimes feared) their priests, obeyed their injunctions to quell a row and pinned a paper Virgin to their wall. The Church might not have kept the Irish poor sober (although there was a Catholic temperance movement led by Father Mather in 1843 which made a great stir) or curbed the truculence of a quick-tempered people, but it helped keep Irish women chaste before marriage and faithful during it – in great contrast, it was said, to the cockney poor.[13]

Religion was one reason for hostility between the Irish and the English in London. The so-called 'papal aggression' of 1850, when the Pope installed a cardinal as archbishop at Westminster and divided the nation into Catholic bishoprics, coincided with the largest ever presence in London of poor Irish people. A 'No Popery' agitation led to fights with staves and brickbats around Guy Fawkes' Night 1850 at Islington, Southwark and no doubt elsewhere. Sectarianism didn't set London alight but it festered uncomfortably from this time on. Irish Catholic labourers violently attacked pro-Garibaldi demonstrations in Hyde Park in September and October 1862. And for the rest of the century militant anti-Catholic propaganda at lecture halls, open-air meetings and among Protestant missionaries seeking converts in Irish streets provoked rows and flare-ups across the capital.[14]

There were other causes of dispute. Alone of London's migrant populations the Irish competed directly with native workers at the lowest-paid end of the labour market. Fears that they would drive down living standards by accepting the lowest possible wage, or by slicing the penny capitalist's profit margins wafer-thin, were reasonably founded. Mayhew discovered that 'next to a policeman, a genuine London costermonger hates an Irishman, considering him an intruder'. And most bitterness was apparently felt by 'Irish cockneys', the second- and third-generation descendants of pre-famine migrants who numbered scores of thousands in London by 1850. They adopted an ironic London slang term and labelled the newcomers 'Grecians' – a 'Grecian accent' was a brogue. 'The [Irish] Cockneys regard the Grecians as coming to take the bread out of their own mouths, and consider their extensive immigration as tending to lower their own wages.' They also felt the newcomers' 'abject poverty and nakedness' as a discredit on their own origins. This antipathy was one cause of a wider distribution from 1850 of the Irish in London, away from the crowded migrant areas: 'There are constant quarrels between the two, and they are so estranged that they will not live even in the same parts of the town, after the first flow of generous hospitality has passed over.'[15]

The numbers of Irish-born in London fell away after the 1860s. There were still 107,000 in 1861, just short of the peak of ten years before, then 91,000 in 1871 and 60,000 in 1901. Even so, the Irish presence in London in the second half of the century was lively enough. And it was to provide a new reason for hostility among the natives.

It was in the 1860s that London was first made a battleground in the struggle for Irish independence, second only to Dublin as a theatre of war. The Irish Revolutionary Brotherhood (IRB) made its first appeal to the 'Irishmen resident in London' in April 1861. The London IRB published the *Irish Liberator* and there were covert Fenian branches in Soho and Finsbury. They made efforts to enlist Irish soldiers at Woolwich barracks around 1866 and shot dead a military bandsman in Holborn in September 1867. But it was the 'Clerkenwell Outrage' of 13 December that year that most forcibly brought Fenianism to Londoners' attention. Richard Burke and Joseph T. Casey, Irish-American gun runners, were awaiting trial at Clerkenwell House of Correction. An attempt at rescue involved rolling a barrel of gunpowder against the prison wall when both men were due in the exercise yard. In fact the prison authorities had been tipped off and they had been moved to fresh cells. A devastating explosion demolished part of the prison wall but had a far greater effect on houses in Corporation Lane. Twelve people were killed and forty injured. Twenty babies were said to have been killed in the womb. Michael Barrett, a Glaswegian by birth, was executed for the crime, the joint work of Dublin men and a band from the London IRB. Barrett's would be the last public hanging in England.[16]

The Clerkenwell explosion produced a great panic in Scotland Yard and the Home Office but it seems to have 'frightened the Fenians quite as much as it frightened the Government'. For the rest of the 1860s and the whole of the 1870s the most audible expression of London Irish nationalism was an occasional Fenian demonstration and the annual St Patrick's Day parade from Trafalgar Square to a rally in Hyde Park. In 1874, for instance, 10,000 London Irish marchers included many 'females' and two brass bands. It was entirely 'orderly and decorous'.[17]

Irish terrorism returned to London with the Home Rule agitation, which gained new boldness from 1880. An attempt by an Irish-American group in March 1881 to dynamite the Mansion House was foiled by an alert City policeman who snuffed out the smouldering fuse. A second try in May 1882 was another half-cocked affair. The police raids that followed led to an arms cache discovery in Clerkenwell – 400 rifles each had their stock 'marked with the shamrock'. Then on one night in March 1883 an abortive attempt to blow up the offices of *The Times* was followed by a more successful explosion at new government offices in Parliament Street. That October the underground railway was bombed at Charing Cross. And on the Metropolitan Railway near Paddington Station a bomb was dropped from a moving tube train, injuring seventy-two passengers travelling in the third-class coaches. In February 1884 a bomb exploded in the left-luggage office at Victoria Station, with no fatalities. Similar devices – assembled in France from American components – were defused at three other London termini. That May sixteen 'cakes' of dynamite were found at the foot of Nelson's

Column. And bombs went off outside the Junior Carlton Club and – cheekily – the offices of the Special Irish Branch at Scotland Yard. In December an attempt to blow up London Bridge killed three bombers. The Fenian campaign continued through 1885 with further attacks on the underground, on the Tower of London, Westminster Hall, the Admiralty and the House of Commons. And a last fling (so to speak) – a foiled bomb plot to assassinate the Queen at the 1887 Jubilee – resulted in the arrests of two Irish-Americans, complete with dynamite, in Islington.[18]

The terror-filled 1880s could not have been a comfortable time for the Irish-born living in London. Anti-Irish sentiment no doubt expressed itself in street or workplace or shop or school. But there is no evidence of any structured backlash. After all, by the 1880s the Irish in London had become so much less strange and more integrated into metropolitan life than the poverty-stricken rural migrants of just thirty or forty years before. There were fewer newcomers, although London continued to exert its magic pull on the ambitious Irish woman and man. Harry Furniss, a brilliant illustrator, began to learn engraving in Dublin around 1872. 'In the studio . . . there hung a huge map of London' which 'I used to pore over'. Within a year he had chosen to take his chances there 'in search of fame and wealth'.[19]

It was not to St Giles or Saffron Hill or Whitechapel that migrants like Furniss looked for lodgings. Indeed, by the end of the century, through demolitions and other migrations, these areas had lost much (but not all) of their Irish character. The riverside concentrations remained, though, especially at Wapping and Rotherhithe. And there were suburban concentrations at the 'Fenian Barracks' near Devons Road, Bow, 'sending, we are told, more police to hospital than any other block in London'; at Putney, where an old colony had matured over fifty years or more; and at Peckham, 'partly a remnant of those who laboured in the potato fields'. By now, though, potato pickers had given way to skilled artisans and tradesmen like stevedores, tailors, engineers and carpenters. In the ever-more desperate search for help in the home, Irish girls had become more acceptable in the servant-keeping areas of west London. And the Irish middle classes had expanded in the law and politics and journalism, in the civil service after competitive examinations were generally applied in 1870, in school teaching and in medicine, where the Irish general practitioner had become a significant London figure. So the Irish at the end of the century were to be found in London 'everywhere – even in places where you never dream of finding them, as any priest will tell you who has ever opened a new mission in London'.[20]

This connection with Roman Catholicism was the strongest integument binding together the cockney Irish at the century's end. In all other respects the 300,000 or so Londoners of Irish descent were more cockney than the cockneys – in speech, in locality, in the types of work they undertook, even in their abstention from religious services, as most London priests bemoaned. But their loyalty to 'Mother Church' continued to distinguish them from other sections of the London working class. And the Church, with its boys' and girls' clubs, its missions and loan societies, and above all its residual power over the imaginations and susceptibilities of a community which believed its teachings to be in some magical sense 'true', had a hold over the London Irish that was uniquely strong.[21]

Or almost. In respect of the numbers affected this was true. But by the 1890s there were other migrant communities, younger in their impact on London life, which had equally strong connections with the Church of Rome. Communities far more 'strange' to the native Londoner than the Irish had ever been.

'Stranded on a Foreign Shore'

Many of these had early origins too. French Catholic priests had been one of the great exports to London of the 1789 revolution and its bloody sequels. By 1801, 5,600 priests and 4,000 lay French Catholics were exiled in England, and probably half of these lived in London. Soho and the area just to the north of Oxford Street, later called Fitzrovia, were favoured locations. The young painters David Wilkie and Benjamin Haydon used frequently to dine at an ordinary (or *prix fixe* restaurant) run by a Frenchman in Poland Street, Soho, around 1805. Here they heard 'all the languages of Europe talked with the greatest fluency' and 'it is a very rare thing to see an Englishman'. It was in these years, too, that Somers Town became a refugee resort, the district half-built and cheap and conveniently near to the Roman Catholic 'burying ground' on Hampstead Road. French migration was one factor in Somers Town's swift decline. Despite rich benefactors like Lady Dorothy Silburn, *'La Mère de Prêtres exilés'*, many priests were desperately poor and a French soup kitchen was established in 1810. But matters improved when the French monarchy was restored five years later and many émigrés returned.[22]

To the native Londoner during the first half of the century, a foreigner was a 'Frenchman' wherever he came from. Yet Wilkie had noted Germans and Italians at the Soho ordinary. For besides refugees from the guillotine, economic migrants from France (among them many shoemakers), from Germany and from Italy had all carved out a livelihood in their chosen districts of the great city by the opening of the nineteenth century.

A small German middle class of merchants and clerks was long established in London. It was enlarged by bankers and others when Napoleon's armies occupied Hamburg and Frankfurt. And an important group of German artisans had for generations dominated the London sugar baking trade, living mainly in the Leman Street area of Whitechapel. In all some 6,000 Germans were thought to be living in London around 1800. They were sufficiently embedded to have their own relief organisations – in 1814, for instance, a 'German committee' was meeting at Baker's coffee house, Exchange Alley, Cornhill, to help distressed migrants with alms or the return fare to Germany.[23]

The most visible European migrants on the streets of London in these early years were the Italians. John Thomas Smith, keeper of prints at the British Museum and a brilliant chronicler and illustrator of London street life before 1820, detected an increase in 'idle foreigners' at the end of the Napoleonic Wars, 'who now infest our streets with their learned mice and chattering monkeys'. 'Italian boys' sold images, artificial flowers, wax birds; played on the 'vertical flute', an assortment of organs and a strange contraption in which strings were bowed over a sounding-board made of an inflated bladder. Besides white mice and monkeys, the dancing 'Italy bear' was a popular attraction. The Italians' main lodging-house district was around Hatton Garden, Holborn, where the organ-building trade clustered. And the Italians seem to have had more volatile relations with the cockneys than did other migrant groups. At the time of the Westminster election of 1806 a row broke out between two Italians and an English mob who objected to the strangers' outlandish dress. An Englishman was stabbed in the mêlée.[24]

Revolutions, wars and rapidly advancing industrialisation all shook and stirred London's European medley from the 1820s on. A rebellion in Spain brought poor but proud refugees to the Polygon, Somers Town, from 1823. In 1827 'great numbers' of Spanish and Italian refugees gathered in Copenhagen Fields, Islington, to play fives matches. The 1830 revolution in France sent another host of priests to London some 150 strong. Within four years it was said that half had died of privation and the survivors petitioned the Lord Mayor for alms. Agitation for Italian unification brought exiles to London from the 1830s, among them Giuseppe Mazzini in June 1836. He had already been expelled from Piedmont, then France, then Switzerland, but London secured him a safe haven on and off for the rest of his life. Spanish, German, Polish and a few Hungarian and Russian political refugees had joined the French and Italians by the early 1840s. But it was 1848 that brought European revolutionaries to London in greater numbers and variety than ever before. Over the next five years, as revolution and reaction waxed and waned, Louis Blanc and Louis Philippe and Louis Napoleon – the most prominent Frenchmen of their generation – Louis Kossuth the Hungarian, the Scalias from Sicily, Alexander Herzen the Russian, Worcell and Darasz the Poles and hundreds of others found their way at some time to London, the most welcoming and least repressive metropolis in Europe. Most famous of all, Karl Marx arrived there on 24 August 1849 following expulsion from Cologne and then Paris. He would live at several north London addresses for the remaining thirty-four years of his life.[25]

When Marx brought his wife and children to join him in April 1850 it was to a hotel in Leicester Square that they first moved. Leicester Square was the very epicentre of refugee life in the 1840s and 1850s, its feel – at least to the English – more French than German. A 'dingy modern France', Thackeray called it. 'There are French cafés, billiards, estaminets, waiters, markers, poor Frenchmen, and rich Frenchmen . . .' And just to its north, Soho and the neighbouring area beyond Oxford Street would provide a congenial milieu for the exiles to work their own way into London society in their own time.[26]

Although there was strong anti-French feeling in London at the time of the 1848 revolution, and although foreigners were fair game for chaff in the streets and for cheating by boarding-house keepers, the political exiles had many English friends in London. Middle-class hostesses, like Mrs Milner Gibson and Mrs James Stansfeld, lionised the exiles at receptions and dinner parties in Brompton and the West End. London intellectuals, like the brilliant Scot David Masson, organised societies to aid refugees in distress and win converts to the cause of European liberty. And militants among London's working men and women found spirited brothers in arms among the foreigners in their midst. London chartists paid for a 'barrack' in Clerkenwell for Hungarian, Polish and Italian refugees, funding it by pay-dances and collections. In his old age the chartist Thomas Frost recalled the night that news of the Paris revolution of 1848 reached London exiles and their comrades. Frost was at a meeting of the Association of Fraternal Democrats in the White Hart, Drury Lane. The Association's motto – 'All Men Are Brethren' – 'was printed in the cards of membership in twelve languages', but its main sections were British, French, German and Polish.

Suddenly the news of the events in Paris was brought in. The effect was electrical. Frenchmen, Germans, Poles, Magyars, sprang to their feet, embraced, shouted, and gesticulated in the wildest enthusiasm. Snatches of oratory were delivered in excited tones, and flags were caught from the walls, to be waved exultingly, amidst cries of '*Hoch! Eljen! Vive la République!*' Then the doors were opened, and the whole assemblage descended to the street, and, with linked arms and colours flying, marched to the meeting-place of the Westminster Chartists, in Dean Street, Soho. There another enthusiastic fraternization took place, and great was the clinking of glasses that night in and around Soho and Leicester Square.[27]

By the early 1850s the numbers of foreigners were swollen not just by revolutionaries but by a small host of working men and women, economic migrants in search of work and a better way of life. French milliners, dressmakers, prostitutes, jewellers and engineers; German clerks, watchmakers, shoemakers, musicians making up 'German bands' in the streets and yet more sugar bakers; Italian plaster-image makers, organ builders and yet more street entertainers – all had come in their many hundreds to London in the 1840s. The city's foreign-born population probably doubled in the decade – from around 13,000 to 26,000 in 1851.

'The Exile-World of London' flourished through the 1860s, its stars Mazzini and Louis Blanc, its main theatrical spectacle the visit of Garibaldi in April 1864, its organisations forming and re-forming in the Soho pubs and coffee houses. The Franco-Prussian War of 1870 and the Commune the year after again sent their harvest of revolutionaries, dispossessed householders and out-of-work artisans. According to some observers, these new arrivals marked a shift in the geography of French London. Many ex-communards settled in the streets between Oxford Street and Fitzroy Square, otherwise best known for its German community. They found Soho too much occupied by French prostitutes, who had moved there in the 1850s and 1860s. So 'to this day', remarked Adolphe Smith at the end of the century, 'we have the political foreign quarter in the Fitzroy Square district, north of Oxford Street, and the non-political foreign quarter south of Oxford Street in the Soho Square District'. A communist soup kitchen was set up in an alley off Rathbone Place in 1871 where exiles were fed a tuppenny meal and English classes were run in the evenings. In Charlotte Street an informal advice centre for refugees was run from a grocer's shop, and Marx and others ate at Andinet's Restaurant just across the street. Here the ranks of the German émigrés were swollen by Bismarck's anti-socialist repressions from 1878.[28]

And here too was the west London centre of anarchism in the 1880s and 1890s. The anarchists were to be found most famously at the Club Autonomie, established in Little Goodge Street around 1885, moving to Rathbone Place and then Windmill Street, until it was closed by the police in 1894. Its members included 'the leader of Italian anarchism' Errico Malatesta, Louise Michel 'the "Red Virgin"' and several who went on to throw or plant bombs in almost every capital city in Europe. One of them, Martial Bourdin, a French tailor working in Soho and living in Fitzroy Street, died in February 1894 while apparently trying to bomb Greenwich Observatory. That same year a bomb attempt on the Mayfair house of Mr Justice Hawkins, a notorious hanging judge who had recently sentenced two anarchists to lengthy imprisonment, seems likely to have been the work of French anarchists: it damaged the wrong house. But otherwise London was left alone. Perhaps the anarchists, hunted down by every continental secret police force, found London a too congenial haven to alienate the British authorities entirely.[29]

London's foreign anarchists were a tiny fraction among the restless milieu of comers and goers in Soho and Fitzrovia. Many would stay for a few months or a few years and then move back to France or Italy or Germany when the economic or political climate seemed more favourable. Some came again and again – like Mazzini, or like Malatesta, whose London years spanned 1881–2, 1889–97, 1900–1913 and 1914–19.[30] Each time they returned to a London home from home,

with its political and charitable and religious institutions, and its shops
and restaurants catering for every migrant taste. What were these
foreign quarters like in the last two decades or so of the nineteenth
century?

Soho remained the cosmopolis of central London at the century's
end. It retained on the surface an essentially French gloss, as it had at
the beginning. In fact, though, by the 1890s the French hold was
starting to slip. The French population of the County of London in
1901 was some 11,300 strong, just over half of them women, and
probably the highest of the century. Numerically the French were not
even the largest minority in Soho in the late 1890s – there were 900
French to over 1,000 Germans. And they had to contend with recent
influxes of Jews (about 700), Italians (650) and Swiss (260). Even
Swedes, Norwegians and Danes had begun to make their presence felt
in the Soho tailoring and shoemaking workshops.[31]

But the French influence in Soho derived less from its numbers than
from its long history of settlement there and from its determination at
all costs to remain French. French London covered a wide class spectrum, from merchants and entrepreneurs, through professionals (especially mechanical engineers), tailors, chefs, waiters, laundresses and
shop assistants, with a large bulge in the middle in retail trade. So a
disproportionate number of businesses in Soho traded under French
names, 'stick foreign bills in their windows' and sold French goods.
The 'place teems with French restaurants' with an 8d or 18d *prix fixe*,
or *à la carte* for 3–5s including wine. Lodging houses advertised
Chambres Garnies. There were nightclubs and gaming houses with
dancing salons and bedrooms above. Shops sold wooden shoes and
berets and everything for the gourmet. There were French pubs and
cafés and hotels; *agents de change* and *agents de renseignements* to
help strangers settle into London's foreign ways; French barbers and
patisseries and *pharmacies* and *blanchisseuses* running some of London's
smartest laundries. Newsagents sold the Paris papers on the day of
publication. The quarter had its own weekly, *La Chronique*, and French
libraries, infamously full of 'light literature'. Lisle Street schools, dating
from 1865, taught émigré children French. The Eglise de Notre Dame
de France in Leicester Place was the largest of four French churches
in London, established in 1868. The *Société Française de Bienfaisance*
(1842), the French Mission (1861) and the French Hospital and
Dispensary in Shaftesbury Avenue (1867) all looked after the poor and

sick. A French Chamber of Commerce (1883) watched out for the petit bourgeoisie. All male children born in London and registered at the consulate were liable to military call-up by the First Arrondissement of Paris, to which they were considered to belong. And the migrants' readiness to return to France meant that 'it is rare to find a second generation of French residents in London'. This was a minority determined never to assimilate. It made Soho more French than in fact it was.[32]

The German minority, on the other hand, or at least the upper middle class within it, had the deserved reputation of becoming in the second generation 'more English than the English'. Germans in London ranged from super-rich merchants and bankers and industrialists (Meinertzhagen, Göschen, Siemens and similar clans) to decrepit artisans in rags at the street corner. There were 27,400 Germans in London in 1901, by far the largest migrant group from Western Europe in the metropolis. Just 37 per cent were women, so men were thrown into the arms of native Londoners much more than were the French. There were marked concentrations in Westminster, St Pancras and Stepney (mainly the Leman Street area of Whitechapel), with the large majority spread pretty evenly over all but the densely cockney parts of London. By the 1890s the better-off East End German tradesmen and artisans had begun to move in their hundreds to Hackney. There were suburban communities of bankers and merchants in Denmark Hill, Forest Hill and Camberwell, and a colony of glass blowers in West Ham near their workplaces at Canning Town and Plaistow.[33]

The East End Germans declined in number from 1861, while the Fitzrovians and Sohoites increased. That marked a shift away from East End trades like sugar baking (which had virtually disappeared as a German occupation by 1899), bootmaking and cigar making, towards commercial clerking in the City (where German language skills were much in demand), towards the restaurant and service trades (especially waiters and barbers) and to West-End tailoring. In all three districts, though, even at the end of the century, the German flavour remained distinctive. Leman Street especially had 'numberless German names over the doors of the shops and [on] the brass plates of German business houses'. And in Soho and the 'Charlottenstrasse' district north of Oxford Street, German restaurants and hotels and provision shops abounded.[34]

More characteristic than all of this, a unique feature of German social life in London, were the *Vereine*. These were clubs based on employment, location or social interest group. There was a famous German Gymnastic Society, with over 1,000 members in 1882, two-thirds of them English. It was founded in 1861 at King's Cross. There was a German Athenaeum for 'artists and literary men' (1869, Mortimer Street); there were *Vereine* for amateur theatricals, cyclists, typographers, chess players, each with its own glee club and concerts and dance nights; smaller clubs among friends for cards, songs and skittles gathered at German-run pubs and cafés. Superimposed on this thriving network of collective endeavour was some attempt at a hierarchy of community leadership. Charitable institutions were founded mainly by rich Germans to aid their compatriots of all classes: the famous German Hospital at Dalston (1845), the German Mission among the German Poor in London (1849), a German YMCA (1860), the German Orphanage and Schools (also at Dalston, 1879). By the end of the century there were more than a dozen German churches – even a German Salvation Army Corps. And the *Londoner Zeitung*, forty-two years old in 1900, was just the longest-running of a stable of metropolitan German newspapers, with the more recent *Die Finanzchronik* catering for City men. With a long tradition of intermarriage between German men of all classes and English women, London's Germans were the most assimilated of all metropolitan minorities in the nineteenth century.[35]

They could not compete for strangeness with the fascinating Italians. In 1901 there were just under 11,000 Italians in London, only one in four of them women. This number had more than doubled in the 1890s. The colony's historic heart was between Saffron Hill and Leather Lane (with Hatton Garden in the middle) to the south of Clerkenwell Road; and Eyre Street Hill, Back Hill and Warner Street to the north. The colony aroused popular indignation on Boxing Day 1863, when an affray between Italians and English in the Golden Anchor Tavern, Saffron Hill, ended in an Englishman stabbed to death, another badly wounded and several cut. There followed three sensational trials, the first sentencing an innocent man to be hanged and the third effectively acquitting him.[36]

From that time the Italian community was pretty much in the public eye, as big a tourist trap as Vesuvius itself. It proved one of the most picturesque sights of London. James Greenwood observed how in just a few steps out of 'the unmistakably English crowd that throngs the

Leather Lane market' he found himself 'stranded on a foreign shore'. Here were 'becowled old women', 'olive-visaged, big-eyed beauties', 'bearded fellows of brigandish attire'. Italian shops sold 'maccaroni, half-yard lengths of crusty bread, all manner of beans in bowls, common sausages in their vulgar brown skins, sausages of genteeler mould smartly coated in tin-foil, and green, yellow, and purple liquids in clumsy glass bottles heavily stopped with coarse wax'. How strange all this was in the 1870s. Strange, too, the trades that centred here. Organ grinders and street musicians still in the majority, just as fifty years before, but now joined by asphalt workers, mosaic and parquet layers, plaster-figure makers, 'piano-organ' builders, picture frame and mirror makers, all stopping up tiny gaps in the London labour market.[37]

So did the Italian ice-cream makers and vendors. Ice cream first appeared on the London streets in the summer of 1850. It was supplied to the street sellers by a Holborn confectioner, probably Italian. The innocent Londoners, trying to chew great mouthfuls of it like toffee, found it all too much for their carious teeth: '"Jasus! I'm kilt,"' exclaimed one of its first victims, an Irishman.[38] But ice cream was irresistible. And by the 1870s it seems to have been exclusively in the hands of the London Italians, the stuff manufactured in some of the capital's most filthy backyards. This was the community's first step into London mass catering and in the 1890s especially the Italian restaurant trade boomed along with the rest of London night-life. It boomed loudest in Soho. It was in the 1890s that the Italians showed the first signs of ousting the French from London's cosmopolis.

The institutions of Italian London reflected a population smaller and less rooted than the French and Germans. The King of Italy established the Italian Benevolent Society at Greville Street in 1861, and Mazzini the Society of Mutual Progress of Italian Workers in Laystall Street, Holborn, in 1864. The Ospidale Italiano was opened in Queen Square in 1884 and there were small educational and dramatic societies, even for a time a 'Cricket Club Italiano'. It never caught on. But as for all the main migrant communities in London there were home-tongue newspapers for the expatriates – the *Londra-Roma* and the *Gazzetta Italiana di Londra*. And the Roman Catholic Church of St Peter's Saffron Hill was the community's cathedral. The mid-July festival of Our Lady of Mount Carmel brought Rome body and soul to Clerkenwell.

Imposing triumphal arches are erected at the entrances of the streets, garlands of flowers upon the roadways, flags wave high and low, coloured lamps reach from house to house, gay tapestries hide the dilapidated walls, transparencies of the Virgin and the Saints appear at the windows, the street-corners are ornamented by large illuminated frames which bear the statue of the Madonna, and even the narrow courts and alleys blaze with flowers and brilliant coloured lights.[39]

But if 'Little Italy' was strange, then London had stranger still to offer. There were the London gypsies, for instance, with their pictur-esque van encampments in Lock's Fields, Walworth, or Wandsworth and Battersea, or at the Potteries, Notting Dale, and a dozen other places in the wintertime. Much like the early nineteenth-century Irish, theirs was a seasonal movement, largely evaporating into the country in the summer, coming back to London in October, making a living selling horses, mending pots and pans, hawking clothes pegs, telling fortunes and begging. Over generations they merged more or less un-noticeably with the cockneys. Gypsy origins were claimed by many in the Nichol Street area of Bethnal Green, in Bangor Street, Notting Dale, Campbell Road, Holloway, and doubtless others.[40]

The most exotic migrants of all, though, were to be found near the port of London and the riverside. Here were the 'blacks' and 'Johnny Chinamen' and 'lascars' – a vague term generally applied to people from the Indian sub-continent – who arrived in London most often as sailors. All these were brought to the port mainly by imperial trade, sometimes by American ships with black men in their crew. And they stayed for a short time before finding another berth or gravitating to the wilderness of city living.

No one knows how many people there were in nineteenth-century London with black or brown or yellow skins, but it is hard to believe that at any time there were more than a thousand or two who made London their home for any lengthy period. And the numbers do not seem to have grown proportionately with London's population over the century. Even so, around the London and West and East India Docks the seamen of the world clustered as nowhere else on earth. Along the London riverside lay a whole sprawling town serving ships and the men who sailed them. So in the back streets of south Whitechapel, St George's, Wapping, Shadwell, Ratcliffe, Limehouse and Poplar were lodging houses accommodating all the peoples under the sun. Most came and went from one berth to another. And most clung tightly to their own kind. There were sufficient 'Lascars of the Mahommedan persuasion' to have their four-day East End festival noted in the *Annual Register* for 1805. A 'multitude of people followed' their processions, complete 'with drums and tambourines' and sword dances. Next year there was a 'dreadful riot' in Ratcliffe Highway between lascars and Chinese sailors, about 200 in all. Four lascars 'just about to be turned off' with cords round their throats were rescued by British tars. In the Napoleonic Wars the numbers of Indian seamen recruited to East India Company ships greatly increased because of impressment of British sailors into the Royal Navy. When in the port they were put up in barracks at Ratcliffe Highway, where a riot between 400 lascars and drunken British seamen took place in 1808. In general, though, there was wary coexistence, usually peaceful but capable of violent outbursts: three Asiatic seamen were 'seriously stabbed' by several 'low characters' at Limehouse in 1877, for instance. And black men, Indians, Malays and others all shared the delights of the riverside brothels, pubs, dining rooms and lodging houses with British and European sailors, as they had done through time out of mind.[41]

There was a slow drift into London from the dockside, a mix of the unfortunate and the talented. So here were men crippled in accidents at sea with no chance now of a ship, alongside others who reckoned they could sell a skill or gift to make their fortune on London's golden pavements. They lived beyond the margins of wage labour at the hand-to-mouth end of economic independence. The cluster of black beggars who shared the Holy Land with the Irish went by the title of 'St Giles black-birds'. Joseph Johnson, a black sailor walking with sticks, sang on the streets with a model sailing ship strapped to his head. Charles McGee, a one-eyed Jamaican and an old man of seventy-one when J. T. Smith sketched him in 1815, swept a crossing at Ludgate Hill and was a devout Methodist. Billy Waters, an African-American sailor with a wooden leg, seems to have made a good living with his fiddle in pubs, even appearing in W. T. Moncrieff's stage version of *Tom and Jerry* at the Adelphi. This 'King of the Beggars' died in St Giles Workhouse just two years later in 1823.

Black beggars declined in numbers as policing grew more effective after 1829. But black men were still to be found on London's streets as musicians and tract sellers. Indian and Arab street musicians playing tom-toms were found by Mayhew around 1856. He noted among the tract sellers 'Malays, Hindoos, and Negroes'. A black woman Christian missionary converted the heathen in City pubs around 1820. Black preachers were not uncommon at a dissenting chapel in Norwood in the 1850s. And in the 1860s a few 'coloured ex-prizefighters' were well known among the night haunts of Leicester Square and around.[42]

It was generally said that black beggars and street sellers and performers did well in London, perhaps because there were few enough of them to remain a novelty. But they no doubt paid a price. Edward Albert, a black crossing sweeper who had lost both legs in an accident at sea, told Mayhew how his Irish neighbours '"chaff me . . . they call me 'cripple'; some says 'Uncle Tom', and some says 'Nigger'; but I never takes no notice of 'em at all"'.[43]

Perhaps the Chinese were the most sensational migrant presence of all, sensational because of their favourite drug. The first Chinese opium dens appear in Shadwell by the mid 1860s; or perhaps it is the same one that gets described over and over again, by Dickens among others from 1865 to 1870, then resurrected unseen by Oscar Wilde and Conan Doyle in the 1890s. The most famous seems to have been 'Johnson's', 'the club house of the Chinese', at Palmer's Folly, Bluegate Fields. The police considered it 'a model of respectability' around 1865, 'when compared with its immediate neighbours', mainly brothels. At that time a few Chinamen were employed in London as shopmen or advertising attractions in large tea retailers', as mercantile clerks and seamen, and jugglers and knife throwers in the music halls. A few more 'dens' were opened up in the 1870s and 1880s. And the roots of a Chinese colony in Limehouse Causeway, to the east of Shadwell, seem to have been planted some time in the 1890s, but with only a few dozen there at most until the new century.[44]

In all, it is hard to accept a recent judgement that 'Up to the mid-nineteenth century a vibrant community of African-Britons lived in London.' There could have been little community among the few score street sellers, crossing sweepers and buskers taking their chances in the common lodging houses of central London and the mill-race of seamen passing through the port. And as far as contemporary evidence takes us, that must have been true for the lascars too. By the end of the nineteenth century historians tell us that there were even fewer black people in London than there were fifty years before, but again the numbers are just not there to state anything with certainty. The 1901 census counted 33,000 Londoners who were born in British colonies or dependencies, but the great majority of these seem likely to have been expatriates or migrants from the white colonies. And although an estimated 20,000 Indian and African sailors shipped in and out of London each year, the stayers among them were few. No doubt some dockside lodging houses in places like Cable Street and Ratcliffe Highway were acquired or tenanted over the years by African, West Indian or lascar seamen. We know that some seamen from these backgrounds married local women: A. J. Mahomet, born in 1858 into dire poverty in Sophia Street, Poplar, had a father from Calcutta and a mother from Norfolk. And doubtless some elderly men settled at the dockside rather than go to sea again, eking out a living or relying on the poor law. Besides the work of Christian missionaries there were few other institutions devoted to their cause. The Strangers' Home for Asiatics, Africans and South Sea Islanders opened in 1858 in the West India Dock Road, with 200 beds for seamen between berths. And an Ayahs' Home at Hackney gave temporary shelter to those Indian women who accompanied families to and from India as nurses and companions. Examples of black or Asian seamen settling down to live cheek-by-jowl with the cockneys are hard to find. Only one 'Negro settlement' has entered the historical record and this was at Canning Town towards the end of the century. Again, the numbers living there seem to have been insignificant.[45]

But numbers were not everything. And from the 1850s on a small black and Asian middle class had been embedding itself in London society. In the law, where the first 'Mahomedan' was admitted as an attorney in 1858; in medicine and academic life; in business and among students training for the Indian civil service – exams were held in London and not in India. A handful entered politics, like Dadabhai Naoroji, elected Liberal MP for Finsbury in 1892. More were called by religion. There were Indian Christian missionaries working near the Victoria Docks at the end of the century, for instance. And perhaps religion was at its most potent in the dissenting Christianity of West Indian intellectuals in London. Celestine Edwards, a brilliant lecturer and editor from Dominica, had begun his London career as a non-conformist temperance advocate in the 1880s. From millenarian Christianity it was but a short step to anti-imperialism and Edwards became the main organiser of the Pan-African Conference, held in London in 1900. It was in London in the 1890s that black and Asian intellectuals, with invaluable contributions from African-Americans, began to articulate an anti-imperialist ideology that would help change for ever world politics in the century to come.[46]

The London 'Ghetto'

Significant as all these strangers were, each in their several ways, there was one group more than any other who most qualified for the title 'alien': the Jews. That at least was the position at the century's end. In 1800, though, London's Jewish community had traditions stretching back 150 years. In some ways it was thoroughly 'assimilated' – economically, for instance, but hardly socially. Intermarriage was uncommon and so were baptisms. Orthodox Judaism kept believers living near the synagogue, and even lax Jews preferred a kosher butcher and a Jewish baker nearby. So separateness was firmly built into the social geography and intellectual outlook of London Jewry from the outset.

London's main Jewish district – 'their metropolis' – at the beginning of the nineteenth century was at the eastern edge of the City of London. This was 'the angular quarter bounded by Bishopsgate, Houndsditch, and the streets of Leadenhall and Aldgate'. But pressure of population in the eighteenth century had already caused overspill into the East End – from Houndsditch in the north, where Petticoat Lane and 'its numerous courts and alleys have long been stigmatized [it was said in 1815] as the resort and residence of Jews and others, of the lowest description', and into Whitechapel south of the High Street around Goodman's Fields, 'mostly inhabited [1806] by rich Jew merchants', and Rosemary Lane, 'that theatre of second-hand commerce, called RAG FAIR'. The City and its overspill accounted for most of London's estimated 20,000 Jews at this period. But there were also some 'western Jews' who had moved along the Strand, with synagogues near the Savoy and Covent Garden, and its own old clothes centre at Holywell Street. There was also a small Jewish community in the Borough south-west of the Obelisk. And some super-rich had taken up residence in the older West End squares in walking distance of a synagogue.[47]

London Jewry in these early years had a distinctive class make-up. The Rev. John Mills, a sympathetic observer, thought in 1853 that only about half of London's Jews were 'lower class', a far smaller proportion than among Londoners as a whole. Bankers (the 'Magnificent Rothschilds' chief among them), merchants, stockbrokers and jobbers made up the plutocracy. The wide middle ranks were filled by a medley of money-lenders, lawyers and small importers; wholesale dealers in jewellery, diamonds, nuts, oranges, second-hand clothing and stolen property; rabbis and ritual slaughterers; and comfortable tradesmen like bakers, pastrycooks and butchers. Some of these engaged with the outside world but many prospered solely from trade within the community. And economic enterprise was strongly characteristic of even the 'lower class', in selling oranges and nuts from a basket or barrow, and in bartering for old clothes. There were said in 1808 to be 1,500 Jewish old-clothes dealers knocking at doors and crying their trade in the streets. Old clo' remained a huge London industry until mass production of ready-made clothing got fully under way in the 1880s. The 'rag fairs' at Rosemary Lane and at the Houndsditch Clothes Exchange seem to have clad rural Ireland for all that time, Irish dealers especially noticeable in the Sunday markets. And new clothing provided the main manufacturing industry in which Jews were involved as masters and workshop hands.[48]

The Jewish community was to some extent split in two. Those of Portuguese and Spanish origin, the Sephardim, had a longer London settlement and separate synagogues from the German, Polish and Russian Jews (the Ashkenazim). But differences in ritual never obscured the fellow-feeling between the two 'nations'. There was considerable institutional cohesion, accepting the leadership of a Chief Rabbi and a Board of Deputies on religious and secular matters involving the whole community. And the great charitable institutions operated without favour since the early years of the nineteenth century. So schools (notably the Jews' Free School, 1817, moving in 1821 to Bell Lane, Spitalfields), burial grounds, refuges for orphans, pregnant mothers, the sick poor, widows and the elderly all produced a fine-mesh safety net of philanthropy through which it was hard for the Jewish poor to fall. From 1859 charity among the London Jews was coordinated by the Jewish Board of Guardians (JBG). The board was a model of its kind, its relative generosity and flexibility far in advance of its English poor law equivalents. They had at least one thing in common, though. Just as the St Giles guardians would 'pass back' the Irish poor to their troubled island, the JBG would 'resettle' those pauper Jews willing to return to their homelands in Holland, Poland, Germany or Russia.[49]

In the first fifty years or so of the century Jewish migration to London was pretty much a trickle. It comprised both rich and poor, mostly from Holland of German origin. It led, though, to some expansion of the Jewish quarter eastwards across Commercial Street. So Tewkesbury Buildings, a slum court in Whitechapel, was described as 'a colony of Dutch Jews' in 1861 and New Court, nearby, was a mix of Irish and Jews.[50] Some Jewish landlords of cheap house property had also emerged by this time. And the suburbanising tendency among better-off Jews to move north and west of the City, establishing new synagogues as they went, strengthened with London's suburban growth.

It was in the 1860s that the character of London Jewry began to change markedly with the first true beginnings of what would later be called 'the ghetto'. In 1861 there had been almost 900 Poles, almost certainly Jews, in Whitechapel and St George's compared to 2,300 'Hollanders'. Migration of Austrian, Prussian and Polish Jews increased in the 1860s, in part to escape military conscription during those years of international friction. These were mainly proletarians. It was in the 1860s that Jewish manu-facturing trades – cigar making and bootmaking, tailoring and shirt-making, cap and slipper making (both 'largely in their hands', it was said in 1867) were consolidated into significant industries. Migration acceler-ated further during the Russian famine of 1869–70 and conscription for the Russo-Turkish War of 1875–6. And as well as proletarian Jews, intel-lectual refugees from Tsarism added to the cultural capacity of the growing Ashkenazi community of the East End. In 1880 Yiddish theatre was being performed by newly settled Russian Jews at the Garrick Theatre in Leman Street. And by 1881 the Russian and Polish population of Whitechapel had risen to 4,500, almost half of them women.[51]

That year marked a crisis for the Jews in Russia that would have an immediate and dramatic effect on the history of London Jewry. On 13 March 1881 Tsar Alexander II was assassinated by a bomb. Jewish nihilists were implicated. Repressive measures against the Jews and state-inspired pogroms in Russia coincided with anti-Semitic agitation in Prussia. Even more onerous clampdowns followed in the Tsar's empire in May 1882. So began the migration of some two million Jews from Russia, Russian Poland and Austria over the next thirty years or so. This was a movement inspired not just by repres-sion. Economic forces, acting ever more strongly to shift Jews away from independent trade and into the workshops as proletarians, gave further reasons to migrate. Just how many came to London is uncer-tain. But the 1881 census recorded 8,700 Russians and Poles in London; in 1901 the figure was 53,500. That excludes German and Austrian Jews who journeyed to London in similar circumstances. In all, historians estimate that some 140,000 Jews (of all origins, and including second and subsequent generations) were living in London at the century's end. That was around three times more than just twenty years before.[52]

Almost all lived first in the East End of London near their co-religionists. And in the East End they could take advantage of some of the cheapest – and humblest – living accommodation that the world's most expensive city had to offer. They burst the bounds of the old Jewish quarter: through Spitalfields and Whitechapel to Mile End New Town; through Goodman's Fields to Shadwell; across Cable Street, from Dock Street to Cannon Street Road.[53]

This massive colonisation over twenty years transformed the character of inner east London. Some of the poorest and roughest of the Londoners were pushed out of places like Flower and Dean Street and Wentworth Street. Landlords spotted the gold to be gleaned from migrants who would of necessity pay a higher rent for less space, and be prepared to work all hours to pay for it. Overcrowding among Jewish migrants scandalised English observers, though it was never so severe as among the Irish at mid-century. So did the rise in rents, affecting Jew and local gentile alike. It was said in 1898 that 'The cost of rent in the Jewish quarter has very nearly doubled during the last ten years.' And a growing number of landlords were Jews themselves. The Chief Rabbi, commenting on the rapacious greed of some Jewish house-farmers, confessed, '"Thank God I live under a Christian landlord."'[54]

In 1901, nearly four out of five Russians and Poles in London – 42,000 people – lived in the western portions of the Metropolitan Borough of Stepney. There was also a notable cluster in Soho, strongly based in the garment industry. And there were already signs of accelerating suburban migration from the inner East End. Hackney, especially Clapton and Stamford Hill, was home to over 1,000 Russians and Poles in 1901. Highbury New Park in east Islington, a smarter address, was known as 'the New Jerusalem' by the late 1890s. And the 'north-west passage' into St John's Wood, West Hampstead and Maida Vale was already thoroughly mapped out.[55]

The 'alien invasion' after 1881 shot fresh venom into that sinew of anti-Semitism which would prove so hard to eradicate from English culture. Jews in London had, on the one hand, much to bear and, on the other, something to be thankful for. There were always those in the City Corporation and in Parliament who stood up for Jewish rights, those in Grub Street who condemned slander, those no doubt in the streets who repelled petty oppression and stood up for its victims. But victims there were. Jews could be assaulted in the streets and taunted with pigs' heads. Anti-Semitic dramas would sometimes raise a storm of counter-protest.

Christian missionaries would harass Jews for their souls. They would have to suffer ridicule and worse from popular journals like *Punch*. And famous writers railed in public – and even more in private – against 'foul Jews'.[56]

It was in the 1880s and 1890s that this sore broke open. The 'flood' of 'pauper aliens' antagonised working people in the East End, less through economic competition (English and Jewish labour hardly ever fished in the same pool) than the struggle for living space and the rise in rents. There was much name calling, many assaults and some affrays in Wentworth Street and other places. In November 1898 Jews trying to move into Ernest Street, Stepney Green, were physically threatened and kept out: '"In essentials, a Judenhetze prevails . . ."' Jews moving into St George's-in-the-East could be met with window breaking. The hostility of the Irish 'has kept Wapping free from Jews . . .' And, reminiscent of the Great Famine migrations, the English Jews of Whitechapel were said to be 'the bitterest enemies of the foreign immigrant'. It was a tense and anxious time. But it is impossible to argue with a later judgement that episodes like Ernest Street and the few that succeeded it 'failed to ignite the East End'.[57]

Nonetheless, the cry of 'pauper alien' seriously alarmed the wealthy and politically sophisticated coterie that claimed spiritual and secular leadership of the Jews in England. 'Our fair fame is bound up with theirs; the outside world is not capable of making minute discrimination between Jew and Jew, and forms its opinion of Jews in general as much, *if not more*, from them than from the Anglicised portion of the Community.'[58] That *Jewish Chronicle* leader from early in the crisis struck home. The response of Anglo-Jewry to the mass migration of the 1880s and 1890s was both swift and wide-ranging.

One response was tragic in the light of subsequent history. The JBG repatriated some 9,250 'cases', probably over 26,000 people, to Eastern Europe between 1880 and 1899. Nearly half that number were shipped on to the USA, Australia, South Africa and later Canada.[59] Help for those determined to stay came by way of charitable gifts to a Mansion House fund from Jewish and non-Jewish sources, as well as donations to the JBG from synagogues and wealthy donors. From 1882 a joint committee of the Mansion House and the JBG coordinated relief in cash (loans, doles and allowances) and kind (boots, medicines and so on), and directed applicants to special charities like the Poor Jews' Temporary Shelter in Leman Street, the Jewish Bread, Meat and Coal Society, or the Jewish Soup Kitchen in Fashion Street, Spitalfields. The

JBG sent out sanitary inspectors to prod the local authorities into action and seek repairs from landlords. Lord Rothschild and others launched a semi-philanthropic company to buy sites and build tenement blocks for respectable artisans among the Jewish poor. The Jews' Free School was expanded to reach more scholars, though most educational responsibilities fell on the local authorities just because of the numbers involved.

So Anglo-Jewry's enlightened self-interest eased the trauma of transition from Eastern Europe to the East End of London. But even more important was the capacity for collective expression of the migrants themselves. All the organisational resources of an infinitely adaptive culture were transplanted fresh cut to Whitechapel. There were the *hebrot* or religious associations, based on *stiebels*, back-street synagogues round which so much of migrant communal life revolved. Associations were based first on *landsleit*, people coming from a particular town or district. Beatrice Potter (later Webb) thought there were thirty or forty *hebrot* in the East End by 1887. They were not just gatherings for worship. Here newcomers could renew old acquaintances, make useful contacts, apply for communal aid. Each had its friendly society, awarding sickness and death benefits from a common pool of *landsleit* donations. Out of the *hebrot* came the *chederim*, the Hebrew schools for boys conducted in Yiddish, the language of the Ashkenazi migrants no matter from which part of Europe they hailed. And for non-observant men, collective life centred on work in the hectic world of Jewish trade unionism; around politics with socialist and anarchist clubs; or around leisure time with Yiddish theatre and gambling clubs set up in rooms of tenement houses or behind back-street cafés.[60]

None of this suited the anglicisation agenda of established Anglo-Jewry. All those features which made the migrants 'alien' had to be tempered. Even religion had to be made to fit English ways. So the *chederim* were attacked for keeping alive a foreign (Yiddish-speaking) culture. Some *hebrot* were shepherded into the Federation of Synagogues to render their sanitary conditions unexceptionable, settle disputes and open them to 'English influences': the Federation banned Yiddish from its councils. And the Jewish Working Men's Club in Great Alie Street, Whitechapel, helped adapt migrant workers to the English proletarian outlook and the politics of the Liberal Party.[61]

All this could provoke fierce resistance. A society calling itself Machzike Hadath – 'Upholders of the Law' – was formed in 1891 to preserve the orthodoxy of the Pale. Its great synagogue in Brick Lane was opened in

1898. Its attack on the alleged laxity of ritual slaughter and kosher butchers rumbled on into the new century. On the one side in these life-and-death debates ranged the great Jewish banking and merchant houses of the Victorian City – the Rothschilds, the Montagus, the Mocattas and Goldsmids – and on the other the rabbis and *shochets* (ritual slaughterers) of the Pale of Settlement and their flock: tailors, cabinet makers, general dealers and shopkeepers who wished to reach some accommodation with English society while trying to resurrect what they'd left behind.[62]

As if this mighty schism within new London Jewry were not enough, religion was cross-cut by politics. It was, after all, revolutionary politics that triggered the mass migration itself, and intellectuals, adventurers and politically minded artisans were among the tens of thousands who ended in London. Just as in other refugee movements across the century, the revolutionary newcomers of the 1880s found that some had got there before them. Russian Jewish socialist refugees had settled in London by the mid-1870s and perhaps before, publishing an anti-Tsarist journal, *Vperyod*. Similarly, the first Jewish trade unions had formed by the early 1870s – among Lithuanian tailors, for instance. With the mass influx after 1881, Jewish socialism, anarchism and trade unionism were swept into a chaos of propaganda and ideas, alliances and feuds, of life at the Berner Street socialist club and meetings at the Sugar Loaf public house in Hanbury Street, of new unions fashioning themselves from the embers of others just a year or two old, of hard-fought strikes and assaults on blacklegs, of demonstrations against employers, landlords, the Tsar, capitalism and observant Judaism itself.[63]

Anglo-Jewry did not merely look on horror-struck. They agitated among Jewish workers, encouraging them to join English trade unions rather than the Yiddish-speaking homespun varieties. Sir Samuel Montagu established and paid for a Jewish tailors' union in 1886 and personally helped negotiate an end to the great tailors' strike of 1889. Boycotts of militant workers were organised by East End employers. And synagogue authorities condemned the bacon-eating atheists who violated Yom Kippur and other holy days.

A final great contradiction was at the heart of the migrants' economic life in London. The dominant trade declared by Jewish migrants as they entered the Poor Jews' Temporary Shelter was tailoring and this was the industry best associated with the newcomers. The 1901 census counted 12,700 Russians and Poles in London calling themselves tailors and a few hundred more shirtmakers, dressmakers and others. Of these a fifth were women. Then boot- and shoemakers, cabinet makers and others, including over 500 street sellers, pounding the same pavements that Jews had trodden for almost 250 years before them.[64]

All these trades had been established in east London for generations. Jews had worked in most of them throughout the nineteenth century. But these newcomers arrived from a culture where the accumulation and manipulation of small capital, mostly through trade, were an important tradition. And the structure of the garment industry, furniture and other workshop trades was such that any 'hand' could, with sufficient ambition, imagine himself a master. With very little capital, using the room he slept in as a workshop, exploiting himself and his family and then a 'greener' (new arrival) or two, with good health and avoiding bad luck, a man could realise profits and grow a business from a tiny seed. And perhaps even more important than the practical possibility was the belief that it *might* be done. In the tailoring trades, 'The ease with which a man may become a master is proverbial at the East End,' Beatrice Potter wrote in 1888. 'Altogether, it is estimated that with £1 in his pocket any man may rise to the dignity of a sweater.' That was enough to hire a sewing machine and a presser's table, the only fixed capital needed to make a start. Little more was required in cabinet making or bootmaking. And ambition was officially stimulated by the JBG, with its system of no-interest start-up loans for traders' stock money and for workshop capital. Between 1881 and 1899 the board made 14,767 loans, averaging under £4 10s each.[65]

So, on the one hand, the collective solidarity of the Jewish proletarian was bolstered by socialist ideology and strong notions of the brotherhood of man. It was made living reality in trade unions and strikes involving thousands. On the other, it had to battle with the enemy within: the daily opportunity to scrabble out of wage labour. And out of the East End. Here, at the very beginning of the great immigration, the origins of the dissolution of the Jewish East End were plain to see.

In some ways, for all their special qualities, the East End Jewish migrants of the last two decades of the century were following paths well marked before them by the Irish, French, Germans and Italians. Each had settled, accommodated but not relinquished, integrated as far as they felt able, prospered, moved on. Or, if not yet by 1900, they would in the decades to come. And when all was said and done, there was one single medium which enabled them to do so. It was that infinitely fluid London economy in which they had chosen to sink or swim.

PART THREE

WORK

'London's River
Feeds the dread Forge, trembling and shuddering along the Valleys.'
William Blake, *Jerusalem*,
c. 1827

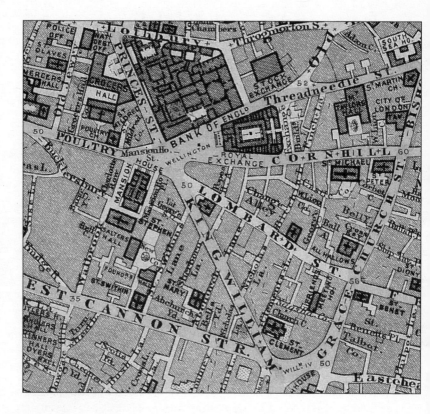

Lombard Street, 1862

LOMBARD STREET:
CAPITAL AND LABOUR

Banker to the World

No one knows how long Lombard Street has been heaped in riches. The oldest property deed bearing something like its modern spelling is dated 1319. But the Bardi or German-Italian Lombards after whom it is named had dwellings thereabouts and loaned money to English kings from the third quarter of the thirteenth century at latest. No tradition weighs heavier than gold, and the clustering of trades that was such a feature of the nineteenth-century London economy might take Lombard Street as an enduring gilt-edged symbol. 'The Grasshopper', 68 Lombard Street, was Martin's Bank at the end of the nineteenth century and a goldsmith's and moneylender's in the time of Henry VIII – maybe long before. The Great Fire of 1666 reduced it to cinders but gold rebuilt it and its gold glistened on. By 1800 Lombard Street, it is no exaggeration to say, was the golden heart which kept world trade in circulation. In 1808 there were twenty-two family and partnership banks in this one short street and the alleys adjoining. Sixty-five years later, despite the rise of joint-stock banking and the demise of the private banks, Lombard Street remained the centre of London finance. For Walter Bagehot, Lombard Street stood as shorthand for global credit based on London, 'by far the greatest combination of economical power and economical delicacy that the world has ever seen'. When the power failed and the delicacy tore asunder it was to Lombard Street that the victims flocked. In December 1825 thousands waited in 'anxious fear' to hear of another bank closing. And 'Black Friday', 11 May 1866, marked 'a single day of wild, ungovernable terror' as white-faced crowds witnessed the smash of Overend, Gurney and Co. at numbers 64–5.[1]

Lombard Street's was no ordinary banking. It was the home of 'the bill on London', of discount houses and that sophisticated industry of 'paper' and 'names' that oiled the wheels of commerce on the one hand and embroiled individuals in ruin and nightmare on the other. A valid bill, or promise to pay, was liquid as a banknote. The bankers of Lombard Street bought paper at a discount – gave cash for a percentage less than the face value of a bill – and then recovered the full sum from those who had incurred the original debt or 'accepted' it by putting their name to it. In essence they loaned money at interest for a fixed (and usually short) term. To raise the cash they loaned they might also sell paper at a discount. This was a credit system that gambled – 'ran a book' in Lombard Street jargon – on the creditworthiness of those who had issued or accepted a bill. In normal times sound merchants and manufacturers honoured their bills and paid up. But if trade was bad the risks could be high, as the failure of Overend, Gurney and Co., the largest of the London discount houses, showed. And sometimes the deck was rigged. In 1868 a bill-forging factory was discovered in Nicholas Lane, Lombard Street, complete with engraved plates and printed bills, signed and endorsed in five languages and pretending to have circulated in every major financial centre in the world.[2]

The London discount market was not the only game in the City. Stock-jobbing, that 'most active and decided spirit of gambling', had come out of the coffee houses into a 'stock exchange' in the last quarter of the eighteenth century. It was given a push with a new building in Capel Court, close to the Bank of England, opened in 1802. Each subsequent decade, but especially from the close of the Napoleonic Wars, brought from all over the world fresh stock to London in which the brokers and jobbers could trade for investors. The young Benjamin Disraeli burned his fingers so badly on Mexican and South American mining shares in 1824–5 that his financial affairs remained encumbered for almost the rest of his life. The 'Spanish panic' of May 1835 ruined many even if they had not personally dabbled in 'Peninsular securities'; those who had, brought their creditors down with them.[3]

But new ventures in this most enterprising and inventive of centuries were always coming along to breathe fresh vigour into Capel Court. None was more lively in the first half of the century than railways and the frantic share-dealing that accompanied proposals for new lines. It all 'perfectly revolutionized' stock exchange business. The 'railway mania' which climaxed on Sunday 30 November 1845 swept the whole City into its maw. Every clerk, engraver, lithographer and printer in London was seemingly engaged on plans and documents in respect of over 800 railway projects. People 'remained at work night after night, snatching a hasty repose for a couple of hours on lockers, benches, or the floor'. Some 400 lithographers were brought over from Belgium to help meet the deadline. Post horses were charged out at two guineas a mile to get couriers to the Board of Trade on time. The commerce in share options on hopeless schemes ruined so many 'stags' that their rendezvous at the Hall of Commerce in Threadneedle Street was christened 'the Refuge for the Destitute'.[4]

The rise in discounting and stock-dealing in the first half of the century was not the only cause of increased City activity and employment. It was matched by growth in insurance and a new City business altogether, joint-stock banking.

Life, fire and marine insurance had long been headquartered in the City of London. Even in 1808, and despite their uncertain legal status at that time, London had twenty-two life and property assurance companies, in addition to Lloyd's as the undisputed centre of marine cover. A clearer legal framework in 1824 produced a surge so that by 1850 there were 126 life assurance companies in London, mainly in the City, with an overspill into the West End. But risk and gamble and desperate failure underwrote insurance as it did discounting and share-jobbing. And again, risk was compounded by 'flagrant long-firm swindles' – companies selling products such as annuities that they had no intention of honouring.[5]

Joint-stock banking took off in the provinces around the same time as the rapid rise in London insurance. The failure of many country and London private banks in 1824–5 gave impetus to ventures raising capital by share issue – and so spreading the risk among many investors – rather than relying on the deep pockets of wealthy families and a few partners. Joint-stock banks were kept out of London until permitted by the Bank Charter Act of 1833. First was the London and Westminster Bank, opening in 1834 and moving to new headquarters at 41 Lothbury four years later. But these new enterprises might also be built on sand. The world's demand for capital and credit brought blackcoated adventurers into joint-stock companies. They fattened directors like pigs for the knife. The Royal British Bank in Tokenhouse Yard, to take one example among several, failed in 1856 after just six years' trading. The first directors, Scottish Presbyterians, opened their board meetings with prayer but went to prison for keeping false accounts and spending their customers' money on grossly luxurious lifestyles.[6]

The growth of London's financial services was phenomenal. Discount business alone was said to have doubled in the five years before 1836. It nearly doubled again between the mid-1840s and the mid-1850s, despite crippling financial crises and scandals almost every year. From the early 1860s an enormous increase in the volume of foreign trade, and the expansion of state-built infrastructure in nations new and old, all made their various calls on loans raised in London. Imperial banking flourished and foreign banks opened City branches. The Franco-German War temporarily dislocated London's two great European financial rivals in the early 1870s, leaving it the unrivalled gold market of the world. The translation of family firms into limited companies led to a fury of share-dealing in the 1880s and after. And by the 1890s the City entered its 'golden age', dominating world finance as never before or since. In the fifty years from 1853 the value of securities on the London stock exchange rose almost sixfold from £1.22 billion to £6.98 billion.[7]

All this hectic activity sucked more and more workers into the City. The numbers travelling to work there in 1866 were 170,000 each day. In 1881 this had risen by more than half to 261,000 and in 1901 to around 332,000. Including those who didn't work there but who came for business, some 1.2 million people entered the City's square mile each working day in 1891. Those Londoners employed in banking and as commercial clerks in merchants' and finance houses more than doubled from 16,700 in 1851 to 38,400 twenty years later. By 1901 the figure for London and Middlesex was 132,100, a more than three-fold increase in thirty years. Employment in insurance rose from 1,700 in 1871 to 11,600 in 1901. At the end of the century London and Middlesex contained fewer than one in six of employed persons in England and Wales but one in three of those employed in financial services and commercial offices.[8]

The large majority of these 180,000 persons worked in the City, making up probably half its workforce. As finance and commerce grew other sorts of City employments, notably manufacturing and retail, were squeezed out. In the process the organisation of financial services changed greatly. Small partnerships amalgamated in large companies. Face-to-face contact between merchants with similar interests reduced in significance. So the old Royal Exchange, with its separate 'Walks' for merchants in the East Indian, Irish, Norway, Spanish, American and other trades, was replaced in 1844 by a new building made up more of offices than circulation space. By the 1860s it and the old specialist coffee houses – the North and South American in Threadneedle Street ('the complete centre for American intelligence'), the Jerusalem at Cowper's Court (for merchants and sea captains in the China, India and Australian trade) and several others – were largely superseded by modern offices receiving instant information by telegraph from all parts of the globe. Even the smells that since time out of mind had demarcated the City's functional specialisms – the 'dry whiff of wheat' in Mark Lane, a taste of wine around Rood Lane, the pungent flavour of drugs in Mincing Lane – would become just memories from the 1860s on.[9]

Even the complexion of the City man changed over time. The expansion of business from the 1820s democratised to some extent this 'world within itself' and brought a new sort of man into the City. D. Morier Evans, the sharpest observer of the City at mid-century, summed it up in the difference between clerks in the old private banks and clerks in the joint stocks that had risen to prominence by the 1840s. The newcomers were a different 'class of people'. Instead of finding, as in the private banks,

cashiers and clerks peering through spectacles, with a steady and staid appearance, whose only inquiries are respecting the weather and the prospects of business, you find yourself in the company of sprightly young gentlemen, who talk about new operas and the other amusements of the town with all the ease of connoisseurs in high life; and whose chief study is to give effect to chequered neckerchiefs, showy chains, and mogul pins.[10]

Here was the forcing frame of what Albert Smith brilliantly characterised in 1847 as 'The Gent' – lascivious, boozy, flash and tasteless, ignorant of all but money and fast horses and the pleasures of town. Here was a new man bred specially for a hubristic money world. Here was an easy-come easy-go existence that had once seemed to be the province only of aristocrats and plutocrats but had now filtered down to the sons of tradesmen and attorneys and quacks. They seemed to be always lolling and lounging in and out of the City, on questions of the Bourse, and Greek and Spanish and India and Mexican and par and premium and discount and three quarters and seven eighths. They were all feverish, boastful, and indefinably loose; and they all ate and drank a great deal; and made bets in eating and drinking.[11]

Men like these – the friends of scheming Alfred Lammle in *Our Mutual Friend* (1864–5) – made the City something like a top-hatted Wild West, especially in the middle decades from the 1840s through the 1860s. Take, for instance, the irrepressible Walter Watts, 'a simple check-clerk' in the Globe Assurance Office earning £200 a year, who defrauded his employers of £70,000 and became by 1850 one of the most fashionable men in the West End – at least at night, for he kept to his humble City clerkship during the day. He leased two London theatres as impresario, combining a passion for the footlights with a backstage enthusiasm for the ballet. His expert eye for upholstery, his perfect equipage for the park, his connoisseur's taste in wine and 'princely hospitality', all made him one of the most sought-after hosts in town. 'But who was he? And what was he? From what source came his apparently inexhaustible means?' Here, in real life, was a true Veneering, more extravagantly drawn than anything even Dickens could describe in fiction.[12]

Indeed, the City was beyond caricature. Boards of directors of fraudulent or just ill-run joint-stock companies or family firms trudged through the dock at the Old Bailey one year after another. The partners of Strahan, Paul and Bates, bankers of the Strand, in 1855; the Royal British Bank directors, 1856; Colonel Waugh, a director of the London and Eastern Bank, who was allowed to draw £250,000 of his depositors' money on the security of a single accepted bill for £2,630, in 1857; the Bank of Deposit and National Assurance Investment Association, 'one of the worst and most sad cases of joint-stock villany [*sic*] ever announced to the London public', which stopped in 1861, owing £363,000 to customers with just £60 cash in hand; and many more.[13]

We get the sense in these middle decades of City men and those who trusted in them walking a narrow ledge between prosperity and ruin, peace of mind and lunacy. It was impossible to tell whether the next step would secure the one or precipitate the other. The sense of desperation was tangible. Suicide was as much in the City air as it was on Waterloo Bridge among the most hopeless of the London poor. Let one stand for all. Commenting in 1862 on a small epidemic of suicides noted in the press, the *Annual Register* highlighted the case of a

managing clerk of a city merchant [who] was apparently engaged in business in the neighbourhood of Mark Lane. Suddenly he left the crowd on the pavement, walked up to a coal-waggon heavily laden and drawn by four horses, kneeled down, and placed his head deliberately in front of the fore-wheel. The next instant the wheel passed over his head, and crushed it completely flat.[14]

The City couldn't quite free itself from this taint of hysteria for the rest of the century. The scandals never entirely abated, even though stock exchange members seem to have become more professional and trustworthy as a breed from around 1870. Insurance and banking frauds, crooked stock-jobbers, wild international speculations in gold and diamond mines, and reckless gambles in domestic company fluctuations, all fuelled City money fever till the century's end. As one critic complained in 1894, 'We are overrun with rotten limited liability companies, flooded with swindling "bucket shops", crashes and collapses rain upon us, and the "promoter" and the "guinea-pig" still and ever enjoy impunity.'[15]

This dark side of the bourse was far from the whole City story. Some private banks – Glyn's, Hoare's, Martin's, Coutts', for instance – remained pillars of rectitude throughout the century. Some great merchant banks – Rothschild, Montagu, Brown Shipley, Kleinwort, Schroeder, for example, but not Barings, who plunged the City into crisis in 1890 – combined entrepreneurial flair with sure-footed intelligence of the soundness of governments and companies from all over the world. Stockbrokers like Cazenove floated on top of the murky waters of Capel Court. And some great joint-stock banks, like the London and Westminster, London and County, National Provincial, and (from 1896) Barclays provided jobs for life for many of that new breed of clerks who came to dominate City employment in the last third of the century.

A City clerkship – indeed a clerk's desk anywhere in a private or public capacity – was a sought after position. In the1850s, when the number of posts available was still small, competition was fierce. Success in recruitment depended on cash and contacts. Commercial and bank clerks at £80-a-year starting salary were expected to produce substantial sureties on joining a firm in case of default. Almost any post required the patronage of a director or a large customer or a father already employed there before a young man could be appointed to it. Until 1871 most of the public service was staffed in this way too. So Dickens, to choose one honourable example, could write unashamedly to acquaintances to get his sons – or friends' sons – placed in government offices. And brazen advertisements could appear without comment in *The Times*.

DOUCEUR – £20 will be immediately given to any person who can legally procure for a married man, age 32, a PERMANENT SITUATION in any public, Government, or railway office as MESSENGER or CLERK . . . The salary must not be less than £80 per annum. Honour and secrecy observed. Address Henry Stanley, 120, Lower Marsh, Lambeth.

Competitive examinations may have sorted out most of these abuses by the 1890s but even then private offices 'commonly give preference to sons of clerks already in their employ'.[16]

Just how hard they had to work when they got there varied from place to place. Hours were nominally long. Nine to seven, with some variation, was customary in the City. Saturdays began to shorten from the late 1850s, but at Glyn's, for instance, 1. p.m. closing didn't come in until 1902.

Discipline varied. Commercial clerks in the City entered a world where strong drink helped them muddle through the hours. Louis Bamberger, a clerk at a timber merchant's in King William Street from 1868, recalled how meeting a friend in the street while on an errand called for a sixpenny glass of sherry ('and good stuff, too'), and beer or wine always accompanied lunch. Drink may not have been such a large part of daily life in the public service but hours were generally shorter and control might be non-existent. 'Not a few of the clerks were habitual idlers,' remembered Sir Robert Anderson of his days in the Home Office around 1870. 'The office hours were from 11 to 5. It was a nominal 11 and a punctual 5; and much of the intervening time was devoted to luncheon, gossip, and the newspapers.'[17]

Pay, in general, was low. In the 1880s the American diarist R. D. Blumenfeld chatted to a Gaiety Theatre barmaid: 'her father is a clerk in a City shipping office . . . he has been there thirty years, and his pay is thirty shillings a week! . . . The brother is a clerk in a shipping office, and receives 21s. a week, out of which he has to buy his top-hats and black coats. These people mystify me.' Ten years' service in the Gas

Light and Coke Co. brought a clerk to the company's maximum of
£150 per annum around 1880. And Booth considered in the 1890s
that 'the great mass of clerks' earned £75–150, broadly the same as
artisans.[18]

Drink and the City's nervy insecurity brought many men low. D.
Morier Evans described in the 1850s its vagabond fringe, a reserve
army of labour hanging on to its blackcoat-tails. The stock exchange
had its '"little-go", or "alley-men"', with a few almost worthless shares
to sell in moribund companies. These were 'broken-down merchants'
clerks' and 'decayed tradesmen' ruined by speculations. The most
derelict of all joined the beggars who jostled round the coffee houses
and City eateries at lunchtime.[19]

Derelict or virile, City clerkdom appeared overwhelmingly male.
Even at the end of the century the City streets were thronged 'by countless tribes of men of all sorts and conditions, but all in black, all in
tall hats, and all . . . swarming, like ants . . .' Even so, in 1901 almost
one in six commercial and bank clerks living in London and Middlesex
were women, over 22,000 of them. 'Typewriters', telegraphists and
telephonists were becoming very much female terrain. Young women
had appeared as commercial clerks, copyists and telegraph operators
by the early 1860s, but this picture at the turn of the century marked
a total transformation in the City even compared to twenty years before.
And these businesswomen were just the upper crust of the City's invisible ranks of women workers. An apron army marched each day across
London and Blackfriars Bridges as the housewives and girls of
Southwark and Lambeth moved in to char for offices and chambers.
They were joined by others 'carrying large bundles of umbrella-frames
home to be covered' or 'wooden cages full of hats, which yet want the
silk and the binding' or 'costergirls, often dirty and sordid, going to
fill their empty baskets', 'above all' the 'sack and bag women of
Bermondsey', carrying on their heads great bundles of canvas out of
the City and finished sacks into it, for the use of grain and other
merchants.[20]

But more than all these were thousands of women manufacturing
workers employed in City factories and workshops. Even at the end
of the century the City was the densest manufacturing quarter of
London, despite the increasing dominance of commerce and financial
services. Some 62,000 manufacturing workers were employed in the
City around 1900 and of these 29,000 (47 per cent) were women. Just

about anything seems to have been made there: arrows, artificial flowers, bells, boots, carpets, carriages, chemicals, clocks, dolls, fireworks, fishing tackle, flags, floorcloth, gas, glass, gloves, hats, jewellery, lamps, nets, paper bags, paper fasteners, pencils, pens, playing cards, pumps, rulers, scales, sealing wax, springs, tarpaulins, toys, turnstiles, valentines and whips, and a hundred others from 'aluminous cake' to writing slates. Yet even this cornucopia was just a drop in the great crucible of London manufacturing.[21]

Made in London

Manufacturing was London's largest employment sector during the nineteenth century. Some 630,000 Londoners, or nearly one in three (30 per cent) workers living in the County of London in 1901, made things in factories, workshops or at home. That compared to one in thirteen employed in commerce, one in eight conveying goods and one in five in domestic and related service. The proportion in manufacturing seems to have been largely constant across the century. In general, though not exclusively, London manufacturing specialised in finished commodities for immediate use and in luxury goods. That befitted London's place as the largest and wealthiest consumer market. And what London couldn't consume was dispatched from its port to every corner of the empire and, indeed, the non-imperial globe. The whole world over, 'the London trade-mark is a guarantee of superior quality; the London article has every where a superior price . . .'[22]

An enduring myth in the historical imagination has cast London as an economic anomaly in the nineteenth century, as somehow bypassed by the industrial revolution, its manufacturing confined to backward modes of production in tiny workshops or at home. In fact London was in one vital regard more advanced than anywhere.

Another marked and decided characteristic of London life, and which must not be passed over without observation, is that of the minute
DIVISION OF LABOUR
observable in the multitudinous avocations of the metropolitan population

wrote John Fisher Murray in 1843.[23] Nowhere else was it observable to such a remarkable degree. Division of labour robbed London artisans of their all-round capacity to envision and construct a commodity in its entirety or nearly so. Instead it split a task into myriad components, each one capable of being undertaken by 'unskilled' hands after training that relied on endless repetition. The traditional London artisan tended to become just another specialist process worker, using his delicate skills on a narrow basis, or was made redundant altogether by mechanisation or cheaper labour. This extreme division of labour in London manufacturing – indeed in London economic life in general – did not need the factory to perfect itself. On the contrary. As land in central London was exorbitantly dear, to fix so much capital in a great building could impede growth rather than encourage it. In London, more often than not, the neighbourhood became the factory. And factory discipline was unnecessary where an endless labour supply had to work long hours to gain a living and as often as not had to find its own heat and light in a workroom that was also home. What looked like industrial backwardness became a model of low-cost, flexible, responsive and competitive enterprise, even if it frequently relied on the super-exploitation of its workforce to remain so.

Having said all that, it is worth pointing our that the absence of large factories in London has been exaggerated. Throughout the century but especially towards its close giant factories were a feature of London's working life. Usually they were put near the river to aid transport of materials and fuel; or at the edge of the built-up area to capitalise on low land values. By the end of the Napoleonic Wars there were Bramah's locks and engine works at Pimlico, and Maudslay and Field, machine makers, in the Westminster Bridge Road, Lambeth; at Battersea there was a soap factory in 'an extensive pile of massy brickwork', with Brunel's army boot factory nearby; there were brewers, maltsters, distillers and mineral water makers all along the south bank of the river, bleaching mills and oil mills and iron foundries along the Wandle at Wandsworth, ropewalks a quarter of a mile long at Shadwell, and the biggest gas works in the world in Westminster, Blackfriars and Shoreditch; there were potteries in Lambeth, Fulham and Mortlake; Smith's silk mill at Hackney Wick employed over 500 workers; Walker's white lead factory at Islington was worked by two monster windmills and employed mainly women; there was Wigram and Green's huge shipyard at Blackwall, and many more.[24]

By the last quarter of the century enormous undertakings were legion. It was only London's vast size that swamped them and rendered them barely visible in the big picture. Clarnico's sweet factory in Hackney Wick employed 2,000 and Bassett's in Wood Green 1,000; Bryant and May had 1,200–1,600 hands at their match factory in Bow; Maudslay and Field were employing 1,500 from the late 1850s on; the Great Eastern Railway works at Stratford kept 3,100 busy in 1880; 3,000 worked at Silver's giant India Rubber and Telegraph Works – Silvertown, West Ham, was named after it; close to Silver's were Tate, the sugar refiner, which employed 1,000, Keiller's jam factory, which employed 1,100, and John Knight's soap works, which employed over 500; across the river at Woolwich Siemens' cable works had 1,700 workers; Frost's rope works at Shadwell was the largest in the world; John Penn's ship boiler works at Greenwich had 1,700 hands; the Royal Army Clothing Depot at Pimlico had 2,000; the London arms industry kept 10,000–14,000 busy at Woolwich Arsenal, the Royal Small Arms factory at Enfield another 2,000 and Eley's cartridge factory in Clerkenwell 1,000 or so; in building, Cubitt's workshops in Gray's Inn Road employed 3,000; in stationery De La Rue's at Bunhill Row, Finsbury, had 1,300 hands and Waterlow and Sons at London Wall 4,000; even in crowded Soho, Crosse and Blackwell's pickle factory in Charing Cross Road had 2,000 hands in the1890s. In all, at the end of the century 560,000 people worked in London County's factories and work-shops; nearly 175,000 of these (31 per cent) worked in factories employing over 100 people.[25]

That left most manufacturing workers employed by small firms, mainly in workshops with fewer than ten people. And a significant minority – around 50,000 in the County of London in 1901 – worked at home. The proximity of workshops and homeworkers employed in a single industry could turn a neighbourhood into one great factory. The London garment industry, for instance, clustered strongly in Stepney (mainly Whitechapel) and in Westminster (mainly Soho). The East End was home especially to extreme subdivision of labour and had been so for generations: 'sweating' was said to have begun around the time of the Napoleonic Wars. But it became scientifically organised with the rise of the great Houndsditch ready-made wholesalers in the 1840s and 1850s. A coat required by Messrs Moses, say, or Hyams, would be cut by the hundred in the wholesaler's, basted or 'fitted up' by the master tailor (the sweater) and sent out to individual homeworkers for pockets, sleeves, velvet lapels, piping, buttonholes and buttons, back to the tailor for finishing and pressing, and then to the wholesaler's for dispatch. Every sundry for the tailor and seamstress could be had within a few yards of the workshop or home: threads and ribbons of all shades of the dyer's art, needles, thimbles, pin cushions, sewing machines (from the 1840s on) for sale or hire by the week. There were more homeworkers available in the garment district than work to put out to them, so there was hardly ever a labour shortage. In an industry neurotically susceptible to changing taste and fluctuating seasonal demand, this was a highly adaptive arrangement. Small runs and large were easily accommodated. The demands of a great state event, like a coronation or funeral or visit from foreign royalty, could be met no matter how short the notice given. Word of mouth and face-to-face transactions ensured that necessary skills at a marketable price were quickly at hand. This competitive flexibility made the clothing industry one of the most robust and profitable in London throughout the century.[26]

There were numerous other industrial clusters which gave to neighbourhoods a distinctive character and which reaped similar advantages. The leather industry had settled in Bermondsey since the middle of the sixteenth century, its tan-pits and curriers' yards and giant hide market importing a special flavour to the Bermondsey air. Depending greatly on skins and fur, hat making located nearby, spreading westward into Southwark from the 1830s. Cabinetmaking was predominantly a Shoreditch and Bethnal Green trade, with another cluster east of Tottenham Court Road. In Clerkenwell, watchmaking was perhaps the finest example of divided labour in London. A watch was made by 'considerably more than one hundred hands', passing along from worker to worker often labouring in his own rooms. Clerkenwell door-plates announced '"escarpment-maker", "engine-turner", "fusee-cutter", "springer", "secret-springer", "finisher", "joint-finisher", &c . . .' In Red Lion Street in the 1840s, sixty out of some eighty houses were occupied by watchmakers.[27] Coachmakers gathered in Long Acre and gunsmiths in the Minories. There were still shoemakers in Shoe Lane in the Napoleonic Wars, but by the 1840s they had largely moved east to Bethnal Green and Stepney. The connection between artists and Newman Street, Soho, well established by 1800, resonated in the cluster of artists' colour-men there a century later even though the painters had long moved away to Fitzroy Square, St John's Wood and Chelsea.[28] Slaughterhouses had herded for centuries in Aldgate and did so till the 1870s at least. Offensive trades like horse knackers and bone and blood boilers made a big stink together in Belle Isle, north of King's Cross, and then from the 1850s in West Ham. Photographers peopled Regent Street in the1860s. Camden Town was the centre of the piano trade from around the same time.

There were, of course, many mixed industrial districts – like the City or Soho or Hoxton, 'the city of the smaller industries and the lesser ingenuities'.[29] The new residential suburbs of the 1850s and 1860s were by the century's end going the same way, seeding a flourishing crop of industries – Islington had workshops and factories employing over 22,000 around 1900 and Kensington nearly 11,000. Even so, the old-established factory networks of London, matching a district to a trade or perhaps two, added value through the ease of direct communication, in the readiness of supplies and spare capacity in a rush, and in the ability to press for longer credit. All helped sharpen a competitive edge; and, once established, inertia kept them in place often for generations.

That would not, though, save a dying trade. London industries might wane as well as flourish. Take silk weaving. Associated with Spitalfields and Bethnal Green since the Huguenot migration of the late seventeenth century, the London silk industry had the protection of the Spitalfields Acts, 1765–1801, which regulated wages and conditions and forbade foreign imports. But smuggled silks, cheap provincial labour in Lancashire, Coventry, Suffolk and elsewhere, and suppressed demand during the Napoleonic Wars brought periodic distress. In 1816 3,000 looms were 'out of employ' and the weavers' condition 'truly wretched'. In the 1820s things only got worse. Some silk imports were permitted from 1826 and Spitalfields weavers became some of the first victims of the shift to free trade. In 1829 there were violent riots against master weavers, with attacks by moonlight on silk in the loom.[30]

Yet silk clung on to Bethnal Green. Thousands of half-idle looms paid starvation wages to a workforce of some 30,000 souls around 1850. The rewards were so low that children were 'quilling' silk from six and put to the loom at twelve. The fabled intellectual vivacity of the eighteenth-century Spitalfields weavers, with their mathematical and microscopical and botanical societies and their passion for caged birds, gave way to an immiserated workforce capable of little but a grinding struggle for survival. In their desperation they resisted every mechanical innovation readily accepted elsewhere. Even the weather was against them: a two-day fog in the freezing December of 1850

The Mint, Southwark, 1825. A view probably of Mint Street, some Tudor houses readily apparent but otherwise remarkable for its ordinariness. The attic-dwellers' washing on poles, and the cages for linnets and other songbirds on the white house to the right, were characteristic of poor London throughout the century. Some of these places were still standing sixty years later when conditions here provoked a campaign for better housing in London.

Pre-Fire Houses in Long Lane, Smithfield, 1810. This 'wretched pile of buildings' was typical of the old London that seemed so out of place to nineteenth-century Londoners. From the beginning, every opportunity was taken to disencumber the city of its ancient legacy, and these were removed in 1811. Demolition men are busy in the street behind and sport on the roof of the house with an elaborately decorated front and prominent birdcage.

Farringdon Road, final period of construction, *c.* 1862. For nearly twenty years the building of Farringdon Road had eaten away at the ancient slums of Clerkenwell along Field Lane, Saffron Hill and the River Fleet. Its final stages were delayed by the decision to run beneath it not just the Fleet but the first underground railway in the world from King's Cross to the City at Farringdon Street.

Wych Street, Strand, *c.* 1899. By the end of the century almost all of London that had survived the Fire of 1666 had been destroyed by public authorities and private developers. Wych Street, and next-door Holywell Street, would not last long past 1900, their overhanging upper stories a rare survivor of tireless redevelopment. Wych Street had been known for its brothels in the 1860s, and Holywell Street its pornographic book trade.

Victoria Embankment looking north to St Paul's, *c.* 1875. The dolphin lamp columns are being raised into position as part of the Embankment's final touches. This was the century's greatest metropolitan improvement. It prevented flooding in Westminster, gave Londoners a view of their river that the old wharves and warehouses had denied them, and carried beneath it the Metropolitan Underground Railway and Bazalgette's low-level intercepting sewer.

Building the Metropolitan District Railway at Victoria, *c.* 1866. The first part of what would become the tube's Inner Circle ran from South Kensington to Westminster Bridge. The mode of construction, cut and cover rather than tunnelling, involved great destruction of property as it came closer to central London. Works like this made London resemble one vast building site throughout the 1860s.

Waterloo Station, *c.* 1895. Railway travel revolutionised the capacity of middle-class Londoners to escape from the smoke for a day or a weekend or longer. The bustle here at London's south-west terminus for the Hampshire and Dorset coasts is aggravated by cabs and buses driving almost up to the platform.

Opening Tower Bridge, 30 June 1894. One of the century's last great public improvements by the City Corporation, a London icon and an important river connection at the City's eastern edge. It was designed by Sir John Wolfe Barry, son of London's greatest architect of the first half of the century, Charles Barry.

Ealing Broadway, *c.* 1890. As London grew with such phenomenal vigour in the second half of the century, villages and country towns were swallowed in its insatiable maw. The metropolitan bustle even of Ealing Broadway, very much an outer suburb, is readily apparent in this summer snapshot.

Charing Cross, looking towards the Strand, 1842. A lithograph of a drawing by Thomas Shotter Boys showing the equestrian statue of Charles I in the right foreground and behind it the Jacobean front of Northumberland House, one of the last great palaces left in London and later demolished to make way for Northumberland Avenue. The dusty way is being watered by a hand-drawn cart.

The Strand from the Golden Cross Hotel, Charing Cross, c. 1897. For nineteenth-century Londoners the Strand, joining the cities of London and Westminster, was the premier street in the world. Here it is on a summer weekday near the end of the century, far busier than in Boys' view but seemingly well ordered and relaxed. And hardly a policeman in sight.

The Jews' Market, Wentworth Street, *c.* 1895. Poor Jewish migrants from Eastern Europe formed by far the largest minority community in London in the nineteenth century. Their biggest street market was in Wentworth Street west of Commercial Street. They called it 'The Lane'. For English observers it was the essence of foreignness, though from this shot it and its customers seem not much different from any other London street market.

Italian street musician, 1877. The Italian community of Saffron Hill on the borders of Holborn and Clerkenwell was well established by the time John Thomson took this photograph of a young 'harper' in England about two years. The piano organ was a more popular instrument among the Italian street musicians but this player earned well: 'His clothes are ample, neat, and clean, his purse well-filled...'

cost one master weaver £100 in damaged silk – '"The blacks (London genuine particular) got into the white satins . . ."' The death blow came in 1860, with a commercial treaty allowing French silks free access to the English market. But the wake lingered on. Around 1900 there were said to be some sixty weaving families left in Spitalfields and Bethnal Green.[31]

London shipbuilding was the other great trade in decline during the nineteenth century. The shift to iron ships, plus the great distance of the Thames from iron and coal, was the true turning point. Yet in the early years, when demand across the world was insatiable for the new vessels, the London trade stood up well. The *Great Eastern* was launched from Blackwall in 1858 and the 1850s and early 1860s saw lively production of warships for governments at home and abroad. But a truculent labour force, wedded to traditional practices and used to higher wages and better conditions than their competitors on the Tyne and Clyde, helped undermine the Thames. It was beset by strikes, employer prosecutions of trade unions and riots against blacklegs. The collapse of Overend, Gurney and Co. in 1866 bankrupted a number of shipbuilders who had depended on the bank for credit. London shipwrights emigrated to the colonies or the northern yards, their numbers falling by nearly three-quarters between 1861 and 1891. Some great firms, like the Thames Iron Works at Blackwall, held on into the early 1880s. But in the 1890s Thames shipbuilding had largely narrowed to torpedo-boat manufacture at Yarrow's on the Isle of Dogs and Thornycroft's at Chiswick, the latter making the fastest boats in the world. The engineers' strike of 1897, and high land and transport costs, drove the remnants north to Newcastle and Glasgow early in the new century.[32]

Some other trades declined too. Thames pollution largely killed off fish and fishing by the 1830s, with numbers of fishermen transferring their skills into river piracy instead. Whitechapel needles – so popular among British housewives in the first decade or so of the century – couldn't survive competition from the Black Country. The London shoemakers' strike of 1812 fatally introduced Northampton goods into the London market: provincial competition suppressed the wages and conditions of metropolitan bootmakers for the rest of the century. Heavy chemical production, especially alkalis, important in London around 1820, had largely moved north by the middle of the century. Belgian and German competition brought London glass blowers 'to starvation' in the 1890s. And German, Swiss and Birmingham competition after 1870 called time on Clerkenwell watchmaking, causing 'great poverty' there in the 1880s and making it an old man's trade by the end of the century.[33]

But Clerkenwell is an interesting case. At the same time as its ancient watchmaking industry entered its last phase, Clerkenwell fostered innovation and helped build new industries for London. Young men who could see no future in cutting fusees might turn their technical ability to new uses. Clerkenwell encouraged them. Its network of enterprises relied on fine skill and encompassed a wide product range. Scientific instruments for surveying, navigation and metrology; surgical instruments and artificial limbs; new developments in electrical instruments like telephones and the first explorings of radio all benefited from a workforce immersed in precision manufacture and workshops that knew how to adapt to changing customer requirements. Clerkenwell and round about was the greenhouse of invention. Hiram Maxim perfected his machine gun there, Sebastian de Ferranti his dynamos, transformers and electric meters, Guglielmo Marconi his electric telegraph and Peter Brotherhood his torpedo engines. When the General Electric Apparatus Co. (later GEC) opened up at a warehouse in Great St Thomas Apostle, City, in 1887 its producers were cabinetmakers, brass workers, glass-shade and globe makers nearby. These were late-century examples but London engineering inventiveness had sparkled in 1800 and long before. The inventors may have been Scottish – as so many were – and from every corner of England and Wales and Ireland. But it was to London – Soho, Millbank, Vauxhall and later Clerkenwell in particular – that they came to perfect their ideas among London's assembly of skilled workers and their unique know-how. In 1901 42 per cent of the 50,000 electrical apparatus makers of England and Wales lived in London and Middlesex. And London proved a fruitful starting point for other new industries, like dyes, margarine, plastics and motor vehicles.[34]

London's enormous and varied labour market allowed new industries to grow and old ones to diversify. But it had ill effects too. Employers confronted with uncontrollable costs higher than elsewhere – rates, coal, transport – constantly sought to pinch wage rates as the only way to secure profits. It was here that the London labour market was at its most flexible and most pernicious. An inexhaustible labour supply, fierce competition even among skilled and blackcoated workers, drove wages down to the lowest tolerable level, frequently lower.

Low wages were a curse on London throughout the nineteenth century. They forced men and women into cripplingly long hours and could enslave their children to help make a living. All classes might be affected. We have glimpsed low wages among clerks and the slow starvation of skilled silk weavers in Spitalfields. But it was unskilled hands who suffered most. Or, rather, workers with a skill that many possessed. The worst wages were paid to women in the garment industry, a byword for shameless exploitation through most of the century.

Women's wages were low in the clothing trades for a number of reasons. Extreme subdivision of labour resulted in a single repetitive task paid by the piece. The work was done often at home, so was easily taken up by journeymen's and labourers' wives to help better the family income. These women competed with the full-time hand for work. With too many workers and seasonal fluctuation, work was often irregular and even a better-paid task couldn't make a living wage because of its infrequency. So those women – spinsters, widows, wives separated from their husbands or caring for a sick man – who relied on their needle for a living were universally poor.

'I could not have believed,' wrote Henry Mayhew in November 1849, 'that there were human beings toiling so long and gaining so little, and starving so silently and heroically, round about our very homes.' That was after at least seven years' exposure of the problem in the public prints, brought home especially to middle-class readers by the plight of respectable widows exploited by the ready-made wholesalers, almost all of them Jewish or reputed to be so. The combination of bourgeois ill-fortune and anti-Semitism was irresistible. Thomas Hood's poem 'The Song of the Shirt', published in the 1843 Christmas number of *Punch*, was inspired by a widow making trousers at 7d a pair, 'for a Jewish slop-seller in the Minories'. She had pawned the material to feed her starving children and the wholesaler had prosecuted.

> Stitch – stitch – stitch,
>   In poverty, hunger, and dirt,
> Sewing at once, with a double thread,
>   A Shroud as well as a Shirt.[35]

Mayhew wrote of a shirtmaker toiling fourteen hours a day for 3s a week and finding 'all her own trimmings, all the thread and cotton';

a waistcoat maker, ill through overwork and with just a penny left in the house – '"nothing to depend upon for an hour"'; and a military uniform maker: '"Sugar", she said, "I broke myself of long ago; I couldn't afford it. A cup of tea, a piece of bread, and an onion, is generally all I have for my dinner, and sometimes I haven't even an onion, and then I sops my bread."' Fifty years on and Beatrice Potter found conditions not that much improved. Around 1890 East End slop shops, now exploiting Jewish immigrant labour, paid just 9d to 1s 6d for a morning coat and 5d to 1s for a lounge jacket. A female 'general hand' in the poorest work earned just 9s for a seventy-two-hour week.[36]

Even skilled wages were pulled down by London's vicissitudes of demand, of weather, of trade. The average London skilled wage for men near the end of the century was around 35s to £2 10s a week. That was about double the unskilled male wage. There was no immense wage inflation in the nineteenth century, so that a plumber could earn 4s 6d a day in 1808 and 7s 6d in the final quarter of the century, a 66 per cent rise in money wages. Real wages, taking into account fluctuations in prices, rose more substantially – 80 per cent between 1850 and 1900. But the rise was unsteady and punctuated by periodic falls in living standards affecting many trades, sometimes all. The combination of a financial crisis and a freezing winter, as in 1866–7, plunged the whole metropolis, skilled men and all, into distress. Even in an average year the building trades lost a sixth of the full-time weekly rate through weather; engineers, bookbinders and piano polishers a quarter through irregular demand; and all but the best tailors had notoriously busy seasons and slack – after the Lord Mayor's Show on 9 November until Easter it was hard to find much work at all.[37]

Low pay was a significant cause of London poverty throughout the century. The figures are uncertain but Booth thought at least a sixth of family poverty was due to wages too low to live on.[38] In fact low pay was a more powerful driver of London poverty than this indicates. Nineteenth-century wages allowed hardly any capacity to save. There was little credit, and no safety net endowed by the state. So a single misfortune – illness, accident, a child's funeral – wiped out any margin between comfort and poverty. Just as in the City, nearly all Londoners lived on a knife-edge. Mr Micawber's formula of 'happiness' for those who lived within their means and 'misery' for the others was literally true. And misery was never far away for those who suffered an unplanned stoppage of work: three months or so for a clerk pawning everything substantial he possessed, three weeks or so for a bricklayer, thirty-six hours for a sempstress.

No wonder, then, that London workers should fight so hard to keep wages as high as they could. And that agreements struck in good years – when employers were hungry for labour – should be so ferociously clung to in the bad. So strikes and lock-outs were constant features of London life. Even when the Combination Acts had punished strikes by transportation, London labour was restless and tough-minded. Builders – especially the masons – seem to have struck on every major construction project that helped transform London into a modern world city: St Katharine's Dock (1827), Trafalgar Square, Nelson's Column and the new Houses of Parliament (1841), the Law Courts (1877, broken by German, Italian and other imported artisans) and no doubt numerous others; and there were widespread builders' strikes and lock-outs in 1859, 1861, 1872, 1891 and 1896. There were momentous tailors' strikes in 1812, 1834 and 1889; and engineers' in 1852, 1879 and 1897. These were just the big events. Around and between them, especially in the last two decades of the century, there was a grumbling war of attrition between masters and workers that might flare up at any time. Pay was always an issue but so was deskilling and the replacement of male artisans by women and boys. In each year from 1889 to 1899, for instance, the Board of Trade returns showed London strikes among upholsterers, bookbinders, furriers and stick makers in one year; cap makers and cigar makers in two; brush makers, French polishers and bakers in three; cabinetmakers in seven, boot makers ten; and tailors in every year of the eleven.[39]

But one of the great strikes of the century, perhaps the very greatest in terms of its effects on the consciousness of London workers and the London middle classes, was not in manufacturing or building but in another industry altogether. An industry synonymous with the degradation of male labour. The docks.

Conveyance Paid

Down the 'silent highway' barges tide-borne floated sideways, with their long thin idle oars projecting from their sides, like fins . . . Then would come a raft of timber, towed by a small boat, and the boatman leaning far back in it as he laboured at the sculls; and presently a rapid river steamer, stuck all over with passengers, would flit past, and you would catch a whiff of music from on board as it hurried by . . . Then came hoys laden with straw and coasting goods, so deep in the water that, as the steamers dashed by, you could see the white spray beat against the tarpaulins that covered their heaped-up cargoes. Next to these, black-looking colliers, and Russian brigs from Memel and Petersburg, lay in a dense mass together . . . Beside the wharf in front of these lay lug-boats and sloops, filled with square cases of wine, while bales of hemp, barrels of porter, and crates of hardware, swung from the cranes, and were lowered into the boats or lifted out of the sloops and 'foreign brigs' below . . . As you beheld the white cloud of the railway engine scudding above the roofs opposite, and heard the clatter of the carts and waggons behind, and looked down the endless vista of masts that crowded each side of the river, you could not help feeling how every power known to man was used to bring and diffuse the riches of every part of the world over this little island.[40]

That was how Henry Mayhew saw the port of London from Custom House roof on a glittering spring morning in 1850. The Thames had been 'the chief river in the world' and London the world's greatest port for at least 150 years before that. But it was only in the nineteenth century that it came of age, properly equipping itself for the role it played at the centre of global trade.

As the nineteenth century dawned, parliamentary sanction was won for companies to build secure docks for the first time in the port's history. Instead of unloading ships at open quays, or by boat and barge from ships moored in deep water, immense wet docks would be gouged out behind the river banks. Ships would be sailed out of the river into a fortress of man-made lakes hemmed in by walls thirty feet high.[41] The first – the West India Docks – were opened at the northern end of the Isle of Dogs in 1802. Their business was restricted to sugar and other imports of the West Indies trade, and they had sole right to export to those fever-stricken islands. To modernise the capacity of the upper port nearer the City, the London Dock Company opened new docks at Wapping in 1805. These London Docks had twenty-one years' exclusive handling of wine, brandy, tobacco and rice, exploiting new warehousing at the dockside and older premises in the City nearby. The East India Docks were opened in 1806 immediately downriver of the Isle of Dogs at Blackwall Point, with exclusive rights in the China and East Indies trade. And south of the river, the Surrey and Commercial Docks at Rotherhithe underwent a massive expansion at the hands of four separate companies between about 1802 and 1815, mainly for the Baltic and Scandinavian timber trade and grain.

This enormous growth of the port during the Napoleonic period allowed more trade into London than ever before. Foreign tonnage rose 22 per cent in the twenty years after 1799, totalling 821,000 tons in 1819.[42] That would prove small beer. As London grew so did the port. The capital's vast rich consumer market, its position at the centre of coastal trade, shipping on to other domestic destinations the world's bounty that sailed up London river, and its place at the hub of an expanding empire depending on London to provide civilisation's most valued commodities all required the port to grow and restructure across the century.

Competition between dock companies resulted in some over-capacity. But the profits to be made on the river meant that investors were never hard to find, even if dividends eventually proved disappointing. St Katharine's Dock, just east of the Tower, competed directly with the London Docks when their twenty-one-year privileges expired, opening in 1828. There was then a lull in dock expansion for two decades, during which the foreign tonnage entering London nearly doubled from a million tons in 1829 to 1,891,000 in 1849. By then it was clear that expansion was again necessary and investors' eyes turned downriver, where land was cheap and demolition unnecessary. The Victoria Dock opened at Plaistow Levels, West Ham, in 1855; the Millwall Dock, specialising in grain and some timber, was dug out of the southern part of the Isle of Dogs, opening in 1868; and in 1880 the Royal Albert Dock linked Victoria Dock to the river at Galleon's Reach. These two 'Royals' made a gigantic artificial waterway across West and East Ham, encouraging industrial development on land the dock company bought and drained around it. Finally in 1886 the East and West India Dock Company leapfrogged the Royals and built giant new deepwater docks twenty-six miles downriver from London Bridge at Tilbury, opposite Gravesend. This 'lower port' was linked by rail to Fenchurch Street Station. With Tilbury's help, foreign tonnage entering London reached 9,245,000 in 1899, a 26 per cent increase in just ten years. Despite fierce rivalry from other UK ports, London more or less held on to its one-third share by value of all imports reaching the nation at the end of the century.

But the port of London was far more than just a place for handling imports and clearing exports. It was closely integrated with some of London's heaviest industry, working on imported goods close to the point of entry, and with a whole town straddling the river devoted to the needs of ships and Jack Tar. Wapping, Limehouse, Shadwell, Ratcliffe and Rotherhithe were all hamlets with seadog traditions going back to Elizabeth and beyond. By 1840 they were submerged in the giant city but they kept their salty tang. Sailors could sell their pets and curiosities at the 'wild-beast shops' of Ratcliffe Highway, especially Jamrach's. At Wapping or Rotherhithe boat builders jostled with 'rope makers, biscuit bakers, mast, oar, and block makers', sailors' outfitters and ships' chandlers, pawnbrokers and 'leaving shops', grog shops and knocking shops. The riverside was a wonderland made more exotic by the strangers from all over the world who rubbed shoulders there. And there were other exotica too. Besides Jamrach's tigers and cobras and camels, it was at Wapping that the fuchsia was first discovered by an inquisitive nurseryman who bought it from a sailor in the West Indies trade, changing the complexion of English gardening in the process.[43]

Sailors were only one small part of the working population of docklands. At the end of the century, when the port had never been busier, about 8,000 sailors were berthing in Bermondsey, Poplar and Stepney on census night 1901. Added to them were all the officials, stevedores, lightermen, artisans and other skilled men in the dock workforce, on regular and reasonable pay. Many of these by the 1880s and 1890s commuted to the docks from the eastern suburbs. And then came the 22,000 or so dock labourers competing daily for work unloading ships at the port. Of these some 8,500 were permanent hands or 'preferred men' – often earning enough to be suburbans too. The other 13,500 'casuals' shared work that, evened out through the year, would have kept about half of them fully employed.[44]

Then there were men who only competed for work at the docks when their own trades were slack, and a host of hangers-on, derelict workmen from other trades or none, who hoped for a day or half a day to supplement poor relief or charity or some hand-to-mouth pursuit. Some of these would 'book off' after doing just enough for a pint of beer and pipe of tobacco and a night's doss. Here in its most shabbily visible form was what contemporaries called the 'residuum', the reserve army of labour, or just the 'scum of the earth'. 'Waiting at the gates' for the dock foreman's early-morning call was one of the sights of

London.[45] Mayhew is our witness again: at the London Docks, 7.30 on an October morning in 1849. He saw

> masses of men of all grades, looks, and kinds; some in half-fashionable surtouts, burst at the elbows, with the dirty shirts showing through; others in greasy sporting jackets, with red pimpled faces; others in the rags of their half-slang gentility, with the velvet collars of their paletots worn through to the canvas; some in rusty black, with their waistcoats fastened tight up to the throat; others, again, with the knowing thieves' curl on each side of the jaunty cap; whilst here and there you may see a big-whiskered Pole, with his hands in the pockets of his plaited French trousers. Some loll outside the gates, smoking the pipe which is forbidden within: but these are mostly Irish.
>
> Presently you know, by the stream pouring through the gates, and the rush towards particular spots, that the 'calling foremen' have made their appearance. Then begins the scuffling and scrambling, and stretching forth of countless hands high in the air, to catch the eye of him whose voice may give them work. As the foreman calls from a book the names, some men jump upon the backs of the others, so as to lift themselves high above the rest, and attract the attention of him who hires them. All are shouting . . . Indeed, it is a sight to sadden the most callous, to see *thousands* of men struggling for only one day's hire, the scuffle being made the fiercer by the knowledge that hundreds out of the number there assembled must be left to idle the day out in want. To look in the faces of that hungry crowd, is to see a sight that must ever be remembered.[46]

Men entered daily this 'brutal fight and struggle' throughout the nineteenth century.[47] This dog-eat-dog world, leavened by the communism of generosity when it came to sharing a pint or a baccy pouch, rendered the condition of dock labour 'hopeless'. Or so it seemed. It appeared to be a workforce incapable of organised self-help. For this reason alone, the Great Dock Strike of 1889 provided the most sensational metropolitan labour dispute of the nineteenth century.

It was a child of the turbulent 1880s, playing on the special circumstances of the port of London. The 'unemployed' had become a feature of metropolitan labour, swollen by trade depression and severe winters. Socialism, preached on street corners and open spaces, scratched away at deference and the acceptance of things as they were. The new lower port at Tilbury stole work from upriver and daily increased the crush at the gates from the Royals westwards. Every hour's pay was harder to get. And it was still worth very little – just 4d or 5d to a casual, who might only get twenty or thirty hours a week.

There had been strikes before, in 1872 and 1880, which had won 5d and then 6d an hour in some docks on contract work, but only a minority of casuals in the port had benefited. The successful match-girls' strike at Bryant and May's in the summer of 1888 and the forma-tion of a gas workers' union in early 1889, quickly winning a reduction in hours without a strike, put heart into the dock casuals. Talks about forming a union of permanent dock men were under way when a dispute at the South West India Dock brought things suddenly to a crisis on Tuesday 13 August. The men walked out. Among other things they sought a minimum of four hours' work when taken on at the gates. And they demanded 6d an hour – 'the docker's tanner'. So began a month of hectic excitement in the East End. Of daily processions to the Mansion House with brass bands and banners flying. Of memor-able oratory from Ben Tillett, Tom Mann and John Burns, the strike's main leaders. Of mass meetings on Tower Hill, attracting thousands. The dock companies were astonished when stevedores and lightermen, the skilled men of the port who in ordinary times would begrudge a nod of recognition to a casual, turned out in sympathy. Within a week the whole port was 'completely paralysed'. Some 75,000 workers were said to be on strike as the world's shipping queued idle in the river. The London press 'rang with the news from day to day'. Donations to the strike fund were telegraphed by Australian dockers and handed in by City stockbrokers and newspaper editors, several of whom opened subscriptions in their papers. The Lord Mayor of London and Cardinal Manning helped broker negotiations between the men and their increas-ingly isolated employers. Eventually the dock companies surrendered. All the men's demands were met. And a new chapter in British trade union history had opened.[48]

When the dockers returned to work on 17 September 1889 goods began to flow once more into the great hinterland of London. They were moved most often by horse and van or wagon. It is a mark of the size and wealth of London that its road haulage industry was disproportionately large compared with the nation as a whole. There were 120,000 road transport workers, including those on omnibuses, living in London and Middlesex in 1901, nearly one in four of the total haulage industry of England and Wales. Some 68,000 of them were carmen and carters employed by a range of enterprises – from huge carrying firms, like Pickford's or Carter Paterson's or the railway companies, to a man running one or more vans for short-haul contract work. These were men (just a handful of women) who knew their way about horses, then such common knowledge that horse handling was hardly a marketable skill at all. Hours were long – ninety-six a week not uncommon – and pay was low. 'There is perhaps no man's employment which yields so small a return per hour.' A man in charge of a one-horse van might take home just 18s a week, 24s at best; larger vans paid more, 30s top rate. In the large firms and well-established small carriers, regularity of employment offered some compensation for low pay. But at the edge of road transport was another casual fringe of 'odd men' who hung around the omnibus and carriers' depots and the carmen's 'pull-ups' – coffee shops for men on the road. 'Of men of this class there is always a surplus in London.'[49]

Carmen and carters didn't only shift goods from the docks. By the end of the century much of their work came from the railway stations. From the 1860s the railways made up the main supply lines from the nation into the metropolis. Employment on railways in London was not disproportionately large, despite the momentous impact the iron way had made on the metropolis and its people. Some 48,000 men (and a couple of hundred women) living in London and Middlesex in 1901 worked on the railways, just over one in six of the nation's railwaymen and roughly in line with London's share of all employment. Here too clustering was evident. A few parts of the capital took on the features of a railway town. Hudson Town at Stratford we have already met. The Delhi Street area of west Islington was known as 'the "Railway barracks"' in the 1890s. And in the streets south of Nine Elms Station, Battersea, lived 'fully 5,000 railway employees', fresh migrants to London with their 'country girl' wives: they had their own Railway Mission, with hellfire stoked by railway preachers.[50]

These armies of men at the docks and on the roads and railways were engaged in bringing goods – and people – to market. For London was not just the world's bank, its greatest manufacturing district for finished commodities, its biggest port. It was the greatest shopping city the world had ever seen.

'The Emporium of the World'

First, though, shopkeepers had to buy before they could sell. And the wholesale markets of London were some of the wonders of the world.

Leadenhall Market was thought to be the largest in Europe at the beginning of the century. Some of its buildings dated from the early 1400s and it comprised three great courts or yards. The 'Beef-market' sold beef, hides, leather, 'Colchester baize' and wool on different days; the 'Green-yard' sold veal, mutton and lamb, with 140 butchers' stalls round its sides and in a central row; and the 'New-market' sold 'herbs, roots, fruit, &c.' Newgate Market was another City meat market, known for its filthy slaughterhouses behind and beneath its butchers' shops, and not abolished until 1868. In both – as at Billingsgate in the early years of the century – porterage was women's work. Around 1840 John Fisher Murray watched the women meat porters, 'many of them old', staggering 'under the weight of a side of beef' or with 'an entire sheep upon their heads'.[51]

Women porters were prominent too at mid-century Covent Garden. This was the largest fruit, vegetable and flower market of the capital and once more wholesale and retail mingled freely. Dating from the seventeenth century, it was rebuilt by the Bedford Estate in 1828–30, the old wooden sheds and standings replaced by Charles Fowler's impressive Market Building. Yet traditional work practices carried on. In the early 1840s, 'Irish basket-women [who 'jabber in Erse'] . . . ply as porteresses, and will carry your purchase' on their heads 'to any part of the town'. By the end of the century women had been entirely edged out of market portering by men.[52]

Like the women porters, a number of London's wholesale markets disappeared over time. They were cleared by street improvements (like Fleet Market and Farringdon Market) or killed by competition (like Newgate Market and Hungerford Market, originally for vegetables and refashioned for fish). Others were renewed over time, like Spitalfields fruit and vegetable market, rebuilt in the 1870s and 1880s by the enterprising Robert Horner, who had begun his working life as a porter there.[53] But of all the London markets it was the cattle market at Smithfield that proved the most controversial, a foul stain on the metropolis for the first half of the century and more.

The Smithfield livestock and horse market had begun in 1615, built and owned by the City Corporation. Then it was in the fields away from London, a great improvement on past arrangements. But London swallowed it up. And by the 1820s, when a select committee reported on the market's 'abominable nuisance', Smithfield was 'in the centre of the metropolis'. Driving thousands of cattle and sheep into the middle of London every Sunday night and away again every Monday brought chaos to metropolitan traffic and danger to life and limb. Bullocks terrorised shoppers and shopkeepers alike, wandering into drapers' and coffee houses and no doubt china shops as well. A wet market day left Smithfield shin-deep in mud and filth. A full day would find the streets around it impassable through tethered beasts, and the Friday horse market was notorious for attracting every thief in London.

But it was the ferocious ill-treatment of animals that won Smithfield true notoriety. Some animals were so infuriated or distressed and exhausted that they had to be slaughtered in the very street on the way to market. But the greatest brutality was meted out at the market itself. On a busy day 4,300 bullocks and thousands of sheep could be driven into the open space at Smithfield. In such a crush, when there was no room to tie them to the rails, the cattle were forced into 'ring-droves' of about twenty apiece. Torturing them with goads, hitting them with thick staves on the head and nose, cracking their hocks and twisting their tails to bring their heads up, almost strangling them with tethers and sometimes breaking off a horn and blinding the animal in blood, the drovers had to use every violent means to get the animals to stand nose to nose in a tight-wedged ring. Despite improvements to the market in the 1830s and 1840s and an increase in the rails, crowded markets inevitably resorted to the terrible ring-droves. There were parliamentary inquiries into the shocking state of Smithfield and the nuisance it caused to London in 1828, 1847, 1849 and 1850. Eventually the City Corporation yielded to nearly thirty years' humanitarian clamour and closed the market in 1855, opening a replacement at Copenhagen Fields, Islington. It took the City another thirteen years to establish a new dead-meat market at Smithfield in 1868. Its preposterous reluctance to abolish the old Smithfield damned the Corporation's reputation, wiping out the memory of its many successes in modernising London.[54]

Cattle and sheep for Smithfield had frequently been driven along the main shopping streets of London. Of these there were two great clusters at the beginning of the century. First, the City, still a residential district of nearly 130,000 people in 1801, which reserved its best shops along the northern cross-route through London at Cheapside and Cornhill, and along the southern at Ludgate Hill and St Paul's Churchyard. Second, the West End had Oxford Street (then Road) 'lined with shops' of a comprehensive variety around 1805, running through into Holborn; and to the south (connected to Oxford Street by Bond Street) Piccadilly, Pall Mall and the Strand. Even in the days before gas, London's great shopping streets were a wonderful draw. 'On winter evenings, till eight or nine o'clock, all the principal streets appear as if partially illuminated; such is the brilliancy that arises from the numerous lamps, &c. with which the shops are lighted up.'[55]

Most spectacular of all were the linen-drapers' – or clothing, cotton- and woollen-goods shops – of St Paul's Churchyard and the Strand. D'Oyley's warehouse at 346 Strand had been an irresistible lure for fashionable women shoppers since the time of Queen Anne. And women were at the heart of the bazaar fashion that set in with John Trotter's Soho Bazaar, entered from Oxford Street and Soho Square. Established in 1816 – and not on its last legs until the late 1890s – the bazaar was run almost entirely for women by women. Some 160 women shop-keepers rented 'a space of counter' or stall there. Each was vetted by Trotter, who encouraged as tenants 'widows and orphans of decayed families who had seen better days'. They sold to women, and were early on patronised by Queen Charlotte and other female royals. In the 1870s the bazaar was 'a fashionable lounge for ladies and chil-dren', especially '"country cousins"'. At that time it boasted an exten-sive labour exchange for domestic servants. The bazaar excluded anyone 'meanly or dirtily addressed'. From the very start of the century we can see how vital were respectable middle-class women to the London shopping experience.[56]

The introduction of gas and plate glass revolutionised London shop-ping from John Trotter's first years onwards. It's possible this passion for display began in the gin palaces and spread to the linen drapers, bakers, chemists and grocers. The craze among linen drapers for pulling down old shopfronts and replacing them with new plate glass and brass had set in by 1821. The change was already pushing up shop rents in London's leading streets. By 1840 'The shops devoted to the sale of wearing apparel are . . . the most remarkable in London.' Even in Whitechapel and Aldgate they were 'glazed with plate-glass, and lighted with a profusion of gas jets', sometimes 'from the ground to the roof'. In St Paul's Churchyard, to avoid stuffiness, the gas lamps were fixed outside the shop windows with reflectors directing the light inside.[57]

These were the last great days of the City as a fashionable shop-ping centre. The haemorrhage of people during the 1850s and after hastened the decline. Drapers hung on in St Paul's Churchyard into the 1880s but the West End had long taken over. From the early 1820s Regent Street had given London shopping a tremendous fillip. The finest street in Europe had the finest shopfronts too. George Swan, who began as a draper in Ludgate Hill but opened in Piccadilly in 1814, moved to the new street when his shop was taken for Regent Circus: it became Swan and Edgar's around 1821. The linen drapers' warehouses of Regent Street included other great names – Peter Robinson's and Dickins and Jones's (from the 1830s), Scott Adie's ('scotch drapers', from the 1850s), Arthur Liberty's (from the 1870s) and Jaeger's (from the 1890s).[58]

The birth of the department store was also predominantly a West End phenomenon. It might reasonably claim parentage from the Soho Bazaar and imitators like the Pantheon in Oxford Street, once more a woman's world behind and in front of the counter. Or from the Pantechnicon, opened near Belgrave Square around 1840, a bazaar with departments for carriages, furniture, wine, toys and no doubt much else. Or even D'Oyley's, much older, which shut up shop in the Strand as part of the westward drift around 1850. It seems to have been the London suburb, though, which proved the nursery of the department store. A smart shop selling a variety of goods of reliable quality in one place appealed especially to suburban housewives, who could avoid a West End trip by bus or tube with all its attendant inconveniences. And to shopkeepers the suburbs offered larger sites on main roads in purpose-built modern premises, all at a cheaper cost than central London would permit. This was a move away from personal service that some, like Anthony Trollope, deplored. But it was already unstoppable. William Whiteley's giant store took root in Westbourne Grove, Bayswater, in 1863; four years later it had seventeen departments. It kept expanding into neighbouring premises for the rest of the century. Charles Harrod established himself in Brompton Road in 1853. With unusual origins as grocer rather than draper, Harrod's seems to have divided into departments from the 1860s, enlarging into neighbouring premises from 1879. In Islington Jones Brothers came to Holloway Road in 1870 and Rackstraw to Upper Street in 1874. Bon Marché opened a purpose-built department store in Brixton in 1877. And so on, culminating in the great store-building period after the turn of the century, especially at the Marble Arch end of Oxford Street.[59]

London didn't just have the largest and smartest shops in the nation. It was the land of the hard sell, of puffs and bills, of barkers and screamers. The lures and entreaties that brought shoppers to London's counters may have gained something in sophistication and artistry by the era of the department store. But for raw energy, the early days when the Soho Bazaar was in short petticoats were hard to beat. 'Tradesmen here lose no opportunity of forcing their notices upon the public,' noted Robert Southey in 1807. 'Wherever there was a dead wall, a vacant house, or a temporary scaffolding erected for repairs, the space was covered with printed bills.' He saw men sent out by rival blacking manufacturers armed with shining boots on poles. One placard claimed 'his blacking was the best blacking in the world; the other, that his blacking was so good you might eat it'. Shopkeepers however situated would keep up to date and puff their wares: one in a filthy alley near the Temple around 1820, a shop 'scarcely big enough to hold three persons at a time', sported a sign with letters a foot or so high declaring 'HAIR CUT AND MODERNIZED!!!' Wall-chalking and whitewashing were the cheapest methods: 'it is scarcely possible to travel ten miles round the metropolis' without seeing 'Dr Eady 32 Dean Street Soho' chalked on walls by agents of that enterprising quack. And barkers or touts paraded outside the old-clothes sellers of Rosemary Lane, and 'She Barkers' did the same for the ladies' dress and bonnet shops of Leicester Fields and Cranbourn Alley:

Woe used to betide the women of the middle classes who passed through Cranbourn Alley with an unfashionable bonnet! It was immediately seen from one end of the place to the other, and twenty barkers beset her, each in turn, as she walked forward . . . Many a one has had her cloak or shawl torn from her back by these rival sisters of trade . . . each pulling a different way.[60]

The last state lottery draw of the nineteenth century on 18 October 1826 provoked an extravaganza of puffing that was not lost on the London retail world. A procession paraded the main streets made up of men in scarlet and gold liveries, of sandwichmen, wind bands and numerous carriages, one carrying a lottery wheel. Men on horseback with long boards strapped to their side went solo through the streets. Most 'pageant-like of all' was an octagonal tower mounted on a cart with a driver and a man behind to keep off urchins. The tower turned as the cart moved and 'had a very *imposing* effect'. A little too imposing on the lively youth of Monmouth Street, Seven Dials – 'that den of filth and rags' – who resolved '"let's sludge it"' with a shower of 'stones, oyster shells, and dirt'.[61]

But London puffery was undeterred. It grew even more fantastic, while keeping away from Monmouth Street. There was an epidemic of bill-posting from the 1830s on, suppressed where there were vigilant property owners by new laws against bill-sticking in 1839; but any abandoned building or empty shopfront or hoarding would be 'brought down to the condition of old cheese' by thick layers of 'rotting paste and rotting paper'. Mr Slum, the poet puffer of *The Old Curiosity Shop* (1840–41) sold jingles to tradesmen at 5s an inspiration – '"Cheaper than any prose"'. Moses and Son at their Holborn slop shop had illuminated signs made up of 'many thousands of gas-flames, forming branches, foliage, and arabesques', with the 'inevitable royal crown' and beneath it 'V. R.' Like moths to the gas jets, the advertisers of London waged war in the street outside. On a huge wagon 'three immense wooden pyramids' advertised a 'panorama of Egypt'; another in the shape of a mosque puffed a London quack's 'most marvellous Arabian medicine'; Vauxhall Gardens screamed its attractions on a dark green chariot, with 'splendid cream-coloured horses' and trumpeters behind. Railway bridges were daubed with 'Buy your clothes of Moses and Son' and on the Thames in 1853 'there is not an arch in a London bridge but has its advertisements painted on it . . .' West End theatres and other entertainments were prominent among the puffers. Around 1860 William Smith, manager at the Adelphi, puffed *Dead Heart* by printing ten million sticky labels in the form of a heart and having them stuck on every object, movable and immovable, in London. And that indefatigable blacking manufacturer at 30 Strand had 'Warren's Jet Blacking' painted at the base of a real Egyptian pyramid in white letters a yard high in the enterprising 1850s.[62]

London's inimitable commercial brashness sought not only Londoners but tourists too. There had alway been a tourist industry in the metropolis, even in coaching days. Modest in scope it may have been, but its inflated self-importance and extortionate prices were notorious. Around 1820 Mrs Hickinbottom, proprietor of the St Petersburgh Hotel, Dover Street, tried her tricks on the wrong man – he was from Aberdeen. He refused to pay charges of 30s a night, plus 6d for a pen, 1s for wax and 3s 6d for extra lights. She retained his luggage and he complained to the magistrates but was told he'd have to sue. Mrs Hickinbottom was one among many. The *Picture of London for 1818* listed eighty-eight 'hotels for families and single gentlemen' and twelve boarding houses, mainly in the West End; and eight large taverns and forty-nine coaching inns, mainly in the City. By 1826 the hotels listed had grown to 111, catering for the prosperous middle classes and above. The 'less wealthy' could 'readily find' 'commodious lodgings' 'at the houses of reputable tradesmen', who advertised rooms over their shops in the leading streets.[63]

The railway age cast a magic wand over this already lively coming and going. It created a ring of giant hotels out of central London at the railway termini or close by. They relied on bus and cab traffic to take residents in and out of the shopping streets. The railway hotels transformed the quality and quantity of accommodation London provided. These were modern purpose-built palaces that the old inns and converted Georgian mansions of Mayfair and the Strand couldn't rival. The first opened at Euston in 1839 and the last at Marylebone (the Great Central) in 1899. The busiest building period was between 1852 and 1872 – the Great Western at Paddington, the Great Northern at King's Cross, the Grosvenor at Victoria, the Charing Cross, and the Midland Grand at St Pancras.

Just what this mutation meant for the London traveller was summed up in 1863 by Andrew Wynter. He looked back to the London coaching inns of Pickwick's time and their 'funereal four-posters', 'the musty old corner washstand, with the cast-iron soap, which had passed through the hands of countless travellers without even raising the ghost of a lather'. The 'public rooms' often didn't even run to a carpet. Now he could walk his readers through the recently opened Grosvenor Hotel: its lift complete with 'lounging sofa', its 180 bedrooms, two-thirds of which had 'private *closets*' – an improvement even on Paris! – its 'magnificent' smoking room as sumptuous as a Pall Mall club. And it was from the 1860s that these 'splendid palaces' stepped out from the railway stations and planted themselves in the heart of the West End. First was the Langham Hotel in Portland Place, opened in 1865 by the Prince of Wales, with 600 rooms and suites and its own fire brigade. It remained a favourite among American tourists till the century's end. And there were numerous others: among them the Hotel Cecil on the Embankment, with 800 rooms the largest in Europe when it opened in 1886; the Savoy (1889); Claridge's (rebuilt from 1895 – it had opened as Minart's in 1808); and the Russell (1898). Baedeker's *London* for 1889 listed 125 top-class hotels in central London, including French, German and temperance premises.[64]

This rise in London tourism and retail worked its way through to the employment structure of London. There were not only more jobs in shops and hotels than ever before but in particular they opened new opportunities for women. The 1871 census for London counted 12,700 male 'servants' in hotels and inns and 4,300 women. In 1901 there were 26,000 men in hotel and inn service (including barmen and domestic indoor servants) and 23,000 women. An American visitor to London in the late 1880s remarked how 'the first thing that strikes . . . most prominently is the employment of women in so many of the public places, where only men are employed by us', and he had in mind especially barmaids and hotel receptionists. Similarly with shop assistants. In the drapers' and mercers' shops 12,700 men and 4,300 women were employed in 1871, but there were 14,800 men and 12,100 women thirty years later. Charles Booth noted in the 1890s how these opportunities marked a shift between the generations in London. The daughters of the respectable working class 'shun the factories, many going to the City to become waitresses in tea-rooms, or to take up some such work. The young people, as a rule, secure better positions than their parents.'[65]

They had, though, to work long hours for low pay to secure them. Barmaids at the railway station buffets worked around eighty hours a week with one Sunday off a month in the late 1880s. They earned 8s a week with 10d-worth of drink a day, and 'lived in', sleeping four or six to a room, often two to a bed, and suffering food that was too poor to serve to the customers. Out of their wages and tips and bits on the side they were made to pay for breakages – their customers' as well as their own. Many shop assistants also lived in, above the shop or in quarters provided by the employer nearby. P. C. Hoffman was apprenticed to the Holborn Silk Market, a large draper's shop, in 1894. He worked from 7.30 a.m. to 10 p.m. and had to take turns to stand at the door of the living quarters to see no strangers entered until lock-up at 11 or midnight on Saturdays. In the dormitory he and his fellows 'hunted for bugs on the walls, cracking them with slipper heels'. Shop assistants commonly worked ninety hours a week. And living in constrained with rules and fines what little leisure time they had left.[66]

It was the dream of many shop assistants themselves to open a place of their own and become independent of the oppression they had suffered. So it also was, apparently, for male domestic servants. Where better to indulge the dream than London? Its streets were popularly said to be 'paved with gold'. And between the cracks there flourished an entire economy outside wage labour and an entire sub-class making some sort of living from it.

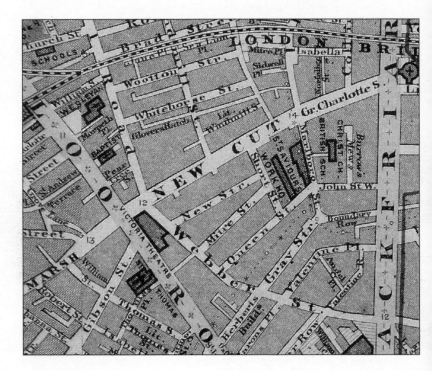

New Cut, 1862

VII

THE NEW CUT: ON THE EDGE

On the Stones

Huge lumps of fine celery at a penny a lot – fried and cured fish at 1d and 2d – tea and sugar at minimum prices – a preparation of shell-fish which was not whelk, and looked in its white saucer like a repulsive surgical study – quack pills for 'wind', and 'worms', and cholera – cauliflowers with heads like bushy white wigs – carrots, such as Gulliver saw in Brobdignag land – walking canes, 'warranted real silver tops or I'll give 'em yer', a penny each, street ballads and 'Chinese puzzles' at a halfpenny, were all eagerly bought up; and despite the opinion of the sergeant of police on duty that 'the place is nothing now to what it was five or ten years ago' . . . it is well worth a visit from any one interested in mastering the social history, and estimating the habits of the poor.[1]

THIS was the New Cut around midnight on a Saturday in 1866. The Cut and its continuation east (Great Charlotte Street) and west (Lower Marsh) was one continuous market of over 200 shops and up to 300 stalls. It was Lambeth's equivalent of Leather Lane (Holborn) or the Brill (Somers Town) or the Sunday morning chaos of Petticoat Lane. As theatregoers disgorged from 'the Vic' at the corner of Waterloo Road and mingled with the shoppers, it became a 'mercantile Pandemonium', crowded 'like a fair'. Mayhew thought that, 'wild as the scene of the London Docks appeared, the confusion and uproar of the New-cut on Saturday night overwhelms the thoughtful mind. Until it is seen and heard, we have no sense of the scramble that is going on through London for a living.'[2]

This was a different sort of scramble. It was a far more subtle jock-eying for position as seller or provider or entertainer or scrounger in an overstocked and highly competitive marketplace where the buyers were as cunning and wary as the sellers themselves. Here on the stones the great game of London life was played out, where brute strength was subservient to wit, quick-thinking, fast hands, a ready tongue and a sharp eye.

The infinite variety of ways in which men, women and children turned a penny in the streets was one of the defining characteristics of London life. On the very edge of wage labour or outside it altogether, tens of thousands of penny capitalists scratched a living by their wits. There was no other place like this in England, maybe anywhere. Daniel Kirwan, an American traveller in London in the 1860s, thought that 'there is not such a city in the world as London for vagrancy and vagabondism . . . No city that I have ever visited will compare with London for the number of its street peddlers, hawkers, booth propri-etors, open-air performers, ballad singers, mountebanks [acrobats], and other street itinerants.' Harold Hardy, one of Charles Booth's assis-tants, wrote in the 1890s that 'The itinerant vendor plays a part in the life of London which has no parallel in any other city with which I am acquainted.' In the census of 1901 the County of London was home to one in five of all the 'costermongers, hawkers and street sellers' of England and Wales, 12,000 of them. But the independent street earners of London were notoriously shy of revealing their livelihoods to census enumerators. Mayhew estimated around 1850 that 'full thirty thousand adults' got a living in the streets where the census recorded just 3,700 hawkers and pedlars and no other street types at all.[3]

Certainly, the street sellers were the largest group. What an amazing mixture they were. Costermongers were the leading fraternity, sellers of fruit, vegetables and fish from a stall or pitch or moving barrow, occasionally a donkey and cart. They seem to have been as important a part of London's penny capitalist economy – and of its street scene – at the end of the century as at the beginning. Even so, tastes in the riotous delicatessen of London street eatables changed over time. Piemen and sellers of saloop (a hot drink made from bark and sold as a tonic) were more common in the first half of the century than later. Coffee-and-bread-and-butter-breakfast sellers, muffin men, vendors of baked potatoes, gingerbread, cakes and sweetmeats, gingerbeer, elder wine and cordial, fried fish, kidney puddings, baked apples, ham sandwiches, pea soup, hot eels, pickled shellfish, roast chestnuts, sheep's trotters, hot green peas, toffee apples – all were common in the middle decades of the century and many survived till the end. They were joined from around 1850 by the ice cream (hokey-pokey) vendors and pineapple sellers. It was possible to breakfast, lunch and dine in the street. Many London children and working men did just that.[4]

It was possible also to buy many household articles and domestic services in the streets. At West Kensington, in the late 1880s Compton Mackenzie recalled knife grinders, fly-paper sellers, chair menders and tinkers calling, "'Any pots, pans, or kettles to mend?'", the tinker's wife wheeling 'the barrow with the furnace and the swinging tools'. There were street sellers of toys and puzzles, songs and ballads, pipe cleaners and pen wipes, stove ornaments and plaster images, cat's meat and dog collars, Staffordshire crockery and Dutch brooms, flowers and lavender, hearthstone and blacking, 'fifty-bladed penknives' and pocket-books, watch guards and toasting forks, pencil cases and sponges, almost every article of necessity or luxury known to the nineteenth-century London housewife.[5]

Then there were numerous sellers of animals. A fancy-dog seller did well among 'young ladies' in Regent Street in the mid-1860s. Others sold birds, songsters and exotics, some of the latter handpainted, as purchasers later discovered. Or tame rats and mice or squirrels; and hedgehogs to keep down black beetles in the home. Street dentists, chiropodists and quack doctors selling cough drops, wonder cures and patent medicines made a ready sale given the primitive state of pain relief and official doctoring. As late as 1885, 'a coach and four used to stand outside the London Hospital, with a footman in livery' and 'a showman resplendent in period costume, shouting to the patients as they approached the dread portals of the hospital: "Don't go in there, they'll cut you up alive."' This graduate of the 'crocus-lay' offered a '"miraculous blood purifier"'. He 'enjoyed considerable success'.[6]

Indeed, street sellers and other earners could make a reasonable living. Some prospered. Others, lacking the right mettle to make a go of it, were prominent among London's starving poor. While energetic costers might make 30s a week, Mayhew thought the average profits were no more than 10s weekly the year round. Three days' continuous rain '"will bring the greater part of thirty thousand street people to the brink of starvation"', a clergyman told him, and earnings in the winter were half those of the summer months. Forty years on, while the run of costermongers might make between £1 and £3 a week, their 'harum-scarum, reckless, random, happy-go-lucky' character meant that earnings ranged from 'quite large sums of money to almost nothing at all'.[7]

There was similar variety among those who worked the streets as buyers or finders and bringers to market. Most prosperous of all were old-clothes collectors and the rag-and-bone men and scrap-metal dealers. They offered small change or a trinket for unwanted articles from householders and domestic servants. With the London dust contractors, it was the dealers in other people's leavings who justified an eloquent metropolitan slang word for money: 'rubbish'. But at the lower levels gleanings were small and hard to come by. J. T. Smith noted in 1817 how 'the streets are constantly looked over at the dawn of day by a set of men in search of sticks, handkerchiefs, shawls, &c. that may have been dropt during the night . . .' Others dug out the cracks between the stones with rusty nails to find a penny. One woman in the early years of the century 'went over London early in the morning to strike out the teeth of dead dogs' for sale to bookbinders and others as burnishing tools. The pure-finders, again mostly women, collected dried-out dog shit for use in the Bermondsey tanning yards, curing morocco for leather-bound Bibles and so on. A Clerkenwell missionary recalled how 'the stench from accumulations of his gatherings' almost beat him out of a pure-finder's room. Bone grubbers scoured the kennels and dustholes for bones to sell to glue and manure makers, sometimes boiling them for a stew first. And men made a living picking up cigar stubs for sale to tobacconists.[8]

Until Bazalgette's embankment was in place, men and boys searched the sewers for valuables scoured out of the gutters. They mostly walked up them from the Thames at low tide. It could be a risky venture. Sewer grubbers might be caught in flash floods or dense pockets of sewer gas. Two lads working their way up the Strand sewer from the river in 1839 came across the skeleton of Robert Stodart of Clerkenwell Green, who had disappeared three years before: he was identified by an 'old shoe' nearby. And the river itself was a source of middling-rich pickings for the mudlarks. Children wallowed in Thames mud searching for anything saleable and so too did women. Some achieved immortality of a kind. Peggy Jones, who disappeared without trace in February 1805, waded at Blackfriars in short petticoats, searching for coals with her toes, filling a bag-like apron round her waist and selling them at

8d a load to the coal merchants: 'In these strange habiliments, and her legs encrusted with mud, she traversed the streets of this metropolis.' And Mary Casey, twenty-five and Irish, was noted in the early 1860s by that interesting *flâneur* Arthur Munby, whom we shall meet again. He saw her, '"naked from the thigh down"', striding into the half-frozen Thames in search of coal, risking any danger and discomfort to win a crust.[9]

More polished – and perhaps a little cleaner – were the hosts of London's street entertainers. The buskers, or musicians and vocalists, were the largest group, though a most disparate lot. The 'English bands' that Dickens recalled playing outside suburban inns in the 1820s were undercut from the 1840s by the German bands, who made up for their painful playing by the pertinacity with which every knocker in a middle-class street was sounded in turn for pennies. By the 1890s the only bands on London's streets seem to have been of this Teutonic order. Of solo artistes the organ grinder – 'music by handle', contemporaries quipped – was almost always an Italian, 1,000 of them in London in 1895, the old barrel organ and hurdy-gurdy having given way to the 'piano organ' on wheels.[10]

The rest of the buskers were divided by Mayhew into 'the skilful and the blind'. The former combined street work with the odd engagement indoors. There were fiddlers, tin whistlers, 'street cornet' players, one-man bands or 'Panharmonicas', Jew's harp players and little groups with a cello and 'clarionet' and other instruments. Of the vocalists, there were full-time ballad singers who sold copies of the music they sang; tone-deaf amateurs whose wailing was the next best thing to begging – or blackmail; and blind Bible readers and reciters, who relied on formidable memories. The banjo-playing 'nigger minstrels' or 'Ethiopian Serenaders', made up with 'lampblack varnish', became popular street performers from the early 1860s. Whatever the turn, it was not an easy life. 'A poor, feeble, half-witted looking' harp player called Foster was hounded to distraction by street boys: '"I'm torn to pieces every day I go out into the streets . . ."' The boys would push him over, howl down his playing, even cut his strings, and in 1851 he petitioned Mayhew's readers for a new harp.[11]

The street exhibitors were just as variegated. Several displayed performing dogs and around 1820 there was a Frenchman with a performing hare. 'Happy families' – mutually incompatible animals trained to tolerate each other in a cage on wheels – were common at mid-century. The great crowd painter William Powell Frith included one in *Ramsgate Sands* (1853). His models were a happy family run by two men; one beat a drum and was 'very ugly'. They addressed a letter to Frith from 'Waterlew Road' and he paid them 30s for two sittings. Peep-show men offered toy-theatre mock-ups of popular murders and melodramas. Walk-in caravan shows at the New Cut and other market streets displayed battle scenes. There were four main sorts of street puppeteers, with Punch at the head, but not making much of a living: 'All Punches die in the workhouse,' a former gentleman's servant and a Punch for twenty-five years told Mayhew. Other men offered to tell your weight by machine, operating mainly at the railway stations. The screevers or pavement artists would seek a niche with trade-mark designs: one specialised in Christ's heads with a crown of thorns – they paid better, he thought, than Napoleons. And a remarkable disabled sailor-artist displayed his 'effigies of the whole British navy' – 800 vessels drawn in chalks – on the wall of Kew Gardens around 1815: it extended about a mile and a half.[12]

And then the street entertainers. There were clowns or 'Billy Barlows'; jugglers, some on stilts, and slack-rope walkers; street dancers like Madeleine Sinclair, who danced the Highland fling to a street organ all over London in the early 1860s, her dress and visage so masculine that audiences disputed whether she was a man or not; strong men, street conjurors, many acrobats who, dozens strong, attracted crowds of idlers to Trafalgar Square on summer evenings in the 1860s. More daring still, the young 'Female Salamander', around 1820, exhibited in a caravan in City Road: she seized red-hot pokers, caught drops of molten lead on her tongue and dipped her feet in boiling oil. More than seventy years later Albert Lieck watched a 'big negro' in the City streets throw giant potatoes high in the air and let them smash to pieces on his forehead. And Mayhew found an acrobat who did 'head-springs'. He ran along for a few yards and then threw himself violently on his head and so turned '"head over heels" without using his hands'. He was aided by 'a large callous lump' at the front of his skull. He could also 'run round his head', resting his scalp on the ground, flinging his trunk around and moving his feet on the floor; and bend over backwards to pick up pins from the ground with his eyelids. Men like this would try anything to strike awe in a crowd and draw a penny from reluctant pockets.[13]

They had other things to contend with besides sprains, ruptures, troublous urchins and the ill-favoured London weather. The capital's streets were contested territory. They had, indeed, always been so, but it seemed the New Police were specially recruited to make things difficult for them. Laws against street sellers using bells and horns were in force from 1839. Writers, Charles Dickens among them, and artists like the morbidly noise-averse John Leech campaigned for a strengthening of the laws against street musicians and won it in 1864, requiring buskers to move on if requested by a householder to do so. Besides the buskers, the police hand against costermongers was hardened by detailed regulations in 1869 which no doubt made some costers' lives a misery. And some vestries moved vigorously against them in the 1880s and 1890s.

Suppression no doubt took its toll. The variety and number of street performers and entertainers certainly seem to have reduced by the century's end, though there are no figures to prove it. But this was probably less due to police action than to changing taste and the rise of indoor amusements, especially cheap theatre and the music hall. Likewise, improvements in London sewerage and official scavenging culled sewer and street grubbers from the 1860s. On the other hand, costermongers seem to have flourished despite the rise of small shops and cheap eating houses.

The London street people most susceptible to police suppression were the beggars. The laws against begging were old indeed, yet here too the New Police from 1829 promised more effective control than ever before. Whether they were successful or not is uncertain. Perception always had greater play on contemporary feeling than fact in this area and perception was volatile. For instance, there was a public outcry over London beggary at the close of the Napoleonic Wars, its ranks apparently swollen by discharged soldiers and sailors, many maimed and others who shammed. Yet experienced magistrates and public men had no hesitation in saying that London beggars were far fewer in 1815 than in the 1780s; even than the careful estimate of 6,000 adults begging there in 1803. Maybe all we can say is that street begging was a constant feature of London life throughout the nineteenth century. It might wax and wane according to migration, economic fortune and seasonal vicissitudes, but its constancy was more important than any periodic fluctuation. Arrests of beggars varied from year to year but there was no discernible long-term decline in numbers. Whatever the year, beggars were unavoidable. Michael Fitzpatrick, clerk to the City justices, met twenty or thirty 'in a morning' as he walked from Goswell Street to Guildhall in 1815. J. C. Parkinson counted thirty-three while walking from the Athenaeum Club, Pall Mall, to Hyde Park Corner in the spring of 1869. Further west, at Cromwell Road, he 'gave up counting out of sheer despair, for beggars seemed to spring up out of the earth whenever ladies or nursemaids came in view'. And at the end of the century George R. Sims counted the 'whining beggar who follows nervous women in the lonely street after nightfall' as one of 'London's little worries'.[14]

There seems little doubt that most London begging was of the professional kind. In general even the very poorest adult workers would not beg in the streets and would rather – this is saying much – turn to the poor law instead. The traditions of London begging were rich in the tricks by which public sympathy could be provoked. Disabled beggars were most readily received. Blind beggars, often led by a dog or child, were said to have been treated well. 'Billies-in-bowls' – men who had lost one or both legs and who moved around on a sledge or cart, sometimes pulled by a helper and one or two by dogs, could frighten off or repel the alms they sought. A few became aggressive and threatening as a result. Men with no arms who cut paper figures or made drawings with their feet won more kindness. Then there were occupations which were merely fronts for alms-getting, like lucifer-match and bootlace selling. The novelist and *Punch* editor Shirley Brooks complained in 1865 of 'those abominable nuisances, the crossing-sweepers'. There were twenty-nine of them between his home in Regent's Park and his office in the Temple. Each one 'either smirks at me, grunts at me, holds a hat at me, whines to me from afar off, runs after me imploring me, scowls at me, or takes some other unpleasant means of begging'.[15]

And then came the shammers, each with their special 'lay' or 'lurk' or unique begging point. The following list comes from 1887, but with tiny variations it can stand for the ingenuity of London's professional beggars throughout the century:

the fire lurk (pretended losses by fire), the shipwrecked or disabled sailors' lurk, the accident lurk, the sick lurk (pretended illness; some tie up their arms in a very clever way, others feign fits, others remain in bed simulating illness while they send out their companions to beg for them), the foreigners' lurk, the frozen-out gardeners' lurk, the servants' lurk (pretended loss of place as a domestic servant), the family man lurk (parading a number of children in a state of feigned destitution), the lucifer, air balloon, picture, or bread-and-butter accident lurk (dropping in the mud or otherwise damaging by an apparent accident boxes of lucifer matches, air balloons, cheap pictures in frames, or slices of bread-and-butter), the deaf and dumb lurk, the colliers' lurk (pretended loss of employment through an explosion), the weavers', the calenderers', and cotton spinners' lurks ('Come all the way from Manchester, and got no work to do'). To these may be added the 'shallow cove' or 'shivering Jemmy', who goes about half naked, the 'cab touter', who begs at cab doors as they are leaving theatres, and the 'high-flier', who simulates the broken-down gentleman, officer, or tradesman.[16]

And we might add, too, the begging-letter writer, who plagued the lives of the rich and famous.

The earnings from all these shifts and shams were unpredictable. No doubt some made a good living out of theatrical skill or literary talent or pathetic handicap, and there was the odd well-attested small fortune. But when arrested, most had just a shilling or two on them. 'I have heard very large sums stated, Sir Nathaniel Conant, the chief magistrate at Bow Street, told the Mendicity Committee in 1815, 'but I disbelieve many of them'. Yet the fabulous wealth made by beggars was a popular delusion throughout the century. And readers of Sherlock Holmes will remember the 'Man with the Twisted Lip' (1891), who gives up a white-collar job to clear his debts by begging in the City.[17]

The most valuable resources for turning a penny in London streets were a combination of natural talent and experience. Numbers of Londoners on the edge of the metropolitan economy were bred to the business. Costermongering – just like the law or politics – was in part a hereditary trade. Similarly, gypsies were prominent among tinkers and chair menders. But others came to the edge by chance, forced out of employment by a disabling accident or kept out by a handicap from birth. Others were newcomers to the metropolis, among them minorities who found paid work hard to come by – the Irish, Germans, Italians and black and brown former seamen whom we've already met as street sellers and entertainers. And others still hovered uneasily between wage labour and economic independence, clamouring for work at the docks one day and pushing a barrow round the streets the next. So between those who inherited a living on the streets and those who chose it or were pushed in that direction there was no shortage of recruits to penny capitalism's opportunities. And disappointments. For an overstocked supply of street sellers, finders, buskers and beggars sharpened competition and depressed earnings for the majority.

There was one other source of recruitment. This was neglected and abandoned children, nineteenth-century London's greatest shame. James Greenwood ranked it first among the 'Seven Curses' of London in 1869 and thought it 'an accepted fact that, daily, winter and summer, within the limits of our vast and wealthy city of London, there wander, destitute of proper guardianship, food, clothing, or employment a *hundred thousand* boys and girls in fair training for the treadmill and the oakum shed . . .' Who knows what the true numbers were? But even in the very pit of destitution – abandoned, ragged, starving, homeless – there were at any time thousands of them. That was the case at least until the 1870s. Thomas Barnardo's early London experiences are salutary. His first close contact with a 'street arab', Jim Jarvis, came around 1868. Jim was ten years old, alone and homeless. On a bitter night he showed Barnardo where he planned to sleep – on a roof where eleven other homeless boys, most aged nine to fourteen, had dossed for the night. Not long after Barnardo took Lord Shaftesbury to Billingsgate fish market after midnight: under a giant tarpaulin covering packing cases they found seventy-three homeless boys, most barefoot, all 'clad in poor and vilely-smelling rags'. The pens at Smithfield were similarly used before the market closed and so were the recesses of Covent Garden.[18]

These numberless children were often victims of the family dislocation involved in mass migration to London, and of working-class family life too frequently poisoned by poverty, overcrowding and brutality. They were largely unprotected by poor law, organised charity or the police. It was not until the 1870s, which brought a new machinery for educating the children of the poor, that the numbers of abandoned and homeless children almost certainly went into decline. Barnardo, too, played his part. But even at the dawn of the twentieth century a 'small colony of homeless boys' was said to live in holes in the giant dust heaps on Hackney Marshes.[19]

Throughout the nineteenth century these children made up a population bred to the streets whose quick wits were honed on the hardest of all whetstones: starvation. We meet them everywhere. Like one of Mayhew's contacts, an apprentice on a fishing smack who had run away through ill-treatment. In the freezing January of 1850 he slept in the streets, lately under a butcher's stall in Whitechapel: 'I am here starving all my time. Last night I was out in the cold and nearly froze to death. When I got up I was quite stiff and could hardly walk . . . (Here the child, still weeping piteously, uncovered his breast, and showed his bones starting through the skin.)' Like the four children locked in one room by their drunken father, also around 1850, 'leaving them to starve'. They broke out and the eldest boy, fifteen, set up home for them in Gee's Court, Oxford Street, and 'took them out singing in the streets, being himself the manager, guardian and steward of the whole party'. Or 'T.S., aged ten (March 5, 1869). – An orphan. Mother died in St George's [-in- the-East] Workhouse. Father killed by coming in contact with a diseased sheep, being a slaughterman. A seller of boxes in the street. Slept last in a bed before Christmas. Slept in hay carts, under a tarpaulin.' And William Locke, secretary to the London Ragged School Union, describing in 1852 how the 13,000 children in his schools were made up, put it all very neatly: 'Many of them are homeless; many of them are entirely neglected by their parents; many are orphans, outcasts, street beggars, crossing sweepers, and little hawkers of things about the streets; they are generally very ignorant, although in some points very quick and cunning.'[20]

Here was the fresh blood that nourished economic individualism at the very edge of London subsistence. Other elements helped pump it round. They included some real capitalists, men and women who'd prospered on the streets through luck and acumen. They employed street sellers on 'half profits' and eventually became bankers and lenders to the trade. Most costermongers and many others depended on borrowed stock money – £1 loan at the start of the week was repaid for 22s 6d at the end. This sort of moneylending could be good business. Mary Robinson, 'Queen of the Costermongers', died in January 1884. A former cats'-meat seller in Somers Town, she left £50,000 amassed from lending stock money to the street trade. Others had fleets of barrows or choirs of organs to hire by the day or week. Scales and weights, baskets and boards, donkeys and carts were all let out on the same basis.[21]

Then there were forms of cooperation even among these fierce individualists. 'Each man has his particular walk and never interferes with that of his neighbour,' it was said of the costers. Beggars too would arrange their 'walks' to avoid competition. Indeed a beggar's walk was considered 'a sort of property', and a coster's or newspaper-seller's pitch was real estate that could be sold on or bequeathed. Information about cheap stock or a generous parson would be shared in coffee houses, common lodging houses and pubs. In the early years of the century the London beggars had some notorious houses of call, the Weaver's Arms (or 'Beggar's Opera') at Church Lane, Whitechapel, and the Rose and Crown and the Robin Hood, both in Church Lane, St Giles, prominent among them. And each fraternity had its argot or secret language, like the costers' back-slang. In these ways news of London's opportunities would spread fast. All the street people would hope to get their penn'orth out of victory celebrations, a royal birth or a potentate's visit, perhaps by turning flag or squirt or balloon seller for the day. Any crowd promised rich pickings. When Oxford rowed against Harvard on the Putney to Mortlake boat race course in August 1869, apparently a million people turned out to watch. The towpath was lined with 'sharpers, players, peddlers, fighting-men, showmen, venders of all kinds of fruit, vegetables, meats, pies, drinks, ices, and all kinds of knick-knacks . . . [B]ack from the river, for fifty or sixty feet, for a distance of three miles, the uproar and sale of questionable merchandise and doubtful provender never ceased for an instant.'[22]

Then there were the institutions of penny capitalist London, market-places bringing together buyer and seller, engorging the money-making possibilities of London's golden pavements. The 'Rag Fairs' – huge part-covered markets of old-clothes stalls and shops – were one of the sights of London right through the century, especially that at Houndsditch, on the eastern borders of the City. 'It was by far, the strangest scene I had ever looked upon,' thought Daniel Kirwan in the late 1860s; 'such a mass of old clothes, grease, patches, tatters, and remnants of decayed prosperity and splendor.' Whole shopping streets were given over to old clothes, like Holywell Street, the Strand, or old shoes, like Monmouth Street, Seven Dials, at least till the 1850s. 'For years, Petticoat Lane "turned me out"', recalled Jerome K. Jerome of his lower-middle-class youth in the 1870s and 1880s. Every district had its rag-and-bottle shop – marine-store dealers, they were often called, though nothing of the sea about them – and its wardrobe dealers for decrepit washstands and bug-ridden bedsteads. Wardour Street, Soho, was the centre of the cheaper London antiques trade. And the beginnings of the Friday festivals of junk at the

Metropolitan Cattle Market, Caledonian Road, were apparent by the early 1870s.[23]

Most exciting of all was the cycle of fairs that clung to the edge of London and in one extraordinary instance penetrated to its very heart. The old town fairs on the borders of London – Barnet, Ealing, Croydon – maintained some liveliness until the last quarter of the nineteenth century, Barnet as a horse fair and meeting place of gypsies into the twentieth. But as a gathering place of showmen, entertainers and exhibitors, as well as of hucksters and street sellers generally, they were on their last legs in the 1840s. By then fairs had faced suppression by the authorities for over a century and a number had already closed. A good deal of energy had no doubt departed from the remainder. But Greenwich Fair was uproarious enough to attract Boz's wry gaze at Easter 1835; and watered-down versions struggled on around the same time at Catford, Camberwell and other places.[24]

It was the great Bartlemy or Bartholomew Fair that brought an annual riot of fun, anarchy, even terror to the City of London every September. William Hone, the radical pamphleteer and publisher, left us the best description of Bartholomew Fair in its last rapturous years. In 1825 he found hundreds of stalls lining the streets around Smithfield. They sold oysters, fruit, toys, gingerbread, wicker baskets, pamphlets, hardware, garters, pocketbooks, trinkets, fried sausages and sit-down hot dinners. Even the open space usually reserved for the cattle market was 'so thronged, as to be wholly impassable'. He counted twenty-two shows. They included John Richardson's famous travelling theatre and Atkins's and Wombwell's menageries. Smaller outfits showed exotica like giants, dwarfs, 'Malays' (who spoke no English but 'three words, "drop o' rum"'), a seven-legged mare ('very fleet in her paces'), the Wild Indian Woman, a performing pig, a mermaid ('manufactured imposture'), the head of a cannibal chief ('might have been some English clod-pole's'), and there were jugglers and acrobats and conjurors to add to the fun in the streets and spaces around. It was a four-day Saturnalia. Richardson's last appearance at Bartlemy was September 1837 – he died soon after at his winter quarters in Horsemonger Lane, Southwark, after more than forty years as a leading attraction in English fairs up and down the land. With his passing Bartholomew Fair entered its final decline. It was already fading away when the City Corporation increased rents for the remaining shows in 1839. Ten years later they were suppressed altogether. By 1855 the fair was just a memory. In truth, though, the old fairs and their showmen were killed off less by civic disapproval than by changing taste. As Thomas Frost, a Chartist leader and historian of the fairs, remarked in 1874, they had lost function as a 'means of popular amusement' to the music hall and theatre.[25]

The same wasn't true of street selling. Despite the growth of retail premises in London, street markets flourished. Most of them were nineteenth-century inventions, rooting in fresh soil with the growth of the town. The New Cut itself, for instance, was new-built from around 1818 as part of the southern expansion that accompanied the building of Waterloo Bridge. Within thirty years it had changed from open country to one of the busiest shopping streets in London. Other markets opened nearby in the expanding suburbs – East Street and Westmoreland Road (Walworth), Lambeth Walk, Southwark Park Road (Bermondsey) and several others. There was never a shortage of costers. Indeed the number of markets seems to have been still rising at the century's end. In official returns around 1900 182 streets were identified by the police as 'Market Streets, etc., habitually used by Costermongers' and a further sixty-seven where they routinely stood, sometimes in the face of police or vestry persecution. The largest street market was Harrow Road, with 300 stalls. The New Cut and Lower Marsh combined had now around 200 at most. There were also specialist markets, like the animal and bird-fanciers' at Sclater Street (Club Row), Bethnal Green, and the gardeners' at Columbia Row nearby. In all, there were over 7,000 stalls at the busiest times in these places. Besides the markets, 600 or so costers wheeled a barrow into the City every day to tempt the hurrying clerks. Uncounted others walked the rest of the metropolis as costers always had. And the busiest markets still attracted that declining number of quacks and strong men and conjurors and buskers who scratched a living from the streets. Every Saturday night all over London a pallid ghost of Bartlemy flickered round the costers' naphtha flares.[26]

But the desire to turn a penny outside wage labour didn't begin and end in the ranks of the London street people. It infected all layers. And it was nurtured by elements that were peculiar, in their range and depth, to the economic life of the metropolis.

On Your Own Account

Several factors inherent in London economic life fostered individual enterprise among all sorts and conditions of men and women. The capital's economic dynamism was one, the frantic growth of London sweeping tradesmen and craftsmen into the great jerry-building jamboree and often into ruin. The London housing problem was another, widespread sub-letting tempting the wily and the unwary into landlordism and its half-promise of easy money. Then the massing together of people in the metropolis, and its unrivalled diversity of luxurious wants, spawned a tradesman or small business to fill every niche: chimney sweeps, as independent-minded as any coster and with as many traditions to their name; odd jobbers like dog doctors – surgeons to the 'fancy' – and bird catchers and birds'-egg painters, and cats'-meat skewer makers and God knew what besides. Firework-making, for instance, was a London cottage industry in the run-up to 5 November, as artisans and their families supplemented their normal livelihood by a few weeks' homework in that risky trade: as late as 1873 eight died in an explosion at a house in Broad Street, Lambeth. Others, like mackerel, lived on the furthest edge of a great industry to pick up what scraps of profit they could – like the trolleymen who might buy a sack of cheap coals and hawk them by the bagful to the city's poorest customers. Or the 'foul hatters', working 'on their own account' to translate old toppers into new. [27]

Then there were the industries in which the London artisan tradition had managed to keep itself alive. In 1901 one in five of the male tailors in the County of London were self-employed or small masters. Of cabinet makers the figure was one in six, of boot- and shoemakers one in four, and watch- and clockmakers one in three. Among women the most independent manufacturing trade was dressmaking, where one in three, nearly 20,000 workers, were self-employed or small 'masters'. Almost certainly the independent portion would have been higher in earlier decades. And the census, from which these figures come, inadequately accounted for the degree of economic individualism in other sectors, most notably building. [28]

Even when working for others, the London artisan had an eye open for how best to work for himself. A skill or hobby might be turned to account. Around 1818 Thomas Carter, a tailor, had a 'workfellow' 'formerly connected with a company of strolling players', who 'often persuaded himself that he could "turn a penny"' away from the bench. He tried his hand at theatrical production and 'verse-making' but settled on life as an 'insect exhibitor', with a large microscope in Hyde Park and other places. Another tailor in the 1850s, with a passion for astronomy, exhibited telescopes for star-gazing after his day job: he commissioned his instruments to his own specification at £80 a time, and he earned well. Another microscope exhibitor around the same time had been a shoemaker, once a master ruined by speculations: his street exhibitions won him over 30s a week. George Wombwell, the great menagerie-keeper, had also been a shoemaker with a shop in Soho. And Mayhew thought that although many coffee-stall keepers had 'been bred to dealing in the streets', others were artisans, even policemen and clerks, who had gathered together the £5 capital needed for a truck and urn.[29]

Probably the insecurity of many employments turned the worker's mind at some time to making his or her own way in the world, especially if a trade could be pursued at home or in the streets. The constant brushing up against better-dressed or more prosperously situated Londoners egged people on. So did the opportunities of improved living conditions in the expanding suburbs, all demanding extra cash to pay for them. So did the daily struggle on a low wage in the face of London's blowsy temptations for purse and pocket. Whatever the source, the culture of making a little bit on the side was deeply bedded in London's working life.

Take the experiences of W. F. Watson, for instance, a young engineer at a variety of workshops in Finsbury and Clerkenwell in the 1890s. He soon discovered that his workmates were as busily engaged on their own account as on their firms'. These sidelines were known as '"contracts", "jobs for the king", or "foreigners"'. '"Contracts" were not confined to [making] small tools. Sets of fire-irons and dogs, toasting-forks, kitchen shovels, and ornaments of novel design and ornate handles, brass, copper, bronze, and gunmetal candlesticks, photo frames and mantelpiece ornaments, door-knockers, model engines for the son, were some of the "foreign orders" executed in the bosses' time.' Government establishments were notorious for 'contracts'. At the Woolwich Arsenal a man was said to have made himself an entire automatic lathe, and occasional scandals broke over 'jobs for the king' there.[30]

Deep-rooted customs of economic individualism also pervaded transport, another giant London industry. On the river, the old watermen had been largely self-employed, and at mid-century 'Most lightermen are occasionally employers, sometimes engaging watermen to assist them; sometimes hiring a lighter, in addition to their own . . .' And on the roads a whole sector was traditionally operated by men who were not employees 'in the ordinary sense'. These were the cabmen – taxi drivers to a later generation – around 15,000 of them by the end of the century. All either owned their cabs or hired them by the day. And with every fare 'a cab and its driver launch out upon a sea of adventure' where the profits depended on chance, certainly, but 'largely on the energy and judgment of the driver'.[31] '"To get on a cab",' Mayhew was told, '"is the ambition of more loose fellows than for anything else, as it's reckoned both an idle life and an exciting one."' Cabbies were a byword for truculent independence of spirit throughout the nineteenth century, especially in its first half. So a palisade of regulation was thrown up to keep them in their place. From 1834 both cabs and cabbies had to be licensed by the government Coach Office. Then, from 1853, the Metropolitan Police took over and pegged and poked away at the cabmen much as they did with the costers. By the 1890s it had all become a war of attrition – or, rather, irritation. In 1894, with 14,672 licensed drivers, the police secured no fewer than 3,985 convictions for offences under the hackney carriage regulations.[32]

In addition, 1,340 cabmen were convicted for drunkenness – scores of them more than once – and the fuddled cabby, falling asleep at the whip, losing his way, obstreperously demanding an inflated fare or a bigger tip was part of middle-class London folklore. Things seem to have been worst early on. 'As a matter of principle the cabman is never satisfied with his legal fare,' complained a German visitor in 1853, and no doubt foreigners and provincials were most at the mercy of the cabby's colourful language and overbearing ways. And in the middle years of the century, when police supervision had not yet tightened its grip, there was a shady periphery of 'bucks' – cabmen who never gained, or had lost, a licence but who took out a cab illegally for a licensed man otherwise engaged or indisposed. Even in the 1890s a low-life fringe still clung to cabbing and we will meet it again in another context.[33]

Over time, though, London cabbing changed. It grew as an employment sector, of course, as the town itself grew. And drawing more men in, it gained in respectability. The rise of the hansom from its primitive origins in 1834 to become the gondola of London, as Disraeli christened it in *Lothair* (1870), brought with it a new class of driver 'more genteel and gifted than the vulgar race of cabmen; he is altogether smarter (in more than one sense) and more dashing, daring, and reckless'.[34]

On the whole, the cabby seems to have earned a reasonable living – though just how reasonable the constitutional reticence of the breed made it impossible to say. The London season – May through July – brought the fattest harvest, but even in the leanest some sort of public event would always touch up demand. The frequently quoted average of 30s a week, as Booth acknowledged in the 1890s, seems far too low. Certainly there were always men queueing up to take the knowledge test of London topography and to get the chance of hiring a cab and horse for 16s a day in peak season; and who might make enough, as over 3,000 did in the 1890s, to buy a cab outright or on hire-purchase. As among the costers, some became cab-masters or providers to the trade, with a yard and several hansoms and 'cattle' for hire. And these opportunities attracted 'all sorts of men . . . Many an educated man, who can do nothing else to earn a living, can drive,' Booth noted. A university-educated cabby kept the trade union's books during the London cab strike of 1891, for instance.[35]

So the middle classes too were lured by London's streets and the other metropolitan opportunities for turning a penny. Hardly anyone was immune from the temptation of 'bunce' or 'cabbage' or making a bit on the side. Certainly not the clerk class or their children. John Williams Benn, for instance, brought up under all the moral strictures of unyielding nonconformism, was drawn into the lucrative swim of philately as a boy-clerk in the City around 1865. Stamp-collecting was a new craze. There were 'wild and remarkable scenes in Birchin Lane' every evening after the six o'clock post, when 'hundreds of youths crowded that thoroughfare, literally going "on 'Change" in this new-born traffic. Youngsters who had previously handled only coppers now "sported" gold and notes, and not a few of them flourished cards and note-headings as "foreign stamp merchants".' Before he was fourteen Benn had made £80 and was in a position to relieve the financial difficulties of his shopkeeper parents.[36]

Adult lives were touched by these youthful experiences. Frank Bullen, born at Paddington in 1857, was a Meteorological Office clerk from 1883. He found that his 'fellow-clerks, with but a few exceptions, had outside employment', mostly of the Grub Street kind.

Bullen didn't trust the worth of his pen and so turned to other shifts. He answered advertisements for door-to-door canvassers and drummed up potential customers in the evenings: but 'I was too sensitive'. Following a friend's example, he bought jewellery and fancy goods cheap at a wholesaler's and sold to workmates by instalment. He acted as agent for insurance companies and photographers, paid on commission. He rented out rooms in his home to lodgers who defaulted on their rent and 'playfully urged me to get it if I could'. He addressed envelopes for advertisers. He subscribed to a monthly publication of prints, framed them and sold them. He was even an artist's model for a time. All this to add extras to his unsatisfactory salary of £100 a year. Around 1890 and still a clerk, his wife was left a small legacy, 'well under £200', which encouraged him to take a shop where he could sell pictures, frames and 'art needlework' in East Dulwich.[37]

The dream of economic independence pushed many in the same direction. Men had to be bred to baking or butchering or fishmongering or milkselling. But being a grocer or a more specialist sort of shopkeeper seemed to demand no more than native wit and a reasonable grasp of sums. These were skills women possessed in abundance and many widows sank their pensions and inheritance into a little 'general' shop to make an independent way in the world. In the 1890s London's inner ring contained one-third of London's population but 58 per cent of its general shopkeepers. The total stock of a general shop in a working-class area might be worth less than £6. Even with a brisk turnover and a mark-up of 50 per cent on many items, it was hard to realise a net profit of 10s to £1 a week, 'a fair living for one person, but not for two'. Shops like these depended on the straitened resources of a poor and shifting population who showed shopkeepers no mercy from theft or bad debts. Competition from a new shop opening nearby might be a killer. Often enough the dream of independence lay shattered at the workhouse door.[38]

Most deadly of all was the tangle of credit in which the small shopkeeper was caught up. She owed cash to suppliers, rent to the landlord, rates to the vestry and water company; and was owed by customers in every direction. Frank Bullen went the way of many. Driven nearly mad by the money he owed and the money he couldn't get in, he declared himself bankrupt for £300. He threw himself on the mercy of Carey Street.

On Your Uppers

There were many ways to go to pot, go up the spout, get hammered, come a cropper and end in Carey Street, the location for many years of the London bankruptcy court, close by Lincoln's Inn Fields. For most Londoners, low wages meant a lack of ready cash, few possessions or 'portable property', and exiguous savings. So credit, even for daily necessities, was essential. Because almost no one owned the house in which he lived, credit was given on the security of a pledge – a material object of some value that the borrower could temporarily do without – or on the security of a name on a bill. Without security the lender had to take on trust the person to whom goods were given on credit. Many did so. Hence the defining importance of 'appearances' in nineteenth-century London – '*appearance* is every thing in London' – and the lengths some went to maintain them, wholly fictional though they might be. And appearances demanded money – and hence more credit – to keep them up.[39]

Throughout the century this fragile credit nexus involved, at some time in their lives, almost the whole population of London in the threat of ruin and a substantial minority in ruin itself. Debt was the stuff of nightmare and suicide and those common 'domestic tragedies' (as the press called them) where a man driven mad by debt slit the throats of wife and children and then his own. A cut-throat razor was the shortest way out of Queer Street. No wonder indebtedness was such a prominent theme in nineteenth-century fiction, especially the novel set in London.[40]

The credit nexus affected different ranks in different ways. For the poor and the working class short-term credit was usually obtainable at the corner shop and from the landlord. Indeed, landlords, wittingly or otherwise, were the main bankers to the poor. Rent arrears were built up in hard times to be worked off in good. Many grocers 'ran a book', totting up purchases made on credit during the week to be redeemed on payday. Some would require a small pledge – an item of clothing, say – as security for the goods passed over the counter. Some wouldn't lend at all, displaying prominent notices accordingly and forgoing the poorest sort of custom as a result.

Besides small shops and landlords, there were two institutions that specialised in allowing credit to the poor. The door-to-door tallyman provided clothing and other drapery for small weekly instalments at high interest. And the ubiquitous pawnbroker – 'Uncle' – loaned cash on the security of possessions, chiefly clothing (sometimes direct from the tallyman), or watches, jewellery, tools and so on. The significance of both institutions in working-class life didn't abate in the nineteenth century, despite the growth of building societies, of savings or loans clubs based on trade unions and church missions and cooperative societies, or the more risky local versions that mushroomed in pubs and working men's clubs. With the growth of the town, there were around 530 pawnbrokers in London at the end of the century compared to about 400 in 1851. Middle-class men would resort to the pawnbroker at times of exceptional difficulty but among working-class Londoners a visit would be a weekly affair. And here women were the primary pilots around the choppy and treacherous waters of credit: 'three-fourths of these attendants on My Uncle', as Dickens put it, were 'nieces'.[41]

But in many ways it was not the London working class who suffered most from the consequences of indebtedness. Their debts were generally small, they might 'flit' without much notice being taken of them, and the costs of action in the courts often outweighed the likely gain to the creditor. This changed somewhat after county court process was simplified for small debts from 1847 and at the end of the century it was mainly workers who ended in prison for short periods when failing to comply with court orders to repay their debts. But until the 1860s, the likelihood of successful pursuit and a far longer period in gaol was greatest in the case of middle-class debtors. Among the London middle classes 'appearances' were often artificially sustained by a small mountain of debt owed to tailor, bootmaker, butcher, baker, landlord, upholsterer, decorator, anyone who could be persuaded or inveigled to part with goods on a promise to pay or a small deposit. As well as put-upon tradesmen, obligations were incurred to friends and relatives touched for ready money or prepared to put their names to a bill. Legal proceedings may have been a last resort after months or years of dunning. But eventually creditors would know that unless they staked their claim others would get in first and nothing would be left from the wreck. In those cases the law since the Middle Ages allowed creditors to lock up a debtor until he, or those who cared for him, paid sufficient for the debt to be accommodated. 'He' is not inappropriate here: almost all imprisoned debtors were men.

An antique choreography had evolved to regulate that merry dance

entwining quarry (the debtor on the one hand) and hunter (the creditor on the other). It was stepped out on the streets of London as much
as in law chambers and courts and compters. And a musty industry
had gathered to call the tune. The whole business broadcast misery in
every direction but one: the lawyers and the crumb-pickers who flocked
around them. They were legion. Bum-bailiffs made arrests and entered
premises to seize goods. Spunging-house keepers made their homes
'provisional prisons' where debtors were held to see if they could be
made to pay and so avoid prison. In the gaols the marshals, wardens,
deputies and turnkeys made a prime living by charging debtors for
lodging expenses and services rendered. 'Little attorneys', too small to
have an office, conducted their business in pub taprooms, acting for
creditors and debtors alike on the cheapest terms. They were 'of a
greasy and mildewed appearance', like Solomon Pell in *Pickwick Papers*
(1836–7), and their 'professional establishment' was 'a blue bag and
a boy', 'generally a youth of the Jewish persuasion'. Around them
huddled the clerks, writers and process servers, like another Solomon,
'an ancient scavenger in the dirty ways of the law', in Blanchard Jerrold's
Cent Per Cent (1869): "'he'll ferret him out, will old Sol: there never
was a man with such a scent. Talk of detectives; I'd back him to beat
them in a search, by miles.'" And one notch up hovered the more
successful solicitors, like Samuel Impey, in the Mayhew brothers' novel
of 1851, *The Image of His Father* – thought to be based on their own,
Joshua Dorset Joseph Mayhew. He 'followed the law principally as a
convenient means of increasing his rate of interest on the bills he loved
to discount' and he increased the rate by piling on legal costs for
recovery of the debt. His house 'had been furnished nearly from top
to bottom by "executions" and "distresses", levied upon the goods
and chattels of the different noblemen and gentlemen whom the moneylender loved to accommodate by cashing their paper for them'.[42]

On the other hand, the debtors had their wicked ways too. They
couldn't be arrested on a Sunday. So 'once-a-week men', 'Sunday-
promenaders' or 'Sunday-men' retired to an 'obscure lodging' –
'somewhere in the neighbourhood of Kilburn', say – and merely showed
their face on one day out of seven. Benjamin Disraeli, in 1836 a Tory
parliamentary candidate, wondered if he could risk appearing at a
Buckinghamshire constituency dinner in case of "'my being nabbed'"
for debts he had juggled for more than a decade. Once, it is said, he
hid in a well to avoid a bailiff. And things could get more desperate

still: he turned for help to Lady Blessington's partner, Count Alfred D'Orsay – fruitlessly, of course, but receiving the most generous refusal one could wish for. D'Orsay himself was better at the borrowing game: poor Disraeli had to take out a loan at 40 per cent in 1843 to pay a bill of £800 he'd backed for that elegant count. Debtors threw up other smokescreens too. Bailiffs could only enter a property by 'invitation', or through an open door or window and in daylight. So when the final crash came for the Blessington D'Orsays in 1848, they locked the gates, bolted the doors and screwed down the window sashes at Gore House, Kensington, 'virtually in a state of siege'. By this time D'Orsay had only been able to venture out, like some confused vampire, after sunset and on Sundays, since 1841. They were apparently undone by a sheriff's officer dressed as a pastrycook in April 1849. The Blessington D'Orsays escaped to France with whatever cash and portable property they could snatch from their creditors. So did others. Boulogne, famously, was 'that blessed retreat where brandy is cheap, and where every day is a Sunday to the despairing debtor!' [43]

Some creditors, though, refused to be beaten. In 1811 at Hoxton, a 'writ of arrest was served upon a dead body' on its way to the grave. The corpse was removed from the coffin by the sheriff's officers and conveyed away in a 'shell' to get the grieving relatives to settle the defunct party's debts. The Lord Chief Justice subsequently ruled the arrest of a dead body for debt unlawful. [44]

Many didn't escape. They ended in quod. London held by far the majority of the nation's prisoners for debt. Until 1842 there were four main debtors' prisons, although in the very early years of the century there had been more. The Fleet and the Marshalsea, north and south of the river, were venerable institutions dating from medieval times and rebuilt on many occasions. The King's Bench in Southwark, from 1837 the Queen's Bench and later just the Queen's Prison, was the most prestigious, home to the richest debtors, those with access to funds that their creditors couldn't reach. And Whitecross Street, the City Corporation's gaol, to which, from 1815, prisoners were moved from the old and ruinous Poultry Compter, from Newgate and from Giltspur Street Compter. All these places held about 1,700 prisoners for debt, though in any year some 7,000 debtors entered their doors. The 'Day Rules', ancient privileges secured by a fee to the marshal or governor of the Fleet and Queen's prisons, enabled a debtor to move, sometimes live, in a prescribed neighbourhood round the gaol. A few lived the 'better' part of their lives there, in that double sense of a life free from the importunities of creditors and a stay of great duration. When the Fleet and the Marshalsea both closed in November 1842, Jeremiah Board had lived in the Fleet since 1814; he was removed to the Queen's Bench, one of 760 or so debtors still in custody after restrictions were imposed on creditors' capacity to imprison for debt. And John Dufrene died at the Queen's Bench in 1856 after forty-four years there. Imprisonment was discontinued altogether for the middle classes only in 1869, when the Queen's Prison and Whitecross Street gaol closed. At Whitecross Street, a 'gentleman who has been in prison for costs 27 years', a 'voluntary prisoner' since 1861, had nowhere else to go but was put on the streets.[45]

For the first four decades of the century the debtors' prison formed 'a little world within itself, a sort of epitome of London'. Here metropolitan class distinctions asserted themselves in new ways. At the King's Bench, debtors with an income or rich friends could hire the best rooms in the 'State House'. The better-off paid 'chummage' to poor prisoners so they could get a room to themselves – destitute 'chums' slept on taproom tables or pews in the chapel. 'Garnish' was levied on new prisoners to pay for a round of drinks. Visitors were charged 'footing' to treat the poorest debtors 'to a more substantial meal than they were accustomed to enjoy'. The prison was a 'college' and the prisoners 'collegians'. Their chairman and officers were elected in accordance with printed rules, handed down by past generations. A man might move in his wife and children, sometimes a mistress. They could be provisioned well. At the King's Bench in 1826 were 'a coffee-house and two public-houses; and the shops and stalls for meat, vegetables, and necessaries of almost every description, give the place the appearance [that word again] of a public market . . .' Samuel Bamford, imprisoned there on a treason charge in 1820, recalled how 'the cobbler's hammer was at work; the barber had stuck out his pole, and displayed his pomatum, tooth powders, and perukes, as if people there had nothing to care about save cosmetics and curls'. Circulating libraries, grocers, bakers, cheesemongers – debtors all – set up shop there for ready money, making better profits than ever they did outside. Prostitutes, gamblers and costermongers seem to have had free run of the place. Rackets or tennis was played in the great courtyard and holidays were celebrated with games and races. On these high days the denizens of the Rules – 'swarming with debtors . . . the haunt of idle, dissipated men; a sort of modern Alsatia' – filled the prison and enjoyed the fun.[46]

All breeds of Alsatians were there. Lord William Pitt Lennox visited a friend at the Fleet Prison around 1830. As he 'entered the racket court . . . I was quite surprised at the number of faces that I recognised. And the number of persons who addressed me.' They included

an officer of one of the smartest hussar regiments in the service, whom I had known by sight, and had once met at dinner. He was at his window, enveloped in a splendid brocaded silk dressing-gown, with a velvet smoking cap on, puffing his cares away under the soothing influence of a handsome hookah. As I passed he dropped me a three-cornered note, written on scented pink paper, and containing the following lines:-

'DEAR LD. W.,
    'Your old friend Frederick T—, whom you knew in Canada, dines with me next Monday week. As, of course, you will be at Goodwood races, if you could get me half a buck of Halnaker venison, or even one of Southdown mutton, four-year old, I should be extremely obliged.
    'Yours truly,
    '—.
    'P.S. —Be careful to pay the carriage, or the authorities may "tap it on the shoulder".'[47]

The cool hussar might have walked straight out of the pages of Thackeray's masterpiece of 1847–8, *Vanity Fair*. There all the shifts and deceits and ruses that enabled fashionable Londoners to 'live well on nothing a year' were faithfully spelled out. Thackeray knew something about it. These were the years of the Blessington D'Orsays' fall and they were his friends. He attended the wreck when the contents of Gore House were sold up after D'Orsay's escape to France. It was 'a dismal sight', the house 'full of Snobs looking at the furniture – foul Jews, odious bombazeen women who drove up in mysterious flies . . .' Indeed, Thackeray knew more than he cared to admit. Some years earlier, having to make his own way in the world, he turned half-heartedly to the law. For a time he worked for a bill discounter at Birchin Lane, wrapped up in that murky world of short-term loans at cent per cent to risky customers. And when he began to write for a living he could only get by with loans from friends and credit from newspaper editors.[48]

Thackeray was not the only one. There was hardly a London writer or artist of the nineteenth century who did not know the credit nexus from the inside. For Grub Street, too, was on the edge of the London economy, at least for the first fifty years. But by the end of the next fifty, publishing had grown to be one of the most important of metropolitan industries. For the world at large, it would be of overwhelming significance.

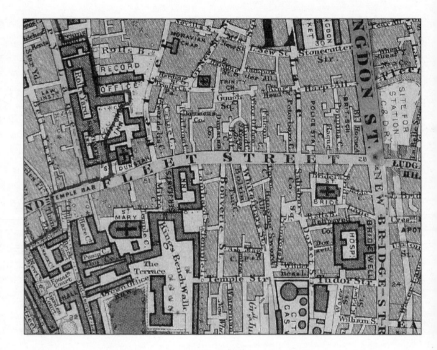

Fleet Street, 1862

VIII

FLEET STREET: CITY OF WORDS

'London News'

MAKING words was a quintessential metropolitan industry. London dominated English newspaper, magazine and book production throughout the nineteenth century. As a centre of intellectual production, London's position in the English-speaking world was scarcely less pivotal than its role as world finance capital. And in England itself no great industry was concentrated more in London than the writing, making and distribution of the printed word.[1]

Like all London's major industries, the manufacture of words clustered in small localities. At its heart was Fleet Street. This ancient way, leading west from Ludgate in the Roman wall, was, by the end of the nineteenth century, 'in a sense, the most famous thoroughfare in London'. No street had been more written about, none had such fertile literary associations, none had more resonance worldwide as the place from which 'London news' – as provincials called any intelligence beyond the local – originated. Fleet Street's connection with the newspaper industry was very much a nineteenth-century product. But its links with print – 'the street of ink' – were venerable indeed. The first book known to have been printed there was produced by Richard Pynson, a pupil of Caxton, in 1493. Wynkyn de Worde moved his printing works from Westminster to Fleet Street a few years later in 1500. Both Pynson (a Norman) and de Worde (an Alsatian) were migrant workers, as befitted an imported industry and Huguenot descendants were prominent among London printers well into the 1800s. There were other shadows from the past. Both Pynson and another Fleet Street man, William de Machlinia (a Belgian), specialised in law books. They could draw their writers, law-French proofreaders and customers from the Temple, entered from Fleet Street and huddled between it and the river. Later, in the time of Elizabeth, Richard Tottell at 7–8 Fleet Street had the sole patent for printing common-law books in England. This ancient association between the city of words and men of the law would be fully alive in the nineteenth century. And so would Fleet Street's position as an intellectual distillery of politics and opinion, of taste and culture high or low. When a motley of Victorian hackney-writers indulged a taste for gin at the Old Cheshire Cheese in Wine Office Court, Fleet Street, they knew that so had Samuel Johnson and Oliver Goldsmith before them. Such a weight of tradition would be a powerful draw for men and women of letters across the whole spectrum of opinion. So we find in and about Fleet Street in the early years of the nineteenth century the king's printer and the printer of the House of Commons rubbing shoulders with publishers like Thomas Hardy, tried for treason, William Hone, tried three times for blasphemous libel, and Richard Carlile, in and out of prison for his atheist and radical pamphlets.[2]

The nineteenth century saw spectacular growth in the manufacture of words. But even at its beginning, print flourished. Book publishing centred just north of St Paul's Churchyard in Paternoster Row, 'the head-quarters of English literature' since the first half of the eighteenth century. When 'bookselling' or publishing grew as an industry, it spread into Fleet Street and other parts of the City or West End. In 1818 eighteen 'publishers and wholesale booksellers' were located in 'the Row' itself, with a further twenty-three in Fleet Street and other parts of the City or West End. And thirteen private 'circulating libraries' kept drawing rooms stocked with new books from the 600–800 or so published in London each year.[3]

But books were just one page in London's city of words. The metropolis had long dominated newspaper and magazine publishing. In 1808 there were nine London morning and seven evening papers published daily; a further seventeen 'evening papers' – three of them in French – were published two or three times a week, sometimes less frequently; and forty-seven 'magazines', many of them catering for specialist tastes like *British Mineralogy*, the *Law Journal* or *Monograph of the Genus Rosa*, were published weekly, monthly or quarterly. Stamp, paper and other duties kept the price of these publications high. But that didn't necessarily put them beyond the means of literate workers hungry for print. Pubs and coffee shops often took in a sheaf of papers and journals. *The Times* and other daily newspapers could be hired by the hour for a penny from news vendors. And old papers had a resale value in an age when it took some days for news to grow stale.[4]

Vigorous though London publishing was in the years before Waterloo, it was dwarfed by the stupendous expansion that set in from the 1820s on, enlarging with each succeeding decade. The reasons for this evergrowing mountain of London print are so intertwined with the nation's social and intellectual history that the story of one is indistinguishable from the other. In no other element did London so entirely overbear the contemporary life of the nation as in the production and distribution of the written word between, say, 1830 and 1890.

A number of factors were in play here. The communications revolution cemented London at the centre of the nation's news. The old road system and post office mail coaches had secured metropolitan superiority in news distribution for generations. We can see this in the Strand-based enterprise of W. H. Smith, which had already captured the bulk of news supply to the great cities of the Midlands and North in the stage coach days of the 1820s. The rail network with London at its hub merely reinforced London's position. So Smith's began to switch to rail as early as 1838 and its railway bookstall empire rolled out to colonise the provinces a decade later. By 1850 'London news' could lay as crisp on breakfast tables from the Isle of Wight to Newcastle as it might in Hampstead or Dulwich.[5]

But it was the telegraph which brought a true revolution in news production and distribution in the nineteenth century. The port had always been a hub of continental and world news. Now it seemed all cable led to London. By 1900 it was connected by a giant steel and rubber web to all the far-flung outposts of the literate world. In England, William Cooke's first insulated telegraph wires began to follow the railway lines out of London from 1838. The first cable under the Channel was laid in 1851 and Paul Julius Reuter moved his news agency from Aachen to London that same year. His office at 5 Lothbury dominated the world supply of telegraphic intelligence for the rest of the century. By 1858 London was connected to Constantinople, by 1865 to Bombay, by 1866 to Washington. And London was the world centre of cable manufacture in Siemens' and other great factories along the Thames at West Ham and Woolwich. It was a London-built ship, Brunel's *Great Eastern*, that laid the first Atlantic cable after years of failed attempts. The telephone, too, spread fastest in London. The first telephone exchange was set up by Thomas Edison in Lombard Street – reminding us how in the City finance and communications depended so much on each other – in September 1879; and *Times* reporters were filing early-morning parliamentary speeches to Printing House Square by 'Edison's loud-speaking telephone' eight months later. These technological developments, so tightly tied by their infant reins to London, utterly transformed the process of news production around the world.[6]

They all interacted, with seismic shifts in social attitudes to education and literacy, and once more the new world showed sharpest in London. The capital could claim higher literacy rates than the rest of England before compulsory education began to take effect, so that 43 per cent of a sample of London bridegrooms in the years 1839–43 could sign their names in the marriage register compared to just 28 per cent in a sample from farming areas; and the proportions in 1869–73 were 75 per cent and 55 per cent respectively.[7]

Decade by decade, all these factors had a dramatic effect on the volume and character of the printed word emerging from London. Despite restrictions on press freedom, tighter and more rigorously enforced than ever in the revolutionary years of 1816–21, the annual production of stamped newspapers in London rose from seven million in 1801 to 16.3 million twenty years later. Similarly, the eighty-eight newspapers and magazines listed in the London guide for 1808 had doubled to 179 in 1826, and were divided into 'ladies', scientific, medical, religious, educational and other categories. There were now twenty-eight circulating libraries, eleven 'reading rooms' and numerous 'newspaper rooms', a feature of London life for the rest of the century where for a small subscription newspapers and journals could be read at leisure and in reasonable comfort. The number of books published in London in 1828 exceeded 1,100. And in 1824 the half-million pamphlets describing a notorious murder that were printed in eight days by Jemmy Catnach of Seven Dials give us some idea of the mass market for sensational literature among the London poor.[8]

All this activity was dwarfed from 1830 with the war of the 'unstamped' press and the first real efforts to create a mass readership for newspapers and journals. This was a concerted attack on the 4d stamp required for each newspaper that kept the price of a London daily at 7d, unaffordable for most households. The campaign emerged

out of a fever for reform among the middle classes and many below
who saw the newspaper stamp and other taxes on knowledge as a
block on reform and education. The war against them was waged on
many fronts. Middle-class campaigners brought out cheap periodicals
agitating for press freedom and mass education. They avoided the
stamp by restricting news. So Charles Knight, of the Society for the
Diffusion of Useful Knowledge, established the *Penny Magazine* in
1832. It quickly reached a weekly circulation of 150,000. Then radicals, a number of them former printers, defied the law by bringing out
real newspapers and ignoring the stamp. They produced hundreds of
titles, most hatching and disappearing like mayflies. Virtually all were
published from London. It was these that felt the weight of the authorities' retribution through the arrest and imprisonment of paper sellers
and the half-dozen or so London publishers responsible for most of
the output.[9]

Between these two groups, and emerging mainly after the newspaper stamp was cut to a penny in 1836, were middle-class entrepreneurs who put a mass audience and profit before politics and
reform. Men like Edward Lloyd, a printer for a time in Shoreditch,
who began publishing immensely popular weeklies from around 1841
and whose office near Fleet Street came to characterise the lurid 'penny
dreadfuls' of the 1840s as 'Salisbury Square fictions'. It was Lloyd
who gave a famous instruction to George Augustus Sala, then an illustrator and engraver: '"The eyes must be larger; and there must be
more blood – much more blood!"' Or like Thomas Lyttleton Holt,
whose 'publications, daily, weekly, and monthly . . . could be reckoned
by the score', but which 'rarely extended beyond a few months, and
. . . in many cases [were] limited to a few weeks'. With Holt we are
reminded that the city of words, despite its vibrancy and growth, was
often on the margins of the London economy. He closed *Holt's Journal*
in 1836 soon after publishing this unheeded advertisement to his
readers:

The appendage of my name to this publication has brought upon me a host
of troubles: beset by bailiffs, hunted by vindictive creditors, harassed by the
harpies of the law, who will have their bond, or else no small number of
pounds of flesh in the shape of my body, I am compelled to throw myself
upon the good feeling of my readers, to raise the price of the magazine one
halfpenny as the readiest means of relieving myself.[10]

The stamp reduction of 1836 unlocked newspaper circulation and gave a huge push to the manufacture of words in London. Sales of the principal London papers nearly doubled from sixteen million a year in 1837 to 31.4 million in 1850. By 1844 there were seventy-nine newspapers of one sort or another published from London, around sixty weekly periodicals and 227 monthlies – 'unequalled by any other commercial operation in Europe' or anywhere else. In 1853 the number of books published in London was almost 3,000. Circulating libraries were joined by Charles Mudie, soon all-powerful, who opened his giant premises at New Oxford Street in 1852: by 1861 he claimed to be buying 180,000 volumes a year for his various outlets in London and beyond. And a mass audience for print found popular authors to match. Charles Dickens inaugurated a new age of bestsellers from the late 1830s on, his monthly numbers selling frequently 50,000 and with immense cumulative sales of his books – 4.24 million in just the twelve years following his death in 1870, for instance.[11]

As technology improved and demand increased, some magazines and journals pushed at the boundaries of what had previously been possible in print. In many ways the most innovative in marking out new directions for journalism was the *Illustrated London News*. Illustrations had accompanied educational and trade publications for some time. But no one had attempted to illustrate the news until Herbert Ingram, a newspaper agent in Nottingham, connected the demand for 'London news' with the high sales that a specially illustrated number of a journal would produce. It took him ten years, and a move to London, to plan and then realise his project. Charles Knight recalled how he was surprised to see at the Old Bailey in early May 1842 an artist sketching 'two Lascars' on trial for their lives.

The mystery was soon explained to me. 'The Illustrated London News' had been announced for publication on the Saturday of the week in which I saw the wretched foreigners standing at the bar. I knew something about hurrying on wood-engravers for 'The Penny Magazine'; but a Newspaper was an essentially different affair. How, I thought, could artists and journalists so work concurrently that the news and the appropriate illustrations should both be fresh? . . . I fancied that this rash experiment would be a failure.[12]

From the start it was an outstanding success. Complications of production and a shortage of engravers were all overcome. A picture could be drawn on wood on Wednesday, engraved on Thursday, printed in the paper on Friday and in people's homes all over the country on Saturday. Even at a distance of more than a century and a half it is easy to see why the *Illustrated London News* triumphed. Its fine drawings, cleanly engraved and set in a format of short, varied and lively articles and paragraphs had great appeal. It brought news alive as nothing before. Its sales at 6d a number around 1850 reached 70,000–100,000 a week, topping 200,000 for the number describing the opening of the Great Exhibition. From 1848 a new political editor, the talented Charles Mackay, gave it a social conscience and a tone of 'advanced public opinion', and from 1852–9 he was manager and editor. And the Crimean War of 1854–6 provided an artists' canvas of unrivalled interest.[13]

Once the penny newspaper stamp was finally abolished in 1855 the *Illustrated London News* was put further on its mettle by a serious rival journal in the *Illustrated Times*. Brought out by a London publisher, David Bogue, and edited by Henry Vizetelly, a former engraver, the *Illustrated Times* sold 200,000 copies of its first number. Other rivals followed, most notably in 1869 the *Graphic*, which allowed its artists to use any medium, not just wood, and brought out two numbers a year in colour. Rather than hurting the *Illustrated London News*, as its projectors apparently intended, 'it only increased the taste for pictorial journalism'. The *Graphic* would go daily from 1890.[14]

When the paper duty, last of the taxes on knowledge, was repealed in 1861 new ventures mushroomed so quickly that printers in London faced a 'type famine'. George Watson, a book and magazine printer at Kirby Street, Hatton Garden, was forced to use old type with a long *s* for cheap books until the foundries could match the demand. Book production fluctuated year on year but showed an underlying steady rise – 4,835 in 1871, 7,567 in 1899, for example. The effect on newspapers, magazines and journals was even more dramatic. In 1883 a guide listed 'the principal newspapers published in London'. There were fifteen morning and nine evening papers, some of them specialist commercial prints. The 'Weekly, etc.' list ran to 383 titles. Of these, fifty were local newspapers meeting the needs of expanded London and its suburbs. The total number of 'registered newspapers' published in London in 1881 was 549; in 1895, 823. This, or something like it, would mark the high point of London publishing in the nineteenth century: English provincial and Scottish houses began to gain ground as the new century approached.[15]

These later years saw another departure as important for English journalism as the birth of illustrated news in the 1840s. The abolition of the paper duty and other taxes enabled *The Times* to reduce its price to 3d, but the *Daily Telegraph* and some others soon began to publish at a penny. They reached a larger than ever audience as a consequence. But the true arrival of the 'popular press' came with the *Star*, a radical evening newspaper addressed to working-class Londoners, which first appeared in 1888 at ½d. The *Star* bypassed London wholesalers and delivered direct to newsagents. By 1892 it had spawned a Liberal morning daily using the same distribution network – the *Morning Leader*, also at ½d. With Alfred Harmsworth's *Daily Mail*, first appearing in 1896, the halfpenny-press augured a new era in democratic journalism for the century to come. All this represented, too, a revolution in reading habits. Before 1855 *The Times* had a circulation of 50,000–60,000 and *Lloyd's Weekly Newspaper* below 100,000. But by the mid-1880s *Lloyd's* was selling 750,000 and *The Times* 100,000. And by 1900 the *Daily Mail* was selling almost a million each day, with the weekly *Harmsworth's Magazine* and the *Royal Magazine* another million each.[16]

There were two other specific effects on London of all this activity. One was on Fleet Street itself. At the early part of the century newspaper and magazine production had centred at least as much on the Strand and the streets and alleys running off it. But from the 1840s and especially the 1850s there was a shift east into Fleet Street and its tributaries. Fleet Street became the preferred location for new titles and for old ones seeking to expand. The reasons are not hard to find: Fleet Street was at the heart of London's printing industry and closer to City intelligence and world news from Reuters. It was the 1850s, too, which first saw the rise of the purpose-built newspaper office, sparking a contagion of redevelopment among titles old and new over the next thirty years. By the 1880s Fleet Street was 'newspaper land', synonymous with news publishing. 'How these . . . newspaper offices are making Fleet Street a palatial thoroughfare in our days!' commented Justin McCarthy, Irish journalist and MP, in 1891: 'The ["Daily News", the] "Telegraph", the "Standard", the "Chronicle" – they are like some of the great American newspaper offices in vastness, in arrangement, and in splendour.'[17]

The second effect was on 'Fleet Street's' role in the nation. Despite the vast growth in news and magazine publishing in the provinces, London continued to exert a whirlpool effect. The establishment of the Press Association in 1868, moving to Wine Office Court, Fleet Street, two years later, anchored telegraphic news production for provincial papers to London. Many felt the need for a London office, frequently on a grand scale and if possible in 'the street of ink' itself. The draw of Fleet Street went further still. It sent its journalists to the provinces as editors and recruited provincial editors as journalists in return. And provincial-grown papers aspiring to national appeal could find the distance from London just too great to overcome. W. E. Henley's *Scottish Observer* (later the *National Observer*), based in Edinburgh, could not avoid moving to London in 1892 to be close to its principal readership and main source of contributors: 'Edinburgh simply did not contain enough writers of stature and authority to fill the columns of the *Scottish Observer* with material of the standard which, from the beginning, the paper set itself.' Similarly the *Clarion*, Robert Blatchford's socialist paper, founded in Manchester in 1891, had to move to Fleet Street (later Worship Street) around 1895 to be nearer the centre of things.[18]

The multiplication of publishing ventures and the steady rise of print runs drew the cream of the nation's printers to the capital and endorsed printing as one of the great metropolitan trades. Compositors, engravers and lithographers were at the very top of the aristocracy of labour in the nineteenth century. There had been a trade union for London compositors since 1801 and possibly since 1785. In 1810 newspaper compositors on full nightwork were guaranteed 48s per week and earnings for the rest of the century were at the top of the artisan tree in London. Working conditions in old print shops could be foul; hours could be long in rushes – nearly forty hours' continuous standing at a composing frame in the 1850s, W. E. Adams remembered; and disconcertingly short in the slack times, especially earlier in the century. But in general printers were envied and apprenticeships sought after for London boys. In the 1890s Booth found that 66 per cent of London printers were London-born, compared to an average of 50 per cent in all London trades combined.[19]

The intelligence and high degree of literacy of compositors put them in the vanguard of the London working class. In the 1820s Pierce Egan found 'very severe critics and first-rate scholars' among the 'typos'. At the *Illustrated Times* in the 1850s the compositors held debates at a Shoe Lane tavern, and spoke 'often about books and pictures and operas. We even formed a magazine club' to share part-numbers of

The Virginians and *Little Dorrit*. Charles Knight thought the intellectual standard of printers fell between the 1820s and the 1860s and no doubt reduced demand for composing in Greek and Latin drove some scholars from the trade. It is also true that printers were notorious for their casual fringe of 'grass hands' degraded by drink, who would work just for the price of the next binge. Even so, printers remained prominent among working-class intellectuals. And they continued to supply the ranks of publishing entrepreneurs – like the Dangerfields of Bouverie Street, highly successful trade publishers, starting with *Cycling* in 1891.[20]

There was another side to the economic power of London compositors and we have seen its like elsewhere. The first composing machines using type keys rather than a stick and frame were introduced to London hesitantly in 1841. They didn't penetrate newspaper production until the 1870s at *The Times*, a non-union shop. Elsewhere they were promptly blacked by the London Society of Compositors, which retained its opposition to the new technology into the 1890s, when improved linotype machines rendered further resistance impracticable. The place of women in composing rooms was held back for a generation and more as a result. Machines had also been opposed in London bookbinding, where women did indeed form the majority of workers by 1871. Resistance to machinery was one reason for London steadily losing its share of the nation's bookbinding from the 1830s on, notably to Scotland.[21]

By the late 1890s, through factors like these and the growth of a provincial press, London's dominance in print was beginning to slip. In the unreliable 1851 census London contained 41 per cent of those in Great Britain engaged in publishing and printing of one sort or another. In 1871 it was 47 per cent of those in England and Wales. By 1901 it had fallen away to 40 per cent, counting both London County and Middlesex. Yet that was still very high for an industry now comprising over 70,000 metropolitan workers. And although we can see a similar trend among authors, in other ways London's superiority in the nation's republic of letters continued to be astonishingly vibrant.[22]

Scribbling for Dear Life

No one knows how big was the constituency of Londoners who filled the pages of London in print. It must certainly have been larger than the 811 'authors, editors and writers' counted in the 1851 census of London; the 1,285 'authors, editors, and journalists' in 1871; and the 4,720 'authors, editors, journalists, reporters and shorthand writers' counted in London County and Middlesex in 1901. These can only have represented the full-time end of a notoriously part-time trade. Few men or women could live by ink alone. Around them were thousands who wrote here and there for the press but gained the better part of their living elsewhere. Even so, the domination of London among the nation's self-described authors is clear: the county contained over 50 per cent of them in 1871 and 1881, and London and Middlesex together nearly 43 per cent in 1901.

The difficulties of writing for a living in London were notorious. The hack writer – driven as hard as the worn-out nag in a hackney carriage – was symbolised by the garret quill-pushers of Samuel Johnson's Grub Street, near Moorfields in the north of the City. By the opening of the nineteenth century the hacks' connection with Grub Street had faded away – it was a filthy colony of poor and hard-drinking shoemakers around 1814. But old echoes were clearly sounding when it was renamed Milton Street some time in the 1820s. And 'Grub Street' lived on in the grinding labour for small reward that characterised much of literary production in London for at least the first three-quarters of the nineteenth century.[23]

As for other London industries, poor reward had much to do with an overstocked labour market in a low-wage economy. The vast expansion of newspapers, reviews, journals, magazines and cheap novels attracted to it a middle-class reserve army of labour whose education and literacy seemed to offer the possibility of earning easy money – even fame and fortune – by writing. Yet despite the ever-spreading shelves of print, there were always more writers than columns to fill. '"A losing trade, I assure you, sir; literature is a drug,"' was the discouraging reply to George Borrow when he asked for commissions from the publisher Sir Richard Phillips in 1824. 'The author did not live who could with any truth say that on the occasion of his first interview Mr Vassett had seemed glad to see him,' wrote Charlotte Riddell of her attempts to get published in London in the 1850s. And thirty years later, when Frank Harris sought something to do at the *Spectator*, he was told, '"We have too many writers . . . Can't find work enough for those we know."'[24]

But still they came. Unemployment for a governess or clerk, too few clients for a professional man, the incapacity or incompetence of a husband, made chancing one's hand a pressing necessity. What alternative could be so easily attempted? As the editor of the *Idler* wrote of the tradesmen and clerks and wives and spinsters who bombarded his in-tray with unsolicited manuscripts, 'Running through all of them, the conviction that literature is the last refuge of the deserving poor.'[25]

A few sources of recruitment for the Grub Street army stand out. Educated women, barred largely from the professions and the public service apart from schoolteaching, took to writing to support themselves and often a husband and family as well. The pen must have seemed so much more attractive than the prospects of governess or teacher or ladies' companion or doll's-house confinement. It offered recognition and independence, in theory at least. So Annie Besant, unhappily married to a young vicar, relieved her mind and her purse by writing short stories for the *Family Herald* from 1868. Charlotte Riddell, a migrant to London from Carrickfergus around 1854, supported herself, her ailing mother and then a husband unlucky in speculations. Eliza Lynn Linton, who wrote when single for the *Morning Chronicle* in the late 1840s, had to go on writing for herself and an improvident husband, and then for herself once again when the marriage ended in separation. Like Linton, Margaret Wilson also married an artist, Francis Oliphant, who earned little and died young. And there are similar echoes in the London life of George Eliot and no doubt many others.[26]

For men, the civil service seems to have offered sufficient leisure, peace of mind and drafting experience to tempt many into the street of ink. 'I wanted to be something more than a clerk in the Post Office,' recalled Edmund Yates. He managed to hold down a senior position while editing some journals and writing copiously in others. His superior Anthony Trollope did famously better still. Somerset House had a whole back-office corps of literary men, among them for a time William Hale White, better known as Mark Rutherford, who moved to the Admiralty later. The War Office, too, bristled with penmen.[27]

Within the professions, a few medical men won literary honours, among them Albert Smith, Somerset Maugham and, most notable of all, Arthur Conan Doyle. But the deepest recruitment pool for Grub Street was the law. It had been for generations. The law had its own middle-class reserve army of men unfitted by birth or wealth for better things. For a good part of the nineteenth century all but the highest reaches of the bar offered second best. 'Even as late as 1860, solicitors were generally regarded by the upper classes as tradesmen, who, if they visited a barrister's house, entered by the back door.' Besides this equivocal status, and sometimes worse reputation, there was never enough law to go round. Briefless barristers, client-shy attorneys, clerks of every grade, law writers or scriveners or copyists, all clung to some shady half-light on the edge of 'legal London', grubbing a living as best they could. Some failed altogether. In January 1827 Robert Bowles, a law writer out of work through an accident, starved to death in a freezing chamber at Johnson's Court, Fleet Street. Poor Bowles 'was completely covered with vermin. He had scratched the skin off almost every part of his body, and consequently the sheets and bed were nearly soaked with blood.'[28]

Generally it was from these outer regions that the law sent its myrmidons to Grub Street. Not all were impecunious. But in the first half of the century the taint of poverty was assumed to fall on every lawyer resorting to print. This and the 'ungentlemanly' status of the press provoked the benchers of Lincoln's Inn to attempt in 1807 to stop anyone who had been paid for writing in the newspapers from being called to the bar. They were voted down. One reason for their failure might have been the rewards to be found in newspaper columns or the drama or cheap fiction which the law could not readily match. Robert Francillon found that his first short story in *Blackwood's Magazine* made him £80, just about as much as the whole of his second year's briefs at the bar; in a few years he took to full-time novel-writing and journalism. And a little later, in the 1870s, 'a considerable number of young barristers – and some old ones – were more or less dependent on their contributions to the Press for an income'. [29]

Wig and pen proved congenial – and fertile – bedfellows. The teenage Dickens spent a year and a half as an attorney's clerk in Gray's Inn. Thackeray, W. S. Gilbert and John Delane (mid-century editor of *The Times*) entered at the Temple, R. D. Blackmore and Wilkie Collins at Lincoln's Inn, W. H. Ainsworth at King's Bench Walk. Benjamin Disraeli, George Borrow, Charles Shirley Brooks and Jerome K. Jerome were articled clerks. A clutch of London police court magistrates combined Bow Street with Grub Street, just as Henry Fielding had done a century before: Gilbert à Beckett (a *Punch* man), Montagu Williams and Joseph Moser (dramatists). Numerous others were the sons (like the Mayhew brothers) or daughters (like M. E. Braddon) of lawyers. In so many ways, of course, the connection was hardly surprising. The ancient partnership of Fleet Street and the Temple had always brought law and literature together in a convivial milieu. Both tended to be worldly wise and cynical. And the law was an excellent articleship for literature and the press. It taught precision of language – though not necessarily brevity of expression – and opened a wide window on others' lives. Disraeli, for one, valued his time at a City solicitors' in the 1820s: 'It gave me great facility with my pen and no inconsiderable knowledge of human nature.'[30]

Disraeli was one of those who did well from literature, although not well enough to keep the bailiffs from his door. But for most, writing proved a hard and largely thankless grind for inadequate reward. 'He was a hack ridden by a printer's devil, with Time barking at his heels,' wrote the biographer of Shirley Brooks. A man of note in his day, Shirley Brooks was an editor of *Punch* and a novelist of some merit. During his last illness, in 1874, he was 'working for *Punch* up to within a few hours, almost a few minutes of his death'. After ceaseless literary work for almost forty years, he left £6,000; a subscription had to be raised for his family and a £100 civil list pension was granted (by Disraeli) to his widow. Angus Reach (pronounced Ree-ack – he was Scottish) worked sixteen hours a day as a shorthand reporter, comic writer and novelist. He died from 'softening of the brain' at thirty-five. His family's dire poverty had to be relieved by theatrical benefits in which Dickens, Thackeray and others took part. Thomas Miller, the basket-maker poet and London novelist, wrote forty volumes and gained a pension from Disraeli, who never forgot an author's dues. But he died destitute and a fund had to be raised for his family: '"it is really a case of starvation"'. Mrs Oliphant, a successful and popular novelist, had to churn out a quite extraordinary flow of volumes to sustain her middle-class lifestyle. The bibliography with her posthumous autobiography runs to 123 titles over a writing career spanning fifty years. In each of twenty-two years she published three books or more, many of two or three volumes in the fashion of the time. The list of articles she published in *Blackwood's* alone, often historical and requiring extensive research, reached almost 300 over the same period. In the year of her death, 1897, were published two novels, three volumes of biography and four contributions to *Blackwood's*. As she justly wrote, 'I have lived a laborious life, incessant work, incessant anxiety'; yet 'Success as measured by money never came to my share.'[31]

Perhaps a final example out of countless numbers might have most resonance to modern ears. George Gissing, the greatest London novelist of the last quarter of the century, with a substantial reputation in his own lifetime, committed to his diary the monthly humiliations of life in and around 'New Grub Street'. March 1889: 'With not one penny to spend on pleasures, I am entirely shut out from the new theatres and places that I should like to see.' March 1890: 'Do not really have enough to eat, but no help for it.' November 1890: 'Sold another lot of books, for £5.' And six months later:

Ordered Hardy's 'Two on a Tower', which I wanted to re-read. Did it with a sense of extravagance, – the cost being 1/8. Look at my position, with a novel succeeding as 'New Grub Street' has done. I cannot buy books, I cannot subscribe to a library; I can only just afford the necessary food from day to day; and have to toil in fear of finishing my money before another book is ready. This is monstrously unjust. Who of the public would believe that I am still in such poverty?[32]

Writing a novel a year brought Gissing an advance of £150 and for a lengthy period little more than that. The conditions under which he and many like him laboured – skimping on necessities to preserve the trappings of gentility – robbed writers of an easy mind and replaced it with endless anxiety. Domestic poverty induced wriggling discomfort. A poor diet left no stomach for sustained concentration. A wonder it is that so much nineteenth-century writing has proved of such lasting worth.

Even when conditions were not so bad as these the competitiveness fuelled by too many publications and an endless supply of penny-a-liners made too great a demand on what talent there was. Shirley Brooks once wrote six songs at three guineas apiece in one day and 'what is worse, [he] was proud of having done it'. But in his defence no opportunity could be ignored when a writer never knew where the next commission was coming from. And for less facile pens a commission might mean hours of laborious study to work up an article. The British Museum reading room as early as the 1840s was 'the great national manufactory of books', where literary grubbers were engaged in 'grinding down the matter of old books in order to make new ones'. Even then, the numbers of women using the reading room was 'ominous of a social revolution'. Gissing called it 'the valley of the shadow of books', its users suffering as much as prisoners on the silent system. So Mr Quarmby in *New Grub Street* (1891), shabby-genteel, a miscellaneous writer for the journals, 'laughed in a peculiar way, which was the result of long years of mirth-subdual in the Reading-room . . . His suppressed laugh ended in a fit of coughing – the Reading-room cough.'[33]

And there were other obstacles to literary endeavour. Publishers and fellow grubbers loomed large among them. There are many salutary instances in the long Grub Street career of Edward Leman Blanchard, 1820–89, dramatist, theatre critic, songwriter, miscellaneous journal-man and genuine hack from the age of sixteen. Some time in the early 1840s he briefly came under the influence of one Olinthus Bostock, 'a small printer and publisher of Holywell Street': '"Why don't you try a novel, sir – something cutting and moral?"' Blanchard set to, using a room of Bostock's in which to pen it and passing copy direct to the compositor for setting. One Saturday, with Blanchard hard at work, Bostock asked for a loan of a pound to pay his paper merchant 'something on account'. No paper, no novel. But no cash either, so Bostock borrowed the obliging Blanchard's coat and waistcoat for pawning, saying he would get them out later in the day. The paper merchant proved unamenable, so Bostock came back for Blanchard's boots, but with the same fruitless result. So Bostock came back a third time. But now Blanchard refused the loan of his trousers as a step too far, and wisely so, for Bostock failed to return with paper, pawn ticket or clothes. Blanchard was eventually rescued from the printer's office on Sunday night with the loan of a watchman's greatcoat and a laundress's carpet slippers. He shuffled off to relieve his feelings at the White Hart, Catherine Street, Strand.[34]

Many others made importunate demands. A Victorian hand has written 'an inveterate cadger' against the name of William Jerdan in the London Library's copy of some mid-century literary reminiscences. Jerdan was editor of the *Literary Gazette* and a founder of both the Royal Society of Literature and the Garrick Club. Edmund Yates's brazen front in demanding a loan was apparently specially difficult to resist. Tom Purnell, a reporter on the *Globe*, was notorious for cadging other men's copy. Perhaps among the worst was W. G. Graham, editor of the *Museum*, a literary cheat and forger of bills. He once handed a parcel of 'copy' to Charles Knight, who passed a cheque in return: 'The outer leaves of each section were the fairest of manuscripts; the inner leaves were blank paper.' Graham was shot dead in a duel in New York around 1826.[35]

The hand-to-mouth rewards of most literary endeavour, that common struggle in which even successful writers had once been engaged, encouraged a high degree of mutuality in Grub Street. Olinthus Bostock aside, publishers more often advanced money than begged it. Writers like Douglas Jerrold, Charles Shirley Brooks and doubtless others committed themselves to collective assistance through Freemasonry. The correspondence of Charles Dickens is full of schemes to relieve destitute writers or their widows and orphans and he was unstinting of time and energy in such ventures. Thackeray had a well-deserved reputation for generosity in cash donations. So too did Disraeli, as we have seen, with the nation's cash more readily, perhaps, than his own.

And fair enough. For Disraeli's official recognition of the obligations the nation owed its writers and artists contributed to one of the great shifts in London literary life, and the conditions of literary production, in the nineteenth century. When he famously declared to Parliament in 1853 that 'I am myself a "gentleman of the Press", and bear no other escutcheon', Disraeli staked a claim for writing and journalism that had been largely at odds with polite society's values during the first half of the century. Grub Street's estimation was low indeed. The poverty and shabbiness and sheer mechanical drudgery of much literary production tarnished the industry as a whole. The boozy libertinism of bohemia – real or imagined – damned it in the eyes of the God-fearing. The unscrupulousness of journalism during the factious years of the Regency and the post-war revolutionary period – where literary talent frequently attached itself to the highest bidder – tainted much of the press as cynical and hypocritical and venal. So did journals like Barnard Gregory's *Satirist*, Grenville Murray's the *Queen's Messenger* and Adolphus Rosenberg's *Town Talk*, scandal sheets that would blackmail a victim into buying off a story before it got into print: '"I'll teach you to call my daughter a w—e"', cried the actor-manager Charles Kemble as he beat Charles Molloy Westmacott, editor of the *Age*, about the head with a thick stick at Covent Garden Theatre in 1830. The taint ran on in the lurid shockers put out by G. W. M. Reynolds – a particular *bête noire* of Charles Dickens – or louche papers like the *Town* under Renton Nicholson, who boasted he knew more of London's brothels and debtors' 'stone jugs' than 'any "flash cove", living or dead'. Sir Walter Scott summed up for polite society when he declared in 1829 that 'nothing but a thorough-going blackguard ought to attempt the daily press . . . I would rather sell gin to the poor people and poison them that way.'[36]

A number of things conspired to raise the status of London literary production in all its forms as the century grew older, some signs already apparent as Scott wrote. That unimpeachable gentleman (at least by birth and appearance) Bulwer Lytton was a popular novelist by the 1820s and was vocal in arguing for higher regard for writers generally.[37] Serious intellectual endeavour found its way into the journals and reviews in that same decade and before. Newspapers like *The Times* and *Morning Chronicle* contributed definitively to questions of politics and social reform.

A corner was turned with Dickens's brilliant arrival, like some shooting star, in the mid-1830s, first with Boz's social reportage and humorous stories, then *Pickwick*, and then the series of novels that sustained such a fierce critique of contemporary society and its institutions. He was not just a novelist, of course. He edited weekly magazines for much of his working life and for a brief moment in 1846 edited the brand-new *Daily News*. Somewhere near the front of his mind in all these ventures lay an ambition: 'I am always possessed with the hope of leaving the position of literary men in England, something better and more independent than I found it.'[38]

Dickens wrote that to Thackeray in 1848 and over the next fifteen years these two came to represent a schism in London's city of words between cockney bohemia (Dickens) on the one hand and gentlemen of letters (Thackeray) on the other. This was a word-war waged more by disciples than by the great men themselves, even though there was considerable rancour between them. The polarity turned on a mixture of snobbery and politics. William Makepeace Thackeray, from a wealthy Anglo-Indian family, tutored at Charterhouse and Cambridge, brought prestige of birth and education to an emerging 'profession' of letters keen to win invitations to the nation's brightest drawing rooms. Charles Dickens, son of a ne'er-do-well clerk, condemned to factory labour before his teens and roughly schooled, who never lost his cockney twang or taste for flashy dressing, seemed to undermine the very status of the literature to which he contributed so gloriously. The politics of their writings were equally at odds. Dickens, 'Mr Popular Sentiment' as Anthony Trollope (a Thackeray-worshipper) dubbed him, was always slashing away at society's ills, while Thackeray in his later years was readily content with his lot and society's too. When Thackeray died suddenly, just fifty-two, on Christmas Eve 1863 a rash of obituaries extolled him as a cool-handed 'gentleman' of letters in contrast to 'the

Gushing School': 'as if the rest of us were of the tinker tribe', complained Dickens privately.[39]

This question of the writer's status was never resolved in the nineteenth century. Nor could it be. The great enlargement of the press and popular writing necessarily drew to it legions of writers who could claim no 'gentlemanly' status at all. But it is true that the old demonisation and social cold-shouldering of writers and journalists as a breed had lost much purchase by the last quarter of the century.

There were some milestones along this rocky path. The *Saturday Review* was one. Established in 1855 by a land-owning Tory MP, it embodied some sort of revolution in weekly journalism. Its writers were 'Cambridge men' and similar (if that's not an impossibility), among them Leslie Stephen (Virginia Woolf's father), Lord Robert Cecil (later Marquis of Salisbury and Prime Minister), John Morley and Walter Bagehot. Aiming high in everything – the Church of England included – the *Saturday* set out to be the scourge of vulgarity, of bohemianism, of Grub Street, of Dickens, and perhaps most of all of religious enthusiasm in the shape of evangelicals and nonconformists. 'Every good man,' according to the hall-rousing preacher C. H. Spurgeon, 'is born for the love of God and the hatred of the *Saturday Review*.'[40]

Another was the *Pall Mall Gazette*. There were strong shades of Thackeray here, for the '*Pall Mall Gazette*' was the imaginary paper, 'written by gentlemen for gentlemen', introduced in *Pendennis* (1849–50) and reappearing near the end of his life in *Philip* (1861–2). The *Pall Mall Gazette* first appeared in 1865 and from the beginning imported the tone of the *Saturday Review* into daily journalism. James Hannay, a cheer-leader for Thackeray and his values, was on the staff and a number of contributors from the *Saturday* found the PMG a convenient vehicle too. Indeed, it brought to the daily press some of the most distinctive voices among London's men and women of letters – George Eliot, Anthony Trollope, John Ruskin and other famous names. 'Its tone has from the first been aristocratic, the tone of the club window, of the smoking-room, of the House of Commons and of the drawing-room', was a verdict of 1882. Within three years, though, it became something else, as we shall see. [41]

Through titles like these the status of ephemeral literary work was transformed during the second half of the century. Earnings improved as a consequence. 'The old bugbear . . . of poverty has vanished,' wrote

Sir Walter Besant at the century's end. 'It is now well known that a respectable man of letters may command an income and a position quite equal to those of the average lawyer or doctor.' Besant was over-optimistic, as the case of Gissing shows. But he went on rightly to point up the hugely expanded range of opportunities for writers compared with fifty years before. He noted simultaneous publication in London and America, even Australia, a first appearance in a journal and then in book form, more books published, sold and read (and reviewed – an important author's perk), larger permanent staff numbers on newspapers, the emergence of a writers' trade union in the Society of Authors (which Besant helped found in 1883), improved copyright laws, and literary agents to haggle the best price from publishers. There might have been still a very wide gap between the earnings of stars like, say, Rudyard Kipling or Conan Doyle and a new writer. Most authors were 'struggling' as they always had. But the revolution in print had brought about a revolution in the terms and conditions of literary production. London's writers reaped benefits accordingly – indeed, all this had worked itself through largely in a metropolitan context. And London was at the centre of things in other ways too.[42]

The Genius of London

London was a comparatively small town, and those who were engaged in the business of amusing the public, however they might hold themselves aloof, lived in a ring fence, and were continually in touch with one another. News spread mysteriously, as it is said to do amongst the Indians, but we must remember that there was a constant intercommunication between authors, artists, engravers, printers, and the like, and anything interesting was contin-ually carried to and fro by a mob of subordinates.[43]

That was how the son of Hablot Browne, the illustrator known as 'Phiz', remembered London literary life in the 1850s and 1860s. The mutuality made necessary by Grub Street's mode of production spilled over into other areas besides charitable relief. And it affected more than just writers. The boundaries between artists and writers was fluid and inclusive. After all, Thackeray, George Augustus Sala, George du Maurier, Richard Whiteing, Watts Phillips and Robert Brough were all writers who had begun their Grub Street careers as illustrators. And

writers like Dickens, for one, was famously close to his illustrators and
valued highly the contribution they made to his work. Writers, artists,
publishers and printers – for them London was indeed a 'small town'
and this feature held as good for the 1890s as it had at mid-century.
Even lonely Gissing circulated among other writers and received more
invitations than he wished to accept.

Gissing lived in Brixton and Camberwell around 1889–91 and
Browne far out in Thornton Heath, but that was no barrier to being
a resident of literary London. Writers and artists could be brought
together by a number of means. They met at the great literary soirée-
giving houses like Gore House under the Blessington-D'Orsays in the
1830s and 1840s, or (also in Kensington) the Samuel Carter Halls in
the 1850s. These places came and went. So too did London's little
'bohemias' – communes in the metropolitan republic of letters. Justin
McCarthy watched a literary and artistic bohemia emerge in the Fitzroy
Square district in the 1870s: Ford Madox Brown, a founding Pre-
Raphaelite, his son Oliver (a novelist), William Rossetti (art critic),
Algernon Swinburne, Eliza Lynn Linton, Kegan Paul (the publisher)
and McCarthy (then on the *Daily News*) were just a few of the person-
alities there among many. At the same time, the publisher William
Tinsley recalled a 'Bohemia at Camden Town'. A decade later and
Mrs Desmond Humphreys, the popular novelist 'Rita', was part of a
cluster of women writers who connected through South Kensington
'At Homes': Marie Corelli (who had hers on the first Sunday of the
month at Longridge Road), Mrs Arthur Frankau ('Frank Danby'),
John Strange Winter, Mrs Campbell Praed and more. At the same time
Joseph Pennell, a brilliant American artist who was one of the century's
finest illustrators of London life, was helping turn the Adelphi into a
'Quarter': his wife's Thursday evenings welcomed artists like Phil May,
James McNeill Whistler, Walter Crane and Aubrey Beardsley and
writers like George Moore, W. E. Henley and Henry James. George
Bernard Shaw, John Galsworthy, J. M. Barrie and the publisher Fisher
Unwin lived close by. A decade later still – the 1890s – and we step
into that

tiny, highly favoured little kingdom bounded to the east by Nash's Regent
Street, and more especially the old Café Royal, and on the west by the
Hogarth Club [Dover Street]. Northwards, it extended perhaps as far as the
Café Verrey [229 Regent Street, corner of Hanover Street] and southwards
scarcely further than Piccadilly. A special light illumined that miniature realm,

in comparison with which all the surrounding tracts were drab and crepuscular . . .

This was the London of Oscar Wilde, Beardsley, the *Yellow Book* and the publisher John Lane of the Bodley Head, Vigo Street.[44]

But the largest and most stable clustering of all was the district north and south of Fleet Street and the Strand, including Covent Garden. This was *the* London bohemia, where Fleet Street was properly renamed 'the Street of Drink'. Here the newspaper, magazine and publishers' offices lay just a raised glass away from the pubs and clubs of literary London. They were legion. The Garrick's Head, Bow Street, where literary men and 'theatricals' formed the Rationals Club in the late 1830s. The Wrekin Tavern, Broad Court (off Bow Street), where an 'ordinary' was held daily at 4 p.m. for 'choice spirits' in the 1840s. The Shakespeare's Head, Wych Street, run in 1840–41 by Mark Lemon, but with Grub Street links, like all these places, long before and for some years after. Clunn's Hotel, Covent Garden Piazza, where the Fielding Club, later Our Club, dined on Saturday evenings in the 1850s with Thackeray and John Leech, the artist, among the company. And other favourite pressmen's pubs around mid-century included the Old Dog, Holywell Street, the Coach and Horses and Edinburgh Castle, the Strand, the Sheridan Knowles, Brydges Street, and any number in Fleet Street itself, like Peel's Coffee House, the Green Dragon, the Cock, and of course the Cheese.[45]

The clubs of this central bohemia may have begun in pub backrooms but with maturity and a growing prosperity they established premises of their own. The great Athenaeum was started in this way by the aristocracy of paper, Sir Walter Scott among them, in the 1820s. Its palatial clubhouse was opened in Waterloo Place in 1830 and its famous library reminds us that such a place had more in it for writers than just good company. It was followed by the Garrick, opened 1831 at King Street, Covent Garden, for 'the "patrons" of the drama and its professors, and also for offering literary men a rendezvous'. So popular did it prove that it moved to purpose-built premises in the newly formed Garrick Street nearby in 1864. But it was the Savage Club, more than any other, that represented the main permanent institution emerging from mid-century bohemia, first in a room at the Crown, Vinegar Yard, Drury Lane, in 1857, and then at some nine pubs and hotels before settling in Adelphi Terrace in 1890.[46]

By then it had fallen into a respectability that some of its original members – among them the radical Robert Brough and George Augustus Sala – wouldn't readily have anticipated. But others, like the Tory James Hannay and another Scot, Andrew Halliday, university man and dramatist, might well have done. All that agonising over status and complaining about the rewards of literature had worth and wealth very much in mind. So the seeds of bohemia's dissolution were there from the start. Writers like Thackeray, and indeed Dickens, entered it to climb out as soon as they could, clinging to fond memories and some acquaintances but firmly rejecting its culture of 'drink, debt and dissipation'.[47]

The heyday of bohemia seems to have been from around 1830 to 1870, most vibrant of all in the 1840s and 1850s. Then it was marked by its strong personalities, its contempt for creditors and bailiffs, its disregard for 'proper' forms of dress and appearance, religious observance and polite speech. It permitted sexual licence and winked at eccentric ménages. And most of all it drank. Indeed, one of the elements of dissolution was bohemians dying young. 'They may see people under the table, but people get their revenge by seeing them under the sod,' quipped James Hannay, himself dying at forty-seven in 1873. Mostly, though, bohemia atrophied as the times changed around it. The defeat of Chartism in 1848 and the demise of men like Douglas Jerrold (1857) and Robert Brough (1860) silenced its small left wing. And the professionalisation of letters, to which so many aspired, brought a civilising of manners in its train.[48]

By 1866, when Richard Whiteing was getting his costermonger pieces into the *Evening Star*,

the Bohemia of the Press was beginning to be a thing of the past. The institution was just kept going by a few convivial clubs all based on the idea that the self-respecting writer was bound to be a bit of a wastrel in his private hours. With most, this was no more than lip service to a social cult in its dotage, and it was consistent with the decorum of the home and wholesome family life.[49]

In fact traces of bohemia in the Fleet Street and Strand neighbourhood were detectable in pubs and club-life, among journalists in particular, till the end of the century. The later bohemias of Vigo Street, or wherever, hardly renounced pleasure. They seem, too, to have had a strong dash of liquor in them. But there was a considerable difference between then and what was thought acceptable behaviour among 'gentlemen of the press' thirty years before. It was summed up by Sir Francis Burnand, editor of *Punch* from 1880, looking back on the time of a former editor, Charles Shirley Brooks. The crucial difference in Burnand's view – for Shirley Brooks as far as we know was a faithful husband and a scrupulous man – was drink:

socially, he belonged to a previous generation of literary men, journalists and theatrical professionals which has very little in common with those of my own time and standing . . . certainly the habits and manners of Shirley and his contemporaries were not congenial to me. Shirley belonged to that period when journalism generally and the profession of lighter literature meant that no matter of business or pleasure could be discussed without it being made, at any time of the day or night, 'an excuse for a glass' . . . They were not drunkards: they were not Teetotallers: they were simply Boozers.[50]

Yet all this conviviality could pay dividends. In an industry not yet beset by conglomerates and monopolies, individual and collective enterprise flourished to a quite extraordinary extent. A printer active in Fleet Street in the 1840s reckoned, 'At that time a literary speculator would start a new journal on a capital of a £10 note.' They might not survive very long but fecundity itself gave writers endless opportunity. We might take George Augustus Sala as an example, one of the most famous of London journalists in the second half of the century. His bottle nose – severely damaged in a dispute with a publican in which he came off by far the worse – proclaimed him 'King of Bohemia', even into the 1890s, when on his last dregs. During his long career from 1848 he wrote for or edited the *Man in the Moon*, *Chat*, *Conservative Magazine*, *Punchinello*, *Daily Telegraph*, *Sunday Times*, *Welcome Guest*, *Illustrated London News*, *Temple Bar*, *Home News*, *Sala's Journal*, *Entertainment Gazette*, *Household Words*, *All the Year Round*, *Banter*, *Belgravia*, *Notes and Queries*, *Bow Bells*, *Train*, *Critic*, *Leader*, *Illustrated Times*, *Everybody's Journal*, *Cornhill Magazine*, *Gentleman's Magazine*, *Graphic*, *London*, *Illustrated London Magazine*, *Literary Gazette*, *London Journal*, *Pan*, *Lloyd's Weekly News*, *Weldon's Register* and no doubt others.[51]

Some bohemian projects, dreamt up over bottles and cigars in one of a hundred London 'haunts', merged real worth with commercial success, like *Household Words*, the *Cornhill*, *Temple Bar*, or the *Strand Magazine*. But one was a work of unparalleled collective genius. That was *Punch*. Its origin was typical of its time, combining happenstance and opportunity well taken, lessons learned from past failures and a coming together of talent, experience and inspiration. Forty and fifty years on, men would argue fiercely over who should bear the palm for inventing what by then was a national institution. It is endearingly apt that so many details were hazy from the beginning. For *Punch* was a love-child of a particularly fruitful bohemian milieu.

It seems as though Ebenezer Landells, a prosperous master wood-engraver who looked to put his capital into newspaper projects, had long thought of establishing in London a version of the Paris *Charivari*, a comic paper that reflected seriously on society and its ills. Early in 1841 he talked over the idea with his friend Joseph Last, a printer of Crane Court, Fleet Street, with whom he was planning to embark on a social review to be called the 'The Cosmorama'. Joseph Last liked the new idea better. His solicitors were the firm headed by Joshua Mayhew, whose talented son Henry was well known to the printer. At this time Henry Mayhew was a dramatist, comic journalist and failed alchemist who for some years had launched a number of papers that would not float. From the start, though, Mayhew identified Landells's idea as one that could be made to work. And Landells as having the necessary 'tin' to do the job properly. 'Come to town,' he wrote to Mark Lemon, 'here's a man with a notion for a comic paper, and he has £2,000 to lose.' Mark Lemon, mine host at the Shakespeare's Head, Wych Street, new to writing but showing comic talent in verse and the drama, had both energy and contacts. The two men put together a slate of writers and artists who could develop Mayhew's notion of humour as a stick to beat jobbery and injustice. They were a remarkable team including Thackeray, Albert Smith, Gilbert à Beckett (who had edited something like a forerunner called *Figaro in London* till it closed in 1839), Douglas Jerrold, W. H. Wills (later to be Dickens's right-hand man in journal editing) and the young John Leech, a medical student and an outstanding draughtsman and caricaturist. Engraving was to be supervised by Landells, the magazine was to be printed by Last, and the agreement was drawn up by Mayhew, Johnston and Mayhew of Carey Street. Henry Mayhew seems to have lighted upon the title, and he and Lemon took editorial responsibility. The first weekly number, at 'the irresistibly comic charge of threepence!!' (a penny more than competitors), was published on Saturday 17 July 1841.[52]

Punch struggled, almost floundered. But in 1842 it was bought by the printers-cum-publishers Bradbury and Evans, of Whitefriars, City. Sole editorial control passed to Mark Lemon and three years later, for reasons that are unclear, Mayhew left the paper he had done so much to establish. On a sounder financial footing, under clearer leadership, *Punch* began to fulfil its potential. There were remarkable coups, like Hood's 'Song of the Shirt', which left the nation reeling. But to modern eyes it is less the quality of its writing than the superbly telling caricatures that give *Punch* its unique appeal. They reveal in startling clarity the spirit of the age. We know, too, that it was this way round for those who steered its course. Once the 'Big Cut' was decided upon, the rest of the number would fall into place. The subjects for this lead cartoon took up most editorial discussion at those famous dinners round the 'mahogany tree'. John Leech, Kenny Meadows, Phiz, Sir John Tenniel, George du Maurier, Harry Furniss and Phil May, among numerous others, provided fifty years' inspiration of blinding brilliance. *Punch* remains among the greatest of Victorian monuments to the printed word.[53]

It was very much a monument sited in London. *Punch* retained its subtitle, *Or the London Charivari*, throughout the century. And its whole character was as metropolitan as the cabby or bobby or skivvy it loved to portray. For London not only brought men and women together in the city of words and made of them more than the sum of their parts. It also gave them a subject for their imaginations. Maybe their main subject. London was an inexhaustible inspiration. And writers couldn't leave it alone.

It is not hard to see why writers caught up in this time and this place found London so fascinating. The inrush of people into the greatest city the globe had ever seen made it an experiment for an urbanising world. Modernisation, driven by steam and electricity, brought the forces of change into conflict with all those counterforces buried deep in the traditions of an old city. But the contrasts of London were not just between old and new. In London the nation's brightest and best confronted every vice and degradation under the sun. And – which was not the same – some of the richest, most glamorous and sophisticated people on earth passed in their carriages some of the poorest, owning nothing, knowing nothing, hoping nothing. Through all this the struggle for life, individual and collective, in its myriad shapes and twists, was won or lost or (more often) called a draw. To a writer, how could this not be an inspiration?

London brought the best out of nineteenth-century writers. Despite all those mealy-mouthed limitations imposed by religion and self-censorship and squeamishness about sex most of all, genius did shine through. In many instances it would not have done so without the raw materials of contemporary London to work upon.

It is difficult to exaggerate the extent to which London and Londoners dominated what found its way into print. What was true of *Punch* was almost as true of the *Illustrated London News*. The metropolitan provenance of a score of magazines declared itself on their mastheads, with London or a place within it reflected in the title. Even the stately *Times* maintained a local feel with its extensive coverage of London police court news. The great men of letters of the early part of the century – Charles Lamb, William Hazlitt, Leigh Hunt, Thomas de Quincey at his best – all looked at life with a cockney squint. Sensational journalism and social reportage threw light into London shadows most of all. Part-works in weekly numbers took the reader on an antiquarian walk through every nook of a city fast disappearing before one's eyes – Knight's *London* (six volumes, 1841–4), Thornbury and Walford's *Old and New London* (six volumes, 1873–8), Walford's *Greater London* (two volumes, 1880s). A ceaseless dribble of London guides and directories and 'handbooks' turned into a flood of plagiarism every time there was an exhibition or jubilee. Much was ephemeral, and intended to be. But London was also, as befitted its experimental character, the largest, and usually the first, subject of serious sociological inquiry: into labour conditions, technological innovation, prostitution, religious observance, poverty.

To a large extent this was true for the early part of the century, but it became indelibly so from the 1840s. The decade was a turning point. There were *Punch*, the *Illustrated London News*, Henry Mayhew's inquiries for the *Morning Chronicle*, the formation of the Statistical Society of London, George Dodd's explorations in London factories, Knight's *London*. Then there were the great London novels – *Martin Chuzzlewit*, *Dombey and Son*, *David Copperfield*, *Vanity Fair*, *Pendennis*; and the not-so-great – *Sybil* (Disraeli), *Godfrey Malvern* (Thomas Miller), *Mr Ledbury* and *Christopher Tadpole* (both Albert Smith), *St Giles and St James* (Douglas Jerrold) and *Alton Locke* (Charles Kingsley, 1850, borrowing greatly from Mayhew) – each with London and its hideous contrasts as an important theme. All this literary endeavour grew out of (and in part influenced) a decade of crisis for London, some of which we've glimpsed and some of which is yet to come. Irish immigration and central demolitions combining to drive living conditions sharply down; starvation and homelessness rife and unprovided for; cholera and revelations of graveyard and other sanitary horrors; financial crashes and desperate panics; Chartism and the fear of revolution at home and abroad. Some of this had been foreshadowed in the decade before. But it was the 1840s in which a crisis of confidence and conscience found a voice. It was – had to be – a London voice. In all its essential elements of social critique and imaginative expression taking London as its muse, it was a voice not stilled for the rest of the century.

Writers absorbed London in many ways – in reading rooms, theatre boxes, drawing rooms and at the dinner table. But most of all they absorbed it in the streets. And we might let a single moment encapsulate its inspirational power. Here is London, with its hideous revelations working on the conscience and imagination of its greatest literary genius of the age. It is Friday 7 January 1853 and Charles Dickens has walked over one of the poorest parts of Bermondsey. He has tried to find a spot for Angela Burdett-Coutts to make a philanthropic investment in the housing of the poor. Later that night he writes telling her what he has seen:

In one corner is a spot called Hickman's Folly (a Folly it is much to be regretted Hickman ever committed) which looks like the last hopeless climax of everything poor and filthy. There is a public house in it, with the odd sign of the Ship Aground, but it is wonderfully appropriate, for everything seems to have got aground there – never to be got off any more until the whole globe is stopped in its rolling and shivered. No more road than in an American swamp – odious sheds for horses, and donkeys, and vagrants, and rubbish, in front of the parlor windows – wooden houses like horrible old packing cases full of fever for a countless number of years. In a broken down gallery at the back of a row of these, there was a wan child looking over at a starved old white horse who was making a meal of oyster shells. The sun was going down and flaring out like an angry fire at the child – and the child, and I, and the pale horse, stared at one another in silence for some five minutes as if we were so many figures in a dismal allegory. I went round to look at the front of the house, but the windows were all broken and the door was shut up as tight as anything so dismantled could be. God knows when anybody will go in to the child, but I suppose it's looking over still – with a little wiry head of hair,

as pale as the horse, all sticking up on its head – and an old weazen face –
and two bony hands holding on to the rail of the gallery, with little fingers
like convulsed skewers.[54]

This *was* a dismal allegory. And it extended well beyond Hickman's
Folly.

PART FOUR

CULTURE

'"My Streets are my Ideas of Imagination . . .
My Houses are Thoughts; my Inhabitants Affections," . . .
So spoke London, immortal Guardian.'
William Blake, *Jerusalem*,
c. 1827

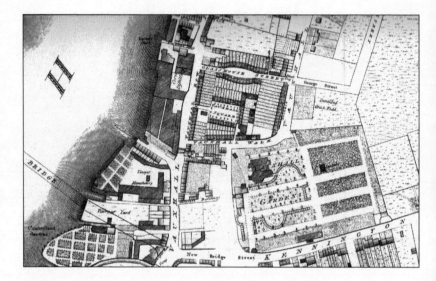

Vauxhall Gardens, 1813

VAUXHALL GARDENS:
SHARED PLEASURES

'The Madness of Crowds'

TUESDAY 27 November 1810 dawned too early for Mrs Tottenham at 54 Berners Street. Around five o'clock the first cry of 'Sweep!' startled that 'lady of property' and her servants. Within minutes it was joined by the shouts of 'crowds of sooty urchins and their masters', and soon by the rumble and roar of 'scores' of heavy wagons carrying chaldrons of coal from the wharves, blocking Berners Street, Castle Street, Charles Street and soon great Oxford Street itself in a bellowing turmoil of horses, iron-shod wheels, cracking shafts and whips and curses. Then came lighter carts bearing 'piano-fortes by dozens', 'gigs, dog-carts, and glass-coaches', spreading confusion into Tottenham Court Road, St Giles High Street and the turnings off. Among the crowds drawn on horse and foot by the excitement were several thousand who had been specially summoned to number 54: 'half-a-hundred pastry-cooks' bearing 2,500 raspberry tarts, bakers with 'massive wedding-cakes', tailors with samples, bootmakers with lasts, surgeons with saws sharpened for amputations, apothecaries with potions, lawyers with brief-paper, clergymen with prayer books, forty fishmongers with 'cod and lobsters', 'lovers to see sweethearts; ladies to find lovers', an undertaker with a coffin made to measure, 'six stout men bearing an organ', every trade and profession, all that exquisite subdivision of labour that the capital of the civilised world could muster. Then there were those most specially summoned of all: the Lord Mayor in his coach, greeted by the 'laughing mob' and the outraged tradespeople, brought there supposedly to release some press-ganged seamen at Mrs Tottenham's behest; the Chairman of the East India Company and the Governor of the Bank of England, led to believe they would be enlightened about frauds that were troubling them; even royalty itself, the Duke of Gloucester anxious to hear the deathbed secrets of a palace attendant. All day the hubbub seethed and boiled, freshly stoked at five in the afternoon by a crowd of 'servants of every description, wanting places' with Mrs Tottenham. The day-long mayhem 'choked up the great avenues of London, and found employment for half the police of the metropolis'.

Such was 'the Great Berners Street Hoax'. It was the brainchild of 22-two-year-old Theodore Hook, a brilliant but flighty Grub Street writer who comprehended his London – and his Londoners – with shrewd affection. The hoax, which took two confederates, some 4,000 letters, a vantage point rented in a house across the road and weeks to plan, seems to have arisen less from spite than from whimsy, in Hook's quixotic desire to make an anonymous genteel house the most talked-about address in town – for nine days or so at least.[1]

Hook's practical joke was a farce specially crafted for the grand open-air theatre that was London's streets. We have seen something of the horror of nineteenth-century London and there is more to come. But we need to counterbalance starvation and ignorance and violence and filth with the boundless fun and ready laughter to be had in London's streets and parks, and the ecstasy derived from a whole world of entertainment in shows and exhibitions and on the stage. In some degree the horror and the ecstasy were inseparable bedfellows. Extremes of deprivation and discomfort and pain provoked extremes of anticipation and enthusiasm and pleasure. Nothing less than stupefaction through drink or transcendental weightless joy could render forgettable the hopeless degradation facing many in London throughout the century.

Pleasure began in the streets. Apart from Berners Street, we have glimpsed some of it already. The popular taunts to raise a laugh, the jeering boys and girls tormenting an ill-favoured street musician, the acrobats and entertainers risking their necks to turn a penny, the riot of Bartlemy. And as at Bartlemy, tradition mingled with happenstance. Out of tradition came children's street games, their rhymes and rules handed down from one urchin generation to another, stamping an invisible history on London's pavements: the writer Norman Douglas could name almost a thousand of them at the century's end. So too the chimney sweeps' Jack-in-the-Green and parades on May Day, pale shabby things in central London by 1820, and Guy Fawkes' Night.[2]

Out of happenstance came the unpredictable. An arrest, an assault, a drunk, a street fight could all attract a crowd, where disgust and mirth might swing one way or another. A barrel organ or blind fiddler would get people dancing in the streets. In Lambeth in the 1890s Somerset Maugham noted girls waltzing to an organ, joined by men 'taking hold of one another in the most approved fashion . . . with all the gravity of judges'; and a 'skirt dance' involving 'difficult steps and motions' executed as well as 'in a trained ballet'.[3] A street accident, when the consequences weren't severe, could be a joy. As with Charles Dickens and his family en route in two cabs to London Bridge and the Margate steamer in August 1865. After heavy rain the horse pulling his children and luggage stumbled on the greasy paving and broke the shafts. The cab 'was drawn to the wharf (about a mile) by a stout man, amid much frightful howlings and derisive yellings on the part of an infuriated populace, as I never heard before'. Dickens's cab followed in procession, 'thereby securing to me a liberal share of the popular curiosity and congratulation . . . [4]

Some fun was less innocent. Torturing animals was a popular pastime among the rougher sections of the London poor throughout the century, but far more so at the beginning than at the end. Bear- and bull-baiting and cockfighting were only outlawed by the Metropolitan Police Act 1839 and by then were very much minority pursuits. Baiting bulls and bears with dogs seems largely to have been confined to Tothill Fields, playground of the old Westminster rookery, and that before 1820, after which the district became increasingly built over. But 'bullock-hunting' was a favourite pastime of Bethnal Green on Sundays and Mondays into the early 1820s, and there are echoes of it into the 1830s. Animals were abstracted from a Smithfield drove and maddened by putting peas in their ears or forcing 'sticks pointed with iron' up their backsides. The beasts were then let loose in a crowded high road and chased by a cheering crowd of men and boys a thousand or two strong. Dog fights, organised for betting purposes, were common among 'flash' men, thieves and costermongers in the fields and waste lands on the shifting edge of London up to 1839. These were often fights to the death. Gratuitous cruelty to cats and dogs by boys and to horses, donkeys and cattle by men was a fact of rough London life until laws were tightened in the twentieth century. At the 'Smithfield races' every

Friday tormented nags were whipped through their paces for the delight of an admiring audience. Mayhew noted tails and ears cropped, owners' initials in 'huge letters burnt into' hind quarters, and one blind horse with 'red empty eye-holes' and head pointed to the sky which 'sent out showers of sparks from its hoofs as it spluttered over the stones, at each blow it received'. When the cattle market moved to Caledonian Road, men and boys followed it for the pleasure of goading with sticks and punches old horses at the costers' sales. And at Barnet Fair in September 1865 Joseph Parkinson watched four or five 'stalwart fellows' torture 'a wretched little pony' with kicks and punches, swinging it in the air by tail or leg and leaving it for dead.[5]

On the other hand it was horses that provided the excuse for one of London's great annual days out. Derby Day, 'that great English festival, at which all London takes a holiday upon Epsom Downs', had been celebrated in Whitsun week since 1780. Even in the 1890s the horse-drawn traffic through Tooting made it the most memorable day of the year for locals. The wagonettes and donkey-carts, victorias and landaus, dog-carts and hansom cabs, brakes and carriers' vans, filled with merry homecomers – 'no ladies' but men and women of every other class and none – playing banjos and concertinas, blowing ticklers and striking coloured matches, were assailed from parapets and top windows by pea-shooters and water-squirts. All 'the houses on the road seem to be turned inside out' as their occupiers enjoyed the fun.[6]

Derby Day was a people's pageant. But then any pageantry in London's streets was turned to popular account. Spectacle drew crowds hungry for novelty, sensation and colour. Any event – the University Boat Race in April, the Lord Mayor's Show in November – was an excuse for shoving and squeezing and poking, shouting and pointing and joking at someone else's expense. Almost every crowd was an unpredictable combination of fun and fear. The unlikeliest event could witness the combination in action. We can take one among scores. The Queen and two princesses opened the new Royal Courts of Justice in the Strand on 4 December 1882. When the doors were opened after the ceremony to let the dignitaries out the enormous crowd of curious onlookers outside rushed in. Men, women and children were swept up in the maelstrom and carried powerless in and out of the great hall. The rule of law was no use here as people fainted and strong men feared for their lives. 'Nothing,' noted Justin McCarthy, who was at the ceremony with his daughter, 'seems to me more pathetic and pitiful in its way than the half-crazy eagerness of the poorer class of Londoners to see any manner of sight. They will fight, struggle, rush, risk their lives, to see anything.'[7]

The greatest sights of all flowed out of the streets and into the parks. Only their wide green spaces could provide for London's largest crowds or for events lasting more than a day. We might glance at two moments, from opposite ends of the century, as revealing how the fun and fury of London crowds could at once celebrate and subvert these public occasions.

The earlier was the gigantic festival for that short-lived peace which drew every crowned head and gilded ambassador to London in the summer of 1814. Two months of 'almost constant succession of grandeur and festivity' climaxed in a civic jubilee commemorating both peace and 100 years of the House of Hanover in England. Hyde Park, Green Park and St James's Park were fitted out as pleasure gardens with Chinese bridge and pagoda, a mock naval battle on the Serpentine, a balloon ascent, fireworks, a wooden castle called the Temple of Concord, and a small town of booths and shows and makeshift inns, including Richardson's theatre and Polito's beasts. It was as if Bartlemy had come early to the Regent's front lawn. On Monday 1 August the 'grand national jubilee' opened – and should indeed have closed. The crowds were immense. The pagoda burned down and 'one or two lives' were lost in the fire or in the crush to witness it. Apart from that blemish the crowd was noted for its good behaviour.

But it was all too much of a good thing. The fair refused to move on. It stayed for a week or more until forced off by magistrates and soldiers after complaints of 'shocking acts of immorality committed in some of the booths or taverns'. The authorities delayed in dismantling the Temple of Concord, fencing it off from an inquisitive multitude. On 12 August a rumour swept London that a second instalment of fireworks had been arranged for the popular delight. That night the parks filled with people and with eager anticipation. When nothing happened the fence was pulled down and burned in lieu of a bonfire and sentry boxes and lop-wood thrown on the flames. These were so high that Londoners-at-home thought St James's Palace was ablaze. The Temple of Concord would have gone the same way had it not been protected by cavalry, who cleared the parks three times before 'the rabble' melted away.[8]

By the end of the century the London crowd was tamer – had been tamed, and tamed itself. Queen Victoria's jubilee celebrations of 1887 (Golden) and 1897 (Diamond) had more of fun in them than fear. The processional streets were decked in flowers and flags and the illuminations were almost as startling to contemporaries as the Regent's own. But on both occasions there were worries over the mood of the vast numbers who thronged the routes. And after the children's fête in Hyde Park on 22 June 1887, where up to 30,000 London schoolchildren were fed and entertained and visited by the Queen, 'the London crowd broke into the enclosure and set fire to the marquees'.[9]

Hyde Park, of course, was 'The Park'. For the whole of the century it was the ostentatious parade-ground of the London rich, more flamboyant at the beginning than at the end because wealth had learned to reign in display in the interim. Even so, the continuities were more noticeable than the contrasts. Captain Rees Gronow of the Foot Guards, sickeningly handsome and the finest pistol shot of his day, looked back from the 1860s on the park he had known in his virile youth around 1815:

The company which then congregated daily about five was composed of dandies and women in the best society; the men mounted on such horses as England alone could then produce. The dandy's dress consisted of a blue coat with brass buttons, leather breeches, and top boots; and it was the fashion to wear a deep, stiff white cravat, which prevented you from seeing your boots while standing . . . Many of the ladies used to drive into the park in a carriage called a *vis-à-vis*, which held only two persons. The hammer-cloth, rich in heraldic designs, the powdered footmen in smart liveries, and a coachman who assumed all the gaiety and appearance of a wigged archbishop, were indispensable.[10]

Gronow thought that since then 'democracy [had] invaded the parks', bringing with it 'a "Brummagem society", with shabby-genteel carriages and servants'. In those days 'the lower or middle classes of London' would not have intruded on 'regions which, with a sort of tacit understanding, were then given up exclusively to persons of rank and fashion'.

It seems true enough that, with the growth of the town and the increase of population on the western side, Hyde Park had become 'emphatically the Park of the People' by 1850. The Great Exhibition a year later, a brief eruption of open class war with the park as battleground in 1855, the sensational parades of courtesans on Sundays in the 1860s, all in their way contributed to the sense that Hyde Park now belonged to every rank of Londoner and not just the rich. In 1864 Charles Knight thought it 'wholly given up to vulgar pedestrians – fashion shuns it'. By the 1880s 'the right people' were said to have forsaken Rotten Row, confining themselves to an ever smaller corner near Stanhope Gate. Even so, during the London season of May to July the self-confident display of wealth in the park remained a brilliant panorama. 'There can be no more wonderful sight anywhere,' the American newspaperman R. D. Blumenfeld confided to his diary in June 1887. 'Certainly there is no place on this earth where there can be seen at one time so many gorgeous equipages, such beautiful horses, and such a display of elegance.' George R. Sims thought this splendour only dimmed with the age of the motor car in the century to come.[11]

By 1900 London's parks had grown as the city moved out. Victoria Park and Regent's Park – the latter with its famous zoo, opened in 1828 and by the end of the century entertaining over half a million visitors a year – were rivals to the great central green spaces. They were home to all sorts of pleasures, more and more of them as the century grew older. By the 1890s there were Saturday and Sunday band concerts, a Babel's tower of spouters, cyclists' picnics and races, football and cricket, early-morning bathing at the Serpentine (men and boys, naked till the 1860s at least, a million a year of them by 1890) and skating on any standing water in winter. In January 1867, when the ice broke on Regent's Park lake, 200 were plunged into the water and forty died, mostly local young men 'apparently in the middle class of life'.[12]

Open-air pleasures did not have to be restricted to those close to home. By the end of the century more and more Londoners were taking advantage of day excursions, an 'enormous business', according to Charles Booth. This was no new phenomenon. Carriers' spring vans were translated on Sundays into the 'landau of the working classes' as early as the 1830s. Artisan trippers from Clerkenwell and Soho and Bethnal Green made their way to Hampton Court and High Beech (Epping Forest) with beer and a fiddler to keep them company. These brake outings remained hugely popular in the 1890s. By then they were greatly extended by the reach of the railways to Windsor, Brighton and Margate. The Maidenhead platform at Paddington Station was said to be packed from eight till noon by a crowd 5,000 strong every summer Saturday and Sunday: 'All of them, men and women, in white, and all wearing "boaters" . . . and every woman carrying a coloured sunshade.' What a sight it must have been.[13]

The river also proved a constant pleasure companion across the century. Steamboats held their own with the railways till the late 1870s at least. They steamed down to Gravesend and Margate and up to Hampton Court and Richmond on Sundays. In 1832 the Margate Steam-Boat Company's three steamers carried 100,000 passengers a year from St Katharine's Dock. The Richmond boats carried 'Very respectable persons . . . very few mechanics.' Rowing and punting had always been popular upstream pursuits: George Eliot's Daniel Deronda kept a boat at Putney and rowed to Richmond for exercise and pleasure in the 1870s, for example. And Henley's famous July regatta, begun in 1839, was one great feature of the London season.[14]

But one tragedy draped a pall over the Thames. On the evening of Tuesday 3 September 1878, the paddle steamer *Princess Alice* was returning to London Bridge from a day excursion to Sheerness. At the Rosherville pleasure gardens, Gravesend, it picked up most of the passengers it had dropped off earlier in the day. In all, including just twenty-three crew, there were thought to be 'about 800' persons on board, mainly women and children. The weather was clear and darkness had not yet set in. At 7.40 p.m., just off Beckton gas works at Tripcock Point, she was struck by the much larger Newcastle-bound steam collier *Bywell Castle* and cut in two. She sank almost immediately. The three boats she managed to launch saved fewer than forty souls. Passengers '"floated round like bees, making the water almost black with their heads and hats and clothes"'. Some 544 bodies were pulled from the water. It's likely that many more, at least another sixty, were lost but never found. The *Princess Alice* disaster remains the worst death toll in a single accident in modern British history. Responsibility seemed to lie with the captain of the *Princess Alice*, who clung to a traditional course against the 1872-determined rule of the river about passing an oncoming vessel on the port side. Within six years her owners, the London Steam Boat Company, were bankrupt. Their successors were in difficulties by 1886, when fourteen Thames steamers went to the breakers. There seems little doubt that the tragedy had some impact – in combination with railway and omnibus competition – in blighting the tidal Thames as a pleasure-ground. Despite some fresh life in the 1890s, when memories may have dimmed, the trade never recovered its mid-Victorian buoyancy.[15]

By that time, too, the lights of some other traditional London pleasure-grounds had guttered. Or gone out altogether.

'The Heptaplasiesoptron'

This splendid exhibition is fitted up with ornamental draperies and presents a fountain of real water illuminated, revolving pillars, palm trees, serpents, foliage, and variegated lamps; and the mirrors are so placed as to reflect each object seven times. This novelty appeared to excite universal admiration, inspiring the company with ideas of refreshing coolness. The bubbling of water, the waving of the foliage, and the seven times reflected effulgence of the lamps, gave the whole an appearance of enchantment, which sets all description at defiance.[16]

The Heptaplasiesoptron was one of the main attractions of Vauxhall Gardens in the 1822 season. The gardens had a long history. As a place of public entertainment they dated back at least to the early 1660s. At the beginning of the nineteenth century they were 'the most celebrated public gardens in Europe'. The Regent had his own 'Prince's Pavillion' facing the splendid orchestra. Here fifty of London's best musicians, reinforced by an organ, played open-air concerts from mid-May to early September, moving into a rotunda and giant saloon when the weather was poor. There was dancing. There was eating – Vauxhall ham, 'shaved' so thin from the bone it 'might answer the purpose of a *sky-light*!' There was drinking – brandy-and-water and 'Vauxhall punch'. There was a theatre. There were lamplit walks and cosy nooks. There were fireworks and balloon ascents and high-wire artistes like Madame Saqui, who descended a sixty-foot tower in a blaze of Roman candles and rockets. And from 1822 there were Indian jugglers, puppet shows, comic songs, mock battles with 1,000 warriors, a Venetian pageant, equestrian shows and operetta – the full cornucopia of nineteenth-century London 'variety'.[17]

Vauxhall Gardens were very much a middle-class pleasure-ground. Fashion required full evening dress even in the 1850s – white trousers and waistcoat and black tailcoat. Vauxhall was smart enough for Thackeray to set an amusing chapter of *Pendennis* there in 1850 and people it with lower aristocrats, gentlemen and gents. The admission charge of 3s 6d, 4s from 1826, deterred the artisan and impecunious-clerk class and necessarily all below. But from the 1820s Vauxhall's push for sensation and spectacle attracted to it an increasingly louche wing of London's diverse middle classes. After a change of management at the gardens in 1841, their fortunes were revived with dubious masquerades or masked balls from eleven at night to five or six in the morning. A puritan backlash threatened Vauxhall's dancing and liquor licences. Barely profitable for many years, overtaken in the 1850s as a fashionable night out by Cremorne Gardens, Chelsea, Vauxhall faded away. It closed on Monday 25 July 1859. Illuminated letters spelled out 'Farewell For Ever': 15,000 turned up to bear witness.[18]

Vauxhall Gardens, as the competition from Cremorne shows, were not unique, though for the first twenty years of the century they were uniquely smart. There had been Ranelagh, at Chelsea, which only just survived the opening years of the century; there were the Surrey Zoological Gardens, laid out by the menagerie-keeper Edward Cross in 1831–2 and lasting till 1877; and North Woolwich Gardens and Rosherville further down the river. Then there were numerous smaller plebeian places largely grown up from country or suburban inns, sometimes connected with a spring or spa. Indeed the pub was a far more fertile progenitor of the London pleasure-ground than the country house from which Vauxhall and Ranelagh had sprung. They make a long list: the Eagle Tavern and Gardens (City Road, Hoxton), the Adam and Eve (Tottenham Court Road), Mermaid Gardens (Hackney Wick), Merlin's Cave Gardens (Finsbury), Jack Straw's Castle (Hampstead Heath), Bowling Green House (Euston), the Yorkshire Stingo (Marylebone), the Red House ('The Red'us', Battersea Fields), Highbury Barn (Islington), Bell Tavern (Kilburn), and numerous others all functioned at some time during the century as tea gardens and refreshment houses. All offered entertainments of one sort or another – in the gardens or in a long room attached to the pub.

One by one most fell victim to London's growth, covered by brick and slate as development offered better returns than beer and sandwiches, and as rival attractions offered greater novelty, luxury and sophistication. Yet despite the submergence of the old tea gardens beneath modern London, the format of country tavern not too far from town remained popular for the artisan and clerk class throughout the century. A London guide of 1843 lists twenty-two 'principal' tea gardens. And as London pushed out, some new country pubs emerged to take the place of those overwhelmed. Notable among them was the Old Welsh Harp at Hendon on the Brent Reservoir of the Regent's Canal. Rescued from near ruin by an enterprising landlord called Warner around 1856, by 1870 there was 'nothing quite like it in the neighbourhood of London, or in the world'. Famous for its formal gardens and statues, its dancing, its angling, pigeon-shooting and steam barge, visited by the Prince of Wales, it was the great 'suburban dining-room' of plebeian north London, home to a hundred annual trade dinners of shopkeepers from Paddington to Whitechapel. 'From noon onwards on any gala day the road [to it] is like a fair', and the Midland Railway was persuaded to plant a station nearby called Welsh Harp. In the old inn itself was 'a varied and horrifying' exhibition of 'stuffed fish'.[19]

The London exhibition had a history even longer than Vauxhall Gardens. Exhibitions were designed for the pockets and tastes of every class. *The Stranger's Guide through London* for 1808 lists art galleries and collections (the biggest at the Royal Academy, then in Somerset House, but most of them in private hands); museums (the British Museum at Montague House, Bloomsbury, then with restricted access, about 12,000 visitors a year); panoramas ('Mountains of the World' at King Street, St James's, and elsewhere views of Paris and Dublin and Weymouth, and Boulogne and St Petersburg); or Maillardet's Automatical Exhibition, Du Bourg's of cork models and a few others. But away from the West End and beneath the *Guide*'s notice lay a back-street industry of waxworks (common in Fleet Street and the Strand, where Madame Tussaud began her illustrious British career in 1802), of freak and monster exhibitions, of juggling and conjuring, of animal shows and menageries (especially at Exeter 'Change, the Strand, where the celebrated Edward Cross was based in the 1820s). Here the link with fairs – and the theatre of London's streets – was complete. For many of the cheapest penny-entry places were run by showmen over-wintering in London; or showed attractions 'let out' by showmen for the winter. That extraordinary entrepreneur of the circus 'Lord' George Sanger, when just twenty and having worked the fairs with his brothers and father (a conjuror), took an empty warehouse in Bethnal Green in 1847. He showed living tableaux and performing birds and mice, and worked conjuring tricks with secret apparatus made for him by a Petticoat Lane tinsmith.[20]

Places like Sanger's flared up and died away as locals tired of familiarity and found novelty elsewhere; and as showmen sought richer pickings on the fairs circuit. But one place in London more than any other took on the semi-permanent aspect of an indoor fair for London's middle classes from the late eighteenth century until the 1860s. That was Leicester Square. It was home to museums, including John Hunter's anatomical collection, from 1771. Miss Linwood's gallery of needlework pictures occupied Savile House from 1806 to 1846. From then till 1865 (when it burned down) Savile House was home to a motley of *poses plastique*, 'Industrious Fleas', giants and giant-esses, arms and armour, a bearded lady, and a 'black opera bouffe, by real negroes direct from the cotton fields of America' (1851). Most of all, Leicester Square was the birthplace of the panorama. Robert Burford's rotunda at the north-east corner of the square opened in 1794, showing Robert Barker's magnificent landscapes and cityscapes. His giant canvases were wrapped round the walls and spectators climbed a central staircase to the top of the building. The rotunda displayed new sensations every year until 1861. It closed in 1863 and was demolished a few years later. Elsewhere in the square, even the scruffy gardens were occupied for ten years from 1851 by James Wyld's Great Globe, sixty feet high in the dome of a building that almost filled the open space. Visitors walked through the world in a series of galleries and were regaled by lecturers, panoramas and ethno-graphic exhibitions that changed each year.[21]

Leicester Square's central importance in London's shared pleasures made it – remarkable though it now seems – the natural choice of loca-tion for the proposed Great Exhibition of the Works of Industry of All Nations of 1851. It was selected but finally rejected as too small and too detrimental to local property. Hyde Park, with all its associations with monarchy and ceremony at the west end of the town, was chosen instead.[22]

Of all the London ventures of this tempestuous and enterprising century, the Great Exhibition was the most stunning: first, for the grandeur of its conception, celebrating for all classes a new world of progress; second, for the revolutionary 'monstrous greenhouse' in which it was placed; and third, for the speed with which the conception was brought to triumphant reality.

The idea originated in early 1848 with Henry Cole, a civil servant, Christ's Hospital scholar, one-time law clerk and member of the Society of Arts. Cole had been involved in local art and industry exhibitions and suggested to Prince Albert, the society's president, a national exhi-bition on a grand scale. Albert was at first lukewarm but experience of something similar in Paris in 1849 made him a convert. The scheme won royal consent in January 1850. Some 250 architects' designs were considered by the royal commission in charge of the project and for a time confusion and doubt held sway. At Albert's urging, Joseph Paxton's plan for a great conservatory, modelled on one he had made earlier for the Duke of Devonshire at Chatsworth, startled the commission into a decision. Begun at the end of September 1850, it was miraculously completed by the following January. Installing 100,000 exhibits from all over the world, fitting out two floors in scores of exhibition halls and courts, occupied just a further three months. The Great Exhibition opened on May Day 1851.[23]

The preparations had been attended by great fears – fear of foreigners, especially French and other socialists, fear the park would be destroyed, fear Paxton's giant structure would collapse. 'But the fear of the working classes caused the most anxiety.' Wellington moved an additional 10,000 troops into London or near it. The Metropolitan Police enlarged its strength by 1,000 constables. A Working Classes Central Committee was formed to win over working men and women to the idea of the exhibition. Dickens, Thackeray, Lord Ashley (Shaftesbury), Joshua Field of Maudslay and Field engineers, Francis Place, John Stuart Mill, Charles Knight, William Lovett the Chartist and other prominent Londoners were members. In the event, the nightmare proved groundless. The Great Exhibition and its Crystal Palace – the happy title was suggested by Douglas Jerrold in *Punch* – was immensely, unprecedentedly popular among all classes. Over 6,170,000 visitors went through the turnstiles. On each of the last few days there were over 100,000, and on the cheapest (shilling) days the workers of London and England came in droves. That they came quietly staggered opinion. 'No circumstance . . . is more remarkable than the conduct of the people.' Even the Queen and Prince Albert visited on shilling days. No previous event in the nineteenth century had brought all sorts and conditions of Londoners together in such numbers or so harmoniously as at Hyde Park from 1 May to 11 October 1851. And this time nothing burned down.[24]

International exhibitions on a smaller scale would be a continuing feature of London pleasure-making until 1874. But the true legacy of 1851 worked itself out in a different direction. The unparalleled richness and variety of the Great Exhibition's exhibits reinforced the commercial attractions of an omnium-gatherum of many things in one space. These things required huge joint-stock investment. And because Hyde Park could not be available for ever, entrepreneurs were forced to turn to cheaper suburban sites to realise their projects. London pleasure gardens – and London variety – would go on. But now they would do so in ways influenced by the events of that astonishing summer.[25]

The Crystal Palace was moved from Hyde Park, sold to a private company, enlarged by half again and re-erected at Sydenham in 1854. The new owners reverted at the Sydenham site to the old pleasure-gardens formula of balancing outdoor attractions with indoor. But the Crystal Palace Company set its sights high. This was to be no reborn Vauxhall. Crystal Palace adopted a superior tone. It offered art, education and beauty to middle-class visitors who would reach it from London on excursion trains to the palace's two railway stations (the second opened in 1865). It would be an 'illustrated encyclopaedia', and an aural one too, with giant classical concerts in the Great Transept. These were a special passion of the company secretary, the great musical lexicographer George Grove. From 1857 Crystal Palace was home to a triennial Handel festival, where some 4,000 performers sang and played to an audience of 16,000. Handel was ruined. But in the first ten years the palace clocked up 15.3 million visitors.

Even by then something of the high tone had begun to slip. London variety, the old pleasure-ground fair-bill, had asserted itself as the only sure way to secure ticket sales among a wide class of customers. The first balloon ascent was 1859. The incomparable Blondin first strode the high-wire there in 1861. Wombwell's Menagerie brought the circus from 1864. Brock's famous fireworks displays began in 1865, and fêtes and 'Fancy Fairs' that same year. Cat, dog, bird and fashion shows followed from 1871. In 1881 a panorama opened in the grounds and by that time Vauxhall had indeed been born again in Sydenham. When the Crystal Palace first opened Saturday entry cost 5s and shilling days were Mondays to Thursdays, Mondays especially popular among workers, who still followed 'Saint Monday' as a traditional extension to the Sunday holiday. By the mid-1870s, all weekdays cost a shilling, while Saturdays (with their popular promenade concerts) now cost just 2s 6d. By the late 1880s the palace was a thoroughly (though not exclusively) proletarian pleasure-ground. George Gissing visited it on Easter Monday 1888 and 'brought back a lot of good notes'. It seems to have confirmed his view of the palace as a workers' saturnalia. A year later he set the wedding-day celebration of a ghastly Clerkenwell slum couple there on August Bank Holiday Monday. The '"Paliss"' regales Bob Hewett and Pennyloaf Candy with swing-boats and merry-go-rounds, coconut shies and test-your-strength machines, with booze and tea and cake. In the Shilling Tea-Room 'there reigned a spirit of imbecile joviality'. In the transept, music dissolves the sentimental Pennyloaf. And at night the fireworks distract her from jealousy as Bob dances with another woman. 'Up shoot the rockets, and all the reeking multitude utters a huge "Oh" of idiot admiration.' Well, at least Gissing enjoyed himself.[26]

Sydenham spawned a number of imitators which, like the Crystal Palace Company itself, found difficulty in attracting sufficient revenue to recoup their enormous outlay. The Agricultural Hall (the Aggie) was opened at Islington Green in 1862. Filling three acres, it was an urban pleasure-ground varying dog and horse and cattle shows with circuses; walking, running and wrestling matches; exhibitions and the Royal Tournament. Like Crystal Palace, it had its own extensive refreshment rooms. Alexandra Palace (Ally Pally) was opened between Muswell Hill and Wood Green in 1873 and reopened in 1875 after a disastrous fire. Like its Sydenham predecessor, there were huge grounds and gardens for strolling and play, and it had its own race course. Olympia opened as the National Agricultural Hall in 1884 but changed its name and purpose in 1886. It was famous for its circuses and (from 1890) the Hungarian-born impresario Imre Kiralfy's spectaculars. They presented variety in three-dimensional panoramas, including 1,000 performers in 'Venice in London' (just like Vauxhall seventy years before), ballets and choruses and plenty to eat and drink. A few hundred yards to the south-east, Earl's Court opened with Buffalo Bill in 1887, and was from 1893 under Kiralfy's inspired direction. It had a theatre, restaurant, dancing and a 'Great Wheel' along the lines of Chicago's: it stuck one night in May 1896 and sixty passengers received £5 each for their elevating experience. Also in 1887 the People's Palace, more educational in tone, brought non-vulgar pleasures to the Mile End Road.[27]

Yet the era of mass entertainment, provided by joint-stock capitalists and brilliant impresarios on a few great sites, never quite annihilated a traditional London taste for small-scale fairground freakery and jiggery-pokery. Into the late 1880s the main streets of working-class London retained their over-wintering showground feel. Blackfriars Road around 1885 was 'dotted with booths, the sort of booths one finds at a fair – Fattest Women in the World, Women with Two Heads, Pig-faced Women and so on'. Up to 1884, when it burned down, the East London Aquarium in Shoreditch held a menagerie and waxworks, including a collection of hangman's implements. And in November that same year Frederick Treves, renowned surgeon at the London Hospital, entered a shop in the Whitechapel Road where cruelly deformed Joseph Merrick, the Elephant Man, was exposed for view for 2d.

> The showman pulled back the curtain and revealed a bent figure crouching on a stool and covered by a brown blanket. In front of it, on a tripod, was a large brick heated by a Bunsen burner. Over this the creature was huddled to warm itself . . . The showman – speaking as if to a dog – called out harshly: "Stand up!"²⁸

The new London County Council seems to have taken an unforgiving line with places like these soon after inheriting London government in 1889. But some doubtless struggled on into the 1890s, merging with the unlicensed 'penny-gaff' or back-room music hall. The novelist Margaret Harkness ('John Law') recorded a 'half-naked youth, whose arm was withered from the shoulder to the wrist', and a man without arms shaving himself and playing the violin with his toes while a girl turned an organ.²⁹ But with this we have stepped over that fine, sometimes imperceptible line between the exhibition and the stage. And the stage was one of the greatest pleasures that London had to offer.

'The O.P. Dance'

On 18 September 1809 the new Covent Garden Theatre Royal opened on the site of the old building that had burned down a year before, killing about twenty-six bystanders and firemen. But the new theatre was not entirely along the lines of the old. Robert Smirke's grand design had been adulterated by 'a meanness in the project'. To maximise profits on an always risky venture, luxurious boxes and a grand private saloon had been constructed at the expense of the plebeian galleries; the galleries themselves were cramped and 'suffocating', with poor views, and each of the lower boxes squeezed in three more playgoers than previously. On top of all this, prices were raised by a shilling in the boxes and sixpence in the pit. Everything seemed calculated to favour the rich, to the detriment of the middling class of theatregoer. The new arrangements were advertised in advance but few understood the depth of public indignation until that first night the theatre opened – with a full bill of *Macbeth* and *The Quaker*, a musical farce.

Neither got a hearing. All was stifled from the pit and galleries by hissing, 'barking, shouting, groaning, cat calls, cries of off! off! old prices' and more. As night followed night the row became more organised and impenetrable. Cockneys and country folk came just to witness this extraordinary theatre-turned-inside-out, where the audience was the only performer who mattered. Protesters with O. P. (old price) stickers in their hats and on their clothes came armed with placards and sticks to beat time to 'the O. P. Dance'. They stood with their backs to the stage shouting 'O. P.!' as loud as they could, stamping or banging the floor in 'strict time and unison', 'one of the most whimsically tantalizing banters or torments that could be conceived'. Orchestral forces were augmented with 'coachmen's horns and trumpets, dustmen's bells, and watchmen's rattles'. For some sixty nights not a word was heard from the stage, the show carrying on in dumb-play or the theatre left dark.

A ferocious climax was reached on 31 October, when Charles Kemble, the theatre's actor-manager, unwisely commissioned a magistrate, constables and prize fighters – prominent among them 'a Jew, nick-named Dutch Sam' – to quell the protesters with the Riot Act, staves and fists. The O. P. rioters, with strength of numbers, gave better than they got and Kemble's strategy was abandoned amid fury and recrimination in the courts. Eventually all demands were met. The pit was restored to the old prices and the private boxes and gilded saloon would be thrown open to the public from the following season. The theatre was permitted to play from 15 December, protesters raising a banner announcing 'We Are Satisfied'. Stupidly, though, Kemble went back on his word and the O. P. row revived briefly the following autumn. A further capitulation followed and finally on 24 September 1810 'the theatre was opened upon the old principle, amidst the applause of an immensely crowded audience'.[30]

Passion for the stage was one of the great facts of London life in the nineteenth century. In the absence of a flourishing provincial theatre it was a uniquely metropolitan passion too. Limelight dazzled Londoners. Theatre-going was as common among certain middle-class families (three or four times a week for the Hain Friswells' in the 1860s) as among boy thieves: 'the largest sum I ever got was £3 7s 6d out of a woman's pocket; I spent it foolishly in sweets, and going to the play . . .' Sensation surrounded the theatre on and off the stage. Frantic scenes attended the appearance at Covent Garden in December 1804 of an actor prodigy, 'scarcely thirteen', known as 'Master Betty' (his surname, lest hares are set running) or '"the young Roscius"'. Hours before admission, 'The multitude stretched out in thick close wedged, impenetrable columns' and soldiers had to clear the crush. Once inside, people dropped from the front boxes into the pit 'by twenties and thirties at a time'. A generation later and the Italian Opera House, Haymarket, was brought to a standstill in April 1840 by a 'riot' in favour of the baritone Tamburini, whom the management refused to engage.[31]

Playgoers at proletarian houses could be just as enthusiastic. Gory melodrama – 'transpontine drama' it was called, as appealing especially to south London tastes – pulled in large crowds to the gallery of the Coburg, later the Victoria (the Vic), in the New Cut. Mayhew noted the 'most frightful rush' as the gallery pay-box opened on any popular night in the 1850s. Around 1870 the Vic still had its own way of enjoying itself:

Five minutes after the doors are opened, it is crammed from the top row of the gallery to the extreme confines of the pit, with a restless, surging, struggling, shouting mob, and the first impression of the visitor is that the evening will be one of unbroken tumult. Boys are rolling bodily over the heads and shoulders of the occupants of the gallery . . . ragged trousers, surmounted by hobnailed boots, wave for a moment in the air, and are then lost in a general mass of heads and limbs, belonging apparently to no one in particular. Fights – some good-tempered, some fierce – are going on in a dozen places at once; orange-peel, oranges, hats, caps, and in one instance boots, are being playfully hurled from one part of the house to the other, and all this is accompanied by a running fire of yells and shrieks, and what would be chaff were it heard by anyone but the utterer. It is an open question whether the boy-rolling is prompted by enmity or friendship . . . Once set in motion, there is no help either for the person rolled or the persons rolled over; and it was one of the most curious experiences of the night, that whenever there was a pause in the proceedings, or a lack of interest on the stage, then might be seen a powerless, struggling form passing rapidly over head after head, until within dangerous proximity to the low railings skirting the gallery in front.[32]

Nor did this enthusiasm abate with time. Nearly twenty years on in 1888 the young Grant Richards – later a prominent publisher, author of *Hasty Marriage* and *Vain Pursuit* – was a first nighter at John Hollingshead's Gaiety Theatre, the Strand. At the Catherine Street entrance the crowd gathered hours before opening, the usefulness of

the queue not yet discovered by Londoners. Medical students allegedly
shoved hardest.

Now and again there would be cheers and a football-players' rush . . . In one
rush my stick or umbrella got in the way and was broken in halves. I was
short at that period and thin . . . [and] when the doors were opened the pressure, bad enough before, increased to such an extent that I fainted. But, as
there was no room for me to slip to the ground, the fainting in no way impeded
my progress. I was carried along and came to just in time to secure one of
the side seats in the front row. [33]

For all the century theatre provided a space in which the classes
mixed to some degree, even though segregated by price and tradition
once inside. J. R. Planché, born in 1796, the playwright son of French
refugees, recalled how in the 1820s HRH the Duke and Duchess of
Gloucester would occupy a box at the little West London Theatre,
Tottenham Court Road, 'as dark and dingy a den as ever sheltered the
children of Thespis'. That was to see 'vaudeville', and forty years on
Charles Dickens noticed how 'all classes' were 'delighted' at Boucicault's
sensational melodrama *The Streets of London* at the Princess's Theatre,
Oxford Street. And it was said that the pit and gallery at the 'patent
theatres' of Drury Lane and Covent Garden in the 1860s were filled
by 'the same class of people' who attended music halls.[34]

Shakespeare was as popular among working-class audiences at
Sadler's Wells, Islington, under the actor-manager Samuel Phelps from
1844–62, as among any gathering in the West End houses. George
Sims recalled the 'wonderful textual knowledge' of Shakespeare at the
Wells in those years: 'If an actor forgot his lines there was always an
amateur prompter in the pit or gallery to give him the missing words.'
At the Effingham Saloon (later the East London Theatre) in Whitechapel
Road *Hamlet* rubbed padded shoulders with *Sweeney Todd*. When the
Shakespeare Commemoration was celebrated in April 1864, mainly at
Stratford-upon-Avon, the 'only public demonstration in honour of
Shakspeare attempted in London' was got up by a committee of working
men. They marched from Russell Square to Primrose Hill, where Phelps
planted an oak tree.[35]

This passion was not merely passive. There was a passion to create
too. What Boz called 'private theatres' charged local youths – clerks
and shopmen in the main – for the privilege of appearing on stage in
character. Shakespeare was popular at the Catherine Street Theatre in

the 1830s and also at the 'Pentonville Thespian Club', which appears in Mark Lemon's novel of 1867, *Golden Fetters*. Here solicitors' clerks and other 'young men of rather respectable exterior' played to a paying audience of their peers. In the London working men's clubs of the 1870s and 1880s, Shakespeare and humbler fare were offered by amateurs among the members or travelling companies who had emerged from a circuit of clubs.[36]

These were all very much local affairs. Dickens noted how 'All the minor theatres of London, especially the lowest, constitute the centre of a little stage-struck neighbourhood.' The Britannia Saloon, later Theatre, at Hoxton Street might stand as supreme example. Anointing itself 'The People's Theatre', it was one of the largest in London, holding 4,000–5,000. It was rebuilt in 1858 by Samuel Lane, losing some of its 'saloon' or public-house character but nothing of its great tradition. By the 1890s it was described by John Hollingshead, a reliable guide, as 'essentially a local house. It is self-supporting and self-supported . . . Its audience, its actors, and its pieces are more or less of native growth . . . [As] a rule, the Britannia company never leaves the Britannia, but lives and moves and has its being in a constant round of dramas that are manufactured on the premises.' Sara Lane, Samuel's widow, who inherited the 'Brit', was known as 'the Queen of Hoxton'. When she and her company appeared on stage at the theatre's yearly Christmas festival they were pelted with presents: 'Not bouquets nor even chocolates . . . but joints of meat, petticoats, ties, stays, boots, stockings . . . umbrellas and walking sticks, baskets of fruit or vegetables . . . I have seen the time when the audience in the stalls had to put up umbrellas to avoid the showers of gifts that poured on to the stage from all parts of the theatre.'[37]

The reckless enthusiasm of the London theatre audiences, their outspoken criticisms rudely expressed, their hugger-mugger mingling of classes, all helped condemn the theatre in some eyes as a place to be avoided. There were other objections too. Until the end of the 1850s gatherings of prostitutes in even the legitimate theatres kept many respectable families away. And the link between stage and sin, inherent in plays of any sort, created an insuperable obstacle to theatre-going among orthodox Christians throughout the century. That feeling was probably at its strongest between about 1850 and 1890.

There were, though, uses of the stage that were unexceptionable. The public lecture was one. It held its interest right across the century.

And 'lecture' was allowed to expand into areas of pure entertainment as long as some educational or moral content remained. Humphry Davy lectured on laughing gas and all things scientific to packed audiences at the Royal Institution, Albemarle Street, in 1802. William Hazlitt dazzled the Rotunda or Surrey Institution south of Blackfriars Bridge with Shakespeare and the poets in 1818. Michael Faraday demonstrated electricity at Albemarle Street in the 1820s. Benjamin Webster combined conjuring tricks and tall stories in Webster's Wallet of Waggeries in the 1830s. Henry Russell lectured on America and sang cotton-picking ditties in the 1840s. Thackeray quipped on 'English Humourists of the Eighteenth Century' at Willis's Rooms in the 1850s. Dickens gave readings from his novels in the 1860s. Professor John Pepper transported his 'Ghost' illusion from the Royal Polytechnic, Regent Street, to the Egyptian Hall, Piccadilly, in the 1870s. John Williams Benn, later a prominent London politician, earned £2,000 a year as a 'lightning sketcher' in the 1880s. And in the 1890s George Grossmith abandoned the Savoy Opera and Gilbert and Sullivan for one-man shows at lecture halls all over London and beyond. These were a few among many. All were hugely popular as family entertainment among every class from artisan and above. And they were astonishingly remunerative, more so than anything an actor could get on the stage or even the most successful of writers could earn in the same time with his pen. We need only remember the enervating toll taken by his readings on Dickens's lifespan to register the lure of ready cash from a lecture tour or one-man show.

Some of these performers provided what a later era would know as a multi-media event. Take one of the most stunning successes in this genre, Albert Smith's lectures on his ascent of Mont Blanc. They began in 1852 and packed out the Egyptian Hall season after season until 1859, shortly before Smith's death at the age of forty-four. The show varied over time but might involve an alpine inn and chalet built by the best wood-carvers in Chamonix; St Bernard dogs padding the aisles for children of all ages to pat; a waterfall, mill-wheel and lily pond; edelweiss on the lampshades and chamois skins round the walls. A painted diorama moved on rollers as Smith described his journey, imitating the voices and donning the dress of travellers and foreigners met along the way. From time to time he 'dropped into verse and song, accompanying himself on the piano, and wound up with a long patter on the topics of the day . . .'[38]

With Albert Smith we are firmly back in the world of London variety, where novelty, sensation and quick-change were indispensable to audience satisfaction. Novelty was not always easy to find. 'There are no fresh sensations to be got,' complained Nelson Lee, manager of the City of London Theatre in Norton Folgate, 'you cannot throw a man off a rock every day.' Yet novelty was what audiences demanded. Even the patent theatres were forced to intersperse legitimate drama with lighter fare to make a living. At the ever-troubled Covent Garden Theatre matters were so dire in the 1856 season that it was leased for six weeks to Professor Anderson, the Wizard of the North, for illusions and pantomimes and the occasional 'monster concert' with forty or fifty musical pieces. A 'Carnival Benefit' involved a fourteen-hour or so extravaganza including a farce, an opera, a drama, a 'squib', a melodrama and a pantomime. It was followed next night, 4–5 March 1856, by a 'grand *bal masqué*', attended by the fast set of all classes. The masquers and onlookers were said to have indulged in 'undisguised indecency, drunkenness, and vice, such as the lowest places of resort have rarely witnessed'. At 4.40 a.m., with some 200 very drunk people still in the house, a gas-fitter noticed a fire in the roof. Covent Garden burned to the ground for the second time in fifty years; this time, miraculously given the circumstances, no lives were lost.[39]

By 1856, though, variety had begun to establish a more congenial home than the patent theatre. The public house had played a large part in the origins of London's pleasure gardens and a significant part through the saloon (the Britannia, the Effingham, the Eagle Tavern) in the spread of London theatre. But the pub played the largest part of all in the rise of music hall. From the 1850s music hall became variety's home. What had begun as an eclectic pick-and-mix entertainment would become a stand-alone art form with a recognised bill of fare in a purpose-made space. In its origins it was an entirely metropolitan institution. It emerged from London's streets, its pleasure gardens, its theatres. And the pub was its midwife.

Music and the public house had always gone together. As long as there had been inns, there had been song. Out of this informal tradition music became professionalised in the public house. In 1815 it was noted how the Ram at Smithfield had 'long been famous' for its 'Glee Club', 'attended by some of the very first professional singers and amateurs in London', and the Cellar in Spring Gardens was similarly famous for its 'chaunt'. By the 1840s places like the Cyder Cellars in

Maiden Lane and Evans's Supper Rooms nearby at Covent Garden Piazza had capitalised on this tradition to become among the most popular resorts for men of the middling classes in London. Thackeray's re-creation of these places in the 'Back Kitchen' (*Pendennis*) and the 'Cave of Harmony' (*The Newcomes*) proved among the most resonant for contemporaries of any London fiction of the century. Here hit singers could cause a sensation. There was a small professional chorus, while sing-alongs and contributions from the audience were all part of the fun. And despite the growth of professional music hall the amateur component of the penny gaff and 'free and easies' in working-class London, where 'the performance [was] conducted by the audience themselves', persisted throughout the century.[40]

'I am the father of the music-halls', claimed Paddy Green, manager of Evans's from 1844, but there were numerous competing paternity suits. The pubs connected with pleasure gardens were the most likely of all. The Grecian Saloon at the Eagle, City Road, had been a home to variety since the 1830s, and it is probably then that the spectrum of street entertainers – acrobats, conjurors, 'head balancers', novelty musicians – began slowly to narrow as performers moved indoors to the saloons and the penny gaffs. But it was south London that seems to have given music hall its name. The Grapes in Southwark was apparently calling itself the Surrey Music Hall in the early 1840s. But for many the Canterbury Arms saloon, Westminster Bridge Road, rebuilt by its enterprising manager Charles Morton around 1854, takes the palm as the first true 'Variety Theatre' in London. Hackney-born Morton is most often remembered as the true 'Father of the Halls'.[41]

The Canterbury in the 1850s had all those characteristics that marked music hall from theatre. Those closest to the stage watched from tables where drink – mainly porter, this was a sober audience – and eatables like sandwiches were consumed. It provided entertainment for 'respectable mechanics, or small tradesmen with their wives and daughters and sweethearts', as well as 'a few fast clerks and warehousemen'. A chairman – Morton himself – kept order with little effort. Yet the combination of drink and entertainment would damn the music hall in puritan eyes for the rest of the century. And things were only made worse when, as often, suggestive songs and patter were delivered by worldly and attractive performers both male and female.[42]

Music hall migrated to central London in 1860 with the Royal Alhambra Palace and Music Hall at 28 Leicester Square. In 1864 it was taken over by Frederick Strange, a former chop-room waiter at Simpson's restaurant in the Strand and one of London's great (but not finally successful) music-hall entrepreneurs. Under Strange the Alhambra prospered – for a time. He spent £25,000 on repairs, decorations and sumptuous furnishings, including 'an acre of valuable carpet' for the ground floor or pit. This marked a transformation in taste that 'sealed the doom of dirt and discomfort in the leading London theatres'. The Alhambra's programme was noted for its extravagant orchestra, chorus and especially ballet. Yet prices were moderate – 6d for the second gallery, 1s for the pit and promenade, 2s in the stalls and a guinea for a private box. According to the chief magistrate at Bow Street in 1866, 'the great majority of the people at the Alhambra were respectable tradespeople and mechanics, with their families, looking at the dancing'. Their favourite tipple was Bass's pale ale and brandy-and-soda. Four metropolitan police officers and six 'private policemen in livery' helped keep order. [43]

But the Alhambra had a troubled history. It lost its dancing licence in a row over the can-can in 1870 and was turned into a theatre. Things improved under Charles Morton's management in the late 1870s until it burned down in 1882. It was rebuilt as a music hall and in 1884 the Alhambra was joined in Leicester Square by the even more luxurious Empire Theatre of Varieties. The Empire boasted private boxes costing eight guineas but the gallery remained at 6d. To a New Yorker in the late 1880s these two places were 'decorated and fitted up on a scale of gorgeousness not to be equalled in any theatres in the world'. [44]

It is impossible to get firm figures for the numbers of theatres and music halls in London across the century. In 1843, there were twenty-five licensed theatres including seven public-house saloons. In 1865 there were in addition thirty-two music halls seating from 500 to 5,000 (the Alhambra). This excluded 'small tavern concert rooms' and that would have been a large number. [45] By 1878 there had been substantial growth – fifty-seven licensed theatres, seventy-eight 'large' music halls and over 300 other places, most of them very small. But from 1878 to the turn of the century there was a drastic reduction in licensed music halls. There were two main reasons. First, licensing passed from the magistrates to the Metropolitan Board of Works (from 1889 the LCC), whose fire regulations closed down many of the smaller saloons and penny gaffs. And second, a taste for luxury fuelled by rising prosperity led to larger, more sumptuous halls providing entertainment for a whole district of London rather than local neighbourhoods. No doubt unlicensed penny gaffs sprang up and died off as opportunity allowed. But by the 1890s they were insignificant as crowd-drawers except among the children of the poor. At the beginning of the new century (1903) there were still fifty-seven theatres, though some were much grander places, with a 'Theatreopolis' emerging at the Drury Lane end of the Strand. But there were now only forty-four music halls compared to nearly 400 a quarter of a century before. In a number of those 'intoxicating drinks' were banned, finally dislocating the halls from their pub origins.[46]

But getting a drink was never that difficult in nineteenth-century London.

'Here's How!'

At the end of the century Londoners of all classes were agreed that the metropolis had grown into a far more sober place than it had started out. Rees Gronow looked back on 1815 and remembered friends staying at Shepherd's Hotel, Bond Street, with their five bottles of wine each a day and how 'three-bottle men' were regular company at fashionable dinner parties. Around the same time, in London's backside so to speak, John Brown was horrified by the shoemakers' colony of Grub Street, the women so drunk they 'dropped their babies in the noisome gutter and rolled over them', the children so 'begrimed with filth and dirt, it was impossible to tell whether they were blacks or whites'. Charles Knight recalled the Christmas of 1824 round Pall Mall and its 'rampant, insolent, outrageous drunkenness'. But in 1834 Francis Place thought sobriety never more widespread. And at the parliamentary inquiry he was addressing, while men could be found with opinions on both sides of the question, the majority thought things had never been better.[47]

If so – and the weight of opinion is hard to ignore – things before 1834 must have been very bad indeed. At that same inquiry reliable witnesses testified to seeing men pawning and selling the shirts off their backs to raise the wind for a glass; a woman who sold her teeth one by one to dentists (no anaesthetic then) to fuel her addiction; a family of six near Worship Street brought low by gin – 'no bed, a few old rags in the corner . . . all occasions of nature in both ways were done in the room'; crowds of customers as the pubs opened at seven on a Sunday morning, among them a woman who beat the crying infant at her breast 'most unmercifully' and then took it in to pacify it with gin.[48]

Indeed, a later generation would look back on the drinking habits of children with horror. All Dickens-lovers will recall that ten-year-old phenomenon demanding to know 'the VERY *best*' ale at a pub in Cannon Street: 'just draw me a glass of that, if you please, with a good head to it'. Dickens was precocious but poor and the year was around 1822. Yet in the early 1860s the middle-class George Sims, then a young teenager accompanying mother and grandfather to his first music hall, found a glass of curaçao pressed in his hand: 'There was nothing remarkable in the spectacle of a small boy taking a liqueur in those days.'[49]

Although the three-bottle man was less commonly met with as the century grew older, drink continued to be a prominent part of the daily routine of all classes throughout the century. Around 1870 Louis Bamberger started the day at one City client's with gin-and-water at 9 a.m. Sir William Fraser, one of the Queen's bodyguards, noted around the same time a woman with the classic symptoms of 'Blue Ruin', the slang name for gin, her face 'an intensely bright, corn-flower, blue', in shocking contrast to the 'black rags' she wore. The 1870s was the decade when per capita consumption of beer and spirits peaked. But old habits clung on in the City, and R. D. Blumenfeld in 1887 thought it a queer custom for 'business men of all ranks to knock off at eleven o'clock in the morning' for a drink, champagne at 6d a glass 'the favourite tipple'.[50]

The worst excesses may have moderated. But throughout the century drink and drunk pervaded London popular culture. Drunken men and women gave the metropolitan police their largest single share of business. There were around 31,000 arrests for drunkenness in 1831 and 31,000 almost exactly in 1875. In the 1880s arrests for drunkenness fell but in the 1890s they rose again. During the whole of that time London's population grew greatly. Even so, what are we to make of the fact that as a proportion of all arrests drink accounted for 43 per cent in 1875 and – at 56,000 – 49 per cent in 1899?[51] In summary we can say this. Drinking to excess was a constant factor in London life in the nineteenth century. That the habit grew less widespread, and the consequences less obnoxious, seems attributable more to changing manners and rising prosperity than to a turning away from drink itself.

One cause (and effect) of changing manners was the changing public house. Of all the institutions of civil society in nineteenth-century London the pub was without question the most versatile and innovative. Certain trends in London pub history are detectable across the century. First, pubs became less accessible to drinkers as their opening hours were curtailed by law. Second, their numbers relative to the population they served declined sharply. Third, those that were left grew bigger and smarter. Fourth, they generated new functions which matured in the pub but then split off from it and formed institutions of their own, clubs, theatres, music halls and restaurants being the most important.

First, then, Sabbath observance ate away at pub hours over the years. In 1839 the 7 a.m. to 11 a.m. slot on Sundays was done away with and there were further restrictions in 1854 and 1865. In 1872 a complete overhaul established the London drinking hours that would remain in place until the First World War: closing at midnight on Saturday, 12.30 a.m. on weekdays; open on weekdays any hour from 5 a.m.; Sundays limited to 1 p.m. to 3 p.m. and 6 p.m. to 11 p.m. And it is difficult to be precise about pub numbers but it seems as though, despite London's enormous growth in area and population, there were no more pubs at the end of the century (10,400 in 1903) than the middle (reputedly 11,000 in 1848).[52]

They were also different places. Pubs modernised as London modernised. Cramped and dirty beerhouses were to be found in the old central districts the century through, but a move to grandiosity could be detected early on. 'Every public-house is now converted into "Wine Vaults",' it was said in 1822. These were the forerunners of the 'gin palace' that was such a feature ('mania', Dickens called it) of the 1830s. What made the palace palatial were gas and brilliant illumination. But even the palaces were designed for drinking not at leisure but at speed. There were often no tables or benches in the main bar – 'done in less than a minute, they depart immediately' was the routine at Thompson and Fearon's gin palace on Holborn Hill. Where tables and chairs were provided at a taproom or saloon, their purpose was more for eating or entertainment than drinking. Here the large coaching inns and City taverns dominated, providing meals and lodgings, some accommodating London's most splendid public meeting rooms well into the second half of the century. And here too were the saloons and cellars out of which variety and the music hall grew. It seems likely that some of the comforts of the music hall were left behind when the saloons split off in the 1850s and after. More luxury – upholstered benches, chairs and small tables, but not carpet – spread into the taprooms and even bars, now mainly for the use of drinkers. By the 1890s they were standard fare, one cause perhaps of the pub's increasing popularity among working-class women: in one Soho pub where drinkers were counted on a Saturday around 1895, half were women, many arriving between 10 p.m. and midnight.[53]

As the pub modernised in form, its function narrowed to become almost entirely a place for drinking. In the first sixty years of the century its role in London's social life had been wonderfully diverse. There were the great coaching inns, London's transport termini, squeezed out of business by the railways from the 1830s on. There were the clubs of literary men and others, establishing a presence in a favoured 'haunt' and then moving out to their own premises as literature grew more profitable. There were the pubs that were labour exchanges for beggars, actors, street entertainers, even bodysnatchers; and most notoriously for the Thames coal-whippers, their gangmasters riverside publicans who required a goodly portion of their men's wages spilled in drink. Pubs were the nurseries of London trade unions until temperance became connected in the radical worker's mind with class discipline. So shoemakers gathered at the Crispin in Grub Street, compositors at the Harlequin, Drury Lane, and brushmakers at the Craven Head in the same street. From connections like these the pub and politics went hand in hand, partly because there were few alternative venues for a lecture or meeting and partly because conviviality and comradeship became each other so well. The radical (and secret at a time of state oppression) Hampden clubs were started at the Thatched House Tavern, St James's Street, in 1812; Robert Owen lectured on socialism in the City of London Tavern, Bishopsgate Street, in 1817; the National Union of the Working Classes originated in meetings at the Argyle Arms, near Gray's Inn Lane, in 1831; debates on issues of the day continued to mid-century at the Temple Forum in the Green Dragon, Fleet Street, and at Cogers Hall, Shoe Lane; and the Reform League's meetings were held in pubs all over London in the 1860s. It was in this decade in particular that the host of working men who had established clubs in a pub back room or upstairs over the bar began to move out to their own premises, rented or purpose-built. The pub also played a role in local government, vestries frequently meeting there to settle the affairs of church or parish until the mid-1850s. Coroners' juries sat in pubs in parts of the East End, for instance, until the 1890s. Even the management committee of the metropolitan dissenters (Presbyterians, Baptists, Independents) met at the King's Head Tavern, Poultry, up to the 1830s at least.[54]

The pub had other associations too. Sport, often with a financial tag, remained a popular pub passion to the end of the century. So we find rat-catching at the King's Head, Compton Street, Soho, in the 1850s, with a gold repeater watch to the dog that killed fifteen rats in the shortest time; foot races for a £50 prize at the White Lion, Hackney Wick; prize-fighting in a twenty-one-foot ring at the Blind Beggar, Whitechapel Road (and a dozen other places too) in the 1860s; a chaffinch-singing match for a £10-purse in Shoreditch in the 1870s. The public-house origins of much London gambling was commemorated by the smartest gaming houses of St James's going in disguise under the name of 'hotels' and sometimes 'saloons'.[55]

Even more than gambling, and just as contentious, the pub was associated with dancing. Once song was accompanied by a fiddle or piano then men and women took to the floor. They needed a special licence over and above one for music alone. For dancing throughout the century was seen as a danger to morality and good order almost as serious as liquor itself. Most threatening of all, despite the 'utmost decorum' prevailing, were the sailors' pubs in Ratcliffe Highway and the turnings out of it.[56] But dancing was not merely a delight of the slums. At all the pleasure gardens and tea gardens, at the saloons and early music halls, dancing was a favourite pastime of respectable tradespeople, artisans, clerks and their families. So it remained in the new music halls until the puritan LCC took hold in the 1890s and confined dancing to the stage. By then dancing for the respectable artisan class and above had moved out of the pubs to 'shilling dancing-rooms', which were 'found in every leading thoroughfare of London'. These were a far cry from the days of the famous Almack's balls at Willis's Rooms (as they later became) at King Street, St James's. In Captain Gronow's day Almack's was 'the seventh heaven of the fashionable world', so exclusive that just a handful of the Foot Guards' 300 officers could gain admission, vouchers restricted by a committee of hawk-eyed lady hostesses. New money eventually penetrated these stout defences, another mark of the democratisation of the times. From the 1840s, the balls were marked by 'plebeian invasions' and Almack's died away in 1863.

Around 1820 it had spawned a cheeky East End analogue, 'All Max', run by a man called Mace.[57]

Much dining, like dancing, emerged from the pub, though not all. The restaurant in London had two origins. One was a foreign import, confined largely to Soho and its neighbour north of Oxford Street. There was much continuity here from the French post-revolution migration of the 1790s: although historians tell us that Regent Street's famous Café Royal first opened in 1864 or 1865, an earlier 'Café Royale', a 'Frenchified' affair, was set up there by 1821 'in the *tip top* stile of elegance'. The other, much older, emerged from the public house, especially the coaching inn and City tavern. Whatever route was followed, the restaurant as a popular institution was a long time coming to London. The very name was hardly used in London guides before 1875. Eating out was largely confined to taverns, inns and coffee houses. In the City there were also 'chop-houses' – 'slap-bangs' they were called because of the speed of service and dispatch. Many City men bought a steak or chop at a butcher's and had it grilled on a pub gridiron. Workers would buy hot food at a pie shop or sheep's-head dealer and take it into a pub taproom to have it with a glass of porter.[58]

From the early 1830s, in that well-established pattern, some working men's dining rooms broke out of the pub and coffee house and concentrated on providing meals, usually offering coffee rather than drink. And the trend to luxury and refinement that split the middle-class club from the public house helped foster more experiment with London's foreign restaurants – Thackeray refers to this as a new habit around 1854, and Charles Verrey's famous French restaurant was established in Regent Street by then. But this was a minority taste, risqué and somewhat declassed even into the 1870s, when Soho's restaurants were said to be frequented by foreigners, 'artists, poets, and other degenerate Englishmen'.[59]

By this time the list of 'Restaurants and Dining-Rooms' in *The Golden Guide to London* (1875) ran to fifteen restaurants, most in Regent Street or nearby, just one in Soho and that apparently English; and a further sixteen City dining rooms, most in taverns. Among them were Spiers and Pond's Ludgate Hill Restaurant and Simpson's Divan Tavern at 103 Strand, and these marked a turning point for middle-class Londoners in the 1860s and 1870s. At Simpson's from 1862, diners were treated to 'Large tables and comfortable chairs in place of the boxes and benches; abundance of clean linen tablecloths and napkins; plated forks and spoons; electro-plated tankards instead of pewter pots; finger-glasses' and more. Here 'things would be done as at the clubs' and the non-club world responded accordingly. Baedeker's 1889 guide to London listed forty-three 'Restaurants at the West End' and in 1905 seventy-two. Among the most famous names the foreign origins of good food in London stand out: the Café Royal, founded by the Burgundian Daniel Thévenon, Gatti's (Charing Cross), Romano's (Strand), Monico's (Tichborne Street). Redevelopment and the continuing modernisation of London gave fresh opportunities to entrepreneurs to exploit these changing tastes. So the Trocadero restaurant opened in 1896 on a site cleared for Shaftesbury Avenue. It was established by a new force in London catering, J. Lyons and Company. And Lyons, who opened their first 'tea-shop' at 213 Piccadilly in September 1894, traded on a new trend identified from the 1880s by the Aërated Bread Company (ABC). That was the commercial woman in the City and the shopping woman in the West End who wished to make a day of her trip. 'They brought with them the modern tea-shop, with its bright tiles and cleanly marble tables,' complained a City man, 'and deprived us of the comfort of the old wooden pews.'[60]

There would be a touch of 'fast' and 'dog' about eating out at night in London's fashionable restaurants till the century's end. For there were, still, so few of them. Bohemia may have dispersed since the 1840s but it might be encountered any evening at Gatti's or the Café Royal or elsewhere. As on Saturday 9 April 1892, at a famous place in the Strand.

Turned in at Romano's for a few minutes to-night and saw the Marquis of Aylesbury, who usually wears coster clothes, with his wife, Dolly Tester, the Brighton barmaid, Charlie Mitchell, the pugilist, Abingdon Baird, the Scottish iron-master who dispenses largesse with a lavish hand, 'Teddy' Bayley, and several convivial spirits dispensing vociferous hospitality to all who entered. Those who refused to drink were playfully tripped up on the sawdust-covered floor.[61]

'At Home'

Shared pleasures at home depended on whether there was a 'home' to share them in. In 1901 – extraordinary to think of – over a million Londoners in the county, almost one in four, lived in just one or two rooms. Over a third of all dwellings were this small. Things were markedly better than ten years before – those in single rooms had fallen from 386,000 to 305,000 (9.1 per cent to 6.7 per cent). Even so, the very overcrowded at three or more persons to a room totalled 325,000.[62]

Not much capacity here then for shared pleasures outside the family. What company could be kept in such conditions where, even if poverty permitted possessions, there was little or no space to seat a guest? The lure of the public house for men and women with coppers or a shilling in pockets and purses was all but irresistible. The lights, the plush, the piano, the laughter and conversation – *there* was life, not in the stifling reek of 'home' with its caterwauling children and wall-to-wall discomfort. Yet in 1901, for the poorest of Londoners, housing conditions had never been better. Comparisons here are statistically unverifiable. But all anecdotal evidence points to the dynamics of the London housing shortage moving something like this: from 1800 to 1840 very severe; from 1840 to 1850 critical; from 1850 to 1870 very severe; from 1870 to 1900 easing slowly to severe.[63]

For the London rich – the aristocracy and the upper middle class by birth or wealth – it was all very different. Here some patterns changed: the move to flats, to the suburbs and to the restaurant habit doubtless affected the frequency and luxury of home entertaining. But here again the constants are more telling than the changes.

Just what constituted London 'Society' altered somewhat over time, influenced as it was by that democratic leavening we have seen in other contexts. 'Society to-day and Society as I formerly knew it are two entirely different things,' complained Lady Dorothy Nevill in 1905. 'Indeed, it may be questioned whether Society, as the word used to be understood, now exists at all.' Her recollections stretched back to the 1840s, when 'Society' was exclusively composed of those eligible for presentation at court, where land, blood and wit were even more important than gold. It was the rise of the new rich, a growing element from railway-mania days she thought, that by the 1880s and 1890s had rendered 'Society' wealth-obsessed and '"on the make"'. Disraeli, looking back in *Endymion* from the 1880s to the 1820s, thought something similar.[64]

Maybe this was just the consciousness of decay that burdens every older generation. Manners changed, though. Louis Simond noted how in some fashionable London houses in 1810 a commode or chamber pot was placed in a corner of the dining room for the use of hard-drinking men: 'The operation is performed very deliberately and undisguisedly, as a matter of course, and occasions no interruption of the conversation.' And conversation itself grew less free and more 'moral'. But the mechanics of the London season stayed pretty much the same. There was the same whirlwind of invitation and counter-invitation each year among a 'mob of competing hostesses'. Hostesses came and went but the competition between them altered little from the early days of Lady Blessington's sumptuous salons at St James's Square (from 1818), Seamore Place (from 1831) and Gore House (from 1836) and Lady Elizabeth Holland at Holland House, both active into the 1840s; and then in the 1880s with the Duchess of Manchester, Lady St Helier, Lady Dorothy Nevill and the formidable clique around the beautiful and brilliant Tennant girls at 40 Grosvenor Square, who basked in the name of 'The Souls', and whose guest lists contained every political star of the day and 'everyone', including 'jockeys, actors, the Prince of Wales and every ambassador in London'.[65]

Those London season guest lists were works of art. 'People always left cards directly they arrived in town.' Private Mayfair circulating libraries arranged for delivery in the case of those with too many to handle. 'It was a fearful breach of etiquette not to leave a card the day after a dinner party and within a few days after a ball.' Invitations to a popular party were shamelessly canvassed in 'what is perhaps the most extraordinary feature of the social life of London, the habit of asking to be asked'. We can glimpse the sheer busyness of it all in a week facing William Makepeace Thackeray at the beginning of the 1850 season.

To day Shakspeare's birthday at the Garrick Club, dinner and speech – lunch Madame Lionel Rothschild – ball Lady Waldegrave. She gives the finest balls in London & I've never seen one yet – tomorrow of 5 invitations to dinner the first is Mr Marshall – The D of Devonshire's Hevening party Lady Emily Dundas's ditto – Thursday Sir Anthony Rothschild – Friday the domestic affections, Saturday Sir Robert Peel, Sunday Lord Lansdowne – Isn't it curious to think . . . that there are people who would give their ears or half their income to go to these fine places.[66]

A great deal of the function of this ceaseless round of entertaining – as Thackeray wryly pointed out at every opportunity in his novels – was matchmaking and marriage between blood, money and beauty: '"I have seen mothers bring their virgin daughters up to battered old rakes, and ready to sacrifice their innocence for fortune or a title."' [67]

If the London season had its virgin sacrifices, then the decoration and ritual round the altar was formidable. Mayfair balls and parties were marked by 'strips of crimson carpet' from door to gutter, striped awnings over the pavement, lines of polished carriages, music drifting through the open windows, little knots of curious bystanders behind wigged and powdered footmen as the guests arrived. Inside were huge buffets 'attended by butlers and men in livery', a 'feminine buttery' for tea and cake and help with a starting seam, brilliant lights – electric by the mid-1890s – glancing in myriad shivers from cut glass, shining silver and burnished gold. And the company was pleasured as often as not by cultural 'lions' like Pablo Sarasate (the violinist), Madame Neruda (the opera singer) and George Grossmith (the Savoy Opera lead and entertainer).[68]

'Society' was marked out from the rest of London by 'the fact that some of the men and practically all the women made the pursuit of pleasure their main occupation in life'. Here 'personal vanity was an "occupational disease"'. 'How well I recollect those first days of my early London seasons' in the 1870s, wrote Beatrice Potter, daughter of a second-generation 'capitalist at large':

the pleasurable but somewhat feverish anticipation of endless distraction, a dissipation of mental and physical energy which filled up all the hours of the day and lasted far into the night; the ritual to be observed; the presentation at Court, the riding in the Row, the calls, the lunches and dinners, the dances and crushes, Hurlingham and Ascot, not to mention amateur theatricals and other sham philanthropic excrescences.[69]

This fever was episodic – sharp but short. London society was active from the recall of Parliament in February, frantic from May to July, somnolent in autumn and winter when society made for the country. The contrasts may have softened somewhat towards the century's end but 'the emptiness of London' (and this a city of 4.5 million in the county alone!) was remarked upon as late as 1898. Those left behind might form themselves into a 'little winter society', hunkering down with whist parties and small dinners like polar explorers in a blizzard.[70]

In the rest of London the season took less of a toll. For the middle classes, entertaining at home was one of the liberating effects of suburbanisation, offering more space to more and more Londoners, especially from the 1850s on. Dinners, musical evenings, amateur theatricals, parties for children and adults had always gone on. But by the end of the century an enlarged middle class, more prosperous and better housed, was able to indulge in more of these activities than ever before.

The middle-class 'At Home' had something about it of the season's invitation whirlwind but with more informality. Jerome K. Jerome's mother would set aside a morning when her friends knew she would be waiting with 'cake and biscuits in a silver basket, and port and sherry on the sideboard. They used to talk about the servants and how things were going from bad to worse.' That was probably Finchley or New Southgate in the 1870s. At a shared house in Queen's Road, Bayswater, in the 1840s, the John Gliddons, the Thornton Hunts and the Samuel Laurences – the wives were sisters or cousins – '"received" on Sundays' in the evenings, their company literary and left-leaning by and large. At the Justin McCarthys', Bedford Place, Bloomsbury, around 1870, 'At Homes' took place on Saturday evenings, the company more political – pro-German and pro-Irish. Others, especially among theatrical and arty sets, might begin at 10 p.m. and Gissing wrote of 'midnight "at homes"' in the late 1890s.[71]

Balls required space that could not always be had and the servant problem constrained much ambition to entertain, but dinner parties were everyday events. And lavish entertainments, almost on Grosvenor Square lines, might be got together by the well-connected and well-heeled. At times the company in these humbler places was as good as could be had anywhere. The actress Ellen Terry recalled 'two or three dinner-parties' at the Shirley Brookses', Kent Terrace, Regent's Park, in the early 1860s, meeting the writers Mark Lemon and Tom Taylor, the artists John Tenniel and George du Maurier, the musicians Joachim, Piatti and Clara Schumann, and many more. At a party placed by George Gissing in Kilburn we find a 'Hungarian band', 'nigger minstrels' and 'an American joker' performing for a 'substantial cheque'.[72] Amateur theatricals were another favourite diversion. At Norwood, for instance, in 1877, where plays put on by the Searle family of Central Hill were 'one of the special attractions' of their 'hospitable house'. And at 37 Kyverdale Road, Stoke Newington, where John Williams Benn knocked down the wall dividing drawing from dining room to give more space for 'dramatic inventions' in the 1880s.[73]

Children's parties could be extraordinary affairs. Edward Draper, an eccentric solicitor, would amuse his children and their friends with a small brass cannon firing holes through the kitchen door. And at

Benjamin Farjeon's sumptuous Christmas parties the giant tree was 'laden with thousands of entrancing gifts' gathered during a year's journeyings at home and abroad: locking the drawing room, he would dress the tree in secret for two weeks before the great day.[74]

Music was the strongest theme in the London middle classes' shared pleasures at home. Some families were intensely musical with many musical connections: like the composer William Horsley at Kensington in the 1830s, who bought his lease from Clementi and for whose glee parties his friend Mendelssohn played the piano. But even in less attuned homes music played a dominant part in domestic entertainments. Musical evenings – songs at the piano – were popular among the 'St John's Wood Clique' of artists in the 1860s and 1870s; they followed lawn-tennis parties in the afternoons. Indeed, the piano seems to have penetrated every bourgeois home by the 1860s. In March 1856 a single issue of the *Illustrated London News* carried thirty-seven advertisements for sheet music for accompanied songs; ten years later it carried 147. English piano production doubled between 1850 and 1890. And by the 1880s musical parties had widened out and were a constant feature of the tradespeople's and clerks' suburbs. At Hackney, for instance, where Henry Wood established the Hackney Orchestral Society around 1889; and where the Lieck family put every member through their musical paces for the delight (or otherwise) of their friends. 'No longer,' recalled Albert Lieck forty years on, 'do the five-finger exercise and the *Maiden's Prayer* come from every open window and through every partition wall.'[75]

By the end of the century the piano had entered the lives of the better-off workers, not only in the suburbs of east London but in the poorer parts too. Hire purchase on the tally system made this possible. And space was found for it even in the 'two rooms and a kitchen' that most working-class London households aspired to by the last quarter or so of the century: even barrows in Lambeth Walk in the 1890s proclaimed, '"Words and music. Four a penny, and all different."'[76] But these small homes were private worlds – or almost always so – in a class for whom privacy was a luxury, perhaps the most desired luxury of all. And that reminds us that London had many private pleasures to offer.

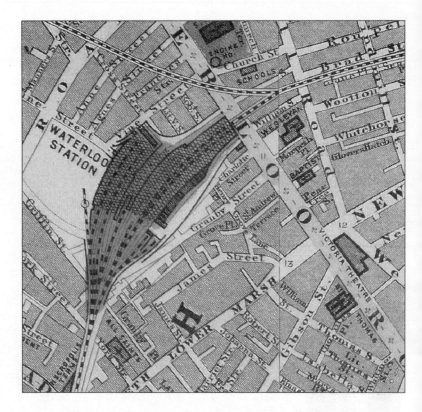

Granby Street, 1862

X

GRANBY STREET: PRIVATE PLEASURES

'The Republic of Vice'

The streets leading out of the Waterloo Road were then occupied much by gay women. Some were absolutely full of them; they were mostly of a class to be had for a few shillings if they could not get more . . . but many a swell have I noticed lingering about there . . . Each woman had generally but one room, but two or three used to sit together in the front room in their chemises. There was the bed, wash-stand, chamber-pot and all complete. Perhaps one lolled out of the window, showing her breasts, and if you gave such a one a shilling, she would stoop so that you could see right down past her belly to her knees, and have a glimpse of her cunt-fringe. Sometimes one would pull up her garter, or another sit down and piddle or pretend to do so, or have recourse to other exciting devices when men peeped in. I used to look in and long . . . Going one Saturday night up Granby Street . . . [a] woman standing at a door seized my hand, asking me in, and at the same time pulling me quite violently into a little passage. I had barely seen her, and upon her saying, 'Come and have me', replied that I had scarcely any money. 'Never mind', said she, 'we will have a fuck for all that'.[1]

So 'Walter', the unidentified author of *My Secret Life*, introduces us to an untypically brazen instance of London prostitution around 1845. Granby Street, running west off the Waterloo Road north of Lower Marsh, contained some ninety two-storey houses in long terraces. Their shuttered windows gave directly onto the pavement and there was a pub, the Royal Oak, and one or two shops. At the time of Walter's visit it was a fairly new suburban development, built between 1831 and 1835. It seems that by the end of the 1830s prostitution was its main cottage industry, though there was a smattering of artisans until the early 1840s. In 1839 Flora Tristan found the district full of prostitutes 'looking out of windows or seated at their doorsteps', and was much struck by their 'fancy men', 'very good-looking, young, tall and strong'. We can get some idea of the numbers of women actually involved from the 1841 census. It shows twenty-four houses where fifty-seven young women were living as separate households: thirty-seven were marked down as 'independent', the others stating a variety of occupations, most with the needle. It's likely that this was the minimum number of prostitutes in the street and that some married women were also active in the trade.[2]

For some thirty years Granby Street and its neighbours comprised one of the most notorious patches of vice in London. A myth would grow up that prostitution in this area, even the construction of Granby Street itself, was brought about by the London and South-West Railway terminus at Waterloo. Nothing like it. Granby Street was already flourishing on the voluminous passing traffic of south London carters, artisans and clerks crossing Waterloo Bridge a decade before the station opened in 1848. Railway passengers encouraged Granby Street's speciality but not, it seems, by much. In 1850 Mayhew noted a concentration there of low cabmen, those who lived on and with 'women of the town', pimping for custom in their cabs at the station and elsewhere. Walter Besant, then still a young City clerk plagued by loneliness, knew it in the mid-1850s: 'There was every day an exhibition of girls dancing up and down, and inviting the young men to come in.' And John Hollingshead in 1861 marked it down as 'perhaps the worst sample of a prostitutes' street' where 'unwashed, drunken, fishy-eyed women hang by dozens out of the windows, beckoning to the passersby'. At that time the census showed sixty-five women living as single households, some with children, and still in twenty-four houses. Thirty-eight were in their twenties, twelve in their teens, the youngest – Emma and Fanny Herriott – just sixteen and fourteen, giving needlework and embroidery as their occupations.[3]

How much longer they or any of their 'fallen sisterhood' were there is uncertain, but probably no more than five or six years. For in 1866 or 1867 the railway company bought up Granby Street and other places for an extension of Waterloo Station. Most of the north side of the street was demolished and in 1868 the remainder was renamed Aubin Street to disguise its old associations. Prostitution was almost certainly cleared out at the same time. By the end of the century what was left of the street was a colony of railway porters: 'Mixed, some fairly comfortable', was the verdict of Charles Booth's investigator. Twenty years on again and another enlargement of Waterloo Station would bury every visible trace of Granby Street and its extraordinary career under London stone.[4]

The abandoned lewdness of the Granby Street neighbourhood was exceptional but not unique. In the 1850s, for instance, the Friar Street area of Southwark, Wych Street off the Strand and Norton Street near Portland Place all had women importuning from doorways and windows. No doubt there were others. Changing manners meant there were more in the early years of the century than later. But these flaunting places were greatly outnumbered by the districts where prostitution went quietly about its business. For prostitution in London throughout the nineteenth century was an enormous and complex industry, affecting to some degree the life of every Londoner. And the prostitute who made up its largely self-employed workforce was one of London's most iconic and troubling figures.[5]

No one knows how many prostitutes there were in London. Estimates varied from 8,000 (the police) to 80,000 (evangelists) and sometimes more. All these numbers were clueless. Most were influenced by self-interest. Even the definition of the prostitute was unclear, enlarged by some to include any women living with a man out of wedlock or any single woman not a virgin. There were few objects of social inquiry that caused more muddle and dishonesty than the prostitute. And that was fitting enough for an industry where lies, deception, extortion, pilfering and brutality were all part of 'the game'.

But there's no doubting one truth. A great industry can only be founded on great demand. Here London was unique in every way. It was the greatest and richest gathering of men on earth and for much of their daily lives they were without women's company. Every working day hundreds of thousands of men walked or rode in and out of the City for work or on business. London was the world's greatest port, home for a short time to sailors from all over the globe. It was a great military encampment, with barracks at Woolwich, the Tower, Knightsbridge, Chelsea, the Palaces and elsewhere. It was the nation's greatest marketplace, with men bringing daily to town meat, fish, vegetables, coal and every other commodity for Londoners' consumption. It was a city of migrant young men coming to London to seek their fortune. It was a city of male visitors for business or pleasure, disgorging daily from railways and steamboats. Its vast size and myriad neighbourhoods made secrecy secure for newcomers and old hands alike. And, for the last seventy years of the century at least, it was the capital of a nation holding puritan notions of sex outside marriage and inside. So that respectable young men of the artisan class and above would expect to marry a virgin and frequently steeled themselves to long courtships involving real or pretended celibacy. Even after marriage, narrow traditions, inadequate birth control and ill-informed innocence could discourage experiment and indulgence in the bedroom.[6]

Weight of numbers and unrequited desire could be made more pressing still by the hubris derived from notions of birth-right and the power that came from possession of gold. 'That shop-girls, work women, domestic servants, and all females in similar positions, were expressly designed for the amusement of gentlemen, and generally serve that purpose' was largely subscribed to by bourgeois men in the 1840s. 'As to servants, and women of the humbler class, that they all took cock on the quiet, and were proud of having a gentleman to cover them. Such was the opinion of men in my class of life and of my age. My experience with my mother's servants corroborated it . . .'[7]

London, then, was a monster of desire. Throughout the nineteenth century, London prostitution ensured that desire need not go unrequited for long. At the beginning of the century there were great clusters of prostitution in the City, the West End, the East End and riverside, the Borough and the poorer suburbs. In other words, virtually the whole metropolis. So we read of disorderly women of the town in the courts around St Martin-in-the-Fields, of a brothel in Surrey Road, Blackfriars, treating its 'very young girls' meanly and of sixteen-year-old 'Ann of Oxford Street' rescuing Thomas de Quincey from starvation (all 1802); of the Key Hotel in Chandos Street, Covent Garden, 'a bagnio of the first description, and the most frequented of any in the metropolis' (1806); of a brothel in Ropemaker Street, Finsbury Square, torn down by an angry crowd when a country girl was abducted there (1807); of the Haymarket as a place where no respectable woman could be immune from indecent approaches (1808); of the 'noise and tumult' of 'unhappy females' disturbing the City in 1810, and of the Liberty of St Martin's-le-Grand 'infested with low women and strumpets'.[8]

At the end of the Napoleonic Wars we hear of 'the crowds of women' in Covent Garden and nearby coming from Southwark, Westminster,

Saffron Hill and St Giles; of riverside pubs in Shadwell with brothels in the back yards, where in any tavern dancing room 150–200 prostitutes would be found of an evening; of brothels catering specially for guardsmen in the Almonry and Duck Lane, Westminster; of one of Mother Cummins's brothels in St Giles having 200 beds; of a brothel-keeper in St Giles called Dancer, clerk to the Bedford Chapel; of a hamlet of bordellos off Fleet Street; of 500–1,000 prostitutes every night in one half of the Strand; of sixty brothels in the parish of St Botolph Without Aldgate, 100 in Shoreditch, 200–300 in St George's Southwark; of the Union Hotel, Dean Street (kept by a sheriff's officer), and close to the notorious White House, a long-lived place of aristocratic lechery in Soho Square.[9]

Second only to the streets as prostitution's main marketplace at this time were the theatres. All London's theatres were parade-grounds for prostitutes of whichever class predominated in the audience. The smartest turned up at Covent Garden and Drury Lane, and at the Italian Opera and Theatre Royal in the Haymarket. At these places, the resort of 'bon ton', the attractions of prostitutes in the saloons (known as 'mutton walks') after 9 p.m. seem to have been as big a draw as anything on the stage. Promenading women handed printed business cards to likely clients, a London fashion till 1870 at least, and the income from commercial sex was a necessary subsidy to dramatic art. The bars at either end of the saloons were said to unite 'the profits of a tavern to those of a brothel'. And the women provided drama of their own. At Covent Garden Theatre in 1810 Louis Simond watched prostitutes in the side galleries of the two upper tiers of boxes 'selling and delivering the articles they deal in under the eye of the public'. Prince Pückler-Muskau, visiting Drury Lane in 1826, complained, 'It is often difficult to keep off these repulsive beings, especially when they are drunk, which is not seldom the case.' Here, the third circle was 'so completely their own, that no women of respectability would ever knowingly enter it'. Here too the lobbies were full of 'women half-dressed, and men half-drunk'. Sometimes things got out of hand. In 1835 'forty or fifty viragos' stripped a young man 'completely naked' in the lobby of Drury Lane Theatre and stole his clothes.[10]

By that last date we can begin to detect some surface changes in the long-established traditions of London prostitution. First, 'strumpets' had been slowly dislodged from the heart of the City through a combination of parish authorities and the Society for the Suppression of Vice prosecuting brothel-keepers, robust watching of the streets at night following citizen pressure especially from 1813, and most of all the demolitions for the new Post Office at St Martin's-le-Grand. Prostitution clung on just inside the City rim and around Fleet Street, the Royal Exchange and St Paul's for some decades to come. But by about 1820 there had begun a decisive shift westwards of prostitution in the same way as City depopulation consolidated the movement of wealth to the West End.

Second, a long campaign to clean up the theatres slowly bore fruit. It began under John Fawcett, the manager of Covent Garden in 1828, who received little more than abuse and 'a torrent of squibs, lampoons, and street ballads' for his pains. It was resurrected in a more hopeful moral climate under William Macready from 1837–9 and was taken to Drury Lane by him in 1841–2. But it was not till 1847 and a belated circular from the Lord Chamberlain that London theatre managers were finally forced to exclude prostitutes from the lobbies and shut down the saloons.[11]

The City removals and the virtual end of theatre prostitution by the close of the 1840s didn't indicate a decline in London's 'Republic of Vice'.[12] It merely shifted its boundaries and changed its haunts.

Boundaries moved out with the town. Prostitution invaded some older suburbs that lost caste as a consequence of more modern development nearby. This seems to have been so in the streets just south of the New Road, east of Portland Place, from the mid-1820s, when Regent's Park and St John's Wood were becoming established. By 1857 80 per cent of houses in Norton Street were brothels, but that was according to the local rector, and Clipstone Street, Great Titchfield Street and Cirencester Place had gone the same way. It was said that some 900–1,000 prostitutes lodged here and round about. On one evening's walk from the Haymarket to Portland Place, an observer counted 185 on the way.[13]

Ten years on and some newer suburbs had almost as dubious reputations. Brompton was one smart London suburb well known for courtesans (prosperous kept women available at a price to men other than their protectors); another was St John's Wood. Neither was known for brothels. But Pimlico was far worse in this respect, apparently from its earliest days. By the 1890s 'the whole district swarms with prostitutes', lodging in every third house, Booth thought, using small hotels there as 'accommodation houses'. The Lisson Grove area near Edgware

Road, the outer circle of Regent's Park, the City Road and Pentonville hill, the main streets from the Angel Islington to Highbury, scores of little suburban slum outcrops from Queensland Road, Holloway, to Sultan Street, Camberwell, and from Grove Avenue, Walham Green, to Goring Street, Haggerston, all reveal prostitution as a thriving element in newly built suburban London.[14]

Some of these areas, most notably Pimlico from 1860, were close to railway stations and there is no doubt that London's new transport hubs were as vitally connected to prostitution as the bridges and old City and West End coaching inns had been for generations before. By the 1890s prostitutes were as embedded in these districts as railway porters or van drivers. Either side of Euston Road 'is terribly cursed with prostitution. Its practice is connected with the presence of the railway termini.' Around the stations 'are a large number of brothels and disreputable houses, making the place notorious'.[15]

Despite these new additions to the spread of London prostitution in the nineteenth century, and despite ceaseless demolitions for roads and railways and model dwellings in the centre, it is striking how prostitution clung on to its traditional haunts. The Strand, for instance, was still 'one of the scandals of London' in the 1890s as it had been in Captain Gronow's day. Regent Street and Piccadilly Circus had not removed prostitution from the old line of Swallow Street, just provided a more gilded playground for its display. The same could be said for Trafalgar Square and the old brothel district around St Martin-in-the-Fields that it dislodged. And where the housebreakers' hammers had left old streets to fester, then conditions in the 1890s seem hardly to have moved on from the evidence to parliamentary committees seventy years before. We can see all this from Booth's survey of Seven Dials, Holborn, around 1889. In the parlour of 6 Parker Street 'a sickly young woman with a child in her arms and shortly expecting another . . . made a trifle by allowing other unfortunates to use her room'. At number 8 'may be seen about twenty women with matted hair, and face and hands most filthy, whose ragged clothing is stiff with accumulations of beer and dirt, their under-clothing, if they have any at all, swarming with vermin . . . These women are thieves, beggars, and prostitutes.' At number 23, 'a mother [lived] on the earnings of her young daughter' in a place where a woman had recently died in a fight over a bed. And much more of the same. A century of progress had largely passed these places and people by.[16]

One street more than any other symbolised the resilience and adapt-
ability of London prostitution in its smartest formation. That was the
Haymarket. There prostitution had long traditions, dating back to the
seventeenth century. Its period of greatest notoriety in the nineteenth
spanned about 1850 to 1870. In and around these twenty years the
Haymarket was 'a cancer in the great heart of the Metropolis', 'the
most infamous thoroughfare in London', 'quite Hogarthian', 'a spectacle such as you can find nowhere else', 'the wicked street', 'the unique
Haymarket', 'the real plague-spot of English society'.[17]

[P]erhaps no sight makes a more striking impression on [a stranger's] mind
than the brilliant gaiety of Regent Street and the Haymarket. It is not only
the architectural splendour of the aristocratic streets in that neighbourhood,
but the brilliant illumination of the shops, cafés, Turkish divans, assembly
halls, and concert rooms, and the troops of elegantly dressed courtesans,
rustling in silks and satins, and waving in laces, promenading along these
superb streets among throngs of fashionable people, and persons apparently
of every order and pursuit, from the ragged crossing-sweeper and tattered
shoe-black to the high-bred gentleman of fashion and scion of society.[18]

Police in the late 1850s thought that from half an hour after midnight
there were about 100 prostitutes on the Haymarket pavements and
another 200 eating and drinking in places nearby. It was in this that
its versatility lay. It was not just a simple promenade. It was the piazza
of an entire district turned over at night to sexual commerce. Here
were cafés and restaurants and 'night houses', here were brothels and
accommodation houses, and here were assembly rooms where buyers
and sellers could freely appraise one another before settling a price. It
was all like a giant bazaar with innumerable counters where the
commodity – at almost every available price but the cheapest – was
women's company.

The most famous of all these places was the Argyll Rooms, 7½
Great Windmill Street, at the top of the Haymarket. Built as an indoor
tennis court in the 1740s, the Argyll had subsequently been used as
a circus, theatre and exhibition hall before being leased in 1849 to
Robert Bignell, an entrepreneur who dabbled extensively in the West
End's seamy side. Bignell converted the old building into a gleaming
dance hall or 'casino' (entrance a shilling), with an upstairs gallery
and bar (another shilling to pay) for lounging on velvet benches,

drinking and watching the dancing below. By the summer of 1850 the Argyll Rooms were sufficiently established as a resort of prostitutes for troubled William Gladstone to wait and watch outside in one of his early efforts to save fallen women – 'save one for me', the old music-hall joke would go.[19]

The Argyll became famous for its band under Laurent, formerly of the Adelaide Gallery, an early casino at the Lowther Arcade, the Strand. By the 1860s it was the premier dance saloon in London, open every night but Sunday, from 8.30 p.m. to midnight. On the dance floor was a strange mix of clerks and women of the town. Above in the gallery were army officers, gentlemen, louche aristocrats all drinking and mingling with London's smartest courtesans. This really was *en haut à bas*. 'The brilliancy of the lights, many times repeated by the panelled mirrors with which the ceiling and walls were lined – the crimson and gilt decorations – the excellent music – the gay dresses – and the gaiety of those who wore them – altogether formed a dazzling *coup d'oeil . . .*'[20]

It was here – and at the Adelaide, the Holborn Casino and others – that the smartest prostitutes in London migrated when the theatre saloons were closed down. Indeed, one was made necessary by the other. But eventually, in their turn, the casinos would also be suppressed. The Argyll Rooms lost their music and dancing licence in 1857 after clerical and parochial agitation. But the closure was thought to have made street prostitution even worse, so the Argyll reopened a year later. It enjoyed another twenty years' dazzle, though year after year the struggle to obtain a licence grew tougher and more expensive, engaging London's top-priced legal minds on either side. It was a struggle finally lost. The Argyll Rooms closed for ever on 30 November 1878.[21]

Other places closed too. In the Haymarket heyday, when midnight struck, 'loose persons of both sexes' swept out of the casinos and into 'the divans and night houses' around the Haymarket for smoke, drink, food, conversation and negotiation. They were known for luxury and exclusiveness. The cigar or Turkish divans had a lounge and bar, the night houses added kitchen and tables, sometimes with a small band and dance floor, all unlicensed; a few had bedrooms over. There were dozens – Kate Hamilton's, the Raleigh, Mott's, Rose Young's, Coney's, Kate Franks's, Sally Sutherland's – in the Haymarket, Jermyn Street (where there was also a notorious Turkish bath), Panton Street, Oxenden

Street and around, shifting location and swapping keepers as the exigencies of trade and repression dictated. The law had tried to deal with them since the Refreshment Houses Act of 1860 ('the One a.m. Act') and in 1872 the licensing laws stipulated a half-past-twelve finish across central London. But the law was one thing, enforcing it another. And the Haymarket night houses, as select and quiet places where prostitutes could gather to eat and drink and meet clients, flourished till 1867 and were not finally stamped out till around 1874.[22]

By that time the Haymarket's accommodation houses had largely disappeared too. These were places where prostitutes took their clients, and vice versa (as distinct from brothels, where clients went to meet women who lived or worked or could be brought there). We can see inside one – 13 James Street, Haymarket – Walter's favourite resort in the 1850s and 1860s. And we can see why. The room he often chose

was handsome throughout, had a big four-post bed with handsome hangings . . . on one side of the room, on another side by a partition was a wash-stand of marble, against the wall on the opposite side a large glass just at the level of the bed; at the foot of the bed a large sofa opposite to the fire; over the chimney-piece a big glass sloping forwards, so that those sitting or lying on the sofa could see themselves reflected in it; in the angle of the room by the windows a big cheval-glass which could be turned in any direction, two easy-chairs and a bidet, the hangings were of red damask, two large gas-burners were over the chimney-piece angles. It was the most compact, comfortable baudy house bed-room I have perhaps ever been in, although by no means a large room. They charged seven and six for its use, and twenty shillings for the night. Scores of times I have paid both fees.[23]

The West End clean up of 1868–74 made the position of the accommodation houses no longer tenable. Their function shifted to 'coffee shops where they wrote up "beds"' in the window, and to small hotels in Pimlico, Chelsea, Brompton and districts near the railway termini. Hotels and coffee shops had always played a part in London prostitution, and in a more vigilant climate their comings and goings attracted less parish attention than private houses in residential streets.[24]

In those same repressive years another great gathering place of the demi-monde was on tired legs. This was Cremorne Gardens, entered from Chelsea's King's Road or from the river, which had replaced Vauxhall as London's premier open-air dancing saloon at the end of the 1850s. For a time the two attractions ran in tandem on either side

Charles M'Gee, crossing sweeper, Ludgate Hill, 1815. Thought to be seventy-three years old and with only one eye, the Jamaican born M'Gee was said to do well at the begging pitch he'd claimed as his own for many years. He was one of numerous black beggars – 'St Giles blackbirds' they were called – in London in the early part of the century. 'Black people, as well as those destitute of sight, seldom fail to excite compassion,' thought John Thomas Smith, that brilliant chronicler of London who drew, etched and published this print.

City traffic outside the Royal Exchange, 1897. This was the third Royal Exchange on the site, the second burning down in 1838 to be replaced by this self-confident statement from Imperial Rome, designed by William Tite. At the time this photograph was taken some 1.2 million people entered the City for business each day, around 300,000 working there in offices and workshops.

The docks, unloading a merchantman, *c.* 1885. London river was a major source of metropolitan wealth and employment, expanding beyond all bounds in the nineteenth century. The docks were notorious for their reliance on poorly-paid casual labour to make good the shifting demands of port work. But they employed a wide range of workers, including officials, clerks and skilled workers, as this picture shows.

Workmen at Liverpool Street Station, Enfield Town platform, 1884. From the 1880s the railways began to attract working-class passengers with 'cheap trains', run especially by the London and North Eastern Railway. Workers could travel, as here, from central London to the Enfield small-arms factories. But as working-class suburbs developed along the tracks, tens of thousands would journey the other way by the century's end.

A good day in the New Cut, c. 1890. The New Cut was one of south London's busiest street markets, especially on Saturday nights. Here, on a sunny weekday, a woman stall-keeper gets ready to pack up after selling all her wares: they seem to have been fruit and veg.

The Cheap Fish of St. Giles's, 1877. John Thomson's wonderful photographs for his *Street Life in London* give a brutally honest picture of some of the poorest in London. He records that the boy with the pitcher is 'Little Mic-Mac Gosling': though just three feet ten inches tall he was seventeen. He went barefoot more through choice than poverty, a habit acquired while at sea on a merchantman. Joseph Carney, the coster on the left, had traded well that day with the best of a barrel of 500 herrings he'd bought for 25 shillings.

London Street Arabs, *c*. 1890. Neglected and abandoned children were London's greatest shame throughout the century. 'I called them human squirrels,' wrote the photographer Paul Martin, 'for when they caught sight of the school inspector, they were over a six-foot paling in a flash, and made off to Lambeth Walk.'

Fleet Street looking east towards St Paul's, *c*. 1899. The century saw the extraordinary rise of the 'street of ink' as centre of the newspaper publishing industry of the nation, provincial as well as metropolitan. The offices of the *Northern Daily Telegraph* advertise themselves from upper windows over the shop on the far right.

Bartholomew Fair, 1808. Swingboats, round-abouts, sausage fryers, a gaming table, accidents, fights, dancing to a fiddler, Thomas Rowlandson's Londoners are among the finest of early nine-teenth-century figures and here they teem in profusion. But all is overshadowed by the fair's travelling theatres, Richardson's to the fore, clowns on the steps drawing paying crowds into the tent. In the original the canvas is painted pink and green.

The Orchestra, Vauxhall Gardens, 1809. Magnificently lit and decorated the orchestra was the centre-point of music and dancing in fine weather at the Gardens, London's main summer attraction in the first three decades of the century. But in the dark walks, away from the oil lamps, more secret pleasures were taken.

Children dancing to a street organ, Lambeth, *c.* 1890. The piece playing is a famous dance-tune from the Gaiety Theatre, 'Pas de Quatre', involving much 'leg-twisting'. Somerset Maugham's Liza, from the same place and period though a bit older, could never resist showing her dancing skills when a street organ played.

Bank Holiday dancing about to begin, Hampstead Heath, *c.* 1897. The music here was provided by a mouth organ and the steps appear to need thought and planning before beginning. The girls are in their Sunday best and probably work in factories or shops during the week.

of the Thames. Cremorne opened for dancing in splendid formal gardens from about 1847, the ubiquitous Laurent playing there in the early seasons. Even then it was a place for men about town and prostitutes, at least from 10 p.m. when respectable couples were replaced as thoroughly as shifts at a factory. Cremorne shrugged off the puritan reaction of 1857–8 that briefly closed the Argyll, and under Edward Tyrrell Smith from 1861–70 it became the liveliest – sometimes the rowdiest – of London's night spots. Here, around midnight, would gather some 700 men and 300 prostitutes. The spectacle could be dull fare for those not dancing and without a particular end in view, but food and drink, lamplit walks and occasional rows could make it all a night to remember. In the 1870s, under John Baum, the rows became just too memorable and the main trade of late-night Cremorne just too brazen for modern tastes. Annual assaults on the music and dancing licence by the Chelsea Vestry, urged on by a prominent clergyman, made things difficult for Baum, and an unsuccessful libel action he brought against one tormentor precipitated closure in 1877.[25]

By the end of the 1870s the surface pattern of London prostitution was beginning to shift once more. The departure of Vauxhall and Cremorne, and of the casinos and night houses round the Haymarket, shepherded the smartest prostitutes into the music halls and a few great West End restaurants, and returned the remainder to the streets. The West End music halls – first the Alhambra, joined later by the Empire – had been associated with prostitution from their beginnings. Outside the Lord Chamberlain's jurisdiction, they revived the old theatre saloons in a more luxurious, decorous and better-behaved environment. When alternative venues for display shut down, the music-hall promenade became more popular among prostitutes. About 100 walked the gallery of the Alhambra every night around 1866, but then there were other opportunities. By the 1880s and 1890s the music-hall promenades were the premier showcase of well-dressed prostitution in London. The numbers might seem far fewer than the absence of rival attractions would suggest: 180 'women of "objectionable character"' at the Empire around 1894, for instance. Even so, scenes were redolent of the Argyll Rooms in their heyday. The Empire's promenade behind the 'Royal Circle' was known as 'the Cosmopolitan Club of Europe'. 'Famous men-about-town, like Col. Newnham-Davis ("The Dwarf of Blood", of "The Pink 'Un" [*The Sporting Times*]) had their favourite seats in the promenade, holding court of their admirers – bearers of famous names in the aristocracy, the Army, the judicial Bench.' The Empire and Alhambra promenades; the Alhambra 'canteen', a basement saloon and bar where ballet girls in costume relaxed in the company of well-heeled admirers; and a few smart eating places like St James's Restaurant ('Jimmy's') and the Café de l'Europe, all carried remnants of the traditions of the 1850s and 1860s through to the century's end.[26]

Street prostitution, though, survived in more than remnants. Its techniques had altered little over time. In the East End and other working-class districts solicitation was obvious, the prostitute gazing at the man or speaking first. '"Johnnie darling, won't you come home with me?"' startled the teenage John Lane one evening at Euston Square: he couldn't understand how she knew his name, and 'incontinently took to his heels'.[27] Cheaper West End prostitutes had similar methods. But the smartest in the West End expected the man to speak first. Some acted and dressed so respectably, adding excitement to the chase, that not even Walter could always recognise such a woman for what she was.

One summer's morning about midday, I was in the Quadrant. It had been raining, and the streets were dirty. In front of me I saw a well-grown woman . . . She was holding her petticoats well up out of the dirt, the common habit of even respectable women then [c. 1860]. With gay ladies the habit was to hold them up just a little higher . . . Just by Beak Street she stopped, and looked into a shop. 'Is she gay?' I thought. 'No.' I followed on, passed her, then turned round and met her eye. She looked at me, but the look was so steady, indifferent, and with so little of the gay woman in her expression, that I could not make up my mind as to whether she was accessible or not.

She turned back and went on without looking round. Crossing Tichborne Street she raised her petticoats higher, it was very muddy there . . . I followed quickly, saying as I came close, 'Will you come with me?' She made no reply, and I fell behind. Soon she stopped again at a shop, and looked in, and again I said, 'May I go with you?' 'Yes, – where to?'[28]

All this could make some streets especially difficult for respectable women. And in 1881, some years after all the closures of night haunts, this is how street prostitution in the West End looked even to the Metropolitan Police:

from 3 o'clock in the afternoon, it is impossible for any respectable woman to walk from the top of the Haymarket to Wellington-street, Strand. From 3 or 4 o'clock in the afternoon, Villiers-street and Charing Cross Station, and the Strand, are crowded with prostitutes, who are there openly soliciting prostitution in broad daylight. At half-past 12 at night [when 20,000 people were on the streets as theatres and pubs closed their doors], a calculation was made a short time ago that there were 500 prostitutes between Piccadilly Circus and the bottom of Waterloo-place.[29]

There is no reason to believe that the volume of prostitution declined much at all between the naughty 1860s and the equally naughty 1890s. But at the turn of the century, when men looked back they did detect changes, most of all in the manners and behaviour of prostitutes. Drunkenness (among West End prostitutes at least) was said to have declined after the polka era of the late 1840s, when vigorous exercise began to take better care of face and figure. Most flaunting lewdness had gone by the late 1860s – there were no more Granby Streets after 1868. Disorder was less frequently met with, even at night in the West End. In all, 'School Board education and an acquired knowledge of the laws of hygiene' had done much for the London prostitute, thought a man of the world in 1913. 'When one compares the toilet, the costume, and the manners, of the *demi-mondaines* who nightly frequent the back of the dress-circle of certain houses of entertainment, with the tawdry, over-painted, giggling, solicitous creature of thirty years ago, then, and only then, can one understand the gratifying change that has taken place.'[30]

'Another Unfortunate'

Who were these women? They came from 'every state in life'. A survey of around 16,000 London prostitutes imprisoned for short periods at Millbank Penitentiary in the late 1880s showed their fathers to be from every imaginable calling, from dock labourer and horsekeeper, through clerk and commercial traveller, to professional man and gentleman. 'Clergyman's daughter' was a favourite origin to claim, but that was just tongue in cheek. In short, there is little to suggest that prostitutes' backgrounds did other than reflect the broad class spectrum of London society as a whole. Around half were London-born and, given all we have seen about migration to the capital, that seems unremarkable too.

There were, though, special factors that might indicate why some rather than others chose prostitution as a career, at least for some periods of their lives. Evidence of a disturbed home life was very common: in 4,558 cases both parents were said to be dead, and in a further 3,540 one parent was no longer living. And the dominance among previous employments of domestic service (40 per cent) and the needle trades (17 per cent) suggests that drudgery and poverty – in work where the contrasts of finery and comfort were daily apparent – provided an important push.[31]

Contemporaries often mistook factors like these for the 'causes' of prostitution. But the largest cause of any was the importunate demands of men. And the lure of easy money that these demands produced was the major reason for individual women choosing prostitution as a career. The opportunities were inexhaustible. The pressures on women to exploit them were enormous, in some cases irresistible. We have seen, in the starvation wages for needlewomen, what scant rewards hard labour might bring. So poverty was a driver for many. Yet just as important was the grinding inability to satisfy material wants even among those who were not poor, in a world where the possibilities of consumption and the expanding sphere of pleasure were increasingly plain to all. What jingled in men's pockets might seem the answer to these unrequited desires. A deal in these circumstances was easily struck. 'My friend has often told me that he has picked up half a dozen virgins in the streets. That a sovereign, offered to lasses looking in at a Linen-drapers [*sic*], will get them to a house, and that the sight of the gold vanquishes them.'[32]

Concerned more with morals than political economy, contemporaries were constantly surprised at how little those traditional morality tales of seduction by means of a broken promise, class deference or *force majeure* actually played in the real-life narratives of London prostitution. Easy money was all the seduction generally needed for women choosing their livelihood on the streets, and who could blame them? They were 'led away by such allurements as, "Nothing to do." "Plenty of money." "Your own mistress." "Perfect liberty." "Being a lady", as they say.' And when they had the chance, indeed how they said so. At a 'Midnight Mission' at the Café Royal around 1875 the first thing that struck the observer was that none seemed hungry. A preacher asked

'What is the great mystery of life?' . . . and was answered, 'Want of money!' which caused shouts of laughter, general disturbance, and complete interruption of the proceedings for several minutes. 'Happiness', he resumed, 'is not

in silks and satins, theatres or champagne.' He was again interrupted by low
fierce hisses, which seemed to come from all parts of the hall.[33]

We can see these influences absorbed into working-class culture and
acting on one young woman in the life history of 'Another Unfortunate',
who spelled it out eloquently in a letter to *The Times* on Christmas
Eve, 1858. Her father had been a brickmaker somewhere on the edge
of London, it seems, and her parents were both drinkers. She had been
a 'very pretty child' and she lost her virginity at thirteen. She grew up
aware of girls moving away and coming back on visits 'with a profusion of ribands, fine clothes, and lots of cash'. Their open-handed prosperity was explained 'by knowing winks and the words "luck" and
"friends"'. It was one of these who introduced Another Unfortunate
to prostitution at the age of fifteen. By eighteen she had a special
'protector' who encouraged her to educate herself. She too returned
on visits, supporting her parents, burying them 'decently', setting up
one brother in trade and helping another with defence lawyers when
caught thieving. Her two sisters followed her into prostitution and
were also kept in part by special friends.

Now, what if I am a prostitute, what business has society to abuse me? . . . I
earn my money and pay my way, and try to do good with it, according to
my ideas of good. I do not get drunk, nor fight, nor create uproar in the
streets or out of them . . . I do not use bad language. I do not offend the public
eye by open indecencies. I go to the Opera, I go to Almack's, I go to the
theatres, I go to quiet, well-conducted casinos . . .

And she patronised milliners and silk mercers and bootmakers who
knew what she was but were glad of her custom.[34]

Here was one success story among many. For prostitution could
provide pretty girls with the quickest possible exit from slums like
Seven Dials throughout the century. It was plain for all to see: 'They
appear dressed, in my division, with a belcher over their shoulders (one
of the coloured handkerchiefs); they come two and two through the
streets, and after a few days they are dressed a little more elaborately;
and at last you see them launch out in silks and satins.' And in
Whitechapel in 1861 John Hollingshead noted how

The best paid occupation appears to be prostitution, and it is a melancholy
fact that a nest of bad houses in Angel Alley, supported chiefly by the farmers'

men who bring the hay and straw to Whitechapel market twice a week, are the cleanest-looking dwellings in the district. The windows have tolerably neat green blinds, the doors have brass plates, and inside the houses there is comparative comfort, if not plenty.[35]

But where did these women end up? No one knows what happened to Another Unfortunate, but there is no reason to suppose that her career brought less chance of a satisfying relationship or marriage and domestic comfort than that of any other woman of the lower middle class, as she had by then become. The upward social mobility offered by prostitution had been acknowledged by commentators as early as 1857, a corrective to older and gloomier prognostications for the 'wages of sin'. There were more bourgeois customers than bourgeois prostitutes to satisfy them and in this hopeful market the opportunities for clever and attractive women from the working classes were legion.[36]

We can take two more examples from the same era as Another Unfortunate. The first comes from that extraordinary diarist Arthur Munby, a minor poet and civil servant who was one of the great *flâneurs* and observers of London life at mid-century. Among his many women acquaintances, some of them prostitutes, was Sarah Tanner. Munby first met her in 1854 or 1855, when she was about twenty-one years old and maid of all work to an Oxford Street shopkeeper. A year or two later she was a prostitute 'in gorgeous apparel' walking Regent Street. She had chosen the life 'of her own accord & without being seduced. She saw no harm in it: enjoyed it very much, thought it might raise her & perhaps be profitable.' Then, in July 1859, he met Sarah again, this time in the Strand. She had been 'taking lessons in writing and other accomplishments' and was dressed 'not professionally as a "lady", but quietly & well, like a respectable upper servant'. She had left the streets with savings after three years and was now running the Hampstead Coffeehouse near the Waterloo Road. A singular insight, he thought, into the surprising consequences 'of the "Social Evil"'.[37]

And then there was 'Kitty', whom Walter met in the Strand on 'a blazing hot day in June', around 1856. She was about sixteen, maybe a little less, and not long a 'gay woman'. Her mother was a widow, a charwoman, living, it seems, close to the Strand, who did not know how Kitty earned her money. She supposed Kitty to be at home looking after two young siblings. In fact she locked them in the family's one room and told them to be quiet while she tried her luck on the streets. She went with Walter for 3s 6d – 'the exact sum' – and despite the hardships of her home life, 'She was beautifully clean in her flesh, her linen was clean, its colour awful.' He asked Kitty what she spent her money on. '"I buy things to eat, I can't eat what Mother gives us ... so I buys food, and gives the others what Mother gives me, they don't know better ..." "What do you like?" "Pies and sausage-rolls", said the girl, smacking her lips and laughing, "Oh! my eye, ain't they prime, – oh!"' Four or five years later Walter met Kitty again in Regent Street. She was 'an elegantly dressed woman with her veil down. Through it I saw her eyes fixed on mine, and knew her at once.' She was no longer on the town.

Kitty told me her recent history, it seemed probable to me then, and not improbable now. She met a gentleman, went to a house with him, then saw him again, and again; he offered to keep her and she had been with him ever since. He kept her mother and lived with Kitty, but could not introduce her into society, and was about to sell his commission and take her abroad to marry her. He was an officer, and on talking with her she was certainly well up in army matters.[38]

That these rags-to-comfort stories were not exceptional a whole constellation of courtesans bears witness. The details of their lives are foggy, obscured in part by invention and misdirection from the women themselves. But the highest shooting stars were most likely to come from that uniquely effervescent, ambitious and enterprising stratum in English society – one especially strong in London – the lower middle class.

So Mary Anne Clarke, mistress of the Duke of York, who scandalised the nation in 1809 by obtaining army commissions at a price from her royal lover, was brought up in obscure circumstances at Ball and Pin Alley, White's Alley, Chancery Lane, and was said to have married first a compositor and second a master builder. Harriette Wilson, whose memoirs (1825) terrorised the aristocracy and political elite, was the daughter of a master stocking cleaner and mender and was raised among the deferential but worldly tradesmen of Mayfair. Catherine Walters – 'Skittles' – the most famous London courtesan of the 1850s and 1860s, was daughter to a Liverpool customs man: Skittles would become the most stunning of the 'horsebreakers', finely skilled riders showing off horses' paces in Hyde Park to sell the mounts and themselves into the pricey bargain. And there were many others whose names have come down to us and who made – and often lost – fortunes from prostitution. Like Agnes Willoughby, whose marriage to a Norfolk squire was attacked by his relatives through a suit to declare him insane. Or Elizabeth Howard, the mistress of Napoleon III, who met him at the Blessington-D'Orsays' in 1839. Or Kate Cooke, who became the Marquess of Euston. Or famous Mabel Gray, a Regent Street shop-girl, who just missed by an eyelash marrying into the English upper classes.[39]

But what went up could also go down. And many began at the bottom and hardly rose at all. Most prostitutes did not stay long in the business: 'every month I find fresh girls come and the old ones disappear,' observed Joseph Dunlap, superintendent of police in the West End, in 1881. They moved out as luck or capacity gave cause – to cohabit or marry or to find an opening in other work. Some, like Helen Gissing, George's first wife, found the life ruinous through drink; others through disease, sometimes worse. These were all occu-pational hazards. And instability was inherent in a trade subject to hyper-competition in an over-stocked labour market. As in many other London trades, a casual fringe of unsuccessful earners – as well as 'amateurs' and part-timers – could make a sale hard to find for those without special appeal. Competition was made worse by foreign women chancing their charms in Europe's greatest city and rising in numbers as London became more cosmopolitan in character towards the century's end. Between 1884 and 1886, of 4,286 pros-titutes arrested in the West End, 769 were French, 641 German and sixty-three Belgian. [40]

In trying to chart these dynamics it's important to put to one side a distortion in the literature. Most writing about London prostitution in these years has highlighted bourgeois clients and the West End trade. But the majority of prostitution was carried on between working-class men and women. Between 1884 and 1886 three times as many pros-titutes were arrested outside the West End as in it. And at society's outer edge there were even tramping prostitutes for tramping men. 'The female vagrants generally consist of prostitutes of the lowest and most miserable kind. They are mostly young girls, who have sunk into a state of dirt, disease, and almost nudity.' That was Mayhew writing of the late 1840s, a desperate decade. But it was still all true fifteen years on. In the summer of 1864 Munby saw many girls sleeping out in the daytime in St James's Park. The park-keeper knew them as 'degraded prostitutes'.

One girl lay in rags at my feet, her face hidden between her outstretched arms. I spoke to her: but it was at least a minute before she heeded. When she did lift her dirty sodden face, she seemed halfmazed: answered, that she was about twenty; a shawlfringemaker; out of work; no father nor mother; no home; comes here to lie down every day . . . [As] soon as I stopped asking, she covered her face again and curled herself up without a word.[41]

Women like these would be lucky to pick up a shilling from homeless men, filthy and louse-ridden like themselves. But moving up the social scale, for labourers and artisans there were streetwalkers galore. It was women in the cheap common lodging houses of Spitalfields and Whitechapel – the East End's west end, as it were – who provided commercial sex for dock and building labourers and market porters. It was women lodging two to a room in houses with understanding landladies who plied Stamford Street, Southwark, or York Road, Lambeth, or the Euston Road, St Pancras, to lure the artisan or clerk. And it was women at these ends of the London trade who seemed to prove most vulnerable to extreme violence at the hands of men who were, or purported to be, their clients.

The underworld of London prostitution took many violent forms. Violence always attended, in one way or another, the exploitation of children. There were a few cases – not many identified as such in the press – of sexual murder of boys and girls. But child prostitution was far less uncommon. There are some hideous instances in Walter's memoirs, the earliest beginning at a masquerade late at night in Vauxhall Gardens, around 1848:

I passed a woman leading a little girl dressed like a ballet-girl, and looked at the girl who seemed about ten years old, then at the woman who winked. I stopped, she came up and said, 'Is she not a nice little girl? . . . Would you like to see her undressed?'. . . The little girl kept tugging the woman's hand and saying, 'Oh! Do come to the fireworks.'

The girl called the woman aunt, but she was a neighbour who had looked after her when her parents died – to save her from the workhouse, she said. Walter paid three sovereigns. The girl was not a virgin. 'She [the "aunt"] was in difficulties, she must live, the child would be sure to have it done to her some day, why not make a little money by her? Some one else would if she did not.'[42]

Some violence also seems to have been a natural part of life in brothels. Abduction and kidnapping were much rarer than reformers led contemporaries to believe: in 1881, Superintendent Dunlap had never, in a long career, come across a case of a young girl 'led into a life of prostitution by any artifice' and had never known of one held in a brothel against her will. But there were certainly a few cases of this kind before about 1830, and more frequently girls were exploited in brothels in ways similar to 'truck' among other elements of the London workforce. They were charged extortionate rent and board and dress hire and were then threatened with ejection in rags if the price were not obtained. These 'dress-lodgers' were not uncommon even into the late 1870s and no doubt many women who took to the life negotiated things to their own satisfaction with the brothel-keeper. But they were usually watched when on the streets by a man or older woman – at least when newly 'out' – to ensure they didn't abscond in their finery. This dress-lodging trade fell away from about 1880, with brothels facing more vigorous action from parish authorities and puritan societies and becoming scarcer in the process.[43]

Then violence was never far away from prostitutes' relations with bullies, fancy men, ponces or pounceys. These were the men kept financially by prostitutes and who offered protection, lust and love in return. Largely scorned by the working-class communities from which they came, more isolated than prostitutes themselves, they could be bitterly fought over by the women who craved their company. One emerges from the Booth notebooks for Islington in 1897. This was 'Jim'. About thirty-eight and with a grown-up son, 'herculean to look at, enormous chest, arms which looked as if they wd burst his coat sleeves and huge hands, about 6ft high', he was 'a "fair terror" in the neighbourhood'. 'Jim seems to be worshipped by women who go for one another tooth and nail whenever he changes the object of his affections.'[44]

Fancy men like these could turn their hand to violence against clients, to blackmail, to robbery and theft. Many prostitutes filched as a matter of course: one unlucky businessman woke up in a Paddington hotel bedroom with everything of value gone, including his false teeth. And robberies with violence, the women decoying and the bully closing in with blows and kicks, were common enough, especially along the riverside. Inevitably bullies would show off their strength against the women who depended on them or who could not escape them. Francis Jones, the '"Terror of the Haymarket"', preyed on West End prostitutes in the 1860s: repeatedly 'convicted for assaulting women of the unfortunate class', he got two years' hard labour for slashing Georgina Evans's throat with a razor in March 1866. The assault took place in the street when Georgina dared intervene to protect another prostitute from him.[45]

Georgina Evans survived. Countless others did not. No one knows the tally of murdered London prostitutes in the nineteenth century. We can assume they died in some numbers every year, their true count disguised by the crude forensic understanding of the time. Sometimes they died so horribly that the visceral hatred of women borne by a few men was plain for all to see. Like poor Elizabeth Winterflood (a.k.a. Ann Webb), just eighteen and 'very handsome', found dying in Higler's Lane (later Friar Street), Borough, in 1806; strangled and beaten about the head, 'a piece of flesh ['the size of a nut'] was also found to be cut and torn away from the lower and secret part of the body!' Like Eliza Grimwood of the Waterloo Road, killed in 1838, apparently by a client with 'the look of a foreigner' whom she'd picked up at the Strand Theatre. She was stabbed in the abdomen and chest and had her throat cut: her watch and seals worth £80 were still about her and robbery seems not to have been the motive. Like the Flower and Dean Street prostitute Sissy Aldridge, beaten to death at Brecker's Hotel near Finsbury Square in 1870 by Jacob Spinass, the hotel's Swiss porter. Her face unrecognisable from her injuries, she was identified by her boots, on loan from another prostitute.[46]

And Flower and Dean Street brings us to the 'autumn of terror' and the 'Whitechapel murders' of Jack the Ripper, so fully documented (and so bizarrely ascribed) over the intervening years that we need do no more here than commemorate the victims: Mary Ann (Polly) Nichols at Buck's Row, 31 August 1888; Annie Chapman in the backyard of 29 Hanbury Street, 8 September; Elizabeth (Long Liz) Stride at Berner Street and Kate Eddowes at Mitre Square, both 30 September; and Mary Kelly at 13 Miller's Court, Dorset Street, 8 November. Most were living in the common lodging houses of Flower and Dean Street and Thrawl Street at the time of their deaths. Their murderer was most likely to have been an anonymous working man frequenting prostitutes thereabout for some time past. The Ripper murders were unique in their unrelenting ferocity and terrible mystery. But horror faced London prostitutes constantly throughout the century. And we need only turn to the years immediately following the Whitechapel killings for our final examples. Among murders that police failed to solve in London in 1889 were those of probably four prostitutes. One was found battered to death in Algernon Road, Lewisham; parts of Elizabeth Jackson's dismembered body were found at Chelsea, Battersea and in the river; Alice McKenzie was found with her throat cut and with abdominal wounds in Castle Alley, Whitechapel, and was conceivably another Ripper victim; and a portion of the body of an unknown woman was found under a railway arch at Pinchin Street, St George's-in-the-East. And the years 1891 and 1892 were rendered vilely memorable by the serial poisonings of at least four south London prostitutes by Thomas Neill Cream, another frequenter of 'fallen women'.[47]

These were the ghastly consequences of a risky profession. They were the counterweight to those more hopeful examples of women for whom prostitution provided a swift and not too taxing way out of rags and hunger. Both remained true, even in those years over which Jack the Ripper cast such a long shadow. We should finally return to this hopefulness as representing more the reality of prostitution than the terrible ill-luck of some, and we can do so in a brief visit to the suburb most associated with upwardly mobile prostitution, St John's Wood. This was 'the Wicked Wood', with 'Naughty North Bank' and a host of shaded and shady locations. Any reference to St John's Wood in a nineteenth-century novel tipped a wink at secret sex, its signs easily deciphered by the knowing reader. So when an American visitor in a novel of 1898 asks saucy Mrs Verulam the whereabouts of St John's Wood she is told, '"Well, where it oughtn't to be, you understand."' Here lived a silken regiment of kept women and high-class prostitutes who walked Bond Street or the Burlington Arcade and came home from Jimmy's in a hansom or hired barouche.[48]

That it still had drawing power in the 1890s is revealed in the extraordinary tale of the confidence trickster Augustus William Meyers, for whom unlucky Adolf Beck was infamously mistaken and twice imprisoned. Meyers's victims were mostly prostitutes, both amateurs and full-timers, whom he met in the streets and persuaded that he wished to install them as his mistress – 'housekeeper', some said – at his fictional second home in St John's Wood. Arranging to visit them at their homes – not professionally, it seems – he would write out a list of clothes they should buy, gave them a false cheque for the approximate amount and then relieved them of rings and jewellery to match for size or copy as a present. Eighteen women were tricked in this way in 1877, at least ten more in 1894–6 and then others still around 1904. A number of his victims lived in Pimlico, Walham Green and Chelsea – they evidently saw St John's Wood as a superior rung on the ladder – and he met several in Bond Street, Charing Cross, Ludgate Hill, Piccadilly and elsewhere. '"I was looking into a jeweller's window when the prisoner spoke to me,"' testified Marion Taylor, a.k.a. Kate Duncan, in 1896. He '"addressed me in the usual way, and asked me if he might call"'.[49]

Throughout the century, scrape away at the surface respectability of London's streets and that potent combination of lust and money fever readily exposes itself. And not just in London's streets.

'Aphrodisiopolis'

On a Saturday afternoon in March 1866, Arthur Munby and a friend called at Lord Houghton's London town house, 16 Upper Brook Street, Mayfair. Drinking brandy-and-seltzer, the trio turned their attention to Houghton's 'favourite subject – venery: he produced out of a secret drawer R. Payne Knight's "Worship of Priapus", a book full of antique obscenities'. Houghton, looking 'sly, sensuous, and potentially wicked', was one of the great erotica collectors of his day. He referred to his country house in Yorkshire, where his main library was held, as 'Aphrodisiopolis'.[50]

Other wealthy men shared similar interests. In 1869 Charles Shirley Brooks, the *Punch* writer and novelist, dined at W. S. Potter's, 1 Adam Street, Adelphi. There were eight at the table, including 'two military types'.

His picture gallery has been enriched with some new abominations, some concealed behind decorous ones, and revealed by a spring . . . In almost any other man than P. the characteristic would be offensive, but he looks such a picture himself that somehow one forgets that a man of 60 ought not to be a showman of lechery . . . Swinburne, Elmore [Alfred, the artist] and Whistler have inspected his collection with much satisfaction. One work, of a whipping by women, was fine in spite of its brutality . . .[51]

Shirley Brooks didn't approve. And there's no doubt that tastes like these were rare, the capacity to indulge them rarer still. But nonetheless there was much material to choose from. London's pornographic book trade was lively throughout the nineteenth century. It centred, for almost all of it, at Holywell Street, the Strand. Until the 1840s the trade ran in tandem with second-hand clothes. But second-hand books began to dominate from around 1850, and Holywell Street soon became synonymous with the London dirty-book trade. The street also contained 'so-called chemists' shops where goods were hidden away inside'. Booksellers spilled over into neighbouring Wych Street, where their shops jostled with brothels. The link was not entirely accidental. Some prostitutes, especially, it seems, French women, enlivened their activities with erotic prints and tattered *Fanny Hills*.[52]

London pornography's most notorious figure was William Dugdale. Born in Stockport in 1800 but in London by the age of twenty, Dugdale was a frustrated revolutionary for whom pornography was a congenial conduit for both protest and profit. His business was conducted under various aliases and at several addresses in Holywell Street and around. Thomas Frost, who jobbed as a printer for Dugdale briefly in the early 1840s, recalled his 'sodden and sensual countenance' following a period of imprisonment when, it was rumoured, Home Office influence secured him an early release on medical grounds. But the laws against obscene publications were tightened in 1857. And Dugdale, a marked man, died in 1868 at the Clerkenwell House of Correction, serving a sentence of hard labour that the court must have known would kill him.[53]

Dugdale and his kind were beyond the pale of respectability even though their guinea publications could only be bought by the wealthy. But pornography penetrated the secret lives of the respectable bourgeoisie, and not just as consumers. John Camden Hotten, a publisher and collector of erotica, was friends with the great, including Lord Macaulay. John Black, a famous editor of the *Morning Chronicle*, friend of James and John Stuart Mill and (less surprisingly) a close companion of lecherous Lord Melbourne, sold off his collection of 'facetiae' 'to provide him with bread in his old age'. Artists, even Dickens's illustrator Phiz in *The Pretty Girls of London*, and writers like George Augustus Sala, would turn their hand to obscene material for the money and the fun of it. Sala was never entirely respectable, it's true, but his writings in Dickens's *Household Words* and elsewhere scrupulously avoided suggestive topics. He had almost nothing to say about prostitution, for instance. But his anonymous pornographic output included, it seems, *Harlequin Prince Cherrytop, and the Good*

Fairy Fairfuck, 'Oxford: Printed at the University Press MDCC-CLXXIX'.[54]

Lively as all this trade was, it was said to be pornographic photography in which London, of all European cities, excelled. Erotic still life had long been a feature of louche West End entertainments. *Poses plastiques* and *tableaux vivants* were shown in casinos and music halls and backstreet theatres. They were said to have been introduced to London by Professor Keller's German troupe at the Adelaide Gallery in 1846. 'Lord Chief Baron' Renton Nicholson quickly adapted them as a suitable end to the evening after a mock divorce trial (with female witnesses played by men in 'drag') at the Judge and Jury Club, Garrick's Head, Bow Street, and later at the Coal Hole off the Strand. The *poses plastiques* involved well-made men and women on a turntable adopting classical poses and wearing only skin-tight fleshings.[55]

Photography, operating in a private sphere, could be more versatile and abandoned. Obscene prints of women were offered to Arthur Munby in 1862 at photographers' shops in Westminster Bridge Road, Lambeth, and in Bloomsbury. The models were from varied backgrounds, including envelope makers, milliners and ballet (or chorus) dancers. A pornographic family enterprise was broken up in Pimlico in 1874 when police raided two studios run by Henry Hayler. They seized 130,000 photos and 5,000 slides, some of which involved Hayler, his wife and two sons. The family was running a worldwide postal business. Hayler escaped the police, absconding to Berlin. And a similar family affair was discovered in Holywell Street in the 1880s. The mail-order business had penetrated to Eton.[56]

Homosexual life in London was also forced more into this private sphere than was commercial sex between men and women. The law saw to that. Sodomy had been a criminal offence since the early sixteenth century. Until 1861 it was punishable by death. Two soldiers were hanged outside Newgate in 1811, with several 'noblemen' looking on among an outraged crowd. But the savage penalty and the difficulty of finding witnesses made convictions rare. Fresh codification of 'unnatural offences' from 1861 still prescribed harsh punishment for sodomy and for 'indecent assault' by one man on another. And in 1885 Henry Labouchere's addition to the Criminal Law Amendment Act punished any act of 'gross indecency' between men whether 'in public or private'.[57]

Despite this victimisation, the culture of homosexuality in London in the nineteenth century had many parallels with patterns of commercial sex between men and women. Despite the risks, young male prostitutes solicited in the West End streets, urged on by the prospects of good earnings. John Saul, later implicated in the Cleveland Street scandal, claimed to be earning £8 a week around 1879. St James's Park, conveniently close to the guards' barracks, was a well-known parade-ground for solicitation. So too were the Alhambra and the Gaiety, just as for men and women. Walter's later encounters with prostitutes sometimes involved homoerotic diversions. In the late 1860s, for instance, Betsy Johnson got him '"a man to frig"' (masturbate). It was '"easy enough"', she said, to find a 'sod' – '"there are plenty of them"'. Betsy introduced Walter to a male prostitute in Soho Square and all three went to the man's 'well-furnished' rooms north of Oxford Street. Walter gave him a sovereign, and Betsy two.[58]

There were numerous brothels and accommodation houses for men. The extraordinary White Swan public house, Vere Street, Clare Market, was home to the 'Sodomitical Club' or the Vere Street Coterie until broken up by police in 1810. Mock weddings – and real consummations – took place mainly on Sundays, though the upstairs rooms were in action all week long. A butcher was known as 'The Duchess of Devonshire', a coal merchant as 'Kitty Cambric', and the clientele was made up of a complete cross-section of London life from West End aristocrats to East End coal-heavers. A few years on and the White Lion public house, St Alban's Place, Haymarket, was a popular resort for guardsmen and their clients: the Honourable and Reverend Percy Jocelyn, Bishop of Clogher, was discovered 'in a situation' there in 1822.[59]

Most famous of all was 19 Cleveland Street, north of Oxford Street, where post office telegraph boys (mostly fifteen to seventeen years old) were brought to be enjoyed by older men. Customers handed over half a sovereign to the brothel-keeper, Charlie Hammond, who kept 6s for himself. Hammond's empire crashed around him in July 1889 and the ensuing trial shocked the nation. Six years later and the Oscar Wilde trials would hear of hotels in Piccadilly, restaurants in Rupert Street, the Café Royal, parties at a rough street near Westminster Abbey, of the Haymarket Theatre and Earl's Court Great Exhibition, and of male brothels at Fitzroy Street. At all these places Wilde met boys brought to him by pimps and friends. And all these places, or round about, were prominent in the sex-for-cash nexus involving men and women in London too.[60]

Prosecutions and trials and punishment remind us that so many of London's private pleasures were illicit. Even though prostitution was not in itself unlawful, it invariably strutted an impossibly narrow line, more often than not transgressing one or other aspect of the criminal law. With homosexual relations the position was clearer: any act, at any time or place, was liable to be labelled a crime and brutally punished as such. So all commercial sex, in one way or another, was drawn close to or into the London underworld. Prostitutes were often thieves or thieves' accomplices. Male prostitutes could add blackmail to their portfolio. But there were many other doors to the London underworld. And many other ways to earn a living once there.

Flower and Dean Street, 1862

FLOWER AND DEAN STREET: CRIME AND SAVAGERY

The Rookery

> Flower and Dean Street, Spitalfields, is associated in most people's minds with vice, immorality, and crime in their most hideous shapes, and rightly so, for as a matter of fact there is no street in any other part of this great Metropolis that has for its inhabitants a like number of the dangerous criminal class. Other streets there are even in its neighbourhood that vie with it in poverty, squalor and vice, but Flower and Dean Street has a character all its own. For to its tenements resort mostly that class of criminals the most daring and the most to be feared – the men who commit robberies accompanied with acts of violence.

THIS was how the local press – usually fiercely defensive of the East End's good name – described in 1881 'perhaps the foulest and most dangerous street in the whole metropolis'.[1]

From the demise of the worst part of the St Giles Rookery in the 1840s, the Flower and Dean Street neighbourhood had as bad a reputation as a 'thief-preserve' as any part of London until around 1895. Developed first in the 1650s by two Whitechapel bricklayers, John Flower and Gowen Deane, rebuilt in parts through the eighteenth century as the original structures decayed, overdeveloped in the early nineteenth century with back gardens cut up for courts and alleys, this was an archetypal London slum. Its main streets were narrow – Flower and Dean Street sixteen feet wide, narrowing to just ten feet at either end. The main buildings were disproportionately tall, three storeys of smoke-blacked brick and timber, some jutting out at first and second floors. The courts behind them were mere shanties of timber frames and brick-and-dirt-mortar infill. All this was to be expected in old London. What marked out this neighbourhood – Flower and Dean Street, Upper and Lower Keate Street, George Street, Thrawl Street, Wentworth Street and the litter of courts between – was the predominance within it of one of the great social institutions of the London poor. This was the common lodging house.[2]

There is no doubt that the Flower and Dean Street rookery was home to large numbers of thieves and the cheap prostitutes who associated with them. Even after Commercial Street 'ventilated' the western end we read of petitions to police in 1858 and 1859, begging protection from 'the frequent robberies and assaults which are committed in and about Commercial Street, and Flower and Dean Street in this parish', especially 'on Females' at 'the close of Evening Service'; of 800 'thieves, vagabonds, beggars, and prostitutes' in the area and adjoining in 1860; of Thomas Barnardo, preaching in lodging houses around 1867, robbed of 'hat, coat, watch and chain and money' by 'four roughs'; of twelve robberies with violence in Flower and Dean Street alone on four successive Saturday nights in 1881, and of 'it being useless for the police to follow beyond a certain point'; of a young Swede in that terrible autumn of 1888, decoyed by Mary Hawkes, eighteen, into a Flower and Dean Street lodging house for couples, set upon by four or five men and robbed of £4 and his trousers. And so on.[3]

There is no doubt, too, that the common lodging house had always played a large part in attracting thieves to the rookery. Here was the densest concentration of lodging-house beds in London. The five main streets had eighty with 2,107 lodgers on census night 1871. There were thirty-one with 902 lodgers in Flower and Dean Street alone. Many of the houses lacked street numbers, not uncommon in slum districts, and some at night were marked out from their neighbours by different coloured lamps as the red house, blue house or white house. Most lodgers were single people renting a bed for the night at 4d – 'doubles', used most by prostitutes and their clients, were 8d. Some paid for a week's lodging in advance, getting Sunday free, and a few were long-term residents. All slept in common dormitories, doubles partitioned off with boarding that didn't reach floor or ceiling. Lodgers cooked and ate in a single basement or backroom kitchen and washed in a trough or under a pump in the yard. There was nothing of even the semi-permanence of a one-room 'home' here. They catered for a mobile population for whom mobility was an aid to avoiding arrest or a summons – thieves, beggars, prostitutes. Just as important, the lodging houses sheltered the very poorest of Londoners, for whom mobility was no choice but necessity. These were people who, when they rose from their straw mattresses in the morning, did not know where the pennies for that night's 'kip' would come from, if come they would at all.[4]

But there was a mixture even in the lodging houses. Wilmott's Chambers, Thrawl Street, in the mid-1860s could put up around 100 lodgers in superior accommodation: a 'gaily-papered passage', a 'well-lit' kitchen with model range, accommodating bricklayers' labourers, navvies, a 'lower grade of artisan' moving between one job and another, 'shabby-genteel figures in rusty cloth' and the odd 'broken-down shopman'. Similarly Smith's in Flower and Dean Street. And besides the dock labourers, general labourers, hawkers and street sellers who made up four out of ten occupations in the Flower and Dean Street area in 1871 were a variety of workers in East End manufacturing (clothing, boot and shoe, furniture, umbrellas and sticks), a few seamen, many laundresses and charwomen, and the odd skilled worker.[5]

Probably all these were 'broken-down' too. A sanitary inspector's conclusion in 1880 that no house in the area was occupied by a 'respectable class of mechanic' could not have been far wrong. And degrading poverty was as great a fact of life here as criminality. 'Shocking Death from Starvation' was a frequent headline from the Flower and Dean Street rookery. Take a few instances from 1875 to 1880. Ellen Munro, twenty-seven, found dead in a doorway in Wentworth Street, 'her bones appeared to be protruding through the skin' – 'Witness had been in the force fifteen years, but had never found anything like it, even in a decomposed body'. Mary Connor, forty, 'nearly in a state of nudity' at 2 Keate Court, two spoonfuls of tea in her stomach, her 'skin adhered to the flesh like parchment'. Ellen Constable, twenty-six, a prostitute living in a common lodging house in Flower and Dean Street, her clothes 'a mass of rags', her stomach and intestines empty, her 'blood pure and liquid'. George Smith, sixty-nine, also at a Flower and Dean Street lodging house, 'had been starving for some very considerable time', his skin 'all colours', his blood 'like water'.[6]

We have here, then, people on the very margins of the metropolitan economy, clustering in the common lodging house with those who chose to be outside it altogether. To call this cluster 'a criminal class' is to accord it a homogeneity it did not possess, even though there were elements about it of class behaviour and of a common culture. The term misleads in another direction too: measured by value, most crime – as we saw in the City – was committed by other social groups entirely. Even so, populations like that of the Flower and Dean Street rookery remained a distinctive feature of London life well into the 1890s. They were marked out by their inexhaustible capacity for dishonest toil and by their disregard for norms and values that the rest of society ostensibly held dear. And they were distinguished by their poverty. Successful thieves, like successful prostitutes, did not stay in Flower and Dean Street – if only because they would not long remain immune from the depredations of their fellows.[7]

There was a ready supply of replacements, though, for those who moved on. Some were migrants from other parts of London and beyond, perhaps already used to the rookery way of life, or drifters down on their luck and ready for anything. Another source of recruitment, already familiar to us, was London's legion of homeless, abandoned or delinquent children. In the Flower and Dean Street lodging houses on census night in 1871 were sixty-eight children aged fourteen or younger, all apparently there as lodgers in their own right and just under half of them girls. According to Dr Barnardo, 'so many' common lodging-house 'inmates' were children even in 1888. This was thought to be especially a London phenomenon. Housing there was so expensive that 'many parents, owing to the want of room at home . . . make growing lads shift for themselves at a very early age'. Unable to afford a room, they ended up in lodging houses, corrupted by 'broken-down, worthless characters'. Others left drunken or violent parents who could provide no home for them. Like the brothers Hart, fifteen, thirteen and twelve, with 'no other resource but to thieve or starve', imprisoned together in the Westminster House of Correction in 1851. Others got into bad company: a fourteen-year-old serving twelve months for picking pockets recalled how 'a lot of boys came and took me from home; I went with them to a lodging-house by Cates-street [Keate Street], Whitechapel, where the little boys are; I paid threepence a night'. Others were orphaned. One boy of sixteen, in prison six times, lost his father at eleven and his mother in the workhouse at thirteen: he 'went a thieving; stealing provisions, and other articles from shops'. Yet others inherited thieving as a birthright. William Frith, the brilliant Victorian realist painter, hired as a model a boy crossing sweeper

who stole a watch-chain from him; a local policeman upbraided Frith –
'"Didn't you notice his 'air with the prison-cut quite fresh? You'll be
having your house robbed, sir. That boy's father is a thief, so's his
mother, and his sister."'[8]

These young recruits were inducted into a world turned upside-
down. Here was no God. Here was no book learning. Here were no
rights, except those derived from might or on sufferance. Here was,
though, a recognition of difference – of exclusion from the good things
of life, of harassment and oppression from those with power, of hunger
and fear on the one hand and reckless insouciance on the other. And
a recognition too of a common cause and a new set of values expressed
in language and behaviour at odds with those of the rest of society.
'"The people there talk backwards,"' a fifteen-year-old pickpocket told
Mayhew of his lodging house in 1850. But even without this self-
conscious exclusiveness, the gulf between the people of the rookeries
and, say, the upper echelons of the London working class was fath-
omless and unbridgeable. Ideas of democracy couldn't touch it. One
of the small ironies of the struggle of the unstamped press in the 1830s
was the horror with which radical printers like Henry Hetherington
and James Watson encountered fellow prisoners at Coldbath Fields and
elsewhere, petitioning desperately for accommodation away from
'"thieves, pickpockets, costermongers and mendicants"', their '"horrid
swearing and . . . grossest licentiousness"', and their remorseless
pilfering of personal possessions. And at the very end of the century,
Will Crooks, MP, himself an East End workhouse child for a time,
knew the difference between the respectable unemployed and 'the
waster': '"I object to loafers at both ends of the scale, whether in Park
Lane or in Poplar."'[9]

Consciousness of separateness was expressed in other ways besides
language. Usually it found a voice in individual or group transgres-
sions of the moral or criminal code. Occasionally, where strength of
numbers gave some immunity from police and retribution, it took on
the appearance of something like civil war. At West End Fair, Hampstead,
in 1819, some 200 'ruffians' on two successive evenings seized and
rifled every person arriving; clothes were cut off to simplify the search
for valuables and men and women alike were 'left nearly naked'. In
1826 a 'lawless gang of thieves' 500–600 strong were said to be terror-
ising Bethnal Green and Spitalfields, plundering shops in 'open day'
and robbing and beating fifty foot-passengers in a fortnight. And when

five pirates from the ship *Flowery Land* were hanged in 1864, the cry of 'Black, black!' would identify by the colour of his coat a well-dressed person in the crowd for a beating and robbery.[10]

Oppositional values, capable of enforcement with collective violence, were underpinned by some rookery institutions with long histories. The 'flash' public house adapted itself to the needs of thieves, prostitutes and others with interests beyond the law. Not all were in the rookeries but many were. The landlords of these places were known '"to be what they term right (*i.e.* a thief's friend), who would screen them from justice, in case of necessity, by all the means in [their] power"'.[11] And an anonymous thief, born at Stamford Hill in 1853 into a respectable family but led astray by freebooting companions, had his underworld schooling finished at 'a pub in Shoreditch' used by 'some of the widest (cleverest) people in London', around 1870.

The following people used to go in there – toy-getters (watch-stealers), magsmen (confidence-trick men), men at the mace (sham loan offices), broadsmen (card-sharpers), peter-claimers (box-stealers), busters and screwsmen (burglars), snide-pitchers (utterers of false coin), men at the duff (passing false jewellery [and other things]), welshers (turf-swindlers), and skittle-sharps. Being with this nice mob (gang) you may be sure what I learned.[12]

Many of these publicans were receivers of stolen property, or fences. So were pawnbrokers, the keepers of coffee shop and lodging houses and 'marine-store' (rag and bone) dealers. The Jewish second-hand clothes dealers of Petticoat Lane (just five minutes from Flower and Dean Street) and Field Lane were notorious receivers. It was said of Field Lane, up to about 1845, that a silk handkerchief could be bought back within an hour or so of being stolen, and that twenty dealers in their 'Hell Houses' handled 4,000–5,000 each week. They were hung out on poles from upper windows or on hooks in the doorframes. Fortunes were made here, it was said, and certainly some fences trading on the edges of the City won fabulous wealth. The 'Great Ikey Solomons', at his heyday in the 1820s, operated from Bell Lane, Spitalfields. He paid the best prices for stolen gold and banknotes in London and was said to have had property worth £18,000 at his house when arrested in 1827. In 1854 Moses Moses was transported for fourteen years for receiving an 'unimaginable variety' of goods from robberies all over London – broadcloth, jewellery, silver plate and more – at his warehouses in Gravel Lane, Houndsditch, and (again) Bell Lane. Moses's disciples included 'an organised gang of cabmen' using false plates who transported plunder by night. And fences prospered on. Around 1899 an 'Aladdin's Cave' of stolen property, mainly clothing, was discovered by police near the Elephant and Castle.[13]

Some of these fences, Fagin-like – Dickens never exaggerated in these matters – combined receiving stolen goods with training the boy and girl thieves who stole them. They generally operated in the sanctity of the rookeries and were more common in the first half of the century than later. Even so, Dr Barnardo claimed to recall three operating in the late 1860s at Houndsditch, Short's Gardens (Seven Dials) and Fullwood's Rents, a notorious turning off High Holborn. Earlier we find Thomas Duggin of St Giles teaching boys to pick pockets around 1817; and Jemima Matthews, of Upper Keate Street in the Flower and Dean Street rookery, sending eight children out to steal daily, around 1820. And in 1855, Charles King, thirty-two, a 'thief-trainer', was transported for fourteen years. He was a former Metropolitan Police detective who had recruited boy pickpockets, running three or four at any one time. They lived well. John Reeves, the thirteen-year-old who gave evidence against him, picked pockets in his best weeks to the value of £100. He had begun thieving before the age of ten, stealing his daily bread in Newport Market, but now 'was able to keep a pony and to ride in the Parks'.[14]

We saw in Chapters 1 and 2 how the assault on old London had targeted the rookeries from the very outset of the nineteenth century but increasingly from the late 1830s on. Road improvements, public building projects, railway demolitions and, from the late 1870s, slum clearance had all sought out the haunts of the 'dangerous criminal class' wherever possible. Yet we have seen, too, how tenacious these places were even in remnants. Their very existence continued in some degree to keep alive the traditions and modes of behaviour that had long made them notorious. Closeted together in thieves' lodging houses, drinking in thieves' pubs, resorting to local fences, relying on neighbours to shelter or rescue them from the police, the less-skilled end of London criminality could tap resources that, without the rookeries, would not have been there for them.

The Rev. John William Horsley, chaplain of Clerkenwell Prison from 1876 to 1889, left some fascinating insights into the significance of the rookery for London criminality as the century entered its final decade. He showed too how prison replicated the exclusiveness of rookery life, translating elements of community from tightly defined neighbourhood into the narrow confines of penitentiary walls. He noted down the graffiti that prisoners scratched or pencilled on the walls of their cells. Many, he thought, 'would certainly puzzle a future antiquarian' because of their strange language. 'Fullied for a Clock and Slang' (committed for trial for stealing a watch and chain). 'Long bil expects bolt' (penal servitude). 'Neddie, from City Road, smugged for attempt up the Grove, expects a sixer' (six months for attempting to steal from the person near Whiteley's, Westbourne Grove). 'Kit, from 7 dials, remanded innocent on 2 charges of pokes [purses], only out 2 weeks for a Drag [robbery from a vehicle], expects to get fulled or else chucked [acquitted]. Got 2 previous convictions. Cheer up all you Dials.'[15]

Many, like Neddie and Kit, gave an indication of their address. So Horsley compiled 'a list of the streets or lodging-houses' whose residents were most likely to pass their days and nights at Clerkenwell:

and these would be – in the Western District; Bangor Street and Crescent Street, Notting Hill: in the South-west district; Pye Street and Peter Street, Westminster: in the East; Flower and Dean Street, Kate [sic] Street, and the Beehive lodging-house in Brick Lane: in the East Central; Whitecross Street and Golden Lane, St. Luke's; Lever Street, New North Road, and the streets between it and Hoxton Street on the east and City Road on the west, and notably Blind Con's lodging-house in Golden Lane: in the West Central division; Eagle Street, Holborn, Short's Gardens, Drury Lane, the Empress Chambers, and Fullwood's (or Fuller's) Rents. Across the Thames, Mint Street and Tabard Street, in the Borough, and East Street, Walworth.[16]

He published this in 1887, at a moment of defining change for the London rookery. Of the streets he mentions, most of those in Westminster, the East End, St Luke's and Southwark were already in the process of demolition. Again, they took time to die, and the Flower and Dean Street rookery might stand as one sample for a whole class. All of Keate Street, the west side of George Street and a quarter of Flower and Dean Street were cleared as slums between 1881 and 1883. Then came the Jack the Ripper murders of 1888. Polly Nichols was living at 18 Thrawl Street, 'Long Liz' Stride at 32 Flower and Dean Street, Catherine Eddowes at 55 Flower and Dean Street, and the other two victims had close connections with the area. *The Times* called for the names of the freeholders of the rookery to be publicly exposed. They were ladies and gentlemen with impeccable links to Church, army and the Conservative Party. Worried by the scandal, they took the first opportunity of some leases falling in to rid themselves of a social embarrassment. Between 1891 and 1894 the rest of Flower and Dean Street, George (by then Lolesworth) Street, Thrawl Street and Wentworth Street were almost entirely destroyed. Even so, two or three lodging houses at the Brick Lane end of Flower and Dean Street contrived to keep a shadow of 'the Flowery's' reputation alive until the Second World War.[17]

The effects of demolition were closely monitored by police. Superintendent James Thompson of E (Holborn) Division recorded that Church Lane, St Giles, had produced sixty-eight police charges in 1875 but in 1885, now it was all commercial property, none at all. The Great Wild Street area of Drury Lane, the Bedfordbury district of Covent Garden and Little Coram Street, Bloomsbury, had between them amassed 203 charges in 1875. Each had largely been demolished and produced a total of just nineteen ten years later.[18]

Demolition from 1879 to 1895 was the main lever of change in the London rookery, but there were other factors too. One was the changing nature of London common lodging houses. They had come under police supervision from 1851, with some control over the character of lodging-house keepers from 1853. The police closed the worst of the thieves' houses and over time numbers fell sharply. In 1875 there were 1,241 registered common lodging houses, but in 1894, when supervision passed from the police to the LCC, 654. In five years the number fell further to 542. It was the smaller privately owned places that were most likely to be shut down, or demolished with the rookeries. They were replaced in the 1880s and 1890s by large hostels run by the Salvation Army and the Church Army and by Rowton Houses, providing more beds in respectable conditions.[19] And there were social factors – better reformatories for delinquent youngsters, improved care for those orphaned or abandoned, and from 1870 better education for all working-class children.

By the end of the century most of inner London's tight-knit clusters of lawless people mixing with the very poor had been destroyed, though Dorset Street, Spitalfields, Bastwick Street, St Luke's, and a couple of dozen or so single streets and small neighbourhoods kept the old way of life going into the 1900s. And the so-called criminal district had not disappeared. Around 1899 it was said that Hoxton in south-west Shoreditch was 'the leading criminal quarter of London, and indeed of all England'. But Hoxton was no rookery. It was too large and mixed a district: 'many decent and worthy people still live in Hoxton', its engineers and compositors some of the most skilled of the London working class. On Booth's revised poverty map of 1898, streets marked 'fairly comfortable' and 'poverty and comfort mixed' substantially outnumber the poor and criminal. It was a place where a successful thief, reasonably prosperous and with family responsibilities, could still choose to settle down. In some parts though – notably Wilmer Gardens ('Kill-Copper Row') – the oppositional traditions of the London rookery remained lively enough.[20]

So the old rookeries had been mostly cleared away by the century's end. But what evidence was there that crime overall had diminished as a consequence? And how had London crime altered its character from one end of the century to the other?

Magsmen, Cracksmen, Hoisters and Fogle-hunters

London for sharpers, Brummagem for thieves, Paris for flymen, Sheffield for pitchers of snyde, signed by Darkey, the gun, from Wandsworth Road, for a bust.[21]

There were other candidates for the archetypal London crook but Darkey's choice of cheat was – all in all, remembering the wiles of City men and Grub Street hacks and costermongers and beggars and street children – the right one. Cheating exploited the Londoners' unique capacity for sharp wit, shrewd psychology and talented tongue. These were abilities that crossed all classes. The little library of London detectives' memoirs that began at the end of the nineteenth century showcased sharpers most of all: Chief Inspector Greenham's of 1904 typically has a chapter headed 'Aristocratic Swindler'.[22]

The guides aimed at visitors to the city warn most against the London cheat. Baedeker, as late as 1905, repeats earlier advice that 'It is even prudent to avoid speaking to strangers in the street.' A hundred years earlier and Barrington's *New London Spy* gave a frightening list of the 'Frauds and Cheats daily practised on the unwary tradesman, mechanic, and deluded countryman'. There were duffers selling false silk at street corners and elsewhere; fortune-tellers and 'conjurors' (astrologers); professional gamblers, 'hangers-on' and 'spungers'; 'intelligencers' giving false information about jobs, insolvents cheating creditors, lottery-office keepers welshing if numbers came up, mock auctioneers dealing in false bargains; 'money-droppers' and 'ring-droppers' (devices to lure into conversation or pass bad money and false jewellery); 'pretended friends' and quack doctors; sharpers and swindlers of 'genteel education' pretending 'to be men of quality, or independent fortunes, many of whom keep their equipages and *filles de joie*, without a foot of land, or shilling in the funds'. A decade or so later and the warnings extended to 'pretended porters or clerks' who haunted the coaching inns watching for new arrivals, to street sellers and hackney coachmen 'ringing the changes' (befuddling the customer with short change) or passing bad money. Throughout the century, any stunning event – the Great Exhibition, say, or the Diamond Jubilee of 1897 – 'brought the aristocracy of the criminal world' to London, including many magsmen, confidence tricksters playing for high stakes or low.[23]

Sharpers tended to stick with the tricks they knew best, and the same was true of thieves in general. Men and women specialised, had been apprenticed perhaps when boys and girls. And as in all trades and professions, some were more skilled and successful than others. Take that other great London terror about which Baedeker warned travellers – pickpockets. They were legion throughout the century. John Binny thought that almost all had 'sprung from the dregs of society'. But there were pickpockets and pickpockets. The most skilled were as adept in sleight of hand as any music-hall magician, and scarcely less well rewarded. No snotter-haulers or fogle-hunters these, to be satisfied with a silk handkerchief or two. Here were men in search of red-toys or red-kettles (gold watches). The best pickings were found in crowds. All crowds were meat and drink to the dip. A plain-clothes policeman in the crowded Strand on the evening of a Lord Mayor's Show around 1883 saw a pickpocket slide his hand over a portly man's waistcoat and pluck a watch from its chain, 'so near that I noticed the excited glitter in his eyes'. He seized the man and took him and his victim from the crowd, but the watch had disappeared, 'no doubt dropped and trampled to pieces'. At Bow Street the policeman searched the pickpocket but found nothing until a 'sage old detective' looking on said, '"That's a good man, sonny; give him another rub down."'

At the back of his trousers he found a secret pocket holding four watches and a gold sovereign case with four sovereigns in it.[24]

This thief worked alone, but usually pickpockets operated in twos and threes – one to jostle, one to dip, one to collect. And in a tumultuous crowd – a hanging, the opening of Bartlemy, a great event when numbers got out of hand – finesse would go to the wall. At the Coronation of George IV in July 1821, Captain Gronow was on duty at a platform for distinguished guests near the Abbey, along with John Townsend, Bow Street runner and sometime bodyguard to the former Prince. Below was a sea of prosperous bystanders mixed up with those not prosperous at all. As the cortège approached and the struggling crowd squeezed together with shrieks and yells, Townsend boomed at the top of his voice, '"Gentlemen and ladies, take care of your pockets, for you are surrounded by thieves."' But with the procession at hand and confusion at its peak, 'in the twinkling of an eye there were more watches and purses snatched from the pockets of his Majesty's loyal subjects than perhaps on any previous occasion'. One Welshman was set upon for protesting to Townsend, 'his hat was beaten over his eyes [a bonneting], and his coat, neckcloth, &c., were torn off his body'. Thefts from the person remained one of the commonest crimes recorded by police in London even in the second half of the century: 1,474 in 1860, 2,281 in 1890, 1,515 in 1899, for instance.[25]

Changing fashions tended to work against the pickpockets' interests. Coats would alter to make pockets less prominent and harder to reach. And there were technical devices like 'thief-proof' chains for watches. For shoplifters or 'hoisters' though the growing volume of London commerce – with bazaars, department stores and the more brazen display of goods – presented more and more opportunities for plunder. This was predominantly a woman's trade, the voluminous drapery of nineteenth-century dress – boosted by pretended pregnancies – providing apparently inexhaustible capacity for concealment. And it was a trade not confined to poor women, the best plunder available to '"women above the mediocrity of rank"'. Most shoplifters around 1860 were said to hail from Hoxton and inner south London, and that was a pattern lasting well into the twentieth century.[26]

There are no statistics to indicate whether shoplifting increased in London in the second half of the century, though there's little room to doubt that it did. But some other crimes fell away. Grave robbing and stealing bodies, for instance, slowly faded out after the Anatomy Act of 1832 began to provide anatomists and medical students with a plentiful supply of legitimate corpses. But not before the terrible murder of Carlo Ferrari, 'the Italian boy', by John Bishop and Thomas Williams at Nova Scotia Gardens, Bethnal Green, in 1831: they sold his body to King's College for nine guineas; his teeth were broken out and sold to a dentist. They confessed to dispatching two others, one a homeless boy, in similar circumstances. Then coining and uttering were more common early in the century than later – 332 arrests in 1860, 100 in both 1890 and 1899. As was dog stealing. In 1844 it had been so prevalent in London – 'no man's dog is safe' – that a parliamentary committee had inquired into its whys and wherefores. Valuable dogs were stolen for ransom or export, the cheaper kind for their skins. The dog stealer was himself a peculiar animal, bred apparently to that class of theft and no other. Yet the breed was not extinct even in the 1890s, when in south London 'a notorious old dog thief' and receiver filled every room in his house with dogs stolen from all over the country: thirty were reclaimed by their owners.[27]

Both housebreaking and burglary, the latter thought by Charles Booth at the end of the century to be 'perhaps the most characteristic London crime', seem to have increased in importance. Together, the police recorded just 259 in 1860, then 453 in 1870, 1,292 in 1880 and 1,768 in 1899. Shop and warehouse-breaking showed a similar rise – fifty-one in 1860, 675 in 1899. All these offences required 'violence' to break into property and were codified by the time of day when committed – burglary, at night, the more serious crime.[28]

There were sophisticated high-value burglaries even early in the century, committed by teams of men attacking well-guarded premises. They used inside knowledge (especially from servants), intelligent planning and the best locksmith knowledge available to them. Young boys, Oliver Twist-like, would be used if the best way to enter was through a small opening: for example, a boy called Palmer, a.k.a., Roberts, who was just seven or eight, his father a transported thief, his mother a prostitute, could enter holes not much bigger than would admit a cat (1821). There were notorious robberies at the Royal Exchange (1808), St Paul's Cathedral (1810), Lambeth Palace (1823), the Custom House (1836). Some domestic burglaries were accompanied by extreme violence, like the bludgeoning to death of elderly Mr Bird and his housekeeper at Greenwich (1818) and the killing of Mrs Donatty, an elderly widow, at her home off Bedford Row (1822). Some involved armed men, as at a goldsmith's and a music dealer's in Oxford Street (1819). And much more of the same.[29]

Despite the arrival of a preventive police force from 1829, and a long tradition of shrewd but compromised detective police before and after, London offered more and more opportunities and temptations for similar offences as the century grew older. Two complementary developments were key: the suburb and the railway. Suburbs pulled people out of the City and thereabouts, leaving shops and warehouses deserted at night and on Sundays. And the outskirts of London filled with detached houses, often in quiet surroundings, occupied by some of London's wealthiest citizens. London thieves had always been prepared to travel and in coaching days had gone out with horse and carts into the country: in 1828 both Camberwell and Brompton were especially troubled in this way, for example. The omnibus had done its bit, too, so that burglaries were so common in west London in 1857 that Edmund Yates had a hit at the Adelphi Theatre with a play on this theme called *A Night at Notting Hill*. But it was the railways that brought the suburbs most easily within the reach of the thieves of St Luke's or Hoxton or the Borough. The anonymous housebreaker who introduced us to the wide pub in Shoreditch took 'the rattler' to rob all over suburban London from the early 1870s on: Sutton, Forest Hill, Blackheath, Croydon, Isleworth, Stoke Newington, Lewisham, Surbiton, St Mary Cray, Malden; and further afield to Slough, Reigate, Maidenhead, even Portsmouth. The various 'swell mobs' of London thieves – top-class pickpockets as well as housebreakers – went even further. Large robberies at Manchester in 1837 and a bank robbery at Aberdeen in 1838 were put down as the work of London men. Trains made all this easier. And we are able to see what some of '"the London Swell Mob"' looked like in the photographs of eight suspected pickpockets arrested at Derby races in the early 1860s. Most could be mistaken for clerks or tradesmen. All were acquitted through lack of evidence.[30]

With street robbery, another common and much-feared crime in London throughout the nineteenth century, we leave the swell mob touring the racecourses of England in the rattler and are back in the slums. This was the heavy-handed offence for which Flower and Dean Street was specially noted. It was often a mob-handed venture too, for this was a crime where there was strength in numbers, and where darkness assisted both surprise and escape. It was, after the early years of the century, almost always an inner-city crime, with robbers – including snatchers of a lady's reticule or gentleman's watch, torn off the waist-coat by force – hunting for prey in main streets close to low neigh-bourhoods.[31]

There were, though, some important changes over time. Highway robbery of coaches and travellers on horseback largely ceased after 1805 with the introduction of the Bow Street 'horse patrole'. Till then, and for a few years more, travellers along Shooters Hill (Greenwich), Wandsworth Road, the Edgware Road near Stanmore, in Golders Green and elsewhere were vulnerable to footpads and horsemen armed with pistols they were willing to fire.[32] But almost in response, it seems, street robberies in central London 'very much increased' and by 1816 were thought to be 'very prevalent now'. Just how prevalent is hard to fathom. Some 'eight or nine within this last two months' in St Giles was thought a 'great number' by the local constable and keeper of the parish lock-up or round-house in 1817. And it is important to remember the experience of that intelligent student of London John Britton, who, in a footnote to a guide to the capital of 1825, affirmed how he 'has lived forty years in London, – has traversed the streets by day and night, frequented all its public places, and consequently mixed with various classes of society, and has never been robbed, ill-treated, or suffered any personal injury'.[33]

But when it happened, street robbery was a fearful crime. And from time to time it caused something like panic in London. Garrotting, seizing a foot passenger round the throat from behind while an accom-plice rifled his pockets, received much attention in the press from around 1849 to 1852. Sometimes the attack was made more terri-fying by strangling with a rope or gag. There was not much new in this, but the very name garrotting struck fear to the heart and the label 'thuggism', from Indian cult followers of Kali who strangled people from behind, added to the scare. There were more outbreaks – or maybe just fresh attention in the press – in 1856–7 and notori-ously in the 'garrotting panic' of 1862. Panic it certainly was. Dr William Gardner, with a rich West End clientele, 'carried an enormous knotted cudgel' when on night calls; military officers at the Tower sported 'knuckle-dusters and short blades' when off duty in the Haymarket; and feisty Miss Louisa Boyd, sister of the first rector of St Mark's, Silvertown, went about parochial visits with a loaded revolver, having 'taken a little quiet [?] practice on the marshes'. Yet even in this tumultuous year the police recorded just 140 robberies (or attempts) with violence. We'll return to this vexed question of criminal statistics in a moment.[34]

To illustrate how brazen and outrageous the London street robber could be around this time we have the testimony of an anonymous *Times* reporter at the hanging of Franz Müller outside Newgate on Monday 14 November 1864. Müller, a German migrant, had committed the first murder in Britain to take place on a train – that of Thomas Briggs, a chief bank clerk, between Hackney Wick and Bow. A great crowd had begun to gather early on the Sunday evening, undeterred by bursts of heavy rain. In the darkness the reporter had been puzzled by a 'peculiar sound', 'like a dull blow . . . sometimes followed by the noise of struggling, almost always by shouts of laughter, and now and then a cry of "Hedge"'. As dawn broke, he understood.

Then, and then only, as the sun rose clearer did the mysterious, dull sound, so often mentioned, explain itself with all its noises of laughter and of fighting. It was literally and absolutely nothing more than the sound caused by knocking the hats over the eyes of those well-dressed persons who had ventured among the crowd, and, while so 'bonneted', stripping them and robbing them of everything. None but those who looked down upon the awful crowd of yesterday will ever believe in the wholesale, open, broadcast manner in which garrotting and highway robbery were carried on . . . There were regular gangs, not so much in the crowd itself within the barriers as along the avenues which led to them, and these vagrants openly stopped, 'bonneted', and sometimes garrotted, and always plundered any person whose dress led them to think him worth the trouble; the risk was nothing. Sometimes their victims made a desperate resistance, and for a few minutes kept the crowd around them violently swaying to and fro amid the dreadful uproar. In no instance, however, could we ascertain that 'police' was ever called. [35]

Those whose panic was most in evidence in the early 1860s were adult middle-class Londoners. But crime affected everyone, the working classes most of all. The poor were at the mercy of the strong and the wily who lived among them. Sailors bewitched by prostitutes were led not to bed but to a beating and a robbery. Possessions and clothes salvaged from fires were looted from the pavement. We hear of a poor dressmaker paid with a gilt sixpence for half a sovereign, who gave change as well as the dress; a 'poor industrious labourer' beaten almost to death and robbed of fifteen years' savings, which he eccentrically kept about him; a couple's rooms stripped of everything while they were attending their child's funeral; an old man from the Nichol Street area knocked down and robbed of his coppers by youths living in the street next door. And wholesale 'pillaging of slot meters' was common in poor streets at the century's end.[36]

The weakest could be preyed on in other ways too. Child stealing – the victim lured from the street and stripped naked or nearly so for their clothes – was a terrifying crime, not uncommon in the early years of the century. As late as 1848, Henry Lazarus, the small son of a Jewish dealer in Tenter Street, Spitalfields, was found strangled (but not sexually molested) with all his outer clothing stolen, in a nearby backyard. The elderly were also vulnerable here. Eliza Cook, thirty-eight, was found guilty of suffocating Caroline Walsh, an old woman, in Cook's room at Goodman's Yard, Whitechapel, in 1832, apparently to sell her clothes to the dealers in Rag Fair, Rosemary Lane.[37]

On the other hand, the cleverest and toughest of those who took to crime could prosper, no doubt from such small beginnings. But perhaps the most successful were those who had already begun life with some advantages. Take two careers, the second better known than the first. William 'Bill' Cauty was remembered as '"the father of all the robbers"' fifty years after his comeuppance at the Old Bailey in June 1851. Even though transported, he was reputed to have died worth £20,000. He seems to have begun his working life as a banker's clerk. 'On leaving that most respectable occupation he did not neglect the interest of bankers, but rather further identified it with his own.' An 'old man' in 1851, his career stretched back to the end of the Napoleonic Wars, when he was associated with the new crime of stealing bankers' parcels en route between the provinces and London. In the 1830s he was a 'notorious' habitué of thieves' pubs like the Sol's Arms and the Bell, near Leicester Square. And he seems to have been a prototype for the London criminal mastermind.

He had all his life been connected with the great gambling houses; but his real occupation was in devising and perfecting robberies upon the grandest scale. He is said to have had in his hands the bills and bank-notes stolen from Messrs. Rogers, Toogood, and Company's banking house [1844]; to have disposed of the gold and bank-notes, the produce of the great robberies on the Great Western Railway [1844]; and of the great gold-dust robberies [1839]. His intervals of leisure he filled up latterly by travelling in the West India steamers to the Gulf of Mexico and the Spanish Main, for the purpose of

fleecing the rich Mexican and Spanish American passengers, who are notoriously addicted to gambling; in these cases he travelled with three confederates, each of whose passage expenses cost £100 per voyage. It is stated that
not less than half a million's worth of stolen property has been traced into
his hands.[38]

Second, more in the public eye, was dreadful Charles Peace, a double
murderer hanged in 1879 at Sheffield, his birthplace. He was a skilled
and daring burglar who lived at Evelina Road, Peckham, conveniently
close to Nunhead railway station, during 1877–8. He occupied a semi-
detached three-storey villa with his wife and son and mistress. He was
an early example of a suburban burglar having no connections at all
with the inner-London underworld. He worked alone, armed with a
revolver. Peace soon made his presence felt. The *Annual Register* noted
for October 1877 'very serious, not to say alarming, state of insecurity' among suburban householders in south London, especially Clapham,
Balham, Dulwich and Putney, with twenty burglaries in the past ten
weeks or so. A month later and Sir Joseph Bazalgette's home at
Wimbledon Park was burgled, among the spoils the silver trowel
commemorating the laying of the first stone on the Thames embankment. Peace prospered. His home was 'beautifully furnished', with
walnut furniture, Turkey carpet and 'bijou piano'. A music-lover, he
amassed 'quite a fine collection of Cremona fiddles' and 'an inlaid
Spanish guitar', all apparently stolen. His career ended in October
1878. Discovered by police at two in the morning in a house at St
John's Park, Blackheath, Peace fired five times at PC Robinson,
wounding him in the arm. It took three officers to overpower him.
When asked his name and address he said, '"Find out."'[39]

It would have been difficult to convince suburban south Londoners
in 1878 that crime in London was reducing. But historians tell us that
crime overall fell proportionate to the population of England and Wales
from around 1842 right through the remainder of the century. Some
crime fell absolutely. Given the universal acceptance that crime everywhere rises as urban populations grow and as prosperity increases, the
Victorian experience has been called 'the English miracle'. And the
statistics of crime in London seem to confirm that metropolis and
nation, in this regard at least, were marching in step.[40]

There is a reasonably complete run of crime figures compiled by
police for London from 1860. They show that the proportion of arrests

per 1,000 of population fell steadily decade on decade from 19.6 in
1861 to 14.8 in 1891, then rising quite sharply to around 17.6 in
1899. Most significantly, felonies against property known to the police
fell absolutely, with some ups and downs along the way, from 21,303
in 1867 to 16,149 in 1899. When the great increase in London's population is taken into account we find a quite astonishing reduction from
6.17 property offences per 1,000 population in 1867 to 2.44 in 1899.
Buried in these figures were the more serious burglaries and house-
breakings mentioned earlier. These rose against the trend, but their
volume in respect of all property crime remained small. At the same
time, most (but not all) informed commentators affirmed what the
statistics indicated, that despite urbanisation, a growing population and
rising prosperity, there was far less crime in the country (and London
within it) after 1850 than before. And the smaller numbers finding
their way into the convict prisons seemed to bear all this out.

To jettison this analysis, marshalled in recent years with such intelligence and care, would be a foolhardy project. But on the other hand
there is no doubt that the criminal statistics enormously understate the
true picture of crime in London. By just how much we can never know.

There are numerous reasons why the offences recorded by police
were such hopeless guides to the real movement of crime in London.
This involves the so-called 'dark figure' of crime which goes unreported
by victims or unrecorded by police even when reported to them. There
is some reason to believe that these were particular problems in London
compared with elsewhere.

Most victims of metropolitan crime were working-class Londoners.
Their losses were often inconsiderable – and bruises quickly healed.
We have seen elsewhere the mobility and anonymity which militated
against making a fuss or bringing a charge. To that can be added much
mistrust and dislike of the police, and the not unreasonable fear of
retribution from perpetrators and neighbours. A good deal of crime,
too, was associated with vice and prostitution, where prosecutors were
famously shy of coming forward. Then again the hopelessness of recovering the property taken deterred complaints to the police. So did the
effort that complaining entailed, for no return: 'In no instance, however,
could we ascertain that "police" was ever called.'

The police themselves were well aware of all this and their reflections throw a little light on the dark figure in London at the end of
the century. Between 1885 and 1899, robbery and attempted robbery

with violence, what a later generation – resurrecting a little-used nineteenth-century slang expression – would call muggings, averaged 131 a year. If we take the 1890s alone, when 'hooliganism' was a matter of considerable press agitation towards the end of the decade, the figure is 139 each year. But how do we reconcile that with this: 'One of the most prevalent crimes which we had to contend with when I was a young constable [Whitechapel, c. 1895] was garrotting . . . or highway robbery'? Or, 'A type of offence very rife in our district [Whitechapel, c. 1892] was the terrible one of garrotting'? Or, 'Garrotting was at this time [Southwark, c. 1895] going on to a most serious extent'? Or the article published in the Pall Mall Gazette in October 1888 detailing the extraordinary extent of robbery, house-breakings and assault in Gray's Inn Road – 222 'robberies' and thirty-eight 'attempts' over roughly the past two years, mostly snatching from tills and shop windows, some burglaries, maybe nineteen robberies with violence, but with the postmaster saying, 'Almost daily street robberies occur'? Or similar accounts for Southwark Park Road and Hackney Road, giving the impression that the picture was the same for every main shopping street of working-class London?

Perhaps one way is offered by the police officers themselves and in the evidence gleaned by reporters. Ex-Detective Sergeant Leeson recalled the garrotting of a man around 1894 who had been lured by a woman from a pub. He had drunk too much and was set upon and robbed by her two associates. But he refused to prosecute, 'being ashamed of himself'; 'I should have done the same myself.' Ex-Chief Inspector Dew recalled how 'In most cases the attacks would be so sudden that the victim never saw the faces of his assailants, and even if he did he was more often than not too scared to give any assistance to the police.' And the Pall Mall Gazette was told, '"I used to keep a record of the robberies, but at last I grew sick of writing it up, and threw it away," said a pawnbroker, who had already been robbed thirty times this year . . . The words of one tradesman, "We never tell the police – it's no good," aptly expresses the state of mind of the residents of Gray's-inn-road and neighbourhood.'[41]

There were other reasons for the under-recording of offences, though. It was noted in the 1890s that police kept the figure artificially low in part because it was not in the interests of senior officers to record crime as either prevalent or undetected. And when in 1932 the Metropolitan Police abandoned the 'suspected stolen book', kept in

London police stations for 'many years', which allowed suspected crimes not to be entered into the 'crimes known' figures, the indictable offences known to the police jumped threefold, the 1931 figure being retrospectively adjusted from 26,000 to 79,000.[42]

Similar influences were at work on the most serious offences against the person, even murder, manslaughter, rape, wounding and so on. These didn't show the secular fall of property crime in London: there was no marked difference between the 1870s and 1890s, for example. But the numbers involved were very small, just over 500 each year between 1897 and 1899, around 8 per 100,000 of the population. Here again, though, under-recording was rife, partly no doubt due to the limited medical jurisprudence of the times. Ex-Chief Constable Frederick 'Weasel' Wensley, recalling the East End in the 1890s, put it well: 'Murder was probably more common than the official statistics showed; for bodies of people, who it is likely had been knocked on the head, were frequently found in the streets, often near disreputable houses. Unless there was obvious evidence of foul play, the inquest verdicts were usually indefinite.'[43]

In 1906, an unexceptional year, London coroners' inquests recorded thirty-two murder verdicts and thirteen manslaughter; there were 531 of suicide and 239 open verdicts, including fifty-one on deaths from injuries and 115 drownings. And the numbers of missing persons in London was always very high – 18,004 in 1887, about half 'absolutely unaccounted for', and countless others not reported at all.[44]

It has been said of late Victorian England that 'the most serious acts of violence were extremely rare'.[45] But it would not have felt much like that in London during the troubled 1880s or even in the decade after. We have already noted the roll-call of butchered prostitutes, which reached a terrible toll in 1888–92. And the 1880s were plagued too by a wave of gun crime of some ferocity. London burglars increasingly went armed.

There had been isolated instances of this in the 1870s, but three or four years after Peace a loaded revolver seemed to be a necessary accompaniment to a suburban burglary. In 1881 shots were fired during a burglary at Kensington and a constable and a postman were wounded – the thief was a Hoxton man; PC Fred Atkins was shot dead by a burglar at a house on Kingston Hill; and an armed burglars' hideout was raided at Addington, Croydon. In 1882 a groom at a big house on Stamford Hill was shot in the back by a burglar with two revolvers; constables were shot and wounded during burglaries at Upper Clapton and Hampstead; and PC George Cole was shot dead on a foggy night in Ashwin Street, Dalston, by Thomas Orrock, a member of the Baptist chapel he had attempted to rob. In 1883, the frequency of shootings was such that police in the outlying districts were permitted to carry revolvers at night. Even so, a constable was shot in the leg at Wimbledon and burglars discovered entering a house at Loraine Road, Holloway, shot and wounded men who gave chase. In 1884 James Wright, one of two armed burglars fleeing police, opened fire and wounded one of them; his gun empty, he scaled a roof at Nile Street, Hoxton, and kept his pursuers at bay for a time by hurling tiles at them. It was discovered that Wright had previously been responsible for shooting a constable at Islington. In 1885 Inspector Simmons of the Essex police was shot dead by one of three men he'd been watching in Romford; and a constable was shot three times by masked burglars on a Kensington roof. In 1886 a constable was shot during an attempted robbery at Marylebone Parish Church, and a sub-postmaster shot dead in Brecknock Road, Archway. These were the sensations, though the list is by no means exhaustive. The peak years were 1881–6. But gun crime was not uncommon for the rest of the century. Revolvers were widely available, for example, to the gangs of blackmailers levying protection money on poor East End shopkeepers in the 1890s. And '"belt and pistol gangs"' were noted in Hoxton around the same time.[46]

Then there was one year near the end of the century when the ferocity of London burglars seemed to know no bounds. This was 1896. First, in February, at Muswell Hill, Henry Smith, nearly eighty and a wealthy retired gas engineer, was murdered by two burglars, Henry Fowler and Albert Milsom. He was beaten to death in horrific circumstances. At least one of the men had a revolver, but it wasn't fired. The two had set off for Muswell Hill from the notorious Southam Street, Kensal New Town. Two months later, on Easter Sunday at Turner Street, Stepney, an elderly Jewish shopkeeper called Levy and his housekeeper were bludgeoned to death during a robbery by William Seaman, a desperate and brutal man. All three were hanged together at Newgate. 'Never were two more savage murders committed than those at Muswell Hill and Stepney, in the spring of 1896,' was the judgment of Sir Melville Macnaghten, head of the London CID. Londoners were entitled to wonder just how much more civilised their city had become in the eighty-five years since one of the great crimes of the century had become a byword for savagery in the metropolis.[47]

'Weltering in His Gore'

It can be deemed no kind of exaggeration to assert, that during the winter of 1811, the [c]ity of London experienced a degree of alarm and apprehension to which it had been a stranger for centuries past.

Not just the capital. Responding to a rumour that the murderer 'had quitted London, the panic which had convulsed the mighty metropolis diffused itself all over the island'. Such was the great fear that followed the murder of the Marrs at their draper's shop, 29 Ratcliffe Highway, near London Dock, in the early morning of Sunday 8 December 1811. Young Timothy Marr, his wife, Celia, their baby of fourteen weeks and their shop boy, James Gowen, were brutally battered to death with a carpenter's maul, a large hammer with a pointed end. The baby had also had his throat slit. All had been murdered in the space of twenty minutes, the time a servant had been out to buy oysters for a late supper. Nothing had been taken from the house but robbery seemed a possible motive. There was a small fortune in cash in an upstairs drawer and the murderer might have been disturbed by the servant's return. But the very savagery of the killings – the 'blood and brains from one end of [the shop] to another', the shop boy 'weltering in his gore', the gratuitous murder of the baby – left a terrible doubt that this was no economic crime at all.

Twelve nights later and a couple of hundred yards away at the King's Arms public house, New Gravel Lane, a second slaughter took three more victims. Mr and Mrs John Williamson, who ran the house, and Bridget Harrington, their servant, were found with their skulls smashed and their throats cut. A lodger and another servant, both in the house at the time, escaped, one having seen the murderer at work. Again, nothing had been taken, though there were money and valuables in easy reach, and now it seemed clear that the motive was some mad bloodlust. Years later, Macaulay the historian recalled 'the terror which was on every face – the careful barring of doors – the providing of blunderbusses and watchmen's rattles'.

The universal outrage, and the ever more pressing calls on the police, produced numerous arrests. Among these, three days before Christmas, was that of John Williams, a sailor. Soon the maul was brought home to him and so, eventually, were a bloodstained knife, stockings and shirt. On 27 December Williams hanged himself in his cell at Coldbath

Fields Prison. Cheated of a public trial and hanging, the authorities gave Williams the burial traditionally reserved for suicides but not commonly carried out. On New Year's Eve his body was displayed on a cart and wheeled past the scenes of the murders through crowded streets. It was buried at the crossroads where Cable Street met the New Road to Whitechapel (later Cannon Street Road). The bloody maul was used to drive a stake through his heart. Each strike was met with exultant shouts from the crowd.[48]

Londoners had always been alive to the horror of crime. There was an enduring, passionate, almost unreasonable fascination with its scenes and details, especially when murder was involved. This was a fascination that seduced all classes, like the Great Exhibition or horse racing or an out-of-town boxing bout. And it expressed itself in a variety of forms. In print, where the radical William Hone '"and my family lived for four months"' on a pamphlet protesting the innocence of Elizabeth Fenning, a servant hanged in 1815 for allegedly poisoning her employers; where Jemmy Catnach's broadsides on the murder of William Weare and the trial and execution of his notorious assailants, John Thurtell and Joseph Hunt, made £500 profit in pennies, printing 500,000 copies in 1824; and where the *People's Police Gazette* proved among the most popular of all the unstamped press, selling 20,000 of each issue in 1834, twice the circulation of *The Times*. On the stage, where 'Boiled Beef' Williams, proprietor of the Surrey Theatre, introduced into a play the very gig in which Thurtell first tried to kill Weare. And most of all in exhibitions. Some were held at the scenes of the murder itself. At 17 Southampton Street, Pentonville, in 1834, the rooms in which a German whip-maker called Steinberg slaughtered his mistress and her four children were thrown open to the public for a fee; wax figures dressed in the victims' real clothes helped reap £50 in a single day. Large numbers tried to view the body of Eliza Grimwood when it lay for a time in the Waterloo Road house where she was murdered in 1838. And 'thousands wished to look over the house' in Bermondsey where Mrs Manning connived with her husband to shoot dead her lover and bury him under the kitchen floor in 1849. Later in the century, penny gaffs and peepshows in the Whitechapel Road portrayed the Jack the Ripper murders in wax and cardboard in 1888. And Madame Tussaud's 'chamber of horrors', established in 1843, translated murderers into wax within a few days of their executions until the century's end and beyond.[49]

In real life, though, most murders – and some of the worst

savagery – took place at home. Most victims were members of the perpetrators' family or household. And in the main they were women and children.

Sarah Pomeroy. – Is landlady of a house in Christopher's-alley, Lambeth-street [Whitechapel], where the prisoner and his wife had lodged for nearly two months. Was at home on Thursday, 10th of May [1827]. In the evening the mother of the child came to witness; she said something which induced witness to go up stairs to the top room, which was occupied by the prisoner. As soon as witness entered the door, she saw a child's head on the table. It stood on the table, on the neck part; it was completely separated from the body.[50]

The rest of Charles William Beadle, about four months old, was found under a counterpane on the bed. He had been murdered by William Sheen, his father or stepfather, who had left his wife and was now being pursued by the parish authorities to maintain the child and mother. This was Sheen's revenge. Through a technical error in the indictment and a blunder at the trial, Sheen walked free.

Cases like this, of savage blind rage, seem to have been more common in the first half of the century than after. But infanticide and the murderous abuse, neglect or torture of children remained not so 'extremely rare' throughout the nineteenth century in London. This was not just a phenomenon of the rookeries. George R. Sims, at the century's end and drawing on cases handled by the NSPCC, recounted how terrible maltreatment was found in suburban villas as well as in the slums. A notorious case that came to public attention in the year of the Great Exhibition concerned the appalling cruelty with which a servant, Jane Wilbred, had been treated by her employers, George and Theresa Sloane. George Sloane was a special pleader at the bar and the cruelty took place at 6 Pump Court, Temple. Jane Wilbred was an orphan brought up in the West London Union workhouse, whom Mrs Sloane approached for a servant-girl. At Christmas 1849 Mrs Sloane's favourite bird had died and for the next fourteen months the Sloanes beat and starved the girl mercilessly. Wilbred – 'emaciated, weak, in want of clothing, and covered with filth' – was rescued by a neighbouring barrister. The Sloanes received two years' imprisonment and some rough handling by the London crowd. And then the Brixton baby farmer Margaret Waters, hanged in 1870, who had murdered by starvation and neglect at least nine infants, had a middle-class Baptist upbringing and a comfortable life until her husband died and she was forced to shift for herself. She offered 'adoption' for a £5 premium, advertising in *Lloyd's Weekly Newspaper* and elsewhere. Baby-farming, a peculiarly south London suburban industry, continued right through the 1890s, fuelled by the large number of illegitimate children whom 'respectable' families wished to disown.[51]

A final extraordinary example of child neglect connects wealthy London to the poorest of the poor. Richard Guinness Hill, a rich Irish brewer, was alleged to have given his wife's newborn baby by another man to a London beggar in 1859, telling her first that he had made satisfactory provision for it but later unable to disclose its whereabouts. In 1861 Mrs Hill asked solicitors to find the boy. They commissioned 'Brett, an experienced detective officer', to track him down. Brett had bills posted offering a £20 reward for information. A tip-off led him to 'a filthy alley in Drury Lane'.

After searching various rooms, Brett proceeded to a small apartment on the second floor. In one corner lay a man, nearly naked, apparently in a dying state, and squatting all over the floor were several women in a most ragged and miserable condition. The whole place was in a dreadful state, the stench from the filth being almost overpowering. On the floor in this horrible den Brett discovered the heir to £14,000 – almost in a state of nudity, and covered with vermin and filth. No shoes were on his feet, and only one dirty rag enveloped the entire body. One of his thighs had been broken and had been badly mis-set, his toes were terribly scarred with wounds, and the head and body generally showed unmistakable marks of neglect and ill-usage. The house, from top to bottom, appeared to be occupied by prostitutes and beggars.[52]

Historians warn us how London's rookeries, seen so often through the journalist's distorting lens, were 'quarters embellished with surreal horror by literary imagination'. No embellishment was needed here. There was nothing so surreal, or so terrible, as reality.[53]

That was 1861 and the behaviour and conditions the story revealed had an anachronistic feel even then, as though a dusty curtain had been briefly drawn aside to reveal again the London of Townsend the Runner or Williams the murderer. Forty years on and even the 1860s would look to some as a bygone era too. Frederick Rogers recalled being brought up then 'in an atmosphere of wife-beating' while yet in 'a street that prided itself on its respectability'. He thought it had now 'all but disappeared'. But he was out of touch. Wives' applications for

summonses against their husbands for assault were meat and drink to
the London police court magistrates right through the 1890s. Drink
and violence in the home played a prominent part in Charlie Chaplin's
memoir of his early life in 1890s Newington. His upbringing was by
no means the poorest and wife-beating and other violence in the home
affected all classes. Yet the details published by Charles Booth of the
Shelton Street area, Drury Lane, around 1890 show that the conditions found by Brett, or something like them, persisted into the last
decade of the century. One story of 'the utmost horror' from 24 Shelton
Street involved a man beating to death the woman who had lived with
him for eleven years. His adult sons beat her too. 'There was no prosecution, the neighbours shielded the man.'[54]

With Shelton Street and its neighbours around 1889–92 we might
pause for a moment to consider the question of continuity and change
as it affected crime and brutality in London. Plainly, the modernising
influences that all could see in London's built environment, its communications, its administration, policing and education were of huge
importance in civilising the Londoner. Too much qualitative evidence
to ignore supports the case that lawlessness and rowdyism reduced as
a consequence. To this extent London was a more law-abiding city in
the third and fourth quarters of the century than before and a less
brutal and savage place as well.[55]

But these civilising influences did not reach everyone. Traditions of
hard drinking and violent behaviour endured, most of all in the remnants
of the rookeries and in the suburban slums that their demolition had
helped nurture. Rowdyism never departed the main shopping streets
of working-class London, taking various forms of bullying and petty
theft and even (just one example) the stoning in 1888 for twenty minutes
in a main Holborn street of a 'poor half-demented woman' who had
somehow aroused bystanders' antagonism.[56] And although crime against
property probably declined in proportion to the growth of population,
the evidence here is not half as optimistic as it seems at first sight.

So we can say with some confidence that London was a safer and
more secure place in 1899 than in 1800, while by no means every
element of rough or savage behaviour had been transformed out of
recognition. And this incomplete revolution in manners was apparent
in the way political protest expressed itself in London. Here too the
transformation was a long time coming.

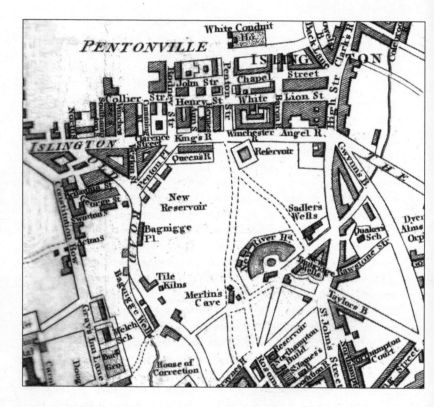

Spa Fields, 1806

XII

SPA FIELDS: PROTEST
AND POLITICS

Spa Fields, 1800–1821

THE meadows between Clerkenwell and Islington south of the New (Pentonville) Road had many names over the generations. Ducking Pond Fields is the oldest that's come down to us. But by 1685 the Islington Spa or New Tunbridge Wells had been set up just south-east of New River Head and from that time Spa Fields was how they were most commonly known. The cockneys pronounced it Spaw, and so it was often written. In the eighteenth century the fields were one of London's great rural attractions. There were prize fights between women, and between women and men. They were home to the Welsh or Gooseberry Fair each Whitsun and part was given over to a cheapskate Vauxhall called the Pantheon, around 1770. On dark nights Spa Fields were notorious for footpads and even in the early years of the nineteenth century playgoers at Sadler's Wells would gather in groups of ten or a dozen with 'two or three linkmen' before hazarding a crossing.[1]

In 1816 the fields around the Spa tea garden, which still retained pretensions of gentility, were just one more frowzy no man's land at the edge of London, ripe for the house-builder's mattock. That year London was in tumult. Revisions to the corn laws had kept the price of bread artificially high by excluding foreign grain. There was a week of window-breaking in March when government ministers' houses were attacked by the aggrieved poor. Economic distress worsened through the summer and autumn as war spending stopped and as soldiers and sailors were discharged by the tens of thousands into a sickly labour market. Important London occupations – shipbuilders and watch-makers, tailors and hatters, coopers and printers, cabinet makers and silk weavers – plunged suddenly into slack time. Mass unemployment combined with dear food to provoke furious discontent.

There were some in London waiting eagerly to put a match to such tinder. And in November a group of north London ultra-radicals, combining the philosophy of Thomas Spence (common ownership of the land) with a Jacobin belief in direct action modelled on revolutionary France, announced a meeting in Spa Fields to petition the Prince Regent to relieve distress in his metropolis. They invited several radicals to address the crowds. Just one agreed. This was Henry 'Orator' Hunt, a Wiltshire gentleman farmer, whose platform was parliamentary reform. The men who called the meeting included Arthur Thistlewood, a Lincolnshire gentleman who had served as an army officer in the West Indies; Dr James Watson, a struggling medical man, and his surgeon son, also James; and an impoverished and hard-drinking shoemaker, Thomas Preston, who organised the group's business from his rooms off Fetter Lane in the City. Hunt noted the strange contrast these men afforded: Preston's 'two or three dirtily dressed, miserable, poor children', Thistlewood's 'handsome dressing-gown and morocco slippers', the elder Watson's 'shabby-genteel black'.[2]

The first Spa Fields meeting was held on 15 November 1816, a Monday – 'Saint Monday', that weekly non-working festival of the London working classes. Spa Fields were close to the distressed artisan district of Clerkenwell and the turnout was staggering. The fields were 'covered by much the largest concourse of people I had ever seen together in my life', recalled Hunt, a man with some ten years' experience of the reformers' hustings. Estimates of the numbers ranged from 20,000–40,000. Numerous resolutions called on the Regent to help the people in their plight.[3]

Though some local bakers' shops were looted by stragglers on their way home, the meeting itself passed peacefully. It was adjourned to 1 p.m. on Thursday 2 December to receive the Regent's reply. In the interval rumours of an insurrection reached government. The authorities sought to deter potential crowds with a display of armed force. Guardsmen and horse artillery guarded nearby Coldbath Fields prison. Cannon, cavalry and foot soldiers were moved to strategic points around Spa Fields and as far south as London Bridge. To no effect: this gathering would prove even larger than the first.

But it was not the second meeting itself that made 2 December 1816 notorious. An hour or two before one o'clock the first arrivals at Spa Fields were met by 'a very inflammatory harangue' from the younger Watson, who, with Thistlewood at his side, seized a tricolour and led some hundred or two agitated demonstrators to the Tower. Their object was to foment mutiny among the soldiers and then seize it as the first step in an English revolution. At Snow Hill they stormed Beckwith's gunshop. When a bystander called Platt tried to stop them, Watson pulled a pistol from his pocket and shot him, apparently with wadding rather than ball, in the groin. Armed with Beckwith's weapons, the Spa Fields demonstrators met a crowd coming from a hanging outside Newgate. Among them were discharged sailors, disgruntled at Admiralty delays in paying prize money and wages. Like most of the Newgate crowd, and apparently like Watson himself, they were primed with drink. Now a few hundred strong, the pocket insurrection surged into the Minories, relieving the gunshops that clustered there of some 400 pistols, muskets and other weapons. It then moved on to the Tower. A man thought to be Thistlewood, who had worked hard for months to sow sedition among his former comrades-in-arms over drinks in several London pubs, jumped on the railings, flourished a cutlass and called on the soldiers to join him in taking the Tower. No one stirred. Reports of cavalry on the move reached the Spa Fields rioters. And satisfied that the moment was not yet ripe for an English Bastille Day they melted into the London throng. Young Watson fled to America. Thistlewood, Dr Watson, Preston and others would later face trial for high treason, but Watson was acquitted by a sympathetic London jury and the attorney general offered no evidence against the rest. A destitute former sailor called John Cashman was hanged on a makeshift gallows outside Beckwith's gunshop for his alleged part in the shooting there. Cashman protested his innocence to the end, probably with justice. '"Now, my lads, give me three cheers when I trip"' were the last words heard from him.[4]

There was a third giant gathering at Spa Fields, once more addressed by Hunt, in February 1817, but no half-cocked attempt at revolution this time. Smaller meetings followed into early 1818. Three years later and the house-builders began to move in. By the mid-1830s Spa Fields was bricked over by the Lloyd Baker Estate and the other streets that stretch from King's Cross Road to Rosebery Avenue.

The Spa Fields meetings were an important moment in the history of protest in London. They were the first great effort to establish a popular platform for parliamentary reform. And it was the beginning of the end of insurrectionary ambitions among metropolitan ultras. For most contemporaries, though, it was just one more dangerous episode in the story of that wayward fury, 'the London mob'.

The excitable London crowd had a long history. It was unpredictable in formation and volatile in action. It shared that passion for excitement and novelty so readily expressed when Londoners gathered in any numbers on the streets. It mobilised to defend its customs from attack, to wreak vengeance on its oppressors, to demand rights it had not yet been granted and to force others to do its bidding. Its targets depended on the cause at issue but almost always involved assaults on the persons or property or servants of the rich and powerful. Its main weapons were window-breaking and stoning, occasionally arson and the 'pulling-down' of houses – usually windows and doorframes yanked out with crows and ropes. It did not disdain opportunities for plunder. And more often than not it swept into its ranks an explosive cocktail of the informed and the inflammable from almost every stratum of metropolitan society – as epitomised in Hunt's observation of 'the Thistlewood gang'.

The inflammable component of the agitated London crowd was mostly made up of dispossessed artisans, labourers, the very poor and the 'rough', those living by a mix of casual work, street selling and petty crime. Here there was love of disorder for disorder's sake.

Under an idea of whim and pleasantry [wrote the London chronicler J. P. Malcolm in 1810] they perpetrate many scandalous actions, amusing themselves by throwing some filthy thing into the thickest part of a crowd, or driving forward till they half suffocate those before them, or hurt others by severe falls. Whenever an illumination takes place, their turbulence becomes seriously mischievous by the firing of pistols and throwing of squibs and crackers . . .[5]

Their numbers and flammability were stoked by economic distress. As episodes of widespread starving destitution grew more rare, so the crowd had less cause for disgruntlement. As other vehicles for expressing discontent on the platform, in the union branch meeting and in the working men's clubs became more readily available, there was less reason to take to the streets. And as manners grew more gentle through the spread of the written word, through religious influences and education, then collective violence attracted fewer as a means of forcing change or venting outrage.

Even so, the London poor stayed quick to anger. Whatever the influence of agitators, a great fact of London life underpinned their readiness to revolt. Francis Place, the reforming master tailor of Charing Cross, described it well. He wrote in 1841, but his analysis would hold good for another fifty years to come. And he didn't let punctuation impede the passion of his words.

A great mass of our unskilled and but little skilled labourers among whom are the hand loom [silk] weavers, and a very considerable number of our skilled labourers are in poverty, if not in actual misery. A large portion of them have been in a state of poverty and great privation all their lives, they are neither ignorant of their condition nor reconciled to it, they live amongst others who are better off than themselves, with whom they compare themselves and they cannot understand why there should be so great a difference . . . To escape from this state is with them of paramount importance, among a vast multitude of these people, not a day, scarcely an hour can be said to pass without some circumstance, some matter exciting reflection occurring to remind them of their condition which notwithstanding they have been poor and distressed from their infancy and however much they may *at times* be cheerful, they scarcely ever cease . . . to feel and to acknowledge to themselves with deep sensations of anguish their deplorable condition.[6]

The first two decades of the nineteenth century combined chronic privation with intolerably sharp economic crises. All that at a time when most forms of political expression were sternly suppressed. Scandal and corruption in Parliament and at court combined with dear food and irregular work to irritate plebeian London from the beginning of the century. Some of this found a political voice among the small Spencean societies and Hampden clubs where radicals of all classes met in a galaxy of London pubs to plot revolution on the one hand or constitutional reform on the other. An insurrectionary conspiracy, apparently led by the Irishman Colonel Edward Marcus Despard, was broken up by a raid on the Oakley Arms, Oakley Street, Lambeth, in November 1802. There were forty-eight arrests in all. Despard and six others were hanged and beheaded as traitors on the roof of Horsemonger Lane gaol in February 1803. Just as at Spa Fields, the revolutionaries' tactics involved encouraging mutiny in the London barracks, with Despard, like Thistlewood, speaking soldier to soldier.[7]

Mostly, though, irritation was expressed in rioting of the flare-up kind. Every election involved a row, even if only at the end, when the giant wooden hustings were taken apart for firewood or building materials, 'agreeably to immemorial custom', in a riot of destruction. There was window-breaking, stoning of unpopular candidates and assaults on their followers at the Middlesex elections of 1804 and 1806. At the Westminster election of 1807 half a million Londoners turned out to watch the victorious Sir Francis Burdett – injured in a duel by a bullet in his thigh – 'chaired' through the streets. The authorities feared a riot, doubled the Foot Guards in Whitehall and issued ball-cartridge, but good humour prevailed. Three years later the indignant fury of the crowd who couldn't save Burdett from the Tower in April 1810 brought London to the brink of civil war, as we have seen.[8]

Then on 11 May 1812 John Bellingham, a madman with a grievance against the government, shot dead Spencer Perceval, evangelical lawyer and Tory prime minister, in the lobby of the House of Commons. Bellingham was held and a hackney coach was summoned to take him to Newgate. But news of the killing caused a crowd to gather, 'at first composed of decent people', then 'swelled by a concourse of pickpockets and the lower orders', who greeted the assassin with 'shouts of applause' and tried to rescue him from the coach. Life Guards restored order and took Bellingham from the Commons by a back gate.[9]

And in March 1815 the Life Guards, to shouts of '"Down with the Piccadilly butchers!"', were in action once more during serious rioting against the continuation of the corn laws. Over three nights windows were broken in Bedford Square, St James's Square and elsewhere in attacks on ministers' residences. Troops with fixed bayonets guarded Parliament after the crowd had swarmed in the lobby and corridors. Two rioters were shot dead in Old Burlington Street during the sacking of Frederick Robinson's house: he had introduced the bill and lost his furniture and some valuable pictures for his pains. Outside his house the 'kennels' ran with blood, 'into which men and women were dipping sticks and handkerchiefs'.[10]

After Spa Fields and the half-drunken pinchbeck insurrection of 2 December 1816, government panic induced the state suppression of meetings, societies and publications. In the metropolis, revolutionaries were driven even more deeply underground, but popular anger was appeased by some return of labour demand. The electors of Westminster and Middlesex made London ring with clamour for reform at the general election of 1818, and at the Westminster election of March 1819 a riotous crowd stoned Lord Castlereagh's London mansion. But the slaughter at Peterloo Fields, Manchester, in August 1819 brought yet more repression, with an unflappable Castlereagh active in turning the screw. And although Londoners sympathised with the Manchester reformers – 300,000, it was said, lined the streets to welcome Henry Hunt, the hero of Peterloo, back to London on 13 September 1819 – they were not moved to riot or revolt.

It would take a provocation of uniquely metropolitan character to push London once more to the brink of civil war in 1820–21. But first there was the last bow of Jacobin insurrection among conspirators who believed a single violent act would bring down the imperial government and crown revolution in its stead. And some of the men of Spa Fields were prominent among the plotters.

The ultras of 1816 had never abandoned their dream of revolution. For all their delusions, these men had courage enough to put themselves at the head of the charge. In 1818 Arthur Thistlewood challenged the repressive Home Secretary, Lord Sidmouth, to a duel and suffered imprisonment as a result. Thistlewood, Dr Watson, Preston and a Deptford shipwright called John Gast planned a simultaneous uprising at four places across London in August 1819, but it came to nothing. Their meetings and organisation were riddled with spies, and with most radicals increasingly adopting the non-violent tactics of Hunt and William Cobbett to press for parliamentary reform, Thistlewood and a handpicked few hatched a desperate plot. They planned to assassinate simultaneously members of the cabinet at their homes late at night. The very night had been chosen when it was learned from the newspapers that a cabinet dinner was to be held at Grosvenor Square that same evening, Wednesday 23 February 1820. Now it could all be done in a single massacre. The heads of Sidmouth and Castlereagh 'were to be brought away in a bag' to encourage others to revolt.

But one of Thistlewood's fellow conspirators was Edwards, a government spy, and the plot's every twist was in the hands of ministers. As Thistlewood and nearly thirty others gathered for the attack over a stable at Cato Street, Marylebone, just east of the Edgware Road, the place was raided by Bow Street runners and a party of Coldstream Guards, though with little cooperation between the parties. The police officers were first in the room, where 'cutlasses, bayonets, pistols, sword-belts, pistol-balls in great quantities, ball-cartridges, &c' lay on tables. In the mêlée, Thistlewood, 'armed with a cut-and-thrust sword of unusual length', stabbed a runner named Richard Smithers through the heart: '"Oh God! I am – "' were his last words. In the confusion most conspirators got away from Cato Street. Nine were arrested that night, and Thistlewood and a few others over the next day or two, while some escaped scot free. Besides Thistlewood, the ringleaders included James Ings, a butcher, Richard Tidd and John Brunt, both shoemakers, and 'a man of colour', William Davidson, a cabinet maker and son of the attorney general in Kingston, Jamaica.

On 1 May 1820 all five were hanged outside Newgate. An enormous crowd, held well back from the scaffold because of fear of a rescue, greeted the men with cheers – there were cries of '"God bless you, Thistlewood!"' After death a medical man in a black mask cut off their heads and the executioner held up each in turn to the crowd: '"This is the head of Arthur Thistlewood, the traitor!"' The decapitations were greeted with 'exclamations of horror and of reproach', with 'hissings and hootings'. Afterwards a rumour gained ground that the surgeon who severed the heads was Thomas Wakley, editor of the *Lancet*, in fact a radical and firm friend to the people. In August Wakley's house at Argyle Street, Euston, was attacked by several men, set on fire and burnt out. Wakley himself was stabbed and bludgeoned and robbed of his watch in a familiar London blend of politics and plunder.[11]

Less than five weeks after the Cato Street conspirators' agony on the gallows, Caroline, the estranged wife of George IV, returned to England to claim her place as queen to the new monarch. Viewed as a victim of George's scandalous neglect, untarnished by revelations of corruption and waste at court that stretched back a decade and more, her cause was hugely popular. It combined factors peculiarly stimulating to the London crowd: the misdeeds of a royal family, an injured woman, revelations of naughtiness in the bedroom. Caroline's arrival on 7 June 1820 made it seem 'as if London had poured out its myriads from every street'. They greeted her with 'exulting shouts' and broke the windows of any house refusing to 'light up' that night. A handbill called for a 'general illumination' for 10 June, when window-breaking brought out the Life Guards. Police used cutlasses on demonstrators in Portman Square, where some 'were desperately wounded'. Sporadic rioting followed through June amid rumours of disaffection among the

London military. Some Foot Guards were removed to the West Country to preserve discipline in barracks. If Thistlewood had held his hand for just four or five months, how different his prospects might have been.

In August 1820 Caroline was put on trial in the House of Lords for adulterous misconduct while abroad. Despite the lurid charges, each day the arrival of her carriage near Parliament brought forth an 'immense multitude' to cheer her on and hiss her enemies. When the trial, drowning in official embarrassment, was abandoned in November there were three successive nights of jubilation and some rioting outside the offices of pro-government newspapers in Fleet Street.

Ten years later, the *Annual Register* would look back to marvel at the hubris of a king who 'wanted to get rid of his wife at the risk of a civil war'. And civil war came closest in the bacchanal of grieving on the Queen's sudden death a year after her return to London; nearest of all during her funeral on 14 August 1821. Caroline had directed that she be buried at Brunswick and her cortège had to pass through or round London on the way from her residence at Brandenburgh House, Hammersmith, to the docks at Harwich. To minimise the expression of popular feeling, the authorities laid on a guard of cavalry and foot soldiers and prescribed a route along the New Road, bypassing the poorest parts of London and the City, where the Corporation had been outspokenly sympathetic to the injured Queen. In spite of heavy rain, the turnout of spectators was 'immense'. They had one object: to force the procession south, '"To the City!" – "the City!"' At strategic points in Kensington and Hyde Park Corner and Tottenham Court Road the procession found the way 'barricadoed' with carts and wagons and great crowds of angry protesters. When the Life Guards tried to force a way through Cumberland Gate they were met with cries of '"Blues for Ever, No Reds, Piccadilly Butchers, No Butchers, Kill the buggers"'. Men and horses were stoned and the Life Guards hit back with cutlasses and musket fire. Two protesters were shot dead and others wounded. But the crowd had its way. Dirty and bedraggled, the cortège found every escape route blocked. It was forced through St Giles, through Drury Lane, along the Strand and – to shouts of '"Victory! Victory!"' – through Temple Bar and the City of London.[12]

This was the last great mobilisation of the London crowd in the nineteenth century. There would be violent moments again. Some would put London in panic-stricken fear of revolution. Yet none would involve such enormous numbers working in concert for an explicit political end, curtailed and short-term though it might have been, such that the civil power of London was helpless in its grasp. And 1821 marked the passing of the radical storm which had kept London at its centre. The storm would return. But when it did its eye settled no longer over the metropolis but over the great cities of the North and Midlands, whose political circumstances were even less tolerable than those of the fickle Londoners.

Kennington Common, 1822–1848

For most of the 1820s prices were low and work relatively plentiful. Throughout the country it was a period of 'quiescence'. From 1824 to 1829 not a single petition on reform reached Parliament. Some of the repressive laws of 1819 had been allowed to lapse. In London trade unionism among the most skilled artisans had strengthened with prosperity. And there were other things to think about. The aspirations of the middle classes were stimulated by fashionable suburbs. A new seriousness of purpose revealed itself in a litany of church building and a hunger for education. In 1823 George Birkbeck founded the London Mechanics' Institute to encourage the general education of the artisan and three years later Birkbeck, Lord Brougham, Thomas Campbell the poet and others founded London University. The first London Co-operative Society was established by Robert Owen at Red Lion Square in 1824. In all these years the London crowd had not much fury to ventilate. But it didn't forget old scores. Lord Castlereagh cut his throat in a fit of depression in August 1822. As his coffin was lifted from the hearse the crowd at Westminster Abbey gave 'a loud and general shout of exultation'.[13]

By the end of 1829 distress was once more 'settling down on the country'. It was worst in the rural districts, but wage cuts and unemployment hit London too. A year on and distress in London was far worse. And now for the first time in the nineteenth century fear of 'the London mob' proved more potent than the thing itself. With nightly arson and rioting in the countryside, the revolution of July 1830 in France, which toppled a monarchy in three days, fixed attention on the metropolis. That London would prove another Paris had been the panic of the powerful and the hope of the powerless since 1789. 'Nothing can exceed the interest and excitement that all these proceedings create here,' Charles Greville confided to his diary. The July days were as much a spur to artisan radicalism as a source of anxiety to government and court. Most of all, they thrust parliamentary reform centre stage: 'fear, sheer fear' was Francis Place's explanation for the Whigs so firmly espousing reform from the summer and autumn of 1830.[14]

A feverish general election, called at the end of July, put the question of reform in front of every active constituency in the country. The new Parliament assembled at the end of October and was opened by a new king, William IV, on 2 November. That weekend, thousands of notices circulated in London, '"not written papers, drawn up by illiterate persons, and casually dropped in the streets,"' Peel told Parliament, '"but printed handbills"' calling for '"*liberty or death!*"' They summoned Londoners to '"come *armed*"' when the King and Queen's carriage journeyed to the City for a dinner in their honour. It was cancelled at the last minute by the Home Secretary, advised by the Lord Mayor that royal safety couldn't be guaranteed. 'This announcement filled the metropolis with doubt and alarm.'

With the timidity of the King's ministers so ridiculed that the Tory administration soon fell, trouble of sorts did erupt. A thousand men marched behind a tricolour over Blackfriars Bridge from an Owenite socialist meeting at the Rotunda, shouting for reform and '"Down with the Police!"' In the City they gathered 'a considerable number of notoriously bad characters'. There was a 'general fight' with the New Police in Downing Street; cavalry paraded but were not engaged. Next night, 10 November 1830, there was a fierce riot at Temple Bar involving, it was said, 'the refuse of the mob . . . consisting principally of boys of the lowest description, vociferating "No Peel – down with the raw lobsters!"' The New Police had no jurisdiction in the City, so Temple Bar offered rioters sanctuary as they stoned police from the Fleet Street side. West End and East End were excited by groups of 200–300 men and boys with tricolours parading up and down and breaking a few windows.[15]

The specifically London grievance of the New Police, quintessential servants of the rich and powerful as they seemed to many, clung to the coat-tails of reform and perpetuated an unholy alliance of the vocal and the violent. London would prove unsteady in the great struggle for the Reform Act, in shaming contrast to Birmingham in particular, and the volatility of the London crowd was one factor in metropolitan light-mindedness. Even so, these were restless days in the capital. Hostility to the New Police and anxieties during 1831 over cholera (many working-class Londoners thought the whole thing a humbug got up by government to impose central control on the people) helped bolster the most uncompromising wing of reform.[16]

The extraordinary fortunes of the Reform Bill, like some madcap game of snakes and ladders, exercised Parliament through 1831 and 1832. At the end of April 1831, defeat of the bill in the House of Commons was marked by a defiant call for an illumination in favour of reform. There was a frenzy of window-breaking in the West End of any building refusing to light up. Aristocratic mansions and club houses suffered severely. The Duke of Wellington, whose out-and-out rejection of reform had made him perhaps the most hated man in London, was a special target. Windows were broken at Apsley House ('Number One, London', his mansion in Hyde Park) and the Duke's servants fired muskets (but no ball) over the heads of the crowd. In May the Queen was frightened when her carriage was mobbed in the streets. In October, when the bill was rejected again, this time in the Lords, there were riotous meetings in the parks, monster demonstrations, a panic among West End shopkeepers, fighting with police, window-breaking and assaults on any aristocrat hostile to reform unwise enough to show his face in the town. Here the military had to come to the aid of police, stretched past breaking point by the shiftless enterprise of the London crowd. Almost every pane of glass in Apsley House was broken once more: for years to come Wellington would order great iron shutters to be drawn over the windows at night. At the end of the month a 'vast crowd' at Lincoln's Inn Fields, addressed by Burdett, Wakley and others, formed the National Political Union 'of the middling and working classes' to campaign for reform. Shortly after, a left-wing caucus split off to form the National Political Union of the Working Classes (NUWC), with William Lovett, a Cornish ropemaker in London since 1821 and now a cabinet maker, its main spokesman.[17]

It was the NUWC which organised the next event to excite the London crowd. The King had proclaimed a 'day of fasting and humiliation on account of the cholera' on 21 March 1832. The union countered the Fast Day with a 'Feast Day'. It called a meeting at Finsbury Square, to be followed by a procession. Bread and meat were to be distributed 'amongst the lower orders'. Some thousands were in the square, 'many of whom appeared to be in the greatest possible distress and destitution', and more were on the streets. The police were stoned at Finsbury Square and near Tottenham Court Road, with injuries on both sides.[18]

Six weeks on and for eleven days in May 1832 London was considered by many to be on the brink of insurrection. A committee of the House of Lords had mutilated the Reform Bill and the government resigned on the King's refusal to create fifty new Whig peers. All classes were swept up in the excitement. Thousands flooded meetings and joined London's political unions. Some factories closed as workers marched in a body to sign up. Resolutions not to pay rates or taxes were passed at householder meetings across London. Reformers organised a run on the banks. No great demonstration was called because the leaders feared, in Francis Place's words, 'the riotous proceedings of a mob'. Even so, he thought, 'We were within a moment of general revolution . . .' And 'the air was charged with talk of pikes and barricades and swords rough-sharpened for the first time since Waterloo'.[19]

There would indeed be a reminder of Waterloo. The Reform Act received royal assent on 8 June 1832. It was Wellington's great defeat. Ten days later was the seventeenth anniversary of his greatest victory and the Duke was spied on a visit to the Royal Mint. A 'crowd of persons collected on Tower-hill to wait his return'. Hissed and booed as he rode west, followed by an angry crowd, he coolly refused the help offered by a Thames police magistrate and his officers. But in Fenchurch Street he had to be rescued from assault by 'a body of the City police'. And in Holborn he was assailed by 'stones and filth', or every kind of shit the London streets could provide. Then he did take shelter, at Mr Speaker Wetherell's chambers at Lincoln's Inn, until a posse of police from Bow Street could escort him home to his iron shutters.[20]

The Reform Act did nothing for the London poor. And it couldn't touch distress, which still pressed hard on the working classes. With its aim realised, the moderate reform union under bourgeois leadership evaporated. But the sense of grievance among artisans reduced to starvation by slack trade burned on. On 7 May 1833 a meeting in Coldbath Fields, near Calthorpe Street, King's Cross, called by the NUWC, was declared illegal by the Commissioners of Police. It went ahead, in part organised by an undercover policeman and agent provocateur, Sergeant William Popay. When the police charged the demonstration they met fierce resistance. Two police officers were

stabbed, one – PC Culley – fatally. The man charged with both knif-
ings was acquitted and an inquest jury brought in a verdict of justifiable homicide on Culley's death – it was overturned later in the
courts.

Only a few hundred had turned up at Coldbath Fields and most of
those active militants. But the conditions that drove some artisans to
desperation in 1833 were clear enough. Shem Shelley, a carpenter from
George Street, Camberwell, and a member of class 83 of the NUWC,
was asked its 'chief objects'.

I do not know I am sure; I am not much of a political man; they were for
the protection of ourselves. Equal rights and equal laws is what we want; we
want no more than that; not to be oppressed quite so much as we are. Work
being scarce and so on, brings people together; if there had been plenty of
work I dare say there never would have been anything of it. If every man
could keep the wolf from his door there would be no meetings of any sort.
It is poverty that has brought the people together. Sometimes we do not have
a day's work for a month. I have been at work now three weeks, and have
not got the money. I only had seven shillings on Saturday night; we work
three or four days, and perhaps get half-a-crown or three shillings; that is not
enough to buy bread for a family, letting alone anything else.[21]

Disillusion with the reforms of 1832 was deepened by the draconian
New Poor Law of 1834, virtually the first legislative act of the reformed
Parliament and an undisguised attack on the living standards of the
poor. It fed an ulcer of discontent that helped keep radicalism alive
among the working classes throughout the 1830s. That was true even
in London, despite the infinite variety of shifts and wheezes that helped
suppress recourse to official relief in the workhouse or outside. And it
was in London that a new coalescence of radical movements first found
a voice.

In politics, London had long been more effective in fomenting ideas
than in putting them into action. Its attractions for intellectuals, politicians and writers had encouraged the one while its inchoate class mix,
its increasing separation between home and work, its absorption 'in
matters of business' and its unpredictable crowd behaviour had all
subverted the other. In London, political life never ceased among a
restless milieu of opinionated activists who were frequently at war with
one another. But politics could not ignite a mass movement in London,
even with the 'music, banners, and equipages' that 'warm the soul of

a Cockney into active life', as one critic of metropolitan 'apathy' put it.[22] All that was notably true of Chartism. It was born in London and died there. But it lived most vigorously elsewhere.

Fresh from winning a reduction to a penny of the newspaper stamp, a miscellaneous alliance of radicals, both bourgeois and working class, saw the opportunity to encourage the formation of a new movement for reform to make good the omissions of 1832. The printers Cleave and Hetherington, Francis Place, Birkbeck, an American medical doctor called J. Roberts Black and William Lovett (among others) were instrumental in carrying the idea forward. On 16 June 1836, at 14 Tavistock Street, Covent Garden, Lovett and other workers started the London Working Men's Association (LWMA), successor to the NUWC. The famous six points of what would become the People's Charter were first resolved at a LWMA meeting at the Crown and Anchor Tavern, the Strand, in February 1837 and first published in May 1838. Francis Place and William Lovett were the authors.[23]

Yet Chartism proved a tender bloom to cultivate in London. There was much branch activity in 1838–40 in working-class districts, especially Clerkenwell, the East End and the south side of the Thames. Its adherents were strong among tailors, shoemakers, silk weavers – all trades susceptible to pressure from semi-skilled labour and periodic distress – and among unionised building craftsmen. But in these years the numbers active weren't large and the Charter never inflamed the London crowd. There were enthusiastic assemblies of 10,000–15,000, but none of the monster gatherings that the six points could summon elsewhere. And none of the fierce rioting of Birmingham, Newport, the Potteries and other places.[24]

But when political agitation coincided with sharp distress, as it did in 1841–2, then thousands would come onto the streets to side with radical aspirations and to show their hurt. Great numbers turned out to cheer on the giant petition in favour of the Charter that was driven to Parliament on 2 May 1842. Some 100,000–150,000 were said to be in the procession; even omnibuses and cabs were decked in tricolours. All was considered good-humoured and 'teetotal'. But in early August, lasting for some days, troops entraining at Euston for the manufacturing districts were booed and hissed and jostled so much that on several occasions the order was given to fix bayonets. There were large meetings at Clerkenwell Green, Stepney Green and Islington Green, and fights between demonstrators and police, notably in Bow Street,

Covent Garden. And a meeting on Kennington Common was charged and routed by a large body of police.[25]

It would be Kennington Common where the last act of Chartism was played out – whether returning as farce or tragedy dependent on the point of view of the spectator. From 1842 to 1847 Chartism slumbered, overwhelmed by a campaign for the repeal of the corn laws, led by the middle classes but involving many workers in the struggle for cheaper bread. Repeal was won in June 1846. By 1847 the pressures of immigration from Ireland and manufacturing distress revived dreams of reform. Efforts were put countrywide into another petition calling on Parliament to grant the six points.

At the end of 1847 the reawakening of European democracy gave heart to radicals of all complexions. In February 1848 the news from Paris of another revolution, and yet another king deposed and exiled, put the threat or promise of insurrection into many minds. It was the Paris events that transformed London and the Londoners from 'apathy' to being at the centre of things. Republicanism and Chartism combined to bring out London's unholy alliance. In early March there were meetings – 'immense', 'tremendous' – at Lambeth, Stepney, Clerkenwell and Bethnal Green. A meeting at Trafalgar Square on 6 March was declared illegal but held nonetheless after fights with police, the London journalist G. W. M. Reynolds taking the chair. There were calls for the Charter and cries of '*Vive la République*' from the radicals. But elements in the crowd had a different agenda. There was 'bonneting' and horseplay. The *Annual Register* characterised the crowd as 'artisans and labourers out of work, idle spectators, and thieves', 'for the most part the refuse of a crowded city'. That night there was window-breaking and some looting of bread and beershops in the West End by 'disorderly persons' who 'joined the crowd'.[26]

For some days isolated disturbances contributed to a panic, most of all among shopkeepers, who organised vigilantes to protect their property. On 13 March a meeting at Kennington Common attracted radicals 'and a predacious crowd of the lowest mob of London'. By now shopkeepers' anxiety had infected the organs of state.

Four thousand police were in attendance; eighty were mounted and armed with sabres and pistols, and amused themselves with riding about the Common . . . Special constables were sworn in. The gun-makers were requested by the authorities to unscrew the barrels of their fire-arms, and the dealers in powder and shot were ordered to be cautious in the sale of those articles.[27]

Even so, as the meeting dispersed street traders were looted and there were attacks on a baker's, a pawnbroker's and other shops. Of eleven people later convicted of riot and other offences, two were 'known thieves' and most were very young.[28]

The alarm fuelled by the events of 6–13 March was kept simmering by metropolitan meetings leading up to the time for delivering the new Chartist petition to Parliament – 10 April 1848. The day was to start with a mass meeting at Kennington Common and then a procession, carrying the enormous petition, over Westminster Bridge to the Commons. To almost all the propertied classes, echoes of Paris ringing loud in their ears, the projected assembly sounded like a tocsin for revolution. The panic was immense. Londoners, as in April 1810, as from June 1820 to August 1821, and as in May 1832, believed themselves on the brink of civil war. At least 85,000 special constables were sworn in. Among them were Edmund Yates, Louis Napoleon, Count D'Orsay, George Augustus Sala, John Leech and the fathers of Richard Whiteing and George R. Sims – to mention names we've already encountered. Over 5,000 police were on duty; over 7,000 troops were posted at Millbank Penitentiary, the Houses of Parliament, Whitehall, the Tower, the Bank of England; artillery was deployed near Buckingham Palace and Westminster Bridge; 1,231 Chelsea Pensioners, armed to the gums, guarded Thames bridges; the aged Duke of Wellington, Waterloo doubtless clear in his mind, rode out with an escort to Kennington Common at six in the morning to take in the lie of the land.

In the event, most Chartists were as frightened of the idea of revolution as anyone else. Around 150,000 were allowed to gather at Kennington Common. They met peaceably and listened to the speeches. But the police outlawed a procession carrying the petition to Parliament and the Chartist leaders put up no fight. Order was maintained in part by heavy rain, the best London policeman of all. Demonstrators attempting to cross the bridges were met by insuperable force and were turned away. As the afternoon wore on they were permitted to draggle home in groups of a score or so at a time. For years after, Kennington Common would be a byword for radical failure, almost farce. Reformers of a later generation would choose a different amphitheatre to parade their demands.[29]

Kennington Common was not the end of London Chartism, but it was the end of its appeal to the London crowd. Branch activism survived. There was even a spasmodic return to London Jacobinism: 'pistols loaded to the muzzle, pikes, three-corner daggers, spear-heads, and swords' were found at a meeting in the Angel Tavern, Webber Street, off the New Cut, not far from Despard's Oakley Arms, and there were seizures of weapons elsewhere.[30] But the capacity of radical politics to bring onto the streets 'the lowest mob of London' had ended. For a time, at least.

Hyde Park, 1849–1879

Parliamentary reform would sleep for another ten years and not be actively pursued until 1865. In the interim, the institutions of working-class association in London strengthened around the workplace and the neighbourhood but not the streets. Cooperation in London was revived by Christian socialists in the wreck of Chartism. Cooperative workshops were established for tailors, shoemakers and others from 1850, with a few fragile retail ventures by the end of the decade. The Christian socialists, middle-class men like Frederick Maurice and Charles Kingsley, established the Working Men's College in 1854 at Red Lion Square, moving later to Great Ormond Street. Workers' clubs prospered sufficiently to move out of the public house and find their own premises. Many were radical and educational in tone – 'the artisan's university', a later historian would call them – and were dotted all over London and the eastern suburbs. Larger establishments, like the Eclectic Hall (Denmark Street, Soho), the John Street Institute (near Fitzroy Square), St Martin's Hall (Long Acre), provided lecture and concert rooms for a working-class audience. Trade unionists, too, were sufficiently self confident to construct a London Trades Council (LTC) in May 1860, following a lengthy strike and lock-out in the building trades. The founding societies included brickmakers, machine sawyers, carpenters, bootmakers, tinplate workers, ropemakers and hatters. All this intellectual and institutional development was erected on a foundation of relative prosperity.[31]

But there was distress enough when the economic dislocations of war and a steep rise in the price of bread precipitated so-called 'bread riots' in the East End in February 1855. 'Mobs of boys and degraded women, under the guidance of stalwart ruffians or desperate Irishmen, paraded the streets and levied contributions.' Some organisation led to disturbances in several places simultaneously. Bakers' and chandlers' shops were plundered of bread and coal.[32]

The summer saw more serious stuff. In June 1855 a Sunday Trading Bill introduced by Lord Robert Grosvenor was debated in Parliament. Its object was to close shops and beerhouses and to shut down public transport all in the name of Sabbath observance. In the week before Sunday 24 June, printed bills from 'A ratepayer of Walworth' called 'artizans, mechanics, and lower orders of the metropolis' to Hyde Park 'to see how religiously the aristocracy observe the Sabbath'. Along the carriage drives between the Serpentine and Kensington Gardens crowds assembled to hoot and hiss the phaetons of the rich and their Sabbath-breaking servants. There were cries of 'Go to Church!' and horses were made to shy and bolt.

Another week and anger was kindled by yet more handbills and posters all over working-class London calling people to Hyde Park on Sunday 1 July to protest against Grosvenor's '"Tyrannical attack upon the liberty of the people"'. By mid-afternoon vast numbers, some said 150,000, had turned up, despite newspaper advertisements taken out by the Commissioner of Police to deter 'well disposed persons' from attending, and banning any meeting in the park or 'assemblage of persons in large numbers'. Henry Beal, a 'table-decker' from Charles Street, Portman Square, was in the crowd that day, listening to the talk around him, and it was clear why many had come.

There seemed to be a general feeling of abhorrence about the [Bill]; that it was a measure to crush the poor; levelled exclusively against the poor, while the rich had their privileges unmolested . . . Tattersall's would be open, where horse-racing and betting could go on all day – that I heard stated – and the clubs, where a gentleman could have any refreshment that he pleased, where he could have his cards or anything he liked, and yet that it was a sin for a man to buy a newspaper or get shaved, and that it was a great piece of hypocrisy – that was the general observation which I heard applied.[33]

The crowds were made up of all ranges of society except the highest, from professionals through clerks and artisans to labourers and below. Most were no doubt exercised by Grosvenor's egregious bill. Many were prepared to catcall and jeer the carriages and riders out for a Sunday display in the park. But some had come for trouble. Sticks, stones, clods of earth and horse dung were thrown and a noisy crowd clung deep along the rails of the drive. It was not just the rich who were abused – '"Down with the Crushers!"' was one cry reported in *The Times*. Around 3.30 the police decided to clear the worst-behaved sections of the crowd. For the next six hours or so there were running skirmishes between police and people. Bystanders, promenaders, peaceful demonstrators and ruffians were all swept indiscriminately into the mêlée. For a time some young guardsmen joined the tumult against 'the crushers' and when eventually they were marched off the crowd followed, stoning their escort and then their barracks until dispersed by a police charge. There was much violence on both sides. Forty-nine policemen were injured. 'I saw all boys, the lowest rabble from the lowest parts of London; it was not working people that made the disturbance,' claimed a master currier injured by police, 'it was the boys that made it.' And among the crowd were a number of well-dressed pickpockets and 'other reckless and disorderly persons, bent on plunder and mischief'.[34]

A week later still, 8 July 1855, and things promised to turn even uglier. Ultra-radicals and former Chartists from Clerkenwell, Bethnal Green, Shoreditch and elsewhere converged on the park to revenge the police assaults of a week before. Among them was Thomas Frost. 'Few of the men who were going the same way as myself were without sticks' and 'several men and lads' inside the park carried 'bundles of stout sticks' for sale. But the carriage folk wisely stayed away from Hyde Park and so, in any numbers, did the police. Without a target, men and boys formed large groups, 'which rushed from one end of the Park to the other'. This proved eventually unsatisfying. And about five o'clock some hundreds left the park and moved to Grosvenor Place, 'where they insulted every person who rode or drove by'. Later there was extensive window-smashing in Belgrave Square, Eaton Square and elsewhere. Later still, the mood briefly infectious, shop windows were broken along the Hampstead Road, a mainly working-class district, to the terror of 'tradesmen, clerks, and small people'.[35]

Next day Lord Robert Grosvenor withdrew his bill. Even so, it would be many weeks before Hyde Park returned to normality and ceased to be the cockpit of class war. And in October and November a revival of the bread riots that had disturbed the East End earlier in the year now chose Hyde Park as a battleground, again on Sundays. On one night windows were broken in Mayfair.[36]

When class feeling next excited the London crowd it would not be to defend plebeian culture but to go on the attack for an extension of political rights. Parliamentary reform would once more provide the touchpaper. Its timing coincided with a temporary deepening of winter distress, especially in the East End. And internationalism once more spurred metropolitan action.

In April 1864 London hosted for two weeks the great Italian freedom fighter Giuseppe Garibaldi. His welcome among London's workers showed that he was a popular hero, unequalled by any other figure at home or abroad. Garibaldi's journey by carriage from Nine Elms, Battersea, to Stafford House, Green Park, witnessed 'the outpouring of the whole population of London'. Hundreds of thousands cheered themselves hoarse. Between Trafalgar Square and Parliament Street Arthur Munby found an impassable crowd 'composed mainly of the lowest classes; a very shabby and foul smelling crowd; and the women of it, young and old, were painfully ugly and dirty & tawdry'. Yet 'this coarse mob behaved with the utmost good humour and peacefulness'. [37]

When Garibaldi's visit was cut short, some London workers blamed the government for hustling this thought-provoking figure out of the country. A protest meeting called by the London Working Men's Garibaldi Committee was broken up by police. Out of that came an agitation to defend and enlarge workers' rights. And in February 1865 emerged the Reform League, London-based, essentially a workers' movement and radical in tone. It would occupy the left flank of a broader-based countrywide campaign for reform that built up strongly over the winter of 1865–6. In response, a Reform Bill was introduced by Gladstone's Liberal government in March 1866. Three months later an amendment on its third reading brought down the government and the bill fell.

Frustration and anger at the setback was soon given full play in London. On 29 June 1866 the Reform League organised a meeting and demonstration in Trafalgar Square. A march from Clerkenwell Green sported red flags and the cap of liberty. A cheering crowd milled round the Reform Club in Pall Mall and Gladstone's house nearby. But there were hooting and groaning outside the Conservative or Carlton Club. And a second meeting on 2 July proved more troubled, with rioting in the West End by 'a fortuitous concourse of the waifs and strays and roughs of a great city'. [38]

The Reform League then called for a giant meeting in Hyde Park on 23 July 1866. It was banned by the Tory Home Secretary, Spencer Walpole, in part because political meetings were considered incompatible with the park's purpose. Even so, vast numbers converged from all parts of London. 'So vast were the numbers' in the main procession 'that when the leading carriage was traversing Bond Street the rear rank had not left Holborn.' But the park's gates were chained and 1,600 constables, on foot and mounted, guarded Marble Arch gate alone. 'Barricades of omnibuses were on every side; the carriages of the wealthy blocked the way.' As one procession halted before the obstruction, other marches joined to swell the numbers and raise the pressure. Thwarted, the Reform League leaders turned the procession towards Trafalgar Square. What happened next – an iconic moment in British labour history – was not the action of reformers at all. Thomas Frost, one of their number, saw how everything was due to the traditional inflammable elements of the London crowd clinging to the reformers' coat-tails.

It was while the Reformers were on their way to Trafalgar Square that the sympathizers with the movement who had not joined the procession, the men and women who were on their way to the park, as on other evenings, and the 'roughs' and idlers whom the throng about the park gates caused to congregate, attempted to force their way into the park, and, after several skirmishes with the police, overthrew the railings, and burst into it like a torrent.[39]

The railings were put down in many places and the police were overwhelmed 'like flies before the waiter's napkin'. Some said that 200,000 invaded the park. Unable to enforce the Home Secretary's order, the police sent for the military. Soon troops of Horse Guards Blue and Foot Guards arrived: '"Three cheers for the Guards – the people's Guards!"' was how the crowd greeted the Blues, the Reds being wisely held in barracks. The military manoeuvred, but for decorative purposes only. The police restrained themselves as they had not done in 1855, despite Sir Richard Mayne, the commissioner, and others being stoned. Speeches were made at various points in the park by men and women reformers and at 10 p.m., as darkness fell, the crowd made its way quietly home.[40]

The leaders of the Reform League were now as fearful of the London crowd as were government and the civil power. With the ban on meetings in Hyde Park still in place, great assemblies were held indoors at

Guildhall, the Agricultural Hall, St James's Hall and in the grounds of Beaufort House, Kensington. Marches to the meeting places were tightly controlled – one was said to have had 10,000 stewards.[41]

Gatherings continued through the winter of 1866–7. And as pressure for reform nationwide became irresistible the Reform League took courage. In April 1867 it once more called a meeting on the forbidden turf of Hyde Park. The government promptly banned it. The league said it would hold it anyway. The government promptly lifted the ban. On 6 May some 200,000 people gathered for speeches in the park and dispersed peacefully. During the final run-up to reform the government vacillated over whether it should take stronger powers to ban all meetings in the royal parks without the Queen's permission. It introduced a bill, but then withdrew it, just as the second Reform Act extended the vote to all male householders in towns. Spencer Walpole resigned as Home Secretary, guilty of preposterous confusion over the question of free speech in Hyde Park. Never again would a government try to establish an in-principle objection to meetings in the London parks.

The 'Hyde Park Railings' affair of 1866 would be almost the last great expression of the traditional London crowd. The second Reform Act stilled clamour for an enlarged franchise and for almost twenty years protest slumbered. The movement of artisans to the suburbs increased the separation between work and home and raised the standard of domestic comfort for many. Most important, many Londoners shared in the general prosperity of the times. There was a steady rise in real wages, until a temporary setback in 1878–9. Some London gains in pay were 'regarded as phenomenal'.[42] Foreign affairs – the Paris Commune of 1871, for instance – failed to generate much passion in London outside committed communists and European émigrés. Even the hustings lost their traditional fun: there had been a near riot on Stepney Green at the general election of 1868, and 50,000 excited people were on the streets in the Southwark by-election of 1870, but all that was stilled by the Ballot Act of 1872 and the introduction of secret voting.[43] The machinery of working-class advancement – the social club, the trade union branch – grew stronger and more sophisticated, gaining self-confidence from the vote and prosperity both. And social reforms – compulsory education, slum clearance, new artisans' dwellings, improved sanitary policing, trade union rights, health and safety at work, shorter hours at the bench, encouragement of friendly societies – contributed something to the well-being of London's working classes, even among many unskilled labourers.

But the very poor and marginal – those casual workers with loose ties to any trade – hardly benefited at all. Some reforms, like slum clearance, were against their interests. For twenty years they bore their lot without collective protest, stilled by the prosperity in which even they to some extent could share. But good times couldn't last for ever. And when economic depression returned to London a new political creed was to hand, inflaming once more the London crowd. That was socialism.

Trafalgar Square, 1880–1899

It was distress and not socialism alone that provoked the final curtain call for the traditional London crowd. But socialism was the trigger.

The third Reform Bill caused brief excitement in London when it stalled in the House of Lords in July 1884. There were marches and monster rallies in Hyde Park that month and in October. London trade unionists were active in planning and taking part – the biggest of all was organised by the London Trades Council. Discipline and close stewarding kept away the rougher elements, held in much loathing by artisan unionists acutely conscious of their own hard-won status and aspirations.[44] The London reformers of 1884 had thoroughly learned the lessons of 1866.

Parliamentary reform, though, was milk-and-water for socialists. Not since the Spenceans of the Napoleonic period had London seen agitation for an out-and-out overturning of society to deliver both political rights and economic equality for all. Socialist agitation became a force in London politics only from 1881. But within just three years events gave new meaning to propaganda. The prolonged deep slump of 1884–7 was one of the worst of the century. It cast men and women out of their jobs and cut the wages of those still in work. Misery in the capital was made more desperate still by bitterly cold winters. And the London housing problem was in crisis through extensive demolitions and as a result of Jewish immigration into the East End. Little wonder that for socialists the moment of revolution seemed at hand. It looked that way to many in London's propertied classes too.[45]

Agitation for an enlarged franchise ended victoriously in December 1884, unskilled male labourers in towns winning the lodger vote. In the new year a different agitation took its place. Economic depression that winter provided socialists with a ready audience among 'the unemployed' – a mix of those out of work through trade dislocation on the one hand and those who existed at the edge of London's casual labour market on the other. The alliance of the politically informed and London's inflammable 'roughs' was resurrected on any scale for the last time. It had lost little of its capacity to shock and terrify.

From January 1885 the Social Democratic Federation (SDF), established four years before by H. M. Hyndman, a barrister's son born into wealth at Hyde Park Square, Tyburnia, began to organise a series of street meetings to attract the unemployed. Meetings were held of 2,000–3,000 outside the Royal Exchange, on the Thames embankment and in Hyde Park. One in May at Trafalgar Square became disorderly, attracting the wrath of the police. By the autumn, police interference with socialist meetings demanding 'work or bread' had become more aggressive. The socialists noted how they were singled out on the grounds of traffic obstruction, while evangelists and teetotallers went unmolested. The battle for free speech in the London streets had its first great encounter at Dod Street, Limehouse, in September 1885. The police moved on or summonsed socialist speakers on successive Sunday mornings. In response the radical and social clubs of the East End rallied to the SDF. When 30,000–40,000 workers marched on Dod Street the police proved powerless to act.[46]

As distress deepened over the exceptionally cold winter of 1885–6 trade unions successfully petitioned the Lord Mayor to open a Mansion House fund for subscriptions to relieve the poor. A few days later, on Monday 8 February 1886, a 'Fair Trade League' meeting in Trafalgar Square – allegedly bringing in East End 'roughs' 'at so much a head' to argue for protection for sugar refineries and other local industries – attracted a protest meeting by the SDF. Aggravation between the two gatherings worried the police. They suggested to Hyndman that he move his meeting to Hyde Park (so much had things changed in twenty years). Hyndman, H. H. Champion and John Williams, with John Burns carrying a red flag, put themselves at the head of 8,000–10,000 men and moved west through Pall Mall. They seem to have been joined by the more adventurous spirits among the Fair Trade East Enders too.

Exactly what happened next is unclear. There appears to have been some provocation from one of the Pall Mall clubs. Hyndman, in reminiscences written twenty-five years later, blamed club servants at the Reform for throwing nail brushes, shoe brushes and so on at the crowd, but his memory was faulty about other events that day and he may also have wished to make a point. But whatever the spark, there was no doubting the blaze. Club windows the length of Pall Mall and St James's Street were shattered with stones. Shop windows in Piccadilly were smashed and their contents looted as the stampeding crowd turned its mind to plunder. Old ladies were pulled from carriages and relieved of their jewellery. Men were 'stripped'. Carriages were 'broken in pieces'. Shop fronts were robbed in South Audley Street and then in Oxford Street, where at last a thin line of police wielding truncheons stopped the crowd's onward rampage. In Hyde Park, where a 'somewhat uproarious' meeting of sorts was indeed held, men with their arms full of looted clothing used the grass as a changing room.[47]

For some two or three hours the West End had been at the mercy of the London crowd. The police, taken by surprise and acting under confused orders, were nowhere to be seen. For the next two days parts of London, especially the West End, looked 'like a city under siege. If the Plague had again been raging in London, men could not have shown more fear or the houses worn a more melancholy look.' Two days after the riot, on 10 February, London witnessed 'an absolute panic' in the words of the *Annual Register*, 'heightened by the all-pervading black fog'. The filthy air throbbed with rumour. It was said that 50,000 vengeful unemployed were marching on London from Deptford and Greenwich – where crowds did indeed gather, but with no other intention than to protest at their lot. Shops put up their shutters from Lambeth to Euston. Club telegraphs reported rumour as press-agency fact. Old men spoke of 1848. At night, in the choking fog, some windows were broken and robberies of middle-class pedestrians who ventured out were more frequent than usual. And pockets were lightened in more ways than one. The Mansion House fund was said to have received donations of £75,000 within forty-eight hours of the great panic of 8–10 February 1886.[48]

Demonstrations of the unemployed continued throughout the year. They were largely peaceful, but not always. London's property-owning classes remained on edge. At the Lord Mayor's Show in November, which the socialists marked by a protest meeting in Trafalgar Square, 'a very large display of police and soldiers was made along the route' and many shops were 'closed or barricaded'. And on 8 February 1887 'the anniversary of "the West End riots"' was celebrated by a meeting and torchlit procession in Clerkenwell. When police broke it up, shop windows were smashed from Clerkenwell Green to Goswell Road.[49]

That summer of 1887, celebrating the first of Victoria's jubilees, was unseasonably hot and sunny. It was marked, as always in the nineteenth century, by homeless men and women sleeping out in the parks, in greater numbers this summer because of the kindness of the weather. Some time between June and August it became the habit of many men to bed down in Trafalgar Square, where the fountains gave a free wash and some relief from the heat. It was a poignant comment on jubilee junkets. Guilt was soon aroused. 'Bread vans' toured the square every night – attracting, in the happy phrase of the local police superintendent, 'the loafer' to take advantage of the largesse.[50]

All this did not long go unnoticed by the socialist propagandists of the unemployed. One morning, 'two or three of them appeared on the Square, unfurled a black banner with the words "We will have work or bread" thereon, and after some difficulty' – no doubt from the very poor state of the men concerned – 'induced about 30' to demonstrate outside the offices of the Local Government Board (responsible for the poor law) in Whitehall. The numbers of agitators, of unemployed demonstrators, of sightseers and of 'those poor creatures on the Square' grew from day to day. As late autumn set in the mood of all concerned grew bitter and determined. Faced with some truculence, and urged to deal with circumstances described in the press as a disgrace to London, the police decided to clear Trafalgar Square of its daily and nightly encumbrance. From 17 October the police dispersed meetings in the square, often resorting to force. There was trouble in streets nearby and in the park. In early November there were more arrests and skirmishes in the square. And the clamour for the unemployed began now to chime with the even more inflammatory cause of Irish Home Rulers, who also chose Trafalgar Square as their meeting place.

On 8 November Sir Charles Warren, Commissioner of Police, banned all meetings in Trafalgar Square. This was Hyde Park all over again. And just as twenty-one years before, the challenge united all London radicals – perhaps all London liberals – in the cause of freedom of speech and the right to voice protest in London's great open spaces.

It all came to a head on 13 November 1887. That day would stand as 'Bloody Sunday' in British labour movement history for the next eighty-five years. A meeting was called by the Metropolitan Radical Federation to demand the release from prison of William O'Brien, MP, an Irish Member. Despite Warren's 'ukase', big marches to Trafalgar Square were projected from all over working-class London. Poisonous splits, years in the making, were patched overnight in this enormous show of unity. William Morris, Annie Besant, George Bernard Shaw, W. T. Stead, John Burns, that attractive adventurer Cunninghame Graham, MP, all were there in various roles. An acute American observer, the journalist George W. Smalley, watched eagerly from the sidelines. The view was 'striking'. Mounted police were in strong numbers at every angle of the square; on the south side a line of policemen 'four deep, elbows touching', on the other sides just two deep, sometimes one.

Marches converged on Trafalgar Square from all directions. But half a mile or so away they were ambushed without warning by police baton charges. There was 'severe fighting' in Shaftesbury Avenue, the Strand and Parliament Street. The organisers had insisted on no violence from the demonstrators 'and we attempted none. Mr Cunninghame Graham and Mr John Burns, arm-in-arm, tried to pass through the police' at the square 'and were savagely cut about the head and arrested'. The police fought as though the battle was for life or death. They were supported by two squadrons of cavalry from the Life Guards, led by a mounted magistrate, the Riot Act proclamation in his pocket. Grenadier Guards formed in front of the National Gallery and fixed bayonets. But in the end no sword was drawn, no bayonet needed. Truncheons proved enough on the day. This was a victory for the police. Some 200 demonstrators were treated in hospital for the injuries they received. Two men died, possibly three. The funeral of Alfred Linnell at Bow cemetery near Christmas was attended by some disturbances at the graveside.

But not all the crowd on 13 November had passively resisted. Some thought that without the Life Guards on hand 'matters might have gone seriously with' the police. Smalley, who had also witnessed the hectic days of February 1886, noted an element in the Trafalgar Square crowd unduly ignored by historians.

There were decent people in the crowd, but they were in the minority and powerless. Most of them disappeared after the first few [mounted police] charges, and sought some less exposed point of observation. The rough of London was in the ascendant, with his dirty white face and his dirty brown raiment, and his general air of being on ill terms with mankind. He caught at the reins of the horses, and struck at them with fists and sticks, and at their riders. Nearly every collision that I saw was between these gentry and the mounted police.[51]

Two police officers were reportedly stabbed in the struggle.

For the next seven years there were isolated instances of fights between police and unemployed demonstrators at Trafalgar Square and Tower Hill. But the events of 1886–7 proved the last great outing for the traditional London crowd, where the mix of reformers and roughs seriously troubled the civil power. The great dock strike of 1889 showed that at last trade unionism had even begun to penetrate, and help civilise, the poorest, roughest, most semi-detached members of London's labour force. Associational life was supplemented in working-class communities by institutions born out of the fears of socialism and what it seemed to have brought to the streets of the capital. Social and educational clubs for men and women, girls and boys, took root in every poor neighbourhood in the capital. The London rough – at the end of the century labelled the hooligan – had far from disappeared. But the pressures which brought a disgruntled population onto the streets and ready for trouble had finally waned.

To that extent the forces of law and order had eventually prevailed. But not just through repression. A desire for law and order became an aspiration of more and more Londoners as the century grew older.

PART FIVE

LAW AND ORDER

'He sat by Tyburn's brook, and underneath his heel shot up
A deadly Tree: he nam'd it Moral Virtue and the Law
Of God who dwells in Chaos hidden from the human sight.'
William Blake, *Jerusalem*,
c. 1827

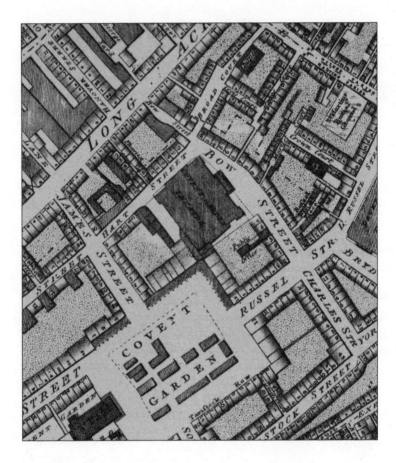

Bow Street, 1813

XIII

BOW STREET: POLICE AND
PUNISHMENT

Redbreasts and Runners: Police, 1800–1828

BOW Street was built 'fitt for the habitaĉons of Gentlemen and men
of abillity' between 1631 and 1636, the eastern edge of a new addition to town with Covent Garden Piazza at its centre. Francis Russell,
Fourth Earl of Bedford, was the suburb's moving spirit and Inigo Jones,
the King's Surveyor, had a hand in its design, but Bow Street never
quite achieved the aristocratic *ton* for which the speculation aimed and
elsewhere secured. It remained respectable enough, though, until a back
alley was cut through to enter the pit at the new Theatre Royal, Covent
Garden, in 1732. Bow Street's long connection with drink and prostitution probably began then. By 1743 there were eight licensed premises in a street of fewer than forty houses. When Smirke's rebuilt opera
house opened at those controversial new prices in 1809, its front portico
now occupied half the west side of Bow Street and the transformation
to a distinctly unrespectable neighbourhood was largely complete.

By then another component in Bow Street's downward slide was
locked in place. In 1740 Sir Thomas De Veil, a prominent Westminster
justice, took 4 Bow Street for both town residence and magistrate's
court. De Veil was mildly corrupt but he was active in the cause of a
more effective police for London and Bow Street Public Office soon
took on itself large responsibility for investigating crime and pursuing
its perpetrators. De Veil was succeeded at 4 Bow Street in 1748 by the
novelist and playwright Henry Fielding, no less active and much less
corrupt. Fielding was the originator of a detective police force in
London. 'Mr Fielding's People', just six of them at the beginning, were

established by 1750 as the only professional thief-takers in London, paid a small retainer from the public purse but relying mainly on rewards from courts and victims as compensation for their dangerous trouble. Over time their successors would become known as the Bow Street runners. 'Bow Street, Covent Garden, is the Office celebrated all over the United Kingdom, and it may be said the whole World, for its execution of the Police . . .'[1]

By 1800 the police of London had enlarged considerably from Henry Fielding's day. A Bow Street night Foot Patrole of sixty-eight men policed the main suburban roads into London and the chief streets of town. Its captains were armed with carbines, a brace of pistols and a cutlass, the men with cutlass only. And a new Thames police office at Wapping patrolled the river and investigated shipboard and dockside crime.[2]

There were further developments in the new century. In 1805 a Bow Street Horse Patrole, mounted and armed, was set up to deter highway robbery at night on the edge of London. In 1821 a Dismounted Horse Patrole was set up for the nearer suburbs, and in 1822 a Bow Street Day Patrole of twenty-seven men. By 1828 the total resources of Bow Street's patrols numbered 288. The Horse Patrole, when 'assembled in a body', had from the outset worn a uniform of blue coat and red waistcoat – the first uniformed police in Britain. This livery was adopted by Peel's Day Patrole and (it appears) by 1828 the Foot Patrole (motto: Be Sober, Be Vigilant). They were all popularly known as Robin Redbreasts.[3]

The runners, though, as detective not preventive police, wore plain clothes. This detective police had also been strengthened since Fielding. In 1792 seven police offices were established at Great Marlborough Street, Hatton Garden, Worship Street, Whitechapel, Shadwell, Union Hall (Southwark) and Queen Square (now Queen Anne's Gate, Westminster). Each was headed by a bench of stipendiary magistrates on the Bow Street model, conducting investigations as well as dispensing justice. At first six police officers, often called runners, were attached to each office. By 1816 there were between seven and ten at each (Bow Street had eight). In 1821 an office was opened in High Street, Marylebone, and Shadwell closed.

Among London's sixty-odd detective police in this first quarter-century were some famous names. There was John Townsend, intimate of George III and the Regent and effectively their bodyguard at public nights in town, reported to have left £20,000 when he died. John Sayers, whose fortune was said to have reached £30,000. George Ruthven, who arrested Thurtell and retired with pensions from the British, Russian and Prussian governments to keep the One Tun Tavern, Chandos Street, Covent Garden. There were notable thief-takers like John Vickery, 'cut all to pieces' when arresting two murderers around 1814, or John Armstrong, beaten almost to death by five highway robbers in Rose Lane, Spitalfields, around 1821. And George Donaldson, who 'never bore a very high reputation for virtue of any sort' but was fearless enough nonetheless. James Hardy Vaux, that racy villain, related how Donaldson and Smith arrested him in 1809 at the thief-filled Butcher's Arms, Clare Market, without a moment's fear for the consequences – '"Mr Vaux, we want you!"'[4]

But these famous men – Townsend, even in an age of eccentrics, was one of the great characters of London until his death in 1832 – were merely the gilded few among a patchwork legion of London parish police, and the police themselves just one diffuse element in an army of peacekeepers.

The parish police of London had origins so archaic and structures so arcane that no complete history has ever been written of them and no accurate record of their organisation or numbers in the early nineteenth century was ever obtained, even at Parliament's request. This alone has obscured some of their importance in London life. Obscurity was made darker still by the glare of Bow Street derring-do and then most of all by the condescension of Sir Robert Peel, his Metropolitan Police and their supporters and chroniclers then and since.[5]

First, take what we know about numbers. These were surprisingly large. In 1822, in the City and the inner districts and suburbs within the jurisdiction of the various police offices, there were at least 3,860 parish peace officers of one kind or another. Some 133 were beadles, paid parish officers with administrative functions and general power of police, like arranging the nightly watch. There were 312 headboroughs and around 474 constables, elected or selected by rote from the rate lists to serve for a year at a time and acting free of charge. Their functions were to arrest wrongdoers and keep the peace. There were then around seventy-two street keepers, parish servants expected to act as constables and quell riot when occasion called. And finally 2,870 or so 'nightly watch', the watchmen or 'charlies' armed with staves and rattles whose nickname has come down to us as a byword for witless incompetence. These numbers didn't include arrangements in the ancient townships incorporated into or close to the metropolis like Greenwich or Deptford or Croydon, for instance. Of the 3,860, 1,040 policed the City, the best-watched part of London. There was some growth in the last ten years or so of the old police, though the numbers must be considered more indicative than accurate: there were said to be between 4,500 and 5,000 by 1828.[6]

There were many serious defects in the organisation of London's parish police. The unpaid duties of headborough and constable were onerous, thankless and dangerous. The job's unpopularity was reflected in the market for 'Tyburn Tickets', until they were abolished in 1818. These were vouchers awarded by the court for bringing a burglar or housebreaker to justice, so facing a capital charge. The ticket absolved the owner from parish duties for life and they could be sold on once. In crowded London parishes a Tyburn Ticket was worth £25 in 1816. Yet although it took a peculiar sort of altruist to discharge this public duty conscientiously, such men could be found. At the other end of the range were a few who saw in the function an opportunity for plunder through rewards or blackmail or bribery. In the middle were the majority who side-stepped harsh responsibility when they could or avoided it altogether by paying a deputy to perform their task for the year. Some of these deputies were of many years' standing and so most likely to be alive to making the most of a bit on the side. A parliamentary inquiry of 1818 called them 'in many instances . . . characters of the worst and lowest description'.[7]

This nightly watch, fragile backbone of London policing, almost deserved the ridicule and opprobrium which continue to blight its reputation. 'Very defective in every respect,' was the view in 1828 of Sir Richard Birnie, Chief Magistrate at Bow Street but himself not without blemish: 'They are good for nothing decrepid old men, who carry a lantern merely to shew a thief where they are.' Stories of the charlies sleeping in the watchhouse, where charges were brought and locked up, or hiding in their watchboxes while riot raged at the other end of the street, were just too common all to be myth. And in St George's Hanover Square in 1826, a newly energised watch committee was horrified to find 'the watchmen invariably consisting of old and wretched creatures, many of them kept there because they would have been a burden to the parish, or from motives of pity'.[8]

But within two years the St George's watch had been replaced by

army pensioners under forty years old. And it is easy to find examples
of watchmen far different from their Tom and Jerry caricature. At
Covent Garden, say, in 1824 we find 'a smart, upright, *Corporal Trim*-
like sort of a watchman' and another a six-foot Irishman, the Irish
very common among watchmen in the 1820s; all 700 men of the City
watch were considered 'able-bodied' in 1822; ex-soldiers only were
generally accepted at Marylebone and there were many ex-sailors at
Spitalfields, where most were in their twenties and hardly any over
forty; and at St James's, Piccadilly, no watchman was under five foot
eight. These last examples come from 1828, when attention to London
policing had received more than sixteen years' anguished scrutiny and
the subject was of abiding interest to many Londoners. In all, the truth
seems to be this: that the parish police had elements of good and bad
but were hopelessly inconsistent; that the reputation of the 'charlies'
was an unfair stereotype; and that when a guide for strangers in London
advised, 'A cry of *"watch"*, three or four times repeated, will instantly
bring up the assistance of several of the watchmen', it was not entirely
whistling in the wind.[9]

Even these significant numbers of parish police, of Bow Street patrols,
of Thames police and runners at the eight police offices didn't exhaust
the resources available to the civil power in the event of a major disturbance of public order or a metropolitan event calling for the supervision of great crowds. In 1830 the City alone could assemble 2,284
variously armed men, not counting the watch, to keep the peace if
need be. They included ward and special constables, firemen, fellow-
ship porters, corn porters, tradesmen with emblems of trade, 'Gentlemen
called Lumber Troopers' (members of 'a respectable smoking club'),
the Honourable Artillery Company Volunteers and the East India
Company Volunteers.[10]

Then the military presence in London was so strong from time to
time that it could take on the appearance of an occupied city. New
barracks were built at Knightsbridge for the Horse Guards (1794–5),
Birdcage Walk, St James's Park (the Wellington Barracks, Foot Guards,
1814), at St George's cavalry barracks behind what would be the
National Gallery around 1818, at Regent's Park (1820–21, cavalry)
and St John's Wood (1832, infantry). In 1814 there were said to be
'upwards of 12,000' soldiers stationed in London and in 1826, calmer
times, 8,200. And two regiments of militia and various volunteer bands
were established in institutions like the Bank of England and the East

India Company and almost every parish in London. They totalled 14,700 in 1803. All these enrolled the merchant, shopkeeping and artisan classes in spare-time military enlistment for any emergency.[11]

Emergencies were rife. The military were used not just for riot control at moments of revolutionary fury or crowd control at great public spectacles. Any large fire could provoke both the excitement and rapacity of the London crowd beyond the powers of parish police or Bow Street Patrole to placate. So a squadron of Lord Cathcart's dragoons was necessary to save 1,000 bags of hops from disappearing into the night when Combe and Shum's brewery at Store Street, Tottenham Court Road, caught fire in September 1802; and Foot Guards had to be summoned to the aid of police when 'Several hundred ruffians formed themselves into bands of ten or a dozen each' and robbed neighbouring houses in the chaos of a fire at a timber yard in Drury Lane in November 1820.[12]

Despite the great numbers of armed men available to magistrates, to government and the crown, the inadequacies of London policing began to press on the public consciousness, particularly in the second decade of the nineteenth century. The ghastly events of Ratcliffe Highway at Christmas 1811 marked a turning point. Later generations would come to know the difficulty of identifying and bringing to justice a cunning homicidal maniac, but the killings of the Marrs and the Williamsons were most of all interpreted as a failure of the police. The entire night watch of Shadwell, forty men, were dismissed overnight and armed patrols took their place. Proposals for reform of the London police cascaded into the Home Department. But the opportunity was missed. Some local strengthening of the watch was effected in various parishes, but the critical weakness of metropolitan coordination was ducked.[13]

Almost every year that passed gave further cause for worry about the inadequacies of the police in London. The serious rioting of 1815, which exposed the insecurity of even government ministers' property, was followed a year later by revelations of rapacious corruption at the head of London policing – Bow Street itself. George Vaughan, a member of the Horse Patrole, was sentenced to five years' hard labour in 1816 for putting up five men to a burglary in Hoxton and then arresting them in the act for a reward of £40 each. Burglary was a hanging offence and this was literally blood money. Two others had been in the conspiracy, one a member of the City police called Robert Mackay.

Vaughan was subsequently also found guilty of burglary and transported. And it seems clear that he had been involved in inveigling dull
men to pass bad money. Vaughan and other officers supplied bad coin
to 'Bubblefoot' Solomons, who passed it on to destitute foreign sailors
and newly arrived Irishmen in the East End. They were arrested in the
moment of spending it. At least eighteen men were trapped in this way.
The Bank of England gave £10 for each conviction.[14]

There followed parliamentary committees reporting in 1816, 1817
(twice), 1818, 1822 and 1828, each with its revelations and criticisms
of various aspects of the police of the metropolis. The runners were
shown to be much out of London, guarding the great or pursuing fat
rewards from banks and wealthy individuals to recover stolen property. Sometimes they were not even in the country, working for foreign
governments and monarchs. They were accused of 'compounding' with
thieves to return stolen goods for a fee, or take 'hush-money' for turning
a blind eye to crime. They were said to wait until a thief 'weighed £40'
before arresting him, allowing less serious crime to go unpunished; to
spend their days in 'flash houses', befriending thieves, drinking at their
expense and 'taxing' the landlords for an expensive 'boxing at
Christmas'. The parish police were also in the pay of thieves and prostitutes, bringing false charges against those who refused to treat. There
were other problems too. Generally the state would prosecute for only
the most serious offences. So preposterous costs and aggravations
attended prosecutions by the victims of crime, doubly victimised by
threats and violence from the friends of those they were proceeding
against and by the depredations of sharp-nailed lawyers.[15]

Most damning of all was exposure of the extreme parochialism of
the current arrangements. The City police couldn't follow stolen goods
beyond Temple Bar, or Westminster and Middlesex police pursue a
thief the other way. Information was kept secret between one police
office and another and there was intense rivalry between Bow Street
and the rest. Jealousies could get out of hand. Joseph Sadler Thomas,
an energetic elected constable, found to his cost that his vigorous
suppression of prostitutes and pickpockets somehow interfered with
the interests of the Bow Street Patroles.

Did you see a sort of spirit of resistance to what you were doing amongst the
established police, as if they were sorry you were exerting yourself? – I saw
a marked spirit of envy, and a determination to do me all the injury they

possibly could . . . I consider they acted as men conscious that every conviction I carried to Bow-street, was a tacit reproach upon them for not doing
their duty; I repeatedly heard of threats made behind my back, and those
threats, in one instance, were carried into execution; while I was clearing the
avenue in front of Drury-lane theatre . . . I was seized by Bond and Nettleton
[and Alderson, all it seems of the Bow Street Day Patrole] and I was struck
and dragged through the streets like a felon . . . I was terribly ill-used, and
pointed out to an exulting set of blackguards as the bloody constable of Saint
Paul's.[16]

The Committee of 1828 to which the indignant Thomas gave evidence
concluded that the present police arrangements for London revealed
the 'absence of all union, of all general control and undivided responsibility'. It called for a central 'Office of Police', 'under the immediate
directions of the Secretary of State for the Home Department'; but day-
to-day executive responsibility should remain with stipendiary magistrates at the police offices.[17]

The committee had been established by that brilliant Tory adminis-
trator Sir Robert Peel. He had reformed the police force in Ireland
between 1812 and 1818, where 'Peelers' and 'bobbies' had first been
christened. His fervent long-term hope was for a national police force
run by the Home Secretary. The committee's recommendations did not
go that far, didn't even contemplate the police of the City being unified
with the police of London, and still left real power with the magistrates rather than the Home Office. But they gave him a toe in the
door. And with one dramatic push Peel changed the police and government of London for ever.

'Peel's Bloody Gang': Police, 1829–1839

Peel's reforms didn't come, as it were, out of the blue. Comprehensive
schemes for a central police authority for London had been devised
since the 1790s, among them two by prominent stipendiary magistrates, Patrick Colquhoun and John Harriott. And although executive
power for the detective police had lain with these stipendiaries since
'Mr Fielding's People', the Home Secretary always had close contact
with the chief magistrate at Bow Street. From 1805 he had directly
paid for and controlled the Horse Patrole. The Dismounted Horse

Patrole in 1821 and the Day Patrole in 1822 were set up and run by Home Secretaries Lord Sidmouth and Peel himself. Whether control of any reformed administration should continue to lie with the magistrates or the Home Office had been the key question facing any proposal for change. Most had sided with the magistrates. But the 1828 committee had decisively cast its vote the other way, at least in respect of strategic oversight. That was in line with Peel's preference. Decisive, intolerant of delay in a hesitant era, Peel turned the bare bones of the committee's recommendations into a bill by April 1829. His proposals went much further in the direction of central government control than the committee had envisaged or public opinion sanctioned. But its originality was masked by the furore surrounding Catholic emancipation. And the bill, despite the sweeping nature of its clauses and their hurt to parish and magisterial interests, raised little opposition. The Act for Improving the Police in and Near the Metropolis became law on 19 June 1829.

Peel's task didn't end there. The act had defined a 'Metropolitan Police District' centred on Charing Cross, had established two 'justices' to run the new police independent of the stipendiaries and a 'Receiver' to collect rates from the parishes to pay for them. But the structure and organisation of the force, its numbers, terms and conditions, build-ings and equipment were to be determined by Peel and whoever he appointed to lead it. Peel's choice of all three was inspired. But even he couldn't have anticipated just how lucky he was in his choice of Lieutenant-Colonel Charles Rowan, a middle-aged former Peninsular War officer and veteran of Waterloo, and Richard Mayne, an Irish barrister just thirty-three and thirteen years Rowan's junior, to be the presiding justices, soon permanently known as commissioners. It is a rare thing to find two men sharing power at the top of any organisa-tion and adding to the sum of their parts, but such was the case with Rowan and Mayne. They neutralised each other's defects and augmented their virtues. For the next twenty-one years, Rowan and Mayne estab-lished and led the New Police in ways that were recognised at the time as exemplary. The judgement of posterity, in the light of everything that has gone since, can hardly be less generous.[18]

Peel, Rowan and Mayne were jointly responsible for getting the new force off the ground. Peel played a determinative role in detailed issues like what sort of man should be recruited (not 'gentlemen' of the retired officer class, even for senior positions), of pay (just a guinea a week for a constable, and help with board and coals), of uniform (a non-military blue, to be worn at all times, even off-duty). Headquarters were established at 4 Whitehall Place, with a rear entrance from Great Scotland Yard. Mayne, it seems, was the drafter of 'New Police Instructions for London', with their famous emphasis on the prevention of crime as chief objective, their injunctions to constables to avoid unnecessary interference or display of authority, their commendation of 'a perfect command of temper' and 'a quiet and determined manner'.[19]

Constables and sergeants were armed with a truncheon but given cutlasses in an emergency, and inspectors carried 'a pocket pistol'. Constables' top hats were strengthened with an iron ring at the crown to forestall 'bonneting' and they wore a stiff stock to ward off the garrotter. Recruits had to be at least five foot seven. Most new policemen were country-born and country-recruited. Many, like one of the commissioners, were Irish – 'red-hot Irishmen', according to one East End critic, 'just imported'. An uncertain but not insignificant number, though, were former members of one branch or other of the London police. Around seventy of the Bow Street Patroles were transferred and younger members of the parish police were accepted into the new force. Joseph Sadler Thomas became Superintendent of Covent Garden Division, Nicholas Pearce of the Daily Patrole was made an inspector, and poor PC Long, the first metropolitan police officer to be murdered on duty, stabbed to the heart by a burglar armed with a shoemaker's knife in August 1830, was one of twelve men recruited from St Luke's watch.[20]

The first thousand or so of Long's comrades took to the London streets on 29 September 1829, in just six of seventeen planned divisions; thirteen were operational in February 1830 and all seventeen in May 1831. That marks the first date of comprehensive policing within roughly a ten-mile radius of Charing Cross. By 1834 the number of London policemen was just short of 3,400. 'I think I may say safely,' affirmed Rowan to a parliamentary committee that year, 'that every street, road, lane, court and alley within the Metropolitan Police District . . . is visited constantly day and night by some of the police.'[21] And at Bow Street, where it had all begun but whose star was eclipsed by what all London would soon call Scotland Yard, the New Police built their own station in 1832, opposite the Public Office where the magistrates and their runners still ran on.

In many ways the new police could not have been established at a more difficult moment. They were the brainchild of a Tory Home

Secretary in an administration led by the Duke of Wellington. Creature of a hated government, the force found itself the most visible target of popular indignation. It was vented not just by the most radical or the poorest but by many sections of press and public. So parish protests against the police were pursued into 1833, with rate strikes and threats of violence against sheriffs enforcing the receiver's writs. The high price of Peel's police was not the only source of resentment. The radical vestry of St Marylebone complained of less effective policing under the new regime and so did Acton, Shoreditch, St Saviour's Southwark ('the policemen are perfect strangers to us'), the Clink Liberty and Christ Church Southwark (where street robberies and shop-window smashing had 'increased considerably'), and St George's-in-the-East (which complained of 'insolence, and inefficiency, their complete inefficiency').[22]

Worse than these complaints, which, however justified, could be brushed aside as self-interested or politically malicious, was the attitude of the London press. The unstamped press and the penny pamphleteers of Seven Dials had a field day with the New Police. Their most potent weapon was ridicule. And there was much to feed on. An early propensity of the stalwart Peelers in their irresistible uniforms to pursue cooks and kitchen maids provoked ribald commentary. One early nickname for the force was 'The Cook's Own'. And when PC John Jones was convicted on a citizen's arrest of stealing a scrag of mutton from a Somers Town butcher in October 1829, the cry of 'Who stole the mutton?' would torment the London policeman for a generation to come.

> Hollo! New Police,
> Who in your blue coats strut on,
> Your fame you won't increase
> By stealing joints of mutton.[23]

More expected, and more bruising of bones than pride, was the response of the truculent London poor. There is no doubt that the crowd 'took on' the New Police, buoyed up by the popular passion for reform and against the government and all its works. A turning point was said to be the truncheon charge led by Superintendent Thomas at Catherine Street, near Temple Bar, on 10 November 1830. Francis Place claimed to have coached Thomas in the tactic before the event. The police proved victor. And the optimistic Place affirmed that afterwards 'there were no more mobs'.[24]

But that was stuff. And so were many claims on behalf of the New Police then and since.[25] Even so, the Metropolitan Police, fledgling and frail and uncertain of survival though it was in its very early days, overcame its tribulations and won general credit. Within just five years of their appointment, Rowan and Mayne had secured some sort of consensus that what was new was measurably better than what had gone before. How?

The response of Londoners to the new police was largely class-determined. The bulk of the metropolitan middle classes and above had been relatively easy to win over. The victory of reform in June 1832 removed for many the taint of reaction's tool that had hung over Peel's force from the beginning. And the killing of PC Culley at the Calthorpe Street riot of May 1833 won sympathy from those who, having gained reform of sorts, now saw the police as a bulwark against more threatening aspirations. Then again, some parishes may have lamented the passing of the nightly watch, but most had suffered from the unreliability and unevenness of the old and saw the new as improvement. And the visibility of the New Police on the streets of London during the day was an entirely new and reassuring development from which all could take comfort. Some instances of bullying and oafishness by individual constables apart, middle-class Londoners in general could welcome a greater feeling of security for property and person. The rector of St Giles in 1832, while bemoaning increased drunkenness among the people and the continuation of 'great outrages' confronting churchgoers in that lively locale, noted, 'There is much less of fighting and tumult than before, owing to the vigilance and zeal and activity of the new police; I feel deeply indebted to them on all occasions for prompt, cheerful and efficient agency.' And there was a similar tale in the suburbs:

of all the improvements which have been effected in our domestic polity during the last half century, the establishment of the police force must undoubtedly be considered as one of the most useful and satisfactory. It has proved a real blessing to this parish [Hammersmith], by the protection which is afforded at all times to the persons and property of the inhabitants, as well as to travellers.[26]

The views of working-class Londoners were more equivocal. To radicals unsatisfied by the Great Reform Act the police remained 'Peel's

Bloody Gang'. The Clerkenwell coroner's jury who handed down the verdict of 'justifiable homicide' over Culley's body were given anniversary dinners for some time after 1833. And William White, a stipendiary magistrate at Queen Square, thought the poor 'very much ill-treated by the police', who acted with 'rather an over-zeal' in pursuing trivial charges to the courts. Policing the London slums would remain arduous and risky throughout the century. And there were some groups of Londoners who were never reconciled to the Metropolitan Police or who had a peculiarly tense relationship with them.

Even so, it would be wrong to see the New Police as a semi-imperialist quasi-military force garrisoned on the poor, or 'P for PEELERS', as *A New Political and Reform Alphabet, with Fables on the Times* put it around 1837: 'A body of great Force. Brave and noble conquerors of an un-armed and peaceable people'. For the poor needed protection too. Most victims of crime were working-class Londoners. Assault, terrorism, theft and mean tricks were as much part of life in Seven Dials or Ratcliffe Highway as mutual assistance and collective solidarity. So the police could be both common foe and helping hand – even saviour – and almost in the same breath. They were helped in their task by that good-tempered determination that Rowan and Mayne had extolled as the constable's cardinal virtue; and by not a little heroism. In this way, the New Police and the London poor reached some sort of accommodation just short of open warfare.[27]

The *New Alphabet*'s 'Q for QUESTION' was 'how long will they last?' But even by 1834 the answer was readily apparent. The Metropolitan Police were here to stay. And as a result, elements of the old regime that had been cautiously untouched by the act of 1829 began to be absorbed into the new force. The Horse Patrole were taken into the Metropolitan's mounted branch from early 1837. Then in 1839 the police district was enlarged to a rough radius of fifteen miles from Charing Cross, and the strength increased to some 4,300 men; the Thames police were merged as a separate branch; and the eight police offices became merely magistrates' courts dispensing justice, no longer investigating crime. The runners went too. They had remained the only detective force in London after 1829, apart from a few police in plain clothes. They had gone on in their old – not entirely ineffective – way. One of the telling anecdotes of John Townsend was his comment on the passing of the Reform Bill: 'It's all up now!' In 1839 it really was. Faced with a life in blue serge, almost all the runners seem to have retired, a few becoming private enquiry agents. For three years until 1842 London had no detective police at all: neglect of the detective function was Rowan and Mayne's one strategic error of judgement.[28]

Not all anomalies were removed. Most notably, the City police were kept out of Metropolitan hands. With typical prudence, the Corporation overhauled its police with one eye on a potential takeover from 4 Whitehall Place and another on the daytime difficulties of prostitutes and beggars finding asylum from the New Police east of Temple Bar. In 1832 the City established a day police of 100 uniformed men. And then in 1839 the City Police Act set up a parallel force to the Metropolitan under a commissioner appointed by the Common Council and not the Home Secretary. The City constable was more statuesque at five foot nine than his London colleague. By the end of the century there were other differences too: 'To-day the police of the City of London constitute a highly efficient body, inferior to no other force in the kingdom. Pay is higher than in the Metropolitan Police, and the stamp of men are frequently superior in intelligence and courtesy. Politeness is the characteristic of the force . . .'[29]

One other difference lay in the City's small detective department, spanning old and new systems without a break and apparently without any damaging rivalries. The famous Forrester brothers had been the City's chief runners from 1817 (John) and 1821 (Daniel). In 1848 the City's New Police formed a detective branch but the Forresters worked side by side with them until 1858, paid a salary by the Corporation and waxing stout on private rewards.[30]

There were important continuities in the Metropolitan force too. They show that the world was not entirely turned upside-down by the great reforms of 1829–39. 'Constables' and 'beats', truncheons and rattles, some personnel and sources of recruitment (like the Irish) and a non-military style of dress were all inherited from the past. Special constables and the armed forces would still help police London, even though it was often said that from October 1829 the army was never again needed to keep the peace. Even in some local emergencies red coats and fixed bayonets were necessary to keep the crowd in order: at fires at Millbank Penitentiary in 1835 and at Her Majesty's Theatre, Haymarket, in 1867, for instance; and to clear Bow Street when the police went briefly on strike in July 1890. And the common informer – that jackal of legal London – would still be encouraged by a trickle of legislation, the last as late as 1895, to spy out offences and bring them to the magistrates for reward.[31]

Then there were all sorts of cultural influences that migrated effortlessly from the old police to the new. A culture of tipping pervaded street policing, despite its absolute prohibition in police rules, carrying the threat of instant dismissal. From innumerable examples, one might serve. Right through the century early-rising workers would book and pay for a wake-up call at the local police station: '"What's the time, please, sir?" "Fourpence a week."' Then, just as in Townsend's day, the Metropolitan Police were for hire by private employers – individuals or companies. So that, for instance, the Argyll Rooms paid the receiver for a sergeant and constable to be on duty there nightly, and constables could be loaned at the discretion of the commissioner to keep order among cabs and coaches at a society party. Freemasonry had been common among the runners and so it would among Metropolitan detectives; former members of both would look to keep a central London pub on retirement as the cosiest of nest-eggs; and nepotism, backbiting, secrecy, betrayal and parochial jealousy were all carried over from old to new. Even worse were those elements which continued to flaw London policing after 1829, despite the rationale they had provided for reform itself: corruption, brutality, swearing false witness. Old John Townsend, verbose and opinionated and revelling in his celebrity, nonetheless gave true evidence to a House of Commons committee in 1816 when he warned against the temptations that led to abuse of police power: 'I have been always of opinion, that an officer is a dangerous subject to the community.' That danger would dog London policing for the rest of the century and beyond.[32]

Bobbies and Rozzers: Police and Public, 1840–1899

The accommodation between police and public achieved by 1834 had more room for respect and fear than affection on either side. In general, and for the rest of the century, the police were not popular in London. In the public imagination, when thought about collectively as a resource available to and needed by Londoners of every complexion, they were valued and admired, even liked. But on the street, in action, as individuals doing a job, they received more brickbats than posies. Cussedness and criticism came not just from those being policed but from observers too, whether journalists or politicians or bystanders, even magistrates and judges. Perhaps things were not made easier by the City and Metropolitan forces' tradition of recruiting strangers to London: just one in six policemen was London-born in 1891, the lowest of any significant employment group in the capital except the armed forces.[33] But whatever the cause, police–public relations in London in the nineteenth century could frequently be harsh and brutal.

Policing was most bruising of all in the slums among the poor. In October 1852 PC Michael Dwyer gave evidence of a murderous assault on him in Southampton Street, Camberwell. Dwyer was helped into court by two PCs. He 'could only move when bent double', and he stood with 'glassy eye, haggard appearance, and death-like countenance'. There had been a fight outside the Bricklayer's Arms and Dwyer said he approached a chimney sweep called Cannon, whose head was bleeding badly, to get him to a doctor. Cannon at first agreed to go. But then he 'rushed in upon me, and, catching me by the small of my legs, threw me with great force on my back. He then jumped on my chest and bowels with all his force three times, which caused me the greatest possible pain, and from the effects of which I am still severely suffering.' Cannon then tried to strangle him. Dwyer got to his feet but Cannon knocked him down and kicked him 'on a delicate part of my person, and inflicted the most serious injury. The upper part of my thighs were quite black, and much swollen by his kicks and brutal violence.' The two had gathered what the police knew as a 'hostile crowd'. 'At this time I heard some person in the crowd exclaim, "Well done, Cannon, give it the –".' Dwyer was thought to be 'probably disabled for life'.[34]

This was suburban Camberwell and poor Dwyer's experience reminds us that edge-of-town shanty-dwellers could be as ferocious to the police as any court or alley community in central London or the East End. Forty years on and the fury was unabated. Charles Booth, writing of Poplar in 1898, noted how 'Nearly everyone speaks well of the police.' But Booth's 'everyone' embraced just clergymen, missionaries, school board visitors and senior police officers themselves. On the street, as the police well knew, things were different. When PC Tom Divall was transferred to Deptford, near the tempestuous Foreign Cattle Market, his inspector's first question was, '"Can you fight?"' He could. '"That will just do for us,"' he was told, and fight he had to. 'I have often seen our charge room at the station more like a slaughter-house than a place for human beings.' And when PC Fred Wensley moved from Lambeth to Whitechapel in 1891 he found that two previous holders of his number (402H) had left the force through serious injury from assault, one proving fatal.[35]

Arrests for assault on police, obstruction and attempted rescue of a prisoner fluctuated year on year (3,259 in 1869, 2,901 in 1879, for instance) but showed no general tendency to abate as the century grew older. Indeed, in the 1890s there were frequently over 4,000 each year. And the police were generally reluctant to bring a charge. PC Leeson recalled his Whitechapel days in the 1890s, when 'Many a time I have been both kicked and punched and have had my charge of assault declined by the inspector. The most loathsome thing I can remember was a man spitting deliberately in my face, but when reporting it to the inspector was told that trivial charges of that nature must be discouraged.'[36]

In an antagonistic culture there were certain elements among the London poor who were especially adamant against the police. Most notable were the costermongers and other London street folk. Here the police were in constant battle to still their noise and keep them moving and so not obstruct pavement or carriageway. Special powers of harassment were provided to the police from 1839. Afterwards, there were no holds barred: 'To serve out [fight and beat] a policeman is the bravest act by which a costermonger can distinguish himself.'[37] But any working-class Londoner was likely to grow up jaundiced against police interference – when playing street games or watching entertainers, when drunk and merry or in a fair fight with rival or enemy. And there's little doubt that some heavy-handedness, understandable or excessive, did not endear the 'rozzers' to the communities they policed.

There was another special case and that was the prostitute. Policemen, young men generally and often unmarried, saw prostitutes as potential lawbreakers (prostitution itself was not unlawful though its frills and tassels were likely to be) and as easy sexual conquests. In this the police competed with working-class (sometimes middle-class) men who didn't have constabulary coercion in their quiver. One of the very earliest scandals of the New Police involved the alleged rape of a prostitute by an inspector and there is much evidence that the police expected cash or sexual favours for not interfering in the flesh trade. This operated across London and so across classes. The first-hand voice of the prostitute is denied us but we hear something authentic from Walter. He cites several instances. From the late 1860s (probably) we have Betsy Johnson: '"the other night I gave a Peeler a treat." – "Where did he have you?" – "Against a shop door," said Betsy . . .' Beautiful Nelly Little (in the early 1870s,' it seems) 'never got into police rows. How she squared the police I don't know. I asked her if she let the constables tail her – "No" – but an Inspector used to have her. He was a married man and came in plain clothes [!]. She never was "run in" that I heard of, when they ran in fifty women a night from the Haymarket and its vicinity.' And around 1858, outside a public house in central London, Walter renewed an acquaintance with Brighton Bessie. He had missed her and asked where she'd been.

'I've been locked up, – it's a damned shame,' she cried out, 'I was marched off without having said a word by a policeman, – blast him! – and all because I would not let the bugger fuck me one night up in **** Street, – I'd never let a policeman touch me – damn them all.' She spoke loud to a man and two or three sympathizing women, a mob began to gather round her, so noisy was she . . . 'I know him,' said a voice, 'he wants every woman in the Strand, and if he don't get them he walks them off . . . Yes, and he quodded Mary Summers last night.' 'And he is a married man with a large family' – and so on.[38]

Episodes like this reminded working-class Londoners that the dynamics of police–public relations were weighted unfairly towards the man in blue. And it was clear that anyone could be victims in the nightly struggle for control of London's streets. The police, of course, could hand out punishment as well as take it. Unsurprisingly, little of this can be gleaned from policemen's memoirs, but honest Tom Divall relates a Deptford incident in the 1890s. He moved on 'a lot of roughs singing and shouting in Stanhope Street' but one 'wouldn't budge, so, being aroused, I gave him a good open-handed smack on the side of his face'. But an inspector had secretly watched it all and gave Divall 'an awful bang on the head, which stunned me for some seconds', and told him, '"I'll teach you better than to hit a man under a street lamp!"' Beatings in police stations were no doubt common enough. Graham Grant was a police surgeon in Shadwell in the late 1890s and recalled dressing the head wounds of a prisoner who asked Grant to accompany him back to his cell. 'We were just passing the door of an empty cell, when a police constable with a mop slipped out and struck the man a blow over the head, which made short work of all my beautiful bandaging.' And it was said around the same time that police frequently gave beatings to male prostitutes soliciting in the parks.[39]

It was not only 'roughs' and outcasts who might get on the wrong side of the London policeman. Middle-class bystanders interfering in an arrest – of a prostitute, for instance – could be severely handled. And it was the false or contested arrests of 'gentlemen' and respectable women that landed the police in hottest water. In the clean-up of the Haymarket in the early 1870s some false charges of drunk and disorderly were brought against obstreperous pedestrians, including some guards officers and a barrister called Bell, which the magistrates threw out with harsh comment on police conduct. Most famous of all was the case of Miss Cass, a respectable dressmaker charged by PC Endacott with soliciting in Regent Street in July 1887. The row made life difficult even for the Home Secretary for a time. Endacott was charged with perjury but acquitted.[40]

It was of course difficult for the police to satisfy everyone. For each voice raised in protest at oppressive zeal another complained that the police were too weak-kneed in ridding the streets of prostitutes, unruly youth or petty thieves. There were other criticisms too. One centred on the force's limited efficiency and intelligence, revealed in its inability to catch criminals or in the dull-witted manner of the constable on the beat. And there is evidence that as the Metropolitan Police matured it grew set in its ways, with early signs of sclerosis that impeded innovation and deterred new ways of thinking.

Colonel Rowan retired in 1850 and died two years later. For the next five years there was an uncomfortable period of bickering and backbiting at the top when Rowan's replacement, Captain William Hay, failed to meld in any way with the increasingly autocratic 'Dickey' Mayne. When Hay died in office in 1855, Mayne was left to reign alone. The long experiment of joint control would never be repeated. As sole commissioner Mayne went on and on – for another thirteen years. By then, public dissatisfaction with the Metropolitan Police festered on several levels, but especially peacekeeping and security. The Hyde Park riots of 1866 and the Clerkenwell explosion of 1867 had begun to wipe out the memory of Mayne's creative contribution of almost forty years before. He died in office on Boxing Day 1868.

After a brief interregnum, Mayne was followed by Colonel Sir Edmund Henderson, another soldier but one with relevant experience in the prison service. Henderson inherited problems of poor pay and morale. In 1872 there was a brief strike, jolting the Home Office into a pay rise. But some problems remained and a further strike would be needed in 1890 before grumbles over police pensions were appeased.

Difficulties with the rank and file were mirrored in the 1880s by crises of leadership. Henderson was scapegoated by Liberal Home Secretary Hugh Childers over the 1886 riot in Pall Mall and resigned. Government thought that anxieties over insufficient vigour on the streets could be soothed by bringing in a notable disciplinarian from the army, Sir Charles Warren. But Warren lasted only two years before he in turn fell out with Tory Home Secretary Henry Matthews, mostly over the gory dance that Jack the Ripper led the police in the East End. And Warren's successor, James Monro, formerly Inspector General of Bengal Police and then Assistant Commissioner in charge of the Criminal Investigation Department (CID) at Scotland Yard, also proved a stopgap. Appointed in 1888, he resigned in 1890 at what he thought to be foot-dragging by the Home Office over police pensions. The fourth commissioner in five years, Sir Edward Bradford, an Anglo-Indian military man, took the force into the new century with some distinction.

Partly because of all these difficulties, the police were held back by sluggish managerial and technological inventiveness. As the Metropolitan Police District enlarged, so some divisions were recast and new ones created. And as the force grew in strength (5,493 in 1849, 10,227 in 1875, 15,765 in 1899) overlong command structures made management remote and cumbersome. Change in any direction proved slow to take. The old reinforced top hats were replaced by the lighter helmet only after thirty-five years in 1864. Police stations were connected by telegraph with Scotland Yard in 1867, ten years after the City police. A better truncheon carried in a hidden pocket was not introduced until about 1885, and the old charlies' rattles were not entirely replaced by the distinctive whistle until 1886. Finally, the cramped warren in Whitehall Place and Scotland Yard was exchanged for a new headquarters on the Embankment, just north of Westminster Bridge, only in 1890, some fifteen years after a move had been actively planned. In much of this inertia lay the dead hand of the Home Office.

That was a result of the great contradiction in Peel's plan, running what was essentially a local service from a great department of state, accountable to a transitory political master. In 1829 Peel had not much alternative if true coordination were to be achieved. Later there would be other options, but the Home Office proved reluctant to relinquish its paralysing grip.[41]

Despite these systemic disabilities, the Metropolitan Police performed their daily and nightly duties on the streets of London and in general performed them well. The force was indeed a formidable instrument of social discipline for the Londoner. In 1861 there were over 63,000 arrests, one to every fifty-one of the London population. Decade on decade, arrests per head of population declined, though actual numbers remained high (83,400, 1:68 in 1891). Then in the 1890s the volume of arrests rose proportionately again (115,550, 1:57 in 1899). As we have already seen, virtually half these were for drunken conduct, testimony that Peel's police throughout the century focused as much on policing London pleasures as on preventing or detecting crime.[42]

Some of those pleasures were a threat to the police themselves. Hard drinking was the force's main vice over the years, and relations with prostitutes a close second. Yet perhaps the most hurtful criticism levelled at police was that they were venal. 'There's sure to be a bobby as is ready for a bob' was a music-hall lyric of the 1860s, and there's little question that the culture of tipping extended beyond the early-morning call. It seems to have been widespread among middle-class Londoners grateful for some small service rendered. Walter gave a constable a shilling (a 'bob') for turning a blind eye and there were countless opportunities for similar gratuities.[43]

But there were more serious allegations of systematic corruption. Under Mayne, 'the whole C Division was corrupt to the very core', with officers and men in the pay of the Haymarket sex industry, according to Sir Henry Smith, later Commissioner of the City Police. It seems certainly true that the night houses had their lives extended by graft, Inspector George Silverton of C Division retiring around 1871 'upon a very snug competence', or so his defence barrister recalled. And it appears that a top-class brothel at Chelsea had protection at a very senior level in Scotland Yard in the 1880s. These things were widely talked about at the time, and occasional trials of police officers for conspiracy or perjury received much attention in the press.[44]

But it was the extraordinary revelations in 1877 of doings in the detective branch that would destroy much public confidence in the London police. There was a comprehensive reorganisation afterwards and a new CID, led by an ambitious young barrister, Howard Vincent. He also established a Special Irish Branch to combat Fenian terrorism, employing mainly Irish detectives.[45] By the end of the century some of Scotland Yard's reputation had been restored. Yet never at any time, before 1829 or after, could anyone effectively supervise detectives whose jobs depended on an intimate connection with London criminals and their secret sources of information.

At Scotland Yard in 1877 there were just fifteen detectives under Superintendent Frederick Adolphus ('Dolly') Williamson. Below him were three chief inspectors, brilliant Nathaniel Druscovich, William Palmer and George Clarke. All three, and a corrupt and manipulative detective inspector called Jack Meiklejohn, a Scot, were charged with conspiracy to pervert the course of justice. The case involved two convicted fraudsters, William Kurr and Harry Benson, who gave evidence against the detectives, and a corrupt solicitor called Edward Froggatt. Three of the four policemen (Clarke was acquitted) were convicted of receiving bribes from Kurr and Benson in return for immunity from police interference. Among the many London pubs used for meetings between the men was the One Tun Tavern, Ruthven's old house, and when ex-Chief Inspector Palmer came out of prison he ended his days 'a prosperous publican'. At least two of the detectives (Palmer and Clarke) were Freemasons, and so were Kurr, Benson and Froggatt. And Kurr's chilling evidence made clear that many others could have stood in the dock had the whole truth been told.

I and my creatures bribed the prisoners and Von Tornow [another Scotland Yard detective] with reference to the cab inquiry at the Midland [railway station], the police in Scotland Yard and in America, the warders in Newgate, in the House of Detention, and at Millbank, as well as the Post Office Inspectors, Jebb and Godwin, and Inspector Bailey of the City Police, and a good many more.[46]

Clearly the fact that Kurr was in prison had not prevented him using money to get his way. And London's prisons, just like its police, would prove a troubled and flawed instrument of repression throughout the nineteenth century. So too would the punishments to which prison was gateway.

The Steel and the Stone Jug: Prison and Punishment, 1800–1899

In August 1810, Bow Street police officers and local constables raided the White Swan public house and its 'Sodomitical Club'. At the Middlesex Sessions that September seven men were convicted of 'unnatural offences' and sentenced to various terms of imprisonment. Six were also required to stand once in the pillory in the Haymarket, opposite Panton Street.

At 12.30 p.m. on Thursday 27 September their journey began in an open 'caravan' from Newgate along Ludgate Hill, Fleet Street, Strand and Charing Cross. They were guarded by 100 mounted constables armed with pistols and 100 on foot. All shops along the route were closed. The pavements and roofs on both sides of the way were thronged with thousands of men, women and children, the women especially prominent, and each person with a missile or more to hand. Near the pillory, carts from slaughterhouses and the butchers' shops at St James's Market had brought offal, guts and dung; fishwomen from Billingsgate brought 'stinking flounders'; dead cats and dogs were scooped from nearby streets; there was vegetable refuse from Covent Garden by the half-ton; balls of street mud, in large part horse dung, were piled up 'like pyramids of shot in a gun wharf'.

Before the caravan left Old Bailey 'the prisoners resembled bears dipped in a stagnant pool'. 'Some of them were cut in the head with brickbats, and bled profusely.' Before they were halfway through their journey 'they were not discernible as human beings. If they had had much further to go, the cart would have been absolutely filled over them.' At the Haymarket four men were put into the pillory together, 'their faces . . . completely disfigured by blows and mud'. Police formed a ring to keep back the crowd but 'Upwards of fifty women were permitted to stand in the ring, who assailed them incessantly with mud, dead cats, rotten eggs, potatoes, and buckets filled with blood, offal, and dung . . .' After an hour they were put back in the cart and conveyed a different way – through fresh crowds and missiles – back to Newgate. The women in the ring were refreshed with 'gin and beer, procured from a subscription made upon the spot'. Then James Cook (the White Swan's landlord) and William Amos (alias Sally Fox, who had a previous conviction) were brought to the pillory for more concentrated attention from the women.[47]

The terrible theatre of public punishment in London would last for two-thirds of the nineteenth century. The sense that events like these brought shame on all involved and not just (perhaps least of all) the suffering victims was slow to dawn on opinion-formers. The use of the pillory after the Vere Street episode was, though, partly discontinued and in 1815 was restricted to perjurers only. The last in London appears to have been held in 1830, though the practice was not abolished until 1837. Public whippings at the cart's tail for men and youths persisted into the 1830s too. George Laval Chesterton, governor of Coldbath Fields House of Correction, Clerkenwell, had to superintend two around 1831. One, in the Commercial Road, used 'a huge cat-o'-nine-tails'. Chesterton was humane but a no-nonsense disciplinarian and he thought that 'I and the police had been degraded, and the public outraged by so savage a spectacle, and I heartily rejoiced when the custom fell into desuetude, or became prohibited, I know not which.'[48]

Public executions proved harder to abolish, despite the degradation and outrage with which they too were attended. They were most common in the first two decades of the century, averaging eight to ten a year at Newgate until 1810, then more in the troubled last years of the Napoleonic Wars and its revolutionary aftermath. The century's peak was forty-three in 1820, the year of Cato Street. A vocal and articulate minority had opposed capital punishment, or at least its public display, since the early years of the century and from the 1830s had much press opinion on their side. After 1836 there were usually just one, two or three executions a year outside Newgate and quite often none at all.[49] But the old arguments that state retribution was most effective when its visible terrors could both awe and deter would hold sway in Parliament for a long time. Public executions were finally abolished by Disraeli's first administration in 1868.

The last person to be publicly hanged in London was the Fenian Michael Barrett for his part in the Clerkenwell explosion. There was official agonising over the extent of his guilt and the day of his execution was postponed twice. At last, on 26 May 1868, Barrett walked onto the scaffold at Old Bailey to face 'the most complete apathy on the part of the London populace'. Just a few thousand were thought to be in the crowd. Some clapped, others 'groaned and hooted', all removed their hats. Barrett 'was remarkably firm' and as the trap dropped 'did not seem to struggle much'. 'His body slowly swung round once or twice, and then all was over.' As the crowd hastened to work or home, the traffic in Ludgate Hill was stopped 'for some minutes'.[50]

Thereafter, all London executions were shuttered away, less grue-some but no less terrifying for that. Indeed, most punishment in London had always taken place behind the iron-shod gates and stout walls of its many prisons. They were among the city's greatest buildings. At the centre, Newgate was a temporal St Paul's, just as awesome and latent with power, just as crushing to the spirit as the other was sublime. They were a stone's throw apart, linking fear and despair with hope and charity at the very heart of London.

Newgate had turned its bleak black front to the whole length of Old Bailey, where most of London's public hangings were presented from the end of the eighteenth century. In 1899 'the Stone Jug' was there still – towering less now in a London two storeys higher and symbolically less central to its rituals of retribution, but fearsome all the same, perhaps more so for carrying such an age of misery on its stalwart arches. Even in the year of Victoria's Diamond Jubilee, 'Black as Newgate' remained a popular metaphor. Its scowling bulk and lurid history still possessed 'a horrible interest' and agitated crowds still gath-ered outside to mark a hanging and watch 'the raising of the "black flag".'[51]

Newgate was London's main prison, but in 1800 it was one of many. There were nineteen, clustered densely in old London – in the City (six), in Southwark (seven), Clerkenwell, Stepney and Westminster (two each), with overspill in the hulks at Woolwich. Eight prisons were entirely or partly dedicated to holding debtors, among them the Fleet, the King's Bench and the Marshalsea. Many of the nineteen were ancient institutions, their origins irrecoverable from the depths of London's past. There had been a prison on the site of Newgate, it was said in 1883, for 'almost a thousand years'. The first documentary reference to the Fleet prison dated from 1197 but the place was older still.[52] Extended and renewed over the years, a few (like Newgate and Coldbath Fields, Clerkenwell) were recognisably modern structures. But most wore their age badly, were slatternly and broken down and epitomised in their ill-connected decrepitude all that the nineteenth century loathed about old London.

A number of forces combined to shift the fashion and topography of London punishment as that century grew older. First, the clearance and rebuilding of old London took down central prisons, whose valu-able sites were now needed for another purpose. So the City Corporation's Giltspur Street Compter made way for street improvements in the 1850s,

Whitecross Street prison (built 1813–15) was replaced by a railway goods yard around 1870, and Tothill Fields House of Correction became an embarrassment to Victoria Street and was demolished in 1884 – Westminster Cathedral stands on the site. Second, the growth of London gave both cause and opportunity for new suburban gaols to be built on the expanding edge of town: all the London prisons surviving beyond 1900 were of this kind, either entirely new or old premises greatly enlarged. Third, changing fashion in law and penology made some prisons obsolete (like the Fleet and the Marshalsea, closed in 1842) and demanded others be built to satisfy the requirements of policy (notably Millbank Penitentiary, opened 1816, and Pentonville Model Prison, 1842). All these forces interacted. And so London's prisons tended to move out from the centre, growing larger in mass but fewer in number. In 1899 there were just six and, when Newgate was finally emptied (by 1901), five. These were Brixton (an old prison dating from 1817 but rebuilt and extended over the years), Pentonville, Wandsworth (commissioned by the Surrey magistrates and opened in 1851), Holloway (the City Corporation's new prison, 1852) and Wormwood Scrubbs (built by convict labour between 1874 and 1890). These vast places didn't dominate a landscape as Newgate or Tothill Fields had done. They were planted in great suburban parks with monstrous walls wrapping much in mystery. But their very vastness invited contemplation nonetheless.

This modernisation of London's prison stock moved in parallel with the reform of prisoners' treatment. For the first thirty years of the century the state of London's prisons was a disgrace, presided over in the main by the City Corporation and by the magistrates of Middlesex, Westminster and Surrey. Around 1815 Elizabeth Fry, the Quaker philanthropist, found the female wards at Newgate '"filthy to excess, and the smell was quite disgusting"'. '"They slept on the floor, at times one hundred and twenty in one ward, without so much as a mat for bedding, and many of them were very nearly naked."' At the Steel (short for Bastille, the Coldbath Fields House of Correction) the cells were so cold men died of hypothermia. And there, before the reforming days of Chesterton from 1829, was suffering perhaps even worse. The previous governor had been John Vickery, the former Bow Street runner. Under Vickery all turnkeys had shared in the danegeld levied on prisoners who had money or could get it. A network of well-connected prisoners helped gaolers garner the spoils and helped themselves at the same time. 'The poor and friendless prisoner was a man wretchedly maltreated and oppressed.' Anyone who complained 'was called "a nose", and was made to run the gauntlet through a double file of scoundrels armed with short ropes or knotted handkerchiefs'. One 'starving wretch' deprived of his prison rations through the chicanery and bullying of another inmate attempted suicide. 'With tears streaming from his eyes, he exclaimed – "While I am a bag of bones, examine him, sir, and you will find him as plump as a lamb!".'[53]

These were just some of the terrors for prisoners in the first thirty years of the century. But terrors for prison authorities and reformers lay in a different direction. Their concerns were free association between prisoners and the control inmates exerted to soften the burden of chastisement. Free association made prisons colleges of crime and spoilers of virtue. And when life in prison was made more comfortable than life outside – cell searches under Chesterton revealed caches of 'wine, spirits, tea and coffee, tobacco and pipes . . . even pickles, preserves, and fish-sauce' – then the object of punishment was defeated and the profligate waste of public funds became an affront indeed.[54]

These abuses prison reformers set out to abolish from the late 1820s and early 1830s, when rising numbers of committals seemed to indicate that London was suffering a crisis of crime. The London prisons would become more civilised as a result but hardly more humane. Two competing orthodoxies took root around this time, their disciples attacking one another with all the zeal and relish of a theological controversy. Both had as their object the repression and deterrence of the London criminal – for although these were national debates London was their first and biggest testing ground. The question at issue was which would prove more effective.

The best that could be made of London's old prisons, with wards and dormitories rather than separate cells, was the 'silent association system'. Here prisoners had to work, eat, pray and sleep together but were required to maintain the strictest silence everywhere except in chapel. Every other form of non-verbal communication was outlawed too. This was the system most famously in place in Coldbath Fields under Chesterton and at Tothill Fields under Lieutenant Augustus Tracey, RN, a particular friend of Charles Dickens who became an able (if unconvincing) advocate for the system. In fact silent association proved utterly incapable of stopping communication among a population bred and nurtured in the street arts of London. So it was a system that depended entirely on punishment to make it work – for a lifted finger, for a wink, for a ventriloquist's whisper that might have come from anywhere. At Coldbath Fields in 1842 nearly 17,000 punishments were given to a daily prison population of 1,500 or so. On any day five in 100 were undergoing punishments ranging from up to thirty-six lashes with a military cat-o'-nine-tails or handcuffing behind the back to solitary confinement on bread and water or docking of rations. Even so, there were myriad means of subversion. Henry Mayhew toured the prison in 1856. At the school a lad was told to read a sentence aloud for the visitor. He couldn't pronounce his r's and the frustrated schoolmaster told him off: 'thereupon there was a shuffling of feet from the other pupils, as if the only method of laughing under the silent system was with the shoes.'[55]

The alternative orthodoxy was the 'separate system'. In essence this was solitary confinement without some of the punitive aspects that made it such a terror in other gaols. The 'New Model Prison' at Pentonville was built on the separate system and was ready for its first model prisoners a few days before Christmas 1842. There were 520 single cells, heated with warm air, lighted with a high window and gas, fitted with a hammock, a WC and materials for labour (a weaver's frame or work bench). The diet was superior to that of other prisons and far richer than that of workhouses – a cause of outrage to Dickens, who objected loud and long to 'pet prisoners'. Exercise was taken with other inmates but all were masked when out of their cells. Solitude was relieved only by visits from chaplain or officials. Pentonville's terrible 'dark cells' punished refractory behaviour. Here prisoners would stay entombed for up to six days on bread and water. At first the normal sentence in Pentonville had been eighteen months, but ten times 'the ratio of insanity' compared with other gaols frightened the authorities, who cut the sentence there by half. By 1856 Pentonville produced just double the normal rate of men driven mad by prison.[56]

For most Victorian penologists, Pentonville won the argument. But its very high running costs and the practical obstacles in the way of converting old stock to the separate system meant that in most places some sort of hybrid involving both solitary confinement and silent association had to be tolerated. In the absence of a completely separate system attention turned to the 'hard labour' that the most vicious or recalcitrant offenders were forced to undergo. Even in the 1850s, before the prison regime actually grew tougher, this could be very hard indeed. It was designed not just to punish men's bodies but to agonise their spirit too.

At Coldbath Fields, reasonably typical, the working day was just over eight hours, excluding meal breaks. Daily labour alternated between various tasks – the treadwheel (treadmill), oakum picking (or tailoring or cobbling for those who could pick up a skill) or shot drill. This last was too heavy for men over forty-five and involved passing cannon balls from one end of a line of men to another: before they passed, each man had to put the shot down, straighten up, then bend to pick it up again. There were twenty treadwheels on which men climbed, 'grinding the wind' for fifteen quarter-hours with fifteen minutes' rest between. At the end of each quarter the air in the compartment in which they laboured became so hot it was '"difficult to breathe"'. For those medically unfit to tread there was the 'crank', an iron drum worked by a handle: a day's labour of 10,000 turns would take eight hours and twenty minutes. A regime like this, on a mean diet, was a death sentence to an elderly prisoner. We might remember William Dugdale, the pornographer, sentenced to eighteen months' hard labour at Coldbath Fields in July 1868: nearly seventy years old, he was dead inside four months.[57]

Despite its terrors, prison could be more attractive for some than life in London outside the walls, especially for homeless or neglected children. Many ragged boys of Westminster in the 1850s looked on Tothill Fields House of Correction as preferable to the deadly hardships of the streets. Of those committed to the gaol in any one year, nearly half were back within the same year, so prison 'is really made an asylum and a home by many of them'. A sample of fifteen prisoners aged eleven to sixteen had been in prison eighty-five times between them (nearly six sentences each) and the chief warder noted how boys committed offences like lamp- and window-smashing '"merely to get another month's shelter"'. The benefits of prison didn't just extend to regular food and a roof. Mayhew watched boys exercising in the yard in their 'heavy prison boots': 'we could tell, by their shuffling noise and limping gait, how little used many of them had been to such a luxury as shoe leather.'[58]

The garrotting panic of 1862 led to a further sharpening of prison discipline in London and elsewhere. Some of these violent attacks had been traced to men on probation or ticket of leave and official reaction produced heavier sentences and harsher treatment of 'habitual criminals'. Long sentences, often served out of London in the great convict prisons of Parkhurst, Portland or Dartmoor, were preceded by nine months' solitary confinement in one of the London prisons equipped on the separate system, like Pentonville or Millbank. From 1877 these were all run by the Home Office. Now cells were furnished with wooden beds rather than hammocks, and a meaner diet was introduced to emphasise the penal in 'penal servitude'. And the treadmill continued to grind the air in London prisons right through the nineteenth century.

Jabez Balfour, a building society fraudster, began a fourteen-year sentence for fraud in 1895 at Wormwood Scrubbs. He was locked up twenty-three hours a day, exercising with other men but in the strictest silence. He sewed mailbags, hard labour at first but easier over time. The daily diet was poor. Breakfast was 'a pint of impossible tea and an eight-ounce brown loaf'; dinner varied, on four out of seven days including meat; supper was the third loaf of the day with skilly – a thin oatmeal gruel – or cocoa for the ailing. Balfour thought prison 'one long hunger'. Deprivation of this thin fare was the chief punishment, sometimes in dark cells. Whipping was held in reserve for violent conduct or persistent insubordination.[59]

In all this there seemed little room for reclamation or moral reform. What there was lay with the prison chaplain, a figure whose influence was most powerful when his views coincided with the disciplinary tendencies of prison government. So one of the consolations for the religious-minded of the separate system, despite all its tendencies to drive men mad, was the opportunity it gave prisoners to dwell upon their sins. Rev. Joseph Kingsmill, chaplain of Pentonville, discovered in its lonely misery a unity of purpose tying together secular policy and the aims of religion: 'the propagation of crime is impossible – the continuity of vicious habits is broken off – the mind is driven to reflection, and conscience resumes her sway.'[60] Kingsmill reminds us that the proximity of Newgate and St Paul's was not merely of topography alone. For state and Church combined in many ways to bring order to London and Londoners in the nineteenth century.

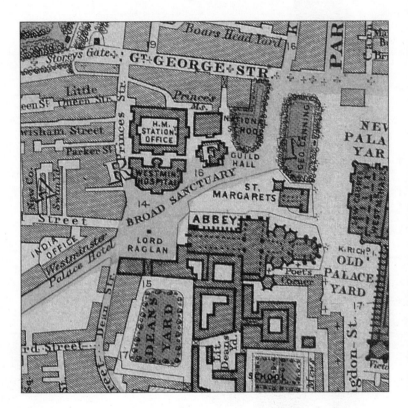

Broad Sanctuary, 1862

XIV

BROAD SANCTUARY: RELIGION AND CHARITY

Order, Authority and Stability, 1800–1834

No place in nineteenth-century London symbolised so eloquently the metropolitan power of organised religion as Broad Sanctuary. More a great funnel than a street, it had for its southern side the Abbey of St Peter, Westminster, completed in the Norman style under Edward the Confessor in 1065. Sanctuary from some penalties of the criminal and civil law could be claimed by people resorting to the shacks and hovels in the Abbey's north shadow and the name lived on centuries after that ancient privilege was swept away. For much of the eighteenth century the street behind Broad Sanctuary to the north was called Thieving Lane. And connections between Westminster Abbey and the ancient slums nearby continued to dog London government almost to the end of the century.[1]

From 1800 Broad Sanctuary began to provide more suitable neighbours for the coronation church for most English monarchs from the Conqueror forwards. The Abbey was now joined by institutions that showed the age-old accord of Church and state branching into wide areas of metropolitan law and order. For London religion and London government were intricately intertwined. When adjudicating standards of morality they seemed indissoluble. During the nineteenth century the knots binding them together would slowly unravel, but not entirely even at the century's end. And for many decades, when we speak of religion and government in London we are dealing with two sides of the same coin.

Facing the Abbey on the west and north sides of Broad Sanctuary for much of the nineteenth century stood three great institutions that epitomised this duality. The oldest, the middle of the three, was the Guildhall or Sessions House, meeting place and courtroom of the Westminster justices. Built in 1805 from a design by Samuel Pepys Cockerell, first architect of Tyburnia, the Guildhall was transferred to the Middlesex justices in 1845. Active among the magistrates dispensing summary punishment and licensing numerous activities, most importantly public houses, were the clerical justices. Here, on all except 'the Lord's day', the Church could wield earthly power in sight of its ancient spiritual home in the Abbey. Here too the Church could put itself in the van of agitation to improve the morals of Londoners by force of law.[2]

East of the Guildhall in 1814 rose the headquarters, book depository and central schools of the National Society for Promoting the Education of the Poor in the Principles of the Church of England (the National Society). Few areas of religious endeavour were more important in London in the nineteenth century than the education of the poor. And none revealed more sharply from the outset the jealousies of Christian sects competing to win precedence over others in the field.

Organised religion of one complexion or another began the movement for working-class schooling in London. We might start with Sunday schools, the idea popularised by an Anglican clergyman in Gloucester from 1780, apparently spreading to London by 1785. In ten years or so Sunday schools had become especially popular among Methodists and it was dissenters of many hues who spurred on popular education early in the new century.

The objectives of most Sunday schools had been limited – reading (so giving access to scripture) but not writing (too potentially seditious and self-aggrandising). But a push to a more rounded curriculum at day schools was given by Joseph Lancaster. He might stand first in a long line of zealous men and women of the nineteenth century who influenced in some degree the lives of their fellow Londoners for the better. With all their flaws – bigotry, arrogance, even megalomania and ruthlessness – many exerted heroic energy on behalf of causes that had much good in them. Lancaster, unworldliness and impracticality his eventual downfall, was one of the most admirable of all these 'honest fanatics', as Mary Ward, herself a late-century London philanthropist, called them.[3]

Born in humble circumstances at Kent Street, Borough, in 1778,

Joseph Lancaster joined the Society of Friends in his teens. In 1801 he opened his first school at a room in Borough Road. The Lancasterian system taught by monitors learning just ahead of their classes and was non-denominational in character, open to all faiths and none. Here was 'Religious principle without sectarian feeling'. Discipline was enforced through humiliation rather than pain. Refractory scholars were never whipped but might be shackled and dangled in cages from the ceiling. In 1805 Lancaster's efforts were recognised by George III, who subscribed funds and urged him to success in a famous pronounce-ment: 'It is my wish that every poor child in my dominions should be taught to read the Holy Scriptures.' Lancaster's schools almost foundered in bankruptcy but were rescued by fellow Quakers. They reconstituted his venture in 1812 as the British and Foreign School Society (the British Society). Its headquarters would later reside in palatial schools in the Borough Road, where Lancaster's work had begun.[4]

By then, though, in what would become a familiar pattern, the Anglican enemies of non-denominational education had resolved to displace Lancaster and the dissenters from their pedestal. An eccentric Scot called Andrew Bell had initiated the monitor system some years before Lancaster in Madras, bringing it to a small charity school at St Botolph Aldgate in 1798, then absorbing himself in other things. Lancaster had duly credited Bell while amending his system. But the Anglican opponents of dissenting influence saw in Bell, now a country rector at Swanage in Dorset, an acceptable alternative standard-bearer to Lancaster. In 1811 the National Society was formed to promulgate Bell's method, its first school in Orchard Street, Westminster, moving to Broad Sanctuary three years later, holding some 600 girl and boy scholars of elementary age.

The British Society and the National Society became opposing powers in the land, especially in London, where their work had begun. By 1816, when the 'Education of the Lower Orders of the Metropolis' had become matter for parliamentary inquiry, hardly a poor district was without its British or National school, operating in new buildings or shabby converted rooms. And the efforts of these great Protestant charities, their funds raised by voluntary subscription, stimulated other parochial, religious or charitable endeavour. So St Giles and St George, Bloomsbury, for instance, was found to have thirteen schools and some 2,000 scholars in 1816, at least 600 of them Irish (mainly Catholic), most places free from any charge of 1d or 2d a week. Surveys in parts of Southwark and Spitalfields showed about 40 per cent of children receiving some education in districts clustered round British or National schools. To all these could be added some 40,000 Sunday scholars in London. In general, though, the inquiry concluded that 'a very large number of poor Children are wholly without the means of Instruction'. And the reformer Henry Brougham called Middlesex 'the worst educated district in Christendom', estimating in 1820 that fewer than 6 per cent had received some learning.[5]

All agreed that this was a defect in the social affairs of the state. The select committee of 1816 noted 'the highly beneficial effects produced upon all those parts of the Population which . . . have enjoyed the benefits of Education'. The spread of schooling was one factor cited in 'the general civilization' of London being 'considerably improved' since the start of the century. The results of schooling at the 'village' of Kingsland, Hackney, according to the Rev. John Campbell, were a 'remarkable alteration' in the 'extremely wicked and riotous' behaviour of the inhabitants and a decline in 'bull fights, men fights, intoxication, and thieving . . .'[6]

In all this, education was no alien imposition on the poor. Even though it was usually accompanied by the taste of religion, like a pill in jam, and sometimes by bitter sectarianism, education was desired at any price. When Elizabeth Fry in 1817 began a school at Newgate for the children of women prisoners, lack of room forced her to 'refuse admission to many of the women, who earnestly entreated to be allowed to share in their instructions'. There was a 'thirst for reading' among the children of the poor such that a 'circulating library' was a welcome attachment to the Borough Road schools. And in the National School at notorious Baldwin's Gardens, Holborn, even 'the lowest orders' had a 'great desire' to school their children. 'An old Irish barrow-woman, with a pipe in her mouth, came into the girls [*sic*] school one day, and said to the mistress, "Good madam, God Almighty has got a place for you in Heaven, for your kindness to my child."'[7]

Close neighbour to the National Society's schools and seat of government in Broad Sanctuary was another institution for which the poor of London had some reason to be grateful, even though they were not allowed to forget it was a 'pious and Christian work'. This was the new Westminster Hospital, built to designs of the ecclesiastical architects William and Henry Inwood and opened in 1834. It had a long and special provenance. Westminster Hospital was begun by 'Good

Henry' Hoare of the Fleet Street banking family in Petty France in 1720. Hoare was a 'staunch Anglican' and this was the first London hospital established for the poor and funded by public subscription. It would prove a model for the next century and a half. Substantial donors were nominated 'governors' and anyone needing treatment, other than accident victims taken off the streets, required a governor's letter before admission. In this way could the giver see the direct result of his or her charity.[8]

At the time Westminster Hospital upped crutches and moved to Broad Sanctuary, all London hospitals were charitable endeavours of one kind or another. The most venerable of all had their origins in medieval abbeys and were rich in endowments over countless generations. Others, like Hoare's, had sprung from the deep pockets of eighteenth-century philanthropy. And from the early years of the nineteenth century charitable hospital foundations and dispensaries multiplied. Not all had explicitly Christian objectives. But all attracted philanthropic givers among churchmen and Christian laity. Notable among these early institutions were the London Fever Hospital (1802), Moorfields Eye Hospital (1805), the first stumbling manifestations of Charing Cross Hospital (1815–18) and a further four dispensaries, making some sixteen giving medicine to the poor by 1817.

By then the Christian churches in London and the charities they endowed had begun to construct a web of aid for almost every disability of the penniless. There were almshouses for the respectable decrepit, Bridewell and Magdalene for the 'penitent' streetwalker, soup kitchens for starving silk weavers, the 'Archbishop's Bounty' for the Lambeth poor, orphanages for abandoned infants, night refuges for the homeless. And so on. All this was conditional, because something was almost always demanded in return, if only lip service to God. In this way charity made frauds out of most of those who benefited.

Not that all was lip service. London was an irreligious city when compared to the nation as a whole, as we shall see. Yet organised religion was a powerful force in London life. As the century grew older it touched in some way every Londoner, even the majority who wouldn't share in public worship. It could not be avoided, no matter what. And the great dynamo forcing religion into Londoners' lives in the nineteenth century was Protestant evangelicalism.

Strongest in the middle four decades of the century, it was a power at both beginning and end. In its heyday at mid-century, religious observance became an overweening middle-class preoccupation. But most important for all London and for all Londoners was the evangelical urge to reform the manners and morals of every class, especially the poor. Just as the Metropolitan Police – itself the brainchild of a Home Secretary raised in an evangelical household – put a constable in 'every street, road, lane, court and alley', the evangelicals would introduce a 'missionary police' into every slum room in London.⁹

Evangelicalism was a passionate and emotional religion of personal salvation through 'conversion'. Accepting a Christ of miracles and devoting one's life to Him would atone for sin in this world and protect from punishment in the next. At the end of the eighteenth century, with the stagnation and decline of Methodism, this was a minority belief at its liveliest in Anglicanism. Its most powerful advocates were the so-called 'Clapham Sect' of wealthy laymen and clerics led by William Wilberforce, a Tory MP who lived in a mansion on Battersea Rise from 1795 to 1808. Concerned to increase the power of evangelicalism in the Church, and involved with a welter of philanthropic causes – notably the abolition of the slave trade – Wilberforce and his allies were also in the van of the movement for the reformation of manners and morals. Those of the poor worried them most. Any improvement was not to disturb the delicate balance of class forces – 'I allow of no writing for the poor', stated the sect's chief propagandist, Hannah More. And Wilberforce strongly believed in the desirability of low wages – that crippling disability of London life and labour – opposing all combinations of workers wanting to raise or protect them. So suppression tended to be at the heart of the sect's social policy, rather than education or political reform.

The sect agitated for the abolition of bull- and bear-baiting, for strict Sabbath observance, for a stronger civil power, for the suppression of dancing, of obscene literature, of brothels, of lotteries and gambling, of astrologers and fortune-tellers. The Society for the Suppression of Vice (SSV), formed in 1802 from a merger of earlier efforts, was the evangelicals' enforcement arm, spying out offenders and prosecuting them in the courts. Their influence had swift impact. In 1805 the Bishop of London prohibited 'Sunday evening routs and concerts in the metropolis'. And a year later the SSV damned Salomon's Sunday concerts and demonstrated outside fashionable mansions 'against the impious conduct of the ladies who patronize the playing of music in their own houses on the Lord's Day'. To some extent, then, fanaticism was not afraid to transcend the interests of class.¹⁰

We can see the new world struggling to emerge from the old, and remind ourselves that evangelicalism was a site of intense struggle within the Church of England in the early years of the century, the laity often in advance of the clergy, in events surrounding the licensing of public houses in darkest Shadwell in 1813–14. The churchwardens and parish officers of Shadwell Vestry, led by a Sabbatarian ship owner called John Fletcher, complained to the licensing magistrates about a number of pubs where prostitutes assembled in large numbers to dance with lascars and other sailors. The licences were taken away for a year but then reinstated by a bench of East End magistrates including Joseph Merceron (the so-called 'boss of Bethnal Green, whom we shall meet again) and two prominent clerical justices, Rev. Edward Robson and Rev. Thomas Thirlwall. It was an ill-tempered fracas, with reverberations in print and public for three years at least, and allegations that the magistrates were unduly influenced by Messrs Hanbury, the Brick Lane brewers. Rev. Robson proved most truculent in combating interference in Shadwell's way of life. Fletcher was given full rein to expose Robson by the evangelical chairman of the parliamentary Committee on the Police of the Metropolis, the Hon. Henry Grey Bennet, in 1816 and again in 1817. Evidence of music and dancing and drinking and interference with churchgoers had all been laid before the justices, Fletcher said.

To this Mr Robson replied, that dancing among sailors and their girls could not be considered as an evil; that such men must have recreation, and it was better that the women should be in the houses than the streets; that he could see nothing in all that had been advanced, and he affected to treat the complaint with levity.[11]

Such opinions among the clergy of the Church of England would not last much longer in London. The era of Robson and Thirlwall was fast ebbing away. Within ten years applications for new licences were met by justices delivering 'A homily upon morals, the profanity of music, the indecency of dancing, and the length of ladies' dresses . . .'[12]

This atmosphere of seriousness and busy evangelical activity began to infect the whole establishment. In 1818 the New Churches Act provided for church building to celebrate victory in the Napoleonic Wars. The act subsidised fine churches in the new suburbs of London, including St John Waterloo Road (not far from where Granby Street would lie), All Souls Langham Place, and St Pancras New Church and Holy Trinity Marylebone at either end of the New Road. The public importance attached to the project was reflected in commissions entrusted to the greatest London architects of the day – Sir John Soane, John Nash, Sir Robert Smirke, Sir Charles Barry and others. Within twenty years from 1815 enthusiasm for church building had erected, it was said, sixty new churches in London.[13]

By the end of the 1820s the evangelical energising of the Church of England had struck a harmonious chord with nonconformism and awoken echoes of its eighteenth-century past. A revival in Methodism was the result and a revival too of open-air preaching in the metropolis. Al fresco preachers risked prosecution as late as 1828, but by 1832 Smithfield was frequently brought to a morning standstill by the Methodist minister George Smith attracting crowds of devoted worshippers. Smith was one among several, the New Police tolerant of what previously had been condemned as a nuisance. These early decades of the century also witnessed a quickening of the charitable impulse. Of 911 London charities active at the end of the century 169 were established before 1800. The first decade of the new century saw twenty-four formed, from 1810–19 thirty-six, in the 1820s thirty-eight and the 1830s sixty-nine. And Protestant London had its own great purpose-built meeting place, free from the taint of public-house assembly rooms, at Exeter Hall, Strand, from 1831.[14]

In all, by 1834 there had been a revolution in Christian feeling in London. More than thirty years of evangelical propaganda and action had helped stimulate a more energetic Protestantism. It was no longer satisfied by the souls of those entering the church doors at the dictate of conscience freely discovered. Now the churches, established and dissenting alike, were more determined than ever before to seek out sinners and convert them to the way of Christ. They demanded a new seriousness towards questions of personal behaviour and morality, of scripture reading and Sabbath observance. They were aided by William IV's succession on the death of George, that unsalvable hedonist, in 1830. Despite a murky past and 'royal bastards', William was a passionate defender of the established Church and a devout man, and some at least of the aristocracy took their tone from him. Most sinful of all, though, were the poor, brought up in dirt and ignorance and infamy, notorious for sexual licence and disrespect for property. Charity and good works would raise them to take advantage of the offer of atonement through Christ. That would guarantee moral behaviour and loyalty to the Church. So conversion would both save souls and contribute '"to the preservation of order, to authority of the law, and the stability of government"'.[15]

Order, authority and stability faced multiple challenges in the early 1830s. When a parliamentary committee on Sabbath Observance, frowning especially on the lax metropolis, noted in 1832 'a systematic and widely-spread violation of the Lord's-day . . . highly injurious to the best interests of the People, and which is calculated to bring down upon the Country the Divine displeasure', they had in mind Asiatic cholera, and perhaps revolution across the Channel and the uncertain consequences of parliamentary reform. Worrisome times gave one more push for all classes to find solace in the ancient verities of scripture. This was the foundation on which the next forty or so years of unparalleled religious exertion were built.

'Moral Courage Beyond All Praise', 1835–1869

The first beginnings of a 'missionary police' probably went back to the closing years of the Napoleonic Wars. We hear in 1812 of a District Visiting Society attached to St John's Chapel, Bedford Row, an early instance of what later would be a widespread parochial mechanism for 'ladies', in particular, to attend to the needs of poor mothers and their families. Around the same time the British and Foreign Bible Society (the Bible Society, established 1804) took up house-to-house visiting in parts of Southwark and Bloomsbury. Its object was to discover who had Bibles (just thirty in one population of 3,600 apparently). The British Society and National Society arranged similar surveys to determine the need for schools in certain poor districts around 1813–14. However, all these seem to have been haphazard efforts arranged by charities or parishes as resources permitted.[16]

That would change from 1835. David Nasmith, an evangelical from Glasgow, brought to London the idea of paid lay visitors to spread the gospel message among the poor. With others, Nasmith formed the London City Mission (LCM), at first operating from his small house in Hoxton. Thirty years later the charity reformer Charles Bosanquet would mark this as a new 'epoch', involving the systematic door-to-door evangelising of the poor of London. The LCM was 'undenomenational'. But Christian goodwill did not extend to Catholics – 'popery' '"The most horrible evil"' of all to a London City missionary. From humble beginnings, the LCM stimulated a uniquely important and (with all faults) impressive movement for social reform. It concerned itself with the very poorest of Londoners in the very worst of slums, undeterred by the filth, brutality and heart-tearing neglect encountered daily. When the historian of the LCM described its first missionaries as 'brave men', he wrote nothing but the truth.[17]

Most were 'little, if at all, above the artisan class'. Funded by voluntary subscription, always scrabbling for support in an over-fished pool of goodwill, the LCM had about 270 missionaries in the field at the end of 1854, 504 in 1890, just 485 in 1895. Three-quarters 'proclaim[ed] the Gospel from house to house, and room to room, day by day'. The rest took Christ to groups in special need like cabmen, dockers, poor Jews – there were even two missionaries to the Metropolitan Police.[18]

Their project was evangelisation. They were instructed to read the scriptures and say a prayer at every visit in every dwelling. Their rules forbade charitable giving, relying on special arrangements to refer cases of starving need to poor law officers, but some (at least) dispensed funds, even depleting their own salaries for pity's sake. But everything was subservient to self-help through redemption. The missionaries taught the gospels alongside temperance, regularity at work, cleanliness in the home, propriety of language and conduct, sexual abstinence outside marriage, the virtues of schooling and saving, faith in an afterlife as consolation for unfairness and poverty and pain in this, obedience to God and his servants in church and chapel. Salvation and respectability were indissoluble. A soul could not be saved without a transformation of manners.[19]

The LCM was an inspiration to evangelical practice in the metropolis. The idea of a missionary police civilising Londoners through Christian conversion, pushed door to door like insurance, spawned a swarm of imitators. Inevitably Anglican separatists, resenting dissenting influence in the LCM, established their own ventures in the Church Pastoral Aid Society (1836) and the Church of England Scripture Readers' Association (1844). And from the 1850s, at least, brave women would be as evident as brave men.

When a London City missionary was first appointed to the potteries and piggeries at Notting Dale in 1850 he was able to draw on support from evangelical Anglicans and nonconformists living in the grand houses a few streets to the east. Among them was Mrs Mary Bayly, who, with his aid, set up a Mothers' Society in 1853. She encouraged self-help through a loan club, adult literacy classes (a compulsory Bible chapter each meeting) and training in domestic skills. Her influence in home visiting was marked in the progress of mothers from 'wretched hovels' and dirty hands and faces to 'white curtains', emblems of thrift and self-respect. Ellen Ranyard, a Congregationalist from Nine Elms, Battersea, recruited working-class women from 1857 to sell Bibles in St Giles for the Bible Society. Eventually she built up a local female mission along the lines of the LCM. The Bible and soap were indivisible parts of Mrs Ranyard's gospel: 'If Jesus makes our hearts clean, our homes will soon be clean too.' In 1868 Ranyard's mission would branch out into district nursing, relieving the sick poor in their homes with medicines, aid and nourishment. A year after Ellen Ranyard began her work Katherine Warburton ('Mother Kate') was one of the first High Anglican nuns at the House of Charity on Rose Street, Soho. There 'we lived *with* the people and *for* the people'. And a couple of years later in 1860 the Rev. William Pennefather at Barnet introduced Low Anglican 'deaconesses' to help secure his aim that 'everyone in his parish should be spoken to individually on the subject of personal salvation'. In 1864 he moved with them to Mildmay, east Islington, setting up from 1877 what became a famous outpost, the Mildmay Mission Hospital, offering medical treatment (and gospel services three days a week) to the poor near Shoreditch church.[20]

The deaconesses, while taking the precaution of visiting in pairs after dark, were never 'molested', according to their historian. If that's true, then they were lucky. Ellen Ranyard, writing in 1860 with the stench of the slums fresh in her nostrils, described the 'vile usage' accorded 'Marian', her first Biblewoman. In one court 'a bucket of filth was emptied upon her from an upper window'; and a drover's wife threatened '"to trample her to pieces if she came canting into her court"'. Hostility to male missionaries was – as far as these things have come down to us – far worse. A missionary called Bullin 'we always considered to have received his death through being thrown down stairs [by Irish catholics] in St Giles's', probably in the late 1840s. Another was ejected from a lodging house in evil George Street, St Giles, his trousers torn to expose him, his mouth filled with powdered mustard and '"then put in a water-butt"'.[21]

Here too, then, a war of attrition was waged against the missionary police around the home as against their uniformed counterparts in the streets. It was not as merciless or as frequent, but it was scarcely more accommodating. For the Catholic Irish, the sight of a Protestant evangelist was a mortal affront. And for the rest of the poor, with charity as essential to their survival as labour, a gospel of love proffered without cash or kind was humiliation aggravated by what looked like hypocrisy. Class-conscious Bosanquet noted how the ungentlemanly upbringing of the missionaries, 'of more energy than cultivation', tended to a common fault of 'self-assertion'. That was a quality made worse when bolstered by a fanatical faith that anaesthetised all sense and feeling. We might envisage R. W. Vanderkiste as a missionary typical of his time, 'rolling about' in agony with cholera cramps in the epidemic of 1849 while 'praising God at the same time'.[22]

Yet some sort of accommodation between the poor and the missionaries was reached over time, just as with the Metropolitan Police. And for something like the same reason. For the London City missionaries and their fellow workers did bring psychic and physical relief to many, and won sympathy and sometimes converts by their unremitting efforts.

One good reason for the LCM gaining credit over the years among the poorest was its work with children, especially education through 'ragged schools'. Compromised as always by the evangelical agenda, so that education was inseparable from religious propaganda, the ragged schools spoke directly to the needs of neglected or abandoned children. Those needs were so dire that, twenty and more years before Thomas Barnardo, several schools set up 'refuges' to take homeless children off the streets and give them some sort of life – even life itself.

No one knows when the first ragged school was established, but it was the LCM that boosted their numbers from about 1837 and which coined the term around 1840.[23] By 1844 there were enough to form a Ragged School Union (RSU) and in five years there were eighty-two in London, with over 17,000 scholars. Numbers fluctuated but in the 1860s pupil numbers ranged from 23,000–36,000 in London. According to the Earl of Shaftesbury, London's greatest evangelical from the death of William Wilberforce in 1833 and a loyal supporter of the RSU, attendance suffered in the summer but '"the chills and rains of winter drive them to the schools for warmth and shelter"'.[24]

It was Shaftesbury too who urged the RSU to '"Stick to the gutter"' and establish schools in the worst (most criminal) of the London slums. This it did. So in the 1840s we find schools in the Mint, Pye Street,

Westminster (close to the Abbey), Thrawl Street, Field Lane, Lisson Grove, and New Cut. The schoolteachers (around one to every ten scholars on the books) were not only missionaries but volunteers from all walks of life. They included some people we've already met, like Thomas Barnardo, George Williams, the founder of the YMCA, and James Hain Friswell, the novelist; and at Ogle Mews Ragged School, Marylebone, the teachers included former Lord Mayor and evangelical stockbroker Sir Robert Carden.[25]

Charles Dickens, instinctively hostile to evangelicals of every stripe, made an exception for ragged school teachers. Even he was staggered by what he found at the Field Lane Ragged School on a Thursday evening in September 1843.

The school is held in three most wretched rooms on the first floor of a rotten house; every plank, and timber, and lath, and piece of plaster in which, shakes as you walk. One room is devoted to the girls: two to the boys. The former are much the better-looking – I cannot say better dressed, for there is no such thing as dress among the seventy pupils; certainly not the elements of a whole suit of clothes, among them all. I have very seldom seen, in all the strange and dreadful things I have seen in London and elsewhere, anything so shocking as the dire neglect of soul and body exhibited in these children . . .

There was one boy, who had been selling Lucifer Matches all day in the streets – not much older than Charley [Dickens's eldest, six and three-quarters] – clad in a bit of a sack – really a clever child, and handsome too, who gave some excellent replies . . . Hardly any of them can read yet. For the masters think it most important to impress them at first with some distinction (communicated in dialogue) between right and wrong. And I quite agree with them. They sell trifles in the streets, or beg (or some, I dare say, steal) all day; and coming tired to this place at night, are very slow to pick up any knowledge. That they *do* come at all, is, *I* think, a Victory.

They knew about the Saviour, & the Day of Judgment. The little match boy told me that God was no respecter of persons, and that if he (the match boy) prayed 'as if he meant it', and didn't keep company with bad boys, and didn't swear, and didn't drink, he would be as readily forgiven in Heaven as the Queen would . . .

The school is miserably poor, you may believe, and is almost entirely supported by the teachers themselves. If they could get a better room (the house they are in, is like an ugly dream); above all, if they could provide some convenience for washing; it would be an immense advantage. The moral courage of the teachers is beyond all praise. They are surrounded by every possible adversity, and every disheartening circumstance that can be imagined. Their office is worthy of the apostles.[26]

These heroic efforts to bring civility to the slums were matched from the 1830s on by an excess of religious enthusiasm in London that would not abate for almost half a century. It was bolstered from 1837 by Victoria's example, in this respect at least William's true heir. Its expression found various public registers. One was a passion for church building, led by Charles Blomfield, Bishop of London from 1828. In 1836 he inaugurated a programme to build fifty new metropolitan churches. In fact voluntary subscriptions far exceeded his aspirations and by the end of his episcopacy in 1856 he had consecrated 107 London churches, almost all in new suburbs. A separate initiative of 1839 to build ten churches in Bethnal Green relied on City money, whipped in by the Leytonstone-born William Cotton, a Limehouse rope and sail maker and director (later Governor) of the Bank of England. The churches were all built by 1850, complete 'with clergy, schools, Scripture-readers, and district visitors in proportion'.[27]

Religion benefited at the same time from a cast of star preachers that attracted huge crowds to church and chapel and elsewhere from the late 1830s on. These included inspirational evangelists like the dissenters Thomas Binney at the King's Weigh House Chapel (Eastcheap, City) and Caleb Morris (a Welsh Independent) at Fetter Lane Chapel; and Anglicans like Thomas Dale at St Bride's, Fleet Street, and Robert Montgomery at Percy Chapel, St Pancras. Most astonishing of all was Rev. Charles Haddon Spurgeon, a Baptist minister from Essex stock, who was 'called to' the New Park Street Chapel, Southwark, in 1854. The 'silver trumpet' of his pulpit oratory was so exciting that he could draw enormous crowds. On the night of 19 October 1856 he hired the Surrey Music Hall which held 10,000, when a false alarm of fire caused seven worshippers to be crushed to death. Undaunted – this an act of man not God, presumably – Spurgeon and his disciples opened the Metropolitan Tabernacle in March 1861 at the Elephant and Castle, its 5,000 seats filled many times a week.[28]

Doubtless stimulated by the anxieties of the age, including the reappearance of cholera, political revolution abroad, Chartism and Irish immigration at home, religious passion revealed itself too in a steep rise in charitable enterprise in London. In the 1840s eighty-five charities were formed that were still active in 1897, in the 1850s 122 and in the 1860s 120. By 1849 Henry Mayhew identified 'the extraordinary change of feeling which has taken place of late years, and which makes the poor of the present day of such moment to us . . .' This concern, what a later generation in the 1880s would call a consciousness of sin, was 'the chief distinction of the present age from the past', more important than steam power, railways or the electric telegraph, Mayhew thought.[29]

It was a 'feeling' that had the reform of manners at its heart. It broke out in many directions: workhouse visiting, bringing the gospel to paupers; Sunday-night services in theatres, claiming the platform for God; working men's clubs, serving coffee and lemonade but no beer; orphanages and children's homes; gospel halls and meeting rooms; rescue homes for prostitutes; evening and debating classes, hot on elocution; industrial schools for reforming thieves; Christmas dinners for children; thieves' suppers; more hospitals and dispensaries; help to the blind, deaf and dumb; infant crèches and nurseries; assisted emigration for discharged prisoners, prostitutes and others; penny banks and loan societies; tracts and cheap wholesome literature; homes for domestic servants between berths; homes for the respectable aged poor; shoe-black battalions and street orderlies; temperance societies; the Young Men's Christian Association (1844) and Young Women's Christian Association (1855); societies for persecuting brothels; night refuges for homeless adults and children; missions to costermongers, police courts, common lodging houses, pubs. A charity for every symptom of collective sin and personal pain was initiated in these decades.[30]

Much of this relied on a few very wealthy givers, like the Hackney-born nonconformist millionaire Samuel Morley and the evangelical Anglican Shaftesbury, who thought 'the great givers of London could be enumerated on the fingers of both hands, and that every subscription list was a repetition of another'. True it is that Shaftesbury and his friends were generous philanthropists: the list of deputations attending his memorial service at Westminster Abbey in October 1885 ran to 185 charities and ended by '&c. &c. &c.' But lavish generosity was underpinned by a base of small sums from large numbers, often for local causes. So that the Anglicans and dissenters of Notting Hill in 1881 were said to pay 'voluntarily about £15,000 a year' for Christian endeavour in their district, and similar activity could doubtless have been uncovered in every other middle-class suburb of London.[31]

The domestic visiting spearheaded by the LCM from 1835 was one factor bringing charitable attention to the 'homes' of the London poor. The revelations of committees of inquiry – the spectre of cholera snapping at their heels – and the daily experience of Christian missionaries and lady visitors in the 1840s and 1850s channelled funds into projects for building 'model dwellings', often on the rubble of former slums. In 1841 the Metropolitan Association for Improving the Dwellings of the Industrious Classes united philanthropy to profit, offering 5 per cent return on shareholders' investments. Similar projects followed in the 1840s and 1850s, but 1862 might stand as *annus mirabilis* for philanthropic intervention in the housing of the poor. In that year Baroness Angela Burdett-Coutts's Columbia Square project in Bethnal Green replaced a notorious slum, the 'Burkers' Ground' of Novia Scotia Gardens, where the Italian boy had been murdered thirty or so years before. Alderman Sydney Waterlow, his wealth derived from printing and stationery, built from his own money model dwellings in Mark Street, Finsbury, and then set up one of the most active 5 per cent ventures, the Improved Industrial Dwellings Society. Finally, the American merchant-philanthropist George Peabody, in London since the late 1830s, made his first gift to the London poor for improved housing – there would be three more, totalling £500,000, by 1873.[32]

None of these initiatives was a mere matter of brick and slate. Model dwellings demanded model tenants. Each tenement estate came with its superintendent enforcing printed rules of conduct and securing respectability under threat of eviction. Drunkenness, sexual laxity and financial fecklessness were outlawed, cleanliness and order were ordained. Intolerance of rent arrears alone ensured that only those workers in stable employment or who were ultra-disciplined home-managers could get and keep their rooms in the 'models'. '[R]esidence in the Peabody Buildings is an undeniable certificate of character', and so it was in other philanthropic dwellings too.[33]

We find the most unashamed expression of improved housing as a reward for better behaviour given voice in the work of Octavia Hill. She was enormously influential in her day in various fields of charitable endeavour (founding with others the National Trust in 1895, for instance), but it was her housing reforms that seized the imagination of contemporaries and has cemented her reputation since. Born in 1838 in Wisbech, Cambridgeshire, into a radical but rich Unitarian family, Hill converted to Anglicanism in London under the influence of the

Christian socialist F. D. Maurice in 1857. Her work with the London poor began at Paradise Place, Marylebone High Street, in 1865. With funding from John Ruskin, she bought three slum houses in a court and refurbished them, evicting irredeemable tenants in the process. Other schemes followed, some bought by or with the help of wealthy women. 'Truly a wild, lawless, desolate little kingdom to come to rule over,' she wrote of one of these places, and rule she did, with the Bible, it seemed, in one hand and a mop in the other. '"Where God gives me authority, this, which you in your own hearts know to be wrong, shall not go on"', and so dirt, rent arrears, drunkenness, neglected children were 'set in order'. The 'main tone of action must be severe. There is much of rebuke and repression needed, although a deep and silent under-current of sympathy and pity may flow beneath.' Sympathy, though, was in short supply. 'She had very little sense of her own humour, and none at all of other people's,' quipped Henrietta Barnett. And 'Among her rare and most attractive [sic] qualities was a disregard of cold, hunger, or other physical discomforts . . . It was this habit of mind which enabled her frequently to disregard the normal sufferings of the poor, and to expect them to feel the same indifference that she felt to petty hardship.'[34]

Arrogance and certainty, the birthright of wealth and education and social structure, were made diamond-hard when acting with God's authority and furthering God's design. Here were the deformities of class and religion in powerful combination. They were most readily apparent in Anglicanism with its rented pews, its livings in the gift of rich men and women, its clergy synonymous with gentry, its close associations with political reaction. This worm in the bud of English Christianity was widely acknowledged by mid-century. Horace Mann's monograph on religious attendance published with the 1851 census lamented the 'alarming' non-attendance at church or chapel of the working classes. They were like 'the people of a heathen country'. Mann attributed this mainly to class distinctions rendering a poor worshipper out of place and uncomfortable, especially in the Anglican church. But he also noted the indifference of 'professed Christians' to the sufferings of the poor, the mistrust of a paid clergy preaching God for money and not necessarily from conviction, and the degradation of the poor which blocked their understanding of the Christian message. In Mann's survey London came out especially badly. It had 13.2 per cent of the population of England and Wales but just 8.4 per cent of church attendances. Apart from Roman Catholics, every important sect (including the Church of England) was under-represented among churchgoers in the metropolis. Ironically, Bethnal Green, despite its ten new churches, appeared the most irreligious of all London's districts: attendances equated to 15 per cent of population compared to 69 per cent in Hampstead, for instance. More than forty years later, '"Remember Bethnal Green" is apt to be thrown in the teeth of those who try to inaugurate any great movement in the City on behalf of the Church.'[35]

In the decades following Mann there would be more reasons for the working classes and others to be repelled by organised religion in London especially. We might recall how Sabbatarianism, with its attack by rich Christian fundamentalists on the amusements and comforts of the poor, led to the Hyde Park riots of 1855. Sabbatarians suppressed Sunday bands in the parks in 1856. It was estimated some 260,000 people turned out to hear them at three locations on a single Sunday, but still the music had to stop.[36] For the rest of the century battle was waged for a brighter Sunday, permitting public pleasures on the workers' sole free day of the week. Year after year, bills to open the London museums and galleries on Sundays were defeated by Christians in Lords or Commons. They were eventually allowed to invade the 'Lord's Day' from April 1896.

Another consequence of religious enthusiasm, especially rampant in London, seemed also designed to foment wry cynicism among the ungodly. This was the furious disputation over ritual in the Church of England. It had accompanied the rising influence of the Oxford Movement from the late 1830s, with its deference to ancient trappings of the mysterious and mystical elements in Christianity. It was a movement that many saw undermining Protestantism and returning the Church to its Catholic roots. The cry of 'No Popery' gathered more urgency from 1850, with 'Papal Aggression' reasserting a Roman Catholic episcopacy in England, at its head the new Archbishop of Westminster.

The first demonstration against ritual in a London church seems to have been that very year at St Barnabas, Pimlico, when elements in a crowded congregation hissed, called out 'no-popery' and 'shame', and threatened to pull down the church. In 1857 the 'Knightsbridge Religious War' brought similar scenes to St Paul's, Wilton Place. But it was when extreme ritualism came to St George's-in-the-East, in godless Limehouse,

A London Swell Mob, *c*. 1865. The railways facilitated country-wide pickings for London thieves. These London pickpockets were all arrested at Derby Races, charged but acquitted for lack of evidence. Dippers, hoisters, fogle-hunters could earn well and these men look and dress much like comfortable tradesmen.

Hustings at Covent Garden, Westminster Election, 1808. Parliamentary elections before the Ballot Act of 1872 were frequently exciting, none more than for Westminster and Middlesex in the Napoleonic Wars. Passion was fuelled by treating with drink and victuals. And the crowd partook in an ancient tradition of demolishing the giant hustings and grandstands, taking away the timber for firewood.

Great Chartist demonstration, Kennington Common, 10 April 1848. This day London felt like a city on the edge of civil war. In the event, it passed peacefully thanks to a massive police presence, backed by the military, tightly controlling the bridges leading to the City and Westminster; thanks, too, to heavy rain. Even so, perhaps 150,000 braved the mud to press for an extension of democracy.

Poultry Compter, Wood Street, 1811. This was one of the two City sheriffs' prisons, rebuilt after the Great Fire and captured here shortly before its demolition around 1815. It had wards for debtors as well as miscreants and was the only London prison with separate accommodation for Jews. Newgate Prison, the City's main gaol designed by George Dance the Younger in the 1770s, was a London landmark familiar throughout the world. It was in use until the century's end, as pictured here, and the main location for London executions.

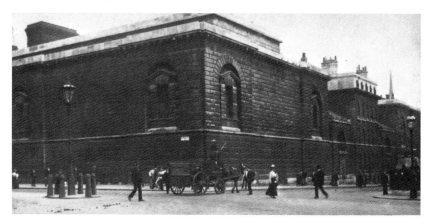

An arrest near Ludgate Hill Station, *c.* 1892. A City policeman, of a breed taller and reputedly smarter than his Metropolitan colleagues, makes an arrest. The difference in size between the country-bred police and the London small-fry they disciplined is eloquently caught here by Paul Martin's hidden 'Facile' camera, disguised as a parcel.

Crowd waiting to see a policeman's funeral, North Lambeth, *c.* 1895. The officer had dropped dead making an arrest. The relationship between police and public in the poorer parts of London was complex: always wary, frequently hostile, sometimes brutally so. But the poor also needed the police for protection from one another and for help in an increasingly complicated world.

Saturday School, Christ Church St George's in the East, July 1900. St George's was an active parish, by this time recovering from its notoriety for Anglo-Catholic ritualism in the 1850s but still very high church. This is a poor district but all these youngsters look clean and well-shod: the church, of course, helped keep them so.

Hoxton Market Mission and Ragged School. The results of a single day's 'booting' in the nineties when bad boots were brought in by poor children and exchanged for good. The Mission was begun in 1881 by the brothers Burtt, former street waifs themselves.

A boys' class at Snowfield Board School, Bermondsey, 1894. From 1870 the School Board for London took on the greatest administrative challenge ever faced by an arm of London government. A large part of the children of the London poor had been without any education. Compulsory schooling was gladly welcomed by many poor parents, fiercely resented by some. Teaching hungry ill-clad boys needed heroic effort: yet the discipline of the boys in this class photograph is some testimony to the School Board's successes.

Offices of the Metropolitan Board of Works, Spring Gardens. Built 1859–61 to an Italian Renaissance design by Frederick Marrable, this was the hub of London government until 1922. Working hours were nine to four, with a ten-minute grace period to sign the hall porter's attendance book.

that things got properly out of hand. Protests against the Rev. Bryan King's ministry ran through much of 1859 and 1860. Every Sunday the church was filled with 'Rits' and antis, for and against King's 'fantastic' altar adornments and other mystical emblems. And it was overrun by locals, many of them drunk, who came to take part in fun more uproarious than an East End music hall. Week after week, indecent responses were made from the gallery and lewd songs bellowed in the pews; hassocks were used as missiles; attempts were made to mob the altar and bring down chandeliers; shouts of 'No Popery', 'Hot Codlins' and 'Pipes all round', and choruses of 'Rule, Britannia' and 'We Won't Go Home Till Morning' drowned out the lessons; firecrackers exploded and peas were shot in clergymen's faces; large bodies of police – sometimes 300 strong – sat through services to keep order; and at worst crowds of 3,000–4,000 invaded the church, battling in the chancel with police for an hour at a time. The Church, so down on the people's exuberant pleasures, especially on Sundays, had itself become a source of riotous joy.[37]

Ritualistic rows rumbled on through the 1860s, 1870s and 1880s, with congregational protests and Church prosecutions from Erith to Knightsbridge. The Rit. Rev. Alexander Heriot Mackonochie at St Alban's, Baldwin's Gardens, Holborn, was at the eye of the storm for twenty years from 1862, his church's lights and warmth and rich colour as much a draw to the poor, apparently, as any superior gin palace. Even at the very end of the century, in 1898–9, frantic disputes over ritual gave further cause for sceptics' mirth in what was by now a more outspokenly secular age.[38]

One final offence was given at the end of the 1860s. Horace Mann had highlighted Christian indifference to the sufferings of the poor and indeed there had been a long tradition in London of conditional philanthropy founded on distrust. From 1818 the Society for the Suppression of Mendicity had initiated 'ticket charity', the society's members equipped with tickets instead of money to hand to beggars. Beggars presenting themselves with a ticket at the society's offices in Red Lion Square would have their circumstances looked into and deserving cases were given relief in cash or kind. Enquiring into what might well be only meretricious destitution seemed a useful check on a public fraud. The idea pressed more urgently as philanthropy multiplied from the 1830s on. For there was nothing to stop ne'er-do-wells hawking their rags from one charity to another and back again. And there was no communication between poor law officers and philanthropists to avoid duplication of relief to wily paupers. On the other hand, a series of shocking exposures in the mid-1860s revealed the starving desperation of the London poor and that relief of any kind was not guaranteed to get to the people who needed it most.

The impulse among Christian social workers that alms-giving was not merely self-defeating but somehow contrary to the spirit of Christ gained ground in the 1860s. By the end of the decade it was an orthodoxy of advanced social work. We see it in Edward Denison, educated at Eton and Christ Church, among the brightest and best of his generation, condemned to an early death from tuberculosis at the age of thirty in 1870. His sickness was made worse, so his friends thought, by a period living among the poor at Philpot Street, Stepney. Denison agonised over his usefulness in improving the workers and their lot. One thing, though, he was clear about. 'I don't believe in those doles of bread and meat.' And he fought against 'the terrible evils of the so-called charity which pours money into the haunts of misery and vice every winter'.[39]

Denison saw charity allowing the state to neglect its proper duties and so become an obstacle to social reform. Others saw it deterring moral reform by rewarding the undeserving – like Octavia Hill, who, despite that inconvenient divine admonition to 'Judge not', believed 'that the distribution of alms irrespective of character is fatal'. And yet others saw it undermining self-help and independence. 'Indiscriminate charity is among the curses of Whitechapel,' wrote the Rev. Samuel Barnett of St Jude's in 1874. 'I would say that "the poor starve because of the alms they receive"': 'Money pauperises the people . . .'[40]

Barnett and Hill, with others including Charles Bosanquet, formed the Charity Organisation Society (COS) in 1869 to put down the evil of indiscriminate giving in London. Its full title was the Society for Organising Charitable Relief and Repressing Mendicity. There were good reasons for establishing local coordination between charities and the poor law, because there was much evidence of cheating. But in the economic climate of mid- to late Victorian London, with its culture of low wages, its slack labour demand and casual employment, and with a desperately low standard of living among the poor, 'charity organisation' seemed harsh, even murderous, and the very antithesis of Christian love. As Frederick Rogers of Whitechapel (a rare working-man Anglican) commented, 'All the thrift in the world will never enable a man to get more than twenty shillings out of a pound, and thrift can never make up for bad wages.' That was a lesson active Christians seemed incapable of learning. All this would not be forgotten as London's numerous religions fought for adherents in the chilly climate to come.[41]

'There Goes the Pennies from the Poor-box!', 1870–1899

When Samuel Barnett came to implement his new close-handed policy in Whitechapel his disgruntled parishioners turned on him.

The people considered that alms were their right and came at all hours to the Vicarage to demand money or tickets, supporting their appeals with lies, noise, and threatened violence. Sometimes after they had been refused, they would tell their grievances to the passers-by, who, collecting into an indignant crowd, would thunder at the door and throw things at the windows, occasionally breaking even the thick glass provided in the Ecclesiastical Commissioners' buildings. At first there was no choice but to stand the siege until the crowd dispersed, but later a door was cut from our house into the Church through which the Vicar could slip out to fetch the police.[42]

Indeed, the early 1870s would prove an uncomfortable time for evangelicals and Christian reformers in London, recalling some of the worst trials of the London City missionaries thirty years before. Open-air preachers offered tempting targets, irresistible when they waged war on the workers' pleasures. Thomas Barnardo had his prating stopped by a pellet of street mud lobbed skilfully into his open mouth, and suffered two broken ribs when young men and women resented his presence in a beerhouse. For some years he campaigned against the Edinburgh Castle public house, a '"flaming gin-palace"', its stage acts using '"filthy *doubles entendres* and questionable gestures"'. He pitched a tent outside for prayer meetings and in October 1872 raised funds to buy the Castle and fit it out as a 'coffee palace' and mission hall. Unsurprisingly, this was resented and Barnardo recalled how '"I and some of my fellow-workers . . . were chased through the streets by people in the neighbourhood"'. John Dunn, preaching temperance outside the Bird Cage public house, Bethnal Green, had refuse and offal thrown at him and his helpers by 'bigoted Romanists and scoffing infidels', who struck 'brimstone matches under our noses'. A Roman

Catholic missionary to Homerton in 1874 was abused and stoned and someone spat in his face. And Rev. C. J. Whitmore around 1876 found his Sunday afternoon open-air praying and hymn-singing disturbing 'the sleep of the drunken', receiving 'an incessant and dangerous shower of brick and stone' in return.[43]

In the face of all this hostility the unstinting efforts of organised Christianity remained robust in London. Missions mushroomed in every dark corner. Charities continued to bloom – of those still there in 1897, 119 were set up in the 1870s and 105 in the 1880s – 'spread[ing] themselves like a network over London'. And individuals, despite the strictures of the COS, continued to give of their money and time. Not least among them were 'lady rent collectors', like the young Beatrice Potter (later Webb), helping the poor and keeping them in order along the lines of spartan Octavia twenty years before.[44]

Nor did the chapels and churches of late Victorian London march in order down the road the COS had mapped out for them. Rev. Whitmore knew the answer to hostility or indifference in the Drury Lane area, home to the very poor and 'the vile'. 'Winter had followed summer, out-of-door work had slackened or ceased, there was nothing to buy or sell in the streets, and the children began to be hungry. Then we tempted them into our Mission-room with some hot nourishing food . . .' Some would call this 'bribery', others Christian charity. And the picture was complicated by competition between churches and missions of different denominations seeking to attract adherents by offering generous relief or superior feeding. Charles Booth was deeply sceptical of the worth of much of this hyperactivity. In some poor parts of London he found missions as thick as flies. At Deptford an exasperated housewife called out to one visitor, '"You are the fifth this morning!"'[45]

Even so, there is no doubt that the poor – even the poorest of all – were helped. The benefits extended not just to relieving hunger and nakedness but to life-expanding opportunities to acquire knowledge and skills, manners and values. Among the Christianising there was much humanising too.

We might take as one fine example the New Court Congregational Chapel's mission to the 'top end' of Campbell Road, Holloway, from 1875. New Court was an old dissenting chapel in Carey Street, Lincoln's Inn Fields, that could date its origins back to 1662. The chapel was needed to make way for the new Law Courts in the Strand, and in any event its congregation had been moving to the suburbs for thirty years. Receiving compensation for its valuable old premises, the chapel authorities could now follow suit and they built a handsome tabernacle at Tollington Way, Holloway, opening in 1871. With a new suburban congregation, much of it middle class and generous, and with contributions from Samuel Morley (£100) among others, New Court sought out the poorest districts nearby for its good works. At Campbell Road the clerks and shop-assistant workers at New Court mission visited every family, 'relieving cases of destitution and illness' among 'the deserving poor [sic]'; they held services in rooms and the open air; set up Sunday schools, popular among parents for providing quiet connubial time at least once in the week; set up a Lads' Institute to teach reading, writing, arithmetic, singing and more; opened a reading room with newspapers, books and games; formed a Band of Hope (temperance), a Self-Help Society (for mutual aid among sick neighbours), a Women's Help-One-Another Society and a Penny Bank; held Sewing Classes and Mothers' Meetings, giving information about childcare and domestic economy; set up a Working Men's Club with subsidised tea, coffee and soup and a proper lavatory; offered tracts room to room; sold halfpenny dinners to children and gave them annual excursions to the country; opened a twice-weekly soup kitchen in bitter weather; and put on free Saturday-night entertainments in the winter. Who could condemn out of hand such efforts as these? And who could deny some positive effects on the lives they touched?[46]

The vigour of places like New Court Chapel and mission in the 1870s reflected a context of unflagging interest in religious affairs that continued to absorb the middle classes, especially middle-class women, until the late 1880s at least. Every Sunday, almost every weeknight, a host of competing theologies and Christian entertainments bustled for attention across the capital – from the Walworth Jumpers to the Plumstead Peculiars; from the Hackney Secularists damning God to Moody and Sankey offering 'intercessary prayer for London'; from 'Tea and Experience Meetings' at Kensal New Town to seances in Old Quebec Street, to unfrocked vicars preaching theism at Langham Place, to reformed Hyde Park 'horse-breakers' advocating charity at the Regent Street Polytechnic; from Bramo Somaj explaining his 'recoil from Brahminism' at Little Portland Street to the emancipated slaves of the American Jubilee Singers' 'Songs of Zion' at Spurgeon's Tabernacle, or the Royal Poland Street Temperance Handbell Ringers. And lest anyone think that the established Church was dull and uniform in comparison, Charles Dickens the Younger's annual *Dictionary of London* from 1879 lavished twelve pages on an elaborate table showing for hundreds of London churches such fine points as which of fifteen hymnals was in use, vestments plain or coloured, tapers lit or unlit, and whether communion was sung or read, in whole or part.[47]

Despite all this work and spiritual energy and all these attractions, most Londoners remained irreligious. This fact was not lost on those concerned daily with the poor, whose infidel state seemed to press ever harder on the enlightened conscience. Of the fresh initiatives launched on the London poor in the 1870s and 1880s two in particular stand out.

The Salvation Army was the most aggressively evangelical of the new ventures. William Booth had been active in London Methodism since his arrival from Nottingham in 1849. He was a man of fixed views and extreme reactions. He was meticulously clean in a grubby age, physically revolted by dirt, would retch at a bad smell, 'whipped' his children and hated 'cricket and football as if they were sins'. For Booth, conversion and the salvation of souls were the only answers to East London's problems. From 1865 he preached hellfire – '"Damnation with the Cross in the middle of it"' – in the open air in the Mile End Road. He seized the chance in 1867 to take over the Effingham Theatre in Whitechapel Road, 'converting' it to 'The Christian Mission'. In 1872 he set up six or seven shops selling cheap 'Food for the Million', but they foundered in financial and managerial confusion. His tendency to dictatorship over God in the East End was finally made plain when he formed the Salvation Army at a Whitechapel 'War Congress' in August 1878, the 'General' commanding with military discipline, uniforms and marching bands.[48]

The Salvation Army had a little success attracting into its ranks some of the poorest of the London poor, among them numerous 'lasses'. Its social work from 1888 with homeless men in the East End, mostly brought low by chronic alcoholism, showed the army unafraid to tackle the most difficult stratum of all and won it some credit. But for its first decade at least the Salvation Army infuriated the East End crowd. There was bad trouble from 1879, local publicans – the General's prime target – apparently organising a 'Skeleton Army' from 'all the flotsam and jetsam of Flower and Dean Street' to attack the Salvationists' street meetings and marches. The army's 'Hallelujah Meetings', where 'the power of the Holy Ghost' both 'prostrated' and 'levitated' worshippers, who 'shouted, wept, clapped . . . and danced', snapped the patience of stolid East End workers. There was much criticism too of the army parading its social work to lever money from the public and then siphoning it into both sectarian religious propaganda and the Booth family's pockets. When, shades of Barnardo, the General secretly raised funds to buy the Eagle Tavern – that venerable pleasure-haunt for workers and clerks in the City Road – a triumphant march announcing its 'conversion' was violently attacked and a police guard had to be kept on the Eagle 'for some months'. That year, 1882, 'William Booth was many times in grave danger of his life'.[49]

At the same time that Booth and the Salvation Army were enlivening spirits in the East End a very different tendency began to assert itself. The 'settlement movement' originated in the conviction that the fundamental evils of society arose from the separation of classes. If the rich really knew about the struggles of the poor, then their consciences would plunge them into social reform to improve things. And if the poor really appreciated the goodwill of the rich, they would abandon class antagonism, strikes and socialism. Religion didn't have to be part of this movement but it helped, because Jesus had preached the brotherhood of man and his churches offered ostensibly the same message to all classes. These were the ideas that had motivated Denison in the late 1860s and many identified him as 'the first settler'. But they now mobilised a generation in the furore provoked in 1883 by Rev. Andrew Mearns's *The Bitter Cry of Outcast London* and *How the Poor Live* by George R. Sims. The 'consciousness of sin' among the wealthy who permitted such things to exist overwhelmed a significant part of the privileged young in particular. Even taking into account all that had gone before, this was the most startling crisis of conscience of the century.[50]

The settlement movement was an instant response. The most famous settlement in London, bringing university men of all denominations and none to Whitechapel from the end of 1884, began in the work of Rev. Samuel Barnett at St Jude's. Its new premises, christened Toynbee Hall, opened in the spring of 1885. The Barnetts left the COS in 1886 and abandoned its most extreme principles. Nevertheless, Toynbee Hall brought to its work the hard-nosed view that charitable assistance demoralised the poor and that the key to salvation was self-help, preferably guided by the gospels. On the other hand, it had something of humility about it, teaching that the rich and educated could learn from the poor. That proved harder to realise in practice than in theology. '"Come and be the squires of East London"' was not a humble call to arms and one cynic noted how, 'From the very nature of its being, Toynbee Hall could not very well help turning out first-class prigs.'[51]

Toynbee Hall's non-denominationalism inevitably provoked a backlash from the Church of England. Toynbee, named after Arnold of that ilk – another saint dying young who undermined his health giving lectures on economics to workers in London and elsewhere – had strong Balliol connections. And it was Keble which established Oxford House, Bethnal Green, in the autumn of 1884. It was mission as well as settlement, proselytising Anglicanism in that ungrateful territory. Other settlements followed, funded by universities or private philanthropists and set up for women as well as men. By the end of the century there were at least fourteen, seven in the East End, five south of the river and two in Bloomsbury.[52]

Much of their work was educational, broadly speaking. It responded to a real hunger. Henry Nevinson, lecturing on *Paradise Lost*, was astonished by the large numbers coming to hear him at Toynbee Hall from Dalston and Hackney Wick. Its Travellers' Club, library, art shows (the Whitechapel Gallery began here), concerts and plays were all well received. Nevinson's conclusion 'that on the whole we did very little harm to others, and in a few instances we may have increased the happiness and intellectual pleasure of those whom we hoped vaguely to benefit' is too self-effacing – but not by much. It was more just than the grandiose claim for Toynbee as 'the working man's university', though it was that to a few. That title might more reasonably go to the People's Palace in Mile End Road, inspired by Walter Besant's *All Sorts and Conditions of Men* (1882) and opened in 1887. But in other areas the settlements had more success, especially in their work for children, organising boys' (and, in the women's settlements, girls') clubs. These exploited what became wryly known as 'muscular Christianity', developing at the same time in Anglican churches in the East End. Well-fed university men apparently overawed the youth of Bethnal Green and Whitechapel, providing object lessons in self-discipline and bodily cleanliness. D. G. Halsted recalled how he and an evangelical friend 'were able to profit [as reformers of manners] from the enormous reverence such boys had for athletes like ourselves', and the boys no doubt profited in turn from lessons in scientific boxing. This club life, building on earlier initiatives but with less forcing of religion down gagging throats, was given a distinctive push in London by the settlement movement, perhaps its most valuable achievement.[53]

Yet even with these late-century initiatives, religion just would not take on in London. We know little of the true dynamics of church attendance in the capital, but we can reasonably speculate on rising numbers (proportions are more difficult to assess) from the 1830s to some time in the 1880s. There was then certainly a falling away, despite a rising population, between 1886 and 1902–3, when results from reasonably scientific counts are available. The latter estimated that of those who could attend a place of worship in Greater London just one in five did so. The working-class bulk of the population remained largely immune to the attractions of public worship, whatever their private opinions might have been.[54]

So every point of the London compass sent up cries of lament when Charles Booth investigated 'religious influences' on metropolitan life and labour between about 1897 and 1901. There were exceptions – Bermondsey stands out, and sumptuous ritualism could draw the poor – but for sixty years of enduring hard work the results in working-class London were pitiful. And in some areas, Wandsworth for instance, worrying signs of a new world emerging from the shadow of orthodox constraints were plainly affecting even those social ranks from whom so many church workers had come.

'Small clerks and City people are almost more stubborn and difficult to reach than the working classes. They make Sunday a day of pleasure simply, and are off rowing and cycling. They won't be visited, and they can't be missionized. They would look upon an open-air service in their street as an insult. [They have] ceased to reckon with the non-material side of life.'[55]

It seems likely, though, that violent hostility to religion had begun to soften by the end of the century. But it left little more than sullenness in its wake. Horace Mann had pointed to suspicion of a paid clergy at mid-century, and Samuel Barnett had been told, '"it's us as pays you"' by a disappointed supplicant forgivably confusing the boundaries of Church and state. For in poor areas clergymen were mistrusted as hypocrites – worse, thieves – skimming the cream from benevolent giving. '"There goes the pennies from the poor-box!" shouted a working man as a clerical friend of mine sped by on his bicycle' somewhere in the East End in the 1890s.[56]

Cultural resistance to organised religion helped wear down evangelical enterprise by the end of the nineteenth century. It was all too much like sculpting granite with a butter knife, and fewer and fewer would spend their best years in the effort. There were numerous other unsympathetic factors in play. Decades of theological controversy had begun to undermine Christianity from within, doubt becoming more normal than conviction in the face of a historical approach to Christian evidence and the expansion of science. Variations on the secularist theme led to almost as many anti-Christian sectlets in the 1870s and 1880s as, say, permutations of Methodism. From the 1880s socialism itself became something like an alternative religion, with all the trappings of schism and sectarianism and a shelf of alternative gospels. And to some extent all that self-help propaganda had undermined evangelicalism from within, the workers' turn to cooperation and trade unionism putting into secular but collective practice what had been preached as a route of individual salvation. This change in mood revealed itself in the social crisis of 1886–9 with its great strikes and nervy riots. It certainly led to a panic-stricken rise in charitable giving. But it was the first crisis of the century not to provoke an explicitly religious response in new missions or churches or enthusiastic revivals.

There were two other elements that helped lead even its disciples to proclaim 'Christianity a failure' by the century's end.[57] One was the narrowing of the evangelical agenda from the salvation of souls to an obsessive campaign for 'purity' in public life. A critical watchfulness on questions of sexual morality had always been a plank of the evangelicals' platform and had brought ribald mirth on their heads in the past. Like the successful campaign, led by the Archbishop of Canterbury, to fix fig leaves to classical statues in the resurrected Crystal Palace in 1854, for example. Or the scandal among evangelicals in 1877 over Thomas Barnardo's use of photographs of half-naked children. But from 1885 sexual purity became the evangelicals' mania.[58]

In that year, the campaigning evangelical editor of the *Pall Mall Gazette*, W. T. Stead, staged an extraordinary stunt. Historians are only now beginning to uncover the sexual politics that drove middle-class men and women to take an active interest in the London poor, much of it hidden away and difficult to get at. With Stead there are no difficulties. He was obsessed by sex, less in the doing than the wondering, it seems. That canny observer Mrs Lynn Linton 'allowed him absolute probity in that [sexual conduct] respect, but, she added, "he exudes semen through the skin."'[59] Stead was convinced that young girls were freely bought and sold in London for use in the metropolitan and continental brothel trade. Proving so would help the passage of the Criminal Law Amendment Bill, which proposed raising the age of female consent from thirteen to sixteen and was then stalled in Parliament. He arranged with Bramwell Booth of the Salvation Army, the General's much-whipped son, together with an army convert who had been a brothel-keeper in a former existence, to 'buy' a girl. In Charles Street, Lisson Grove, Booth and his contacts found a chimney-sweep's daughter called Eliza Armstrong, just turned thirteen, and 'bought' her from her mother for £5. The money paid over, poor Eliza was taken to a hotel, where she was examined by a French procuress who was also a midwife to ensure the girl was a virgin – Stead wanted no 'little harlot' palmed off on him. She was then taken to a brothel at 32 Poland Street, out of sound of the handbill ringers, one hopes, where she was sedated with chloroform and Stead visited her, in her bedroom. After a further medical examination to show that Stead had not tampered with her Eliza was shipped to Paris by the Salvation Army.

The publication of Stead's 'Maiden Tribute to Modern Babylon' in five numbers of the *Pall Mall Gazette* during July 1885 was the newspaper sensation of the century. It served its purpose. The Criminal Law Amendment Act was duly passed in August, with its infamous section 11 outlawing homosexual acts in private. Its passage was celebrated by a monster purity demonstration in Hyde Park. Slowly, though, Stead's plot unravelled. Eliza's mother claimed she had received the £5 for putting the girl to service in the country; and her father's permission had never been given for Eliza's removal. Stead, Booth, the former madam and others were prosecuted for abduction and criminal assault; an 'obscene and raging mob' at Bow Street and the Old Bailey greeted the evangelicals with abuse and stones; and Stead endured the happy martyrdom of a three months' prison sentence, first at Coldbath Fields and then Holloway.[60]

Whether Stead was just unbelievably reckless or caught out fabricating a dishonest illusion divides commentators on the Eliza Armstrong case to this day. Whatever the truth, Stead was not alone in his fanaticism. During the feverish excitement of July and August 1885 a National Vigilance Association (NVA) was formed at meetings in St James's Hall,

Piccadilly, at the very heart of London vice. The NVA's secretary, William Coote, was born of poor Irish parents in 1843 at Norfolk Street, the Strand, and was one of the few Christians ever to claim conversion by a tract. For the rest of the century Coote, the NVA and its imitators persecuted any public expression of sexual dubiousness that offended their sensitive feelings. They pursued the closure of brothels and pornographic booksellers wherever they found them. They prosecuted the Vizetelly brothers for publishing Emile Zola, 69-year-old Henry receiving three months' imprisonment. They forced posters of female acrobats to be torn down from London hoardings because '"extending the arms . . . exhibit[ed] in the most unpleasant manner portions of the arms that can hardly be called delicate"' – this in 1890. They forced 'living pictures' out of the music halls and opposed a licence to the St James's Restaurant because it 'harboured' prostitutes. The brewing philanthropist Frederick Charrington did similar work in the East End, and Mrs Ormiston Chant, of the Britishwoman's Temperance Association, forced the temporary closure of the Empire and its famous promenade in October 1894. Seeing evil everywhere, Coote and the others were ridiculed in the London press as 'prudes on the prowl'.[61]

Coote, Charrington and Chant secured many of their victories by lobbying the London County Council, where a body of Christian councillors made a significant force. And the growth and strengthening of local government provide more reasons for the crisis of metropolitan Christianity at the end of the century. Whereas at the beginning London government had often relied on the Church to get things done, by the end churchmen anxious for progress in their parishes turned to vestries and County Hall instead. By 1900 the settlers of Toynbee Hall knew where the power to change things lay: '"there are three of us on the Stepney Borough Council, and two on the Board of Guardians, one on the County Council, and one on the School Board . . ."' In the established Church, the clergy of St Anne Soho secured three anti-vice councillors on Westminster City Council, and at Walworth 'rectors pose as radicals, and curates become Borough Councillors'. Charles Booth considered all this 'one symptom of religious desperation'.[62] Gradually the local state would begin to offer the advantages that had previously been solely the Church's domain. It would do so without the compromise that religion had demanded in return.

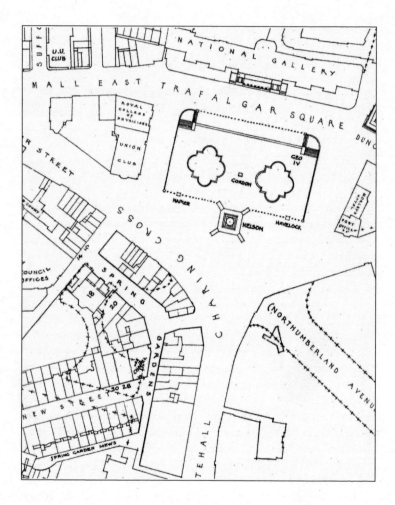

Spring Gardens, 1874

XV

SPRING GARDENS: GOVERNMENT

'From Time Immemorial', 1800–1833

THE records are doubtful about how Spring Gardens came by its name or just when it took on an identity worth marking on the map of London. Some say Spring refers to its 'jet or spring of water', but this may have been introduced artificially at a later date, and others say it describes a copse of trees on this spur of high ground rising up from the Thames. It became gardens when laid out as an enlargement of St James's Park to improve the environs of Whitehall Palace some time in the reign of Elizabeth, perhaps before. By the 1620s it had lost many of its royal connections and taken on the mantle of a pleasure garden. Stopped by the Puritans from opening on Sundays, then 'put down' altogether for a time, the pleasure garden had largely given way to house-building by the Restoration. It became known as 'Old Spring Garden' to differentiate it from the New, across the river at what would become Vauxhall. From the 1750s there was some revival of its jolly past in a Great Exhibition Room. The boy Mozart played here in 1764 and the Society of Artists exhibited. Up to 1825 it was Wigley's Promenade Rooms, for auctions and displays of mechanical wonders and *objets d'art*.

From the latter half of the seventeenth century, though, Spring Gardens was most notable for grand residences occupied by the highest reaches of the political and official classes. So it continued into the nineteenth century. Lord Sidmouth, Home Secretary in the most reactionary years of the century, lived here and so did his fellow Tory George Canning. Later, in the 1880s and 1890s, it was home to George

Shaw-Lefevre, a reforming Liberal First Commissioner of Works under Gladstone. Through all this Spring Gardens remained a backwater. By the 1840s it had become – as it is still – an almost secret turning off the south side of Trafalgar Square, shielded from bustle and traffic.

Its proximity to Whitehall and Parliament, though, made it a prime site for official relocation. In 1858 Berkeley House, a mansion in substantial grounds dating from the time of Queen Anne, was bought by the Metropolitan Board of Works (MBW) for its new offices. Set up in 1855, the board had first been accommodated at 1 Greek Street, Soho, in the premises of the defunct Metropolitan Commissioners of Sewers, but it had outgrown them. So Berkeley House was demolished in 1859 and in its place came palatial new offices on six floors, designed in the popular Italian Renaissance style by the board's own architect, Frederick Marrable. There were just five departments, with fewer than eighty officials in all. The largest, suited to London's great need of the day, was the engineer's under Joseph Bazalgette, on the principal floor above the entrance. From 1861 and for the half-century that followed, Spring Gardens was the centre of London government.[1]

It was fitting that a fresh start for London government should have its headquarters planted in a place steeped in the capital's indecipherable past. For of all the weight of history pressing on metropolitan institutions, the past proved especially disabling for the machinery of London local government as it grappled with nineteenth-century circumstances. It left a legacy of chaos and misrule that the century never entirely shook off.

That past was rooted deep in the parish. So deep, indeed, that the origins and structure of parish government are irretrievably obscure, in London as for the nation. Parishes and their governance evolved – as said, for instance, of St Botolph Without, Aldgate – 'from time immemorial'. At first, parish machinery ran Church affairs – the basis of the parish clergyman's 'immemorial participation in local government' – and then became the secular power for the collective good of the inhabitants. Within parishes, some districts – liberties, precincts, extra-parochial places – devised their own patchy governance or were connected through ownership to other parishes near or far away. In 1801 the total of London parishes in the City and around was 172. By 1851 the metropolis within what would later be the County of London contained 200 parishes and districts with some element of local self-government.[2]

But London local government for much of the first fifty-five years of the nineteenth century was far more complicated even than this. Superimposed on parishes was an untraceable network of local bodies. Some dated back hundreds of years. So for sewers and drainage, London and its environs had been divided since Tudor times into eight Metropolitan Courts of Sewers, one in the City and seven around. The administrative arrangements for each court had diversified over time under bodies of commissioners renewed by cooption among local landlords and developers. The Westminster Court of Sewers, for instance, had nominally 200 commissioners, but not more than a dozen or so showed active interest in the work.[3] There were Turnpike Trusts responsible for London's main roads outside the City, the fourteen Middlesex trusts merging in 1826 into the Metropolitan Roads Board.[4] Then more than fifty Incorporated Guardians of the Poor were set up by local acts to administer the poor law.[5] And Improvement Commissioners or Paving Boards improved pavements and arranged for street sweeping and watering, rubbish collection and street lighting, sometimes for a new estate (like Belgravia) or for a few better-off streets in a generally poor parish. As late as 1855 it was said that some 250 acts had created no fewer than 300 London boards involving over 10,000 local commissioners of one kind or another. That was on top of the 200 self-acting parishes and local areas.

The resulting confusion was perverse beyond belief. The Strand's three-quarters of a mile was the responsibility of seven different paving boards. St Mary Newington (Southwark) had two paving boards and four lighting boards acting solely in the parish and another five which crossed the parish boundary. And St Pancras was 'one of the greatest instances of abuses that had ever existed in a civilised country'. It had sixteen paving boards containing 427 commissioners, 255 of them 'self-elected': even so, 'a great portion of the parish was without paving, and without any jurisdiction whatever'.[6]

This preference for intense and fractured localism reflected the intricate class geography of London. In almost every part of London localism had supervened by the early nineteenth century. In the City of Westminster, for instance, a constitution dated from 1585. It had set up city rule under the Abbey's dean and chapter, with a high steward and Court of Burgesses appointed for life and various juries of parish representatives to stifle nuisances and appoint officials. But it was undermined from below by assertive local vestries. By the early nineteenth century it had mouldered away to a largely ceremonial husk.[7]

The one part of the metropolis which maintained an extra-parochial machinery of real import was the City of London. Resting on ancient charters rather than founding statutes, the City Corporation claimed a constitution of unique complexity and infinite flexibility. Over time it had spread its jurisdiction across much of Southwark, along the Thames from Staines to the Medway, and over London-wide matters like fairs and markets. But just as important as a constitution that seemed to afford legitimacy for whatever it wished to do, the City's endowments and acquisitions, underpinned by the wealthiest revenue base in the country, gave it inexhaustible means. Organised on precincts of a hundred or so houses grouped into twenty-six wards, City freemen (effectively most ratepayers, including 'free sisters') chose the 206 members of the Court of Common Council, the City's main representative body. From there one councilman for each ward was elected for life to a Court of Aldermen. These twenty-six were also the City's justices, their wealth rendering them the most incorruptible magistrates in London. Finally, a Court of Common Hall had a constituency of some 10,000 'liverymen' working in any of the City's trades or 'guilds', whether in London or outside. Common Hall's main function was to elect a Lord Mayor each year, and then the important paid officials of the Corporation when posts fell vacant.[8]

In all, the City Corporation was the most representative 'ratepayer democracy' in the country before 1835. Its worldview was that of the lower middle classes engaged in trade – shopkeepers, wholesalers, rentiers, and 'little-go' money-men of every shade. With all the confidence of its ancient democracy based on privilege and means, the City had long stood forth 'as a sort of unofficial mouthpiece of the people of England, as against their National Government'. And until the Great Reform Act of 1832 we find the Corporation sending outspoken – even insolent – demands to the king and his ministers: to stop the war, to feed the people, in praise of Burdett, to condemn the butchers of Peterloo, to support injured Queen Caroline, to reform the House of Commons on Corporation lines.[9]

A radical ratepayer democracy did not, however, render the City immune from the besetting sin of London local government in the nineteenth century. As if byzantine structures, incomplete or overlapping jurisdictions and inadequate powers and resources were not enough, there was corruption in all its grubby forms. It reached from top to bottom of London local administration. In this, London government reflected London life.

The City's Mayor and Corporation had long been notorious for gluttonous junketing at London's expense and appetites didn't diminish in the nineteenth century. Even worse was jobbery, where Common Councilmen let lucrative contracts to their friends and relatives without competition and at high prices. And the elections of Lord Mayor, sheriffs and paid officials were routinely attended by 'bribery and corruption' – indeed the City's lawyers considered bribery no offence in law at Common Hall elections.[10]

Outside the City things were no better. The Westminster Commissioners of Sewers were in thrall to big contractors, allowed to set their own prices without competition 'year after year'. The poor law guardians of St Luke's let contracts to their shopkeeper friends without tendering at prices sometimes 40 per cent over what the market would supply. Two parish officials of St Leonard's Shoreditch were discovered fraudulently converting an order for paupers' shoes to secure four pairs of 'best wax' for themselves. And for years a baker who was poor law guardian to St Margaret's and St John's Westminster supplied bread to the workhouse, naming his own price. Small wonder that truculent paupers, starved of their due deserts, blamed the '"supposed cupidity and mercenary tricks"' of the overseers, responding with '"outbreakings of violence"'. In aristocratic St James's Westminster in 1808, the rate collector absconded with over £10,000 – an extraordinary fortune – and was arrested by Bow Street officers in Truro. And at lowly Bethnal Green around the same time the intricate machinations of Joseph Merceron became the stuff of legend. Vestryman, parish treasurer, tax commissioner, justice of the peace and publican (so especially interested in licensing sessions, as we have seen), rack-renting landlord, sword in the side of the suffering rector, who tried unsuccessfully to curb his depredations, Merceron was the robber baron of this substantial suburban township. Imprisoned for misappropriating parish funds in 1818, he was back at the helm by 1820. Never short of supporters, he died reputedly worth £300,000, though appearing always to be '"in poor circumstances"', and the local reputation that survived him was as a public-spirited worthy.[11]

The hopelessly muddled local government of London, hidebound and venal, was catastrophically ill-equipped to face the challenges of the early nineteenth century. These came swift and potent. Most stemmed from the massing of people in the metropolis, an exaggerated instance of a national phenomenon. Between 1801 and 1831 the population of London inside what would become the county boundary rose from 959,000 to 1,655,000, an increase of 73 per cent. Many of the newcomers crowded into old London immediately round the City. So the population of the area defined by the Bills of Mortality of 1626 rose from 566,000 to 748,000. London contained 92,000 more inhabited houses in 1831 than thirty years before, a rise of over two-thirds.[12]

The totally inadequate response of the Metropolitan Courts of Sewers led to conditions we've already glimpsed. And the London water supply fell far short of the rising population's needs for drinking, cooking, washing and sewage disposal: just over half London's houses had access to any piped supply in 1810 and still less than two-thirds in 1821.[13] The flood of people into London pressed in other directions too. The perception of rising crime and lawlessness helped lead, as we have seen, to parish government losing its ancient police and night-watch role from 1829. But the parishes were overwhelmed by the tasks still left to them. Primitive road surfaces turned into impassable ruts, pavements were neither swept, repaired nor kept free from obstruction, sometimes not laid at all. The law here was improved by Michael Angelo Taylor's Metropolitan Paving Act of 1817, and by the 1830s London proudly claimed to be better paved than Paris. But in many poorer parts of London the act was a dead letter for lack of means or lack of will.[14]

Efforts were made in 1818 and 1819 to do something about the lack of will. The rampant democracy of some open vestries – capable, like Bethnal Green's, of capture by corrupt oligarchs – seemed a vice to be suppressed, like seditious speeches, meetings and newspapers. Sturges Bourne's Vestries Act of 1818 and Poor Relief Act of 1819 sought order in local administration and prudence in parish expenditure. They relied on taking power from the ratepayers as a body and removing it to a select vestry or executive committee on the lines of St George's Hanover Square, where Bourne had been a vestryman. A select vestry had to be voted in. But the Vestries Act gave rich property owners up to six votes each, and some open vestries welcomed the chance to put their affairs on a sounder footing. There were benefits for a time. But by the end of the 1820s the new bodies had led to as many abuses as they had been formed to correct. Spiteful battles in St Giles, St Paul's Covent Garden and several other places signalled a return to ratepayer democracy. And in 1831 plural voting was abolished by John Cam Hobhouse's Vestries Act, restoring almost all the Sturges Bourne select vestries to their previous open forms.[15]

All this infighting proved a mere distraction from London's real problems. For the massing of people brought disease and death. And it was a feature of the times that when confronted by metropolitan mortality on a fearsome scale, London local government's first priority was the state of the streets and not what festered beneath them. Epidemics year after year brought Londoners low: louse-borne typhus fever hit the poorest districts hard in 1816–19; there was a typhoid epidemic after the long dry summer of 1826; influenza or 'catarrhal fever' struck in 1803, 1831 and 1833; measles in 1808, 1810, 1816 and 1824; rabies in 1830; and smallpox in 1801–3, 1805–10, 1812, 1817 and 1825. In and around these fearful outbreaks infant diarrhoea, costing thousands of lives, was endemic in London year on year.[16]

In November 1830 Charles Greville noted in his diary rumour of a 'sort of plague . . . raging in Russia' and a year later Asiatic cholera made its first appearance in north-east England, spreading to London in February 1832. For the first time government recognised the inadequacy of local arrangements to deal with a potential killer on this scale. It established a Central Board of Health for the whole country and encouraged local boards led by the clergy (this, after all, an act of God) and involving medical men. But the boards floundered in apathy as soon as it became clear that cholera was a disease of the slums. When fear left London the health boards evaporated in its wake.[17]

What did not disappear, though, was parsimony. And the critical push for change in London local government was one more symptom deriving from the massing of population. That was the ever-rising numbers of the poor. And how best to pay for them.

'Morality Outraged and Deranged', 1834–1854

The principle of compulsory assessment of ratepayers to raise money for the local poor was established by the Poor Relief Act of 1603, still law in 1800. But just who the London ratepayers should relieve was a question that became ever more troubled as 'strangers' flocked to the metropolis in unprecedented numbers. The stream of beggars and vagrants, the ragged regiments of orphaned or abandoned children left, as it were, at the vestry door, the aged widows and decrepit industrial workers too old to wield a spokeshave or weave fine silk, all fell as paupers on the ratepayers to relieve out of their own mean pickings. Many, of course, were not 'local' people at all. And the ratepayers knew or suspected that not a few of the calls on their cash were fraudulent, and that their money was wasted or worse by those in charge of poor law machinery.

Pressure on ratepayer pockets weighed heaviest from 1817 to 1820, when the Sturges Bourne acts sought to provide some assistance, and again from 1825 to 1832.[18] High poor rates, though, never indicated proper aid to the poor themselves. There were, it is true, instances of luxurious and obstreperous paupers standing out for white bread and flock beds. But – in general – the treatment of the poor in London was scandalously bad throughout the nineteenth century. That was as true for the years before the New Poor Law as after.

Perhaps the plight of one defenceless group might stand for many. That was pauper children. We have already witnessed as one of the most piteous social problems of the age the desperate straits of those London children whom the poor law passed by, left to fend for themselves in doorways and common lodging houses. But the condition of those in parish care was scarcely better, sometimes worse. 'Parish apprentices' were set to work at a tender age. Some thousands were sent '"by waggon loads at a time"' to factory masters in the North. It was said in 1807 that mill owners in Lancashire and Yorkshire took the largest numbers of their pauper children from London and Westminster workhouses, one contract apparently undertaking to '"receive one idiot with every twenty sound children"'. In 1816 the law was tightened to stop children under nine from being sent more than forty miles from London.[19]

But pauper apprentices didn't have to be sent far to receive dreadful treatment. In 1803 Ann Harris, an eleven-year-old put out by the Bishopsgate Without overseers to Ann Brown, a pin-head maker, was thrashed by her mistress with a cane and a lead weight, had pins run into her arms and body, was beaten about the head with steel files until two broke and was tortured 'on the hob of the grate, with a log of wood suspended from her feet, and her arm extended up the chimney, holding a brick-bat'. And in 1829 came the terrible murder of Frances Colpit, about nine years old, apprenticed with five other children by St Martin's-in-the-Fields workhouse to Esther Hibner the elder, a tambour (silk embroidery) worker. All the children were starved, forced to pick morsels from the waste Hibner gave to her dog. They had no bed but lay on the floor with one blanket to cover them. Frances was specially picked on – frequently beaten and suspended upside-down in a pail of slops so that she half-drowned: '"Damn her, dip her again and finish her"', Ann Robinson, on trial with Hibner and her daughter Esther, was heard to say. Frances died of starvation and an abscess on her lung. Another, Margaret Howse, also died. Hibner was hanged at the Old Bailey in front of a huge exulting crowd, mostly women.[20]

But it was not to correct abuses such as these that the Poor Law Amendment Act of 1834 was made law. This was an act to protect the ratepayer from the importunate and feckless pauper. Doing so involved the second great central intervention in London's local government following the New Police of five years earlier. The New Poor Law established government commissioners for England and Wales to issue instructions on the relief to be given to the poor. Those instructions would be implemented, with some important scope for freedom of action, by local Boards of Guardians, set up for single large parishes or 'unions' of smaller ones. All resident justices (including many clergymen) were automatically members of the boards for their areas. The remainder of the guardians were elected on a ratepayer and freeholder franchise, including women. London was divided into thirty-six Boards of Guardians, rising to thirty-nine and then falling to thirty from 1869 till the end of the century. Ten, governed by Incorporated Boards of Guardians, resented (and sometimes ignored) the pretensions of the Poor Law Commissioners to influence local affairs, among them important parishes like St Pancras, Marylebone, Islington and St George's Hanover Square. They wouldn't come under complete central control till 1867.[21]

Each board was responsible for its own workhouse, nurseries for infants (often put in the country), pauper school and infirmary. The workhouse was generally to be offered an applicant for relief rather than a money dole or help in kind, like bread and coals. 'Out-relief' was discouraged, especially for the 'able-bodied' temporarily unemployed by trade depression or sickness. It was thought to spawn dependency and stifle self-help. And in poor districts an economic downturn would mean that most ratepayers were 'little better off than the applicants for help'. For those in the workhouse, conditions were to be 'less eligible' than those the poorest labourer might obtain outside. And besides a starveling diet were rules designed to make life in 'the house' as uncomfortable as possible. Married couples, for instance, were separated. When, in 1847, the law was relaxed to allow couples over sixty to stay together, even twenty years later it was a concession 'very rarely acted on in London'. Deterrence, punishment and parsimony were the watchwords of the new regime. And the poor of London went on suffering as they always had.[22]

So the major shift in London local government of 1834 had nothing to do with the cholera of two years before and everything to do with ratepayer outrage as the cost of poor relief edged upwards. The New Poor Law did indeed drive down ratepayer costs dramatically for a time.[23] But in London the burden on ratepayers of other tasks proved remorseless. For the next twenty years the pressure of numbers cranked up relentlessly. Between 1831 and 1851 the population of London increased by over 700,000 (42.7 per cent) to 2,362,000. Another 150,000 crowded into the slums of old London, despite road clearances and the commercialisation of the City and its outskirts. The 1840s also saw the famine influx from Ireland, weighing most heavily on St Giles and Whitechapel.

There is much evidence to indicate that the condition of London and the Londoner deteriorated between 1832 and 1848, when cholera threatened its second, most devastating appearance. The influenza epidemic of 1837 brought scenes of mass funerals – no fewer than 1,000 on a single Sunday, the *Annual Register* thought – that even the oldest Londoner had never witnessed before. Yet that was at a time when the condition of the inner-London burial grounds was so scandalously foul that pressure to close them entirely was becoming irresistible. And despite investment in London sewerage, the capital seemed no better off for filth. The Metropolitan Sanitary Commission of 1847–8 heard that in Lambeth the courts and alleys where the poor lived 'are not improved; indeed, being more crowded, they are even worse, and the quantity of decomposing animal and vegetable matter about them is greater'. The same was said for St Giles (especially Church Street) and the 'lower parts of Westminster'. And John Phillips, chief surveyor to the Westminster Court of Sewers, battling insuperable problems with inadequate means, let his frustration spill out in evidence to the commissioners.

I have visited very many places where filth of all kinds was lying scattered about the rooms, vaults, cellars, areas, and yards, so thick and so deep, that it was hardly possible to move for it. I have also seen in such places human beings living and sleeping in sunk rooms, with filth from overflowing cesspools exuding through and running down the walls and over the floors . . . I should be ashamed to keep pigs in so much filth as I have seen human beings living amongst.

It is utterly hopeless to expect to meet with either civilization, benevolence, religion, or virtue, in any shape, where so much filth and wretchedness abounds . . . Morality, and the whole economy of domestic existence, is outraged and deranged by so much suffering and misery.[24]

What of the poor themselves in the midst of all this? It was a 'popular notion' of the time that the poor 'love dirt' and 'cannot be trained to habits of cleanliness'.[25] In fact the evidence to the contrary was both overwhelming and pathetic. We are reminded here of the thirst for self-improvement through literacy and education, the readiness to adopt from missionaries the acquirements of civility (if not the religion that went with them), even the guarded acceptance of the New Police and their promise of order and protection of the weak. And some years before a 'sanitary police' joined the preventive and missionary police in a fine-meshed intervention in the lives of the London poor, the poor themselves demonstrated their own hatred of dirt and their desire to escape from it if only they could.

Most eloquent testimony of all was the phenomenal success of London's public baths and washhouses, first established tentatively in the 1840s. The idea originated in a meeting at the Mansion House, the Lord Mayor's palace, in 1844. Among the prime movers was the Bank of England director William Cotton, he of the Bethnal Green churches. This would prove a happier venture. The first baths, a small affair, were opened in 1846 at George Street, Euston Square. But the 'Model' public baths and washhouses were those opened in 1847 in Goulston Square, Whitechapel, a few minutes west of Flower and Dean Street. A Baths and Washhouses Act that same year enabled vestries to build and run similar enterprises. By 1851 seven parishes had persuaded their ratepayers in a referendum to take advantage of the act, though some proposals were voted down. A teetotal coalwhipper told Henry Mayhew that every fortnight he went to Goulston Square for a warm bath costing a penny: '"This is one of the finest things that ever was invented for the working man. Any persons that use them don't want beer."'[26]

He was not alone. At George Street in 1848 no fewer than 111,788 baths and 246,760 laundry washes were bought by the poor. In 1850 over half a million bathers went to the three baths at Whitechapel, St Martin's-in-the-Fields and Marylebone. And if it be thought that baths only attracted the artisan class, the Glasshouse Yard refuge for the destitute and homeless poor near London Docks proves us wrong. It opened a bath and laundry in May 1845 and in its first year gave 27,662 baths and 35,840 washes.[27]

But all the baths in Christendom couldn't stop cholera reaching London again in the pandemic of 1848–9. It remained a disease of the poor but this time it killed nearly 15,000 Londoners, almost three times as many as 1832. Among them were 150 starved and neglected pauper children at a private 'home' in Tooting run by Peter Drouet, who farmed at any one time the astonishing number of 1,400–1,600 children on behalf of various Metropolitan Boards of Guardians. An inquest jury at Holborn returned a verdict of manslaughter against him but Drouet was acquitted at the trial.[28]

Among all the horror, just as in 1832, government once more realised that the nation's defences needed buttressing, London's most of all. Its local government had not been amended in 1835, as had that of other cities and towns. The Public Health Act 1848 exempted London because it had no mechanism to take advantage of its powers. And the General Board of Health, managing the nation's crisis from Whitehall, had most of its time taken up by those places that could operate the act. Two changes in London, however, were of importance. The seven Courts of Sewers outside the City were merged into a single Metropolitan Commission of Sewers, up and running from 1849. But the more important change emerged in a surprising quarter. The City Sewers Act of 1848, for all the Corporation's antique ways, began to build a model sanitary administration in the City of London. It would be seven years ahead of the rest of the capital in doing so.[29]

The Sewers Act was radical – for London. It outlawed all new private sewers, vesting old ones in a modernised City Commission of Sewers. House owners could be ordered to drain to a sewer and the City was given wide powers to condemn cesspools or privies that were a nuisance. For the first time there were powers to inspect and cleanse common lodging houses and suppress overcrowding in them. And there was a general power to cleanse any house certified as unwholesome or filthy. All this and more would be enforced by a staff of inspectors of nuisances (later called sanitary inspectors); and to supervise them the Commissioners of Sewers could appoint a medical officer of health. The City's Act leaned heavily on similar legislation adopted by Liverpool Corporation in 1846. Liverpool had appointed the famous Dr William Henry Duncan as their officer of health a year later. The City of London would not be left behind. And in a fierce contest, no doubt with bribes and counter-bribes on the side, it elected John Simon, FRCS, to be its medical officer at a salary of £500 a year. Just thirty-two, Simon – of London Huguenot origins, he insisted on pronouncing his surname in the French manner – would become the most famous medical man of the age.[30]

The City, then, was to have the first sanitary police in London. For the rest of the century it would be the best. Simon and his six inspectors concentrated first on suppressing the City's 5,000–6,000 cesspools and enforcing proper drainage – all flowing into the Thames, of course, but at least getting it from under people's feet. The City's courts and alleys were 'systematically visited', scavenged daily and properly paved. And the City's poorest houses were frequently inspected room by room for nuisances. Some 7,000 houses, rising during epidemics to 9,000, were subject to this 'methodical sanitary superintendence'. Simon's weekly and annual reports to the City Commissioners created an extraordinary sensation. Some were printed verbatim in *The Times*. And when the disappearance of cholera in 1849 allowed public health to slip from political consciousness, Simon's reports were one medium sustaining popular interest.[31]

Outside the City sanitary matters stalled. In 1851 an act provided for the registration and supervision of common lodging houses in London outside the City, the function given (in the absence of any alternative) to the Metropolitan Police. This was a sanitary act that recognised the traditional linkage between common lodging houses and crime. But it also built on an early function of the New Police that had by this time largely fallen into disuse, for in the early days 'the superior officers' were generally 'appointed inspectors of nuisances under the local [improvement and paving] Acts'.[32] The police also retained through the century the unpleasant duty of removing stray dogs from London's streets during frequent rabies epidemics. And in 1853 an attempt was made to improve the quality of the capital's air with the Smoke Abatement (London) Act, which again fell to the police to enforce. Only factory and workshop emissions were countered, while London's great problem was in fact the domestic grate. Even so, the

police did good work within the limits of their resources and the technological possibilities of the time. Outside police or any other jurisdiction, an act of 1852 sought to impose duties on the metropolitan
water companies to improve the quality and quantity of London water,
but, in the absence of any effective regulator, to little effect.

It seemed an extraordinary dereliction of parliamentary duty almost
twenty years after provincial town government was put on a proper
footing that London remained in the Dark Ages, with little better than
eighteenth-century machinery facing nineteenth-century challenges. The
increasingly vile state of the Thames provided a pungent reminder to
the Houses of Parliament that London's difficulties were fast becoming
literally intolerable. But it would take yet another cholera outbreak in
1853-4, killing over 11,000 and taking some victims just a stone's
throw from fashionable London on the other side of Regent Street, to
help force government's hand at last.

A New Beginning, 1855-1869

The Metropolis Local Management Act ('Sir Benjamin Hall's Act') of
1855 at last devised a multi-functional governing body for the whole
of that part of London which had far outgrown the ancient City. This
was the Metropolitan Board of Works, its title and tasks urged by a
Royal Commission on the City Corporation, reporting in 1854.
Underpinning the MBW a revamped parish government would continue
to administer the local areas of London. Organisation would be along
similar lines to that of the New Poor Law. Twenty-two parishes were
large enough to stand alone as self-acting 'municipal vestries' in their
own right. There were then fifteen district boards of works (like poor
law unions), comprising small parishes whose primary function was to
elect members onto the district board. The numbers of boards and
vestries changed over time as the population of suburban London
swelled ever larger. At the end of the century there would be thirty
'municipal vestries' and twelve district boards.[33]

The municipal vestries could have as many as 120 vestrymen elected
by ratepayers on a household suffrage excluding lodgers. In general,
vestrymen were found from the 'shopocracy' and other lower middle
classes. Even in aristocratic St James's Piccadilly most vestrymen were
'small tradesmen, in the back streets of the parish . . . I think there is

no dignity conferred upon any individual by electing him as a vestryman'. That was generally true but not exclusively. In the early enthusiastic years of public endeavour Henry Hoare the banker was a vestrymen at St Martin's-in-the-Fields and Lord Elcho and the Hon. Frederick Byng at St James's. And the involvement of the parish clergyman, still claiming his ancient right to act as chairman of the vestry, might raise the tone of parochial business. In general, though, the lower-middle-class vestry membership had most in its mind the ratepayers' burdens. Vestry and district board business was run 'Always with too great a regard to economy'. 'They are the class most interested in keeping in check proper and legitimate improvements.'[34]

From the beginning, then, there was a contradiction built into the new parish government of London. Bodies elected on a parsimonious ratepayer ticket had new powers and duties on City lines. In particular, they had to appoint a medical officer of health and inspectors of nuisances, and a surveyor to secure paving and lighting. All these cost the ratepayers dear, either through the rates or through being forced to pay for drainage and other improvements to their property.

Each municipal vestry and each district board elected one or two of their number onto the London-wide MBW. So its forty-five members were indirectly elected and not held to account by electors for their action on the board. This was one element in the MBW's enduring unpopularity, despite its achievements over the years. And it could recruit members only from the overwhelmingly petty-bourgeois vestrymen of London. Its more outspoken members lamented the board's inability to attract sufficient men of 'the higher class'. Yet it seems as though the elite of metropolitan vestrymen found their way onto the MBW. In 1861 its membership comprised an architect, three engineers, three barristers, five solicitors, a member of the stock exchange, two builders, a manufacturer, two former civil servants, three law stationers and booksellers, a wharfinger, a surgeon, fourteen in trade or commerce and eight retired from business. Among them were the Lord Mayor, two other City aldermen, four more justices and two MPs, one of whom was the outstandingly able W. H. Smith, the rich bookseller and Conservative politician.[35]

It's also worth pointing out, lest later events obscure the fact, that the board's small permanent staff included some brilliant and honourable men. Joseph Bazalgette was the most eminent engineer of his day and Frederick Marrable a talented London architect. Among its younger staff were Edgar Harper (valuer and land economist, later one of the first lecturers at the London School of Economics) and G. Laurence Gomme (later chief clerk to the London County Council and a historian of note): both were subsequently knighted. And recruitment, even for low-paid posts in the first two decades or so, was from the widest social background: from 'York' Whitworth in the accountant's department, who shocked a newcomer with his 'quite phenomenal lack of culture', to Thomas Bell (Cheltenham College and Exeter College, Oxford), a classics teacher appointed third-class clerk in March 1866, later private secretary to the chairman of the board and then to the chairman of the LCC.[36]

This reform of London government provided a solid foundation on which to rest new machinery to fight old ills. So in 1865, for instance, the MBW seemed the right place to establish a Metropolitan Fire Brigade, fashioned from previous incomplete arrangements that had grown from London's insurance companies and outmoded parish provision. As late as Christmas 1860 a fire at Dickens's *All the Year Round* offices in Wellington Street, the Strand, had summoned the 'Parish Engine', 'like a drivelling Perambulator – *with the Beadle in it* – like an Imbecile Baby. Popular opinion, disappointed in the fire having been put out, Snowballed the Beadle. God bless it!' But the Metropolitan Board's new brigade, under the dashing Irishman Captain Eyre Massey Shaw, became the greatest in the world and Shaw would be knighted for his successes in 1891.[37]

The fresh foundation for London local government cast in relief some of the shortcomings of the New Poor Law of 1834. The great question of the public health embraced not only sewerage, water supply and sanitary inspection but also the treatment of those – most often the poor – sick with fever and contagious. They were the responsibility of the local poor law authorities. Yet the poor law had no overarching London-wide body to match the capacity of the MBW. It would be the last resurgence of cholera – that fatal stimulus to administrative action – which brought this element of the poor law up to date. The cholera outbreak of 1866, especially pernicious in the East End, at last prompted government to provide for regional isolation hospitals at a level above the local guardians, whose workhouses and infirmaries proved so crowded and inadequate that they were themselves a large source of infection.

The Metropolitan Poor Act of 1867 constructed a sort of MBW for the poor law. The Metropolitan Asylums Board (MAB) was funded by a precept on the local rates called the Metropolitan Common Poor Fund. This was the first limited redistribution from rich to poor in London, wealthy districts helping pay for services that would, in the nature of things, benefit poorer parts most. The MAB had sixty members, forty-five elected by the Boards of Guardians and fifteen nominated by central government's Poor Law Board. Its first meeting was at the MBW's offices in Spring Gardens in June 1867, but it soon relocated to its own offices at Norfolk Street, Strand.[38]

The MAB was the first great authority for state hospitals in London – indeed, in England. It had responsibility for fever hospitals and for lunatic asylums for the pauper 'insane' and 'imbeciles', whose only previous sanctuary had been the general workhouse. The MAB moved with exemplary swiftness for those sluggardly times. It opened two giant asylums at Leavesden (Hertfordshire) and Caterham (Surrey) by the end of 1870. Brand-new buildings at Hampstead, Homerton and Stockwell were in place to meet the fearsome smallpox epidemic of 1871–2 that killed nearly 10,000 Londoners. Two more in Deptford and Fulham opened in early 1877. By 1880 more asylums for children and adults were operating at Darenth (Dartford). As early as 1876 a forthright critic of most things municipal in London could declare the Metropolitan Asylums Board 'one of the best if not the very best organization ruling the whole of London for any purpose'. And around the same time the development of the local workhouse infirmary was becoming the most successful part of parish poor law provision, extending the range of public hospitals in London from 1867 faster and further than at any time since the middle of the eighteenth century. Between the MAB and the thirty Boards of Guardians, the local state would own some three-quarters of London hospital beds by 1900, with charitable hospitals large and small providing the remainder.[39]

This improvement in poor law infirmary provision only came about after a number of scandals highlighting the treatment of the sick in the general workhouse. St Pancras in the mid-1850s was the epitome of neglect of the sick poor, though it was much improved apparently by 1862. And from 1864 exposés of appalling treatment of those unlucky enough to have to resort to the guardians filled the columns of the daily press. A couple of notorious deaths from neglect in Holborn and St Giles in 1865 were followed by a series of exposures in the *Lancet*, with more to come in 1867. And the fate of the vagrant, whether begging or thieving from one workhouse to the next or whether (as two-thirds of them were reckoned to be) genuinely tramping for work, became a special focus of press inquiry. With mounting distress caused in part by the economic dislocations of the American Civil War, vagrancy had increased from the early 1860s. The response of the central Poor Law Board was to deter admission to local workhouse casual wards and so cut numbers and 'cure' the tramp problem; or rather, cure it for the ratepayer. Conditions for 'casuals' became even more uncomfortable. 'The bath test' introduced a new element of degradation, men having to bathe in public under the eye of workhouse officials.[40]

A steady trickle of investigations in the papers suddenly came alive with James Greenwood's three revelatory articles for the *Pall Mall Gazette* in January 1866. Greenwood and a friend posed as casuals at the Lambeth workhouse and underwent what for civilised Londoners was little short of purgatory – stripping naked among strangers, plunging into water 'like [a] weak mutton broth' of 'filth, floating and liquefied', lying promiscuously with foul-mouthed men smoking and spitting, and with the threat or promise of secret sex among those sharing their 'doss'.[41]

Greenwood's 'amateur casual' narratives mark a sensational turning point in metropolitan journalism. They had less effect, however, on the poor law. For the rest of the century one scandal would tread close on the heels of another. Little would change to benefit the pauper. The poor fought desperately to keep out of the workhouse and all it stood for. Old Betty Higden in *Our Mutual Friend* (1864–5) had any number of real-life counterparts. '"I'd rather live on a penny a day, I'd rather die in this sorry place, than go to the house,"' a widow told the north London missionary James Hillocks in 1865. She was hungry and cold in a 'wretched hovel', 'being slowly but effectually killed, inch by inch, and day by day'.[42]

Not all local government worked so much against the interests of the poor. Sanitary inspection varied in vigour from place to place, sometimes thorough, sometimes a sham. It depended less on the quality of the men involved than in the numbers appointed and the freedom to act with which penny-pinching vestries endowed them. Generally, though, when act they did, the poor saw them as on their side against landlord neglect. Only in the enforcement of weak overcrowding powers, largely ignored because of the hardship an eviction would cause, did the sanitary police provoke bitterness and anger.

Sanitary inspection involved room-by-room visiting in the poorest areas, just as Simon had initiated in the City. In Whitechapel in 1870, for instance, 'Every house in our district has been systematically visited.' Entry was rarely refused, 'for every poor person in my district is exceedingly anxious to admit the sanitary officer'. And after ten years' or so routine inspection in this poor area, with thousands of cesspools closed and houses drained, a member of the Whitechapel District Board of Works thought he could detect a notable difference in the people.

I do think that the public mind even in its lowest grade is being educated to a better condition . . . I saw in a back street an advertisement by a landlord, to the effect that the supply of water was abundant in his houses of the poorest description . . . I am quite certain that a few years ago such a thing would not have been mentioned as recommendatory to the premises. But the poor people themselves are becoming more alive to their wants in sanitary matters than they were before.[43]

Here again we find that desire for betterment we saw evidenced with the spread of baths and washhouses. Most – not all – struggled against insuperable odds not of their own making to maintain some basic level of humanity. William Rendle, Medical Officer of Health of St George-the-Martyr Southwark, who resigned in frustration at his vestry's parsimony and jobbery – eight vestrymen were owners of 'poor property', 'some of them obstructors' of sanitary work – told how he visited a court that had been without water for nearly two years. 'I saw a woman on her knees washing up privy soil from the yard. Those are the people who are charged with being unclean.'[44]

But if sanitary inspection was almost universally welcomed as a means of help and improvement – examples of sanitary inspectors being assaulted by tenants appear to be non-existent or at least very rare – one great reform in the final third of the century would prove more problematic.

'A Genuine Zeal', 1870–1888

Of all the great civilising influences on the Londoner in the nineteenth century compulsory schooling was the most momentous. It was a monument to procrastination. Its delay in coming was almost intolerable after more than fifty years' public concern about London's ignorant poor and their over-representation in prisons and juvenile reformatories. And its arrival marked more than fifty years' failed attempts by private bodies and organised religion to carry out a function better filled by the local state.

The Elementary Education Act of 1870 was administered by an entirely new arm of local government, the School Board for London, more popularly known as the London School Board (LSB). Interest in the new body was phenomenal. And 1870 might mark the true arrival of party politics in London local government, as both political and religious influences combined and manoeuvred to have their say over how and what the London child should be taught in school. Elected on ratepayer suffrage, voting on proportional representation, women ratepayers were allowed not only the vote but to stand as candidates too. Far ahead of its time, the LSB became a triumph of democratic representation. 'The great event of to-day for this country,' wrote *The Times* on the morning of the poll, 'will be the election of the first London School Board. No equally powerful body will exist in England outside Parliament, if power be measured by influence for good or evil over masses of human beings.' From the outset the board was a microcosm of metropolitan talent. Some of the richest men in London (like Samuel Morley, Charles Mudie, W. H. Smith) would sit over the years alongside proponents of London labour like the radical journalist Hepworth Dixon or the Christian socialist Stewart Headlam. And prominent intellectual men like T. H. Huxley, the scientist, and the educationist Edward Lyulph Stanley would find themselves more than matched by a long list of bluestockings and prominent female suffragists: the educationist Helen Taylor, the poet Augusta Webster, Dr Elizabeth Garrett Anderson, Dr Florence Fenwick Miller ('Young, good-looking, brilliant' and packing halls in Bethnal Green 'to suffocation when she lectured on physiology').[45]

The first board sat at the City's Guildhall on 15 December 1870. There were forty-nine members, just two of them women, though that proportion would grow in subsequent elections. The board set up offices at New Bridge Street, City, and later enlarged to fifty-five members. In these early years religious sectarianism was submerged in 'a genuine zeal' for education first and Bible instruction second. The task was huge. Some 455,000 London children needed elementary education in the LSB's area (what would become the county boundary), of whom 176,000 (39 per cent) were receiving no education at all or a 'mere pretence' of one. In addition, London was short of over 100,000 school places if every child who should be in school was to find a desk.[46]

From December 1871 the school board required parents to send to school all children aged five to thirteen. Neglect or refusal to do so would result in prosecution, fines, even prison. But given the shortage of schools, compulsion had to be phased in, district by district, as places became available. Emergency measures put schools under railway arches, in houses, in basements under workshops. The shortage was worst in the East End. It was there that most of the first board schools were built, in that distinctive three-decker style that eventually emerged from the pencil of the board's architect, E. R. Robson. First of all was the Old Castle Street Board School, Whitechapel, ready from 1873. By the end of March 1875 no fewer than fifty-three schools had been completed for over 50,000 children, and another eighty were under construction. The least efficient ragged and voluntary schools were taken over, and grants paid to the best of the church schools to help them reach board standards. This was a display of municipal self-confidence and energy matched only by the MAB in the century so far.[47]

The LSB's enforcers of compulsory schooling were the school board visitors. Here was yet another imposition of house-to-house visitation on the poor. So ubiquitous were they in the poorest districts of London that 'School Board Man' remained the popular name for the school attendance officer seventy years and more after the board had ceased to exist. By 1877 there were 206 visitors, mostly men (often of a military background) but a few women among them. In 1891 there were 271. They were never popular. Children in the poorest families were needed for childcare, housework, errands and odd jobs. Earnings from child labour in workshops, at home and in shop employment, even begging, kept families from the workhouse, and no priority was greater than that. Compulsory full-time schooling cut across a culture where children were an economic resource. Education, for all its acknowledged value, had to play second fiddle. Even for those who wished to attend, the cost of boots and clothes to cover bare nakedness was beyond the poorest of all.[48]

So school board visitors were abused and insulted '"in the most dreadful language"'. Occasionally they visited in pairs for protection. Things got better as compulsion bedded down decade by decade, but even at the end of the century school attendance still showed a significant shortfall at 81.2 per cent. In those early years, too, assaults by the roughest parents and children on board school teachers were 'commonplace'. Although resistance never entirely abated, there's no doubt it was worst in the 1870s when the most intractable elements within the London working classes were dragged into school. For that generation compulsory education had come too late.[49]

The LSB marked a huge expansion in London's public sphere and a consequent diminution of charitable and religious endeavour in the life of the metropolis: 1870 was the moment when the balance tipped from Church to state in the organisation of public affairs. For the rest of the century London local government would grow in confidence.

Partly, too, that was a recognition of early problems overcome. So drainage and the worst of the London nuisances were conquered by 1870, twenty-five years' effort by MBW and vestry government making John Phillips's Westminster just a thing of vile memory. Now attention could turn to the irredeemable condition of much old housing, with primitive slum-clearance measures in place from 1875, and to the far more intractable problem of overcrowding. Burial grounds shut up in the 1840s were resurrected by vestries and district boards as public gardens and recreational spaces in the 1870s. Public baths and washhouses blossomed all over poor London. Public libraries, the first opened far ahead of its time in 1856 by the combined parish of St Margaret and St John, Westminster, couldn't become a local priority until matters of life and death had been attended to first. But in the 1880s they were a passionate object of local patriotism, later aided by the charitable endeavours of John Passmore Edwards and Andrew Carnegie. Wandsworth's public library was the next to follow Westminster's in 1883, and the revival was first of all suburban in impetus. But by 1891 twenty-eight local authorities had built libraries or were in the process of constructing them, including poor districts like Christ Church Southwark, Shoreditch, Clerkenwell and Bermondsey.[50]

Infant life protection, the supervision of explosives, the organisation of tramway routes and operators, the production and distribution of electricity were among new tasks entrusted to London government in this period. One important function, though – the police – stayed firmly outside local government despite some advocates of restoration of the local link from the 1860s if not earlier. By 1888, just before the LCC would make more vocal and convincing claims, a local democrat could complain, 'The action of the Imperial Government in keeping the

Metropolitan Police in the hands of the Home Office is a very serious infraction of the rights of the London people.'[51] But that claim fell on deaf ears. And would for more than a century to come.

Besides the LSB's noble efforts, the other great success of local government in this period came from an unlikely direction: the City Corporation. The City of London went through fluctuating fortunes in the nineteenth century. Its absurdities were manifold and its neglect at times abominable. Newgate and the debtor prisons, the vile excesses of Smithfield Market, the delay in removing Temple Bar, the state of the Thames under its stewardship, its resistance to change that seemed to hold back better local government in London, the ignorant pomposity of aldermen magistrates like Sir Peter Laurie, Guildhall gluttony and the taint of jobbery – all these made justified targets for radical contempt. And because outrage found voices of unparalleled force, most notably that of *The Times* and of Charles Dickens, the real value of the Corporation to London in the nineteenth century has been obscured. In fact we've already glimpsed numerous instances: street improvements (including Holborn Viaduct), Thames bridges, the City police, eventually a new prison and cattle market, and the first sanitary inspection in London. And perhaps its greatest achievement of all: the preservation for Londoners in perpetuity of open space wrenched from landlord enclosure and the house-builder. A lawsuit brought by the Corporation in 1871 against various lords of the manor trying to enclose Epping Forest eventually resulted in 5,600 acres saved for the public and opened in 1882. Significant acquisitions at Burnham Beeches and Coulsdon Common were opened in 1883 and there were other smaller schemes in this period at Highgate Wood, Queen's Park, West Ham Park and West Wickham Common.[52]

In general, though, London local government in the 1880s disappointed public expectations. Some problems may have been solved but opinion was impatient of others now coming to the fore. So cholera had disappeared from London. But smallpox, rabies, measles, scarlet fever, diphtheria, whooping cough, typhoid and tuberculosis were all endemic in the 1880s and would be for the rest of the century. In 1888, too, frustration with the modest achievements of thirty years or so of sanitary administration turned to bitter indignation. Daily stories of horrors from Whitechapel revealed living conditions 'neglected by those whose duty it was to make the surroundings of the poor at least healthy and safe by a fitting supply of light, air, and water'. And each week through the 1880s brought its miserable crop of coroners' jury verdicts condemning London poor law authorities for ignoring the needs of starving poverty – ninety-five in 1880, for instance.[53]

Despite manifestations of municipal pride in new town halls and public meeting rooms, and despite substantial achievements in sanitation especially, the image of London local government in the 1880s was generally tarnished. It received no bouquets from the Royal Commission on the Housing of the Working Classes of 1884–5, with famous men like the Marquess of Salisbury, Samuel Morley, Cardinal Manning, even the Prince of Wales among its number. Its inquiry was intended to be national and wide-ranging. But it spent much of its time pursuing the byways of metropolitan malfeasance and inaction, led there by its chairman Charles Wentworth Dilke, MP for Chelsea, president of the Local Government Board and himself once a local vestryman. Much fire was turned on St Pancras, St Luke's (Finsbury) and Clerkenwell. Fourteen of the seventy Clerkenwell vestrymen were said to be 'interested in bad or doubtful property'. How much influence they actually wielded against reform was disputed by those who knew best. But the lurid glare of the royal commission's examination left public opinion understandably scandalised.[54]

Worse was to come. After nearly thirty years' effort the Metropolitan Board of Works had done great things for London. Its achievements, according to a robust commentator in 1888, 'must have far exceeded the expectations of those who were responsible' for its creation. Even in 1907 its main drainage scheme and embankment were still 'the finest thing that modern London has to show'. When it faltered, as it sometimes did, then government was frequently as much to blame as the board. When imagination or courage failed at the cry of extravagant spending, the MBW saw over its shoulder the spectre of the London ratepayer and his empty purse. Within the limitations of its time it had done well.[55]

But it could have done better. For elements in the board were irredeemably corrupt. This was, indeed, one of the limitations of the time. The standards of even late Victorian public life were lax and low and largely uncodified. And much of the work of the MBW inevitably encountered that fatal combination of property owners, speculators and predatory professionals (architects, surveyors, valuers, solicitors), who could spot the main chance where most were blind.

In 1888 the bubble burst. At the eye of the scandal was Frederick

William Goddard, the board's chief valuer and deputy to the superintending architect, George Vulliamy. Goddard had joined the MBW's staff in 1862 as temporary assistant in the architect's department earning £3 3s a week. A year later he was made permanent. By 1873 he was chief assistant surveyor and valuer and in 1882 his salary was raised to £1,000 a year. His salary, though, was academic. A clever and amusing colleague – he once sent to measure Buckingham Palace a credulous messenger who was only deterred at the point of a bayonet – Goddard combined Sunday preaching in a nonconformist chapel with a legendary talent for telling blue stories. 'He had the best furnished house in Brixton, and knew how to entertain.' He could afford it. From 1868 if not before he had been soliciting and receiving bribes on a large scale. A favourite trick was to tip the wink to developers to buy up property soon to be affected by street improvements or slum clearance and then give them more in compensation than the London ratepayer should justly have paid. The crash came over something similar. With 'Tommy' Robertson, Vulliamy's other deputy on the architectural side, Goddard let a prime site at the Piccadilly Circus end of the new Shaftesbury Avenue to an entrepreneur called Villiers. The lease premium and rent were much less than the market would bear. Villiers's architect was Alderman Saunders, a member of the MBW. And Goddard had already been receiving £50 a quarter from Villiers since 1878, when Goddard helped him rent from the MBW the London Pavilion music hall, acquired for demolition as part of Shaftesbury Avenue. The pickings here were rich indeed. When Villiers sold on the site lease in 1886 he paid Goddard £1,000 in cash and £5,000 in debentures. Londoners were thought to have been cheated of £20,000 on the deal.[56]

'From Cradle to Grave', 1889–1899

By 1888 the MBW's demise was already foreshadowed. There had been years of frustrated campaigns for reform of the 1855 structure at both vestry and central levels. Now the Local Government Act 1888 provided the opportunity for a directly elected county council for London. Elections for the first London County Council took place in January 1889. On 21 March the new council expelled the MBW from Spring Gardens. Discovering that the unrepentant board was preparing to let contracts to dig the Blackwall Tunnel rather than leave them to the new body, government ordered the dissolution of the MBW eleven days sooner than planned.[57]

The formation of the LCC gave Londoners an opportunity to follow the footprint put down by the LSB nearly twenty years before in attracting to it a galaxy of metropolitan talents. In fact the first council was dominated by the vestryman class from which many had hoped it would mark a clean break. Even so, it included a clutch of eminent and powerful individuals, among them John Burns (Battersea), the dockers' leader; F. N. Charrington (Mile End), the puritan brewer; J. F. B. Firth, MP (Haggerston), unrivalled expert on London government, who died before the year was out; John Williams Benn (East Finsbury), publisher of the *Cabinet Maker*, who would later lead the dominant Progressive Party on the council; Sir John Lubbock (City), banker and popular scientific writer; and, most impressive of all, Lord Rosebery (City), aristocratic racehorse owner and future Liberal prime minister (1894–5). There were 118 members and nineteen aldermen, among the latter numerous other aristocrats too shy to stand for election. Two women were elected and others chosen as aldermen; but litigation determined that, unlike the LSB, women ratepayers could vote but not stand.[58]

Rosebery was the council's first chairman, and keen to keep party politics out of the council chamber. But some seventy of the 118 councillors were 'Progressives', on the left of the Liberal Party, and the LCC from the outset showed a stronger spirit of party and faction than the indirectly elected MBW had ever done. In this it was a true descendant of the London School Board. On the LCC politics were paramount. And politics combined with religion to make the council chamber at Spring Gardens a cockpit of moral contention.

Over the first decade or so of its existence the LCC would stake out large claims for local government in the life of the Londoner. Its ambitions proved more grandiose than Parliament would bear. It sought control of London's water supply and the Metropolitan Police but got nowhere, although the role of the police in public health did diminish – they lost smoke control to the vestries and district boards in 1891 and control of common lodging houses to the LCC in 1894. By the end of the century John Williams Benn could claim a role for the council as 'guardian – may I say "the guardian angel" –' of the Londoner. 'Indeed it now follows and guards him from the cradle to the grave.'

Among a long list of services, Benn cited council housing, personal health, public safety, transport, heritage, open spaces, municipal music and adult education.[59]

Benn's biblical metaphor was not inapt. More than a trace of sanctimoniousness wafted into the council chamber from low church and chapel. The evangelicals' turn in frustration from fruitless missionary effort to the earthly claim of political power had begun in the LSB. It found new life in the LCC. 'Cleaning up' the music halls and theatres and obliterating public-house licences were expressions of the strong evangelical tendency – the 'nonconformist conscience' – among Progressive Liberals and the early representatives of labour. Their leader was John McDougall, Progressive member for Poplar. 'MuckDougall', some called him. He became 'one of the best-known and worst-abused men in London'. 'The Progressive Boa-Constrictor', as Conservative municipal reform dubbed the overweening desire for state control and stifling moralism of this powerful element in the radical party, saw evil everywhere and sought to squeeze much life out of London in retribution.[60] And the spirit of party quickly seeped into every pore of the council's business, even extending to the treatment of officials. So in 1891 Eyre Massey Shaw, a man-about-town much lionised by society hostesses and at home in high Tory circles, was eased out as chief officer of the fire brigade as guilty by association.

By the 1890s, too, party and sectarianism had begun fatally to undermine the London School Board. The Progressives were the dominant party on the LSB throughout the decade. Bitterness penetrated debate inside the boardroom and social relations outside. At its heart was the teaching of religion. A clique of orthodox Christians on the board wished London schoolchildren to be taught 'the Divinity of Christ and the doctrine of the Trinity' and so 'transform Bible instruction into the teaching of dogma . . .' According to the Rev. Stewart Headlam, a Progressive anti-puritan who opposed the dogmatists, it was religious controversy '"which killed the Board."'[61]

These elements of fanaticism on the LSB and the LCC, diversions though they proved from Londoners' real problems, at least could claim to be the product of democracy. The operation of the poor law in London, however, with all its woeful shortcomings, was run primarily by Whitehall command and control. Local Boards of Guardians could magnify or minimise oppressions but the system was government's own. Just how rotten it was Charles Booth showed in the 1890s. He calculated that

30.7 per cent of all Londoners were in poverty, 'living under a struggle to obtain the necessaries of life and make both ends meet; while the "very poor" [about 8 per cent] live in a state of chronic want'. In all, this made up nearly 1.3 million people. Yet in the 1890s the average proportion of those receiving any official relief at all was around just 2.7 per cent. That was some 122,000 people, fewer than one in ten of those below Booth's poverty line. About two-thirds were forced to wear recognisable workhouse garb ('brown coats and corduroy trousers' in Fulham apparently) and obey workhouse rules. Restriction of out-relief went furthest in the East End, but Booth's verdict on the effects was sour: 'The people are no less poor, nor much, if at all, more independent. There are fewer paupers, but not any fewer who rely on charity in some form.' The harvest of deaths from starvation and neglect rolled on. And workhouse scandals continued to horrify. Epidemic diarrhoea, probably food poisoning, infected 234 inmates of Greenwich workhouse in 1893, killing nine; that same year 130 children at Forest Gate industrial schools were poisoned by bad potatoes and two of them died.[62]

In other elements of London's public services expectations continued to outstrip delivery right through the 1890s. The metropolitan water supply remained irregular in many parts of the city, stopped for periods during each day and subject to long interruptions during drought and hard frost. And the smoke nuisance in London had got worse as the century grew older, smoky fogs ever more common until they peaked in the early 1890s. Vestrydom also failed to keep pace with modern requirements. But there was some improvement after the Local Government Act 1894 extended the franchise to lodgers and abolished the property qualification for vestrymen and guardians. From then on, Charles Booth thought, 'power passed into the hands of the working classes'. London local government was much invigorated, in part through a more strident party politics in the vestry hall.[63]

So in Shoreditch, for instance, a place of 'jobbery and corruption' and 'feasting and drinking' gave way to a Progressive '"model vestry"' with its electricity works powered by a dust incinerator, its public housing and its macadamised and asphalted streets. Similar improvements were noted in infamous Clerkenwell, at Rotherhithe and no doubt elsewhere. An expansion of the parochial sphere was already flourishing through libraries, art galleries, museums and open spaces some years before vestries and district boards were replaced by the new Metropolitan Borough Councils in 1900. And the influence of working men on local Boards of Guardians like Poplar, Bermondsey, Battersea, Camberwell and elsewhere was politicising poor relief, favouring the outdoor poor and beginning to humanise the workhouse.[64]

The LCC of course played its part in the new municipal world emerging at the end of the 1890s. Its outstanding achievement was the Boundary Street Estate on the site of the ghastly Nichol Street area. It continued to build stone by stone on the foundation laid by the MBW, while casting the memory of that body into hellfire. That was unfair. But there was much in the LCC's self-confident, even self-righteous, aggrandisement that appealed to many ratepayers of the time. Despite the cost and the ever-growing draw on their pockets, they saw London improving and took pride in the betterment. And even the LCC's *bête noire*, that unreconstructed palaeolith the City Corporation, played its part in London pride: it opened its flamboyant London icon, Tower Bridge, on 30 June 1894.

But of all the civilising influences on the Londoner at the century's end it seemed the London School Board was the biggest. In 'humanizing' the 'poor and degraded people', wrote Charles Booth, 'the influence of the schools is greater than that of the churches'.[65] He might truly have said, greater than anything else too. Most certainly greater than the poor law. And the police, their reprimands more resented than respected. Greater too than the hospitals, their humanity not yet throwing off the taint of charity and the pauper's dues; and even the ever-enlarging public sphere, civilising the smell and sight of London through sewerage, street improvements, public buildings, transport, greenery, amusements.

So we might fittingly leave the final word to 'the Headmaster of a poor Board School' in inner south London whom Booth's investigators asked for his views on changes in London schoolchildren and their parents between 1882 and 1900. He shows the distance travelled. And the distance still to go.

Parents in relation to teachers: – Much more friendly; hostility, insolence, violence or threats, common in 1882, now hardly ever occur. No personal case experienced for the last three years.

   Parents in relation to children: – Less violent ill-treatment as shown by bruises and wounds; more effort that the children shall appear respectable, especially noticeable among the girls.

Parental responsibility: – An increasing tendency to shirk troublesome duties; to say of a child 'he won't come to school,' or to request punishment of children for insubordination at home.

The boy of 1880 [sic] as compared with the boy of 1900: – Much more docile; insubordination, then endemic, now almost unknown, and if it occurs very likely to be the fault of the teacher. Cheerful and eager now, then often sullen and morose. Relations with teachers generally friendly, often affectionate – no street-calling after them or stone-throwing as there used to. All this, the result of discipline and control at school, reacts beneficially on the home. Truancy almost extinct and when occurring there is generally something in the blood to explain it. Theft rather common, but perhaps more often detected owing to better supervision.

Personal cleanliness: – Greatly improved; verminous cases among boys rare, but among girls almost universal, due to their long hair. Out of thirty examined, twenty-eight required attention. As to dirt it is necessary to distinguish between recent dirt got at play and the ancient kind that gives the tramp smell. Swimming is taught and has a good effect. The really dirty, seen when stripped, would not be allowed to bathe, but would be sent home to wash there first. This now seldom happens. The vermin referred to are lice; bugs are rarely seen; but fleas are common, especially on children coming from homes where there is a baby.

Obscene language: – Common both in the street and in the home, but not common in the school where, if disagreeable words are heard, they are checked.

Obscene conduct: – Very rare. As to boys and girls, the latter are the aggressors.[66]

AFTERWORD: LONDON, 1900

THE most striking feature of London at the end of the nineteenth century was its modernity. So much of it was the product of the century itself. There was the great belt of suburbs in a ring some eight or nine miles from Charing Cross, most less than fifty years old. At the centre, London's ancient core had been in large part done away with, a modernising century showing utter disrespect for what had gone before. The Thames embankments, all the bridges, all the docks were either new or rebuilt almost within living memory. Churches, concert and meeting and exhibition halls, palaces of leisure, museums, galleries and ceremonial spaces were mainly conceived and constructed within a lifetime. Most staggering of all was a revolutionary quickening in the pace of life through steam travel above and below ground and on the river, all entirely new. It seemed as though the whole living edifice was a creation of the past 100 years. To a great extent it was.

Londoners too had been brought up to date. They were used to a faster life where distance was no longer an impediment to commerce or pleasure. They could be cleaner than ever before in their homes and persons. They had wider knowledge and sharper life skills, able to take advantage of an ever-expanding universe of information. They were better behaved, more civil, more respectful of the privacy and needs of others around them. They were more cosmopolitan in outlook, a little more cosmopolitan in make-up. And they took a larger share through the ballot box in the running of their affairs, both local and London-wide. When people looked back over their own lives, or at the fictions and histories from fifty, even thirty, years before, they wondered how they and their city could have come so far, or could ever have had so far to go. There was one overwhelming feeling, and it was this: that there had been stunning progress and that London and Londoners were progressing still.

But as Londoners stood expectantly on the brink of a new century they knew they had not shaken off all the burdens of the past. One in particular the nineteenth century had done little to solve. The vast numbers of London's poor may have made modest advances in housing conditions and risen one step up from the lowest depths of starving degradation. But vast numbers they remained. And the prospect of raising themselves out of their condition in London's chronically low-wage low-demand economy seemed hopeless. This was the great failure of the age. Here lay the roots of incivility and brutality and stunted opportunity, persisting among a minority of Londoners, that daily undermined the rhetoric of progress.

Some problems, too, were the creation of this age of advancement. Many difficulties associated with the massing of people had been overcome but some – air pollution, the separation of home and work, alienation of neighbour from neighbour – had arguably got worse. Religion had been a critical driver in the establishment of order. And a puritan backlash against pleasures like drink or gambling or the stage or (especially) sexuality in all its manifestations frustrated the inclinations and cramped the leisuretime of all Londoners.

So this was a mixed legacy left by the nineteenth century to the twentieth. Much would eventually be valued (like domestic and public architecture) and much taken for granted (like infrastructure in transport and the rest of the public sphere). And the new century would provide its own challenges, unanticipated by what had gone before. But among the enduring themes of the 100 years to come would be Londoners shaking free from mass poverty and pursuing pleasure not order. For there was much unfinished business as one century closed and another opened.

NOTES

Abbreviations

Darlington	*Darlington's London and Environs*
DNB	*Dictionary of National Biography*
ILN	*Illustrated London News*
Industries	*Great Industries of Great Britain*
ISBG	Islington Board of Guardians
LCC	London County Council
LTR	*London Topographical Record*
ODNB	*Oxford Dictionary of National Biography*
PP	Parliamentary Papers
RC	Royal Commissions
RG	Registrar General
SC	Select Committees
Starvation	*Deaths from Starvation (Metropolis)*

Preface

1. Edward Wedlake Brayley and others, *London and Middlesex . . .*, 1810–16, Vol. III, pp. 10–20; Louis Simond, *Journal of a Tour and Residence . . .*, 1817, Vol. I, pp. 99–101; Lord William Pitt Lennox, *Drafts on My Memory*, 1866, Vol. I, pp. 25–9; J. R. Planché, *Recollections and Reflections*, 1872, p. 22; Graham Wallas, *The Life of Francis Place 1771–1854*, 1918, pp. 49–55; M. W. Patterson, *Sir Francis Burdett and His Times (1770–1844)*, 1931, Vol. I, Ch. XII; George Rudé, *Hanoverian London 1714–1808*, 1971, p. 253.

Chapter 1 The Mint: Old London 1800–1855

1. Thomas Miller, Thomas, *Godfrey Malvern*, 1842–3, pp. 226–7. That Miller was writing of the Mint, which he first knew around 1835, see his *Picturesque Sketches of London*, 1852, p. 251.

2. There are many references to the Mint in contemporary literature, but see David Hughson, *London...*, 1805–9, Vol. IV, pp. 498–500; Watts Phillips, *The Wild Tribes of London*, 1856, pp. 95ff., and John Hollingshead, *Ragged London in 1861*, 1861, p. 168, from whom the last two quotes come; Walter Thornbury and Edward Walford, *Old and New London*, 1873–8, Vol. VI, pp. 60ff., where there is a good engraving of Mint Street in 1825. The memories of cholera there in 1832 were given in evidence to the Metropolitan Sanitary Commission 1848 (PP, *Metropolitan Sanitary Commission: First Report of the Commissioners Appointed to Inquire Whether Any and What Special Means May be Requisite for the Improvement of the Health of the Metropolis*, 1848, pp. 108ff., 117–8). The Mint figures largely in Harrison Ainsworth's *Jack Sheppard*, 1839. On the collapse of houses in Lombard Street see *Annual Register 1814*, Chronicle p. 37.

3. Thornbury and Walford, *Old and New London*, Vol. III, p. 32.

4. For the frequent flooding of Pitt's Place, Bankside, in the 1830s see Ned Wright, *Ned Wright*, 1873 pp. 1–2.

5. Edward Wedlake Brayley and others, *London and Middlesex...*, 1810–16, Vol. III, p. 254.

6. Thomas de Quincey, *Autobiography*, 1950, p. 139.

7. *Annual Register 1803*, Chronicle, p. 387.

8. For the drowned sailors see *Annual Register 1811*, Chronicle, p. 89. George Borrow, *Lavengro*, 1851, pp. 192–3, writing of April 1824. See also Louis Simond, *Journal of a Tour and Residence...*, 1817, Vol. II, pp. 342–3, and Cyrus Redding, *Fifty Years' Recollections...*, 1858, Vol. I, pp. 22–3, who both tell of personal experiences shooting the bridge. The best history of old London Bridge remains Gordon Home, *Old London Bridge*, 1931, a massive and elegant study.

9. Borrow, *Lavengro*. The census is quoted in Brayley and others, *London and Middlesex...*, Vol. III, pp. 641–2. A census from October 1810 in Sholto and Reuben Percy, *London*, 1823, Vol. II, p. 136, gives figures one-third lower, so there was clearly considerable seasonal fluctuation.

10. Simond, *Journal of a Tour and Residence...*, Vol. I, pp. 34–5. The number of vehicles is given in Brayley and others, *London and Middlesex...*, Vol. II, pp. 14–15.

11. See Robert Southey, *Letters from England*, 1807, p. 69; Brayley and others, *London and Middlesex...*, Vol. II, p. 5.

12. Simond, *Journal of a Tour and Residence...*, Vol. I, p. 32. For estimates of size see LCC, *London Statistics*, 1912–13 Vol. XXIII, p. xxv.

13. De Quincey, *Autobiography*, p. 135.

14. For Cornwall see William Lovett, *Life and Struggles...*, 1876, Vol. I, p. 24; William Jerdan, *The Autobiography of William Jerdan*, 1852–3, Vol. I, pp. 25–7; Alexander Bain, *Autobiography*, 1904, p. 141 and see also pp. 148–9, 161 and 165 for faster journeys by rail just a few years later.

15. Mrs Lynn Linton, *The Autobiography of Christopher Kirkland*, 1885, Vol. I, pp. 18–9; for overcrowding on coaches see T. Fairman Ordish, 'History of

Metropolitan Roads', *LTR*, 1913, pp. 19–20. A man was killed when the Hertford coach carrying fourteen outside passengers overturned on fresh gravel at Stamford Hill in May 1802: *Annual Register 1802*, Chronicle, p. 392.

16. De Quincey, *Autobiography*, p. 143, spoke of St Paul's. For oil lamps see Brayley and others, *London and Middlesex . . .*, Vol. II, pp. 7–8. Though street lighting by gas was introduced to London in 1807, Brayley writes in 1814 of oil lamps as still the general mode of lighting in London. For London letters see Redding, *Fifty Years' Recollections . . .*, Vol. II, p. 138.

17. Anon [An Amateur]: *Real Life in London . . .*, 1821, Vol. I, p. 3. Jerdan, *Autobiography*, Vol. I, pp. 25–7. Redding, *Fifty Years' Recollections . . .*, Vol. I, p. 45.

18. Reginald R. Sharpe, *London and the Kingdom*, 1899, Vol. III, pp. 218–9. Hughson, *London*, Vol. III, pp. 628–30.

19. Ibid. Brayley and others, *London and Middlesex . . .*, Vol. III, p. 618.

20. Charles Dickens, *Bleak House*, 1852–3, Ch. 1.

21. The description of Butcher Row is in John Thomas Smith, *An Antiquarian Ramble in the Streets of London . . .*, 1846, Vol. I, p. 375. Henry B. Wheatley and Peter Cunningham, *London Past and Present*, 1891, give the date for the removal of Butcher Row as 1813, but for once seem not to be trusted here. Smith gives 1802 and B. Lambert, *The History and Survey of London and Its Environs*, 1806, Vol. III, p. 457, says, 'Butcher-row, which has been lately pulled down . . .' For the Westminster improvements of 1801–6 see Rev. Mackenzie E. C. Walcott, *Westminster*, 1849 p. 24, and *Annual Register 1804*, Chronicle p. 397.

22. Cited in G. E. Bentley, *The Stranger from Paradise*, 2001, p. 257; the Vitruvius quote is in Thomas H. Shepherd and James Elmes, *Metropolitan Improvements*, 1827, p. 7.

23. On these demolitions see Rev. R. H. Hadden, *An East-End Chronicle*, 1880, p. 35 and J. Bird, *The Geography of the Port of London*, 1957 pp. 83–4.

24. See Stirling Everard, *The History of the Gas Light and Coke Company 1812–1949*, 1949, Pt I; Lynda Nead, *Victorian Babylon*, 2000, Pt II. According to Robert Chambers (ed.), *The Book of Days*, 1862–4, Vol. II, Grosvenor Square was about the last place in London to accept gas in 1842, 'a curious instance of aristocratic self-sufficiency' (p. 411).

25. Their full stories are conveniently told in Charles Knight (ed.), *London*, 1841–4, Vol. III, Ch. lxi.

26. John Britton (ed.), *The Original Picture of London*, 1826, p. 202.

27. *Survey of London* Vol. XXV: *The Parishes of St George the Martyr, Southwark and St Mary, Newington*, 1955 p. 46.

28. On Swallow Street see Shepherd and Elmes, *Metropolitan Improvements*, p. 7, and William Hone, *The Table Book*, 1827, pp. 107–8. On the evictions see Rev. J. H. Stallard, *London Pauperism Amongst Jews and Christians*, 1867, p. 271.

29. Shepherd and Elmes, *Metropolitan Improvements*, p. 2.

30. Nash, George IV, Regent's Park and Regent Street are best surveyed in Summerson, *John Nash*, 1935, and *Georgian London*, 1945, and Hermione Hobhouse, *A History of Regent Street*, 1975.

31. Hone, *The Table Book*, pp. 107–8.

32. Britton (ed.), *The Original Picture of London*, p.xiii.

33. William Hone, *The Every-Day Book*, 1825–7, Vol. I, p. 703ff. For statistics

of the demolitions see Charles Capper, *The Port and Trade of London*, 1862, pp. 158–9, and the story of the dock construction Joseph G. Broodbank, *History of the Port of London*, 1921 Vol. I, pp. 153ff. I have seen other statistics quoted, but Capper seems to have been followed most generally.

34. On the pub and the lodging houses see Smith, *An Antiquarian Ramble in the Streets of London . . .*, Vol. I, p. 181. See also the *Survey of London* Vols. XIII and XIV: *The Parish of St Margaret, Westminster (Parts II and III)*, 1930 and 1931; and J. Mordaunt Crook and M. H. Port, *The History of the King's Works*, Vol. VI, *1782–1851*, 1973, pp. 541ff.

35. On the condition of the area before demolition see Brayley and others, *London and Middlesex . . .*, Vol. III, pp. 404–5. The story of the project is in Crook and Port, *The History of the King's Works*, Vol. VI, *1782–1851*, pp. 430ff. They say 131 houses were demolished; at a typical average of nine persons per house that would mean about 1,200 were made homeless.

36. The select committee's judgement of 1831 cited ibid., pp. 176–7.

37. SC, *Second Report from Select Committee on Metropolis Improvement; with the Minutes of Evidence, Appendix and Plans*, 1838 p. iii.

38. Charles C. F. Greville, *A Journal of the Reigns of King George IV and King William IV*, 1875, Vol. II, pp. 279–80 (1 April 1832).

39. SC, *Second Report from Select Committee on Metropolis Improvements; with the Minutes of Evidence, Appendix and Plans*, 1838 p. iv.

40. See B. R. Mitchell and Phyllis Deane, *Abstract of British Historical Statistics*, 1962, pp. 392ff.

41. There is a good description of St Giles before demolition, drawn from the memories of a police officer who knew it from 1844, in Henry Mayhew, *London Labour and the London Poor*, 1861–2 Vol. IV, pp. 299–301; see also Vol. II, pp. 103–4, written about 1851 and describing Church Lane after the clearances nearby. See also Charles Dickens, *The Dent Uniform Edition of Dickens' Journalism*, 1994–2000, Vol. I, pp. 182–3 (February 1835); Flora Tristan, *Flora Tristan's London Journal*, 1840, pp. 134ff.; Knight (ed.), *London*, Vol. I, pp. 254ff., and Vol. III, pp. 263ff.; and SC, *Second Report from Select Committee on Metropolis Improvements; with the Minutes of Evidence, Apendix and Plans*, 1838, qq.. 1235ff. On unclaimed houses left to fall of their own accord see *Annual Register 1842*, Chronicle, pp. 21–2.

42. See Geoffrey Tyack, *Sir James Pennethorne and the Making of Victorian London*, 1992, pp. 50ff.

43. The statistics of Church Lane are cited in M. W. Flinn (ed.), *Report on the Sanitary Condition of the Labouring Population of Great Britain . . .*, 1965, pp. 5–6. Dickens, *The Dent Uniform Edition of Dickens' Journalism*, Vol. II, p. 363 (14 June 1851).

44. *Report of the Commissioner of the Police of the Metropolis for 1874*, p. 85. Thornbury and Walford, *Old and New London*, Vol. III, p. 202. See also Edward C. W. Grey, *St Giles's of the Lepers*, 1905, pp. 87ff.

45. See SC, *First Report from Select Committee on Metropolis Improvement; with the Minutes of Evidence, Appendix and Plans*, 1840, qq. 77–8, 296ff., evidence of James Pennethorne; SC, *Report from Select Committee on the Health of Towns*, 1840 qq. 182, 259, evidence of Samuel Byles, Medical Officer Whitechapel Union; and qq. 2797–810 (Pennethorne again).

46. See SC, *Report from Select Committee on the Health of Towns*, 1840, q. 2030, evidence of James Peeke, Surveyor of the Tower Hamlets Division of

the Commissioners of Sewers; ibid., q. 2883 (Pennethorne); and SC, *Second Report from Select Committee on Metropolis Improvements; with the Minutes of Evidence, Appendix and Plans*, 1838 q. 1337 (Rev. William Stone).

47. On the building of Commercial Street see *Survey of London*, Vol. XXVII: *The Parish of Christ Church and All Saints (Spitalfields and Mile End New Town)*, 1957, Ch. XIX.

48. Charles Dickens, *The Letters of Charles Dickens*, 1965–2002, Vol. VI, pp. 141–2 (1 August 1850), by when demolitions for Victoria Street were just about complete. *ILN*, Vol. X, p. 144 (27 February 1847). Henry Mayhew, *The* Morning Chronicle *Survey of Labour and the Poor*, 1849–50, Vol. IV, pp. 55ff. *Census of Great Britain, 1851: Population Tables Vols. I and II*, Vol. I, Division 1, p. 11.

49. There is a good account of Victoria Street in Clunn, *The Face of London*, 1934, pp. 214ff. But he dates the demolitions from 1845, whereas the *ILN* says they first began in February 1847. And he appears to say that 3,000–4,000 houses were demolished, which seems fancifully high. The 1851 Census shows just 228 houses fewer in St Margaret's Westminster in 1851 than 1841. The Victoria Street demolitions figure in William Gilbert, *De Profundis*, 1864, Vol. I, a social novel from the City Corporation's fiercest critic.

50. SC, *Report from Select Committee on the Health of Towns*, 1840, qq. 2797, 2816; SC, *First Report from Select Committee on Metropolis Improvements; with the Minutes of Evidence, Appendix and Plans*, 1840, qq. 296–8 (all Pennethorne). For backland development in Clerkenwell in the 1820s see RC, *Report of Her Majesty's Commissioners for Inquiring into the Housing of the Working Classes: Vol. II Minutes of Evidence and Appendix as to England and Wales*, 1885, qq. 588–92, evidence of Lord William Compton.

51. Hector Gavin, *The Habitations of the Industrial Classes*, 1851 p. 31.

Chapter 2 Victoria Embankment: Modern London, 1855–1899

1. They are helpfully listed, with opening dates, in Alan A. Jackson, *London's Termini*, 1969 p. 345.

2. For the London and Greenwich Railway see G. A. Sekon, *Locomotion in Victorian London*, 1938 pp. 128ff.; Edwin Course, *London Railways*, 1962, pp. 19ff.; T. C. Barker and Michael Robbins, *A History of London Transport*, 1963, Ch. XII. Barker and Robbins' study of London transport in the nineteenth century remains definitive.

3. Clearances from Blackwall to the Minories, just inside the City boundary, threatened an estimated 2,850 people, and I've added some more for the extension to Fenchurch Street. I've erred on the cautious side. See H. J. Dyos, 'Railways and Housing in Victorian London', *Journal of Transport History*, Vol. II, No. 1, 1955, p. 12.

4. This period is fully explored in John R. Kellett, *The Impact of Railways on Victorian Cities*, 1969; Jackson, *London's Termini*; Barker and Robbins, *A History of London Transport*; Course, *London Railways*. On the 1846 Royal Commission in particular see Susan Ryley Hoyle, 'The First Battle for London: The Royal Commission on Metropolitan Termini, 1846', *London Journal*, Vol. 8, No. 2, 1982, pp. 140–55.

5. For the changes in the City at this time see John Summerson, *The London Building World of the Eighteen-Sixties*, 1973, 'The Victorian Rebuilding of

the City of London', *London Journal*, Vol. 3, No. 2, 1977, and 'London, the Artifact' in H. J. Dyos and Michael Wolff (eds.), *The Victorian City*, 1973, Vol. I, pp. 311–32; and there is an excellent overview in Simon Bradley and Nikolaus Pevsner, *London I: The City of London*, 1997, pp. 101–20.

6. They are listed in Sir Walter Besant, *London in the Nineteenth Century*, 1909 p. 8. See also Bradley and Pevsner, *London I*, pp. 101–2.

7. See Edward Wedlake Brayley and others, *London and Middlesex . . .*, 1810–16, Vol. III, pp. 298–302, where they are listed, complete with coach destinations. For their later ill-fortunes see Edward Callow, *Old London Taverns*, 1899 (p. 56 for the Old Bull).

8. For traffic into Fenchurch Street see Barker and Robbins, *A History of London Transport*, pp. 51–2; for London Bridge see David J. Johnson, 'Parliament and the Railways of London in 1863', *LTR*, 1980, pp. 147–65. On through-travellers see City, *Report on the City Day-Census . . .*, 1881, pp. 46–7, citing a report of 1854.

9. Censuses, *Population Tables, Vol. I 1851*, Vol. I, Division 1, pp. 38–9.

10. Censuses, *Census of England and Wales, 1871. Population Tables, Vol. I*, p. 3.

11. See Kellett, *The Impact of Railways . . .*, pp. 45–6; Henry Hewitt Bridgman in William Westgarth (ed.), *Essays on the Street Re-Alignment, Reconstruction, and Sanitation of Central London . . .*, 1886, pp. 166ff.

12. *ILN*, Vol. XXV pp. 293–4, 30 September 1854.

13. Charles Dickens, *Charles Dickens' Uncollected Writings from* Household Words *1850–1859*, edited by Harry Stone, 1968, Vol. I, p. 104, 'The Heart of Mid-London' (with W. H. Wills), May 1850.

14. On the solid mass see Hepworth Dixon, *The London Prisons*, 1850, pp. 224–8. On the cats and besom see John Wykeham Archer, *Vestiges of Old London . . .*, 1851 plate XXXIV, pp. 1–6. See also George Godwin, *Town Swamps and Social Bridges*, 1859, pp. 9ff.; Charles Dickens, *The Dent Uniform Edition of Dickens' Journalism*, 1994–2000, Vol. III, pp. 49ff. (March 1852). On cats being skinned alive for fur caps see John Fisher Murray, *The World of London*, 1843 Vol. I, p. 66: the skin was easier to remove, and so of better quality, if the animal was alive. The same was true for dogs apparently.

15. William Gilbert, *The City*, 1877, pp. 18–19.

16. Cited in Barker and Robbins, *The History of London Transport*, p. 106.

17. On the Metropolitan Railway see Sekon, *Locomotion in Victorian London*, pp. 158ff.; Barker and Robbins, *The History of London Transport*, pp. 99ff.

18. See Johnson, 'Parliament and the Railways of London in 1863', pp. 147–65; Kellett, *The Impact of Railways*, pp. 49ff. See also SC, *Report from the Select Committee Appointed to Join with a Committee of the House of Lords on Railway Schemes (Metropolis); together with the Proceedings of the Committee, Minutes of Evidence, and an Appendix*, 1864, passim.

19. Charles Knight, *Passages of a Working Life During Half a Century*, 1864–5, Vol. III, pp. 240–41. *ILN*, Vol. XLVIII, p. 403, 21 April 1866.

20. Charles Welch, *Modern History of the City of London*, 1896, pp. 261–2.

21. On Queen Victoria Street see Percy J. Edwards, *History of London Street Improvements*, 1898, pp. 33–4; on the City's hub see Summerson, 'The Victorian Rebuilding of the City of London', p. 165.

22. Besant, *London in the Nineteenth Century*, p. 6.

23. Walter Thornbury and Edward Walford, *Old and New London*, 1873–8, Vol. III, pp. 129–30, citing an unidentified illustrated newspaper.

24. Gilbert, *The City*, pp. 17–8. On the effects of the Metropolitan Railway demolitions for Farringdon Street Station on housing and population in the parish of St Giles Cripplegate see the evidence of Rev. William Denton at the RC, *Report of Her Majesty's Commissioners for Inquiring into the Housing of the Working Classes. Vol. II Minutes of Evidence and Appendix as to England and Wales*, 1885, qq. 10654ff.

25. The crowding figures for St James Clerkenwell are calculated from the 1851 *Population Tables, Vol. I*, Division 1, pp. 16–7, and 1871 *Population Tables Vol. I* p. 5. The mixture of workers is described in Godwin, *Town Swamps and Social Bridges*, p. 20. The railway clearance figures were calculated in Dyos, 'Railways and Housing in Victorian London', pp. 13–4. There is an excellent discussion of demolitions and overcrowding in central London in David R. Green, *From Artisans to Paupers: Economic Change and Poverty in London, 1790–1870*, 1995, pp. 181ff.

26. Charles Dickens, *The Letters of Charles Dickens*, 1965–2002, Vol. XI, p. 116, to W. W. F. de Cerjat, 30 November 1865.

27. Daniel Joseph Kirwan, *Palace and Hovel: or, Phases of London Life*, 1870, p. 26; Thornbury and Walford, *Old and New London*, Vol. III, p. 323.

28. See John Gwynn, *London and Westminster Improved . . .*, 1766. On Trench (1775–1859) see *DNB*, *Annual Register 1824*, Chronicle, pp. 86–7, and John Hogg, *London As It Is*, 1839 pp. 357–60.

29. See Ibid., pp. 360–2.

30. On Walker's scheme see Benjamin Scott, *A Statistical Vindication of the City of London*, 1867, pp. 151ff.; see also RC, *Report of the Commissioners Appointed to Inquire into the Existing State of the Corporation of the City of London, and to Collect Information Respecting its Constitution, Order, and Government etc. together with the Minutes of Evidence and Appendix*, 1854, qq. 5510ff., evidence of James Wortley MP, City Recorder. Dickens approved of the Millbank embankment too: see Dickens, *The Letters of Charles Dickens*, Vol. IX, p. 383, also to W. W. F. de Cerjat, 1 February 1861.

31. On Mrs Wennels see *Annual Register 1829*, Chronicle, p. 129. On cesspools under living rooms see John Simon, *Public Health Reports*, 1887, Vol. I, p. 4 (First Report, 1849); and RC, *Report of Her Majesty's Commissioners for Inquiring into the Housing of the Working Classes. Vol. II Minutes of Evidence and Appendix as to England and Wales*, 1885, q. 37, for the Earl of Shaftesbury recollecting a graphic example. On the West End cesspools see PP, *Metropolitan Sanitary Commission: First Report*, 1848, pp. 159–60, Lewis Cooke Hertslet, chief clerk, Westminster Court of Sewers. On Bethnal Green see Hector Gavin, *Sanitary Ramblings*, 1848 pp. 9–10.

32. On the drainage of Buckingham Palace see Henry Mayhew, *London Labour and the London Poor*, 1861–2 Vol. II, p. 456; on the Queen's rats see ibid., Vol. III, p. 23; and Lankester is cited in Henry Mayhew, *The Morning Chronicle Survey of Labour and the Poor*, 1849–50, Vol. VI, p. 196. All the evidence comes from 1848–52.

33. On the use of the wc in London see RC, *Royal Commission on Metropolitan Sewage Discharge: First Report*, 1884, p.xi–xii. On more water in the sewers see SC, *Report from the Select Committee on the Supply of Water to the*

Metropolis, 1821, pp. 51–2, evidence of John Dowley, surveyor of the Westminster sewers.

34. The 1832 figures are in PP, *Metropolitan Sanitary Commission: First Report*, 1848, p. 133. Figures for all the epidemics after that are neatly set out in Registrar General 1868, pp. 60–1. Strangely, though, the 652 cholera deaths recorded by the Registrar General for 1848 are omitted.

35. See [John Snow] *Snow on Cholera . . .*, 1936, pp. 38ff.

36. *ILN*, Vol. XXV, pp. 293–4, 30 September 1854.

37. On the Thames near Blackfriars Bridge see Robert Southey, *Letters from England*, 1807, pp. 408–10; on the sturgeon see *Annual Register 1802*, Chronicle, p. 388.

38. On the sixty sewer outlets into the Thames see Mayhew, *London Labour and the London Poor*, Vol. II, p. 459. Dickens, *The Letters of Charles Dickens*, Vol. VIII, p. 598 to W. W. F. de Cerjat, 7 July 1858.

39. SC, *Report from the Select Committee on the River Thames; together with the Proceedings of the Committee, Minutes of Evidence, Appendix and Index*, 1858, qq. 1112. The report's Appendix has a chart showing the extent of the mud banks along the river.

40. The full story, including Hall's machinations, is told in RC, *Royal Commission on Metropolitan Sewage Discharge, First Report*, 1884; it is available in an attractive modern version by Stephen Halliday, *The Great Stink of London*, 1999, who also gives much biographical information about Sir Joseph Bazalgette. For a similar view on Hall to mine see Geoffrey Tyack, *Sir James Pennethorne and the Making of Victorian London*, 1992, pp. 132ff.

41. See Percy J. Edwards, *Street Improvements*, 1898 pp. 125–7.

42. The full story is in Barker and Robbins, *A History of London Transport*, 1963, pp. 148ff., 225ff.

43. By the time Shaftesbury Avenue replaced it the street had been renamed Dudley Street. The present Monmouth Street, close by, is a confusing tribute to the original. See Dickens, *The Dent Uniform Edition of Dickens' Journalism*, Vol. I, pp. 76ff.

44. Charles Booth, *Life and Labour of the People in London*, 1892–1902, Series 3, Vol. II, p. 163. For all these street improvement schemes see Edwards, *Street Improvements*.

45. See Thornbury and Walford *Old and New London*, Vol. III, pp. 16ff. On the number of people evicted see SC, *Minutes of Evidence Taken Before the Select Committee on the Courts of Justice Concentration (Site) Bill; with the Proceedings of the Committee*, 1865: 4,175 were evicted, of whom 3,082 were of the 'labouring class'. On the vacillation between the Embankment and Carey Street sites see Michael Port, 'From Carey Street to the Embankment – And Back Again!', *LTR*, 1980, pp. 167–90; and M. H. Port, *Imperial London*, 1995, Ch.7.

46. See 1871 census, *Population Tables, Vol. I*, pp. 3ff.; *Census of England and Wales 1891. Area, Houses, and Population. Vol. II Registration Areas and Sanitary Districts*, pp. 3ff., 21ff.; *Census of England and Wales 1901: County of London*, p. 59. Because of enumeration disparities over how to classify tenement blocks – they were classed as one house in 1891, though that was not always adhered to – comparisons of 'inhabited houses' between 1891 and 1901 can't be trusted. On the spread of commercial property from the City see RC, *Report of Her Majesty's Commissioners for Inquiring into the*

Housing of the Working Classes. Vol. II Minutes of Evidence and Appendix as to England and Wales, 1885, qq. 672, 1348, 2266, 3222. This change of use would go into reverse in the late twentieth century: see Jerry White, *London in the Twentieth Century: A City and Its People*, 2001 pp. 81–2.

47. Preamble to the Artisans' and Labourers' Dwellings Improvement Act 1875, 38 & 39, Vict. c36.

48. See, for instance, Hansard, Third Series, Vol. CCXXII, cols. 104, 106, where Cross cites the number of brothels in Edinburgh and Glasgow that similar powers had abolished.

49. See Jerry White, *Rothschild Buildings: Life in an East End Tenement Block, 1887–1920*, 1980, Ch. 1 and pp. 91ff.

50. See LCC, *The Housing Question in London, 1855–1900*, 1900, pp. 294–5, 308–9; the dates of evictions are usually given in the details of individual schemes.

51. On the slum clearance area in the Mint see LCC, *Housing*, 1900, pp. 123ff.; on Marshalsea Road see Edwards, *Street Improvements*, p. 73; and on Mearns' and Sims's experience of the Mint see RC, *Report of Her Majesty's Commissioners for Inquiring into the Housing of the Working Classes. Vol. II Minutes of Evidence and Appendix as to England and Wales*, 1885, qq. 5346ff., 5726ff. See also [Andrew Mearns] *The Bitter Cry of Outcast London*, 1883, pp. 58–61; George R. Sims, *How the Poor Live and Horrible London*, 1889, pp. 45, 119ff., 126–30. As for 'shady', Mearns absconded with the London Congregational Union's funds some time in the 1880s.

52. On the 1860s see Thomas Archer, *The Pauper, The Thief, and The Convict*, 1865, pp. 10ff.; see also Henry Morley, *Gossip*, 1857, pp. 91–103. Booth, *Life and Labour of the People in London*, Series 3, Vol. II, p. 67. On where people went when they were evicted, and indeed for the whole story of Boundary Street, see J. A. Yelling, *Slums and Slum Clearance in Victorian London*, 1986, Ch.8; and LCC, *Housing*, 1900, pp. 190ff.

53. Hansard, Third Series, Vol. CCXXIV, cols. 454–5.

54. In 1891 there were 8,505 one-roomed dwellings in Clerkenwell and St Luke's; in 1901, in the new Borough of Finsbury covering the same ground, there were 6,364. In 1881 the number of persons per house in St James Clerkenwell was 9.1 persons per house, substantially down on 1871 (10.6). The figure then shoots up to 13.1 in 1891. But this is a statistical mirage because the great tenement blocks that had arisen in the district were each counted in the Census as one house.

55. Booth, *Life and Labour of the People in London*, Series 3, Vol. III, p. 74 (Westminster); Vol. II, p. 160 (Clerkenwell); Vol. IV, p. 8 (the Mint).

56. On the Gaiety see John Hollingshead, *My Lifetime*, 1895, Vol. II, pp. 126–9. The résumé at the century's end is in Besant, *London in the Nineteenth Century*, p. 325, in an article by George Turnbull.

57. Henry James, *English Hours*, 1905 p. 11, from an article first published in 1888. On the inner London parks and gardens see J. J. Sexby, *The Municipal Parks, Gardens, and Open Spaces of London*, 1905; Mrs B. Holmes, *The London Burial Grounds*, 1896; the acreage is calculated from LCC, *London Statistics*, Vol. XXIII, 1912–3, pp. 220–7.

58. For figures for the volume of passenger travel in London and traffic speeds see ibid., Vol. XVIII, 1907–8 pp. 388, 398.

59. Cited in Bradley and Pevsner, *London I*, p. 101.

60. On block dwellings see LCC, *Housing*, 1900; on class change in tenement blocks compared with the slums they replaced see White, *Rothschild Buildings*, p. 92. On the Portman Estate see Frank Banfield, *The Great Landlords of London*, 1888, pp. 36ff.

61. On Stevenson's as the first Queen Anne revival see Alistair Service, *The Architects of London*, 1979, p. 133. On Thackeray's house see Gordon N. Ray, *Thackeray*, 1958, Ch. XIII. For a new reading of the Queen Anne revival see E. B. Weiner, *Architecture and Social Reform in Late-Victorian London*, 1994, pp. 69-80.

62. Arnold Bennett, *The Journals of Arnold Bennett*, edited by Newman Flower, 1932, Vol. I, pp. 49-50, 6 October 1897.

63. Justin McCarthy, *Charing Cross to St Paul's*, 1891, p. 7; George Gissing, *London and the Life of Literature in Late Victorian England*, edited by Pierre Coustillas, 1978, p. 335, 14 April 1894; Percy Fitzgerald, *Picturesque London*, 1890, p.x; for the Georgian revival among proto-gentrifiers in the Barton Street area of Westminster in the early 1890s see Grant Richards, *Memories of a Misspent Youth 1872-1896*, 1932, pp. 148-9.

Chapter 3 New Road: London Growing, 1800-1899

1. Leigh Hunt, *Autobiography*, 1850, Vol. II, pp. 157-8.

2. Charles Dickens, *Dombey and Son*, 1846-8, Ch. xxxiii. The state of the fields in Bloomsbury was recollected in Rowland Dobie, *The History of the United Parishes of St. Giles in the Fields and St. George Bloomsbury*, 1829, p. 176n. On the Five Fields see Henry George Davis, *The Memorials of the Hamlet of Knightsbridge*, 1859, pp. 216ff.; on Tomlin's New Town see William Robins, *Paddington*, 1853 pp. 190-92 and Charles Knight, *Passages of a Working Life During Half a Century*, 1864-5, Vol. I, p. 119. On the gravel pits see SC, *Reports from Select Committee on the Education of the Lower Orders in the Metropolis: with Minutes of Evidence taken before the Committee*, 1816, pp. 220-1, evidence of Rev. Basil Woodd, minister of Bentinck Chapel, Marylebone. On Bethnal Green's self-built 'villas' in the 1850s see Margaret Llewellyn Davies (ed.), *Life as We Have Known It*, 1931, pp. 1-2. On the Battle Bridge mountains see William J. Pinks, *The History of Clerkenwell*, 1880, p. 501; and Walter Thornbury and Edward Walford *Old and New London*, 1873-8, Vol. II, p. 278.

3. Charles Dickens, *Our Mutual Friend* 1864-5 Ch. iv.

4. On Bethnal Green see Hector Gavin, *Sanitary Ramblings*, 1848, pp. 22, 26 and passim. For Waterlow see George Smalley, *The Life of Sir Sydney H. Waterlow Bart . . .*, 1909, p. 7.

5. See Thomas Miller, *Godfrey Malvern*, 1842-3, pp. 139-44, who gives a memorable picture of the Lock's Fields district.

6. *Annual Register 1808*, Chronicle, p. 29. Richard Phillips, *A Morning's Walk from London to Kew*, 1820, pp. 11-13. SC, *Report from the Select Committee on the Police of the Metropolis*, 1828, pp. 64-5.

7. William Cobbett, *Rural Rides*, 1830-53 Vol. I, p. 52 (4 December 1821 and subsequently). On suburban Kensington see *Survey of London*, Vol. XLI: *Southern Kensington: Brompton*, 1983 pp. 4-5. On rural Camberwell see R. P. Gillies, *Memories of a Literary Veteran*, 1851, Vol. III, pp. 254-6.

8. On Edgware see SC, *Report from the Select Committee on the Police of the Metropolis*, 1828, p. 214. Charles Dickens, *The Letters of Charles Dickens*, 1965–2002, Vol. I, July 1838, to Richard Bentley. On Chelsea's mixed population in the 1820s see [Thomas Bell Ellenor] *Rambling Recollections of Chelsea . . .*, 1901.

9. The work of Donald J. Olsen on this period (*Town Planning in London*, 1964, and *The Growth of Victorian London*, 1976, which covers the period after 1835) remains indispensable here.

10. RC *Report of the Royal Commission on London Squares*, 1928, pp. 10–11.

11. See especially Frank Banfield, *The Great Landlords of London*, 1888.

12. On early Bloomsbury and the legal profession, see Sir Frederick Pollock (ed.), *Personal Remembrances of Sir Frederick Pollock*, 1887, Vol. I, pp. 1–2. Thomas Adolphus Trollope, *What I Remember*, 1887–9, Vol. I, p. 2. William Makepeace Thackeray, *Vanity Fair*, 1847–8, Ch. xiv. See also Olsen, *Town Planning in London*, pp. 113–4.

13. For the development of St John's Wood see John Summerson, *Georgian London*, 1945, p. 157ff.; Malcolm Brown, 'St John's Wood: The Eyre Estate Before 1830', *LTR*, 1995, pp. 49–68; for early residents and reputation see Alan Montgomery Eyre, *Saint John's Wood*, 1913.

14. Summerson, *Georgian London*, pp. 165–7.

15. On Belgravia see Henry George Davis, *The Memorials of the Hamlet of Knightsbridge. With Notices of Its Immediate Neighbourhood*, 1859, Ch. iv; Summerson, *Georgian London*, pp. 176–9; Hermione Hobhouse, *Thomas Cubitt: Master Builder*, 1971, Chs. vi–viii.

16. On Tyburnia see Robins, *Paddington*, Pt I, Ch. v, and Pt II, Ch. v; Gordon Toplis, 'The History of Tyburnia', *Country Life*, 1973; Olsen, *The Growth of Victorian London*, pp. 162ff. See also D. A. Reeder, 'A Theatre of Suburbs: Some Patterns of Development in West London, 1801–1911', in H. J. Dyos, (ed.), *The Study of Urban History*, 1968, pp. 253–71.

17. William Makepeace Thackeray, *The Letters and Private Papers of William Makepeace Thackeray*, edited by Gordon N. Ray, 1945–6, Vol. II, pp. 96–7 (punctuation and abbreviations amended); Dickens, *The Letters of Charles Dickens*, Vol. XII, p. 268, to Mrs Charles Eliot Norton, an American friend, 5 November 1868; William Makepeace Thackeray, *The Newcomes*, 1854–5, Ch. 8. By the 'Indian world' he meant the returned officers of the East India Company, notorious for their vulgarity and their wealth.

18. See T. Fairman Ordish, 'History of Metropolitan Roads', *LTR*, 1913, pp. 1–92. The Metropolitan Road Board is Ordish's shorthand for the Commissioners of the Metropolis Turnpike Roads North of the Thames. On the origin of the Commissioners see Sidney and Beatrice Webb, *English Local Government: The King's Highway*, 1913, pp. 176–80, and *English Local Government: Statutory Authorities for Special Purposes*, 1922, pp. 228–30.

19. T. C. Barker and Michael Robbins, *A History of London Transport*, 1963 Chs. i–iii, remains entirely authoritative in this area, but see also G. A. Sekon, *Locomotion in Victorian London*, 1938, Ch. ii. There is also a fascinating and accurate account of the early omnibus days in Henry Mayhew, *The Morning Chronicle Survey of Labour and the Poor*, 1849–50, Vol. VI, p. 37ff. On the assertion that Parisian omnibuses were seen in London before Christmas 1828 see [Henry Crabb Robinson] *Diary, Reminiscences, and*

Correspondence of Henry Crabb Robinson . . ., edited by Thomas Sadler, 1869 Vol. II, p. 396.

20. Cited in Francis Sheppard, *London 1808-1870*, 1971, p. 135.

21. Thomas Frost, *Forty Years' Recollections*, 1880, pp. 5-6, 28, 197.

22. See Barker and Robbins, *A History of London Transport*, p. 165; Alan A. Jackson, *London's Termini*, 1969 p. 346.

23. David R Green, *From Artisans to Paupers*, 1995, pp. 46-50.

24. Louis Bamberger, *Memories of Sixty Years in the Timber and Pianoforte Trades*, 1929 p. 106.

25. On the growth in bank and savings bank deposits during these years, and the fluctuations in interest rates which bear very little relationship to the London building boom, see B. R. Mitchell and Phyllis Deane, *Abstract of British Historical Statistics*, 1962, pp. 444, 453, 456-7.

26. Mayhew, *The* Morning Chronicle *Survey of Labour and the Poor*, Vol. V, pp. 110-11. The 'Field Rangers' are in Louis Bamberger, *Bow Bell Memories*, 1931, p. 237.

27. On the numbers of houses small builders built see Olsen, *The Growth of Victorian London*, p. 155. On bankruptcy of builders see Mayhew, *The* Morning Chronicle *Survey of Labour and the Poor*, Vol. V, p. 115. On Rotten Hill and Holloway see Bamberger, *Memories of Sixty Years in the Timber and Pianoforte Trades*, pp. 105-6. For the speculative builder more generally see Olsen, *The Growth of Victorian London*, pp. 154ff. For similar arrangements at an earlier period in Somers Town see Linda Clarke, *Building Capitalism*, 1992.

28. W. S. Clarke, (ed.), *The Suburban Homes of London*, 1881, pp. 194-202.

29. See Arthur Philip Crouch, *Silvertown and Neighbourhood (including East and West Ham)*, 1900, and Edward G. Howarth and Mona Wilson, *West Ham*, 1907. For a modern overview see John Marriott, '"West Ham: London's Industrial Centre and Gateway to the World". 1: Industrialisation, 1840-1910', *London Journal*, Vol. 13, No. 2, 1987-8, pp. 121-42.

30. Clarke (ed.), *The Suburban Homes of London*, pp. 74ff.

31. See, for instance, R. Andom, *We Three and Troddles*, 1894 p. 207.

32. Ibid., pp. 56ff.

33. On the estate see Henry S. Simmonds, *All About Battersea*, 1882, pp. 141-3.

34. On the growth of suburban railway stations after 1860 see Peter Hall, 'The Development of Communications', in J. T. Coppock and Hugh C. Prince (eds.), *Greater London*, 1964, pp. 52-79.

35. On Pimlico see Hermione Hobhouse, *Thomas Cubitt*, 1971 Chs. ix-xi.

36. See *Survey of London*, Vol. XXXVIII: *The Museums Area of South Kensington and Westminster*, 1975, and Hermione Hobhouse, *The Crystal Palace and the Great Exhibition*, 2002, Chs. IV-V.

37. See Clarke, (ed.), *Suburban Homes of London*, where, in district after district in outer London the railway is identified as the motor of development and as a selling-point for middle-class settlement. On the impact of railways on development in north-west London see Hugh C. Prince, 'North-West London 1864-1914', in Coppock and Prince (eds.), *Greater London*, pp. 120-41.

38. On overbuilding see RC, *Report of Her Majesty's Commissioners for Inquiring into the Housing of the Working Classes. Vol. II Minutes of Evidence and Appendix as to England and Wales*, 1885 qq. 6546ff., evidence of Ralph Clutton, agent for the Ecclesiastical Commissioners. See also Charles Booth,

Life and Labour of the People in London, 1902, Vol. 17, p. 165. There will also be some other examples from Booth cited later in this chapter.

39. On Campbell Road, see Jerry White, *The Worst Street in North London*, 1986; on Sultan Street see H. J. Dyos, *Victorian Suburb*, 1973, pp. 109–113; on Litcham Street see Gillian Tindall, *The Fields Beneath*, 1980, pp. 198–9.

40. SC, *Report from the Select Committee on the Police of the Metropolis*, 1828, p. 133, evidence of the Hon. Frederick Byng, speaking for the watch committee of the parish of St George's Hanover Square.

41. Booth, *Life and Labour of the People in London*, Series 3, Vol. III, pp. 122–3.

42. See Jerry White, *London in Twentieth Century*, 2001, pp. 119, 237.

43. *Survey of London* Vol. XXXVII: *Northern Kensington*, 1973, Ch. xiii. For the upper Westbourne Park tag see Frank T. Bullen, *Confessions of a Tradesman*, 1908, p. 1. For Soapsuds Island see Booth, *Life and Labour of the People in London*, Series 3, Vol. III, pp. 138–41. See also the wonderful photographs of Roger Mayne, who made a special study of Southam Street when it was on its last legs in the late 1950s.

44. See *Survey of London*, Vol. XXXXVII: *Northern Kensington*, Ch. xiv; Booth, *Life and Labour of the People in London*, Series 3, Vol. III, pp. 151–8; and Kensington MOH, *The Annual Report on the Health, Sanitary Condition . . . 1896*, pp. 144–58. On the gypsies see George Borrow, *Romano Lavo-Lil*, 1874 pp. 228–9.

45. Wilkie Collins, *Basil*, 1852 pp. 31–2.

46. Phillips, *A Morning's Walk from London to Kew*, pp. 100–101, for Wandsworth's 'mushroom aristocracy of trade'.

47. Thackeray, *Vanity Fair*, Ch. 17. Anthony Trollope, *The Three Clerks*, 1858, Ch. XXXVI.

48. John Fisher Murray, *World of London*, 1843, Vol. I, p. 73.

49. Booth, *Life and Labour of the People in London*, Series 3, Vol. V, pp. 158–9; see also Series 3, Vol. I, p. 150.

50. George Gissing, *The Nether World*, 1889, Ch. XXXIX. Booth, *Life and Labour of the People in London*, Series 3, Vol. I, p. 214.

51. Ibid., p. 208.

52. Compton Mackenzie, *My Life and Times: Octave One 1883–1891*, 1963, pp. 114–15.

53. Barker and Robbins, *A History of London Transport*, Ch. vi.

54. Clarke (ed.), *The Suburban Homes of London*, p. 282.

55. Many of these places are listed in Sir Walter Besant, *London in the Nineteenth Century*, 1909 p. 188.

56. See Olsen, *The Growth of Victorian London*, pp. 18–9, 232–3.

57. Percy Fitzgerald, *London City Suburbs*, 1893, pp. 10, 12.

58. Booth, *Life and Labour of the People in London*, Series 3, Vol. I, pp. 78–9, 151, 154, 183; Vol. III, pp. 74, 87, 108–9, 114, 119.

59. See for instance, ibid. Vol. V, pp. 190, 207; Vol. VI, pp. 12, 38–9, 81–2, 88, 146, 152.

60. Ibid. Vol. VI, coloured map between pp. 96 and 97; George Gissing, *In the Year of Jubilee*, 1894, Part the First, section III; RG 12/465–6. See also Dyos, *Victorian Suburb*, pp. 96–9.

61. George and Weedon Grossmith, *The Diary of a Nobody*, 1892, p. 157.

62. Bullen, *Confessions of a Tradesman*, 1908 pp. 93–9.

63. R. D. Blumenfeld, *R.D.B.'s Diary 1887–1914*, 1930, pp. 6–7.
64. Compton Mackenzie, *My Life and Times: Octave Two 1891–1900*, 1963, p. 264.
65. See the table in LCC, *London Statistics* Vol. XVIII 1907–8, p. 398.

Chapter 4 Charing Cross: The London Whirlpool

1. The American novelist Nathaniel Hawthorne wrote of 'the vast London whirlpool' in *Our Old Home*, 1863, Vol. II, p. 81. Thomas Campbell, the Glasgow poet, who first came to London in 1801, called Charing Cross the 'roaring vortex'. For that, Dr Johnson and much else see Henry B. Wheatley and Peter Cunningham, *London Past and Present*, 1891, Vol. I, pp. 353–9. For the hub of the empire see J. Holden Macmichael, *The Story of Charing Cross and Its Immediate Neighbourhood*, 1906, Ch.1. On the Golden Cross see Edward Wedlake Brayley and others, *London and Middlesex . . .*, 1810–16, Vol. III, p. 300. The old Hotel was demolished to make way for Trafalgar Square in the late 1820s, but a replacement was built not far away in the Strand: see B. W. Matz, *The Inns and Taverns of 'Pickwick' with Some Observations on their Other Associations*, 1921, p. 18. On the Admiral Duncan see Walter Thornbury and Edward Walford *Old and New London*, 1873–8, Vol. III, p. 128.
2. See H. A. Shannon, 'Migration and the Growth of London, 1841–91', *Economic History Review*, Vol. V, No. 2, 1935, pp. 79–86.
3. Anon, *Tempted London*, 1888, pp. 1–3.
4. Robert Plumer Ward, *Tremaine, or The Man of Refinement*, 1825, Vol. I, pp. iii–iv. See Charles Booth, *Life and Labour of the People in London*, 1892–1902, Series 1, Vol. 3, pp. 58ff. and 123ff. The penny whistle is in Richard Whiteing, *My Harvest*, 1915, p. 124; the theatre in Arthur Machen, *Far Off Things*, 1922, p. 71, and amusements for the body in Frank Harris, *My Life and Loves*, 1964, pp. 334–5, both writing of London in the 1880s.
5. See G. M. Young, (ed.), *Early Victorian England 1830–1865*, 1934, Vol. I, pp. 212ff., Vol. II, p. 310.
6. Justin McCarthy, *Charing Cross to St Paul's*, 1891, pp. 15–16. On the later draw of Dickens see Jerry White, *London in the Twentieth Century*, 2001, pp. 92, 144.
7. Calculated from *Census of England and Wales 1881 Vol. III Ages, Condition as to Marriage, Occupations, and Birth-Places of the People*, p. 20.
8. Provincial-born outnumbered the London-born in Paddington and Kensington in 1881; women in Paddington outnumbered men by 1,507 to 1,000 and in Kensington by 1,493 to 1,000. The local breakdown of provincial-born is not available in the census but was given as a special calculation in Booth, *Life and Labour of the People in London*, Series 1, Vol. 3, pp. 150ff. He gave no figures for Hampstead. The age-range comparison is given ibid., p. 71. For migration in the first half of the century see Arthur Redford, *Labour Migration in England, 1800–50*, 1926 p. 157 and passim.
9. On Wilkie see Allan Cunningham, *The Life of Sir David Wilkie*; 1843, Vol. I, pp. 98–9. Mrs Lynn Linton, *My Literary Life*, 1899, pp. 14–21. On George Eliot see Frederick Karl, *George Eliot*, 1995 Pts II and III.
10. Mrs Lynn Linton, *Christopher Kirkland*, 1885, Vol. II p. 90: this novel is heavily autobiographical. On George Williams see H. E. Hodder Williams,

The Life of Sir George Williams, 1906, p. 51; and on William Booth see Harold Begbie, *Life of William Booth,* 1920, Vol. I, p. 99.

11. On London's demand for skilled country labour generally see Booth, *Life and Labour of the People in London,* Series 1, Vol. 3, pp. 96–7, and 141. John Brown, *Sixty Years' Gleanings from Life's Harvest,* 1858, p. 23. W. E. Adams, *Memoirs of a Social Atom,* 1903, pp. 332–3. Robert Blatchford, *My Eighty Years,* 1931, pp. 70–71. See also Henry Mayhew, *The Morning Chronicle Survey of Labour and the Poor,*1849–50, Vol. V, pp. 67, 84, and 108 for country-bred sawyers and carpenters.

12. On Elizabeth Jones see *Annual Register 1830,* Chronicle pp. 25–6. On Susan Bartrup see Frederick Rogers, *Labour, Life and Literature,* 1913, p. 103. On Lucy Luck see John Burnett, (ed.), *Useful Toil,* 1974, pp. 67–77.

13. James Burn, *James Burn,* 1882, pp. 22–6.

14. Sam Shaw, *Guttersnipe,* 1946, pp. 29–30.

15. On the Welsh gold smelters see Charles Dickens, *Charles Dickens' Uncollected Writings from* Household Words *1850–1859,* edited by Harry Stone, 1968, Vol. II, pp. 443ff., 'Discovery of a Treasure Near Cheapside', *Household Words,* 13 November 1852. Sir Harold Bellman, *Cornish Cockney,* 1947, p. 16.

16. On the 1840s and Scottish bakers see Charles Knight, (ed.), *London,* 1841–4, Vol. III, pp. 321–2. On Millwall see [Thomas Wright] *Some Habits and Customs of the Working Classes,* 1867, pp. 251–4. On the early Scottish institutions see John Britton (ed.), *The Original Picture of London,* 1826, pp. 255–6, and on the later see George R. Sims (ed.), *Living London,* 1902–3, Vol. I, pp. 179–80, 219; Vol. II, pp. 267–9.

17. Harry Gosling, *Up and Down Stream,* 1927 p. 1.

18. On the vitiation theory see Booth, *Life and Labour of the People in London,* Series 1, Vol. 3, pp. 58, 65; it seems to have originated in James Cantlie, *Degeneration Amongst Londoners,* 1885, especially pp. 19–25. Thomas Okey, *A Basketful of Memories,* 1930 passim. G. K. Chesterton, *Autobiography,* 1936, p. 11.

19. Raphael Samuel, *East End Underworld,* 1981, pp. 12–14. See also Bryan Magee, *Clouds of Glory,* 2003, pp. 87ff. – the Magees had lived in Clerkenwell and Hoxton from the early years of the nineteenth century, Magee's paternal grandparents both Hoxton-born in the 1870s; but his grandmother's father was born in Manchester in the 1850s.

20. The census breaks birthplaces down by London district only in 1851 and 1861. Charles Booth obtained private information from the Registrar General to make a similar analysis in 1881, and his presentation of the material is broadly comparable with 1851 and 1861. He obtained similar information for the 1891 census but grouped it idiosyncratically, rendering it meaningless for comparison with earlier years. The 1881 data are in *Life and Labour of the People in London,* Series 1, Vol. 3, pp. 113ff., and 150ff.

21. Ibid., Vol. 1, pp. 50–1.

22. Geoffrey Holden Pike, *Byeways of Two Cities,* 1873 p. 19.

23. On the fertility rates see Booth, *Life and Labour of the Poor in London,* Vol. 17, pp. 16ff.; the birth rate for London County is in Registrar General *Annual Summary of Births, Deaths, and Causes of Death in London and Other Large Towns,* 1895, p.ii.

24. The ranking of districts by poverty is given in Booth, *Life and Labour of*

the People in London, Vol. 17, pp. 16ff. See also ibid. Series 1, Vol. 3, pp. 142–3.

25. The Campbell Road figures are from the 1881 census RG.11.259–60; 'adults' here refers to heads of households, spouses and lodgers (so not adult children living with their parents).

26. The number of London-born in 1881 for the whole county is in the 1881 *Census*, p. 20; the numbers in the inner arc (St Saviour and St Olave Southwark, Lambeth Church, Holborn, Shoreditch, Mile End Old Town, Bethnal Green, Whitechapel, St George's-in-the-East, Stepney) are in Booth, *Life and Labour of the Poor in London*, Series 1, Vol. 3, pp. 113ff., and 150ff.

27. See Gareth Stedman Jones, 'The "Cockney" and the nation, 1780–1988', in David Feldman and Gareth Stedman Jones (eds.), *Metropolis London*, 1989, pp. 272–324.

28. Samuel Bamford, *Passages in the Life of a Radical*, 1844, Vol. I, pp. 146–7.

29. The best survey of cockney dialect remains William Matthews, *Cockney Past and Present*, 1938. See also the interesting early discussion in Sholto and Reuben Percy, *London*, 1823, Vol. I, pp. 163–7. For w for v in the 1890s see John Hollingshead, *My Lifetime*, 1895, Vol. I, pp. 48–9. An example of 'axed' is in Mayhew, *The Morning Chronicle Survey of Labour and the Poor*, Vol. IV, p. 192.

30. Chesterton, *Autobiography*, p. 15.

31. Bamford, *Passages in the Life of a Radical*.

32. On back slang see, for instance, Henry Mayhew, *London Labour and the London Poor*, 1861–2, Vol. I, pp. 25–6; and Anon.,*Toilers in London*, 1889, p. 27 for the girl flower-sellers of Seven Dials. William Makepeace Thackeray, *The History of Pendennis*, 1849–50 Vol. II, Ch. 25.

33. John S. Farmer and (from Vol. III) W.E. Henley, *Slang And Its Analogues, Past And Present*, 1890–1904.

34. Charles Mackay, *Memoirs of Extraordinary Popular Delusions and the Madness of Crowds*, 1852, p. 619ff. 'Walker' gets a mention in Charles Dickens, *Pickwick Papers*, 1836–7, Ch. xxvii.

35. Rogers, *Labour, Life and Literature*, pp. 6–7. Jerome K. Jerome, *Paul Kelver*, 1902, p. 209 (writing of his own youth around 1880). On the cockney levellers, see William Hazlitt, *The Plain Speaker*, 1826, pp. 156–7 (italics in original).

36. William Makepeace Thackeray, *The Newcomes*, 1854–5, Vol. II, pp. 142–3.

37. Jessie Aitken Wilson, *Memoir of George Wilson*, 1860, p. 244.

38. George Gissing, *The Whirlpool*, 1897, Part the Second, Ch. VI; Booth, *Life and Labour of the People in London*, Series 3, Vol. 5, p. 149, and Vol. 3, p. 170; Arthur Machen, *Far Off Things*, 1922, p. 65.

39. Booth, *Life and Labour of the People in London*, Series 3, Vol. 3, p. 179; Vol. 1, pp. 153, 169.

40. See Anon., *The Picture of London, for 1818*, 1818, pp. 88–9; K. Baedeker, *London and Its Environs*, 1889, pp. 10–11. On the influence of railways in swelling the numbers of those who found the season indispensable see Andrew Wynter, *Subtle Brains and Lissom Fingers*, 1869, pp. 268–9.

41. See Raphael Samuel, 'Comers and Goers', in H. J. Dyos and Michael Wolff (eds.), *The Victorian City*, 1973, Vol. I, pp. 123–60; and Mayhew, *The Morning Chronicle Survey of Labour and the Poor*, Vol. II, pp. 66–7.

42. ISBG London Metropolitan Archives, 253/11 15 October 1889, 17 December 1889 (two).

43. The school board visitor is cited in Booth, *Life and Labour of the People in London*, Series 1, Vol. 1 pp. 26–7. There is an exemplary discussion of the reasons for excessive mobility among the late-nineteenth-century London poor in Anna Davin, *Growing Up Poor*, 1996, pp. 31ff.

44. ISBG, London Metropolitan Archives, 253/11 4 February 1890; *Daily Telegraph*, 27 March 1890. Seckford Street was renamed Sekforde subsequent to these events.

45. Dickens, *Pickwick Papers*, Ch. XXXII – Dickens lodged in Lant Street while his parents were in the Marshalsea Prison, probably 1824. R. Andom, *Martha and I*, 1898, pp. 136–8. I am grateful to Peter Bowen for biographical information relating to Barrett. The artisans' village is in Farmer and Henley, *Slang and Its Analogues*, Vol. VI, pp. 255–6. There seem to have been many Sloper's Islands: Frank Bullen remembered this as the sarcastic title given to east Dulwich in the 1890s – *Confessions of a Trademan*, 1908, p. 110. On the aristocratic moonshooters see Michael Sadleir, *Blessington-d'Orsay*, 1933.

46. Eleanor Farjeon, *A Nursery in the Nineties*, 1935, p. 218; Laura Hain Friswell, *In the Sixties and Seventies*, 1905, p. 308; on White see Catherine MacDonald Maclean, *Mark Rutherford*, 1955, pp. 162–6, 172–3, 177–8.

47. Ernest Benn, *Happier Days*, 1949, p. 38.

48. Okey, *A Basketful of Memories*, 1930, p. 103; RC, *Report of Her Majesty's Commissioners for Inquiring into the Housing of the Working Classes. Vol. II Minutes of Evidence and Appendix as to England and Wales*, 1885, qq. 3925–6; P. G. Patmore, *My Friends and Acquaintances*, 1854, Vol. I, p. 49.

49. The title of a collection of short stories about London working-class life by H. W. Nevinson, 1895.

50. Pierce Egan, *Life in London*, 1821, pp. 22–3; Hazlitt, *The Plain Speaker*, p. 177; the provincial experience is from a novel by Thomas Miller, *Godfrey Malvern*, 1842–3, p. 211, the speaker a worker-poet much like Miller; Mrs Vowles's testimony is in W. Teignmouth Shore, (ed.), *Trial of Thomas Neill Cream*, 1923, p. 75. See also White, *London in the Twentieth Century*, pp. 116–17.

51. Max Schlesinger, *Saunterings in and About London*, 1853, p. 155; for the puppies see Anon., *Real Life in London . . .*, 1821, Vol. I, pp. 418–20; Anon., *Picture of London 1818*, p. 67; Adams, *Memoirs of a Social Atom*, pp. 312–13.

52. Thomas de Quincey, *Autobiography*, 1950, p. 138; B. L. Farjeon, *Great Porter Square*, 1884, Ch. XLIII; Sir Walter Besant, *Autobiography*, 1902, pp. 71–2.

53. Dickens, *The Dent Uniform Edition of Dickens' Journalism*, 1994–2000, Vol. I, p. 211 (April 1835); George Gissing, *London and the Life of Literature in Late Victorian England* edited by Pierre Coustillas, 1978, p. 32 (17 June 1888). There is a good picture of loneliness for a young City clerk around 1880 in Jerome K. Jerome's autobiographical novel *Paul Kelver*, pp. 196–9.

54. Mary Eleanor Benson, *Streets and Lanes of the City*, 1892, pp. 21–2. Ms Benson was the Archbishop of Canterbury's daughter and a social worker in the City.

55. John Fisher Murray, *The World of London*, 1843, Vol. I, Chs. VI and VII.

Dickens, *The Dent Uniform Edition of Dickens' Journalism*, Vol. I, p. 261 (November 1834).

56. Hazlitt, *The Plain Speaker*, 1826, p. 178; Mrs Henry Ward, *A Writer's Recollections*, 1918, p. 197 (italics in originals).

57. Thomas Hardy, *Jude the Obscure*, 1895, Part Fifth, Ch. 6. Margaret Wynne Nevinson, *Life's Fitful Fever*, 1926, pp. 60, and 62-3. On eccentrics see Murray, *The World of London*, Vol. I, p. 24. Booth, *Life and Labour of the People in London*, Series 1, Vol. 3, p. 75; Lord Snell, *Men, Movements, and Myself*, 1936, pp. 68-9.

58. The 'no neighbours' tag is from M. Vivian Hughes, *A London Family 1870-1900*, 1946, p. 77, recalling suburban Canonbury, 1870-85. For Wilkie see Allan Cunningham, *David Wilkie*, 1843, Vol. I, p. 97. Alexander Somerville, *The Autobiography of a Working Man*, 1848, p. 254.

59. Robert R. Hyde, *Industry Was My Parish*, 1968, p. 5; Hughes, *A London Family 1870-1900*, p. 77; Alfred Grosch, *St. Pancras Pavements*, 1947, pp. 13-14; Linton, *Christopher Kirkland*, Vol. I, pp. 249-56; Farjeon, *A Nursery in the Nineties*, p. 428.

60. The Lady Resident is in Booth, *Life and Labour of the People in London*, Series 1, Vol. 3, pp. 40-42. On settlement and mobility coexisting in the roughest streets see Jerry White, *The Worst Street in North London*, 1986, Chs. 2 and 3.

61. For charges made to lying-in mothers see W. Somerset Maugham, *Of Human Bondage*, 1915, p. 866. St Stephen Street is cited in RC, *Report of Her Majesty's Commissioners for Inquiring into the Housing of the Working Classes. Vol. II Minutes of Evidence and Appendix as to England and Wales*, 1885, q. 4932; Our Court is in [Thomas Wright] *The Great Unwashed*, 1868, pp. 144-8; the Clerkenwell cleric is in RC, *Report of Her Majesty's Commissioners for Inquiring into the Housing of the Working Classes. Vol. II Minutes of Evidence and Appendix as to England and Wales*, 1885, qq. 1328ff.; the old inhabitants are in Booth, *Life and Labour of the People in London*, Series 3, Vol. 4, p. 158, describing Rotherhithe, but applicable to similar places. For more information on neighbouring in working-class London more generally see Ellen Ross, *Love and Toil*, 1993, and Davin, *Growing Up Poor*, both illuminating studies.

62. Rogers, *Labour, Life and Literature*, pp. 16-20.

63. *East London Advertiser*, 2 January 1892.

64. On the windows see Rev. J. H. Stallard, *London Pauperism Amongst Jews and Christians*, 1867, p. 78. On Susan Snellgrove see *Annual Register 1872*, Chronicle, pp. 32-3. Jerome, *Paul Kelver*, p. 51. Grosch, *St Pancras Pavements*, pp. 11-12; see also White, *London in the Twentieth Century*, p. 313.

65. T. A. Jackson, *Solo Trumpet*, 1953, p. 13. On litigious low-class London, a glance at the court reports of any nineteenth-century London local newspaper will show this to be the case. See also White, *The Worst Street in North London*, pp. 90ff.

Chapter 5 Wentworth Street: The London Medley

1. Henry Walker, *East London*, 1896, pp. 62-5.

2. On the Australian restaurants – named Spiers and Ponds – see Louis

Bamberger, *Bow Bell Memories*, 1931, p. 36. On London society see Anon., *Society in London*, 1886, p. 23; see also T. H. S. Escott, *Social Transformations of the Victorian Age*, 1897, pp. 222-9.

3. For an irreverent view of the 'high' and 'middling' Irish in London see John Fisher Murray, *The World of London*, 1843, Vol. I, pp. 211ff.; on the general point of Irish migration representing more than the poor see Graham Davis, *The Irish in Britain 1815-1914*, 1991, p. 3.

4. *Annual Register 1804*, Chronicle, p. 409. On the remittance system where money was sent to Ireland, sometimes through a London agent who would arrange for the landlord to make payments at home, see SC, *Report from the Select Committee on the Laws Relating to Irish and Scotch Vagrants*, 1828, pp. 7-8.

5. For the estimates of Irish in St Giles and elsewhere see SC, *Reports from Select Committee on the Education of the Lower Orders in the Metropolis: with Minutes of Evidence taken before the Committee*, 1816, pp. 1, 4, 52; on the suburban colonies see John Thomas Smith, *Vagabondiana . . .*, 1817, p. 49; SC, *Report from the Select Committee on the Police of the Metropolis*, 1828, pp. 192ff., 198. For the riot see *Annual Register 1822*, Chronicle, p. 91. For Calmel Buildings see SC, *Reports from the Committees on the State of Mendicity in the Metropolis*, 1815-16, evidence of Montague Burgoyne, pp. 10ff.; SC, *Reports from Select Committee on the Education of the Lower Orders in the Metropolis: with Minutes of Evidence taken before the Committee*, 1816, Burgoyne again, p. 260; Louis Simond, *Journal of a Tour and Residence . . .*, 1817, Vol. II, pp. 337-9.

6. For the Mendicity Society statistics see *Annual Register 1824*, Chronicle, p. 31. Mrs Keefe is in SC, *Reports from the Committees on the State of Mendicity in the Metropolis*, 1815-16, p. 87.

7. For the estimate of Irish street seller numbers and their taking over in oranges and nuts see Henry Mayhew, *London Labour and the London Poor*, 1861-2, Vol. I, p. 108, and *The Morning Chronicle Survey of Labour and the Poor: The Metropolitan Districts*, 1849-50, Vol. I, p. 262; for Covent Garden market see ibid., Vol. VI, pp. 228-9; information on Field Lane shoemakers comes from RG, 1841, HO/107; and on Monmouth Street see Mayhew, *The Morning Chronicle Survey of Labour and the Poor*, Vol. III, p. 201. Norah Connor is in Henry and Augustus Mayhew, *The Greatest Plague of Life*, 1847, p. 47.

8. See Lynn Hollen Lees, *Exiles of Erin*, 1979, pp. 39ff. On landlords subsidising the passage to England see Mayhew, *The Morning Chronicle Survey of Labour and the Poor*, Vol. III, pp. 19-21.

9. See Davis, *The Irish in Britain 1815-1914*, p. 117.

10. Cited in Mayhew, *The Morning Chronicle Survey of Labour and the Poor*, Vol. III, pp. 19-21.

11. The St Giles clergyman was Rev. Samuel Garratt, cited in John Garwood, *The Million-Peopled City*, 1853, p. 258; Thomas Beames, *The Rookeries of London*, 1852, pp. 60-61.

12. Mayhew, *The Morning Chronicle Survey of Labour and the Poor*, Vol. II, pp. 298-301.

13. On the priest's role in charity see Mayhew, *London Labour and the London Poor*, Vol. I, p. 121, and on female morality see ibid., pp. 108-9. On relations more generally between the Church and the Irish poor in London see

Hugh McLeod, *Class and Religion in the Late Victorian City*, 1974, pp. 72ff.; Lees, *Exiles of Erin*, Ch. 7; Raphael Samuel, 'The Roman Catholic Church and the Irish Poor', in Roger Swift and Sheridan Gilley (eds.), *The Irish in the Victorian City*, 1985, pp. 267–300; Davis, *The Irish in Britain 1815–1914*, pp. 138–48.

14. On Guy Fawkes' night 1850 see Mayhew, *London Labour and the London Poor*, Vol. III, p. 77; Owen Chadwick, *The Victorian Church*, Pt I, 1966, p. 294. On the Garibaldi riots see John Ashton, *Hyde Park*, 1896, pp. 187–93. On the treatment of Protestant missionaries by the Irish poor see Garwood, *The Million-Peopled City*, 1853, pp. 270ff.

15. Mayhew, *London Labour and the London Poor*, Vol. I, p. 108. On the Grecians see Garwood, *The Million-Peopled City*, pp. 303–4.

16. See K. R. M. Short, *The Dynamite War*, 1979, pp. 7–12, a brilliant survey of the hidden world of Irish terrorism in nineteenth-century Britain; and also John Denvir, *The Irish in Britain from the Earliest Times to the Fall and Death of Parnell*, 1892, p. 243; George Augustus Sala, *The Life and Adventures of George Augustus Sala*, 1895, Vol. II, pp. 165–7; John George Littlechild, *The Reminiscences of Chief-Inspector Littlechild*, 1894, passim; John Sweeney, *At Scotland Yard*, 1904, Chs. II, III, VII and VIII; and Sir Robert Anderson, *The Lighter Side of My Official Life*, 1910, pp. 18–25.

17. For frightened Fenians see ibid., p. 25; on the parade see Charles Maurice Davies, *Heterodox London*, 1874, Vol. II, pp. 319ff.

18. See Short, *The Dynamite War*, passim.

19. Harry Furniss, *The Confessions of a Caricaturist*, 1901, Vol. I, pp. 18–21.

20. See Charles Booth, *Life and Labour of the People in London*, 1892–1902, Series 3, Vol. 2, pp. 35–9 for Wapping; Vol. 4, p. 143 for Rotherhithe; Vol. 2, p. 178 for Clare Market; Vol. I, p. 47, for the Fenian Barracks; Vol. 6, pp. 32–3 for Peckham. On the Irish everywhere in London see Denvir, *The Irish in Britain from the Earliest Times to the Fall and Death of Parnell*, pp. 389–401.

21. See the discussion in Hugh McLeod's exemplary study *Class and Religion in the Late Victorian City*, pp. 72–80. The numbers of London-born of Irish descent can only be a guess. Paul Thompson, *Socialists, Liberals and Labour*, 1967, p. 25, says there were probably 350,000 Irish in London in 1900 but that includes 60,000 Irish-born.

22. See for the migration of French priests Douglas Newton, *Catholic London*, 1950, pp. 276–7; on the Poland Street ordinary see Allan Cunningham, *The Life of Sir David Wilkie*, 1843, Vol. I, p. 80, and [Benjamin Robert Haydon] *Life of Benjamin Robert Haydon, Historical Painter, from his Autobiography and Journals*, edited by Tom Taylor, 1853, Vol. I, p. 29; on Somers Town see Edward Wedlake Brayley and others, *London and Middlesex. . .*, 1810–16, Vol. IV, p. 185.

23. On a foreigner being a Frenchman see Flora Tristan, *Flora Tristan's London Journal*, 1840, p. 15; Denis Mack Smith, *Mazzini*, 1994, p. 28. On German migrants in the early nineteenth century and before see the excellent Panikos Panayi, *German Immigrants in Britain During the Nineteenth Century, 1815–1914*, 1995, pp. 9–27. On the German committee see *Annual Register 1814*, Chronicle, p. 98.

24. See John Thomas Smith, *The Cries of London*, 1839, pp. 50–52, 65–6, 92–5, the information and engravings all dating from 1818–20. See also Lucio

Sponza, *Italian Immigrants in Nineteenth-century Britain*, 1988, Ch. 1. On the election spat see *Annual Register 1806*, Chronicle, pp. 453, 459.

25. On the Spanish in Somers Town see Charles Dickens, *Bleak House*, 1852-3, Ch. XLIII, and Humphry House, *The Dickens World*, 1941, pp. 31-2. On Copenhagen Fields see Thomas Coull, *The History and Traditions of Islington*, 1861, p. 59. On the 1830 priests see *Annual Register 1834*, Chronicle, pp. 89-90. On Mazzini coming to London see Smith, *Mazzini*, pp. 20-31. On Marx see David McLellan, *Karl Marx*, 1973, pp. 221-6.

26. William Makepeace Thackeray, *The Adventures of Philip*, 1862, Ch. XXI.

27. On the hostesses see Mrs Lynn Linton, *Christopher Kirkland*, 1885, Vol. II, pp. 15-16; Margaret J. Shaen (ed.), *Memorials of Two Sisters*, 1908, pp. 79-93; G. L. M. Strauss, *Reminiscences of an Old Bohemian*, 1882, Vol. II, pp. 48-9. David Masson, *Memories of London in the 'Forties*, 1908, Ch III. On the Clerkenwell barrack see R. W. Vanderkiste, *Notes and Narratives of a Six Years' Mission, Principally Among the Dens of London*, 1854, pp. 79-80. Thomas Frost, *Forty Years' Recollections*, 1880, pp. 125-9.

28. On 'The Exile-World of London' in the 1860s see Justin McCarthy, *Reminiscences*, 1899, Vol. I, pp. 177-84. Adolphe Smith is in Sir Walter Besant, *London in the Nineteenth Century*, 1909, pp. 399-400.

29. On the Club Autonomie see W. C. Hart, *Confessions of an Anarchist*, 1906, Ch. X; on the Greenwich and Hawkins explosions see Hermia Oliver, *The International Anarchist Movement in Late Victorian London*, 1983, pp. 99-116, which provides the best account of foreign anarchists in London more generally; and also Sweeney, *At Scotland Yard*, Chs. IX-XI; Anderson, *The Lighter Side of My Official Life*, pp. 175-6.

30. See Carl Levy, 'Malatesta in Exile', *Annali della Fondazione Luigi Einandi* (Turin), Vol. XV, 1981, pp. 245-80.

31. The numbers of each group were given in Arthur Sherwell, *Life in West London*, 1897, p. 172. On the Scandinavians see Rev. J. H. Cardwell (ed.), *Twenty Years in Soho*, 1911, p. 27; Sherwell counted 162 in 1897, mainly Swedes.

32. On the French in London see especially Anon., *Wonderful London*, 1878, pp. 143-68; George R. Sims (ed.), *Living London*, 1902-3, Vol. I, pp. 241-7 (Count Armfelt), and Vol. II, pp. 133-8 (Paul Villars); I have also quoted from Emily Constance Cook, *London in the Time of the Diamond Jubilee*, 1897, p. 298.

33. For a memoir of a German upbringing in Hackney see Albert Lieck, *Narrow Waters*, 1935. On the suburban bankers and the 'more English' tag see Booth, *Life and Labour of the People in London*, Series 3, Vol. 6, p. 53. On West Ham see Edward G. Howarth and Mona Wilson, *West Ham*, 1907, p. 143.

34. See Sims (ed.), *Living London*, Vol. III, pp. 57-62 (Count Armfelt).

35. On the German community as a whole see above all Panayi, *German Immigrants in Britain During the Nineteenth Century*, 1995.

36. On the murders and the extraordinary trials that followed, recalled by lawyers involved in them, see Mr Serjeant Ballantine, *Some Experiences of a Barrister's Life*, 1882, Vol. II, pp. 16-21; Montagu Williams, *Leaves of a Life*, 1890, Ch. IX.

37. James Greenwood, *Low-Life Deeps*, 1876, pp. 109-14.

38. Mayhew, *London Labour and the London Poor*, Vol. I, pp. 218-20.

39. Sims (ed.), *Living London*, Vol. I, pp. 183-9. The best study of Italian London

is Sponza, *Italian Immigrants in Nineteenth-century Britain*, 1988.

40. On the 'Metropolitan Gypsyries' see George Borrow, *Romano Lavo-Lil*, 1874, pp. 207ff., his information gathered in 1864-5; Greenwood, *Low-Life Deeps*, pp. 212ff.; James Ewing Ritchie, *Days and Nights in London – or, Studies in Black and Gray*, 1880, pp. 217ff.; Sims (ed.), *Living London*, Vol. III, pp. 319-23 (T. W. Wilkinson); and Raphael Samuel, 'Comers and Goers', in H. J. Dyos and Michael Wolff (eds.), *The Victorian City*, 1973, Vol. I.

41. *Annual Register 1805*, Chronicle, p. 376; *1806*, Chronicle, pp. 450-51; *1808*, Chronicle, p. 13. Commissioner of the Metropolitan Police, *Annual Report for 1877*, p. 43. See also Michael Banton, *The Coloured Quarter*, 1955, p. 25.

42. On Billy Waters see Anon., *Real Life in London . . .*, 1821, Vol. I, p. 118; Charles Hindley, *The Life and Times of James Catnach (Late of Seven Dials), Ballad Monger*, 1878, pp. 135-8; J. C. Reid, *Bucks and Bruisers*, 1971, p. 80. Mayhew, *London Labour and the London Poor*, Vol. III, p. 195. On the missionary John Brown, *Sixty Years' Gleanings from Life's Harvest*, 1858, p. 280. On Norwood, reconstructed from family papers, see Eric Bligh, *Tooting Corner*, 1946, p. 53. And on Leicester Square see Captain Donald Shaw, *London in the Sixties (with a Few Digressions)*, 1909, pp. 44-7.

43. Mayhew, *London Labour and the London Poor*, Vol. II, pp. 556ff.

44. On the opium dens see Philip Collins, *Dickens and Crime*, 1964, pp. 300-301; Joseph Charles Parkinson, *The Poor*, 1864-6, 'An Opium Smoking House in London', p. 15b; Charles Dickens, *The Mystery of Edwin Drood*, 1870, Ch. 1; Rev. Harry Jones, *East and West London*, 1875, pp. 240, 282-3; Ritchie, *Days and Nights in London – or, Studies in Black and Gray*, pp. 170ff.; Richard Rowe, *Life in the London Streets, or Struggles for Daily Bread*, 1881, pp. 38ff., written in 1870 and claiming Dickens's original was in Victoria Court, Bluegate Fields; James Greenwood, *In Strange Company*, 1883, pp. 216ff.; Oscar Wilde, *The Picture of Dorian Gray*, 1891, pp. 72, 222-5; Arthur Conan Doyle, *The Adventures of Sherlock Holmes*, 1892, 'The Man with the Twisted Lip'. On the 'myth of the opium den' see Virginia Berridge, *Opium and the People*, 1999, Ch. 15.

45. The recent judgement is in the generally excellent Jonathan Schneer, *London 1900*, 1999, p. 203. For Mahomet see A. J. Mahomet, *From Street Arab to Pastor*, 1894. The estimate of sailor numbers is in Sims (ed.), *Living London*, Vol. III, pp. 279-85 (Alec Roberts). The Canning Town settlement is in Banton, *The Coloured Quarter*, 1955, p. 27; but it gets no mention in the most exhaustive social study of West Ham, Howarth and Wilson, *West Ham*.

46. See Schneer, *London 1900*, pp. 205ff., for Edwards and his contemporaries.

47. The old quarter is described in Charles Knight (ed.), *London*, 1841-4, Vol. VI, p. 46; and the overspill in Brayley and others, *London and Middlesex . . .*, Vol. III, p. 151, and David Hughson, *London*, 1805-9, Vol. II, pp. 188-9.

48. Mills is cited in the excellent David Feldman, *Englishmen and Jews*, 1994, p. 21. The numbers of Jewish old-clothes dealers is in William Carey, *The Stranger's Guide through London*, 1808, p. 339. On the rag fairs see Mayhew, *The Morning Chronicle Survey of Labour and the Poor*, Vol. II, pp. 33ff.; Brown, *Sixty Years' Gleanings from Life's Harvest*, pp. 172-86, is especially good on the tricks of the old-clothes dealers around 1817; Anon., *Wonderful London*, pp. 426ff; and V. D. Lipman, *Social History of the Jews in England*, 1954, pp. 32-4.

49. On the organisation of charity and the Jewish Board of Guardians see Rev. J. H. Stallard, *London Pauperism Amongst Jews and Christians*, 1867, pp. 1–27; Maurice Freedman (ed.), *A Minority in Britain*, 1955, Part I; and especially V. D. Lipman, *A Century of Social Service 1859–1959*, 1959.

50. John Hollingshead, *Ragged London in 1861*, 1861, pp. 44–8.

51. Stallard, *London Pauperism Amongst Jews and Christians*, p. 9; see also James Ewing Ritchie, *The Religious Life of London*, 1870, pp. 17–41, and Lloyd P. Gartner, *The Jewish Immigrant in England, 1870–1914*, 1973, pp. 38–41. On the Garrick theatre see *Annual Register 1880*, Chronicle, p. 28.

52. There is a full debate on conflicting numbers, which range from 97,000 to 150,000, in Lipman, *Social History of the Jews in England*, 1954, pp. 98–100; for the best background to the great migration and after see Feldman, *Englishmen and Jews*, pp. 147ff., and Gartner, *The Jewish Immigrant in England, 1870–1914*, pp. 41ff.

53. See the map of the Jewish East End in C. Russell and H. S. Lewis, *The Jew in London (a Study of Racial Character and Present-day Conditions)*, 1900.

54. Cited in Jerry White, 'Jewish Landlords, Jewish Tenants: An Aspect of Class Struggle within the Jewish East End, 1881–1914', in Aubrey Newman (ed.), *The Jewish East End 1840–1939*, 1981, pp. 208–10.

55. See Booth, *Life and Labour of the People in London*, Series 3, Vol. 1., pp. 152, 213.

56. On pigs' heads see Anon., *Real Life in London . . .*, Vol. II, pp. 248–50n. On the drama see *Annual Register 1839*, Chronicle, p. 119, for *Gold Dust* at the Garrick Theatre; and Henry Saxe Wyndham, *The Annals of Covent Garden Theatre from 1732 to 1897*, 1906, Vol. I, pp. 290–91, for *Family Quarrels* at Covent Garden, December 1802. On Christian missionaries see, for example, Geoffrey Holden Pike, *Byeways of Two Cities*, 1873, pp. 169–77. On *Punch* see M. H. Spielmann, *The History of 'Punch'*, 1895, pp. 103–5. *Punch* also had a strong anti-popery bias and routinely ridiculed the Irish. For the 'foul Jews' see William Makepeace Thackeray, *The Letters and Private Papers of William Makepeace Thackeray*, edited by Gordon N. Ray, 1945–6, Vol. II, p. 532 (4 May 1849). For more on the background and on other aspects of anti-Semitism see Feldman, *Englishmen and Jews*.

57. For some assaults and affrays see the local press: for example, *East London Advertiser*, 16 May 1891, 26 November 1892; *East London Observer*, 1 September 1894; see also Bernard Gainer, *The Alien Invasion*, 1972, pp. 56–9. Ernest Street is in *East London Observer*, 26 November 1898. Wapping and trouble generally is in Russell and Lewis, *The Jew in London . . .*, pp. xxxix–xiii, and see p. 24 for the English Jews. The judgement is in Gainer, *The Alien Invasion*, p. 58.

58. *Jewish Chronicle*, 12 August 1881, cited in William J. Fishman, *East End Jewish Radicals 1975–1914*, 1975, p. 55.

59. See Lipman, *A Century of Social Service 1859–1959*, pp. 94ff.; my figures are calculated from the data on pp. 278–83.

60. On the *hebrot* or *khevras* see Beatrice Potter writing in Booth, *Life and Labour of the People in London*, Series 1, Vol. 3, pp. 171ff.; Gartner, *The Jewish Immigrant in England, 1870–1914*, pp. 197ff.; Fishman, *East End Jewish Radicals 1975–1914*, pp. 55ff.; Feldman, *Englishmen and Jews*, pp. 312ff.

61. See Gartner, *The Jewish Immigrant in England, 1870–1914*, pp. 181–2, 203ff.

62. On the slaughter controversy see Albert M. Hyamson, *The London Board for Shechita 1804–1954*, 1954, Ch. IX. On all this and more see Feldman, *Englishmen and Jews*, pp. 335ff. and passim.

63. See Rudolf Rocker, *The London Years*, 1956; Fishman, *East End Jewish Radicals 1975–1914* (especially); and Gartner, *The Jewish Immigrant in England, 1870–1914*, Ch. IV.

64. On the trades claimed by newcomers see ibid., pp. 57–8.

65. Beatrice Potter is in Booth, *Life and Labour of the People in London*, Series 1, Vol. 4, p. 60. The loans are calculated from Lipman, *A Century of Social Service 1859–1959*, pp. 278–83.

Chapter 6 Lombard Street: Capital and Labour

1. On the Grasshopper see John Biddulph Martin, '*The Grasshopper' in Lombard Street*, 1892, Book I, Ch. 1, Book III, Ch. 1. For the numbers of banks see William Carey, *The Stranger's Guide through London*, 1808, pp. 123–5. On Lombard Street and discount see Walter Bagehot, *Lombard Street*, 1873, p. 3, and the very helpful W. T. C. King, *History of the London Discount Market*, 1936, pp. xv–xix. On the panics see *Annual Register 1825*, History of Europe, p. 123; and *ILN*, Vol. XLVIII, January–June 1866, pp. 477–8.

2. *Annual Register 1868*, Chronicle, pp. 142–4.

3. On stock-jobbing as gambling see Rudolph Ackermann, *The Microcosm of London*, 1808–10, Vol. III, p. 103. On Disraeli see Robert Blake, *Disraeli*, 1966, pp. 24–5. On the Spanish panic see David Morier Evans, *City Men and City Manners*, 1852, pp. 39–40.

4. On the effect of railways on stock exchange business see ibid., pp. 49–50. On the railway mania see *Annual Register 1845*, Chronicle, pp. 177–8; Edward Callow, *Old London Taverns*, 1899, pp. 28–9 (Callow was a stockbroker's clerk at the time); Robert Chambers (ed.), *The Book of Days*, 1862–4, Vol. II, pp. 637–8. See also David Kynaston, *The City of London*, Vol. I, 1994, pp. 151–3.

5. On 1808 see Carey, *The Stranger's Guide through London*, pp. 162–3, and on 1850 see John Weale, *A New Survey of London*, 1853, Vol. I, pp. 240–42. On the swindles see D. E. W. Gibb, *Lloyd's of London*, 1957, p. 80.

6. On the early days of joint-stock banks see T. E. Gregory, *The Westminster Bank Through a Century*, 1936, Vol. I, Chs. II and III. On the Royal British Bank see David Mories Evans, *Facts, Failures, and Frauds*, 1859, pp. 268ff.; Callow, *Old London Taverns*, pp. 22–3.

7. See King, *History of the London Discount Market*; Ronald C. Mitchie, *The City of London*, 1992; Kynaston, *The City of London*, Vol. I and Vol. II, 1995.

8. On the City's day population see City, *Day-Census 1881*, p. 8, and *Ten Years' Growth of the City of London*, 1891, pp. 24, 47. There was no City day census in 1901 but it is customary to split the difference between the 1891 and 1911 figures. It is likely that the earlier figures understate City employment and so make the rise seem steeper than it was, by discounting (!) the numbers resident in the City: 93,000 in 1866, 51,000 in 1871, 38,000 1891 and 27,000 in 1901. The employment figures are calculated from *Census of Great Britain, 1851: Population Tables II. Ages, Civil Condition, Occupations, and Birth-Place of the People, Vol. I*, pp.

cxxviiiff., 8ff.; *Census of England and Wales, 1871. Population Abstracts. Ages, Civil Condition, Occupations, and Birth-Places of the People. Vol. III*, pp. xxvff., 12ff.; *Census of England and Wales 1901: County of London*, pp. 76ff.; *Census of England and Wales 1901: County of Middlesex. Area, Houses and Population*, pp. 42ff.; *Census of England and Wales 1901: General report with Appendices*, pp. 256ff.

9. On the coffee houses see Evans, *City Men and City Manners*, pp. 116ff.; and Callow, *Old London Taverns*, pp. 37ff. Bryant Lillywhite, *London Coffee Houses*, 1963, provides an exhaustive directory. See also Kynaston, *The City of London*, Vol. I, pp. 244–5. On the smells see Charles Dickens, *The Dent Uniform Edition of Dickens' Journalism*, 1994–2000, Vol. IV, p. 115, 'City of London Churches', *All the Year Round*, 5 May 1860.

10. Evans, *City Men and City Manners*, p. 13; the phrase 'world within itself' is his too (p. 1).

11. See Albert Smith, *The Natural History of the Gent*, 1847. Dickens describes the friends of Alfred Lammle in *Our Mutual Friend*, 1864–5, Book 2, Ch. IV.

12. See Evans, *Facts, Failures, and Frauds*, pp. 74ff. Veneering is the fraudulent merchant-financier whom nobody knows in *Our Mutual Friend*.

13. See Evans, *Facts, Failures, and Frauds*, pp. 392ff. for Robson and passim for the 1855–7 events; *Annual Register 1861*, Chronicle, pp. 222–4.

14. *Annual Register 1862*, Chronicle, p. 67.

15. On the increasing professionalisation of share dealing see Ronald C. Mitchie, *The London Stock Exchange*, 1999, pp. 99–111; the critic was the publisher and Zola fan E. A. Vizetelly, cited in Mitchie, *The City of London*, 1992, pp. 2–3. A bucket-shop was 'A stock-gambling den carried on in opposition to regular exchange business; usually of a more than doubtful character'. And a guinea-pig was a company director who had his guinea and a substantial lunch for attending board meetings (John S. Farmer and W. E. Henley, *Slang and Its Analogues, Past and Present*, 1890–1904).

16. See Charles Dickens, *The Letters of Charles Dickens*, 1965–2002, Vol. X, pp. 194–5, 17 January 1863, to Lord Henry Brougham; Vol. XI, pp. 379–80, 16 June 1867, to Benjamin Disraeli. The advertisement is in *The Times*, 14 November 1849 (Supplement, p. 1). For numerous similar examples see James Pope-Hennessy, *Monckton Milnes*, 1951, pp. 63ff. For the 1890s see Charles Booth, *Life and Labour of the People in London*, 1892–1902, Series 2, Vol. 3, pp. 274–5.

17. On Glyn's see Roger Fulford, *Glyn's 1753–1953*, 1953, p. 169. Louis Bamberger, *Memories of Sixty Years in the Timber and Pianoforte Trades*, 1929, pp. 4–5. Sir Robert Anderson, *The Lighter Side of My Official Life*, 1910, pp. 42–3.

18. R. D. Blumenfeld, *R.D.B.'s Diary 1887–1914*, 1930, pp. 7–8 (23 June 1887). See Stirling Everard, *The History of the Gas Light and Coke Company 1812–1949*, 1949, p. 268. Booth, *Life and Labour of the People in London*, Series 2, Vol. 3, p. 277. See also the thorough review in F. D. Klingender, *The Condition of Clerical Labour in Britain*, 1935, Ch. 1.

19. Evans, *City Men and City Manners*, pp. 52–3, 168–72.

20. The City's men in black are in *Darlington's London and Environs*, 1902, p. 236. On the spread of women in the 1890s see, for instance, George R. Sims, *My Life – Sixty Years' Recollections of Bohemian London*, 1917, p. 97. For

an early reference to 'young women' in 'an Electric Telegraph Office' see Dickens, *Our Mutual Friend*, Chapter the last. On the women on London Bridge see Derek Hudson (ed.), *Munby*, 1972, p. 99, 5 June 1861. For Bermondsey sack women see Charles Knight (ed.), *London*, 1841-4, Vol. III, pp. 31-2.

21. For figures of factory and workshop employment in the City and elsewhere in 1904 see LCC, *London Statistics*, Vol. XVIII, 1907-8, p. 66. On what was made in the City see the formidable list in City, *Ten Years' Growth of the City of London*, 1891, pp. 101-29.

22. Census for 1901, *County of London*, pp. 76ff. For the middle decades see Peter G. Hall, *The Industries of London Since 1861*, 1962, pp. 22-3; L. D. Schwarz, *London in the Age of Industrialisation, 1700-1850*, 1992, pp. 11-14; David R. Green, *From Artisans to Paupers*, 1995, p. 18; P. Johnson, 'Economic Development and Industrial Dynamism in Victorian London', *London Journal*, Vol. 21, No. 1, 1996, pp. 27-37.

23. John Fisher Murray, *The World of London*, 1843, Vol. I, p. 189. See also Schwarz, *London in the Age of Industrialisation, 1700-1850*, p. 231.

24. These come from Edward Wedlake Brayley and others, *London and Middlesex . . .*, 1810-16, and Sir Richard Phillips, *A Morning's Walk from London to Kew*, 1820 (whose evidence is from 1813-16).

25. Information from George Dodd, *Days at the Factories*, 1843; *Industries*, 1878; R. Andom, *Industrial Explorings in and Around London*, 1895; Arthur Philip Crouch, *Silvertown and Neighbourhood (including East and West Ham*, 1900; Edward G. Howarth and Mona Wilson, *West Ham*, 1907; and a variety of other sources. The figures for factory and workshop employment in London County in 1904 are in LCC, *London Statistics*, Vol. XVIII, 1907-8, p. 66; the numbers employed in large factories are in RC, *Report of the Royal Commission on London Traffic*, 1905-6, Vol. VII, p. 14.

26. See, for instance, Hall, *The Industries of London Since 1861*; James A. Schmiechen, *Sweated Industries and Sweated Labor*, 1984; Schwarz, *London in the Age of Industrialisation, 1700-1850*, 1992; Green, *From Artisans to Paupers*, 1995; Andrew Godley, 'Immigrant Entrepreneurs and the Emergence of London's East End as an Industrial District', *London Journal*, Vol. 21, No. 1, 1996, pp. 38-45.

27. On Clerkenwell see Charles Knight (ed.), *London*, Vol. III, pp. 132-43. See also Booth, *Life and Labour of the People in London*, Series 2, Vol. 2, pp. 26ff. A fusee was the cogged wheel in a watch or clock round which the chain was wound.

28. On London's artists' quarters, including Newman Street, see Kit Wedd, *Artists' London*, 2001, Chs. 3-5.

29. Sir Walter Besant, *Children of Gibeon*, 1886, Book II, Ch. II.

30. *Annual Register 1829*, History of Europe, pp. 116-19, 131; Chronicle, pp. 99-100.

31. In general see George Dodd in Knight (ed.), *London*, Vol. II, pp. 386ff.; Henry Mayhew, *The Morning Chronicle Survey of Labour and the Poor*, 1849-50, Vol. I, pp. 51ff.; the blacks are in 'Spitalfields' by Charles Dickens and W. H. Wills, *Household Words*, 5 April 1851, reprinted in Charles Dickens, *Charles Dickens' Uncollected Writings from* Household Words *1850-1859*, edited by Harry Stone, 1968, Vol. I, pp. 227ff.; Sir Frank Warner, *The Silk Industry of the United Kingdom*, 1921; M. Dorothy George, *London Life in the XVIIIth Century*, 1925, pp. 178ff.

32. For an instance of strife see *Annual Register 1856*, Chronicle, pp. 161–3. Booth, *Life and Labour of the People in London*, Series 2, Vol. 5, p. 60, gives the declining number of shipwrights. On Thornycroft's fast boats see *Annual Register 1887*, Chronicle, p. 18. On Yarrow's move from London see Eleanor C. Barnes, *Alfred Yarrow*, 1923, pp. 181–93.

33. On pirate fishermen see SC, *Report from the Select Committee on the Police of the Metropolis*, 1828, qq. 267–8 (Captain Thomas Richbell, Thames magistrate). On London boot makers see Mayhew, *The* Morning Chronicle *Survey of Labour and the Poor*, Vol. III, p. 147; Booth, *Life and Labour of the People in London*, Series 2, Vol. 3, p. 19. On glass-blowers see Esme Howard, *Theatre of Life*, 1935, p. 171–3 – Howard worked on the Booth survey. On Clerkenwell poverty and the decline of the watch trade see RC, *Report of Her Majesty's Commissioners for Inquiring into the Housing of the Working Classes. Vol. II Minutes of Evidence and Appendix as to England and Wales*, 1885, qq. 1088 (Henry Boodle, solicitor to the Marquess of Northampton) and 1353ff. (Rev. Benjamin Sharp, Vicar of St Paul's, Clerkenwell); and Booth, *Life and Labour of the People in London*, Series 2, Vol. 2, pp. 26ff.

34. On the beginnings of GEC see Adam Gowans Whyte, *Forty Years of Electrical Progress*, 1930, pp. 22–4; on the early days of London engineering see Charles Wilson and William Reader, *Men and Machines*, 1958, introduction and Ch. I. Generally see J. E. Martin, *Greater London*, 1966, pp. 13–17.

35. Mayhew, *The* Morning Chronicle *Survey of Labour and the Poor*, Vol. I, p. 110. For the background to Hood's poem see Alfred Ainger (ed.), *Poems of Thomas Hood*, 1897, Vol. I, pl. xiv–v. He reports cases in *The Times* at the end of 1843, but an earlier example of a middle-class spinster relying on her needle and starving in the process appears in the *Annual Register 1842*, Chronicle, pp. 178–80.

36. Mayhew, *The* Morning Chronicle *Survey of Labour and the Poor*, pp. 115–16, 122, 157. See also Sally Alexander, *Women's Work in Nineteenth-century London*, 1983. Potter is in Booth, *Life and Labour of the People in London*, Series 1, Vol. 4, Ch. III.

37. On the lucky plumbers see Raymond Postgate, *The Builders' History*, 1923, p. 455. On the shift in money and real wages see B. R. Mitchell and Phyllis Deane, *Abstract of British Historical Statistics*, 1962, pp. 343–4.

38. Booth, *Life and Labour of the People in London*, Series 1, Vol. 1, p. 147.

39. *Annual Reports on Strikes and Lock-Outs, and on Conciliation and Arbitration Boards in the United Kingdom*, 1889–99.

40. Mayhew, *The* Morning Chronicle *Survey of Labour and the Poor*, Vol. IV, pp. 98–100.

41. For detailed histories of the growth of the port in the nineteenth century see Charles Capper, *Port and Trade of London*, 1862; RC, *Report of the Royal Commission on the Port of London*, 1902, Vol. I (Report); Joseph G. Broodbank, *Port of London*, 1921, Vol. I.

42. Tonnage figures, here and subsequently, come from RC, *Report of the Royal Commission on the Port of London*, 1902, Vol. III, pp. 232ff.

43. See Walter Thornbury and Edward Walford, *Old and New London*, 1873–9, Vol. II, pp. 134–7, on wild beasts, Wapping and fuchsias; George Dodd in Knight (ed.), *London*, Vol. III, pp. 22–3, on Bermondsey's 'maritime quarter'; on 'leaving shops' see Dickens, *Our Mutual Friend*, Book II, Ch. XII; see also Rev. Harry Jones, *East and West London*, 1875, pp. 123ff.

44. Booth, *Life and Labour of the People in London*, Series 2, Vol. 3, pp. 412ff.

45. See Beatrice Potter in ibid., Vol. 4, Ch. 1; Beatrice Webb, *My Apprenticeship*, 1926, pp. 296ff., and *The Diary of Beatrice Webb: Vol. I*, edited by Norman and Jean MacKenzie, 1982. And, more generally, Gareth Stedman Jones, *Outcast London*, 1971.

46. Mayhew, *The Morning Chronicle Survey of Labour and the Poor*, Vol. I, pp. 71-2.

47. Webb, *My Apprenticeship*, p. 298. See also Jerry White, *London in the Twentieth Century*, 2001, p. 173.

48. See *Annual Register 1889*, English History, pp. 177-81, Chronicle, pp. 40, 45; Hubert Llewellyn Smith and Vaughan Nash, *The Story of the Dockers' Strike . . .*, 1889; Terry McCarthy (ed.), *The Great Dock Strike 1889*, 1988.

49. Booth, *Life and Labour of the People in London*, Series 2, Vol. 3, pp. 322ff.

50. Ibid., Series 3, Vol. 1, p. 159, and Vol. 6, pp. 10-11.

51. On Leadenhall Market see B. Lambert, *The History and Survey of London and Its Environs*, 1806, Vol. II, pp. 402-3; Rudolph Ackermann, *The Microcosm of London*, 1808-10, Vol. II, pp. 176-80. For Billingsgate's women porters see Rowlandson's wonderful figures ibid., Vol. I, opp. p. 63. Murray, *The World of London*, Vol. I, p. 64.

52. For the Irish basket-women see Knight (ed.), *London*, Vol. V, pp. 137-41. The 1851 census records 550 women aged twenty or over employed as 'messenger, porter, errand-girl'. The 1901 census had just ninety-nine of the same age employed as 'messengers, porters, watchmen'.

53. *Survey of London*, Vol. XXVII, *Spitalfields*, 1957, pp. 134-5.

54. For ghastly details of tortured animals and nuisance see the evidence to the various select committees and other inquiries: for instance, SC, *Second Report from the Select Committee on the State of Smithfield Market*, 1828; *Report from the Select Committee on Smithfield Market; together with the Minutes of Evidence, Appendix, and Index*, 1847; *Report from the Select Committee on Smithfield Market; together with the Proceedings of the Committee, Minutes of Evidence, Appendix, and Index*, 1849; PP, *Report of the Commissioners Appointed to Make Inquiries Relating to Smithfield Market, and the Markets in the City of London For the Sale of Meat*, 1850. For a representative criticism of the Corporation see Dickens, *Charles Dickens' Uncollected Writings from* Household Words *1850-1859*, Vol. I, pp. 101ff., 'The Heart of Mid-London' (with W. H. Wills), *Household Words*, 4 May 1850.

55. On early Oxford Street see Richard Bowden, 'Oxford Street Two Hundred Years Ago: The Portland Estate Block Plans, *c.* 1805-1870', *LTR*, 2001, pp. 79-89. On the lamps see Brayley and others, *London and Middlesex . . .*, Vol. II, pp. 13-14.

56. On D'Oyley's see David Hughson, *London*, 1805-9, Vol. IV, pp. 194-5 and fn. On the Soho Bazaar see William Jerdan, *The Autobiography of William Jerdan*, 1852-3, Vol. II, pp. 216-20; Thornbury and Walford, *Old and New London*, Vol. III, p. 190; Charles Hindley, *The Life and Times of James Catnach (Late of Seven Dials), Ballad Monger*, 1878, p. 193; Soho, 1898, pp. 90-95.

57. On the move of gas and glass from gin palace to emporium see George Dodd in Knight (ed.), *London*, Vol. V, pp. 389-93; Anon., *Real Life in London . . .*, 1821, Vol. I, pp. 126-7n.

58. On Regent Street see Hermione Hobhouse, *A History of Regent Street*, 1975, pp. 82ff.

59. On the Pantheon see John Weale, *A New Survey of London*, 1853, Vol. I, p. 264; and the Pantechnicon see Knight (ed.), *London*, Vol. V, p. 397. On Harrod's see *Survey of London*, Vol. XLI, *Southern Kensington*, 1983, p17ff. For Edwardian developments see White, *London in the Twentieth Century*, p. 11. For an overview see Michael Ball and David Sutherland, *An Economic History of London, 1800–1914*, 2001, pp. 138–41; and Erika Diane Rappaport, *Shopping for Pleasure*, 2000, which deals with suburban and West End shopping from 1850 to 1914 from the woman's point of view. For Trollope's criticisms see Anthony Trollope, *London Tradesmen*, 1927, especially Michael Sadleir's introduction, p x.

60. Robert Southey, *Letters from England*, 1807, p. 51; see Anon., *Real Life in London . . .*, Vol. I, p. 51n, and Vol. II, pp. 156–7, for the sign and chalking; and for the barkers see John Thomas Smith, *An Antiquarian Ramble in the Streets of London . . .*, 1846, Vol. I, pp. 124–5, writing probably of the 1820s.

61. William Hone, *The Every-Day Book . . .*, 1825–7, Vol. II, pp. 703, 750–51.

62. On the old cheese see Dickens, *The Dent Uniform Edition of Dickens' Journalism*, Vol. II, p. 340, 'Bill-Sticking', *Household Words*, 22 March 1851. See also Knight (ed.), *London*, Vol. V, pp. 31ff. For Mr Slum see especially Ch. XXVIII. On Moses and his followers see Max Schlesinger, *Saunterings in and About London*, 1853, pp. 17–24. On the railway bridges, Smith and the pyramid see Andrew Wynter, *Subtle Brains and Lissom Fingers*, 1863, pp. 44ff. On later theatrical enterprise see John Hollingshead, *My Lifetime*, 1895, Vol. II, p. 16.

63. For Mrs H see Anon., *Real Life in London . . .*, Vol. II, p. 3n; Anon., *The Picture of London, for 1818*, 1818, pp. 412ff.; John Britton (ed.), *The Original Picture of London*, 1826, pp. 364ff.

64. Wynter, *Subtle Brains and Lissom Fingers*, pp. 82ff. For an overview see Ball and Sutherland, *An Economic History of London, 1800–1914*, pp. 154–6; on building the Langham Hotel see Willert Beale, *The Light of Other Days*, 1890, Vol. II, pp. 294–300. Karl Baedeker, *London and Its Environs*, 1889, pp. 6–10.

65. The American was T. C. Crawford, *English Life*, 1889, pp. 7–8. Booth, *Life and Labour of the People in London*, Series 3, Vol. 4, p. 145, writing of south London but true generally.

66. On the barmaids see Anon., *Toilers in London*, 1889, Ch. XIX. P. C. Hoffman, *They Also Serve*, 1949, pp. 5–6 and Ch. III.

Chapter 7 The New Cut: On the Edge

1. Joseph Charles Parkinson, *The Poor*, 1864–6, p. 12b (*Daily News*, n.d., but the reference to cholera places it probably in 1866).

2. Henry Mayhew, *The Morning Chronicle Survey of Labour and the Poor*, 1849–50, Vol. I, p. 251. The Pandemonium is cited in Walter Thornbury and Edward Walford, *Old and New London*, 1873–8, Vol. VI, pp. 411–13. Mayhew gives 300 stalls in 1849 but Parkinson thought the number had declined seventeen years or so later. At the end of the century there were 220 stalls on a Saturday night, the market's busiest time: RC, *Report of the Royal Commission on London Traffic*, 1905–6, Vol. III, pp. 341ff.

3. Daniel Joseph Kirwan, *Palace and Hovel*, 1870, pp. 208–9, 391; Charles Booth, *Life and Labour of the People in London*, 1892–1902, Series 2, Vol. 3, p. 260; Henry Mayhew, *London Labour and the London Poor*, 1861–2, Vol. I, pp. 6–8; *Census of Great Britain, 1851: Population Tables*, Vol. II, *Ages, Civil Condition, Occupations, and Birth-Place of the People*, 1854, pp. 8ff.

4. See Mayhew, *London Labour and the London Poor*, Vol. I, pp. 166ff.

5. Compton Mackenzie, *My Life and Times: Octave One 1883–1891*, 1963, pp. 208–10. Besides Mayhew, *The* Morning Chronicle *Survey of Labour and the Poor* and *London Labour and the London Poor*, see also John Thomas Smith, *The Cries of London*, 1839, Charles Hindley, *A History of the Cries of London, Ancient and Modern*, 1881, and Andrew W. Tuer, *Old London Street Cries and the Cries of To-Day*, 1885.

6. On the dog dealer in Regent Street see *ILN*, Vol. XLVIII, January–June 1866, pp. 397–8. On the London Hospital see D. G. Halsted, *Doctor in the Nineties*, 1959, p. 25 – Halsted was a medical student there at the time.

7. Mayhew, *London Labour and the London Poor*, Vol. I, pp. 57–9; Booth, *Life and Labour of the People in London*, pp. 269–70.

8. John Thomas Smith, *Vagabondiana . . .*, 1817, pp. 41–4. On the pure-finders see Mayhew, *The* Morning Chronicle *Survey of Labour and the Poor*, Vol. II, pp. 69ff., and *London Labour and the London Poor*, Vol. II, pp. 160ff.; and R. W. Vanderkiste, *Notes and Narratives of a Six Years' Mission . . .*, 1854, p. 43. On bone stew see James Greenwood, *The Wilds of London*, 1874, pp. 59–60.

9. On Stodart see *Annual Register 1839*, Chronicle, p. 175; on Jones see Anon., *Real Life in London . . .*, 1821, Vol. II, pp. 156–7n; on Casey see Diane Atkinson, *Love and Dirt*, 2003, pp. 83–4, 28–9, and Derek Hudson (ed.), *Munby Diaries*, 1972, pp. 89–90, which reveals an interesting excision from Munby's diary by Atkinson.

10. For Dickens's memories see Charles Dickens, *The Dent Uniform Edition of Dickens' Journalism*, 1994–2000, Vol. III, pp. 241ff.: 'An Unsettled Neighbourhood', *Household Words*, 11 November 1854. For organ grinders and German bands in the 1890s see Booth, *Life and Labour of the People in London*, Series 1, Vol. 4, pp. 142ff.

11. There is a nice account from 1863 of Ethiopian serenaders in Hudson (ed.), *Munby Diaries*, pp. 157–9. Foster's petition is in 'Answers to Correspondents' published with the weekly parts of the 1851–2 edition of Mayhew, *London Labour and the London Poor*.

12. W. P. Frith, *My Autobiography and Reminiscences*, 1887, Vol. I, pp. 249–51. Mayhew, *The* Morning Chronicle *Survey of Labour and the Poor*, Vol. IV, pp. 192ff., on the Punches and Vol. III, p. 92, and Vol. V, pp. 18–19. On the disabled sailor artist see Sir Richard Phillips, *A Morning's Walk from London to Kew*, 1820, p. 379.

13. For Madeleine Sinclair see Hudson (ed.), *Munby Diaries*, p. 131. The Female Salamander is in Anon., *Real Life in London . . .*, Vol. II, pp. 478ff. Albert Lieck, *Narrow Waters*, 1935, pp. 118–19. Mayhew, *The* Morning Chronicle *Survey of Labour and the Poor*, Vol. IV, pp. 214ff.

14. For 1815 and earlier comparisons see SC, *Reports from the Committees on the State of Mendicity in the Metropolis*, 1815–16, pp. 37–9: John Stafford, chief clerk Bow Street police office since 1803; Sir Nathaniel Conant, chief

magistrate Bow Street. For Fitzpatrick see ibid., p. 15. [Joseph Charles Parkinson] *Daily News*, 19 April 1869. George R. Sims (ed.), *Living London*, 1902–3, Vol. II, p. 363.

15. Cited in George Somes Layard, *A Great 'Punch' Editor*, 1907, pp. 236–7.

16. C. J. Ribton-Turner, *A History of Vagrants and Vagrancy and Beggars and Begging*, 1887, pp. 311–12. See also Smith, *Vagabondiana*...; James Greenwood, *The Seven Curses of London*, 1869, Pt. III; Mayhew, *The* Morning Chronicle *Survey of Labour and the Poor*, Vols. I, II and III passim, and *London Labour and the London Poor*, Vol. II, pp. 572ff., and Vol. IV, pp. 399ff.; Tuer, *Old London Street Cries and the Cries of To-Day*, 1885.

17. For Conant see SC, *Reports from the Committees on the State of Mendicity in the Metropolis*, 1815–16, p. 41. Arthur Conan Doyle, *The Adventures of Sherlock Holmes*, 1892.

18. Greenwood, *The Seven Curses of London*, pp. 1–2: oakum was tarred and knotted rope that convicts were set to unpick by hand, taking a heavy toll of the fingers. On Barnardo and Jim Jarvis see Gillian Wagner, *Barnardo*, 1979, pp. 30ff., 50; and Mrs Barnardo and James Marchant, *Memoirs of the Late Dr Barnardo*, 1907, Appendix B. There is considerable doubt about the date of this incident, which could have been at any time between 1866 and 1870. On the night out with Shaftesbury see ibid., pp. 84–5: Shaftesbury had been involved in similar excursions twenty years before – see Mayhew, *The* Morning Chronicle *Survey of Labour and the Poor*, Vol. IV, p. 45.

19. Sims (ed.), *Living London*, Vol. III, p. 332.

20. Mayhew, *The* Morning Chronicle *Survey of Labour and the Poor*, Vol. III, p. 109. SC, *Select Committee on Criminal and Destitute Juveniles: Report, together with the Proceedings of the Committee, Minutes of Evidence, Appendix and Index*, 1852, q. 331, Rev. Sydney Turner, chaplain to the Philanthropic Society's Farm School for Boys, Redhill; and q. 3280, William Locke. TS is cited in Charles Maurice Davies, *Mystic London*, 1875, p. 14. The numbers of children in the London ragged schools is in C. J. Montague, *Sixty Years in Waifdom*, 1904, p. 97.

21. On Mary Robinson see *Annual Register 1884*, Chronicle, p. 3. For other capitalists among the street folk see Charles Knight (ed.), *London*, 1841–4, Vol. V, pp. 142–3, and Booth, *Life and Labour of the People in London*, Series 2, Vol. 4, p. 143.

22. On the costers' walks see Mayhew, *The* Morning Chronicle *Survey of Labour and the Poor*, Vol. II, p. 36. On the beggars' walks and pubs see SC, *Reports from the Committees on the State of Mendicity in the Metropolis*, 1815–16, pp. 18–19, 29–30, 46–8, 65–6, and Sholto and Reuben Percy, *London*, 1823, Vol. II, pp. 270–71. On the boat race see Krwan, *Palace and Hovel*, p. 355.

23. Ibid., pp. 140–41; Jerome K. Jerome, *My Life and Times*, 1926, p. 38; and on the pedlars' market at Caledonian Road see Greenwood, *The Wilds of London*, p. 286, and, for its twentieth-century inter-war heyday, Jerry White, *London in the Twentieth Century*, 2001, pp. 251–2.

24. For Boz at Greenwich see Dickens, *The Dent Uniform Edition of Dickens' Journalism*, Vol. I, pp. 112ff.

25. William Hone, *The Every-Day Book* . . ., 1825–7, Vol. I, pp. 583ff.; see also Henry Morley, *Memoirs of Bartholomew Fair*, 1859, passim. On Richardson see Thomas Frost, *The Old Showmen, and the Old London Fairs*, 1874, pp. 337–52, and *DNB*. Frost's final judgement is on pp. 376–7. For a superb

modern study see Richard D. Altick, *The Shows of London*, 1978.

26. For the detailed market returns and City costers see RC, *Report of the Royal Commission on London Traffic*, 1905-6, Vol. III, pp. 341-53, 512-13; see also Booth, *Life and Labour of the People in London*, Series 2, Vol. 2, pp. 262-3.

27. A female birds'-egg painter (or forger) has a prominent part in Shirley Brooks's novel *Sooner or Later*, 1868. On the fireworks explosion see *Annual Register 1873*, Chronicle, pp. 107-8. Any year prior to this notched up similar accidents. On foul hatters see Mayhew, *The Morning Chronicle Survey of Labour and the Poor*, Vol. VI, p. 153.

28. See *Census of England and Wales 1901: County of London*, 1903, pp. 76ff. Booth, *Life and Labour of the People in London*, Series 2, Vol. 5, pp. 54-5, makes the point about under-enumeration in the 1891 census and there seems to have been no improvement ten years on. Booth emphasises at pp. 57-8 that London is 'the stronghold of small industries' compared to England and Wales as a whole. In fact, though, the proportion of employers and self-employed in the industries I have selected here (the most 'independent' of the London workshop trades) were *higher* in England and Wales without London than in London alone. This re-emphasises, I think, that the small-industry view of London's economy has been overdone by historians.

29. [T. Carter] *A Continuation of the Memoirs of a Working Man*, 1850, pp. 105-11. Mayhew, *The Morning Chronicle Survey of Labour and the Poor*, Vol. II, p. 5, and Vol. III, pp. 87ff., 91ff. On Wombwell see Robert Chambers (ed.), *The Book of Days*, 1862-4, Vol. II, p. 586.

30. W. F. Watson, *Machines and Men*, 1935, pp. 21-3.

31. On the lightermen see Mayhew, *The Morning Chronicle Survey of Labour and the Poor*, Vol. VI, p. 105. On the cabbies see Booth, *Life and Labour of the People in London*, Series 2, Vol. 3, p. 289.

32. Ibid., pp. 298-9. See also G. A. Sekon, *Locomotion in Victorian London*, 1938, Ch. IV.

33. Max Schlesinger, *Saunterings in and About London*, 1853, pp. 158-60. On the bucks see Mayhew, *The Morning Chronicle Survey of Labour and the Poor*, Vol. VI, pp. 56ff.

34. Schlesinger, *Saunterings in and About London*, p. 160.

35. Booth, *Life and Labour of the People in London*, pp. 300-301. Trade unions among the cabbies rose and fell, often beginning and ending in a strike, as in 1853, 1871, 1891, 1894 and 1896.

36. Cited in A. G. Gardiner, *John Benn and the Progressive Movement*, 1925, p. 21.

37. Frank T. Bullen, *Confessions of a Tradesman*, 1908, passim.

38. For a good survey of the life of small shopkeepers see Booth, *Life and Labour of the People in London*, Series 2, Vol. 3, pp. 250ff.

39. On *appearance* see Anon., *Real Life in London . . .*, Vol. I, p. 47. Portable property is an obsession of Wemmick, Mr Jaggers's confidential clerk in Charles Dickens, *Great Expectations*, 1860-61.

40. For an excellent modern overview with London as a main theme see Margot C. Finn, *The Character of Credit*, 2003. See also, on the writers, Nigel Cross, *The Common Writer*, 1985, pp. 38-47.

41. Charles Dickens, *Charles Dickens' Uncollected Writings from Household Words 1850-1859*, edited by Harry Stone, 1968, Vol. II, pp. 372-3 (Charles

Dickens and W. H. Wills, 'My Uncle', *Household Words*, 6 December 1851).
That gives 'upwards of 400' in London and in 1906–7 the LCC's *London
Statistics* says 536.

42. 'Provisional prisons' is from Anon., *The Picture of London, for 1818*, 1818,
p. 227. On Solomon Pell see Charles Dickens, *Pickwick Papers*, 1836–7, Ch.
xliii. Blanchard Jerrold, *Cent Per Cent*, 1869, p. 139. Henry and Augustus
Mayhew, *The Image of His Father*, 1851, pp. 50, 130. For Joshua Mayhew
see Anne Humpherys, *Travels into the Poor Man's Country*, 1977, Ch. 1.

43. On Sunday-men see Anon., *Real Life in London . . .*, Vol. I, pp. 44–5. On
the Blessington D'Orsays see Michael Sadleir, *Blessington D'Orsay*, 1933,
pp. 317–47. On Disraeli see William Flavelle Monypenny and George Earle
Buckle, *The Life of Benjamin Disraeli, Earl of Beaconsfield*, 1929, Vol. I,
pp. 350ff., and Robert Blake, *Disraeli*, 1966, pp. 134, 145, 160. On Boulogne
see Jerrold, *Cent Per Cent*, p. 218; and James Pope-Hennessey, *Monckton
Milnes*, 1949, p. 28, writing of the Monckton Milnes family from 1828. See
also Renton Nicholson, *Rogue's Progress*, 1860, passim.

44. See Edward Wedlake Brayley and others, *London and Middlesex . . .*,
1810–16, Vol. III, Pt. I, p. 45.

45. On Dufrene see Nicholson, *Rogue's Progress*, pp. 160–66; [Joseph Charles
Parkinson] 'Prisoners for Debt', *Daily News*, 30 September 1869.

46. For the epitome see Anon., *Real Life in London . . .*, Vol. II, p. 56. On chummage and garnish see Finn, *The Character of Credit*, 2003. On footing see
Lord William Pitt Lennox, *Drafts on My Memory*, 1866, Vol. II, p. 366. On
the joys of the King's Bench see John Britton (ed.), *The Original Picture of
London*, 1826, p. 229; and E. M. Butler (ed.), *A Regency Visitor*, 1957, pp.
226–7, for a visit by Prince Pückler-Muskau. The barber's pole is in Samuel
Bamford, *Passages in the Life of a Radical*, 1844, Vol. II, pp. 163–4. And
for Alsatia see Rev. J. Richardson, *Recollections, Political, Literary, Dramatic,
and Miscellaneous, of the Last Half–Century . . .*, 1856, Vol. II, pp. 1–26,
writing of the period around 1820.

47. Lennox, *Drafts on My Memory*, Vol. II, pp. 360–67. He didn't oblige.

48. The Gore House sale is in William Makepeace Thackeray, *The Letters and
Private Papers of William Makepeace Thackeray*, edited by Gordon N. Ray,
1945–6, Vol. II, p. 532, to Mrs Brookfield. On Thackeray's early life in the
moneylending business see Gordon N. Ray, *Thackeray: The Uses of Adversity,
1811–1846*, 1955, pp. 159–60.

Chapter 8 Fleet Street: City of Words

1. On this last point see Charles Booth, *Life and Labour of the People in
London*, 1892–1902, Series 2, Vol. 2, p. 190.

2. See for Fleet Street generally E. Beresford Chancellor, *The Annals of Fleet
Street*, 1912, who provides the 'most famous' tag, p. 1, and Susie Barson
and Andrew Saint, *A Farewell to Fleet Street*, 1988; and for further details
of its early connection with printing see Elic Howe and Harold E. Waite,
The London Society of Compositors, 1948; P. M. Handover, *Printing in
London*, 1960; and J. H. Baker, 'English Law Books and Legal Publishing',
in John Barnard and D. F. McKenzie (eds.), *The Cambridge History of the
Book in Britain*, 2002 (disappointingly uninformative on London topography, however); and Robin Myers et al. (eds.), *The London Book Trade*,

2003, Chs. 1 and 6. For 'London news' see Arthur A. Adrian, *Mark Lemon*, 1966, p. 90. The Old Cheshire Cheese gets a book to itself in R. R. D. Adams (ed.), *The Book of the Cheese*, 1901.

3. The status of the Row is in John Thomas Smith, *An Antiquarian Ramble in the Streets of London . . .*, 1846, Vol. II, pp. 210–12, written at an earlier period. For numbers and addresses see Anon., *The Picture of London, for 1818*, 1818, p. 299.

4. The publications are listed in William Carey, *The Stranger's Guide through London*, 1808, pp. 254ff.

5. On W. H. Smith see Charles Wilson, *First with the News*, 1985, pp. 36–49, 99–100 and passim.

6. On the telegraph and London news see, for example, Knight, *Passages of a Working Life During Half a Century*, Vol. II, pp. 219–21, and Vol. III, pp. 156–7; and Sir John R. Robinson, *Fifty Years of Fleet Street*, 1904, pp. 164ff. For some intimate revelations of the early years of Reuter in London see Valentine Williams, *The World of Action*, 1938, pp. 25ff. On *The Times* see *Annual Register 1880*, Chronicle, p. 43.

7. David F. Mitch, *The Rise of Popular Literacy in Victorian England*, 1992, pp. 54–8.

8. Numbers of stamped newspapers are in *Annual Register 1822*, Appendix to Chronicle, pp. 350–52. The 1826 lists are in John Britton (ed.), *The Original Picture of London*, 1826, pp. 342ff. The changes over time of numbers of books published in London are given in Knight, *Passages of a Working Life During Half a Century*, Vol. III, p. 194. For Catnach see Charles Hindley, *The Life and Times of James Catnach (Late of Seven Dials), Ballad Monger*, 1878, p. 143: he gives the date as 1823 but the trial of the murderers of Mr Weare did not come on at Hertford till January 1824. Street vendors of the pamphlet rioted outside Catnach's shop in Monmouth Street when he failed to satisfy the demand.

9. See Richard D. Altick, *The English Common Reader*, 1957, p. 393n for circulation figures for the *Penny Magazine*. On the war of the unstamped, and its metropolitan focus, see Patricia Hollis, *The Pauper Press*, 1970, which remains unrivalled in the field.

10. On Lloyd see Thomas Frost, *Forty Years' Recollections*, 1880, pp. 84ff.; George Augustus Sala, *The Life and Adventures of George Augustus Sala*, 1895, Vol. I, pp. 208–9. On Holt see ibid., pp. 236–41; the advertisement is in An Old Printer, *A Few Personal Recollections*, 1896, pp. 46–7.

11. On newspaper sales see Wilson, *First with the News*, pp. 72–3; on the position in 1844 and numbers of books published in London see Knight, *Passages of a Working Life During Half a Century*, Vol. II, pp. 278–9, and Vol. III, pp. 194–5. On Dickens's sales see Altick, *The English Common Reader*, pp. 383–4.

12. Knight, *Passages of a Working Life During Half a Century*, Vol. III, p. 244.

13. For circulation figures see *ILN*, Vol. XVIII, p. 451 (24 May 1851). On the *ILN* generally see Charles Mackay, *Forty Years' Recollections of Life, Literature, and Public Affairs from 1830 to 1870*, 1877, Vol. II, pp. 64ff., and *Through the Long Day, or, Memorials of a Literary Life During Half a Century*, 1887, Vol. I, pp. 353–7; and Joseph Hatton, *Journalistic London*, 1882, pp. 221ff. On the *Illustrated Times* see Sala, *The Life and Adventures of George Augustus Sala*, Vol. I, pp. 324ff.

14. See Hatton, *Journalistic London*, pp. 221ff.

15. For Watson see H. J. Keefe, *A Century in Print*, 1939, p. 46. Books published (in Great Britain) and newspapers registered as published in London are in *Haydn's Dictionary of Dates*, 1904 edn, 'Book' and 'Newspapers', although the 1881 figure for the latter comes from Hatton, *Journalistic London*, p. 128. The list of titles is in *Dickens's Dictionary of London*, 1883, 'Newspapers'.

16. On the *Daily Mail* see H. Simonis, *The Street of Ink*, 1917, Ch. 2.; for circulation figures see Altick, *The English Common Reader*, 1957, pp. 394–6.

17. Justin McCarthy, *Charing Cross to St. Paul's*, 1891, p. 44. See also W. J. Loftie, *London City*, 1891, pp. 233–4; Emily Constance Cook, *London in the Time of the Diamond Jubilee*, 1897, pp. 274–80; and Barson and Saint, *A Farewell to Fleet Street*, 1988, pp. 19–26.

18. See Hatton, *Journalistic London*, pp. 27–30, for Fleet Street providing provincial editors, and J. A. Hammerton, *Books and Myself*, 1944, pp. 118–22, for a provincial editor doing well-paid freelance work for Fleet Street in the 1890s. On the *Scottish Observer* see John Connell, *W. E. Henley*, 1949, pp. 142–3; and *The Clarion* see Alex Thompson, *Here I Lie*, 1937, pp. 123ff.

19. A stinking print shop is in T. A. Jackson, *Solo Trumpet*, 1953, pp. 2–3, 7ff. Other foul conditions are recalled in the 1830s in a shop that was probably Hansard's, in Charles Manby Smith, *The Working Man's Way in the World*, 1853, pp. 241–4; he remembers the slack times, too, at pp. 165–73. W. E. Adams, *Memoirs of a Social Atom*, 1903, p. 377. Charles Booth, *Life and Labour of the People in London*, Series 2, Vol. 5, p. 28.

20. Pierce Egan, *The Life of an Actor*, 1825, pp. 25ff. The *Illustrated Times* is remembered in Adams, *Memoirs of a Social Atom*, p. 334. Knight, *Passages of a Working Life During Half a Century*, 1864–5, Vol. III, p. 135. On the casual fringe see An Old Printer, *A Few Personal Recollections*, pp. 32–4, and Adams, *Memoirs of a Social Atom*, pp. 332–3. On the Dangerfields see Arthur C. Armstrong, *Bouverie Street to Bowling Green Lane*, 1946, passim.

21. On London opposition to composing machines see Howe and Waite, *The London Society of Compositors*, pp. 225–33. On bookbinding see Handover, *Printing in London*, Ch. VIII; on opposition to machinery see Knight, *Passages of a Working Life During Half a Century*, Vol. II, pp. 161–2.

22. See Peter G. Hall, *The Industries of London Since 1861*, 1962, pp. 104ff., for comments on the proportionate decline of printing in London at the end of the century.

23. For Grub Street in 1814 see John Brown, *Sixty Years' Gleanings from Life's Rich Harvest*, 1858, pp. 25–6.

24. On Phillips see George Borrow, *Lavengro*, 1851, Ch. XXX, and Herbert Jenkins, *The Life of George Borrow*, 1912, pp. 40ff.; Mrs J. H. Riddell, *A Struggle for Fame*, 1883, Vol. I, p. 108 – an autobiographical novel, Mr Vassett is a fictional character but true enough; Frank Harris, *My Life and Loves*, 1964, p. 299 – this was around 1883.

25. Jerome K. Jerome, *My Life and Times*, 1926, p. 122, writing of the 1890s.

26. See Annie Besant, *An Autobiography*, 1893, p. 84. Biographical details are otherwise very usefully summarised in John Sutherland, *The Longman Companion to Victorian Fiction*, 1988, on which I've drawn greatly.

27. See Edmund Yates, *His Recollections and Experiences*, 1884, Vol. I, pp. 217–18. On White see Catherine Macdonald Maclean, *Mark Rutherford*,

1955. See also Arthur William à Beckett, *Recollections of a Humourist*, 1907, pp. 33ff. (a War Office clerk in the 1860s, naming several others) and Anthony Trollope, *An Autobiography*, 1883.

28. On the status of lawyers see Brian Abel-Smith and Robert Stevens, *Lawyers and the Courts*, 1967, p. 187. On Bowles see *Annual Register 1827*, Chronicle, p. 21.

29. On Lincoln's Inn see Elie Halévy, *England in 1815*, 1949, p. 23. R. E. Francillon, *Mid-Victorian Memories*, 1913, pp. 134-5. A Journalist, *Bohemian Days in Fleet Street*, 1913, pp. 49-50.

30. Cited in William Flavelle Monypenny and George Earle Buckle, *The Life of Benjamin Disraeli, Earl of Beaconsfield*, 1929, Vol. I, pp. 36-7.

31. For Brooks see George Somes Layard, *A Great 'Punch' Editor*, 1907, pp. 176, 585-90; on Reach see Sala, *The Life and Adventures of George Augustus Sala*, Vol. I, pp. 199ff., and Nigel Cross, *The Common Writer*, 1985, pp. 112-13 – Cross provides a thorough and illuminating survey of nineteenth-century Grub Street; on Miller see Thomas Cooper, *The Life of Thomas Cooper*, 1872, p. 124, and Thomas Frost, *Reminiscences of a Country Journalist*, 1886, pp. 282-4; Mrs M. O. W. Oliphant, *The Autobiography and Letters of Mrs. M. O. W. Oliphant*, 1899, pp. 4, 83, 441ff.

32. George Gissing, *London and the Life of Literature in Late Victorian England*, edited by Pierre Coustillas, 1978, pp. 143, 211, 229, 247. See also Jacob Korg, *George Gissing*, 1965, p. 157.

33. For the 1840s see Charles Knight (ed.), *London*, 1841-4, Vol. IV, pp. 385ff. George Gissing, *New Grub Street*, 1891, Chs. II and VII.

34. Clement Scott and Cecil Howard, *The Life and Reminiscences of E. L. Blanchard, with notes from the Diary of William Blanchard*, 1891, Vol. I, pp. 45-6n.

35. On Jerdan see the London Library's copy of Rev. J. Richardson, *Recollections, Political, Literary, Dramatic, and Miscellaneous, of the Last Half-Century . . .*, 1856, Vol. II, p. 196; see also the *DNB* and William Jerdan, *The Autobiography of William Jerdan*, 1852-3. On Yates see Edmund Downey, *Twenty Years Ago*, 1905, pp. 105-6: again a turn-of-the-century London Library reader has identified 'the distinguished literary man' of the tale as Yates. On Purnell see Francillon, *Mid-Victorian Memories*, pp. 156ff. On Graham see Knight, *Passages of a Working Life During Half a Century*, Vol. II, pp. 20-22.

36. For Disraeli see Monypenny and Buckle, *The Life of Benjamin Disraeli, Earl of Beaconsfield*, Vol. I, p. 1,301. On Kemble see *Annual Register 1830*, Chronicle, pp. 170-71. On Nicholson see Renton Nicholson, *Rogue's Progress*, 1860, Chs. XXIV; Scott and Howard, *The Life and Reminiscences of E. L. Blanchard . . .*, Vol. I, pp. 256-8n. Scott is cited in Gordon N. Ray, *Thackeray: The Uses of Adversity, 1811-1846*, 1955, pp. 194-5.

37. See Leslie Mitchell, *Bulwer Lytton*, 2003, p. 127 and passim.

38. Charles Dickens, *The Letters of Charles Dickens*, 1965-2002, Vol. V, pp. 227-8, 9 January 1848, to W. M. Thackeray.

39. This is all well and fairly covered in Gordon N. Ray, *Thackeray: The Age of Wisdom, 1847-1863*, 1958, pp. 154-5, 304ff. Dickens, *The Letters of Charles Dickens*, Vol. X, pp. 346-7, 25 January 1864, to Wilkie Collins: see also the (as always) illuminating notes to the letter.

40. On the *Saturday Review* see Sir Walter Besant, *Autobiography*, 1902, pp.

91-5; J. W. Robertson Scott, *The Story of the Pall Mall Gazette, of its first editor Frederick Greenwood and of its founder George Murray Smith*, 1950, pp. 8, 26-7; and Cross, *The Common Writer*, pp. 97ff. Spurgeon is cited in E. E. Kellett, 'The Press', in G. M. Young (ed.), *Early Victorian England 1830-1865*, 1934, Vol. II, pp. 56-7.

41. On the early history of the *Pall Mall Gazette* and its first editor, Frederick Greenwood, see the very informative Robertson Scott, *The Story of the Pall Mall Gazette* . . . – the quote cited is at pp. 125-6.

42. See Sir Walter Besant, *The Pen and the Book*, 1899, pp. vi-vii and passim, and *Autobiography*, pp. 91-5, 216-21.

43. Edgar Browne, *Phiz and Dickens*, 1913, p. 102.

44. Justin McCarthy, *Reminiscences*, 1899, Vol. I, pp. 308ff. William Tinsley, *Random Recollections of an Old Publisher*, 1900, Vol. II, pp. 102-3. Mrs Desmond Humphreys, *Recollections of a Literary Life*, 1936, pp. 55-6. Joseph Pennell, *The Adventures of an Illustrator*, 1925, pp. 162-9. For John Lane see J. Lewis May, *John Lane and the Nineties*, 1936, pp. 122-3.

45. The 'Street of Drink' is in Simonis, *The Street of Ink*, p. 7.

46. On the Garrick Club see J. R. Planché, *Recollections and Reflections*, 1872, Vol. I, pp. 164-6, John Timbs, *Clubs and Club Life in London*, 1872, pp. 218ff., and Ralph Nevill, *London Clubs*, 1911, p. 285. On the Savage see Aaron Watson, *The Savage Club*, 1907, passim.

47. The phrase is in McCarthy, *Reminiscences*, Vol. I, p. 311, rather differently formulated.

48. Cited in Francis Espinasse, *Literary Recollections and Sketches*, 1893, p. 303. On Hannay generally see the excellent George J. Worth, *James Hannay*, 1964.

49. Richard Whiteing, *My Harvest*, 1915, p. 67.

50. Cited in Layard, *A Great 'Punch' Editor*, pp. 250-51.

51. On the capital for literary speculations see An Old Printer, *A Few Personal Recollections*, p. 24; see also Sala, *The Life and Adventures of George Augustus Sala*, Vol. I, p. 112. On Sala himself see Ralph Straus, *Sala*, 1942.

52. The whole story is told in M. H. Spielmann, *The History of 'Punch'*, 1895, Ch. 1. See also Arthur William à Beckett, *The à Becketts of 'Punch'*, 1903, Ch. 1; Adrian, *Mark Lemon*, Ch. 3; and Athol Mayhew, *A Jorum of 'Punch'*, 1895.

53. On *Punch* as the spirit of the age, see Charles L. Graves, *Mr. Punch's History of Modern England*, 1922 – a social history drawn largely from its files and by no means to be sniffed at. On the significance of the Big Cut see Layard, *A Great 'Punch' Editor*, passim.

54. Dickens, *The Letters of Charles Dickens*, Vol. VII, p. 2.

Chapter 9 Vauxhall Gardens: Shared Pleasures

1. See *The News*, 2 December 1810; *Annual Register 1810*, Chronicle, pp. 291-2; Theodore Edward Hook, *Gilbert Gurney*, 1836, Vol. I, pp. 298-9; R. H. Dalton Barham, *The Life and Remains of Theodore Edward Hook*, 1849, Vol. I, pp. 72-7; Anon., *Real Life in London* . . ., 1821-2, Vol. II pp. 7-8n; E. Beresford Chancellor, *London's Old Latin Quarter*, 1930, pp. 186-8. Mrs Tottenham is also given as Tottington and Tottingham. The *DNB* and Barham give 1809 as the date. Henry B. Wheatley and Peter Cunningham,

London Past and Present, 1891, following the *Annual Register*, give [Monday] 26 November as the date. But *The News*, published the Sunday following, states clearly that it was Tuesday, and I've followed that. All the trades in my list are mentioned in the sources.

2. On children's street games see Norman Douglas, *London Street Games*, 1931: he began collecting around 1911, and in the nature of things, if there were any changes between 1899 and then it would have been in favour of restriction, not expansion. On Jack-in-the-Green see John Thomas Smith, *The Cries of London*, 1839, p. 91, writing of 1819; Charles Dickens, *The Dent Uniform Edition of Dickens' Journalism*, 1994–2000, Vol. I, pp. 168ff., 'The First of May', first published May 1836; Sir Francis C. Burnand, *Records and Reminiscences*, 1904, Vol. I, pp. 16–17, recalls similar scenes in Bond Street in 1842; and one draggled specimen was recalled by George Sims as late as around 1890 at Charing Cross, in George R. Sims, *Glances Back*, 1917, p. 150. On Guy Fawkes' night see Henry Mayhew, *London Labour and the London Poor*, 1861–2, Vol. III, pp. 73–7.

3. W. Somerset Maugham, *Liza of Lambeth*, 1897, Ch. 1.

4. Charles Dickens, *The Letters of Charles Dickens*, 1965–2002, Vol. IV, p. 358, to John Foster, 19 August 1845.

5. The last episode of bull-baiting on the remnants of Tothill Fields that I have found dates from 1817: SC, *Second Report from the Committee on the State of the Police of the Metropolis*, 1817, p. 375, James Bly, senior police officer at the Queen Square office. On bullock-hunting see SC, *Report of the Committee Appointed to Inquire into the State of the Police of the Metropolis*, 1816, pp. 151–2, Rev. Jonathan King, rector of Bethnal Green; and p. 161, Rev. Edward Robson, for bullock-hunting in Whitechapel, apparently by then less of a problem than formerly. The SC, *Report from the Select Committee on the Police of the Metropolis*, 1822, pp. 11–12, received a petition from Bethnal Green parishioners against the practice, but there was evidence to the SC, *Report from the Select Committee on the Police of the Metropolis*, 1828, p. 92, that it had 'been put a stop to': Richard Gregory, treasurer of the watch, Spitalfields. On dog fights see, for instance, SC, *Report from the Select Committee on the Petition of Frederick Young and Others, (Police)*, 1833, where dog fights were reported on waste ground near Calthorpe Street, Gray's Inn Lane: evidence of Richard Stallwood, 13 Calthorpe Street, q. 271. Mayhew, *London Labour and the London Poor*, Vol. I, p. 30; the cruelty at Caledonian Road is reported in Anon., *Wonderful London*, 1878, pp. 434ff. [Joseph Charles Parkinson] 'Barnet Fair', *Daily News*, 5 September 1865.

6. The great English festival is in William Makepeace Thackeray, *Pendennis*, 1849–50, Vol. II, pp. 193ff. – the cross-class cast list all assemble for the event. Tooting in the 1890s is recalled in Eric Bligh, *Tooting Corner*, 1949, pp. 100–102, and the houses turned inside out are in Charles Dickens, *Charles Dickens' Uncollected Writings from* Household Words *1850–1859*, edited by Harry Stone, 1968, Vol. I, p. 310, 'Epsom', with W. H. Wills, *Household Words*, 7 June 1851. The 'no ladies' point is in Percy Armytage, *By The Clock of St James's*, 1927, p. 48.

7. Justin McCarthy, *Charing Cross to St Paul's*, 1891, p. 35.

8. *Annual Register 1814*, Chronicle, pp. 67–9; Edward Wedlake Brayley and others, *London and Middlesex . . .*, 1810–16, Vol. III, pp. 114–15; diary of

Luke Graves Hansard in J. C. Trewin and E. M. King, *Printer to the House*, 1952, pp. 110-11; William Jerdan, *The Autobiography of William Jerdan*, 1852-3, Vol. I, pp. 203-7, which is very good on the state visits before the fête; Jacob Larwood, *The Story of the London Parks*, 1877, pp. 293ff.; John Ashton, *Hyde Park*, 1896, pp. 68-74.

9. J. Hall Richardson, *From the City to Fleet Street*, 1927, p. 137. There is fine observation of the 1897 jubilee by the American writer Mary H. Krout, *A Looker on in London*, 1899, Chs. XXIII-XXV.

10. Captain Gronow, *Reminiscences and Recollections*, 1862-6, Vol. I, pp. 52-3.

11. The 'Park of the People' tag was from Col. Charles Sibthorp, MP, in the House of Commons in July 1850, cited in Ashton, *Hyde Park*, p. 104. Charles Knight, *Passages of a Working Life During Half a Century*, 1864-5, Vol. II, pp. 275-6. For Stanhope Gate see George W. Smalley, *London Letters and Some Others*, 1890, Vol. II, pp. 31-2. R. D. Blumenfeld, *R. D. B.'s Diary 1887-1914*, 1930, pp. 18-19, 29 June 1887. Sims, *Glances Back*, pp. 173-4. See also T. H. S. Escott, *Social Transformations of the Victorian Age*, 1897, pp. 1-5.

12. For the Regent's Park disaster see *Annual Register 1867*, Chronicle, pp. 3-11; Ann Saunders, *Regent's Park*, 1969, pp. 187-8.

13. Charles Booth, *Life and Labour of the People in London*, 1892-1902, Series 3, Vol. 1, p. 15. On the vans see Henry Mayhew, *The Morning Chronicle Survey of Labour and the Poor: The Metropolitan Districts*, 1849-50, Vol. VI, pp. 84-7. For the Maidenhead platform see Blumenfeld, *R. D. B.'s Diary 1887-1914*, p. 13, 26 June 1887.

14. George Eliot, *Daniel Deronda*, 1876, Ch. 17. On steamers in the 1830s see SC, *Report from the Select Committee on the Observance of the Sabbath Day: with the Minutes of Evidence, and Appendix*, 1832, qq. 2868ff., John Miller, Secretary Margate Steam-Boat Co.; 3267ff., Lewis Gibson, Secretary New Gravesend Co.; 3321ff., Squire Knight, agent for the Richmond Steam Boat Co.

15. *Annual Register 1878*, Chronicle, pp. 91-6; Frank L. Dix, *Royal River Highway*, 1985, pp. 96ff., discounts the effect of the *Princess Alice* disaster on the troubles of the 1880s, contrary to common sense, it seems to me. The Commissioner of the Metropolitan Police (*Annual Report*, 1878, p. 30) says 544, with a total loss of 'at least 582 *and upwards of* 600'. But *Haydn's Dictionary of Dates* says over 900 on board and that some 700 were probably lost.

16. Anon., *Real Life in London . . .*, 1821-2, Vol. II, p. 515.

17. The finest in Europe is in B. Lambert, *The History and Survey of London and Its Environs*, 1806, Vol. IV, p. 160. There is a fine illustration of the Orchestra in Rudolph Ackermann, *The Microcosm of London*, 1808-9, Vol. III, pp. 202ff. The ham (much written about until the 1850s, when the chefs were more generous) is in Pierce Egan, *Life in London*, 1821, p. 337n.

18. On Vauxhall dress see Walter, *My Secret Life*, 1888-94, Vol. II, pp. 290-91. Thackeray, *Pendennis*, Vol. II, Ch. VIII. See generally H. H. Montgomery, *The History of Kennington and its Neighbourhood*, 1889, Ch. X; Warwick Wroth, *The London Pleasure Gardens of the Eighteenth Century*, 1896, pp. 286-326; E. Beresford Chancellor, *The Pleasure Haunts of London during Four Centuries*, 1925, pp. 205-27. And for the last night see Derek Hudson (ed.), *Munby*, 1972, p. 40.

19. The guide is E. Mogg, *Mogg's New Picture of London*, 1843, p. 105. On the Welsh Harp see [Joseph Charles Parkinson] 'Cockney Pleasures', *Daily News*, 27 May 1870.

20. The guide is William Carey, *The Stranger's Guide through London*, 1808, Chs. XXII and XXV. For all the rich history of London's shows see the epic Richard D. Altick, *The Shows of London*, 1978. Chancellor, *The Pleasure Haunts of London during Four Centuries*, is also a useful but more general survey. 'Lord' George Sanger, *Seventy Years a Showman*, 1910, pp. 134ff. And for showmen letting out their exhibitions see John Hollingshead, *Ragged London in 1861*, 1861, p. 182.

21. Tom Taylor, *Leicester Square*, 1874, Ch. XVI; Altick, *The Shows of London*, Ch. 10 and pp. 329-31.

22. See Sir Henry Cole, *Fifty Years of Public Work . . .*, 1884, Vol. I, pp. 124-5, for the debate over Leicester Square; see also Hermione Hobhouse, *The Crystal Palace and the Great Exhibition*, 2002, p. 9.

23. For a comprehensive modern overview see Jeffrey A. Auerbach, *The Great Exhibition of 1851*, 1999. On the royal commission and its work from 1850 on see Hobhouse, *The Crystal Palace and the Great Exhibition*.

24. On the fears see Cole, *Fifty Years of Public Work . . .*, Vol. I, pp. 185-93. On Jerrold and the Crystal Palace see Michael Slater, *Douglas Jerrold (1803-1857)*, 2002, p. 243. The conduct of the people was noted in *Frazer's Magazine*, January 1852, cited in Auerbach, *The Great Exhibition of 1851*, p. 147.

25. Altick, *The Shows of London*, Chs. 33-4, argues for a sudden shift in taste in the 1850s in which the Great Exhibition played a large part. But the continuities post-1851 are stronger than the changes. These took much longer to work themselves through. The real revolution came with the cinema, the final transformation only taking place in the 1930s.

26. On Saint Monday at Crystal Palace in the 1860s see [Thomas Wright] *Some Habits and Customs of the Working Classes*, 1867, p. 116. For Gissing's suspicions of the Palace see the letter to his sister Margaret of 29 May 1882 in Algernon and Ellen Gissing, *Letters of George Gissing to Members of His Family*, 1927, pp. 115-16; for the brief note of his visit see George Gissing, *London and the Life of Literature in Late Victorian England*, edited by Pierre Coustillas, 1978, pp. 25-6. George Gissing, *The Nether World*, 1889, Ch. XII, 'Io Saturnalia!' For a full history of the Palace at Sydenham see the excellent J. R. Piggott, *Palace of the People*, 2004; I am grateful for Jan Piggott's help on some points of detail.

27. For a nice recollection of 'Venice in London' (December 1891) see Compton Mackenzie, *My Life and Times: Octave Two 1891-1900*, 1963, p. 35.

28. On Blackfriars Road see Grant Richards, *Memories of a Misspent Youth*, 1932, p. 41; on the Aquarium see *Annual Register 1884*, Chronicle, pp. 17-18. Sir Frederick Treves, *The Elephant Man and Other Reminiscences*, 1923, Ch. 1. The showman, Tom Norman, gets a better press in the deservedly popular Michael Howell and Peter Ford, *The True History of the Elephant Man*, 1980.

29. John Law [Margaret Harkness], *Captain Lobe*, 1889, pp. 5-6, 69.

30. *Annual Register 1809*, Appendix to Chronicle, pp. 404ff.; Brayley and others, *London and Middlesex . . .*, Vol. III, pp. 4ff.; David Hughson, *London*, 1809-10, Vol. VI, pp. 615-18; John Ashton, *The Dawn of the XIXth Century*

in England, 1906, Ch. XL; Henry Saxe Wyndham, *Covent Garden Theatre*, 1906, Vol. I, pp. 339ff. The number of deaths is given at about twenty-six in *Annual Register 1808*, Chronicle, pp. 106-9.

31.   Laura Hain Friswell, *In the Sixties and Seventies*, 1905, p. 118; SC, *Select Committee on Criminal and Destitute Juveniles: Report, together with the Proceedings of the Committee, Minutes of Evidence, Appendix and Index*, 1852, App. I, p. 391 – see also pp. 392, 394-5. On Master Betty see *Annual Register 1804*, pp. 437-9, 791ff.; and Ashton, *The Dawn of the XIXth Century in England*, Ch. XXXVIII. Roscius, according to *Brewer's Dictionary of Phrase and Fable*, is a 'first-rate actor', after Quintus Roscius, who died around 62BC. On the Tamburini see *Annual Register 1840*, Chronicle, pp. 45-7.

32.   Mayhew, *London Labour and the London Poor*, Vol. I, p. 20. Joseph Charles Parkinson, *Literary Scraps*, 1865-70, pp. 147-8; cutting headed 'Victoria' from *Daily Telegraph*, n.d., *c.* 1870.

33.   Richards, *Memories of a Misspent Youth*, pp. 93-4.

34.   J. R. Planché, *Recollections and Reflections*, 1872, Vol. I, pp. 93-4. Dickens, *The Letters of Charles Dickens*, Vol. X, pp. 433-4, to John Forster, ?5 October 1864. The music hall point is made in SC, *Report from the Select Committee on Theatrical Licenses and Regulations; together with the Proceedings of the Committee, Minutes of Evidence and Appendix*, q. 195, Hon. Spencer Cecil Brabazon Ponsonby, Lord Chamberlain's office.

35.   George R. Sims, *My Life – Sixty Years' Recollections of Bohemian London*, 1917, p. 13. On Phelps and Sadler's Wells more generally see Michael Williams, *Some London Theatres*, 1883, pp. 1-32. On the Effingham see Frederick Rogers, *Labour, Life and Literature*, 1913, pp. 7-10; Erroll Sherson, *London's Lost Theatres of the Nineteenth Century*, 1925, pp. 47-8. On the Shakespeare celebrations see *Annual Register 1864*, Chronicle, pp. 58-67.

36.   Dickens, *The Dent Uniform Edition of Dickens' Journalism*, Vol. I, Ch. 13, 'Private Theatres', reprinted from the *Evening Chronicle*, 11 August 1835. Mark Lemon, *Golden Fetters*, 1867, Vol. I, pp. 215-16. On the clubs see Rogers, *Labour, Life and Literature*, pp. 133-6.

37.   John Hollingshead, *My Lifetime*, 1895, Vol. I, pp. 30-31. Sherson, *London's Lost Theatres of the Nineteenth Century*, pp. 363ff. See also Dickens, *The Dent Uniform Edition of Dickens' Journalism*, Vol. II, pp. 193ff., 'The Amusements of the People', *Household Words*, 13 April 1850, and Vol. IV, pp. 52ff., 'Two Views of a Cheap Theatre', *All the Year Round*, 25 February 1860.

38.   On Smith and Mont Blanc see Raymund Fitzsimons, *The Baron of Piccadilly*, 1967, Pt 3; Altick, *The Shows of London*, pp. 473-8. The patter is in Edgar Browne, *Phiz and Dickens*, 1913, pp. 138-40.

39.   SC, *Report from the Select Committee on Theatrical Licenses and Regulations; together with the Proceedings of the Committee, Minutes of Evidence and Appendix*, 1866, q. 4949, Nelson Lee. On the tribulations of Covent Garden see *Annual Register 1856*, Chronicle, pp. 45-53; Wyndham, *Covent Garden Theatre,* Vol. II, pp. 199-217.

40.   For the Ram see Brayley and others, *London and Middlesex . . .*, Vol. III, p. 479; for the Cellar see Egan, *Life in London*, p. 34. The point about the audience as their own performers is in SC, *Report from the Select Committee on Metropolis Management and Building Acts Amendment Bill; together*

with the Proceedings of the Committee, Minutes of Evidence, and Index, q. 1071ff., Inspector George Steed, K Division Metropolitan Police (Stepney). Karaoke, I suppose, is the most recent manifestation of an enduring tradition.

41. On the Grecian see Hollingshead, *My Lifetime*, Vol. I, pp. 26-7; on the Grapes see Archibald Haddon, *The Story of the Music Hall*, 1935, p. 19; on the Canterbury see Sir Walter Besant, *London in the Nineteenth Century*, 1909, p. 194 (John Hollingshead). For music hall generally see Walter Macqueen-Pope, *The Melodies Linger On*, n.d., *c.* 1950.

42. The description of the Canterbury is in James Ewing Ritchie, *The Night Side of London*, 1858, pp. 67ff.

43. See SC, *Report from the Select Committee on Theatrical Licenses and Regulations; together with the Proceedings of the Committee, Minutes of Evidence and Appendix*, 1866, q. 856, Sir Thomas Henry, chief magistrate Bow Street; q. 1354ff., Frederick Strange, managing director, Alhambra. See also Besant, *London in the Nineteenth Century*, p. 195 (John Hollingshead); H. G. Hibbert, *Fifty Years of a Londoner's Life*, 1916, passim; Sims, *Glances Back*, pp. 90ff.; *Survey of London*, Vols. XXXIII-IV: *The Parish of St. Anne Soho*, 1966 Vol. XXXIV, pp. 495-9.

44. T. C. Crawford, *English Life*, 1889, p. 123.

45. SC, *Report from the Select Committee on Theatrical Licenses and Regulations; together with the Proceedings of the Committee, Minutes of Evidence and Appendix*, 1866, appendices, pp. 293, 313.

46. The 1878 figures are given in SC, *Report from the Select Committee on Metropolis Management and Building Acts Amendment Bill; together with the Proceedings of the Committee, Minutes of Evidence, and Index*, 1878, qq. 1035-48, John Hollingshead, lessee of the Gaiety Theatre, Strand. The 1903 figures are in LCC, *London Statistics*, Vol. XIV, 1903-4, pp. 405ff. The number of music halls in London rose somewhat, reaching fifty-two in 1907.

47. Gronow, *Reminiscences and Recollections*, Vol. I, pp. 54-5, Vol. II, p. 76. John Brown, *Sixty Years' Gleanings from Life's Harvest*, 1858, pp. 25-6. Knight, *Passages of a Working Life During Half a Century*, Vol. II, pp. 25-6. SC, *Report from the Select Committee on Inquiry into Drunkenness, with Minutes of Evidence, and Appendix*, 1834, q. 2006ff., Francis Place; see also Maurice J. Quinlan, *Victorian Prelude*, 1941, pp. 174-5, citing Place's similar opinions in 1826.

48. SC, *Report from the Select Committee on Inquiry into Drunkenness, with Minutes of Evidence, and Appendix*, 1834, q. 19, Mark Moore, Queen Street Place, member of improvement societies; q. 3340, Samuel Herapath, hatter, Holborn Hill; q. 217ff., Robert Edwards Broughton, Worship Street magistrate; q. 3196 George Wilson, grocer, 8 Tothill Street.

49. John Forster, *The Life of Charles Dickens*, 1872-4, Vol. I, p. 43; Charles Dickens, *David Copperfield*, 1849-50, Ch. XI. Sims, *Glances Back*, pp. 81-2.

50. Louis Bamberger, *Memories of Sixty Years in the Timber and Pianoforte Trades*, 1929, p. 36. Sir William Fraser, *Hic et Ubique*, 1893, pp. 101-2. Blumenfeld, *R. D. B.'s Diary 1887-1914*, 1930, p. 4, 22 June 1887.

51. Figures for arrests are in the annual reports of the Commissioner of the Metropolitan Police. The proportion of arrests for drunkenness per 1,000 population was 20.6 in 1831 and just 7.6 in 1875; but this latter propor-

tion, or thereabouts, had been relatively constant since 1840.

52. The 1903 figure is in *London Statistics*, the 1848 is from *Chambers's Journal* and cited in Rev. Frederick Meyrick, *The Outcast and the Poor of London*, 1858, pp. 45-6.

53. The wine vaults are in Anon., *Real Life in London* . . ., 1821-2, Vol. II, pp. 204n. The illustration shows very similar premises to those in Cruikshank's illustration of a gin palace in *Sketches by Boz* around 1835: see Dickens, *The Dent Uniform Edition of Dickens' Journalism*, Vol. I, p. 181. Habits on Holborn Hill are in SC, *Report from the Select Committee on Inquiry into Drunkenness, with Minutes of Evidence, and Appendix*, 1834, q. 236off., Henry Bradshaw Fearon, spirit and wine dealer of Holborn Hill and Bond Street. On women in pubs see Booth, *Life and Labour of the People in London*, Series 3, Vol. 1, p. 54. The pub is in Arthur Sherwell, *Life in West London*, 1897, pp. 131-2: more women than this went in but about a third of them went to fill jugs. See in general that fine survey Mark Girouard, *Victorian Pubs*, 1984; and Brian Harrison, 'Pubs', in H. J. Dyos and Michael Wolff (eds.), *The Victorian City*, 1973, Vol. I, pp. 161-90.

54. On pubs and workers' club life see Stan Shipley, *Club Life and Socialism in Mid-Victorian London*, 1983, pp. 21ff.

55. For the gaming houses see Brayley and others, *London and Middlesex* . . ., Vol. III, Pt II, p. 640; Mr Serjeant Ballantine, *Some Experiences of a Barrister's Life*, 1882, Vol. I, pp. 58-60.

56. The 'utmost decorum' is Bracebridge Hemyng in Mayhew, *London Labour and the London Poor*, Vol. IV, pp. 228-9.

57. On shilling dancing rooms see Anon., *Tempted London*, 1888, Ch. XII. Gronow, *Reminiscences and Recollections*, Vol. I, p. 31; Almack's gets a bad notice in 1827 from Prince Pückler-Muskau (E. M. Butler (ed.), *A Regency Visitor*, 1957, pp. 198-9); for its later history see Walter Thornbury and Edward Walford *Old and New London*, 1873-8, Vol. IV, pp. 196-200; Wheatley and Cunningham, *London Past and Present*, Vol. I, pp. 37-8. On All Max see, among others, Egan, *Life in London*, pp. 284ff.

58. On slap-bangs see Edmund Yates, *His Recollections and Experiences*, 1884, Vol. I, pp. 154-5; Sims, *Glances Back*, p. 196.

59. On the new eating houses of the 1830s see Charles Knight (ed.), *London*, 1841-4, Vol. IV, pp. 315-19. William Makepeace Thackeray, *The Newcomes*, 1854-5, Vol. I, p. 240. On the degenerates see A Journalist, *Bohemian Days*, 1913, p. 247, recalling the 1870s.

60. On Simpson's see Yates, *His Recollections and Experiences*, Vol. I, pp. 156-7; *Illustrated London and Its Representative of Commerce*, 1893, p. 193. On the Trocadero see *Survey of London*, Vols. XXXI-II: *The Parish of St. James Westminster Pt II North of Piccadilly*, 1963, Vol. XXI, pp. 83-4. The City man was Ernest Benn, *Happier Days*, 1949, p. 126. See also Erika Diane Rappaport, *Shopping for Pleasure*, 2000, pp. 101ff.

61. Blumenfeld, *R. D. B.'s Diary 1887-1914*, pp. 55-6.

62. Calculated from *Census of England and Wales, 1891: Area, Houses, and Population*, Vol. II, *Registration Areas and Sanitary Districts*, 1893-4, pp. 20-24, and *Census of England and Wales 1901: County of London*, 1903, p. 58. The total in the County of London in one or two rooms in 1891 was 1.076m (25.4 per cent) and in 1901 1.006m (22.2 per cent).

63. The only census indicator with apparently comparative value is 'persons per

inhabited house'. But because of definitional difficulties the run is misleading. For what it is worth, the figures for the registrar-general's definition of London (the County after 1889) run 1841 7.42; 1851 7.72; 1861 8.03; 1871 7.79; 1881 7.85; 1891 7.73; 1901 7.93. The last two demonstrate the problem because more detailed data in the census returns show that crowding certainly diminished in the 1890s.

64.   Dorothy Nevill, *The Reminiscences of Lady Dorothy Nevill*, edited by Ralph Nevill, 1905, pp. 99–106. See also Percy Armytage, *By the Clock of St. James's*, 1927, p. 45; and, generally, Peter Thorold, *The London Rich*, 1999, Chs. 9 and 10.

65.   Louis Simond, *Journal of a Tour and Residence . . .*, 1817, Vol. I, pp. 62–3. The 'mob' is Beatrice Webb's term in her *My Apprenticeship*, 1926, p. 54, recalling the 1860s and 1870s. On Blessington see Michael Sadleir, *Blessington D'Orsay*, 1933, passim; on Holland see Princess Marie Liechtenstein, *Holland House*, 1874, Vol. I, Ch. IV. On the 1880s see Ralph Nevill, *The Life and Letters of Lady Dorothy Nevill*, 1919, Ch. V, and Margot Asquith, *Autobiography*, 1920, pp. 139–41, 173–5, 161–201.

66.   On the cards see Armytage, *By the Clock of St. James's*, pp. 46–7; on the canvassing see Smalley, *London Letters and Some Others*, Vol. II, p. 21. William Makepeace Thackeray, *The Letters and Private Papers of William Makepeace Thackeray*, edited by Gordon N. Ray, 1945–6, Vol. II, p. 665, to Mrs Brookfield, 26–30 April 1850 (some punctuation added).

67.   William Makepeace Thackeray, *Philip*, 1862, Ch. VI.

68.   On the view from the outside see George R. Sims (ed.), *Living London*, 1902–3, Vol. I, p. 217; W. Somerset Maugham, *On Human Bondage*, 1915, p. 242, describing the 1890s. On the inside see, for instance, the Grosvenor Square party in Anthony Trollope, *Can You Forgive Her?*, 1864–5, Ch. XLIX; George Grossmith, *A Society Clown*, 1888, pp. 140–41.

69.   Webb, *My Apprenticeship*, pp. 3, 47–9.

70.   On the 'emptiness' see Sir Algernon West, 'A Walk Through Deserted London', *Nineteenth Century*, Vol. XLIII, January–June 1898, pp. 35–46. Things may have changed a few years from then: see G. W. E. Russell, *Seeing and Hearing*, 1907, pp. 70–71. On 'winter society' see Sir Henry Drummond Wolff, *Rambling Recollections*, 1908, Vol. I, pp. 100–103, recalling the 1870s and 1880s.

71.   Jerome K. Jerome, *My Life and Times*, 1926, p. 70. The Bayswater ménage is in Mrs Lynn Linton, *My Literary Life*, 1899, pp. 14ff., the McCarthys' in Friswell, *In the Sixties and Seventies*, pp. 204ff. George Gissing, *The Whirlpool*, 1897, Pt II, Chs. IV and X.

72.   Ellen Terry is cited in George Somes Layard, *A Great 'Punch' Editor*, 1907, p. 182. George Gissing, *In the Year of Jubilee*, 1894, p. 227.

73.   For Norwood see Bligh, *Tooting Corner*, p. 145; for Benn see A. G. Gardiner, *John Benn and the Progressive Movement*, 1925, p. 49.

74.   Draper is in Friswell, *In the Sixties and Seventies*, pp. 61–2. Eleanor Farjeon, *A Nursery in the Nineties*, 1935, p. 202; see also Mackenzie, *My Life and Times: Octave Two 1891–1900*, p. 111, for similar events in West Kensington in the early 1890s.

75.   On the Horsleys see Rosamund Brunel Gotch (ed.), *Mendelssohn and His Friends in Kensington*, 1934, p. 35, and passim. For the Wood Clique see M. H. Stephen Smith, *Art and Anecdote*, 1927, pp. 120–24, 132–42. *ILN*, Vol. XXVIII, 29 March 1856, and Vol. XLVIII, 24 March 1866. On English

piano production see Asa Briggs, *Victorian Things*, 1988, p. 217. On Hackney see Henry J. Wood, *My Life of Music*, 1938, pp. 51–3; Albert Lieck, *Narrow Waters*, 1935, pp. 52, 69.

76. Clarence Rook, *The Hooligan Nights*, 1899, p. 4.

Chapter 10 Granby Street: Private Pleasures

1. Walter, *My Secret Life*, 1888–94, Vol. I, Chs. X and XI, pp. 147–8, 173–4, order of excerpts reversed. There are almost no dates in these eleven volumes and those I give are estimates based on a close reading.

2. Flora Tristan, *Flora Tristan's London Journal*, 1840, pp. 74–5; RG, *Census Enumerators' Record Books, Parish of St Mary Lambeth*, 1841, HO/107/1061/4–5.

3. For the myth see 'The Reasons for Granby Street' in Michael Sadleir's fictional reconstruction of Victorian lowlife of the 1860s, *Forlorn Sunset*, 1947. Sadleir was so schooled in these matters that it is disconcerting to find him wrong in so many details. Maps show it partly built in 1831 and wholly by 1835. The street directories show no entry in 1835, six in 1836, fourteen in 1838 and 1840 but just five in 1845 and two in 1850 – the pub continuously and artisans and tradesmen in the best years. For some information about the development of the area – though nothing of its outcast character – see *Survey of London*, Vol. XXIII, *South Bank and Vauxhall: The Parish of St Mary Lambeth Pt. I*, 1951, Ch. 4. For further evidence of the district's notoriety for prostitution before the railway see Renton Nicholson, *Dombey and Daughter*, 1847, pp. 1–2, 30. Henry Mayhew, *The* Morning Chronicle *Survey of Labour and the Poor*, 1849–50, Vol. VI, pp. 64ff.; see also Henry Mayhew, *London Labour and the London Poor*, 1861–2, Vol. I, p. 430 (written 1851), and Vol. IV, pp. 266, 358 (written about 1860–61). Sir Walter Besant, *Autobiography*, 1902, p. 278. John Hollingshead, *Ragged London in 1861*, 1861, pp. 166–7, 179. RG, *Census Enumerators' Record Books, Parish of St Mary Lambeth*, 1861, RG/9/349/97 and 230; it is sadly impossible to check whether it was the same twenty-four houses in both 1841 and 1861, but much that we know of London prostitution suggests it was likely, lodgings passing from one generation of prostitutes to another.

4. Daniel Joseph Kirwan, *Palace and Hovel*, 1870, pp. 128–9, mentions Granby Street in the same breath as the dangerous area around the New Cut, and his information seems to come from 1866–7, but that's the latest reference I've found to any continuing notoriety. Charles Booth, *The Streets of London*, edited by Jess Steele, 1997, p. 19; it seems to have had the same character at the time of the first Booth poverty maps in 1889.

5. For some recent fine studies of various aspects of London prostitution, especially its cultural representation in the nineteenth century, see Lynda Nead, *Myths of Sexuality*, 1988; Judith R. Walkowitz, *City of Dreadful Delight*, 1992; Michael Mason, *The Making of Victorian Sexuality*, 1994.

6. Some of these points are well made by Eric Trudgill in 'Prostitution and Paterfamilias', in H. J. Dyos and Michael Wolff (eds.), *The Victorian City*, 1973, Vol. II, pp. 693–705.

7. Charles Astor Bristed, an American visitor writing in 1852, cited in Gordon N. Ray, *Thackeray: The Uses of Adversity, 1811–1846*, 1955, p. 135. Walter, *My Secret Life*, Vol. II, Ch. I, p. 219.

8. *Annual Register 1802*, Chronicle, pp. 381, 453–4; *Annual Register 1806*, Chronicle, pp. 415–16; *Annual Register 1807*, Chronicle, p. 432; *Annual Register 1808*, Chronicle, p. 78. Thomas de Quincey, *Autobiography*, 1950, pp. 274ff. For 1810 and thereabouts see *The Times*, 29 November 1810, citing a letter from 'Civis' to the Lord Mayor; and Edward Wedlake Brayley and others, *London and Middlesex . . .*, 1810–16, pp. 404–5.

9. See SC, *Report of the Committee Appointed to Inquire into the State of the Police of the Metropolis*, 1816; *First Report from the Committee on the State of the Police of the Metropolis: with Minutes of Evidence taken before the Committee; and an Appendix*, 1817; *Second Report from the Committee on the State of the Police of the Metropolis*, 1817; *Third Report from the Committee on the State of the Police of the Metropolis: with Minutes of the Evidence taken before the Committee; and an Appendix*, 1818, passim. On the White House see E. Beresford Chancellor, EB *The Romance of Soho*, 1931, pp. 50ff.

10. 'Mutton walks' are recalled in Charles Hindley, *The True History of Tom and Jerry*, 1888, p. 191. The business cards at Covent Garden are in Pierce Egan, *Life in London*, 1821, pp. 172–3. The profits quip is in Rev. J. Richardson, *Recollections, Political, Literary, Dramatic, and Miscellaneous, of the Last Half-century . . .*, 1856, Vol. II, pp. 218–19, writing of the early years of the century. Louis Simond, *Journal of a Tour and Residence in Great Britain, During the Years 1810 and 1811 . . .*, 1817, Vol. I, p. 115. The German prince is in E. M. Butler (ed.), *A Regency Visitor*, 1957, pp. 83–4 – it's possible to read the sentences in two ways but is not meant, I think, lubriciously; see also another German visitor, Frederick von Raumer, *England in 1835*, 1836, Vol. II, p. 218. On the grades of old Drury see George Smeeton, *Doings in London*, 1828, pp. 99ff. And the 1835 shocker is in Tristan, *Flora Tristan's London Journal*, p. 179.

11. On Fawcett see Charles Hindley, *The Life and Times of James Catnach (Late of Seven Dials), Ballad Monger*, 1878, pp. 166–7; on Macready see *Annual Register 1842*, Chronicle, pp. 115–16, and Sir Frederick Pollock (ed.), *Macready's Reminiscences, and Selections from His Diaries and Letters*, 1875, Vol. II, pp. 187ff.; on the circular see SC, *Report from the Select Committee on Theatrical Licenses and Regulations; together with the Proceedings of the Committee, Minutes of Evidence and Appendix*, 1866, App. 2, p. 282.

12. The term is Kirwan's, *Palace and Hovel*, p. 588.

13. On the Norton Street (including Upper Norton Street) area see Renton Nicholson, *Rogue's Progress*, 1860, pp. 31–2 (Clipstone Street, around 1827); William Acton, *Prostitution, considered in Its Moral, Social, and Sanitary Aspects, in London and other Large Cities*, 1857, pp. 114–15; *The Times*, 4 January 1858; James Ewing Ritchie, *Here and There in London*, 1859, pp. 155ff.; Cyril Pearl, *The Girl with the Swansdown Seat*, 1955, p. 34.

14. On Pimlico see Booth, *Life and Labour of the People in London*, 1892–1902, Series 3, Vol. 3, pp. 87–8.

15. See ibid., Vol. 1, pp. 186, 195, and Vol. 2, p. 174.

16. On the Strand see Abraham Flexner, *Prostitution in Europe*, 1914, p. 304. Booth, *Life and Labour of the People in London*, Series 1, Vol. 2, pp. 62–7.

17. Albert Smith writing in September 1857 and cited in Acton, *Prostitution . . .*, pp. 21–2n; Edward Callow, *Old London Taverns*, 1899, p. 333; B. L. Farjeon, *Great Porter Square*, 1884, p. 51; Derek Hudson (ed.), *Munby*, 1972, p. 35

(2 June 1859 and describing a Hogarthian scene); James Ewing Ritchie, *The Night Side of London*, 1869, p. 226; George Augustus Sala, *Twice Round the London Clock*, 1878, pp. 318–19, both wicked and unique; Hippolyte Taine, *Notes on England*, 1872, p. 30.

18. John Binny in Mayhew, *London Labour and the London Poor*, Vol. IV, pp. 356ff.

19. Sometimes 'Argyle', but not to be confused with the Argyle (sometimes also Argyll) Rooms at Argyle Street, Regent Street, built by Nash and used as a concert hall and assembly rooms, opened 1818, burnt down 1830. Bignell also ran, for a time at least, the Piccadilly Saloon – the Pic – in the Haymarket and the Café Riche, Great Windmill Street, both notorious for their gatherings of prostitutes. [William Ewart Gladstone] *The Gladstone Diaries*, edited by M. R. D. Foot and H. C. G. Matthew, 1974, p. 228, 22 July 1850.

20. Lieut. John Blackmore, *The London by Moonlight Mission*, 1860, pp. 313ff., the account of a 'Lady' rescue worker.

21. On the move here from the theatre saloons see SC, *Report from the Select Committee on Theatrical Licenses and Regulations; together with the Proceedings of the Committee, Minutes of Evidence and Appendix*, 1866, qq. 815ff., evidence of Sir Thomas Henry, Chief Magistrate Bow Street. For more on the Argyll Rooms see *Survey of London, St James Westminster*, 1963, Vol. XXXI, pp. 46–7; and, for example, Acton, *Prostitution . . .*, pp. 99–102, and 1870, pp. 19ff.; Anon., *London by Night*, 1868, pp. 36ff.; Kirwan, *Palace and Hovel*, pp. 476ff.; Callow, *Old London Taverns*, p. 328. On the licensing battles see Montagu Williams, *Round London*, 1892, pp. 66–8.

22. On the Haymarket night houses see Captn Donald Shaw, *London in the Sixties (with a Few Digressions)*, 1909, passim; Sir Henry Smith, *From Constable to Commissioner*, 1910, Ch. XXI; and Ronald Pearsall, *The Worm in the Bud*, 1969, Pt 2. On the end of the night houses see Commissioner of Police, *Annual Report for the Year 1874*, p. 4; and Edward J. Bristow, *Vice and Vigilance*, 1977, pp. 56–7. There is an imaginative reconstruction of Panton Street in Michael Sadleir's *Fanny by Gaslight*, 1940, pp. 33–123.

23. Walter, *My Secret Life*, Vol. III, Ch. XII, pp. 527–8 (punctuation as in the 1966 edn).

24. On the coffee shops see ibid., Vol. V, Ch. XIX, p. 1055.

25. See Warwick Wroth, *Cremorne and the Later London Gardens*, 1907, pp. 1–23. There is an excellent recent survey in Nead, *Victorian Babylon*, Pt 2, Ch. 4.

26. Numbers of prostitutes in the Alhambra are in SC, *Report from the Select Committee on Theatrical Licenses and Regulations; together with the Proceedings of the Committee, Minutes of Evidence and Appendix*, 1866, qq. 1566ff., Frederick Strange, managing director of the Alhambra; and for the Empire see John Stokes, '"Prudes on the Prowl": The View from the Empire Promenade', in *Victorian England*, Folio Society, 1999, pp. 365–96. See also Susan D. Pennybacker, *A Vision for London 1889–1914*, 1995, pp. 210ff. For the Dwarf of Blood quote see Archibald Haddon, *The Story of the Music Hall*, 1935, p. 86; and for more on the Dwarf (all six foot of him) and his times see J. B. Booth, *Old Pink 'Un Days*, 1924, and its innumerable successors – well, at least five of them. On the move into fashionable West End restaurants as a new phenomenon see Commissioner of Police, *Annual Report for the Year 1879*, p. 32.

27. J. Lewis May, *John Lane and the Nineties*, 1936, pp. 18–19.

28. Walter, *My Secret Life*, Vol. III, Ch. XII, pp. 524–5.

29. SC, *First Report from the Select Committee of the House of Lords on the Law Relating to the Protection of Young Girls; together with the Proceedings of the Committee, Minutes of Evidence, and Appendix*, 1881, q. 593, CE Howard Vincent, Director of Criminal Investigations, Metropolitan Police. For the 20,000 on the West End streets see Commissioner of Police, *Annual Report for the Year 1887*, p. 49.

30. A Journalist, *Bohemian Days*, 1913, pp. 161–3. See also Besant, *Autobiography*, p. 285; A. R. Hope Moncrieff, *London*, 1910, p. 105; Flexner, *Prostitution in Europe*, p. 304.

31. 'Every state in life' is in Smeeton, *Doings in London*, p. 92. The 16,000 are in Rev. G. P. Merrick, *Work Among the Fallen*, 1890, pp. 23ff. Blackmore, *London by Moonlight*, p. 6, giving details of previous employment for just 107 prostitutes, has almost exactly the same proportions.

32. Walter, *My Secret Life*, Vol. V, Ch. XVI, p. 1,035.

33. The list of reasons are in Merrick, *Work Among the Fallen*, p. 39. Rev. C. J. Whitmore, *Seeking the Lost*, 1876, pp. 103ff.

34. Letters to *The Times* about subjects like this are always suspect because not a few were the work of clever hoaxers. We can imagine them chuckling over their handiwork in club coffee-rooms. There is something suspect, I think, about the long letters from 'One More Unfortunate' in the issues of 4 and 11 February 1858 which followed reports of parochial excitement over brothels in the West End and elsewhere. No one can be sure but to me 'Another Unfortunate' has the ring of truth about her.

35. SC, *First Report from the Select Committee of the House of Lords on the Law Relating to the Protection of Young Girls; together with the Proceedings of the Committee, Minutes of Evidence, and Appendix*, 1881, q. 746, Joseph Henry Dunlap, Superintendent C Division, Metropolitan Police. Hollingshead, *Ragged London in 1861*, pp. 49–50.

36. Acton, *Prostitution . . .*, 1857, pp. v–vi, and passim, was the first commentator to view prostitution as a temporary career choice not inhibiting marriage and domesticity. For an early reference to prostitutes falling in love and marrying (though not exactly into respectability) see that extraordinary memoir James Hardy Vaux, *Memoirs of James Hardy Vaux*, 1819, Vol. II, pp. 26ff.

37. Hudson (ed.), *Munby*, pp. 40–41, 30 July to 4 August 1859.

38. Walter, *My Secret Life*, Vol. III, Chs. III–IV, and Vol. IV, Ch. I, pp. 650ff. See also the similar case of Nelly Turner related by Munby in Hudson (ed.), *Munby*, pp. 213–15, 14 November 1865.

39. For Clarke, see DNB. For Wilson see Frances Wilson, *The Courtesan's Revenge*, 2003, Chs. 1–3; and Harriette Wilson, *The Memoirs of Harriette Wilson, Written by Herself*, 1825. For Skittles see Henry Blyth, *Skittles*, 1970. And for a useful and hard-working overview see Pearl, *The Girl with the Swandown Seat*, pp. 112ff., 154–62.

40. On Helen Gissing's death in 1888 not far from Granby/Aubin Street see George Gissing, *London and the Life of Literature in Late Victorian England*, edited by Pierre Coustillas, 1978, pp. 22–3. Dunlap was giving evidence to SC, *First Report from the Select Committee of the House of Lords on the Law Relating to the Protection of Young Girls; together with the Proceedings*

of the Committee, Minutes of Evidence, and Appendix, 1881, q. 772. On the arrests see Commissioner of Police, *Annual Report for the Year 1887,* p. 49.

41. Mayhew, *The* Morning Chronicle *Survey of Labour and the Poor,* Vol. III, pp. 27–8. Hudson (ed.), *Munby,* pp. 199–200, Wednesday 20 July 1864.

42. Walter, *My Secret Life,* Vol. II, Ch. IX. On child murder for sexual purposes see for instance *Annual Register 1833,* Chronicle, pp. 68–70 (three men acquitted of murdering a thirteen-year-old boy who had been sexually assaulted and terribly injured); and *Annual Register 1890,* Chronicle, p. 9, for what appears to be a serial killer of young girls after sexual assault in West Ham: one girl found murdered and two others missing.

43. For Dunlap see SC, *First Report from the Select Committee of the House of Lords on the Law Relating to the Protection of Young Girls; together with the Proceedings of the Committee, Minutes of Evidence, and Appendix,* 1881, qq. 735–6, 787. On Lock see *Annual Register 1821,* Chronicle, pp. 95–6. On dress lodgers more generally see Acton, *Prostitution . . .,* 1857, pp. 97–4; SC, *First Report from the Select Committee of the House of Lords on the Law Relating to the Protection of Young Girls; together with the Proceedings of the Committee, Minutes of Evidence, and Appendix,* 1881, q. 570, CE Howard Vincent, Director of Criminal Investigations, Metropolitan Police; and for an extraordinary adventure with a dress lodger in a brothel near Drury Lane Theatre, around 1857, see Walter, *My Secret Life,* Vol. III, Ch. II, pp. 444–9.

44. Charles Booth (Booth MSS), Group B, Vol. 349, pp. 91ff., 11 December 1897, George Duckworth reporting.

45. On the businessman see J. Kenneth Ferrier, *Crooks and Crime,* 1928, pp. 44–5: Scotland Yard recovered the teeth unharmed – those were the days. On Jones see Montagu Williams, *Later Leaves,* 1891, pp. 2–3.

46. *Annual Register 1806,* Chronicle, pp. 415–16, and *Annual Register 1807,* Chronicle, pp. 412–14. *Annual Register 1838,* Chronicle, pp. 81–3, 89–90. *The Times,* 7 April, 16 May and 3 June 1845. *Annual Register 1870,* Chronicle, pp. 6–8; Commissioner of Police, *Annual Report for the Year 1870,* p. 44.

47. The most useful account of the Ripper murders I've come across is Philip Sugden, *The Complete History of Jack the Ripper,* 1994; see also William J. Fishman, *East End 1888,* 1988, pp. 209–29. On 1889 see Commissioner of Police, *Annual Report for the Year 1889,* p. 4. On Cream see W. Teignmouth Shore (ed.), *Trial of Cream,* 1923, and the excellent Angus McLaren, *A Prescription for Murder,* 1993.

48. Mrs Verulam is in Robert Hichens, *The Londoners,* 1898, p. 18; see also Shirley Brooks, *Sooner or Later,* 1868, Vol. I, pp. 24–7, and Robert Patrick Watson, *Louise Reignier,* 1895, p. 19.

49. See Eric R. Watson (ed.), *Adolf Beck (1877–1904),* 1924, passim.

50. Hudson (ed.), *Munby,* pp. 219–20, 17 March 1866. On Houghton see James Pope-Hennessy, *Monckton Milnes,* 1949, p. 84, and 1951, pp. 114ff., 132–4.

51. Shirley Brooks's MS Diary, held at the London Library, 1869, Thursday 21 January 1869. See also George Somes Layard, *A Great 'Punch' Editor,* 1907, p. 333.

52. On Holywell Street see, for an early reference to pornography there, Martin Farquhar Tupper, *My Life as an Author,* 1886, p. 17, writing of 1818–21;

for the chemists see Louis Bamberger, *Bow Bell Memories*, 1931, p. 25; and generally see Nead, *Victorian Babylon*, Pt 3, Ch. 2. On prostitutes' use of erotica see Walter, *My Secret Life*, Vol. XI, Ch. II, pp. 2,192-3, and there are several other examples in his memoirs.

53. Thomas Frost, *Reminiscences of a Country Journalist*, 1886, pp. 52-5. On Dugdale see Henry Spencer Ashbee, *Index Librorum Prohibitorum*, 1877, p. 127; Donald Thomas, *The Victorian Underworld*, 1998, pp. 140ff.; and especially Iain McCalman, *Radical Underworld*, 1988, passim.

54. On Hotten see Ashbee, *Index Librorum Prohibitorum*, pp. 249-56; on Black see Charles Mackay, *Forty Years' Recollections of Life, Literature, and Public Affairs from 1830 to 1870*, 1877 Vol. I pp. 92-3; on *Harlequin* see Henry Spencer Ashbee, *Catena Librorum Tacendorum*, 1885 pp. 319-21 – the ascription to Sala is not certain, and is made in a referenced annotation to my copy.

55. On *poses plastiques*, etc. see Callow, *Old London Taverns*, pp. 304-6; and on the Judge and Jury see Nicholson, *Rogue's Progress*, 1860, passim.

56. For Munby see Hudson (ed.), *Munby*, pp. 117-18, and Diane Atkinson, *Love and Dirt*, 2003, pp. 96-7. On Hayler see Ashbee, *Index Librorum Prohibitorum*, p. xixn. On Holywell Street see Inspector Maurice Moser and Charles F. Rideal, *Stories from Scotland Yard*, 1890, pp. 36-45.

57. *Annual Register 1811*, Chronicle, p. 28. For an excellent recent review of homosexuality in London in the nineteenth century, especially from 1885, see Matt Cook, *London and the Culture of Homosexuality, 1885-1914*, 2003.

58. On Saul's earnings see H. Montgomery Hyde (ed.), *The Cleveland Street Scandal*, 1976, p. 144. Walter, *My Secret Life*, Vol. VI, Ch. VI, pp. 1,149ff.; see also, for instance, Vol. VIII, Ch. II, and Vol. IX, Ch. VIII.

59. On Vere Street see *The News*, 30 September 1810; and Ashbee, *Index Librorum Prohibitorum*, pp. 328-38. For the Bishop see *Annual Register 1822*, Chronicle, p. 126, Appendix pp. 425-32.

60. On Cleveland Street see Hyde (ed.), *The Cleveland Street Scandal*; and on Wilde see H. Montgomery Hyde (ed.), *The Trials of Oscar Wilde*, 1948.

Chapter 11 Flower and Dean Street: Crime and Savagery

1. *Tower Hamlets Independent*, 19 November 1881. The 'foulest' tag is James Greenwood, *In Strange Company*, 1883, pp. 158-60.

2. For overviews of the Flower and Dean Street neighbourhood see *Survey of London*, Vol. XXVII, *Spitalfields*, 1957, Chs. XVII and XIX; and Jerry White, *Rothschild Buildings*, 1980, Ch.1.

3. Spitalfields Vestry Minutes (in London Borough of Tower Hamlets, Local History Library), 29 September 1858, 10 June 1859; for 1860 see John Binny in Henry Mayhew, *London Labour and the London Poor*, 1861-2, Vol. IV, pp. 311-24; for Barnardo see Mrs Barnardo and James Marchant, *Memoirs of the Late Dr Barnardo*, 1907, pp. 39-40 – when he was identified the articles were returned, apparently; *Tower Hamlets Independent*, 4 February 1882 (the robberies were 'twelve months ago'). According to ex-Chief Inspector Walter Dew, writing of the 1888-9 period, Flower and Dean Street was 'always "double-patrolled" by the police. A single constable would have been lucky to reach the other end unscathed' (*I Caught Crippen*, 1938, p. 88).

For the poor Swede see *Daily Telegraph*, 9 October 1888, and *The Star*, 12 October 1888.

4. Figures for lodgers etc. in the Flower and Dean Street area are from the 1871 *Census Enumerators' Record Books*. On the houses' distinctive colours see Greenwood, *In Strange Company*, p. 160, which notes red, blue and yellow houses: and one on the corner of Brick Lane was known as 'the white house' into the 1930s. On the absence of street numbers see, for instance, *Daily News*, 2 October 1888.

5. On Wilmott's and Smith's see Joseph Charles Parkinson, *The Poor*, 1864–6, p. 14b (from the *Daily News, c.* 1865).

6. The sanitary inspector's comments are in the Whitechapel District Board of Works Minutes (in London Borough of Tower Hamlets, Local History Library), 27 September 1880. The starvation cases are in *Tower Hamlets Independent*, 21 August and 9 October 1875; 7 September 1878; 16 October 1880. See also PP, *Deaths from Starvation (Metropolis): Return of the Number of all Deaths in the Metropolitan District . . .*, 1880, pp. 6–7, showing eight deaths from the Flower and Dean Street area out of a total of thirty-seven for East London as a whole.

7. For overviews of the London criminal class and criminality in general see J. J. Tobias, *Crime and Industrial Society in the 19th Century*, 1967, especially Ch. 4; Kellow Chesney, *The Victorian Underworld*, 1970, especially Ch. 4; Sir Leon Radzinowicz and Roger Hood, *A History of English Criminal Law and Its Administration from 1750*, 1986, pp. 73–84; an excellent recent survey is Donald Thomas, *The Victorian Underworld*, 1998.

8. A letter from Dr Barnardo is in *Pall Mall Gazette*, 9 October 1888; the London housing problem and juvenile crime are discussed in William Douglas Morrison, *Crime and Its Causes*, 1891, pp. 86–7; the three boy thieves' stories are in SC, *Select Committee on Criminal and Destitute Juveniles: Report, together with the Proceedings of the Committee, Minutes of Evidence, Appendix and Index*, 1852, Appendix 1, pp. 389, 391, 393. W. P. Frith, *My Autobiography and Reminiscences*, 1887, Vol. II, pp. 215–19.

9. Henry Mayhew, *The* Morning Chronicle *Survey of Labour and the Poor*, 1849–50, Vol. III, p. 82. On the radical prisoners see W. J. Linton, *James Watson*, 1880, pp. 2–4; Patricia Hollis, *The Pauper Press*, 1970, pp. 184–5. On Crooks see George Haw, *From Workhouse to Westminster*, 1907, pp. 223–4, 229.

10. *Annual Register 1819*, Chronicle, pp. 55–6; *Annual Register 1826*, Chronicle, pp. 140–41. For more on the extraordinary outbreak of 1819 see Rev. J. Richardson, *Recollections, Political, Literary, Dramatic, and Miscellaneous, of the Last Half-century . . .*, 1856, Vol. I, pp. 38–42. On the pirates see *Daily News*, 23 February 1864 (Joseph Charles Parkinson).

11. On the landlords see George Laval Chesterton, *Revelations of Prison Life*, 1856, Vol. I, p. 137, citing a paper by a prisoner at Coldbath Fields, *c.* 1830. There is an excellent discussion on flash houses in Leon Radzinowicz, *A History of English Criminal Law and Its Administration from 1750*, Vol. 2, 1956, pp. 297–306.

12. Rev. John William Horsley, *Jottings from Jail*, 1887, p. 9.

13. On Field Lane see Charles Dickens, *Oliver Twist*, 1837–9, Ch. XXVI; Flora Tristan, *Flora Tristan's London Journal*, 1840, pp. 147–8; Henry Vizetelly, *Glances Back Through Seventy Years*, 1893, Vol. I, p. 122; and for the hand-

kerchiefs on display see 'The Last of Field Lane' facing p. 63 in Thomas
Beames, *The Rookeries of London*, 1852; and 'Field Lane about 1840' in
Walter Thornbury and Edward Walford, *Old and New London*, 1873-8,
Vol. II, p. 499; on the Hell Houses see SC, *Second Report from the Committee
on the State of the Police of the Metropolis*, 1817, pp. 355-6, John Barnley,
beadle, St Andrew's Holborn, Hatton Garden and Ely Rents Division. On
Solomons see J. J. Tobias, *Prince of Fences*, 1974, Ch. 3 and passim. On
Moses see *Annual Register 1854*, Chronicle, pp. 62-3; *ILN*, Vol. XXIV, 29
May 1854, p. 391; *The Times*, 14 April 1854. On the south London discovery
see Arthur Fowler Neil, *Forty Years of Man-Hunting*, 1932, pp. 98-104.

14. The good doctor is cited in Barnardo and Marchant, *Memoirs of the Late
Dr Barnardo*, p. 242. For Duggin see SC, *First Report from the Committee
on the State of the Police of the Metropolis: with Minutes of Evidence taken
before the Committee; and an Appendix*, 1817, p. 152, evidence of John
Smith, special constable and beadle, St Giles. Ms Matthews is noted in Anon.,
Real Life in London . . ., 1821-2, Vol. II, pp. 390-91n; the text gives 'Upper
Cato-street, Spitalfields', but there was no such place and the Upper gives it
away. And for King see *Annual Register 1855*, Chronicle, pp. 61-4.

15. Horsley, *Jottings from Jail*, pp. 23-4.

16. Ibid., pp. 24-5; see also his evidence to the RC, *Report of Her Majesty's
Commissioners for Inquiring into the Housing of the Working Classes. Vol.
II Minutes of Evidence and Appendix as to England and Wales*, 1885, q.
2235; and Rev. John William Horsley, '*I Remember.*', 1911.

17. See LCC, *Housing*, 1900, pp. 118-23; White, *Rothschild Buildings*, pp. 24-30.

18. Commissioner of Police *Annual Report for the Year 1885*, p. 41.

19. For numbers of registered common lodging houses see ibid., *Annual Report
for the Year 1875*, p. 6, and LCC, *Housing*, 1900, p. 66. On Rowton Houses
see Michael Sheridan, *Rowton Houses 1892-1954*, 1956.

20. Charles Booth, *Life and Labour of the People in London*, 1892-1902, Series
3, Vol. 2, pp. 111-30, and map facing p. 168.

21. Horsley, *Jottings from Jail*, p. 31. Flymen here, I think, are beggars ('To take
on the fly' was to beg on the streets, according to Mayhew: see John S.
Farmer and W. E. Henley, *Slang and Its Analgoues, Past and Present*), but
possibly clever or artful criminals; pitching snyde (snide) was passing fake
coinage; gun was short for gonoph, Yiddish for thief.

22. G. H. Greenham, *Scotland Yard Experiences*, 1904, pp. 9ff. See also Inspector
Maurice Moser and Charles F. Rideal, *Stories from Scotland Yard*, 1890,
passim.

23. George Barrington, *Barrington's New London Spy for 1805 . . .*, 1805, p. iii
and passim; Anon., *The Picture of London, for 1818*, 1818, pp. 64-7; Charles
Arrow, *Rogues and Others*, 1926, pp. 120ff., for the Diamond Jubilee. On
magsmen generally see John Binny in Mayhew, *London Labour and the
London Poor*, Vol. IV, pp. 385ff.

24. Arrow, *Rogues and Others*, pp. 34-6.

25. Captain Gronow, *Reminiscences and Recollections*, 1862-6, Vol. II, pp.
313-14. Crime statistics for London here and in the rest of this chapter are
taken from the Commissioner of Police, *Annual Reports*, for various years.

26. The hoisters' rank is in Anon., *Real Life in London. . .*, Vol. II, pp. 212-13.
The 1860 picture is from John Binny in Mayhew, *London Labour and the
London Poor*, Vol. IV, p. 311.

27. On the Anatomy Act see Ruth Richardson, *Death, Dissection and the Destitute*, 1987, passim. The London resurrectionists' crimes are detailed in *Annual Register 1831*, Law Cases, etc., pp. 316–35; Camden Pelham, *The Chronicles of Crime*, 1887, Vol. II, pp. 274–305; and Sarah Wise, *The Italian Boy*, 2004. SC, *Report from the Select Committee on Dog Stealing (Metropolis); together with the Minutes of Evidence taken before them*, 1844, passim. The south London episode is in Neil, *Forty Years of Man-Hunting*, 1932, pp. 110–11.

28. Booth, *Life and Labour of the People in London*, Vol. 17, p. 139.

29. On the boy Palmer see *Annual Register 1821*, Chronicle, pp. 187–8.

30. On suburban burglaries before the train see SC, *Report from the Select Committee on the Police of the Metropolis*, 1828, p. 187, evidence of Richard Widrington, former beadle of Camberwell, and p. 220, Hugh Stock, residing near Brompton. See also SC, *Report from the Select Committee on the Police of the Metropolis*, 1822, p. 20, Sir Richard Birnie, chief magistrate, Bow Street; and p. 35, William Day, 'conductor of the horse and dismounted horse patroles', Bow Street Police Office. For Notting Hill see Edmund Yates, *His Recollections and Experiences*, 1884, Vol. I, p. 289. For the thief on the rattler see Horsley, *Jottings from Jail*, pp. 8ff., 16–17. On the burglaries outside London in the 1830s see Henry Goddard, *Memoirs of a Bow Street Runner*, 1956, pp. 117, 154. For the photographs see F. D. Klingender, 'A Victorian Rogues' Gallery', *Pilot Papers*, Vol. 1, No. 1, January 1946, pp. 55–9.

31. See SC, *First Report from the Committee on the State of the Police of the Metropolis: with Minutes of Evidence taken before the Committee; and an Appendix*, 1817, pp. 153–4, evidence of John Smith, special constable and beadle, St Giles; ibid., p. 166, Samuel Roberts, watch-house keeper, St Giles and St George, Bloomsbury; SC, *Second Report from the Committee on the State of the Police of the Metropolis*, 1817, p. 363, Thomas Goodwin, constable, St Giles.

32. On the decrease in highway robberies from 1805 see SC, *Report of the Committee Appointed to Inquire into the State of the Police of the Metropolis*, 1816, pp. 143–4, evidence of John Townsend, Bow Street police officer since 1782, p. 173, John Vickery, similar since 1799, and p. 195, William Day, conductor of the horse patrole.

33. On the increase in street robberies see ibid., p. 226, evidence of John Gifford, magistrate, Worship Street, and p. 228, John Armstrong, police officer, Worship Street, since 1778. On the numbers in St Giles see SC, *Second Report from the Committee on the State of the Police of the Metropolis*, 1817, p. 360, Samuel Fuzman [!], constable and round-house keeper, St Giles and St George, Bloomsbury. John Britton (ed.), *The Original Picture of London*, 1826, p. xn, Preface to the 1825 edition.

34. Fitzroy Gardner, *Days and Ways of an Old Bohemian*, 1921, p. 21; Captn Donald Shaw, *London in the Sixties (with a Few Digressions)*, 1909, p. 19; Arthur Philip Crouch, *Silvertown and Neighbourhood (including East and West Ham)*, 1900, p. 72. See also George R. Sims, *Glances Back*, 1917, p. 20; and Anthony Trollope, *Phineas Finn*, 1867–9, Ch. XXX. See also Jennifer Davis, 'The London Garrotting Panic of 1862: A Moral Panic and the Creation of a Criminal Class in mid-Victorian England', in V. A. C. Gatrell et al. (eds.), *Crime and the Law*, 1980, pp. 190–213.

35. *The Times*, 15 November 1864, reprinted in H. B. Irving (ed.), *Trial of Franz Müller*, 1911, pp. 169–79. 'Hedge', in this context, I think means 'get out of it' or 'get away'. Joseph Parkinson, who reported the Müller execution for the *Daily News*, thought the crowd less venomous than at the *Flowery Land* pirates' execution nine months before.

36. On looting after fires see *Annual Register 1803*, Chronicle, pp. 427–8: forty houses in Felix Street, Southwark, were destroyed by fire spreading from Astley's Amphitheatre. In the *Annual Register* the street is wrongly given as Phoenix Street. The dressmaker is in SC, *Report from the Select Committee on the Petition of Frederick Young and Others (Police)*, 1833, q. 1217, evidence of Andrew McLean, Superintendent P Division, New Police. The labourer is in *Annual Register 1816*, Chronicle pp. 103–4, and the funeral in *Annual Register 1822*, Chronicle, p. 82. The poor woman is in Tom Divall, *Scoundrels and Scallywags (and Some Honest Men)*, 1929, p. 46, recalling the mid-1890s. The old man is in Rev. A. O. Jay, *Life in Darkest London*, 1891, pp. 104–5, and the gas meters in B. Leeson, *Lost London*, 1934, recalling Shadwell in the mid-1890s.

37. *Annual Register 1848*, Chronicle, p. 62; *Annual Register 1832*, Law Cases, etc., pp. 264–71. Wise, *The Italian Boy*, pp. 172–3, says the motive was to sell the body to the dissectors and that may well be right.

38. *Annual Register 1851*, Chronicle, pp. 86–7. See also Renton Nicholson, *Rogue's Progress*, 1860, pp. 136–8; Arthur Griffiths, *Mysteries of Police and Crime*, 1901–2, Vol. III, pp. 188–90; Goddard, *Memoirs of a Bow Street Runner*, 1956, p. 168. Nicholson associates the early stealing bankers' parcels with Cauty, on which see SC, *Report of the Committee Appointed to Inquire into the State of the Police of the Metropolis*, 1816, p. 173, evidence of John Vickery, Bow Street police officer.

39. On the burglaries see *Annual Register 1877*, Chronicle, pp. 96, 117; on Peace see Montagu Williams, *Leaves of a Life*, 1890, pp. 257ff.; Griffiths, *Mysteries of Police and Crime*, Vol. II, pp. 33–40; W. Teignmouth Shore (ed.), *Trials of Charles Frederick Peace*, 1926, passim.

40. See, definitively, V. A. C. Gatrell, 'The Decline of Theft and Violence in Victorian and Edwardian England', in Gatrell et al. (eds.), *Crime and the Law*, pp. 238–370; and Radzinowicz and Hood, *A History of English Criminal Law and Its Administration from 1750*, Ch. 5.

41. The three police officers were Ex-Supt G. W. Cornish, *Cornish of the 'Yard'*, 1935, p. 6; Leeson, *Lost London*, pp. 70–72; Divall, *Scoundrels and Scallywags (and Some Honest Men)*, p. 46 (see also pp. 95, 99–100). *Pall Mall Gazette*, 10, 11 and 12 October 1888; see also the article on 13 October 1888 on the bandit gangs of London. Leeson, *Lost London*, but see similar comments in the Commissioner of Police, *Annual Report for the Year 1870*, p. 57. Dew, *I Caught Crippen*, p. 89, recalling Whitechapel *c*. 1887–9; *Pall Mall Gazette*, 11 October 1888.

42. See Hermann Mannheim, *Social Aspects of Crime in England Between the Wars*, 1940, pp. 35–9, 72–3.

43. Frederick Porter Wensley, *Detective Days*, 1931, pp. 13–14.

44. The inquest verdicts are in LCC, *London Statistics*, Vol. XVIII, 1907–8, pp. 270–71. The missing persons are given in Moser and Rideal, *Stories from Scotland Yard*, pp. 86–7.

45. Gatrell in Gatrell et al. (eds.), *Crime and the Law*, p. 286.

46. For all this see the Commissioner of Police, *Annual Reports*, 1881-6; Charles Tempest Clarkson and J. Hall Richardson, *Police!*, 1889, pp. 306-11. On protection rackets see Wensley, *Detective Days*, pp. 13-14; Cornish, *Cornish of the 'Yard'*, pp. 7-8; Leeson, *Lost London*, pp. 113-18. On Hoxton see Booth, *Life and Labour of the People in London*, Series 3, Vol. 2, p. 111.

47. On the Muswell Hill murder see Griffiths, *Mysteries of Police and Crime*, Vol. III, pp. 158-68; on Stepney see Wensley, *Detective Days*, Ch. III. Sir Melville L. Macnaghten, *Days of My Years*, 1914, Ch. XIII.

48. Leon Radzinowicz, *A History of English Criminal Law and Its Administration from 1750*, Vol. 3, 1956, Ch. 11; T. A. Critchley and P. D. James, *The Maul and the Pear Tree*, 1971; Edward Wedlake Brayley and others, *London and Middlesex . . .*, Vol. III, pp. 46ff.; Thomas de Quincey, 'On Murder, Considered as One of the Fine Arts', 1854, *The English Mail-Coach and Other Essays*, 1912, pp. 47-133. See also *Annual Register 1811*, Chronicle, pp. 138-9,141-2; *Annual Register 1812*, Chronicle, pp. 5-6, 16-7. Williams's body was rediscovered during sewerage works in July 1886.

49. For Hone see Frederick F. M. Hackwood, *William Hone*, 1912, p. 101; for Catnach see Charles Hindley, *The Life and Times of James Catnach (Late of Seven Dials), Ballad Monger*, 1878, pp. 142ff.; for the *Gazette* see Hollis, *The Pauper Press*, p. 122; see also Mayhew, *The Morning Chronicle Survey of Labour and the Poor*, Vol. II, pp. 57-8, for the popularity among the street sellers of literature for broadsides about murder trials and executions. On the Surrey Theatre see Nicholson, *Rogue's Progress*, pp. 149-50, and Eric R. Watson (ed.), *Trial of Thurtell and Hunt*, 1920, pp. 26-7, 29-30. On Steinberg see Thornbury and Walford, *Old and New London*, Vol. II, pp. 287-9. On Grimwood see *The Times*, 31 May 1838; on the Mannings see *ILN*, Vol. XV, 1 September 1849, p. 147. On Jack the Ripper exhibitions see Montagu Williams, *Round London*, 1892, pp. 6-8, and L. Perry Curtis, Jr, *Jack the Ripper and the London Press*, 2001, pp. 248-9. On the chamber of horrors see Richard D. Altick, *The Shows of London*, 1978, pp. 333-8; and Martin L. Friedland, *The Trials of Israel Lipski*, 1984, pp. 203-4, shows how Israel Lipski was on display just six days after his execution in August 1887.

50. *Annual Register 1827*, Law Cases, etc., pp. 326-31.

51. George R. Sims, *The Black Stain*, 1907, especially Ch. II; for an excellent overview of infanticide see Lionel Rose, *The Massacre of the Innocents*, 1986. On the Sloanes see *The Times*, 6 February 1851. On the south London baby farmers see Rose, *The Massacre of the Innocents*, pp. 96ff.

52. *Annual Register 1861*, Chronicle, pp. 175-80.

53. Gareth Stedman Jones, *Outcast London*, 1971, pp. 178-9.

54. Frederick Rogers, *Labour, Life and Literature*, 1913, pp. 303-4. On magistrates see, for instance, Montagu Williams, *Later Leaves*, 1891, Ch. XXVI; and Cecil Chapman, *The Poor Man's Court of Justice*, 1925, passim. Charles Chaplin, *My Autobiography*, 1964, pp. 33ff. Booth, *Life and Labour of the People in London*, Series 1, Vol. 2, p. 57.

55. On the change in manners see, for instance, Rev. R. H. Hadden, *East-End Chronicle*, 1880, pp. 110-14, looking back on St George's-in-the-East since 1850 with the help of the local Medical Officer of Health.

56. *Pall Mall Gazette*, 11 October 1888.

Chapter 12 Spa Fields: Protest and Politics

1. For the history of Spa Fields see William J. Pinks, *Clerkenwell*, 1880, pp. 141–2, 151–2, 398ff. The linkmen are in John Britton, *The Auto-Biography of John Britton*, 1849–50, Vol. I, p. 103.

2. Henry Hunt, *Memoirs of Henry Hunt, Esq., Written by Himself*, 1820–22, Vol. III, pp. 329–30.

3. Ibid., p. 335.

4. Ibid., pp. 459–61. There are detailed modern accounts of the meetings and riot in E. P. Thompson, *The Making of the English Working Class*, 1963, pp. 606–7, 631–5; David Johnson, *Regency Revolution*, 1974, Ch. 1; I. J. Prothero, *Artisans and Politics in Early Nineteenth-century London*, 1979, pp. 90ff.; John Belchem, *'Orator' Hunt*, 1985, pp. 58ff. See also the invaluable Henry Jephson, *The Platform*, 1892, Vol. I, pp. 383ff.; and S. Maccoby, *English Radicalism 1786–1832*, 1955, pp. 323ff.

5. James Peller Malcolm, *Anecdotes of the Manners and Customs of London During the Eighteenth Century . . .*, 1810, Vol. II, p. 408.

6. D. J. Rowe (ed.), *London Radicalism 1830–1843*, 1970, pp. 148–9. Place, while writing in the present tense, was analysing the causes behind the formation of the London Working Men's Association in 1836.

7. See Thompson, *The Making of the English Working Class*, pp. 478–84.

8. The old custom, indulged in at the Westminster election 1802, was noted in *Annual Register 1802*, Chronicle, pp. 427–7. On the chairing of Burdett see M. W. Patterson, *Sir Francis Burdett and His Times (1770–1844)*, 1931, Vol. I, pp. 215–18.

9. *Annual Register 1812*, Chronicle, pp. 71–2.

10. For the Life Guards see Captain Gronow, *Reminiscences and Recollections*, 1862–6, Vol. I, pp. 220–21. See also *Annual Register 1815*, Chronicle, pp. 19–25; J. R. Planché, *Recollections and Reflections*, 1872, p. 22; Frederick W. M. Hackwood, *William Hone*, 1912, p. 102. The *Annual Register* gives one man dead at Robinson's but Hackwood says two and that William Hone served on inquest juries into both.

11. See *Annual Register 1820* (the Wakley incident – his name is variously spelled but I've followed the *DNB* – is in Chronicle, pp. 441–2, and *Annual Register 1821*, Appendix to Chronicle, pp. 433–45); George Theodore Wilkinson, *An Authentic History of the Cato-Street Conspiracy*, 1820, passim; Thompson, *The Making of the English Working Class*, pp. 693–705; Johnson, *Regency Revolution*, passim; Prothero, *Artisans and Politics in Early Nineteenth-century London*, pp. 127–31.

12. *Annual Register 1820*, passim, and *Annual Register 1821*, History of Europe, pp. 127–8, for the funeral. On the mutinous state of the army over Caroline see Leon Radzinowicz, *A History of English Criminal Law and its Administration from 1750*, Vol. 4, 1968, pp. 155–6. For an excellent modern account see Prothero, *Artisans and Politics in Early Nineteenth-century London*, Ch. 7. The verdict ten years on is in *Annual Register 1830*, History of Europe, p. 143.

13. On the 1820s and reform see Jephson, *The Platform*, Vol. II, p. 40. For Castlereagh see John Thomas Smith, *An Antiquarian Ramble in the Streets of London . . .*, 1846, Vol. I, p. 69.

14. Charles C. F. Greville, *A Journal of the Reigns of King George IV and King*

William IV, 1875, Vol. II, p. 19. The anniversary of the 1830 revolution would be kept by London radicals as a feast day for some years to come: see SC, *Report from the Select Committee on the Petition of Frederick Young and Others (Police)*, 1833, qq. 1ff., evidence of James Burrell of East Street, Walworth. Place is cited in Jephson, *The Platform*, Vol. II, p. 71n.

15. See *Annual Register 1830*, English History, pp. 158–63, Chronicle, pp. 188–92; Greville, *A Journal of the Reigns of King George IV and King William IV*, Vol. II, pp. 53–6; J. R. M. Butler, *The Passing of the Great Reform Bill*, 1914, pp. 34–5.

16. On these early harbingers of the cholera see Greville, *A Journal of the Reigns of King George IV and King William IV*, Vol. II, pp. 57–8.

17. *Annual Register 1831*, Chronicle, pp. 68–9, 161–3, 170–71; Greville, *A Journal of the Reigns of King George IV and King William IV*, Vol. II, pp. 141–2; William Lovett, *Life and Struggles of William Lovett in His Pursuit of Bread, Knowledge, and Freedom*, 1876, Vol. I, Ch. IV – the 'Political' was soon dropped, and at the beginning 'and Others' followed 'Working Classes'; Jephson, *The Platform*, Vol. II, Ch. XV; Butler, *The Passing of the Great Reform Bill*, pp. 219–20, 292–4.

18. *Annual Register 1832*, Chronicle, pp. 40–41, 60; Rowe (ed.), *London Radicalism 1830–1843*, pp. 73–7.

19. Place is ibid., pp. 81–96; the Waterloo reference is Butler, *The Passing of the Great Reform Bill*, p. 377.

20. *Annual Register 1832*, Chronicle, p. 76.

21. SC, *Report from the Select Committee on the Petition of Frederick Young and Others (Police)*, 1833, Cd 627, q. 868. See also *Annual Register 1833*, Chronicle, pp. 79–83, and Law Cases, etc., pp. 319–27; Gavin Thurston, *The Clerkenwell Riot*, 1967, passim.

22. R. G. Gammage, *History of the Chartist Movement 1837–1854*, 1894, p. 47.

23. The six points were: universal suffrage, no property qualification for MPs, annual parliaments, equal representation of electoral districts, payment of MPs and vote by ballot. See Lovett, *Life and Struggles of William Lovett in His Pursuit of Bread, Knowledge, and Freedom*, passim; Rowe (ed.), *London Radicalism 1830–1843*, pp. 146ff.

24. There is a fine modern account of London Chartism in David Goodway, *London Chartism 1838–1848*, 1982.

25. See ibid., pp. 50–53, 106–8.

26. See *Annual Register 1848*, History, pp. 124–8, Chronicle, pp. 35–6; Gammage, *History of the Chartist Movement 1837–1854*, pp. 294–5; and Rodney Mace, *Trafalgar Square*, 1976, Ch. 6.

27. Gammage, *History of the Chartist Movement 1837–1854*, p. 296.

28. *Annual Register 1848*, Chronicle, pp. 39, 48–50.

29. For the 'ever memorable' 10 April 1848 see *Annual Register 1848*, Chronicle, pp. 50–54; John Tanswell, *The History and Antiquities of Lambeth*, 1858, pp. 215–19; Charles Mackay, *Forty Years' Recollections of Life, Literature, and Public Affairs from 1830 to 1870*, 1877, Vol. II, pp. 50–63; H. H. Montgomery, *The History of Kennington and its Neighbourhood*, 1889, pp. 35–48; Gammage, *History of the Chartist Movement 1837–1854*, pp. 312ff.; Goodway, *London Chartism 1838–1848*, pp. 68ff. The numbers of both demonstrators and special constables are impossible to pin down accurately, though I have generally followed Goodway.

30. *Annual Register 1848*, Chronicle, pp. 103–4.

31. On London cooperation see W. H. Brown, *A Century of London Co-operation*, 1928, Chs. I–VI. On the Working Men's College see J. F. C. Harrison, *A History of the Working Men's College 1854–1954*, 1954, Chs. I–II; it would not move to Crowndale Road, St Pancras, until January 1906. On the clubs see Stan Shipley, *Club Life and Socialism in Mid-Victorian London*, 1983, whose phrase I've quoted. On the LTC see London Trades Council, *Short History of the London Trades Council*, 1935, and *London Trades Council 1860–1950*, 1950.

32. *Annual Register 1855*, Chronicle, pp. 32–3.

33. PP, *Report of Her Majesty's Commissioners appointed to inquire into the Alleged Disturbance of the Public Peace in Hyde Park on Sunday, July 1st, 1855; and the Conduct of the Metropolitan Police in Connexion with the Same. Together with the Minutes of Evidence, Appendix, and Index*, 1856, qq. 1324–5; a table-decker set tables at great parties and balls for the rich.

34. See ibid., q.3777, evidence of Thomas Cannon of Earl Street, Seven Dials; the *Report*, pp. v–xxxiv, and evidence of Sir Richard Mayne, qq. 16156ff. For the pickpockets see qq. 13622ff. and 13777ff., evidence of Detective Sergeant Henry Smith.

35. Thomas Frost, *Forty Years' Recollections*, 1880, Ch. XVI; *Annual Register 1855*, Chronicle, pp. 106–9; see also Maccoby, *English Radicalism 1853–1886*, 1938, pp. 46–7.

36. *Annual Register 1855*, Chronicle, pp. 157–8. A good modern account is in Phillip Thurmond Smith, *Policing Victorian London*, 1985, Ch. 6.

37. *Annual Register 1864*, Chronicle, pp. 44–58. Derek Hudson (ed.), *Munby*, 1972, pp. 186–7.

38. *Annual Register 1866*, Chronicle, pp. 74–5; Jephson, *The Platform*, Vol. II, pp. 442–3.

39. Frost, *Forty Years' Recollections*, p. 310. The report in the *Annual Register* backs up Frost's account and Disraeli, ever acute and ever pejorative, told Parliament that the rioters were '"not of the working classes"' but '"all the scum of a great city"', cited in Jephson, *The Platform*, p. 466.

40. *Annual Register 1866*, Chronicle, pp. 98–102; Frost, *Forty Years' Recollections*, pp. 308–11; Jephson, *The Platform*, Vol. II, pp. 443–4; Henry Broadhurst, *Henry Broadhurst, MP*, 1901, pp. 34–40. See also Smith, *Policing Victorian London*, Ch. 8.

41. At Beaufort House: see *Annual Register 1866*, Chronicle, pp. 188–92.

42. George Howell, *Labour Legislation, Labour Movements and Labour Leaders*, 1902, p. 237, writing of the context for the Beckton gas workers' strike of 1872.

43. See Commissioner of Police, *Annual Report for the Year 1870*, p. 49, and 1874, p. 90.

44. See Gareth Stedman Jones, *Outcast London*, 1971, pp. 337ff.

45. Ibid., pp. 344–5.

46. See Ernest Belfort Bax, *Reminiscences and Reflexions of a Mid and Late Victorian*, 1918, pp. 76–7.

47. See *Annual Register 1886*, English History, pp. 45–7, Chronicle, pp. 6–7; George W. Smalley, *London Letters and Some Others*, 1890, Vol. II, pp. 368–87; Henry Mayers Hyndman, *The Record of an Adventurous Life*, 1911, pp. 400–404; Bax, *Reminiscences and Reflexions of a Mid and Late Victorian*, pp. 84–6.

48. See Hyndman, *The Record of an Adventurous Life*, pp. 402–3. See also Stedman Jones, *Outcast London*, pp. 290–94, for the best modern account. Hyndman, Champion, Williams and Burns were prosecuted for sedition but acquitted on 10 April 1886, the thirty-eighth anniversary of Kennington Common.

49. *Annual Register 1886*, Chronicle, p. 52; *Annual Register 1887*, Chronicle, p. 7.

50. Commissioner of Police, *Annual Report for the Year 1887*, p. 47.

51. Smalley, *London Letters and Some Others*, Vol. II, pp. 388–95. See also Commissioner of Police, *Annual Report for the Year 1887*, p. 47; *Annual Register 1887*, English History, pp. 175–7, Chronicle, pp. 54, 61; Annie Besant, *An Autobiography*, 1893, pp. 318–28; William Kent, *John Burns*, 1950, pp. 28ff.; E. P. Thompson, *William Morris*, 1955, pp. 482–95. Thompson says that Linnell's injuries were received after Bloody Sunday but all other sources I've seen puts him there; his first name is variously given as Alfred, William and John.

Chapter 13 Bow Street: Police and Punishment

1. Anon., *The Picture of London, forn 1818*, 1818, p. 61. For the development of Bow Street see *Survey of London*, Vol. XXXVI, *The Parish of St. Paul Covent Garden*, 1970, Chs. I and VIII. On its connection with the police see Percy Fitzgerald, *Chronicles of Bow Street Police Office with an Account of the Magistrates, 'Runners', and Police*, 1888; Patrick Pringle, *Hue and Cry*, 1955, passim; Leon Radzinowicz, *A History of English Criminal Law and Its Administration from 1750*, Vol. 2, 1956, pp. 263ff.; Douglas G. Browne, *The Rise of Scotland Yard*, 1956, Chs. 2–5; and Peter Pringle's introduction to Henry Goddard, *Memoirs of a Bow Street Runner*, 1956. In this last Pringle gives 1739 for De Veil's appearance in Bow Street but I've followed the *Survey of London*, which gives his first listing in the ratebooks as 1740.

2. The Thames police were regularised by an act of 1800 and sometimes this is given as the date of their formation. For their earliest days see John Harriott, *Struggles Through Life, exemplified in the Various Travels and Adventures in Europe, Asia, Africa, and America, of John Harriott, Esq.*, 1815, Vol. III, pp. 108ff.

3. For numbers in 1821 see PP, *Police Establishments of the Metropolis: Return of the Establishments of the Several Police Offices, on the Fifth January, 1821, Including the Horse and Foot Patrole*, 1821, p. 3. And for 1828 see SC, *Report from the Select Committee on the Police of the Metropolis*, 1828, App. G, pp. 326–34. Few things are more confused in the literature of Bow Street police office than this question of uniform. Dickens, in an often quoted letter of June 1862 to Walter Thornbury misremembered the Runners in 'a bright red cloth waistcoat . . . and the slang name for them was "red-breasts" in consequence'. His error persisted until the works of Pringle in the 1950s. In fact it seems likely that the 'uniform' was a hit and miss affair for the Horse, Dismounted and Foot Patroles until the late 1820s and possibly throughout their existence. See, for instance, SC, *Report from the Select Committee on the Police of the Metropolis*, 1822, p. 34, evidence of William Day, Conductor of the Horse and Dismounted Horse Patroles.

4. On Vickery see his evidence to the SC, *Report of the Committee Appointed to Inquire into the State of the Police of the Metropolis*, 1816, p. 177. On Armstrong see Fitzgerald, *Chronicles of Bow Street Police Office with an Account of the Magistrates, 'Runners', and Police*, Vol. I, pp. 116-17. On Donaldson see Rev. J. Richardson, *Recollections, Political, Literary, Dramatic, and Miscellaneous, of the Last Half-century . . .*, 1856, Vol. II, p. 220-23, and James Hardy Vaux, *Memoirs of James Hardy Vaux*, 1819, Vol. II, p. 72-82, 93. For others see Radzinowicz, *A History of English Criminal Law and Its Administration from 1750*, Vol. 2, p. 268.

5. The best account is Elaine A. Reynolds, *Before the Bobbies*, 1998; see also Radzinowicz, *A History of English Criminal Law and Its Administration from 1750*, Vol. 2, which is too prone, I think, to side with the post-Peel view of the parish police. Phillip Thurmond Smith, *Policing Victorian London*, 1985, pp. 3ff., puts the problem well. For a modern overview of these issues and more see Clive Emsley, *The English Police*, 1996.

6. The figures for 1822 are in SC, *Report from the Select Committee on the Police of the Metropolis*, 1822, pp. 96-140. For 1828 see SC, *Report from the Select Committee on the Police of the Metropolis; with the Minutes of Evidence, Appendix and Index*, 1834, pp. 443-4, its figures now including Deptford and Greenwich but excluding the City, and possibly incomplete returns.

7. On Tyburn Tickets see SC, *Report of the Committee Appointed to Inquire into the State of the Police of the Metropolis*, 1816, p. 138, evidence of John Townsend, citing a case from St Paul's, Covent Garden. The judgement on deputies is in SC, *Third Report from the Committee on the State of the Police of the Metropolis: with Minutes of the Evidence taken before the Committee; and an Appendix*, 1818, p. 26.

8. Birnie is in SC, *Police*, 1828, p. 37; pp. 126-7, evidence of Hon. Frederick Byng, watch committee, St George's Hanover Square.

9. SC, *Report from the Select Committee on the Police of the Metropolis*, 1828, p. 128 (Frederick Byng on St George's); on Covent Garden and Irishmen in the watch see John Wight, *Mornings at Bow Street*, 1824, pp. 44ff., and passim; the City watch is in SC, *Report from the Select Committee on the Police of the Metropolis*, 1822, pp. 4-6 (Report). The 1828 examples are all from SC, *Report from the Select Committee on the Police of the Metropolis*, 1828, p. 50, H. M. Dyer, magistrate, Great Marlborough Street; pp. 92ff., Richard Gregory, treasurer of the watch, Spitalfields; p. 124, William Chadwell, inspector of the watch, St James's. The guide is Anon., *Picture of London, for 1818*, p. 67.

10. See *Annual Register 1830*, Chronicle, pp. 188-90.

11. See Edward Wedlake Brayley and others, *London and Middlesex . . .*, 1810-16, Vol. II, pp. 12n; John Britton (ed.), *The Original Picture of London*, 1826, p. 80; William Carey, *The Stranger's Guide through London*, 1808, pp. 28-31.

12. *Annual Register 1802*, Chronicle, pp. 452-3; *Annual Register 1820*, Chronicle, pp. 483-4.

13. See Leon Radzinowicz, *A History of English Criminal Law and Its Administration from 1750*, Vol. 3, 1956, pp. 324ff.

14. See *Annual Register 1816*, Chronicle, pp. 168-9; Appendix to Chronicle, pp. 314-18. See also Camden Pelham, *The Chronicles of Crime*, 1887, Vol.

II, pp. 1-3; Fitzgerald, *Chronicles of Bow Street Police Office with an Account of the Magistrates, 'Runners', and Police*, Vol. I, pp. 165ff.; Charles Tempest Clarkson and J. Hall Richardson *Police!*, 1889, p. 47; Radzinowicz, *A History of English Criminal Law and Its Administration from 1750*, Vol. 2, pp. 333ff. Bubblefoot Solomons was not the Ikey Solomons we met in Chapter xi: he was so called for a deformed foot.

15. A bad case was that of Mr Fuller of Bethnal Green, recalled in George Laval Chesterton, *Revelations of Prison Life*, 1856, Vol. I, pp. 27-9.

16. SC, *Report from the Select Committee on the Police of the Metropolis*, 1828, pp. 76-7.

17. Ibid., p. 22 (Report).

18. See Norman Gash, *Mr. Secretary Peel*, 1961, pp. 487-507; Browne, *The Rise of Scotland Yard*, Ch.8; David Ascoli, *The Queen's Peace*, 1979, Chs. 2 and 3; Smith, *Policing Victorian London*, pp. 20-27, 33ff.; Emsley, *The English Police*, Ch. 2.

19. The Instructions are given in full in *Annual Register 1829*, Public Documents, pp. 377-94. An excellent account of these early days is in Leon Radzinowicz, *A History of English Criminal Law and Its Administration from 1750*, Vol. 4, 1968, Ch. 5; Browne, *The Rise of Scotland Yard*, is also very good.

20. On the arms carried in these early days see SC, *Report from the Select Committee on the Police of the Metropolis; with the Minutes of Evidence, Appendix and Index,* 1834, q. 180, evidence of Col. Rowan. On the Irish see ibid., q. 4379 (Thomas Morris, straw-hat manufacturer, St George's-in-the-East); see also Clarkson and Richardson, *Police!*, p. 68. On the St Luke's watch and the new police see Reynolds, *Before the Bobbies*, p. 153. On the murder of Long see *Annual Register 1830*, Chronicle, pp. 6-8; Browne, *The Rise of Scotland Yard*, p. 95.

21. SC, *Report from the Select Committee on the Police of the Metropolis; with the Minutes of Evidence, Appendix and Index*, 1834, qq. 4-47.

22. On rate protests see *Annual Register 1833*, Chronicle, pp. 151-2, 155-7; Radzinowicz, *A History of English Criminal Law and Its Administration from 1750*, Vol. 4, pp. 167-9. For vestry criticism see SC, *Report from the Select Committee on the Police of the Metropolis; with the Minutes of Evidence, Appendix and Index*, 1834, qq. 3154ff., 3172ff., 3234ff., 3330ff., 3350ff., 3411ff., 3525ff., 3998ff., 4296ff., 5084ff.

23. Charles Hindley, *The Life and Times of James Catnach (Late of Seven Dials), Ballad Monger*, 1878, p. 203. See also Henry Vizetelly, *Glances Back Through Seventy Years*, 1893, Vol. I, p. 25. Collective memory would, though, play tricks. In Albert Smith's *The Adventures of Mr Ledbury and His Friend Jack Johnson*, 1844 (Ch. XXVII), a drunken reveller asks a policeman, '"Who stole the lobster?"' And at the Hyde Park Sabbath observance riots of 1855, PC 380A was seen to 'beat in a very severe manner over the back and shoulder with his truncheon a little boy who had called out to him, "Who stole the goose?"' The Home Office Commissioners, it should be said, found the case against the PC not proven – the boy, wisely enough, didn't come forward: see PP, *Report of Her Majesty's Commissioners appointed to inquire into the Alleged Disturbance of the Public Peace in Hyde Park on Sunday, July 1st, 1855; and the Conduct of the Metropolitan Police in Connexion with the Same. Together with the Minutes of Evidence, Appendix, and Index*, 1856, Report, p. xxix.

24. Place is cited in Graham Wallas, *The Life of Francis Place 1771–1854*, 1918, pp. 248–9n.

25. See, for instance, J. F. Moylan, *Scotland Yard and the Metropolitan Police*, 1929, p. 150, who claimed without citing an authority that from 1829 to 1839 the runners 'took the jewel robberies and left the murders to the Metropolitan police. All the murderers were traced, but only a sixth of the jewel thieves were brought to justice.' In fact, there were numerous cases of unsolved murders in these years, among them that of PC Culley at Calthorpe Street in 1833.

26. For St Giles see SC, *Report from the Select Committee on the Observance of the Sabbath Day: with the Minutes of Evidence, and Appendix*, 1832, q. 4047, Rev. J. E. Tyler. For Hammersmith see Thomas Faulkner, *The History and Antiquities of the Parish of Hammersmith . . .*, 1839, p. 226.

27. For Clerkenwell see Gavin Thurston, *The Clerkenwell Riot*, 1967, Ch. XVI. White was giving evidence to SC, *Report from the Select Committee on the Police of the Metropolis; with the Minutes of Evidence, Appendix and Index*, 1834, qq. 1822, 1868–9. The *New Alphabet* is cited in Hindley, *The Life and Times of James Catnach (Late of Seven Dials), Ballad Monger*, p. 284.

28. On Townsend see Clarkson and Richardson, *Police!*, p. 56; he died in July 1832, just a month after the Reform Act passed. The famous Inspector Charles Field of the Detective Department was said to have been a former runner: see Charles Dickens, *The Letters of Charles Dickens*, 1965–2002, Vol. VI, p. 689n, and Vol. X, pp. 71–2, to Walter Thornbury, 18 April 1862.

29. Clarkson and Richardson, *Police!*, pp. 108–9.

30. See Peter Pringle's introduction to Goddard, *Memoirs of a Bow Street Runner*, pp. xxv–vii.

31. On Millbank see Browne, *The Rise of Scotland Yard*, p. 109; on Her Majesty's see Alfred Rosling Bennett, *London and Londoners in the Eighteen-fifties and Sixties*, 1924, p. 311; and on Bow Street see *Annual Register 1890*, Chronicle, p. 35. On the common informer see Radzinowicz, *A History of English Criminal Law and Its Administration from 1750*, Vol. 2, pp. 147–55.

32. The early-morning knock-up is in B. Leeson, *Lost London*, 1934, pp. 92–3, recalling the East End in the 1890s; see also Charles Booth, *Life and Labour of the People in London*, 1892–1902, Vol. 17, p. 134. For the Argyll Rooms and a list of other premises and events for which police were hired see the Commissioner of Police, *Annual Reports*. On the society parties see SC, *Report from the Select Committee on the Police of the Metropolis; with the Minutes of Evidence, Appendix and Index*, 1834, qq. 618–21, evidence of Colonel Rowan. On freemasonry among the runners see Goddard, *Memoirs of a Bow Street Runner*, p. 209. Townsend is in SC, *Report of the Committee Appointed to Inquire into the State of the Police of the Metropolis*, 1816, p. 139.

33. Booth, *Life and Labour of the People in London*, Series 2, Vol. 5, p. 29.

34. *Annual Register 1852*, Chronicle, pp. 164–6. Cannon was sentenced to death for attempted murder, probably commuted to life imprisonment.

35. Tom Divall, *Scoundrels and Scallywags (and Some Honest Men)*, 1929 pp. 11–13; Frederick Porter Wensley, *Detective Days*, 1931, p. 8. See also Leeson, *Lost London*, pp. 29–31, 69–70.

36. Phil Cohen, 'Policing the Working-class City', in National Deviancy

Conference and Conference of Socialist Economists, *Capitalism and the Rule of Law*, 1979, p. 121, counted 146 affrays against police in just four Islington streets reported in the local press between 1880 and 1920. Figures for arrests for assault on police, etc., are in the Commissioner of Police, *Annual Reports*. Leeson, *Lost London*, p. 72.

37. Henry Mayhew, *London Labour and the London Poor*, 1861–2, Vol. I, pp. 15–16.

38. Walter, *My Secret Life*, 1888–94, Vol. VI, p. 1,166; Vol. VIII, pp. 1,682–3; Vol. III, p. 493 (quodded is imprisoned, but perhaps here means locked up). For an excellent modern discussion of this aspect of London policing see Stephan Petrow, *Policing Morals*, 1994.

39. Divall, *Scoundrels and Scallywags (and Some Honest Men)*, pp. 16–17; Graham Grant, *The Diary of a Police Surgeon*, 1920, pp. 15–16. For the male prostitutes see Robert Patrick Watson, *Memoirs of Robert Patrick Watson*, 1899, p. 174.

40. For the Bell case and some others see *Annual Register 1873*, Chronicle, pp. 113–15; and for similar cases in the 1890s see Cyril Pearl, *The Girl with the Swansdown Seat*, 1955, pp. 210–11. On Miss Cass see *Annual Register 1887*, English History, pp. 145–6.

41. On all these developments from 1839 see Moylan, *Scotland Yard and the Metropolitan Police*; Browne, *The Rise of Scotland Yard*; and Ascoli, *The Queen's Peace*. On the City police's use of the telegraph from 1857–8 see George Smalley, *The Life of Sir Sydney H. Waterlow Bart . . .*, 1909, pp. 39–42.

42. Figures for arrests are in the Commissioner of Police, *Annual Reports*.

43. The lyric is cited by a character in Shirley Brooks, *Sooner or Later*, 1868, Vol. II, p. 360; Walter, *My Secret Life*, Vol. IV, p. 806 (about 1866).

44. Sir Henry Smith, *From Constable to Commissioner*, 1910, pp. 194–6. On Silverton see Montagu Williams, *Leaves of a Life*, 1890, pp. 148–9, and *Later Leaves*, 1891, pp. 31ff. See also Anon., *London by Night*, 1868, p. 43; Captn Donald Shaw, *London in the Sixties (with a Few Digressions)*, 1909, pp. 37–8. On the brothel see London Committee for Suppressing the Traffic in British Girls for Purposes of Continental Prostitution, *Six Years' Labour and Sorrow; being the Fourth Report . . .*, 1885, pp. 49ff.

45. See John George Littlechild, *Reminiscences of Chief-Inspector Littlechild*, 1894, and John Sweeney, *At Scotland Yard*, 1904, for the Special Irish Branch.

46. George Dilnot (ed.), *The Trial of the Detectives*, 1928, p. 113. Dilnot's remains the most thorough account of this scandalous episode. See also Andrew Lansdowne, *A Life's Reminiscences of Scotland Yard*, 1890, pp. 6–15; and, for the CID after 1877, see Sir Robert Anderson, *The Lighter Side of My Official Life*, 1910, pp. 124–32. Remarkably, Frederick Williamson continued in charge as Howard Vincent's chief detective.

47. Henry Spencer Ashbee, *Index Librorum Prohibitorum*, 1877, pp. 328–38, citing 'a newspaper of the time'; the same account is given verbatim in *The News*, 30 September 1810.

48. Chesterton, *Revelations of Prison Life*, Vol. II, pp. 135–6.

49. There appears to be no comprehensive series of statistics for executions in London including the Surrey side, just those for Newgate. I have relied on V. A. C. Gatrell, *The Hanging Tree*, 1994, pp. 616–17, and *Haydn's Dictionary of Dates* (1904 edn).

50. *Annual Register 1868*, Chronicle, pp. 63-5.
51. Emily Constance Cook, *London in the Time of the Diamond Jubilee*, 1897, pp. 237-9.
52. On Newgate see Arthur Griffiths, *The Chronicles of Newgate*, 1883, p. 1; on the Fleet, John Ashton, *The Fleet*, 1888, pp. 233-4.
53. Fry is cited in Joseph Adshead, *Prisons and Prisoners*, 1845, p. 153n; see also Katherine Fry and Rachel Elizabeth Cresswell, *Memoir of the Life of Elizabeth Fry, with Extracts from Her Journal and Letters*, 1848, Vol. I, pp. 200-202, 255ff., 291ff. On the cold cells at Coldbath Fields see Henry Mayhew and John Binny, *The Criminal Prisons of London and Scenes of Prison Life*, 1862, p. 325, written about 1856 and referring to a case 'some time since'. Chesterton, *Revelations of Prison Life*, Vol. I, pp. 41-55.
54. Ibid., pp. 49-50.
55. On Dickens and prison see Alfred Trumble, *In Jail with Charles Dickens*, 1896, and the indispensable Philip Collins, *Dickens and Crime*, 1964, passim. On Coldbath Fields punishments see Adshead, *Prisons and Prisoners*, pp. 176ff., and Hepworth Dixon, *The London Prisons*, 1850, who called it 'In many respects . . . the best of our metropolitan gaols'. Mayhew and Binny, *The Criminal Prisons of London and Scenes of Prison Life*, p. 320.
56. Ibid., pp. 135-6, 168.
57. On labour in Coldbath Fields around 1856 see ibid., pp. 303ff. For a personal recollection of hard labour at Wandsworth around 1854 see Ned Wright, *Ned Wright*, 1873, pp. 20-21. For Dugdale see the *ODNB*.
58. Mayhew and Binny, *The Criminal Prisons of London and Scenes of Prison Life*, pp. 409ff.
59. For garrotting and its effect on penal policy see Jennifer Davis, 'The London Garrotting Panic of 1862: A Moral Panic and the Creation of a Criminal Class in mid-Victorian England', in V. A. C. Gatrell et al. (eds.), *Crime and the Law*, 1980, pp. 190-213; there is also much useful discussion of this and the earlier panic of 1830-31 in Arthur Griffiths, *Memorials of Millbank and Chapters in Prison History*, 1875, Chs. VIII, XXII-III. Jabez Spencer Balfour, *My Prison Life*, 1907, Chs. V and XV (Scrubbs dropped a 'b' some time by the 1930s); there is a thorough modern overview of prison punishment after 1862 in Sir Leon Radzinowicz and Roger Hood, *A History of English Criminal Law and Its Administration from 1750*, Vol. 5, 1986, pp. 526-67.
60. Cited in Mayhew and Binny, *The Criminal Prisons of London and Scenes of Prison Life*, pp. 100-105.

Chapter 14 Broad Sanctuary: Religion and Charity

1. According to the antiquarian Rev. Mackenzie E. C. Walcott, *Westminster*, 1849, pp. 80-87, sanctuary persisted here from 1198 to 1623.
2. On the significant reforming role of the clerical justices from the eighteenth century on see Sidney and Beatrice Webb, *English Local Government from the Revolution to the Municipal Corporations Act: The Parish and the County*, 1906, pp. 350-60.
3. Mrs Humphrey Ward, *Robert Elsmere*, 1888, Ch. XXII.
4. For the details of Lancaster's work see *DNB*. Its non-sectarian feeling is noted in Charles Knight (ed.), *London*, 1841-4, Vol. VI, pp. 20-21. On

George's proclamation, the *DNB* gives 'Bible' but 'Holy Scriptures' was the text under the portrait of George III hung in the Borough Road school in the 1820s: see James Bonwick's memoir cited in John Burnett (ed.), *Destiny Obscure*, 1982, p. 171 – Bonwick was a pupil and then teacher at the school. There is a good picture of the Borough Road school in 1808 in A. Highmore, *Pietas Londinensis*, 1810, pp. 773–80.

5. On St Giles and St George see SC, *Reports from Select Committee on the Education of the Lower Orders in the Metropolis: with Minutes of Evidence taken before the Committee*, 1816, First Report, pp. 8–9, evidence of Frederick Augustus Earle, vestry clerk, St Giles; on Southwark, p. 2, John Pickton, master of Borough Road British School, and Third Report, p. 229, James Millar, assistant secretary of the British and Foreign School Society; on Spitalfields, see Third Report, p. 185, William Crawford, Spitalfields Lancasterian School; for the Sunday Schools see First Report, p. 76, William Freeman Lloyd, Secretary, Sunday School Union. The conclusion is in First Report, p. iii. For Brougham see *Annual Register 1820*, History of Europe, pp. 49–57.

6. On the general improvement of London see SC, *Reports from Select Committee on the Education of the Lower Orders in the Metropolis: with Minutes of Evidence taken before the Committee*, 1816, Third Report, p. 221, Rev. Basil Woodd, rector of Bentinck Chapel, Marylebone since about 1785; and Francis Place, p. 269. See p. 236 for the Rev. John Campbell's evidence. The good reverend lives on in John Campbell Road, Stoke Newington. His charity schools were established in Kingsland in 1808.

7. For Fry see Katherine Fry and Rachel Elizabeth Cresswell, *Memoir of the Life of Elizabeth Fry, with Extracts from Her Journal and Letters*, 1848, Vol. I, p. 256. For the Borough Road schools see SC, *Reports from Select Committee on the Education of the Lower Orders in the Metropolis: with Minutes of Evidence taken before the Committee*, 1816, Third Report, p. 181, John Pickton. The Irishwoman is ibid., pp. 6–7, Rev. Tindall Thompson Walmsley, Secretary of the National Society.

8. 'Pious and Christian' is part of the citation hanging in the Secretary's room at the Westminster Hospital, quoted in Walter Thornbury and Edward Walford, *Old and New London*, 1873–8, Vol. IV, pp. 33–4. Dates for the formation of the hospital are disputed. It moved to James Street, presumably Haymarket, around 1724, which the *ODNB* entry for Hoare gives as the foundation date. But I have followed Henry B. Wheatley and Peter Cunningham, *London Past and Present*, 1891, and Thornbury and Walford, *Old and New London*, which agree on 1720 for the first premises, though the charity was projected and first subscribed in 1719.

9. The term comes from Leon Radzinowicz, *A History of English Criminal Law and Its Administration from 1750*, Vol. 3, 1956, p. 181.

10. Hannah More's injunction is in the *DNB*. On the activities of the sect, the SSV and evangelicalism more generally see Maurice J. Quinlan, *Victorian Prelude*, 1941, pp. 117ff.; Radzinowicz, *A History of English Criminal Law and Its Administration from 1750*, Vol. 3, pp. 141ff., 504–6; Kathleen Heasman, *Evangelicals in Action*, 1962, pp. 20–23; Ian Bradley, *The Call to Seriousness*, 1976, Ch. 1; and Edward J. Bristow, *Vice and Vigilance*, 1977, Ch.2. The early examples come from *Annual Register 1805*, Chronicle, p. 394, and *Annual Register 1806*, Chronicle, p. 388.

11. The story, very much from Fletcher's point of view, is extensively set out in SC, *Report of the Committee Appointed to Inquire into the State of the Police of the Metropolis*, 1816, especially pp. 81–4 (John Fletcher), 157–62 (Rev. Edward Robson), and *Second Report from the Committee on the State of the Police of the Metropolis*, 1817, pp. 130–47 (John Fletcher). For allegations of the corrupt influence of brewers on the justices in the 1820s see Mr Serjeant Ballantine, *Some Experiences of a Barrister's Life*, 1882, Vol. I, pp. 45–7.

12. See ibid., Vol. I, pp. 44–5.

13. The number of new churches is in Baptist Wriothesley Noel, *The State of the Metropolis Considered, in a Letter to the Rt. Honourable and Rt. Reverend the Lord Bishop of London*, 1835, p. 5; see also Charles B. P. Bosanquet, *London*, 1869, pp. 58–60.

14. On the rise of street preaching see Noel, *The State of the Metropolis Considered, in a Letter to the Rt. Honourable and Rt. Reverend the Lord Bishop of London*, pp. 49–54, and SC, *Report from the Select Committee on the Observance of the Sabbath Day: with the Minutes of Evidence, and Appendix*, 1832, qq. 2236ff. (John Cowton, Superintendent of City Police). For the binding over of two street preachers whom 'the Lord had sent into the vineyard' of New Street, Westminster, among 'a most wicked and sinful race', see *Annual Register 1828*, Chronicle, pp. 97–8. The charity count is from *Low's Handbook to the Charities of London . . . 1896–97*. These figures are indicative only, based on charities for which dates of foundation are given. They probably over-represent newer charities, some older institutions having fallen by the wayside or been subject to merger by the Charity Commission after 1853. For Exeter Hall see F. Morell Holmes, *Exeter Hall and Its Associations*, 1881.

15. From an appeal for the British and Foreign Bible Society in the *Christian Observer*, July 1812, cited in Quinlan, *Victorian Prelude*, p. 128; see also his helpful analysis of the religious and moral significance of these first three decades of the century summarised at pp. 117–18 and 254–60.

16. An overview of these early initiatives is in Bosanquet, *London*, pp. 67–70.

17. Bosanquet's characterisation of the LCM is ibid., pp. 70–71. On Popery, citing a St Giles missionary, probably in the 1840s, see John Matthias Weylland, *These Fifty Years*, 1884, p. 59. The 'brave men' tag is in John Matthias Weylland, *Round the Tower*, 1875, pp. 15–16.

18. The reference to artisan class is in Bosanquet, *London*, pp. 71–2. The shabby missionary was R. W. Vanderkiste, *Notes and Narratives of a Six Years' Mission, Principally Among the Dens of London*, 1854, pp. 2–3, where he also describes the 'day to day' work of the LCM.

19. See James Dunn, *Modern London – Its Sins and Woes and the Sovereign Remedy*, 1906, p. 68, for the prayer at every visit. On the work of the LCM generally see Vanderkiste, *Notes and Narratives of a Six Years' Mission, Principally Among the Dens of London*; Weylland, *Round the Tower* and *These Fifty Years*; John Hunt, *Pioneer Work in the Great City*, 1895; Dunn, *Modern London . . .*, and *From Coal Mine Upwards, or, Seventy Years of an Eventful Life*, 1910; and for similar experiences with the Home Missionary Society see James Inches Hillocks, *My Life and Labours in London, a Step Nearer The Mark*, 1865.

20. Mary Bayly, *Ragged Homes and How to Mend Them*, 1860, passim. For

Ranyard see *ODNB*; Lydia N. Ranyard, *L. N. R.*, 1860; Elspeth Platt, *The Story of the Ranyard Mission 1857-1937*, 1937. Mother Kate, *Old Soho Days and Other Memories*, 1906, p. 7. On Mildmay see Harriette J. Cooke, *Mildmay*, 1893, passim. For evangelical missions more generally in this period see Heasman, *Evangelicals in Action*, pp. 30-47.

21. Ranyard, *L. N. R.*, pp. 30-31. Poor Bullin is recalled in Vanderkiste, *Notes and Narratives of a Six Years' Mission, Principally Among the Dens of London*, pp. 59-60. The episode in George Street is relayed in Henry Mayhew, *London Labour and the London Poor*, 1861-2, Vol. I, p. 267. See also Hunt, *Pioneer Work in the Great City*, pp. 45-6, 78-9. Dunn, *From Coal Mine Upwards; or, Seventy Years of an Eventful Life*, pp. 109-10.

22. Bosanquet, *London*, pp. 71-2; Vanderkiste, *Notes and Narratives of a Six Years' Mission, Principally Among the Dens of London*, pp. 269-70.

23. See C. J. Montague, *Sixty Years in Waifdom*, 1904, Ch. III, for the early days of the movement. Bosanquet, *London*, p. 74, gives 1837 for the first London City Missionaries' school. On the other hand, the *ODNB* entry for John Pounds, a Portsmouth cobbler, shows what were essentially ragged schools developed by him in that city from 1818. And it's likely that the very first, even though not named as such, flowed naturally out of the Sunday School movement of the last twenty years of the eighteenth century.

24. Cited in Henry Mayhew, *The* Morning Chronicle *Survey of Labour and the Poor*, 1849-50, Vol. IV, p. 40. Surprisingly, Mayhew opposed the ragged schools, seeing them as nurseries of crime, good children corrupted by the bad. But it's possible he was reacting against their evangelical origins, feeling unable to oppose their extreme Christianising openly.

25. Mayhew lists ragged school addresses in March 1850, ibid., pp. 44-5. On Carden see C. J. Montague, *Sixty Years in Waifdom*, 1904, p. 312.

26. Charles Dickens, *The Letters of Charles Dickens*, 1965-2002, Vol. III, pp. 562-4 (to Angela Burdett-Coutts, 16 September 1843).

27. For Blomfield's and Cotton's efforts see *ODNB*. See also Bosanquet, *London*, p. 61.

28. On the star preachers, there is an interesting list from two London Sundays in 1839 in Thomas Cooper, *The Life of Thomas Cooper*, 1872, pp. 127-8. Morris and Binney inspired William Hale White in the late 1840s and 1850s – see Catherine Macdonald Maclean, *Mark Rutherford*, 1955, pp. 66-8, 85-6; and Binney also inspired George Williams – see J. E. Hodder Williams, *The Life of Sir George Williams*, 1906, pp. 36-41. On Spurgeon see Ernest W. Bacon, *Spurgeon*, 1967, passim.

29. Mayhew, *The* Morning Chronicle *Survey of Labour and the Poor*, Vol. I, pp. 41-2.

30. See for evangelical social work generally in this period Heasman, *Evangelicals in Action*, pp. 48-68; there is also a useful overview of London charity at this period in Daniel Joseph Kirwan, *Palace and Hovel*, 1870, Ch. XXVIII.

31. Shaftesbury is quoted in Edwin Hodder, *The Life of Samuel Morley*, 1887, p. 301; the deputations to the memorial are listed in Edwin Hodder, *The Life and Work of the Seventh Earl of Shaftesbury, K.G.*, 1887, Vol. III, pp. 525-8. Notting Hill is in W. S. Clarke, *The Suburban Homes of London*, 1881, pp. 400-401; and for the amount of voluntary giving for church building in the period see Owen Chadwick, *The Victorian Church*, Part II, 1970, p. 241.

32. See David Owen, *English Philanthropy, 1660–1960*, 1960, Ch. XIV; Anthony S. Wohl, *The Eternal Slum*, 1977, Ch.6.

33. The Peabody character reference is in Edward Bowmaker, *The Housing of the Working Classes*, 1895, p. 101. See also Jerry White, *Rothschild Buildings*, 1980, pp. 54–60.

34. For Hill's views the best source is her own writings gathered in Octavia Hill, *Homes of the London Poor*, 1875, but mostly collected from the 1860s: see especially pp. 17–18, 20–21, 26–7, 33, 41, 43. Henrietta Barnett, *Canon Barnett, His Life, Work and Friends*, 1918, pp. 30–31. For more sympathetic views of Hill see E. Moberley Bell, *Octavia Hill*, 1942, and Gillian Darley, *Octavia Hill*, 1990, passim.

35. *Census of Great Britain, 1851: Population (Great Britain): Religious Worship (England and Wales)*, pp. clviii–xi. The figures of church attendance in London are calculated from pp. 3–9. These figures do not show the numbers actually attending church but are based on all attendances at three Sunday sittings (morning, afternoon and evening). They thus count numerous twicers, and no doubt a few thricers, in the total. This, together with the fact that Mann's figures derive from the churches' own estimates or 'counts', have rightly tended to undermine his figures which clearly tend to overstate the numbers of worshippers. On the other hand they can be useful in constructing the sorts of comparisons I've given here, I think. And his text seems to have been unduly ignored, for it is a powerful call for more evangelical activity by the churches, a call answered over the next three decades in particular. 'Remember Bethnal Green' is in Charles Booth, *Life and Labour of the People in London*, 1892–1902, Series 3, Vol. 2, pp. 76–7.

36. *Annual Register 1856*, Chronicle, pp. 92–4.

37. On St Barnabas see Chadwick, *Victorian Church*, Part I, 1966, pp. 301–2; on Lowder see *ODNB*. On St George's see *Annual Register 1859*, Chronicle, pp. 125ff.; *Annual Register 1860*, Chronicle, pp. 110–13; *ILN*, Vol. XXXVI, January–June 1860, passim; Rev. Harry Jones, *East and West London*, 1875, pp. 60–63; Chadwick, *Victorian Church*, Part I, pp. 497–501.

38. For Mackonochie see *ODNB*. On ritualism at Erith in the 1860s see Rev. Theodore Wood, *The Rev. J. G. Wood*, 1890, pp. 28–31; and for police having to intervene at St James's, Hatcham, see Commissioner of Police, *Annual Report for the Year 1877*, p. 45.

39. Edward Denison, *Letters and Other Writings of the Late Edward Denison, M.P. for Newark*, edited by Sir Baldwyn Leighton, 1872, pp. 20–21, 58–9.

40. Hill, *Homes of the London Poor*, p. 37, written 1869; Samuel cited in Barnett, *Canon Barnett, His Life, Work and Friends*, pp. 83–4.

41. For the COS see in particular Helen Bosanquet, *Social Work in London, 1869–1912*, 1914, and C. Loch Mowat, *The Charity Organisation Society, 1869–1913*, 1961.

42. Barnett, *Canon Barnett, His Life, Work and Friends*, p. 84.

43. Barnardo is cited in Mrs Barnardo and James Marchant, *Memoirs of the Late Dr Barnardo*, 1907, pp. 96–9. Dunn, *From Coal Mine Upwards, or, Seventy Years of an Eventful Life*, pp. 115ff. No-popery in Homerton is recalled in Langton George Vere, *Random Recollections of Homerton Mission*, 1912, p. 48. Rev. C. J. Whitmore, *Seeking the Lost*, 1876, pp. 186–91.

44. The network is from Arnold Bennett, *The Journals of Arnold Bennett*, edited by Newman Flower, 1932, Vol. I, p. 92 (18 April 1899). For lady rent collec-

tors see Beatrice Webb, *My Apprenticeship*, 1926, pp. 259–79; Ellen Chase, *Tenant Friends in Old Deptford*, 1929, passim; and Margaret Wynne Nevinson, *Life's Fitful Fever*, 1926, pp. 76–101. For recent discussion of this work see Judith R. Walkowitz, *City of Dreadful Delight*, 1992, pp. 52–8 and Seth Koven, *Slumming*, 2004, Ch. 4.

45. Booth, *Life and Labour of the People in London*, Series 3, Vol. 5, p. 14; there are examples too numerous to list throughout the first six volumes of the Religious Influences series.

46. For Booth, the Congregationalists here and elsewhere were among the 'most complete and successful religious organizations in North London': see ibid., Vol. 1, pp. 120–24. For the history of New Court Chapel see William Pierce, *Old New-Court*, 1892; on the mission see E. F. Heaven, *Lennox Road Mission Hall 1874–1934*, 1934 (at Islington Local History Library); the New Court Chapel Manuals and issues of the *New Court Congregational Magazine* are in the London Metropolitan Archive.

47. I have sampled just a few London offerings described with wonderful wit and humanity by the broad-church Rev. C. Maurice Davies in the mid-1870s, his collected newspaper pieces running to some seven volumes, viz. *Unorthodox London* (2 vols., 1873–5); *Orthodox London* (2 vols., 1874–5); *Heterodox London* (2 vols., 1874) and *Mystic London* (1875).

48. These elements in Booth's character are described in Harold Begbie, *Life of William Booth*, 1920, Vol. I, pp. 347–51. Begbie's two-volume hagiography remains a useful source for Booth and his army.

49. The Skeleton Army is recalled in George Lansbury, *My Life*, 1928, p. 84. The indecisive power of the Holy Ghost is described in Bramwell Booth, *Echoes and Memories*, 1925, pp. 53–6. The Eagle episode is in Begbie, *Life of William Booth*, Vol. II, pp. 10–13; Booth was dispossessed of the Eagle in the courts, unable to comply with covenants requiring its permanent use as a public house. For some interesting reflections on the Hallelujah Lasses see Walkowitz, *City of Dreadful Delight*, pp. 73–6. See also John Law, *Captain Lobe*, 1889: Harkness remained a life-long supporter of the army's objectives, eventually preferring them to socialism.

50. The comment on Denison is in J. A. R. Pimlott, *Toynbee Hall*, 1935, pp. 11–12. On the influence of the *Bitter Cry* see ibid., pp. 24ff.; Anthony S. Wohl's introduction to the 1970 Victorian Library edn of Andrew Mearns, *The Bitter Cry of Outcast London*; Wohl, *The Eternal Slum*, Ch. 8.

51. The call was by Canon Scott Holland for settlers in Oxford House, though the spirit was generally applicable, cited in James Adderley, *In Slums and Society*, 1916, p. 48; the cynic was Horace Wyndham, *The Nineteen Hundreds*, 1923, p. 18. There is a large literature on settlements, especially Toynbee Hall: see, e.g., John M. Knapp (ed.), *The Universities and the Social Problem*, 1895; Philip Whitwell Wilson, 'The Settlement Ideal', in Richard Mudie-Smith (ed.), *The Religious Life of London*, 1904; Pimlott, *Toynbee Hall*, 1935; Asa Briggs and Anne McCartney, *Toynbee Hall*, 1984; Standish Meacham, *Toynbee Hall and Social Reform 1880–1914*, 1987; Deborah E. B. Weiner, *Architecture and Social Reform*, 1994, pp. 157–79; see also useful early recollections in Barnett, *Canon Barnett, His Life, Work and Friends*, Ch. XXIVff.; Adderley, *In Slums and Society*, passim; Henry W. Nevinson, *Changes and Chances*, 1923, pp. 78ff. For an enlightening study of the sexual politics of these settlements see Koven, *Slumming*, Ch. 5.

52. There is a list in Karl Baedeker, *London and Its Environs*, 1905, p. 88.

53. Working man's university is the title of Ch. IV in Pimlott, *Toynbee Hall*. On the People's Palace see Weiner, *Architecture and Social Reform*, pp. 180–203. For those who did find it a university see Thomas Okey, *A Basketful of Memories*, 1930, pp. 50ff., and Frederick Rogers, *Labour, Life and Literature*, 1913, Ch. XV. D. G. Halsted, *Doctor in the Nineties*, 1959, pp. 30–31; see also Sir Wilfred Thomason, Grenfell, *The Story of a Labrador Doctor*, 1928, pp. 56ff. Boys' clubs gained strength in the 1890s and matured as a national movement in the first three decades of the twentieth century.

54. See Mudie-Smith (ed.), *The Religious Life of London*, especially pp. 17–18 on the one in five worshippers and 280ff. on the decline since 1886. The best overview on the London working classes and religion in the last quarter of the century remains Hugh McLeod, *Class and Religion in the Late Victorian City*, 1974. One in five worshippers was how some informed observers interpreted Mann's results for London: see Robert Gregory, *Sermons on the Poorer Classes of London, preached before the University of Oxford*, 1869, pp. 8–9.

55. Booth, *Life and Labour of the People in London*, Series 3, Vol. 5, p. 201, citing (I think) the vicar of St Anne's, Wandsworth.

56. For a comment on declining violent hostility see Percy Alden, 'The Problem of East London', in Mudie-Smith (ed.), *The Religious Life of London*, p. 28. Barnett, *Canon Barnett, His Life, Work and Friends*, p. 142. The cycling cleric is recalled in Richard Free, *Seven Years' Hard*, 1904, pp. 227–8.

57. A chapter heading in ibid. Free was an Anglican vicar in the Isle of Dogs.

58. See J. R. Piggott, *Palace of the People*, 2004; and Koven, *Slumming*, for Barnardo.

59. Cited in Grant Richards, *Memories of a Misspent Youth 1872–1896*, 1932, p. 307. Richards worked with Stead on the *Review of Reviews*, 1890–97. See too the revealing recollections of Stead by Havelock Ellis in Frederic Whyte, *The Life of W. T. Stead*, 1925, Vol. II, pp. 341–2.

60. A great deal has been written about this celebrated event over the years but I have condensed this account especially from *Pall Mall Gazette 'Extra'*, No. 20, 1885; Whyte, *The Life of W. T. Stead*, Vol. I, pp. 159–86; J. W. Robertson Scott, *The Story of the Pall Mall Gazette, of its First Editor Frederick Greenwood and of Its Founder George Murray Smith*, 1952, pp. 125–35; Horace Wyndham, *Victorian Sensations*, 1933, pp. 121–64 (a sceptic's view); Michael Pearson, *The Age of Consent*, 1972, Chs. 7–11; Walkowitz, *City of Dreadful Delight*, Chs. 3–4. See also Edward J. Bristow, *Vice and Vigilance*, 1977, Pts 2 and 3.

61. Coote's childhood is in William Alexander Coote and Miss A. Baker (eds.), *A Romance of Philanthropy*, 1916, pp. 20–25, and the improper arms are ibid., p. 59. On this whole movement see, for instance, Susan D. Pennybacker, *A Vision for London 1889–1914*, 1995, pp. 210–40; and John Stokes, '"Prudes on the Prowl": The View from the Empire Promenade', in *Victorian England*, Folio Society History of England, 1996, pp. 365–95.

62. Toynbee Hall is in George R. Sims (ed.), *Living London*, 1902–3, Vol. I, p. 268; the Soho clergy are in Rev. J. H. Cardwell (ed.), *Twenty Years in Soho*, 1911, pp. 61–3; Booth, *Life and Labour of the People in London*, Series 3, Vol. 4, p. 58. See also Percy Alden in Knapp (ed.), *The Universities and the Social Problem*, pp. 74–5.

Chapter 15 Spring Gardens: Government

1. For Spring Gardens see Henry B. Wheatley and Peter Cunningham, *London Past and Present*, 1891, Vol. III, and *Survey of London*, Vol. XX, *Trafalgar Square and Neighbourhood (The Parish of St. Martin-in-the-Fields, Pt. III)*, 1940, Chs. 6 and 7. On the fraught move of the Board from Greek Street to Spring Gardens see SC, *Second Report from the Select Committee on Metropolis Local Taxation [together with the Minutes of Evidence, Appendices, Proceedings of the Committee and Index]*, 1861, especially the evidence of Sir John Thwaites, MBW chairman, qq. 3383-3510. Marrable's building gets an appreciative, if brief, notice in Nikolaus Pevsner, *London I. The Cities of London and Westminster*, 1957, p. 575.

2. The description of St Botolph is Sir Benjamin Hall's in Hansard, Third Series, Vol. CXXXVII, col. 703. For the clergymen in local government see Sidney and Beatrice Webb, *English Local Government: The Parish and the County*, 1906, p. 255. The steady growth of parishes in the Bills of Mortality from 1603, subsumed within the Registrar-General's definition of London from 1831, is charted in *Census 1851, Population Tables Vol. I*, Division 1, pp. 42-4.

3. See Webb, *English Local Government: Statutory Authorities for Special Purposes*, 1922, Ch. I.

4. For the Turnpike Trusts see ibid., Ch. III; on the continuation of trusts in south London until 1865 see Janet Roebuck, *Urban Development in 19th-century London*, 1979, pp. 111-12. On the operation of the Metropolitan Roads Board, under-regarded generally by historians of London, see T. F. Ordish, *London Topographical Record*, 1913, pp. 1-92.

5. See Webb, *English Local Government: Statutory Authorities for Special Purposes*, 1922, Ch. II.

6. See ibid., Ch. IV. For Belgravia see Hermione Hobhouse, *Thomas Cubitt*, 1971, pp. 109ff. Sir Benjamin Hall's verdict on St Pancras and others is in Hansard, Third Series, Vol. CXXXVII, cols. 709-13. See also Joseph F. B. Firth, *Municipal London*, 1876, Ch. VII.

7. See Sidney and Beatrice Webb, *English Local Government: The Manor and the Borough*, 1908, Part 1, pp. 212ff. See also David Hughson, *London*, 1805-9, Vol. IV, pp. 138ff., for a reasonably clear explanation of Westminster's theoretical constitution.

8. For the incorruptible justices see Webb, *English Local Government: The Manor and the Borough*, Part 2, p. 667.

9. See especially ibid., Part 2, Ch. 10. See also William Ferneley Allen, *The Corporation of London*, 1858, passim; RC, *Report of the Commissioners Appointed to Inquire into the Existing State of the Corporation of the City of London, and to Collect Information Respecting its Constitution, Order, and Government etc. together with the Minutes of Evidence and Appendix*, 1854 (*Report*); and David Owen, *The Government of Victorian London 1855-1889*, 1981, Ch. 11.

10. On gluttony see John Hogg, *London As It Is*, 1837, pp. 328-9; on elections see RC, *Report of the Commissioners Appointed to Inquire into the Existing State of the Corporation of the City of London, and to Collect Information Respecting its Constitution, Order, and Government etc. together with the Minutes of Evidence and Appendix*, 1854, qq. 309-30 (James Acland, electoral agent).

11. On the Westminster commissioners see Webb, *English Local Government: Statutory Authorities for Special Purposes*, 1922, pp. 78ff.; on St Luke's see PP, *Extracts from the information received by Her Majesty's Commissioners as to the Administration and Operation of the Poor-Laws*, 1833, Edwin Chadwick's Report, pp. 224ff., and for Shoreditch see pp. 274–5; St Margaret's and St John's is in Webb, *English Local Government: The Parish and the County*, 1906, pp. 237–8; the angry paupers were described in PP, *Extracts from the information received by Her Majesty's Commissioners as to the Administration and Operation of the Poor-Laws*, 1833, Chadwick's Report p. 334, citing Superintendent T. Y. Smith, K Division, New Police; the absconding rate collector is in *Annual Register 1808*, Chronicle, pp. 126–7. For Merceron see Webb, *English Local Government: The Parish and the County*, 1906, pp. 79–90, and *ODNB* (leaning heavily on the Webbs). His activities were extensively enquired into by the SC, *Report of the Committee Appointed to Inquire into the State of the Police of the Metropolis*, 1816, and *First Report from the Committee on the State of the Police of the Metropolis: with Minutes of Evidence taken before the Committee; and an Appendix*, 1817, mainly in respect of his licensing and rate-collecting ventures.
12. See *Census 1851, Population Tables Vol. I*, Division I, pp. 40–43.
13. SC, *Report from the Select Committee on the Supply of Water to the Metropolis*, 1821, p. 246, Table L.
14. On the Paving Act see Webb, *English Local Government: Statutory Authorities for Special Purposes*, 1922, pp. 293ff.; on the comparison with Paris see Hogg, *London As It Is*, pp. 178–9, 206–7.
15. See Webb, *English Local Government: The Parish and the County*, 1906, pp. 152ff., 262ff.
16. See the still invaluable Charles Creighton, *A History of Epidemics in Britain*, 1891–4, Vol. II, passim; SC, *Report from the Select Committee on Contagious Fever in London*, 1818; PP, *Report from the Committee on the Bill to prevent the Spreading of Canine Madness*, 1830. For the health of London compared to that of England at this period see Hogg, *London As It Is*, Chs. II–VI.
17. On the local boards' difficulties see PP, *Copies of Certain Papers Relating to Cholera; together with the Report of the Central Board of Health thereupon*, 1832, pp. 3–4, 9; see also PP, *Metropolitan Sanitary Commission*, 1848, *First Report*, pp. 2–6.
18. For the changing cost of poor relief in these years see Sir George Nicholls, *A History of the English Poor Law*, 1854, Vol. II, pp. 302ff.
19. See M. Dorothy George, *London Life in the XVIIIth Century*, 1925, pp. 257–8; Arthur Redford, *Labour Migration in England 1800–50*, 1926, pp. 28–9; Sidney and Beatrice Webb, *English Poor Law History: Part I, The Old Poor Law*, 1927, pp. 196–206. All these cite the 2,026 pauper apprentices identified by a House of Commons Committee on Parish Apprenticeships reporting in 1815 as having been sent out of London between 1802 and 1811. But this figure cannot be definitive because the parish returns were incomplete and they do not cover the years 1812–15.
20. *Annual Register 1803*, Chronicle, p. 368. For the Hibner case see the Proceedings of the Old Bailey (www.oldbaileyonline.org.uk); *Annual Register 1829*, Chronicle, pp. 71–4; *The Times*, 11, 13 and 14 April 1829. Colpit is also rendered Colpitts.
21. For difficulties between the Commissioners and local incorporated boards

see PP, *Report of the Poor Law Commissioners, upon the Relief of the poor in the Parishes of St. Marylebone and St. Pancras. With Appendix*, 1847.

22. See Charles B. P. Bosanquet, *London*, 1869, pp. 184–7.

23. Sidney and Beatrice Webb, *English Poor Law History*, 1929, Vol. II, pp. 1,038–9. Cost per head of poor relief, England and Wales, 10s 2d 1832, 9s 1d 1834, 5s 5d 1837.

24. For the flu see *Annual Register 1837*, Chronicle, pp. 8–10. For worsening conditions see PP, *Metropolitan Sanitary Commission*, 1848, *First Report*, p. 81; p. 115, evidence of Matthew French Wagstaffe, police and parish surgeon, Lambeth; p. 119, William Simpson, surgeon, High Street, Bloomsbury, for St Giles; p. 131, John Wright, MD, poor law surgeon St Margaret and St John, Westminster; and John Phillips's heartfelt cry is on pp. 203–4: when he said filth he meant shit.

25. As described by the Metropolitan Sanitary Commissioners in a question to a witness, ibid., p. 92. A year later and Albert Smith could write, '"The People", we regret to say, are naturally fond of dirt . . .' in *Gavarni in London*, 1849, 'Acrobats', n.p.

26. Henry Mayhew, *The* Morning Chronicle *Survey of Labour and the Poor*, 1849–50, Vol. II, p. 203.

27. Early statistics are to be found in John Simon, *Public Health Reports*, 1887, Vol. I, pp. 40–41, citing his 1849 report; John Weale, *A New Survey of London*, 1853, Vol. I, pp. 254–64; some baths were cold 1d, warm 2d. For the failure in 1846 to persuade the ratepayers of St George's-in-the-East that baths and washhouses were a good thing see William J. Quekett, *'My Sayings and Doings', with Reminiscences of My Life*, 1888, pp. 174–8. Glasshouse Yard and its baths are described in PP, *Metropolitan Sanitary Commission*, 1848, *First Report*, pp. 98–108, by R. Bowie, surgeon, East Smithfield.

28. *Annual Register 1849*, Chronicle, pp. 1–2.

29. On the background to the 1848 Sewers Act see John Simon, *English Sanitary Institutions, reviewed in their course of development, and in some of their political and social relations*, 1890, Chs. X and XI; and Royston Lambert, *Sir John Simon 1816–1904 and English Social Administration*, 1963, Chs. 4 and 5.

30. Ibid., Ch. 5.

31. See Simon, *Public Health Reports*, Vol. I, passim; Simon, *English Sanitary Institutions . . .*, pp. 247–53; Lambert, *Sir John Simon 1816–1904 and English Social Administration*, Chs. 6–9. See also Simon's evidence to the RC, *Report of the Commissioners Appointed to Inquire into the Existing State of the Corporation of the City of London, and to Collect Information Respecting its Constitution, Order, and Government etc. together with the Minutes of Evidence and Appendix*, 1854, qq. 7391ff.

32. SC, *Report from the Select Committee on the Police of the Metropolis; with the Minutes of Evidence, Appendix and Index*, 1834, qq. 454ff., Col. Rowan and Richard Mayne, Commissioners of the Metropolitan Police.

33. The best overview of the post-1855 arrangements is Owen, *The Government of Victorian London 1855–1889*.

34. SC, *Second Report from the Select Committee on Metropolitan Local Government, &c; [together with the Minutes of Evidence, Appendices, Proceedings of the Committee and Index]*, 1866–7, qq. 1780ff., q. 1819 (James Beal, land agent and auctioneer of 209 Piccadilly, St James's

Vestryman); qq. 2630–31 (Thomas Begg, mechanical engineer, Vestryman of St Paul's Covent Garden and Member of Strand District Board of Works).

35. For criticism of the MBW from within see SC, *First, Second and Third Reports from the Select Committee on Metropolis Local Taxation [together with the Minutes of Evidence, Appendices, Proceedings of the Committee and Index]*, 1861, Second Report, qq. 2537–44, Major William Lyon, MBW member for St George's Hanover Square 1856–8; qq. 2709ff., Charles Mills Roche, MBW member for Paddington since 1859. On the membership see ibid., Appendix 11, p. 227.

36. For Whitworth see LCC, *London County Council Staff Gazette*, Vol. I, No. 6, June 1900, pp. 68–9; and for Bell, LCC, *London County Council Staff Gazette*, Vol. II, No. 20, August 1901, pp. 92–3. For a full study, including social origins of the staff of the MBW, see Gloria C. Clifton, *Professionalism, Patronage and Public Service in Victorian London*, 1992, especially Ch. 7. And generally see Owen, *The Government of Victorian London, 1855–1889*.

37. Charles Dickens, *The Letters of Charles Dickens*, 1965–2002, Vol. IX, p. 354, to Mary Boyle, 28 December 1860. On Massey see *ODNB* and Jack While, *Fifty Years of Fire Fighting in London*, 1931, passim.

38. The MAB moved to Norfolk House, at the Embankment end of Norfolk Street in 1881 and to purpose-built offices on Victoria Embankment in 1900. See Sir Allan Powell, *The Metropolitan Asylums Board and Its Work, 1867–1930*, 1930, Ch. II; see also Firth, *Municipal London*, Ch. XI.

39. For an excellent history of the MAB and its hospitals see Gwendoline M. Ayers, *England's First State Hospitals and the Metropolitan Asylums Board, 1867–1930*, 1971; see also Powell, *Metropolitan Asylums Board and Its Work, 1867–1930*, and G. C. Cook, *From the Greenwich Hulks to Old St Pancras*, 1992, Chs. 1 and 3. The critic was Firth, *Municipal London*, p. 497. For workhouse infirmaries see the magisterial overview in Ruth Hodgkinson, *The Origins of the National Health Service*, 1967, Ch. 14. The proportion of state-run hospital provision is calculated from LCC, *London Statistics*, Vol. XXIII, 1912–13, section XII.

40. For workhouse infirmary scandals see Hodgkinson, *The Origins of the National Health Service*, Ch. 14. For the cases of Timothy Daly and Richard Gibson see *Daily News*, 16 January 1865 (Joseph Charles Parkinson). For the rise of vagrancy in the 1860s and the Board's response see Webb, *English Poor Law: Pt II, The Last Hundred Years*, 1929, Vol. I, pp. 406–10.

41. See especially Seth Koven, *Slumming*, 2004, pp. 31ff.

42. James Inches Hillocks, *My Life and Labours in London, a Step Nearer the Mark*, 1865, pp. 128–9; see also Charles Dickens, *Our Mutual Friend*, 1864–5, 'Postscript in lieu of a preface', dated 2 September 1865.

43. See RC, *Second Report of the Royal Sanitary Commission*, 1871, qq. 12282 and 12290, Dr John Liddle, Medical Officer of Health Whitechapel District Board of Works (he gave evidence on 23 June 1870); the member was Robert Gladding, bookseller, in SC, *Metropolitan Local Government*, 1866–7, *First Report*, q. 3208; see also qq. 5044ff., Daniel Birt, Vestry Clerk, St George-the-Martyr Southwark.

44. SC, *Metropolitan Local Government*, 1866–7, *First Report*, q. 6923. Rendle was also an impressive historian of Southwark. For highlights from his lively reports see Henry Jephson, *The Sanitary Evolution of London*, 1907, pp.

142–51, and Chs. II and III for this period generally. See also Anthony S. Wohl, *Endangered Lives*, 1983, Ch. 7. On the unevenness of sanitary inspection in London see Firth, *Municipal London*, pp. 307–15.

45. *The Times* is cited in Thomas Alfred Spalding, *The Work of the London School Board*, 1900, p. 29. The comment on Miller is Frederick Rogers, *Labour, Life and Literature*, 1913, p. 51.

46. For these early years see Spalding, *The Work of the London School Board*, Part II; Hugh B. Philpott, *London at School*, 1904, Chs. I–III (the genuine zeal is on p. 20); and Stuart Maclure, *One Hundred Years of London Education 1870–1970*, 1970, Chs. 1–4.

47. On the temporary schools and compulsion generally see Spalding, *The Work of the London School Board*, pp. 54, 120ff. For the early statistics of school-building see Firth, *Municipal London*, pp. 446, 459ff.

48. For the difficulties posed by school for the poorest Londoners see the discussion in Anna Davin, *Growing Up Poor*, 1996, especially Parts 2 and 3; and David Rubinstein, *School Attendance in London 1870–1914*, 1969, Ch. IV. See also George R. Sims, *How the Poor Live and Horrible London*, 1883, 'How the Poor Live', Chs. III–IV.

49. For the difficulties of the visitors see Rubinstein, *School Attendance in London 1870–1914*, Ch. IV and p. 112 for the truancy figures. For teachers' problems see Maclure, *One Hundred Years of London Education 1870–1970*, p. 42; and P. A. Heard, *An Octogenarian's Memories*, 1974, pp. 83ff., 109. For a very useful study of a single board school see W. E. Marsden, *Educating the Respectable*, 1991. The nine years' hard labour are to be found in Spalding, *The Work of the London School Board*, pp. 165–6.

50. See Thomas Greenwood, *Public Libraries*, 1891, Ch. XVI.

51. Joseph F. B. Firth, *Reform of London Government and of City Guilds*, 1888, pp. 74–6. For earlier advocacy of local control of the police under an improved and more accountable MBW see SC, *First, Second and Third Reports from the Select Committee on Metropolis Local Taxation [together with the Minutes of Evidence, Appendices, Proceedings of the Committee and Index]*, 1861, *Second Report*, q. 1221, James Beal, former vestryman, St James's Piccadilly.

52. There's a balanced appraisal of the City Corporation after 1854 in Owen, *The Government of Victorian London 1855–1889*, Ch. 11. See also Webb, *English Local Government: The Manor and the Borough*, 1908, Part 2, pp. 689–92.

53. *Annual Register 1888*, English History, pp. 174–5. See also PP, *Starvation*.

54. See, for instance, RC, *Report of Her Majesty's Commissioners for Inquiring into the Housing of the Working Classes. Vol. II Minutes of Evidence and Appendix as to England and Wales*, 1885, q. 2947ff. (Thomas Jennings, Chairman, Sanitary Committee, Clerkenwell Vestry). For action taken by the vestries against their own members see qq. 4666 (John Dixon, MOH Bermondsey Vestry) and 9567 (John William Tripe, MOH Hackney District Board of Works).

55. The critic was Firth, *Reform of London Government and of City Guilds*, p. 43; the judgement twenty years on, politically biased against the successor LCC it should be said, is in *The Times, The Story of the London County Council*, 1907, p. 4.

56. See RC, *Interim Report of the Royal Commissioners appointed to inquire into certain matters connected with the working of the Metropolitan Board*

of Works, 1888; Owen, The Government of Victorian London 1855–1889, Ch. 8; John Davis, Reforming London, 1988, Ch. 4; Clifton, Professionalism, Patronage and Public Service in Victorian London, Ch. 13; on Goddard and Robinson see LCC, London County Council Staff Gazette, Vol. I, No. 5, May 1900, pp. 57–9, 'Spring Gardens Thirty Years Ago' by C. W. N. [C. W. Nairn].

57. The best overview of the struggles for London government reform after 1855 is the masterly Davis, Reforming London.

58. On the first council, including disappointment over the calibre of members, see Annual Register 1889, English History, pp. 4–5; William Saunders, History of the First London County Council, 1889–1890–1891, 1892; The Times, The Story of the London County Council, 1907, pp. 4–6; A. G. Gardiner, John Benn and the Progressive Movement, 1925, Ch. VI; Davis, Reforming London, Chs. 5 and 6.

59. LCC Annual Report, 1904, p. 3.

60. See George R. Sims, My Life – Sixty Years' Recollection of Bohemian London, 1917, p. 116; Edward J. Bristow, Vice and Vigilance, 1977, pp. 209–11; Susan D. Pennybacker, A Vision for London 1889–1914, 1995, pp. 210–48.

61. F. G. Bettany, Stewart Headlam, 1926, pp. 149–52.

62. See Charles Booth, Life and Labour of the People in London, 1892–1902, Series 1, Vol. 2, Ch. II; his comment on the East End is in Series 3, Vol. 2, pp. 51–2. For Fulham see Arnold Bennett, The Journals of Arnold Bennett, edited by Newman Flower, 1932, Vol. I, p. 10 (15 June 1896). For instances of the inadequacy of poor relief in hard winters in the East End see Montagu Williams, Round London, 1892, pp. 226–9, and 1892, pp. 34–7. The workhouse scandals are from Annual Register 1893, Chronicle, pp. 39, 67.

63. On water see the RC, Report of the Royal Commission Appointed to Inquire into the Water Supply of the Metropolis, 1893; e.g. Vol. I, q. 343 (New River Co.); q. 883 (East London Water Co.); qq. 1697ff., 1784ff. (West Middlesex Water Co.); qq. 2224–5 (Grand Junction Water Co.); qq. 2400ff. (Southwark and Vauxhall Water Co.), qq. 2809ff. (Kent Water Co.); and Vol. II, Appendix A.1, Table C, and Appendix A.12. For smoke see Anthony S. Wohl, Endangered Lives, Ch.8; Peter Brimblecombe, The Big Smoke, 1987, especially Chs. 5 and 6; and for a fascinating recent overview of smoke and the London atmosphere's special attraction for painters in the late nineteenth century see Jonathan Ribner, 'The Poetics of Pollution', in Katharine Lochnan (ed.), Turner, Whistler, Monet, 2005, pp. 51–63. Booth, Life and Labour of the People in London, Series 3, Vol. 1, p. 60.

64. On the vestries see ibid., Vol. 2, pp. 155–9, 161, and Vol. 4, p. 161. For the guardians see ibid., Vol. 1, pp. 66–8, Vol. 2, pp. 138–9, Vol. 5, p. 217, and Vol. 6, p. 86.

65. Ibid., Vol. 1, p. 156; see also Vol. 2, p. 53.

66. Ibid., Vol. 4, pp. 202–3.

BIBLIOGRAPHY

The books listed are only those referred to in the notes. Unless indicated otherwise, the place of publication is London and the first edition is always cited.

À Beckett, Arthur William, *The à Becketts of 'Punch': Memories of Father and Sons*, 1903
—*Recollections of a Humourist: Grave and Gay*, 1907
Abel-Smith, Brian, and Stevens, Robert, *Lawyers and the Courts: A Sociological Study of the English Legal System 1750–1965*, 1967
Ackermann, Rudolf, *The Micorcosm of London; or, London in Miniature*, 3 Vols., 1808–10
Acton, William, *Prostitution, considered in Its Moral, Social, and Sanitary Aspects, in London and other Large Cities. With Proposals for the Mitigation and Prevention of its Attendant Evils*, 1857
—*Prostitution, considered in Its Moral, Social, and Sanitary Aspects, in London and other Large Cities and Garrison Towns. With Proposals for the Control and Prevention of its Attendant Evils*, 1870
Adams, R. R. D. (ed.), *The Book of the Cheese: Being Traits and Stories of 'Ye Olde Cheshire Cheese', Wine Office Court, Fleet Street, London, E.C., Complied by the Late T. W. Reid*, 4th edn, 1901
Adams, W. E., *Memoirs of a Social Atom*, 1903
Adamson, John and Hudson, Len (eds), *The London Town Miscellany. Vol. 1 1900–1939*, 1992
Adderley, James, *In Slums and Society: Reminiscences of Old Friends*, 1916
Adrian, Arthur A., *Mark Lemon: First Editor of 'Punch'*, 1966
Adshead, Joseph, *Prisons and Prisoners*, 1845
Ainger, Alfred (ed.), *Poems of Thomas Hood*, 2 vols., 1897
Ainsworth, William Harrison, *Jack Sheppard*, 1839

Alexander, Sally, *Women's Work in Nineteenth-Century London: A Study of the Years 1820–50*, 1983

Allen, William Ferneley, *The Corporation of London: Its Rights and Privileges*, 1858

Altick, Richard D., *The English Common Reader: A Social History of the Mass Reading Public, 1800–1900*, Columbus, Ohio, 1957 (2nd edn, 1998)

—*The Shows of London*, Cambridge, Mass., 1978

Anderson, Sir Robert, *The Lighter Side of My Official Life*, 1910

Andom, R. [Alfred Walter Barrett], *We Three and Troddles: A Tale of London Life*, 1894

— *Industrial Explorings in and Around London*, 1895 (2nd edn, 1896)

—*Martha and I: Being Sketches from our Suburban Life*, 2nd edn, 1898

Anon., *The Picture of London, for 1818; being a Correct Guide . . .*,1818

—[An Amateur], *Real Life in London or, The Rambles and Adventures of Bob Tallyho, Esq., and His Cousin, the Hon. Tom Dashall, Through the Metropolis; Exhibiting a Living Picture of Fashionable Characters, Manners, and Amusements in High and Low Life*, 1821–2

—*London by Night: By the Author of Skittles, Anonyma &c*, n.d., c. 1868

—*Wonderful London: Its Lights and Shadows of Humour and Sadness*, 1878

—[A Foreign Resident], *Society in London*, 1886

—*Tempted London: Young Men*, 1888

—[British Weekly Commissioners] *Toilers in London; or Inquiries Concerning Female Labour in the Metropolis: Being the Second Part of 'Tempted London'*, 1889

Annual Register, The . . ., various years

Archer, John Wykeham, *Vestiges of Old London, a Series of Etchings from Original Drawings . . . with Descriptions and Historical Notices*, 1851

Archer, Thomas, *The Pauper, the Thief, and the Convict; Sketches of Some of their Homes, Haunts, and Habits*, 1865

Armstrong, Arthur C., *Bouverie Street to Bowling Green Lane: Fifty-Five Years of Specialized Publishing*, 1946

Armytage, Percy, *By the Clock of St James's*, 1927

Arrow, Charles, *Rogues and Others*, 1926

Ascoli, David, *The Queen's Peace: The Origins and Development of the Metropolitan Police 1829–1979*, 1979

Ashbee, Henry Spencer [Pisanus Fraxi], *Index Librorum Prohibitorum: being Notes Bio-Biblio-Icono-graphical and Critical on Curious and Uncommon Books*, 1877

—*Centuria Librorum Absconditorum: being Notes Bio-Biblio-Iconographical and Critical on Curious and Uncommon Books*, 1879

—*Catena Librorum Tacendorum: being Notes Bio-Biblio-Icono-graphical and Critical on Curious and Uncommon Books*, 1885

Ashton, John, *The Fleet: Its River, Prison, and Marriages*, 1888 (popular edn, 1889)

—*Hyde Park: From Domesday-Book to Date*, 1896

—*The Dawn of the XIXth Century in England: A Social Sketch of the Times*, 5th edn, 1906

Asquith, Margot, *Autobiography*, 1920

Atkinson, Diane, *Love and Dirt: The Marriage of Arthur Munby and Hannah Cullwick*, 2003

Auerbach, Jeffrey A., *The Great Exhibition of 1851: A Nation on Display*, 1999

Ayers, Gwendoline M., *England's First State Hospitals and the Metropolitan Asylums Board, 1867–1930*, 1971

Bacon, Ernest W., *Spurgeon: Heir of the Puritans*, 1967

Baedeker, Karl, *London and Its Environs: Handbook for Travellers*, 1889 and 1905

Bagehot, Walter, *Lombard Street: A Description of the Money Market*, 1873 (new edn, 1931)

Bain, Alexander, *Autobiography*, 1904

Balfour, Jabez Spencer, *My Prison Life*, 1907

Ball, Michael, and Sunderland, David, *An Economic History of London, 1800–1914*, 2001

Ballantine, Mr Serjeant, *Some Experiences of a Barrister's Life*, 2 vols., 1882

Bamberger, Louis, *Memories of Sixty Years in the Timber and Pianoforte Trades*, 1929

—*Bow Bell Memories*, 1931

Bamford, Samuel, *Passages in the Life of a Radical*, 2 vols., 3rd edn, 1844

Banfield, Frank, *The Great Landlords of London*, 1888

Banton, Michael, *The Coloured Quarter: Negro Immigrants in an English City*, 1955

Barham, R. H. Dalton, *The Life and Remains of Theodore Edward Hook*, 2 vols., 1849

Barker, T. C., and Robbins, Michael, *A History of London Transport: Passenger Travel and the Development of the Metropolis*, Vol. I, *The Nineteenth Century*, 1963

Barnard, John, and McKenzie, D. F. (eds.), *The Cambridge History of the Book in Britain*, Vol. IV, *1557–1695*, Cambridge, 2002

Barnardo, Mrs [Syrie Louise], and Marchant, James, *Memoirs of the Late Dr Barnardo*, 1907

Barnes, Eleanor C., *Alfred Yarrow: His Life and Work*, 1923

Barnett, Henretta, *Canon Barnett, His Life, Work and Friends*, 2 vols., 1918 (single vol. edn, 1921)

Barrington, George, *Barrington's New London Spy for 1805 . . .*, 1805

Barson, Susie, and Saint, Andrew, *A Farewell to Fleet Street*, 1988

Bax, Ernest Belfort, *Reminiscences and Reflexions of a Mid and Late Victorian*, 1918

Bayly, Mary, *Ragged Homes and How to Mend Them*, 1860

Beale, Willert, *The Light of Other Days: Seen Through the Wrong End of an Opera Glass*, 2 vols., 1890

Beames, Thomas, *The Rookeries of London: Past, Present, and Prospective*, 2nd edn, 1852

Begbie, Harold, *Life of William Booth: The Founder of The Salvation Army*, 2 vols., 1920

Belchem, John, *'Orator' Hunt: Henry Hunt and English Working-Class Radicalism*, Oxford, 1985

Bell, E Moberley, *Octavia Hill: A Biography*, 1942

Bellman, Sir Harold, *Cornish Cockney: Reminiscences and Reflections*, 1947

Benn, Ernest, *Happier Days: Recollections and Reflections*, 1949

Bennett, Alfred Rosling, *London and Londoners in the Eighteen-Fifties and Sixties*, 1924

Bennett, Arnold, *The Journals of Arnold Bennett*, edited by Newman Flower, 3 vols., 1932–3

Benson, Mary Eleanor, *Streets and Lanes of the City*, 1892

Bentley, G. E., Jr, *The Stranger from Paradise: A Biography of William Blake*, New Haven, 2001

Berridge, Virginia, *Opium and the People: Opiate Use and Drug Control Policy in Nineteenth and Early Twentieth Century England*, revised edn, 1999

Besant, Annie, *An Autobiography*, 1893 (1908 edn)

Besant, Sir Walter, *Children of Gibeon*, 1886

—*The Pen and the Book*, 1899

—*Autobiography*, 1902

—*London in the Nineteenth Century*, 1909

Bettany, F. G., *Stewart Headlam: A Biography*, 1926

Bird, J., *The Geography of the Port of London*, 1957

Blackmore, Lieut. John, *London by Moonlight: Missionary Enterprise, or the First Report of the Female Temporary Home*, n.d., c.1853

—*The London by Moonlight Mission: being an account of midnight cruises on the streets of London during the last thirteen years*, 1860

Blake, Robert, *Disraeli*, 1966

Blatchford, Robert, *My Eighty Years*, 1931

Bligh, Eric, *Tooting Corner*, 1946

Blumenfeld, R. D., *R.D.B.'s Diary 1887–1914*, 1930

Blyth, Henry, *Skittles: The Last Victorian Courtesan*, 1970

Booth, Bramwell, *Echoes and Memories*, 1925

Booth, Charles, *Life and Labour of the People in London*, 17 vols., 1892–1902

—(Booth MSS) Booth Manuscripts at the British Library of Political and Economic Science, London School of Economics

—*The Streets of London: The Booth Notebooks – South East*, edited by Jess Steele, 1997

Booth, J. B., *Old Pink 'Un Days*, 1924

Borrow, George *Lavengro: The Scholar, the Gypsy, the Priest*, 1851

—*Romano Lavo-Lil. Word-Book of the Romany or, English Gypsy Language*, 1874 (1923 edn)

Bosanquet, Charles B. P., *London: Some Account of Its Growth, Charitable Agencies, and Wants*, 1869

Bosanquet, Helen, *Social Work in London, 1869–1912*, 1914

Bowmaker, Edward, *The Housing of the Working Classes*, 1895

Bradley, Ian, *The Call to Seriousness: The Evangelical Impact on the Victorians*, 1976

Bradley, Simon, and Pevsner, Nikolaus, *London I: The City of London*, 1997

Brayley, Edward Wedlake and others, *London and Middlesex; or an Historical, Commercial, and Descriptive Survey of the Metropolis of Great Britain . . .*, 5 vols., 1810–16

Briggs, Asa, *Victorian Things*, 1988 (Folio Society edn, 1996)

Briggs, Asa, and Macartney, Anne, *Toynbee Hall: The First Hundred Years*, 1984

Brimblecombe, Peter, *The Big Smoke: A History of Air Pollution in London since Medieval Times*, 1987

Bristow, Edward J., *Vice and Vigilance: Purity Movements in Britain since 1700*, Dublin, 1977

Britton, John (ed.), *The Original Picture of London*, 25th edn, 1826

—*The Auto-Biography of John Britton*, 2 vols., 1849–50

Broadhurst, Henry, *Henry Broadhurst, MP: The Story of His Life from a Stonemason's Bench to the Treasury Bench. Told by Himself*, 1901

Broodbank, Joseph G., *History of the Port of London*, 2 vols., 1921

Brooks, Shirley, *Sooner or Later*, 2 vols., 1868

—MS Diary, 1869 (London Library)

Brown, John, *Sixty Years' Gleanings from Life's Harvest: A Genuine Autobiography*, 1858

Browne, Douglas G., *The Rise of Scotland Yard: A History of the Metropolitan Police*, 1956

Brown, W. H., *A Century of London Co-operation*, 1928

Browne, Edgar, *Phiz and Dickens*, 1913

Bullen, Frank T., *Confessions of a Tradesman*, 1908

Burn, James, *James Burn; the 'Beggar Boy': An Autobiography*, 6th edn, 1882

Burnand, Sir Francis C., *Records and Reminiscences: Personal and General*, 2 vols., 1904

Burnett, John (ed.), *Useful Toil: Autobiographies of Working People from the 1820s to the 1920s*, 1974 (1975 edn)

—*Destiny Obscure: Autobiographies of Childhood, Education and Family from the 1820s to the 1920s*, 1982

Butler, E. M. (ed.), *A Regency Visitor: The English Tour of Prince Pückler-Muskau Described in His Letters 1826–1828*, 1957

Butler, J. R. M., *The Passing of the Great Reform Bill*, 1914 (2nd edn, 1964)

Callow, Edward, *Old London Taverns: Historical, Descriptive and Reminiscent. With Some Account of the Coffee Houses, Clubs, Etc.*, 1899

Cantlie, James, *Degeneration Amongst Londoners*, 1885

Capper, Charles, *The Port and Trade of London: Historical, Statistical, Local and General*, 1862

Cardwell, Rev. J. H. (ed.), *Twenty Years in Soho: A Review of the Work of the Church in the Parish of St Anne's, Soho from 1891 to 1911*, 1911

Carey, William, *The Stranger's Guide through London; Or, a View of the British Metropolis*, 1808

[Carter, T.] *A Continuation of the Memoirs of a Working Man; illustrated by some Original Sketches of Character*, 1850

Censuses:

Census of Great Britain, 1851: Population Tables, Vols. I and II, *Numbers of Inhabitants in the Years 1801, 1811, 1821, 1831, 1841, and 1851*, 1852

Census of Great Britain, 1851: Population Tables, II, *Ages, Civil Condition, Occupations, and Birth-Place of the People*, 1854

Census of Great Britain, 1851: Population (Great Britain): Religious Worship (England and Wales), 1853

Census of England and Wales, 1871: Population Tables, Vol. I, 1872

Census of England and Wales, 1871: Population Abstracts. Ages, Civil Condition, Occupations, and Birth-Places of the People, Vol. III, 1873

Census of England and Wales, 1881: Ages, Condition as to Marriage, Occupations, and Birth-Places of the People, Vol. III, 1883

Census of England and Wales, 1891: Area, Houses, and Population, Vol.

II, *Registration Areas and Sanitary Districts*, 1893–4

Census of England and Wales 1901: County of London, 1903

Census of England and Wales 1901: County of Middlesex. Area, Houses and Population, 1902

Census of England and Wales 1901: General report with Appendices, 1904

Chadwick, Owen, *The Victorian Church*, Part I, 1966; Part II, 1970

Chambers, Robert (ed.), *The Book of Days: A Miscellany of Popular Antiquities in Connection with the Calendar . . .*, 1862–4 (2 vols., 1886 edn)

Chancellor, E. Beresford, *The Annals of Fleet Street: Its Traditions and Associations*, 1912

—*The Pleasure Haunts of London during Four Centuries*, 1925

—*London's Old Latin Quarter: Being an Account of Tottenham Court Road and Its Immediate Surroundings*, 1930

—*The Romance of Soho*, 1931

Chaplin, Charles, *My Autobiography*, 1964 (Penguin edn, 1966)

Chapman, Cecil, *The Poor Man's Court of Justice: 25 years as a Metropolitan Police Magistrate*, 1925

Chase, Ellen, *Tenant Friends in Old Deptford*, 1929

Chesney, Kellow, *The Victorian Underworld*, 1970

Chesterton, G. K., *Autobiography*, 1936

Chesterton, George Laval, *Revelations of Prison Life; with an Enquiry into Prison Discipline and Secondary Punishments*, 2 vols., 1856

City:

Report on the City Day-Census, 1881, by the Local Government and Taxation Committee of the Corporation of London, 1881

Ten Years' Growth of the City of London, 1891

Clarke, Linda, *Building Capitalism: Historical Change and the Labour Process in the Production of the Built Environment*, 1992

Clarke, W. S. (ed.), *The Suburban Homes of London: A Residential Guide to Favourite London Localities, their Society, Celebrities, and Associations with notes on their Rental, Rates, and House Accommodation*, 1881

Clarkson, Charles Tempest, and Richardson, J. Hall, *Police!*, 1889

The Clergy of St Anne's, Soho, *Two Centuries of Soho: Its Institutions, Firms, and Amusements*, 1898

Clifton, Gloria C., *Professionalism, Patronage and Public Service in Victorian London: The Staff of the Metropolitan Board of Works 1856–1889*, 1992

Clunn, Harold, *The Face of London: The Record of a Century's Changes and Developments*, 1932 (1934 edn)

Cobbett, William, *Rural Rides*, 1830–53 (2 vols., 1908)

Cohen, Phil, 'Policing the Working-class City', in National Deviancy

Conference and Conference of Socialist Economists, *Capitalism and the Rule of Law: From Deviancy Theory to Marxism*, 1979

Cole, Sir Henry, *Fifty Years of Public Work of Sir Henry Cole, KCB, Accounted for in His Deeds, Speeches and Writings*, 2 vols., 1884

Collins, Philip, *Dickens and Crime*, 2nd edn, 1964

Collins, Wilkie, *Basil: A Story of Modern Life*, 1852 (World's Classics edn, 2000)

Colqhoun, Patrick, *A Treatise on the Commerce and Police of the River Thames . . .*, 1800

Commissioner of Police of the Metropolis, *Report of the Commissioner of Police of the Metropolis*, various years

Connell, John, *W. E. Henley*, 1949

Cook, Emily Constance, *London in the Time of the Diamond Jubilee*, 1897

Cook, G. C., *From the Greenwich Hulks to Old St Pancras: A History of Tropical Disease in London*, 1992

Cook, Matt, *London and the Culture of Homosexuality, 1885–1914*, Cambridge, 2003

Cooke, Harriette J., *Mildmay; or, The Story of the First Deaconess Institution*, 1893

Cooper, Thomas, *The Life of Thomas Cooper: Written by Himself*, 1872

Coote, William Alexander, and Baker, Miss A. (eds.), *A Romance of Philanthropy: Being a Record of Some of the Principal Incidents Connected with the Exceptionally Successful Thirty Years' Work of the National Vigilance Association*, 1916

Coppock, J. T., and Prince, Hugh C. (eds.), *Greater London*, 1964

Cornish, Ex-Supt G. W., *Cornish of the 'Yard': His Reminiscences and Cases*, 1935

Coull, Thomas, *The History and Traditions of Islington*, 1864

Course, Edwin, *London Railways*, 1962

Crawford, T.C., *English Life: Seen Through Yankee Eyes*, New York, 1889

Creighton, Charles, *A History of Epidemics in Britain*, 2 vols., Cambridge, 1891–94

Critchley, T. A., and James, P. D., *The Maul and the Pear Tree: The Ratcliffe Highway Murders 1811*, 1971

Crook, J. Mordaunt, and Port, M. H., *The History of the King's Works*, Vol. VI, 1782–1851, 1973

Cross, Nigel, *The Common Writer: Life in Nineteenth-Century Grub Street*, Cambridge, 1985

Crouch, Arthur Philip, *Silvertown and Neighbourhood (including East and West Ham): A Retrospect*, 1900

Cunningham, Allan, *The Life of Sir David Wilkie; with His Journals,*

Tours, and Critical Remarks on Works of Art; and a Selection from His Correspondence, 3 vols., 1843

Curtis, L. Perry, Jr, *Jack the Ripper and the London Press*, New Haven, 2001

Darley, Gillian, *Octavia Hill*, 1990

Darlington's London and Environs, 4th edn, 1902

Davies, Charles Maurice, *Unorthodox London: or, Phases of Religious Life in the Metropolis*, 2 vols., 1873–5

—*Heterodox London: or, Phases of Free Thought in the Metropolis*, 2 vols., 1874

—*Orthodox London: or, Phases of Religious Life in the Church of England*, 2 vols., 1874–5

—*Mystic London: or, Phases of Occult Life in the Metropolis*, 1875

Davies, Margaret Llewellyn (ed.), *Life as We Have Known It: By Co-operative Working Women*, 1931 (Virago edn, 1977)

Davin, Anna, *Growing Up Poor: Home, School and Street in London, 1870–1914*, 1996

Davis, Graham, *The Irish in Britain 1815–1914*, Dublin 1991

Davis, Henry George, *The Memorials of the Hamlet of Knightsbridge: With Notices of Its Immediate Neighbourhood*, 1859

Davis, John, *Reforming London: The London Government Problem, 1855–1900*, Oxford, 1988

Deaths from Starvation (Metropolis): Return of the Number of all Deaths in the Metropolitan District . . ., various years

Denison, Edward, *Letters and Other Writings of the Late Edward Denison, M.P. for Newark*, edited by Sir Baldwyn Leighton, 2nd edn, 1872

Denvir, John, *The Irish in Britain from the Earliest Times to the Fall and Death of Parnell*, 1892

De Quincey, Thomas, *The English Mail-Coach and Other Essays*, Everyman edn, 1912

—*Autobiography*, Cresset Press edn, 1950

Dew, Walter, *I Caught Crippen: Memoirs of Ex-Chief Inspector Walter Dew of Scotland Yard*, 1938

Dickens, Charles, *The Pickwick Papers*, 1836–7

—*Oliver Twist*, 1837–9

—*The Old Curiosity Shop*, 1840–41

—*Dombey and Son*, 1846–8

—*David Copperfield*, 1849–50

—*Bleak House*, 1852–3

—*Great Expectations*, 1860–61

—*Our Mutual Friend*, 1864–5

—*The Mystery of Edwin Drood*, 1870

—*The Letters of Charles Dickens*, 12 vols., Oxford, 1965–2002

Charles Dickens' Uncollected Writings from Household Words 1850–1859, edited by Harry Stone, 2 vols., Bloomington, 1968

—*The Dent Uniform Edition of Dickens' Journalism*, 4 vols., 1994–2000

Dictionary of National Biography

Dilnot, George (ed.), *The Trial of the Detectives*, 1928

Divall, Tom, *Scoundrels and Scallywags (and Some Honest Men)*, 1929

Dix, Frank L., *Royal River Highway: A History of the Passenger Boats and Services on the River Thames*, Newton Abbot, 1985

Dixon, Hepworth, *The London Prisons: with an Account of the More Distinguished Persons who have been Confined in them. To which is added, A Description of the Chief Provincial Prisons*, 1850

Dobie, Rowland, *The History of the United Parishes of St. Giles in the Fields and St. George Bloomsbury*, 1829

Dodd, George, *Days at the Factories; or, The Manufacturing Industry of Great Britain Described: Series I – London*, 1843

Douglas, Norman, *London Street Games*, 1931

Downey, Edmund, *Twenty Years Ago: A Book of Anecdote Illustrating Literary Life in London*, 1905

Doyle, Arthur Conan, *The Adventures of Sherlock Holmes*, 1892

Dunn, James, *Modern London – Its Sins and Woes and the Sovereign Remedy*, 1906

—*From Coal Mine Upwards, or, Seventy Years of an Eventful Life*, 1910

Dyos, H. J., 'Railways and Housing in Victorian London', *Journal of Transport History*, Vol. II, Nos. 1 and 2, May and November 1955, pp. 11–21 and 90–100

—*Victorian Suburb: A Study of the Growth of Camberwell*, Leicester, 1961 (1973 edn)

Dyos, H. J. (ed.), *The Study of Urban History*, 1968

Dyos, H. J. and Wolff, Michael (eds.), *The Victorian City: Images and Realities*, 2 vols., 1973

Edwards, Percy J., *History of London Street Improvements, 1855–1897*, 1898

Egan, Pierce, *Life in London; or, the Day and Night Scenes of Jerry Hawthorn, Esq. and his elegant friend Corinthian Tom . . .*, 1821

—*The Life of an Actor*, 1825

Eliot, George, *Daniel Deronda*, 1876

[Ellenor, Thomas Bell] An Old Inhabitant *Rambling Recollections of Chelsea and the Surrounding District as a Village in the Early Part of the Past Century*, 1901

Emsley, Clive, *The English Police: A Political and Social History*, 1991 (2nd edn, 1996)

Escott, T. H. S., *Social Transformations of the Victorian Age: A Survey of Court and Country*, 1897

Espinasse, Francis, *Literary Recollections and Sketches*, 1893

Evans, David Morier, *City Men and City Manners: The City; or, The Physiology of London Business; with Sketches on 'Change, and at the Coffee Houses*, 1852

—*Facts, Failures, and Frauds: Revelations, Financial, Mercantile, Criminal*, 1859

Everard, Stirling *The History of the Gas Light and Coke Company 1812–1949*, 1949

Eyre, Alan Montgomery, *Saint John's Wood: Its History, Its Houses, Its Haunts and Its Celebrities*, 1913

Farjeon, B. L., *Great Porter Square: A Mystery*, 1884

Farjeon, Eleanor, *A Nursery in the Nineties*, 1935 (2nd edn, 1960)

Farmer, John S., and Henley, W. E., *Slang and Its Analogues, Past and Present*, 7 vols., 1890–1904

Faulkner, Thomas, *The History and Antiquities of the Parish of Hammersmith . . .*, 1839

Feldman, David, *Englishmen and Jews: Social Relations and Political Culture 1840–1914*, 1994

Feldman, David, and Stedman Jones, Gareth (eds.), *Metropolis London: Histories and Representations since 1800*, 1989

Ferrier, J. Kenneth, *Crooks and Crime*, 2nd edn, 1928

Finn, Margot C., *The Character of Credit: Personal Debt in English Culture, 1740–1914*, Cambridge, 2003

Firth, Joseph F. B., *Municipal London; or, London Government As It Is, and London under a Municipal Council*, 1876

—*Reform of London Government and of City Guilds*, 1888

Fishman, William J., *East End Jewish Radicals 1975–1914*, 1975

—*East End 1888: A Year in a London Borough among the Labouring Poor*, 1988

Fitzgerald, Percy, *Chronicles of Bow Street Police Office with an Account of the Magistrates, 'Runners', and Police; and a selection of the most interesting cases*, 2 vols., 1888

—*Picturesque London*, 1890

—*London City Suburbs: As They Are To-Day*, 1893

Fitzsimons, Raymund, *The Baron of Piccadilly: The Travels and Entertainments of Albert Smith 1816–1860*, 1967

Flexner, Abraham, *Prostitution in Europe*, 1914

Flinn, M. W., (ed.), *Report on the Sanitary Condition of the Labouring Population of Great Britain, by Edwin Chadwick*, 1965

Forster, John, *The Life of Charles Dickens*, 3 vols., 1872–4

Francillon, R. E., *Mid-Victorian Memories*, 1913

Fraser, Sir William, *Hic et Ubique*, 1893

Free, Richard, *Seven Years' Hard*, 1904

Freedman, Maurice (ed.), *A Minority in Britain: Social Studies of the Anglo-Jewish Community*, 1955

Friedland, Martin L., *The Trials of Israel Lipski*, 1984

Friswell, Laura Hain, *In the Sixties and Seventies: Impressions of Literary People and Others*, 1905

Frith, W. P., *My Autobiography and Reminiscences*, 2 vols., 1887

Frost, Thomas, *The Old Showmen, and the Old London Fairs*, 1874

—*Forty Years' Recollections: Literary and Political*, 1880

—*Reminiscences of a Country Journalist*, 1886

Fry, Katharine, and Cresswell, Rachel Elizabeth, *Memoir of the Life of Elizabeth Fry, with Extracts from Her Journal and Letters. Edited by Two of Her Daughters*, 2 vols., 1848

Fulford, Roger, *Glyn's 1753–1953: Six Generations in Lombard Street*, 1953

Furniss, Harry, *The Confessions of a Caricaturist*, 2 vols., 1901

Gainer, Bernard, *The Alien Invasion: The Origins of the Aliens Act of 1905*, 1972

Gammage, R. G., *History of the Chartist Movement 1837–1854*, 1894

Gardiner, A. G., *John Benn and the Progressive Movement*, 1925

Gardner, Fitzroy, *Days and Ways of an Old Bohemian*, 1921

Gartner, Lloyd P., *The Jewish Immigrant in England, 1870–1914*, 2nd edn, 1973

Garwood, John, *The Million-Peopled City; or, One-Half of the People of London made known to the Other Half*, 1853

Gash, Norman, *Mr. Secretary Peel: The Life of Sir Robert Peel to 1830*, 1961

Gatrell, V. A. C., *The Hanging Tree: Execution and the English People 1770–1868*, Oxford, 1994 (pb edn, 1996)

Gatrell, V. A. C., Lenman, Bruce and Parker, Geoffrey (eds.), *Crime and the Law: The Social History of Crime in Western Europe since 1500*, 1980

Gavin, Hector, *Sanitary Ramblings: Being Sketches and Illustrations of Bethnal Green*, 1848

—*The Habitations of the Industrial Classes*, 1851

George, M. Dorothy, *London Life in the XVIIIth Century*, 1925

Gibb, D. E. W., *Lloyd's of London: A Study in Individualism*, 1957

Gilbert, William, *De Profundis: A Tale of the Social Deposits*, 2 vols., 1864
—*Contrasts: Dedicated to the Ratepayers of London*, 1873
—*The City: An Enquiry into the Corporation, its Livery Companies, and the Administration of their Charities and Endowments*, 1877
Gillies, R. P., *Memories of a Literary Veteran; including Sketches and Anecdotes of the most Distinguished Literary Characters from 1794 to 1849*, 3 vols., 1851
Girouard, Mark, *Victorian Pubs*, 2nd edn, 1984
Gissing, Algernon and Ellen, *Letters of George Gissing to Members of His Family*, 1927
Gissing, George, *The Nether World*, 1889
—*New Grub Street: A Novel*, 1891
—*In the Year of Jubilee*, 1894
—*The Whirlpool*, 1897
—*London and the Life of Literature in Late Victorian England: The Diary of George Gissing, Novelist*, edited by Pierre Coustillas, Cranbury, NJ 1978
[Gladstone, William Ewart] *The Gladstone Diaries*, Vol. IV, *1848–1854*, edited by M. R. D. Foot and H. C. G. Matthew, Oxford, 1974
Goddard, Henry, *Memoirs of a Bow Street Runner*, 1956
Godley, Andrew, 'Immigrant Entrepreneurs and the Emergence of London's East End as an Industrial District', *The London Journal*, Vol. 21, No. 1, 1996, pp. 38–45
Godwin, George, *Town Swamps and Social Bridges*, 1859
Goodway, David, *London Chartism 1838–1848*, 1982
Gosling, Harry, *Up and Down Stream*, 1927
Gotch, Rosamund Brunel (ed.), *Mendelssohn and His Friends in Kensington: Letters from Fanny and Sophy Horsley Written 1833–36*, 1934
Grant, Graham, *The Diary of a Police Surgeon*, 1920
Graves, Charles L., *Mr Punch's History of Modern England*, 4 vols., 1921
Great Industries of Great Britain, 3 vols., 1878
Green, David R., *From Artisans to Paupers: Economic Change and Poverty in London, 1790–1870*, Aldershot, 1995
Greenham, G. H., *Scotland Yard Experiences: From the Diary of G. H. Greenham*, 1904
Greenwood, James, *The Seven Curses of London*, 1869
—*The Wilds of London*, 1874
—*Low-Life Deeps: An Account of the Strange Fish to be Found There*, 1876
—*In Strange Company*, 2nd edn, 1883
Greenwood, Thomas, *Public Libraries: A History of the Movement and a Manual for the Organization and Management of Rate-Supported Libraries*, 4th edn, 1891

Gregory, Robert, *Sermons on the Poorer Classes of London, preached before the University of Oxford*, 1869

Gregory, T. E., *The Westminster Bank Through a Century*, 2 vols., 1936

Grenfell, Sir Wilfred Thomason, *The Story of a Labrador Doctor*, 1920 (abridged edn, *c.* 1928)

Greville, Charles C. F., *A Journal of the Reigns of King George IV and King William IV*, 3 vols., 3rd edn, 1875

Grey, Edward C. W., *St. Giles's of the Lepers*, 1905

Griffiths, Arthur, *Memorials of Millbank and Chapters in Prison History*, 1875 (1884 edn)

—*The Chronicles of Newgate*, 1883 (new edn, 1884)

—*Mysteries of Police and Crime*, 3 vols., 1901–2

Gronow, Captain [Rees Howell], *Reminiscences and Recollections*, 2 vols., 1862–66 (1889 edn)

Grosch, Alfred, *St Pancras Pavements: An Autobiography*, 1947

Grossmith, George, *A Society Clown*, Bristol, 1888

Grossmith, George and Weedon, *The Diary of a Nobody*, 1892

Gwynn, John, *London and Westminster Improved, Illustrated by Plans . . .*, 1766

Hackwood, Frederick W. M., *William Hone: His Life and Times*, 1912

Hadden, Rev. R. H., *An East-End Chronicle: St George's-in-the-East Parish and Parish Church*, 1880

Haddon, Archibald, *The Story of the Music Hall: From Cave of Harmony to Cabaret*, 1935

Halévy, Elie, *England in 1815: A History of the English People in the Nineteenth Century – 1*, 2nd revised edn, 1949

Hall, Peter G., *The Industries of London Since 1861*, 1962

Halliday, Stephen, *The Great Stink of London: Sir Joseph Bazalgette and the Cleansing of the Victorian Capital*, 1999

Halsted, D. G., *Doctor in the Nineties*, 1959

Hammeron, J. A., *Books and Myself: Memoirs of an Editor*, 1944

Handover, P. M., *Printing in London: From 1476 to Modern Times*, 1960

Hansard, *Parliamentary Debates*, various years

Hardy, Thomas, *Jude the Obscure*, 1895

Harriott, John, *Struggles Through Life, exemplified in the Various Travels and Adventures in Europe, Asia, Africa, and America, of John Harriott, Esq.*, 3 vols., 3rd edn, 1815

Harris, Frank, *My Life and Loves*, 1964

Harrison, J. F. C., *A History of the Working Men's College 1854–1954*, 1954

Hart, W. C., *Confessions of an Anarchist*, 1906

Hatton, Joseph, *Journalistic London: Being a Series of Sketches of Famous Pens and Papers of the Day*, 1882

Haw, George, *From Workhouse to Westminster: The Life Story of Will Crooks M. P.*, 1907

Hawthorne, Nathaniel, *Our Old Home*, 2 vols., 1863

[Haydon, Benjamin Robert] *Life of Benjamin Robert Haydon, Historical Painter, from his Autobiography and Journals*, edited by Tom Taylor, 1853 (2 vols., 1926 edn)

Hazlitt, William, *The Plain Speaker: Opinions on Books, Men, and Things*, 2 vols., 1826

Heard, P. A., *An Octogenarian's Memories*, Ilfracombe, 1974

Heasman, Kathleen, *Evangelicals in Action: An Appraisal of Their Social Work in the Victorian Era*, 1962

Heaven, E. F., *Lennox Road Mission Hall 1874–1934: Diamond Jubilee Celebration Souvenir*, 1934

Hibbert, H. G., *Fifty Years of a Londoner's Life*, 1916

Hichens, Robert, *The Londoners: An Absurdity*, 1898

Highmore, A., *Pietas Londinensis: The History, Design, and Present State of the Various Public Charities in and near London*, 1810

Hill, Octavia, *Homes of the London Poor*, 1875 (2nd edn, 1883)

Hillocks, James Inches, *My Life and Labours in London, A Step Nearer The Mark*, 1865

Hindley, Charles, *The Life and Times of James Catnach (Late of Seven Dials), Ballad Monger*, 1878

—*A History of the Cries of London, Ancient and Modern*, 1881

—*The True History of Tom and Jerry*, 1888

Hobhouse, Hermione, *Thomas Cubitt: Master Builder*, 1971 (2nd edn, 1995)

—*A History of Regent Street*, 1975

—*The Crystal Palace and the Great Exhibition: Art, Science and Productive Industry. A History of the Royal Commission for the Exhibition of 1851*, 2002

Hodder, Edwin, *The Life of Samuel Morley*, 2nd edn, 1887

—*The Life and Work of the Seventh Earl of Shaftesbury, K. G.*, 3 vols., 1887

Hodgkinson, Ruth, *The Origins of the National Health Service: The Medical Services of the New Poor Law, 1834–1871*, 1967

Hoffman, P. C., *They Also Serve: The Story of the Shopworker*, 1949

Hogg, John, *London As It Is; being a Series of Observations on the Health, Habits, and Amusements of The People*, 1837

Hollingshead, John, *Ragged London in 1861*, 1861

—*My Lifetime*, 2 vols., 1895

Hollis, Patricia, *The Pauper Press: A Study in Working-class Radicalism of the 1830s*, Oxford, 1970

Holmes, Mrs Basil, *The London Burial Grounds: Notes on their History from the Earliest Times to the Present Day*, 1896

Holmes, F. Morell, *Exeter Hall and Its Associations*, 1881

Home, Gordon, *Old London Bridge*, 1931

Hone, William, *The Every-Day Book . . .*, 2 vols., 1825–7 (1878 edn)

—*The Table Book*, 1827 (1878 edn)

Hook, Theodore Edward, *Gilbert Gurney*, 3 vols., 1836

Horsley, Rev. John William, *Jottings from Jail: Notes and Papers on Prison Matters*, 1887

—*'I Remember.' Memories of a 'Sky Pilot' in the Prison and the Slum*, 1911

House, Humphry, *The Dickens World*, 1941

Howard, Esme [Lord Howard of Penrith], *Theatre of Life: Life Seen from the Pit 1863–1905*, 1935

Howarth, Edward G., and Wilson, Mona, *West Ham: A Study in Social and Industrial Problems*, 1907

Howe, Ellic, and Waite, Harold E., *The London Society of Compositors: A Centenary History*, 1948

Howell, George, *Labour Legislation, Labour Movements and Labour Leaders*, 1902

Howell, Michael, and Ford, Peter, *The True History of the Elephant Man*, 1980 (Penguin edn, 1980)

Hoyle, Susan Ryley, 'The First Battle for London: The Royal Commission on Metropolitan Termini, 1846', *The London Journal*, Vol. 8, No. 2, 1982, pp.140–55

Hudson, Derek (ed.), *Munby: Man of Two Worlds. The Life and Diaries of Arthur J. Munby 1828–1910*, 1972

Hughes, M. Vivian, *A London Family 1870–1900*, 1946

Hughson, David, *London; Being an Accurate History and Description of the British Metropolis and its Neighbourhood to Thirty Miles Extent, From an Actual Perambulation*, 6 vols., 1805–9

Humpherys, Anne, *Travels into the Poor Man's Country: The Work of Henry Mayhew*, Firle, Sussex, 1977

Humphreys, Mrs Desmond ('Rita'), *Recollections of a Literary Life*, 1936

Hunt, Henry, *Memoirs of Henry Hunt, Esq., Written by Himself. In His Majesty's Jail at Ilchester, in the County of Somerset*, 3 vols., 1820–22

Hunt, John, *Pioneer Work in the Great City: The Autobiography of a London City Missionary*, 1895

Hunt, Leigh, *Autobiography: With Reminiscences of Friends and Contemporaries*, 3 vols., 1850

Hyamson, Albert M., *The London Board for Shechita 1804–1954*, 1954

Hyde, H. Montgomery (ed.), *The Trials of Oscar Wilde*, 1948

—*The Cleveland Street Scandal*, New York, 1976

Hyde, Robert R., *Industry Was My Parish*, 1968

Hyndman, Henry Mayers, *The Record of an Adventurous Life*, 1911

Illustrated London and Its Representatives of Commerce, 1893

Islington Board of Guardians, Records, London Metropolitan Archive

Irving, H. B., (ed.), *Trial of Franz Müller*, 1911

Jackson, Alan A., *London's Termini*, Newton Abbott, 1969

Jackson, T. A., *Solo Trumpet: Some Memories of Socialist Agitation and Propaganda*, 1953

James, Henry, *English Hours*, 1905 (Readers' Union edn, 1962)

Jay, Rev. A. O., *Life in Darkest London*, 1891

Jenkins, Herbert, *The Life of George Borrow: Compiled from Unpublished Official Documents, His Works, Correspondence, Etc.*, 1912

Jephson, Henry, *The Platform: Its Rise and Progress*, 2 vols., 1892

—*The Sanitary Evolution of London*, 1907

Jerdan, William, *The Autobiography of William Jerdan*, 4 vols., 1852–3

Jerome, Jerome K., *Paul Kelver: A Novel*, 1902

—*My Life and Times*, 1926 (Folio Society edn, 1992)

Jerrold, Blanchard, *Cent Per Cent: A Story Written upon a Bill Stamp*, 1869

Johnson, David, *Regency Revolution: The Case of Arthur Thistlewood*, 1974

Johnson, Paul, 'Economic Development and Industrial Dynamism in Victorian London', *The London Journal*, Vol. 21, No. 1, 1996, pp. 27–37

Jones, Rev. Harry, *East and West London: Being notes of a common life and pastoral work in St. James's, Westminster and in St. George's-in-the-East*, 1875

Journalist, A, *Bohemian Days in Fleet Street*, 1913

Karl, Frederick, *George Eliot: A Biography*, 1995

Keefe, H. J., *A Century in Print: The story of Hazell's 1839–1939*, 1939

Kellett, John R., *The Impact of Railways on Victorian Cities*, 1969

Kensington MOH:

The Annual Report on the Health, Sanitary Condition, &c., &c., of the Parish of St. Mary Abbotts, Kensington, various years

Kent, William, *John Burns: Labour's Lost Leader*, 1950

King, W. T. C., *History of the London Discount Market*, 1936

Kirwan, Daniel Joseph, *Palace and Hovel: or, Phases of London Life*, Hartford, Conn., 1870

Klingender, F. D., *The Condition of Clerical Labour in Britain*, 1935

Knapp, John M. (ed.), *The Universities and the Social Problem: An Account of the University Settlements in East London*, 1895

Knight, Charles, *Passages of a Working Life During Half a Century: with a Prelude of Early Reminiscences*, 3 vols., 1864–5

Knight, Charles (ed.), *London*, 6 vols., 1841–4

Korg, Jacob, *George Gissing: A Critical Biography*, 1965

Koven, Seth, *Slumming: Sexual and Social Politics in Victorian London*, Princeton, 2004

Krout, Mary H., *A Looker on in London*, 1899

Kynaston, David, *The City of London*, Vol. I, *A World of Its Own 1815–1890*, 1994

—*The City of London*, Vol. II, *Golden Years 1890–1914*, 1995

Lambert, B., *The History and Survey of London and Its Environs: From the Earliest Period to the Present Time*, 4 vols., 1806

Lambert, Royston, *Sir John Simon 1816–1904 and English Social Administration*, 1963

Lansbury, George, *My Life*, 1928

Lansdowne, Andrew, *A Life's Reminiscences of Scotland Yard*, 1890

Larwood, Jacob, *The Story of the London Parks*, one-volume edn, 1877

Law, John [Margaret Harkness], *Captain Lobe: A Story of the Salvation Army*, 1889

Layard, George Somes, *A Great 'Punch' Editor: Being the Life, Letters, and Diaries of Shirley Brooks*, 1907

Lees, Lynn Hollen *Exiles of Erin: Irish Migrants in Victorian London*, Manchester, 1979

Leeson, B., *Lost London: The Memoirs of an East End Detective*, 1930

Lemon, Mark, *Golden Fetters*, 3 vols., 1867

Lennox, Lord William Pitt, *Drafts on My Memory: Being Men I Have Known, Things I Have Seen, Places I Have Visited*, 2 vols., 1866

Liechstenstein, Princess Marie, *Holland House*, 2 vols., 2nd edn, 1874

Lieck, Albert ['Authorship Unacknowledged'], *Narrow Waters: The First Volume of the Life and Thoughts of a Common Man*, 1935

Lillywhite, Bryant, *London Coffee Houses: A Reference Book of the Seventeenth, Eighteenth and Nineteenth Centuries*, 1963

Linton, Mrs Lynn., *The Autobiography of Christopher Kirkland*, 3 vols., 1885

—*My Literary Life*, 1899

Linton, W. J., *James Watson: A Memoir of the Days of the Fight for a Free Press in England and of the Agitation for the People's Charter*, 1880

Lipman, V. D., *Social History of the Jews in England*, 1954

—*A Century of Social Service 1869–1959: The Jewish Board of Guardians*, 1959

Littlechild, John George, *The Reminiscences of Chief-Inspector Littlechild*, 1894

Lochnan, Katharine, *Turner, Whistler, Monet*, 2005

Loftie, W. J., *London City: Its History – Streets – Traffic – Buildings – People*, 1891

London Commitee for Suppressing the Traffic in British Girls for Purposes of Continental Prostitution, *Six Years' Labour and Sorrow; being the Fourth Report. . . .*, 1885

London County Council, *London Statistics*, various years

—*The Housing Question in London, 1855–1900*, 1900

London Trades Council, [A Delegate] *Short History of the London Trades Council*, 1935

—*London Trades Council 1860–1950*, 1950

Lovett, William, *Life and Struggles of William Lovett in His Pursuit of Bread, Knowledge, and Freedom*, 1876 (2 vols., 1920)

Low's Handbook to the Charities of London. . . .1896–97

McCalman, Iain, *Radical Underworld: Prophets, Revolutionaries and Pornographers in London, 1795–1840*, Oxford, 1988 (pb edn, 2002)

McCarthy, Justin [vignettes by Pennell, Joseph], *Charing Cross to St Paul's*, 1891

—*Reminiscences*, 2 vols., 1899

McCarthy, Terry (ed.), *The Great Dock Strike 1889*, 1988

Maccoby, S., *English Radicalism 1853–1886*, 1938

—*English Radicalism 1786–1832: From Paine to Cobbett*, 1955

Mace, Rodney, *Trafalgar Square: Emblem of Empire*, 1976

Machen, Arthur, *Far Off Things*, 1922 (1974 edn)

Mackay, Charles, *Memoirs of Extraordinary Popular Delusions and the Madness of Crowds*, 2nd edn, 1852

—*Forty Years' Recollections of Life, Literature, and Public Affairs from 1830 to 1870*, 2 vols., 1877

—*Through the Long Day, or, Memorials of a Literary Life During Half a Century*, 2 vols., 1887

Mackenzie, Compton, *My Life and Times: Octave One 1883–1891*, 1963

—*My Life and Times: Octave Two 1891–1900*, 1963

McLaren, Angus, *A Prescription for Murder: The Victorian Serial Killings of Dr Thomas Neill Cream*, Chicago, 1993

Maclean, Catherine Macdonald, *Mark Rutherford: A Biography of William Hale White*, 1955

McLellan, David, *Karl Marx: His Life and Thought*, 1973 (Paladin edn, 1976)

McLeod, Hugh, *Class and Religion in the Late Victorian City*, 1974

Maclure, Stuart, *One Hundred Years of London Education 1870–1970*, 1970

Macmichael, J. Holden, *The Story of Charing Cross and Its Immediate Neighbourhood*, 1906

Macnaghten, Sir Melville L., *Days of My Years*, 1914

Macqueen-Pope, Walter, *The Melodies Linger On*, n.d. [*c.*1950]

Magee, Bryan, *Clouds of Glory: A Hoxton Childhood*, 2003

Mahomet, A. J., *From Street Arab to Pastor*, 1894

Malcolm, James Peller, *Anecdotes of the Manners and Customs of London During the Eighteenth Century. . . .*, 2 vols., 2nd edn, 1810

Mannheim, Hermann, *Social Aspects of Crime in England Between the Wars*, 1940

Marriott, John, '"West Ham: London's Industrial Centre and Gateway to the World". 1: Industrialisation, 1840–1910', *The London Journal*, Vol. 13, No. 2, 1987–8, pp. 121–42.

Marsden, W. E., *Educating the Respectable: A Study of Fleet Road Board School, Hampstead, 1879–1903*, 1991

Martin, J. E., *Greater London: An Industrial Geography*, 1966

Martin, John Biddulph, *'The Grasshopper' in Lombard Street*, 1892

Mason, Michael, *The Making of Victorian Sexuality*, Oxford, 1994

Masson, David, *Memories of London in the 'Forties*, 1908

Matthews, William, *Cockney Past and Present: A Short History of the Dialect of London*, 1938 (1972 edn)

Matz, B. W., *The Inns and Taverns of 'Pickwick' with Some Observations on their Other Associations*, 1921

Maugham, W. Somerset, *Liza of Lambeth*, 1897

—*Of Human Bondage*, 1915 (collected edn, 1937)

May, J. Lewis, *John Lane and the Nineties*, 1936

Mayhew, Athol, *A Jorum of 'Punch': With Those Who Helped to Brew It. Being the Early History of 'The London Charivari'*, 1895

Mayhew, Henry, *The* Morning Chronicle *Survey of Labour and the Poor: The Metropolitan Districts*, [1849–50], 6 vols., 1980

—*London Labour and the London Poor*, 4 vols., 1861–2

Mayhew, Henry, and Augustus [The Brothers Mayhew], *The Greatest Plague of Life: or The Adventures of a Lady in Search of a Good Servant. By One Who Has Been 'Almost Worried to Death'*, 1847

—*The Image of His Father; or, One Boy is More Trouble Than a Dozen Girls. Being a Tale of a 'Young Monkey'*, 1851

Mayhew, Henry, and Binny, John, *The Criminal Prisons of London and Scenes of Prison Life*, 1862

Meacham, Standish, *Toynbee Hall and Social Reform 1880–1914: The Search for Community*, 1987

[Mearns, Andrew] *The Bitter Cry of Outcast London: An Inquiry into the Condition of the Abject Poor*, 1883 (Victorian Library edn, 1970)

Merrick, Rev. G. P., *Work Among the Fallen: As Seen in the Prison Cell*, 1890

Meyrick, Rev. Frederick, *The Outcast and the Poor of London; or, Our Present Duties Towards the Poor: a Course of Sermons preached at The Chapel Royal, Whitehall*, 1858

Miller, Thomas, *Godfrey Malvern*, 1842–3

—*Picturesque Sketches of London: Past and Present*, 1852

Mitch, David F., *The Rise of Popular Literacy in Victorian England: The Influence of Private Choice and Public Policy*, Philadelphia, 1992

Mitchell, B. R., and Deane, Phyllis, *Abstract of British Historical Statistics*, Cambridge, 1962

Mitchell, Leslie, *Bulwer Lytton: The Rise and Fall of a Victorian Man of Letters*, 2003

Mitchie, Ronald C., *The City of London: Continuity and Change, 1850–1990*, 1992

—*The London Stock Exchange: A History*, 1999

Mogg, E., *Mogg's New Picture of London; or Strangers' Guide to the British Metropolis. . . .*, 6th edn, 1843

Moncrieff, A. R. Hope, *London*, 1910

Montague, C. J., *Sixty Years in Waifdom: or, The Ragged School Movement in English History*, 1904

Montgomery, H. H., *The History of Kennington and its Neighbourhood*, 1889

Monypenny, William Flavelle, and Buckle, George Earle, *The Life of Benjamin Disraeli, Earl of Beaconsfield*, 2 vols., complete revised edn, 1929

Morley, Henry, *Gossip*, 1857

—*Memoirs of Bartholomew Fair*, 1859

Morrison, William Douglas, *Crime and its Causes*, 1891

Moser, Inspector Maurice, and Rideal, Charles F., *Stories from Scotland Yard*, 1890

Mother Kate [Katherine Anne Egerton Warburton], *Old Soho Days and Other Memories*, 1906

Mowat, C Loch, *The Charity Organisation Society, 1869–1913: Its Ideas and Work*, 1961

Moylan, J. F., *Scotland Yard and the Metropolitan Police*, 1929

Mudie-Smith, Richard, *The Religious Life of London*, 1904

Murray, John Fisher, *The World of London*, 2 vols., Edinburgh, 1843

Myers, Robin, Harris, Michael, and Mandelbrote, Giles (eds.), *The London Book Trade: Topographies of Print in the Metropolis from the Sixteenth Century*, 2003

Nead, Lynda, *Myths of Sexuality: Representations of Women in Victorian Britain*, Oxford, 1988

—*Victorian Babylon: People, Streets and Images in Nineteenth-Century London*, 2000

Neil, Arthur Fowler, *Forty Years of Man-Hunting*, 1932

Nevill, Dorothy, *The Reminiscences of Lady Dorothy Nevill*, edited by Ralph Nevill, 1906

Nevill, Ralph, *London Clubs: Their History and Treasures*, 1911

—*The Life and Letters of Lady Dorothy Nevill*, 1919

Nevinson, Henry W., *Neighbours of Ours*, 1895

—*Changes and Chances*, 1923

Nevinson, Margaret Wynne, *Life's Fitful Fever: A Volume of Memories*, 1926

Newton, Douglas, *Catholic London*, 1950

Nicholls, Sir George, *A History of the English Poor Law*, 2 vols., 1854

Nicholson, Renton, *Dombey and Daughter: A Moral Fiction*, 1847

—*Rogue's Progress: The Autobiography of 'Lord Chief Baron' Nicholson*, 1860

Noel, Baptist Wriothesley, *The State of the Metropolis Considered, in a Letter to the Rt. Honourable and Rt. Reverend the Lord Bishop of London*, 1835

Okey, Thomas, *A Basketful of Memories: An Autobiographical Sketch*, 1930

Oliphant, Mrs M. O. W., *The Autobiography and Letters of Mrs M. O. W. Oliphant*, 1899

Oliver, Hermia, *The International Anarchist Movement in Late Victorian London*, 1983

Olsen, Donald J., *Town Planning in London: The Eighteenth and Nineteenth Centuries*, New Haven, 1964

—*The Growth of Victorian London*, 1976

Owen, David, *English Philanthropy, 1660–1960*, 1965

—*The Government of Victorian London 1855–1889: The Metropolitan Board of Works, the Vestries, and the City Corporation*, Cambridge, Mass., 1982

Oxford Dictionary of National Biography

Pall Mall Gazette 'Extra' No. 20. The Eliza Armstrong Case: being a Verbatim Report of the Proceedings at Bow Street. With Mr Stead's Suppressed Defence, 1885

Panayi, Panikos, *German Immigrants in Britain During the Nineteenth Century, 1815–1914*, Oxford, 1995

Parkinson, Joseph Charles, *The Poor: Articles from* Daily News *Etc. 1864-5-6*, 1864–6 [Parkinson's cuttings book, in author's possession]

—*Literary Scraps: Cuttings from Newspapers, Extracts, Miscellanea, Etc.*, 1865–70 [Parkinson's cuttings book, in author's possession]

Parliamentary Papers, Reports of Commissioners, etc.:

Copies of Certain Papers Relating to Cholera; together with the Report of the Central Board of Health thereupon, 1832

Extracts from the information received by Her Majesty's Commissioners as to the Administration and Operation of the Poor-Laws, 1833

Report of the Poor Law Commissioners, upon the Relief of the Poor in the Parishes of St. Marylebone and St. Pancras. With Appendix, 1847

Metropolitan Sanitary Commission: First, Second and Third Reports of the Commissioners Appointed to Inquire Whether Any and What Special Means May be Requisite for the Improvement of the Health of the Metropolis, 1848

Report of the Commissioners Appointed to Make Inquiries Relating to Smithfield Market, and the Markets in the City of London for the Sale of Meat, 1850

Report of Her Majesty's Commissioners appointed to inquire into the Alleged Disturbance of the Public Peace in Hyde Park on Sunday, July 1st, 1855; and the Conduct of the Metropolitan Police in Connexion with the Same. Together with the Minutes of Evidence, Appendix, and Index, 1856

Patmore, P. G., *My Friends and Acquaintances: Being Memorials, Mind-Portraits, and Personal Recollections of Deceased Celebrities of the Nineteenth Century*, 3 vols., 1854

Patterson, M. W., *Sir Francis Burdett and His Times (1770–1844)*, 2 vols., 1931

Pearl, Cyril, *The Girl with the Swansdown Seat*, 1955

Pearsall, Ronald, *The Worm in the Bud: The World of Victorian Sexuality*, 1969

Pearson, Michael, *The Age of Consent: Victorian Prostitution and Its Enemies*, Newton Abbot, 1972

Pelham, Camden, *The Chronicles of Crime; or, The New Newgate Calendar*, 2 vols., 1887

Pennell, Joseph, *The Adventures of an Illustrator: Mostly in Following His Authors in America and Europe*, Boston, Mass., 1925

Pennybacker, Susan D., *A Vision for London 1889–1914: Labour, Everyday Life and the LCC Experiment*, 1995

Percy, Sholto and Reuben, *London: or Interesting Memorials of its Rise, Progress and Present State*, 3 vols., 1823

Petrow, Stefan, *Policing Morals: The Metropolitan Police and the Home Office 1870–1914*, Oxford, 1994

Pevsner, Nikolaus, *London I. The Cities of London and Westminster*, 1957

Phillips, Sir Richard, A Morning's Walk from London to Kew, new edn, 1820

Phillips, Watts, The Wild Tribes of London, 1856

Philpott, Hugh B., London at School: The Story of the School Board, 1870–1904, 1904

Pierce, William, Old New-Court: The Story of an Old London Nonconformist Church, 1892

Piggott, J. R., Palace of the People: The Crystal Palace at Sydenham 1854–1936, 2004

Pike, Geoffrey Holden, Byeways of Two Cities, 1873

Pimlott, J. A. R., Toynbee Hall: Fifty Years of Social Progress 1884–1934, 1935

Pinks, William J. (with additions by Edward J. Wood), The History of Clerkenwell, 2nd edn, 1880

Planché, J. R., Recollections and Reflections, 2 vols., 1872

Platt, Elspeth, The Story of the Ranyard Mission 1857–1937, 1937

Pollock, Sir Frederick (ed.), Macready's Reminiscences, and Selections from His Diaries and Letters, 2 vols., 1875

—Personal Remembrances of Sir Frederick Pollock, 2 vols., 1887

Pope-Hennessy, James, Monckton Milnes: The Years of Promise 1809–1851, 1949

—Monckton Milnes: The Flight of Youth 1851–1885, 1951

Port, M. H., Imperial London: Civil Government Building in London 1850–1915, 1995

Postgate, Raymond, The Builders' History, 1923

Powell, Sir Allan, The Metropolitan Asylums Board and Its Work, 1867–1930, 1930

Pringle, Patrick, Hue and Cry: The Birth of the British Police, 1955

Printer, An Old, A Few Personal Recollections, 1896

Prothero, I. J., Artisans and Politics in Early Nineteenth-century London: John Gast and His Times, 1979 (pb edn, 1981)

Quekett, William J., 'My Sayings and Doings', with Reminiscences of My Life, 1888

Quinlan, Maurice J., Victorian Prelude: A History of English Manners 1700–1830, New York, 1941

Radzinowicz, Leon, A History of English Criminal Law and Its Administration from 1750, Vol. 2, The Clash Between Private Initiative and Public Interest in the Enforcement of the Law, 1956

—A History of English Criminal Law and Its Administration from 1750, Vol. 3, Cross-currents in the Movement for the Reform of the Police, 1956

—A History of English Criminal Law and Its Administration from 1750, Vol. 4, Grappling for Control, 1968

Radzinowicz, Sir Leon, and Hood, Roger, *A History of English Criminal Law and Its Administration from 1750*, Vol. 5, *The Emergence of Penal Policy*, 1986

Ranyard, Lydia N. [Ellen Henrietta Ranyard], *The Missing Link; or, Bible-Women in the Homes of the London Poor*, 1860 (1st US edn, New Brunswick, 1861)

Rappaport, Erika Diane, *Shopping for Pleasure: Women in the Making of London's West End*, Princeton, 2000

Raumer, Frederick von, *England in 1835: being a Series of Letters Written to Friends in Germany during a Residence in London and Excursions into the Provinces*, 3 vols., 1836

Ray, Gordon N., *Thackeray: The Uses of Adversity, 1811–1846*, 1955

—*Thackeray: The Age of Wisdom, 1847–1863*, 1958

Redding, Cyrus, *Fifty Years' Recollections, Literary and Personal, with Observations on Men and Things*, 3 vols., 1858

Redford, Arthur, *Labour Migration in England, 1800–50*, 1926

Registrar General, *Annual Summary of Births, Deaths, and Causes of Death in London and Other Large Towns*, various years

—*Census Enumerators' Records*, various years

—*Report on the Cholera Epidemic of 1866 in England*, 1868

Reid, J. C., *Bucks and Bruisers: Pierce Egan and Regency England*, 1971

Reynolds, Elaine A., *Before the Bobbies: The Night Watch and Police Reform in Metropolitan London, 1720–1830*, 1998

Ribton-Turner, C. J., *A History of Vagrants and Vagrancy and Beggars and Begging*, 1887

Richards, Grant, *Memories of a Misspent Youth 1872–1896*, 1932

Richardson, Rev. J., *Recollections, Political, Literary, Dramatic, and Miscellaneous, of the Last Half-century . . .*, 2 vols., 1856

Richardson, J. Hall, *From the City to Fleet Street: Some Journalistic Experiences*, 1927

Richardson, Ruth, *Death, Dissection and the Destitute*, 1987

Riddell, Mrs J. H., *A Struggle for Fame*, 3 vols., 1883

Ritchie, James Ewing, *The Night Side of London*, 2nd edn, revised 1858

—*Here and There in London*, 1859

—*The Night Side of London*, new edn, revised and enlarged, 1869

—*The Religious Life of London*, 1870

—*Days and Nights in London – or, Studies in Black and Gray*, 1880

Robertson Scott, J. W., *The Story of the Pall Mall Gazette, of its First Editor Frederick Greenwood and of Its Founder George Murray Smith*, 1950

Robins, William, *Paddington: Past and Present*, 1853

[Robinson, Henry Crabb] *Diary, Reminiscences, and Correspondence of*

Henry Crabb Robinson, Barrister-at-Law, F.S.A., edited by Thomas Sadler, 3 vols., 1869

Robinson, Sir John R., *Fifty Years of Fleet Street*, 1904

Rocker, Rudolf, *The London Years*, 1956

Roebuck, Janet, *Urban Development in 19th-century London: Lambeth, Battersea and Wandsworth 1838–1888*, 1979

Rogers, Frederick, *Labour, Life and Literature*, 1913

Rook, Clarence, *The Hooligan Nights: Being the Life and Opinions of a Young and Impertinent Criminal Recounted by Himself and Set Forth by Clarence Rook*, 1899 (1979 edn)

Rose, Lionel, *The Massacre of the Innocents: Infanticide in Britain, 1800–1939*, 1986

Ross, Ellen, *Love and Toil: Motherhood in Outcast London, 1870–1918*, Oxford, 1993

Rowe, D. J. (ed.), *London Radicalism 1830–1843: A Selection from the Papers of Francis Place*, 1970

Rowe, Richard, *Life in the London Streets, or Struggles for Daily Bread*, 1881

Royal Commissions:

Report of the Commissioners Appointed to Inquire into the Existing State of the Corporation of the City of London, and to Collect Information Respecting its Constitution, Order, and Government etc. together with the Minutes of Evidence and Appendix, 1854

Second Report of the Royal Sanitary Commission, 1871

Royal Commission on Metropolitan Sewage Discharge. First Report, 1884

Report of Her Majesty's Commissioners for Inquiring into the Housing of the Working Classes. Vol. II Minutes of Evidence and Appendix as to England and Wales, 1885

Interim Report of the Royal Commissioners appointed to inquire into certain matters connected with the working of The Metropolitan Board of Works, 1888

Report of the Royal Commission Appointed to Inquire into the Water Supply of the Metropolis, 5 vols., 1893

Report of the Royal Commission on the Port of London, 3 vols., 1902

Report of the Royal Commission on London Traffic, 8 vols., 1905–6

Report of the Royal Commission on London Squares, 1928

Rubinstein, David, *School Attendance in London 1870–1914: A Social History*, Hull, 1969

Rudé, George, *Hanoverian London 1714–1808*, 1971

Russell, C., and Lewis, H. S., *The Jew in London (a Study of Racial Character and Present-day Conditions)*, 1900

Russell, G. W. E., *Seeing and Hearing*, 1907

Sadleir, Michael, *Blessington-d'Orsay: A Masquerade*, 1933

—*Fanny by Gaslight*, 1940

—*Forlorn Sunset*, 1947

Sala, George Augustus, *Twice Round the London Clock*, 1878 edn

—*The Life and Adventures of George Augustus Sala*, 2 vols., 1895

Samuel, Raphael, *East End Underworld: Chapters in the Life of Arthur Harding*, 1981

Sanger, 'Lord' George, *Seventy Years a Showman*, 1910 (1935 edn)

Saunders, Ann, *Regent's Park: A Study of the Development of the Area from 1086 to the Present Day*, Newton Abbot, 1969

Saunders, William, *History of the First London County Council, 1889–1890–1891*, 1892

Schlesinger, Max, *Saunterings in and About London*, 1853

Schmiechen, James A., *Sweated Industries and Sweated Labor: The London Clothing Trades 1860–1914*, 1984

Schneer, Jonathan, *London 1900: The Imperial Metropolis*, New Haven, 1999

Schwartz, L. D., *London in the Age of Industrialisation: Entrepreneurs, Labour Force and Living Conditions, 1700–1850*, Cambridge, 1992

Scott, Benjamin, *A Statistical Vindication of the City of London; or, Fallacies Exploded and Figures Explained*, 1867

Scott, Clement, and Howard, Cecil, *The Life and Reminiscences of E. L. Blanchard, with notes from the Diary of William Blanchard*, 2 vols., 1891

Sekon, G. A., *Locomotion in Victorian London*, Oxford, 1938

Select Committees:

Reports from the Committees on the State of Mendicity in the Metropolis, 1815–16

Reports from Select Committee on the Education of the Lower Orders in the Metropolis: with Minutes of Evidence taken before the Committee [4 reports, continuously paginated], 1816

Report of the Committee Appointed to Inquire into the State of the Police of the Metropolis, 1816

First Report from the Committee on the State of the Police of the Metropolis: with Minutes of Evidence taken before the Committee; and an Appendix, 1817

Second Report from the Committee on the State of the Police of the Metropolis, 1817

Third Report from the Committee on the State of the Police of the Metropolis: with Minutes of the Evidence taken before the Committee; and an Appendix, 1818

Report from the Select Committee on Contagious Fever in London, 1818

Report from the Select Committee on the Supply of Water to the Metropolis, 1821

Report from the Select Committee on the Police of the Metropolis, 1822

Report from the Select Committee on the Laws Relating to Irish and Scotch Vagrants, 1828

Report from the Select Committee on the Police of the Metropolis, 1828

Second Report from the Select Committee on the State of Smithfield Market, 1828

Report from the Committee on the Bill to prevent the Spreading of Canine Madness, 1830

Report from the Select Committee on the Observance of the Sabbath Day: with the Minutes of Evidence, and Appendix, 1832

Report from the Select Committee on the Petition of Frederick Young and Others (Police), 1833

Report from the Select Committee on Inquiry into Drunkenness, with Minutes of Evidence, and Appendix, 1834

Report from the Select Committee on the Police of the Metropolis; with the Minutes of Evidence, Appendix and Index, 1834

Second Report from Select Committee on Metropolis Improvements; with the Minutes of Evidence, Appendix and Plans, 1838

First Report from Select Committee on Metropolis Improvements; with the Minutes of Evidence, Appendix and Plans, 1840

Report from Select Committee on the Health of Towns, 1840

Report from the Select Committee on Dog Stealing (Metropolis); together with the Minutes of Evidence taken before them, 1844

Report from the Select Committee on Smithfield Market; together with the Minutes of Evidence, Appendix, and Index, 1847

Report from the Select Committee on Smithfield Market; together with the Proceedings of the Committee, Minutes of Evidence, Appendix, and Index, 1849

Select Committee on Criminal and Destitute Juveniles: Report, together with the Proceedings of the Committee, Minutes of Evidence, Appendix and Index, 1852

Report from the Select Committee on the River Thames; together with the Proceedings of the Committee, Minutes of Evidence, Appendix and Index, 1858

First, Second and Third Reports from the Select Committee on Metropolis Local Taxation [together with the Minutes of Evidence, Appendices, Proceedings of the Committee and Index], 1861

Report from the Select Committee Appointed to Join with a Committee of the House of Lords on Railway Schemes (Metropolis); together with the Proceedings of the Committee, Minutes of Evidence, and an Appendix, 1864

Minutes of Evidence Taken Before the Select Committee on the Courts of Justice Concentration (Site) Bill; with the Proceedings of the Committee, 1865

Report from the Select Committee on Theatrical Licenses and Regulations; together with the Proceedings of the Committee, Minutes of Evidence and Appendix, 1866

First, Second and Third Reports from the Select Committee on Metropolitan Local Government, &c; [together with the Minutes of Evidence, Appendices, Proceedings of the Committee and Index], 1866–7

Report from the Select Committee on Metropolis Management and Building Acts Amendment Bill; together with the Proceedings of the Committee, Minutes of Evidence, and Index, 1878

First Report from the Select Committee of the House of Lords on the Law Relating to the Protection of Young Girls; together with the Proceedings of the Committee, Minutes of Evidence, and Appendix, 1881

Second Report from the Select Committee of the House of Lords on the Law Relating to the Protection of Young Girls; together with the Proceedings of the Committee, Minutes of Evidence, and Appendix, 1882

Service, Alistair, *The Architects of London: And Their Buildings from 1066 to the Present Day,* 1979

Sexby, J. J., *The Municipal Parks, Gardens, and Open Spaces of London: Their History and Association,* 1905

Shaen, Margaret J. (ed.), *Memorials of Two Sisters: Susanna and Catherine Winkworth,* 1908

Shannon, H. A., 'Migration and the Growth of London, 1841–91', *Economic History Review,* Vol. V, No. 2, 1935, pp. 79–86

Sharpe, Reginald R., *London and the Kingdom,* 3 vols., 1894–5

Shaw, Captn Donald [One of the Old Brigade], *London in the Sixties (with a Few Digressions),* 3rd edn, 1909

Shaw, Sam, *Guttersnipe,* 1946

Shepherd, Thomas H., and Elmes, James, *Metropolitan Improvements; or London in the Nineteenth Century,* 1827

Sheppard, Francis, *London 1808–1870: The Infernal Wen,* 1971

Sheridan, Michael, *Rowton Houses 1892–1954,* 1956

Sherson, Erroll, *London's Lost Theatres of the Nineteenth Century: With Notes on Plays and Players Seen There,* 1925

Sherwell, Arthur, *Life in West London: A Study and a Contrast,* 1897

Shipley, Stan, *Club Life and Socialism in Mid-Victorian London,* 2nd edn, 1983

Shore, W. Teignmouth (ed.), *Trial of Thomas Neill Cream,* 1923

—*Trials of Charles Frederick Peace,* 1926

Short, K. R. M., *The Dynamite War: Irish-American Bombers in Victorian Britain*, Dublin, 1979

Simmonds, Henry S., *All About Battersea*, 1882

Simon, John, *Public Health Reports*, 2 vols., 1887

—*English Sanitary Institutions, reviewed in their course of development, and in some of their political and social relations*, 1890

Simond, Louis [A French Traveller], *Journal of a Tour and Residence in Great Britain, During the Years 1810 and 1811 . . .*, 2 vols., 2nd edn, Edinburgh, 1817

Simonis, H., *The Street of Ink: An Intimate History of Journalism*, 1917

Sims, George R., *How the Poor Live and Horrible London*, 1889

—*The Black Stain*, 1907

—*Glances Back*, 1917

—*My Life – Sixty Years' Recollections of Bohemian London*, 1917

Sims, George R. (ed.), *Living London*, 3 vols., 1902–3

Slater, Michael, *Douglas Jerrold (1803–1857)*, 2002

Smalley, George, *The Life of Sir Sydney H. Waterlow Bart. London Apprentice, Lord Mayor, Captain of Industry, and Philanthropist*, 1909

Smalley, George W., *London Letters and Some Others*, 2 vols., 1890

Smeeton, George, *Doings in London; or Day and Night Scenes of the Frauds, Frolics, Manners, and Depravities of the Metropolis*, 1828 (10th edn, *c.* 1840)

Smith, Albert, *The Adventures of Mr. Ledbury and His Friend Jack Johnson*, 1844

—*The Natural History of the Gent*, 1847

Smith, Albert (ed.), *Gavarni in London: Sketches of Life and Character, with Illustrative Essays by Popular Writers*, 1849

Smith, Charles Manby, *The Working Man's Way in the World*, 1853

Smith, Denis Mack, *Mazzini*, 1994

Smith, Sir Henry, *From Constable to Commissioner: The Story of Sixty Years, Most of Them Misspent*, 1910

Smith, Hubert Llewellyn, and Nash, Vaughan, *The Story of the Dockers' Strike, told by two East Londoners*, 1889

Smith, John Thomas, *Vagabondiana or, Anecdotes of Mendicant Wanderers through the Streets of London; with portraits of the most remarkable, drawn from the life*, 1817

—*The Cries of London: Exhibiting Several of the Itinerant Traders of Antient and Modern Times*, 1839

—*An Antiquarian Ramble in the Streets of London, with Anecdotes of their More Celebrated Residents*, 2 vols., 1846

Smith, M. H. Stephen, *Art and Anecdote: Recollections of William Frederick Yeames, R.A., His Life and His Friends*, 1927

Smith, Phillip Thurmond, *Policing Victorian London: Political Policing, Public Order, and the London Metropolitan Police*, Westport, Conn., 1985

Snell, Lord [Harry], *Men, Movements, and Myself*, 1936 (1938 edn)

[Snow, John] *Snow on Cholera, being a reprint of two papers by John Snow, M.D. together with a Biographical Memoir by B.W. Richardson, M.D. and an Introduction by Wade Hampton Frost, M.D.*, Cambridge, Mass., 1936

Somerville, Alexander, *The Autobiography of a Working Man*, 1848 (1951 edn)

Southey, Robert, *Letters from England: by Don Manual Alvarez Espriella. Translated from the Spanish*, 1807 (Cresset Press edn, 1951)

Spalding, Thomas Alfred, *The Work of the London School Board*, 1900

Spielmann, M. H., *The History of 'Punch'*, 1895

Sponza, Lucio, *Italian Immigrants in Nineteenth-century Britain: Realities and Images*, Leicester, 1988

Stallard, Rev. J. H., *London Pauperism Amongst Jews and Christians: An Inquiry into the Principles and Practice of Out-Door Relief in the Metropolis and the Result Upon the Moral and Physical Condition of the Pauper Class*, 1867

Stedman Jones, Gareth, *Outcast London: A Study in the Relationship between Classes in Victorian Society*, Oxford, 1971

Straus, Ralph, *Sala: The Portrait of an Eminent Victorian*, 1942

Strauss, G. L. M., *Reminiscences of an Old Bohemian*, 2 vols., 1882

Sugden, Philip, *The Complete History of Jack the Ripper*, 1994 (pb edn, 1995)

Summerson, John, *John Nash: Architect to King George IV*, 1935

—*Georgian London*, 1945

—*The London Building World of the Eighteen-sixties*, 1973

'The Victorian Rebuilding of the City of London', *The London Journal*, Vol.3, No. 2, 1977, pp. 163–85

Survey of London

Vol. XIII: *The Parish of St. Margaret, Westminster (Part II) (Neighbourhood of Whitehall, Vol. I)*, 1930

Vol. XIV: *The Parish of St. Margaret, Westminster (Part III) (Neighbourhood of Whitehall, Vol. II)*, 1931

Vol. XXIII: *South Bank and Vauxhall. The Parish of St. Mary Lambeth Pt. I*, 1951

Vol. XXV: *The Parishes of St. George the Martyr, Southwark and St. Mary, Newington*, 1955

Vol. XXVII: *The Parish of Christ Church and All Saints (Spitalfields and Mile End New Town)*, 1957

Vol. XXXI–II: *The Parish of St. James Westminster Pt. II North of Piccadilly*, 1963

Vol. XXXIII–IV: *The Parish of St. Anne Soho*, 1966

Vol. XXXVI: *The Parish of St. Paul Covent Garden*, 1970

Vol. XXXVII: *Northern Kensington*, 1973

Vol. XXXVIII: *The Museums Area of South Kensington and Westminster*, 1975

Vol. XLI: *Southern Kensington: Brompton*, 1983

Sutherland, John, *The Longman Companion to Victorian Fiction*, 1988

Sweeney, John, *At Scotland Yard*, 1904

Swift, Roger, and Gilley, Sheridan (eds.), *The Irish in the Victorian City*, 1985

Taine, Hippolyte, *Notes on England*, New York, 1872

Tanswell, John, *The History and Antiquities of Lambeth*, 1858

Taylor, Tom, *Leicester Square: Its Associations and Its Worthies*, 1874

Thackeray, William Makepeace, *Vanity Fair*, 1847–8

—*The History of Pendennis*, 2 vols., 1849–50

—*The Newcomes: A History of a Most Respectable Family*, 2 vols., 1854–5

—*The Adventures of Philip*, 1862

—*The Letters and Private Papers of William Makepeace Thackeray*, edited by Gordon N. Ray, 4 vols., 1945–6

Thomas, Donald, *The Victorian Underworld*, 1998

Thompson, Alex, *Here I Lie: The Memorial of an Old Journalist*, 1937

Thompson, E. P., *William Morris: Romantic to Revolutionary*, 1955 (Merlin Press edn, 1977)

—*The Making of the English Working Class*, 1963

Thompson, Paul, *Socialists, Liberals and Labour: The Struggle for London, 1885–1914*, 1967

Thornbury, Walter, and Walford, Edward, *Old and New London: A Narrative of Its History, Its People, and Its Places*, 6 vols., 1873–8

Thorold, Peter, *The London Rich: The Creation of a Great City, from 1666 to the Present*, 1999

Thurston, Gavin, *The Clerkenwell Riot: The Killing of Constable Culley*, 1967

Timbs, John, *Clubs and Club Life in London: With Anecdotes of its Famous Coffee-Houses, Hostelries, and Taverns, from the Seventeenth Century to the Present Time*, 1872

Tindall, Gillian, *The Fields Beneath: The History of One London Village*, 1977 (1980 pb edn)

Tinsley, William, *Random Recollections of an Old Publisher*, 2 vols., 1900

Tobias, J. J., *Crime and Industrial Society in the 19th Century*, 1967

—*Prince of Fences: The Life and Crimes of Ikey Solomons*, 1974

Toplis, Gordon, 'The History of Tyburnia', *Country Life*, 15, 22 and 29 November 1973

Treves, Sir Frederick, *The Elephant Man and Other Reminiscences*, 1923

Trewin, J. C., and King, E. M., *Printer to the House: The Story of Hansard*, 1952

Tristan, Flora, *Flora Tristan's London Journal: A Survey of London Life in the 1830s*, 1980 (first published in French, 1840)

Trollope, Anthony, *The Three Clerks*, 1858

—*Can You Forgive Her?*, 1864–5

—*Phineas Finn: The Irish Member*, 1867–9

—*An Autobiography*, 1883

—*London Tradesmen*, 1927

Trollope, Thomas Adolphus, *What I Remember*, 3 vols., 1887–9

Trumble, Alfred, *In Jail with Charles Dickens*, 1896

Tuer, Andrew W., *Old London Street Cries and the Cries of To-Day*, 1885

Tupper, Martin Farquhar, *My Life as an Author*, 1886

Tyack, Geoffrey, *Sir James Pennethorne and the Making of Victorian London*, Cambridge, 1992

Vanderkiste, R. W., *Notes and Narratives of a Six Years' Mission, Principally Among the Dens of London*, new edn, 1854

Vaux, James Hardy, *Memoirs of James Hardy Vaux: Written by Himself*, 2 vols., 1819

Vere, Langton George, *Random Recollections of Homerton Mission*, Barnet, 1912

Vizetelly, Henry, *Glances Back Through Seventy Years: Autobiographical and Other Reminiscences*, 2 vols., 1893

Wagner, Gillian, *Barnardo*, 1979

Walcott, Rev. Mackenzie E. C., *Westminster: Memorials of the City, Saint Peter's College, the Parish Churches, Palaces, Streets, and Worthies*, 1849

Walker, Henry, *East London: Sketches of Christian Work and Workers*, 1896

Walkowitz, Judith R., *City of Dreadful Delight: Narratives of Sexual Danger in Late-Victorian London*, 1992

Wallas, Graham, *The Life of Francis Place 1771–1854*, revised edn, 1918

Walter, *My Secret Life*, 11 vols., 1888–94 (Grove Press edn, 2 vols., New York, 1966)

Ward, [Mary] Mrs Humphry, *Robert Elsmere*, 1888

—*A Writer's Recollections*, 1918 (3rd edn, 1919)

Ward, Robert Plumer, *Tremaine, or The Man of Refinement*, 3 vols., 1825

Warner, Sir Frank, *The Silk Industry of the United Kingdom*, 1921

Watson, Aaron, *The Savage Club: A Medley of History, Anecdote and Reminiscence*, 1907

Watson, Eric R. (ed.), *Trial of Thurtell and Hunt*, 1920

—*Adolf Beck (1877–1904)*, 1924

Watson, Robert Patrick, *Louise Reignier: The Communion of Crime and Criminals. A True Story*, 1895

—*Memoirs of Robert Patrick Watson: A Journalist's Experience of Mixed Society*, 1899

Watson, W. F., *Machines and Men: An Autobiography of an Itinerant Mechanic*, 1935

Weale, John, *A New Survey of London*, 2 vols., 1853

Webb, Beatrice, *My Apprenticeship*, 1926

—*The Diary of Beatrice Webb: Vol. I, 1873–1892. Glitter Around and Darkness Within*, edited by Norman and Jean MacKenzie, 1982

—*The Diary of Beatrice Webb: Vol. II, 1892–1905. 'All the Good Things of Life'*, edited by Norman and Jean MacKenzie, 1983

Webb, Sidney and Beatrice, *English Local Government from the Revolution to the Municipal Corporations Act: The Parish and the County*, 1906

—*English Local Government from the Revolution to the Municipal Corporations Act: The Manor and the Borough*, 2 vols., 1908

—*English Local Government: The King's Highway*, 1913 (1920 edn)

—*English Local Government: Statutory Authorities for Special Purposes*, 1922

—*English Poor Law History: Pt. I, The Old Poor Law*, 1927

—*English Poor Law History: Pt. II, The Last Hundred Years*, 2 vols., 1929

Wedd, Kit, with Lucy Peltz and Cathy Ross, *Artists' London: Holbein to Hirst*, 2001

Weiner, Deborah E. B., *Architecture and Social Reform in Late-Victorian London*, Manchester, 1994

Welch, Charles, *Modern History of the City of London: A Record of Municipal and Social Progress from 1760 to the Present Day*, 1896

Wensley, Frederick Porter, *Detective Days: The Record of 42 Years' Service in the Criminal Investigation Department*, 1931

Westgarth, William (ed.), *Essays on the Street Re-Alignment, Reconstruction, and Sanitation of Central London, and on the Re-Housing of the Poorer Classes*, 1886

Weylland, John Matthias, *Round the Tower: or, The Story of the London City Mission*, 2nd edn, 1875

—*These Fifty Years: Being the Jubilee Volume of the London City Mission*, 1884 (3rd edn, 1895)

Wheatley, Henry B., and Cunningham, Peter, *London Past and Present: Its History, Associations, and Traditions*, 3 vols., 1891

While, Jack, *Fifty Years of Fire Fighting in London*, 1931

White, Jerry, *Rothschild Buildings: Life in an East End Tenement Block, 1887–1920*, 1980

—*The Worst Street in North London: Campbell Bunk, Islington, Between the Wars*, 1986

—*London in the Twentieth Century: A City and Its People*, 2001

Whiteing, Richard, *My Harvest*, 1915

Whitmore, Rev. C. J., *Seeking the Lost: Incidents and Sketches of Christian Work in London*, 1876

Whyte, Adam Gowans, *Forty Years of Electrical Progress: The Story of the G.E.C.*, 1930

Whyte, Frederic, *The Life of W. T. Stead*, 2 vols., 1925

Wight, John, *Mornings at Bow Street: A selection of the most humorous and entertaining Reports which have appeared in the Morning Herald*, 1824

Wilde, Oscar, *The Picture of Dorian Gray*, 1891 (Penguin Classics edn, 1985)

Wilkinson, George Theodore, *An Authentic History of the Cato-Street Conspiracy; with the Trials at Large of the Conspirators, for High Treason and Murder . . .*, 2nd edn, 1820

Williams, J. E. Hodder, *The Life of Sir George Williams*, 1906

Williams, Michael, *Some London Theatres: Past and Present*, 1883

Williams, Montagu, *Leaves of a Life*, 1890 (2nd edn, 1899)

—*Later Leaves*, 1891

—*Round London*, 1892

Williams, Valentine, *The World of Action*, 1938

Wilson, Charles, *First with the News: The History of W.H. Smith 1792–1972*, 1985

Wilson, Charles, and Reader, William, *Men and Machines: A History of D. Napier & Son, Engineers, Ltd. 1808–1958*, 1958

Wilson, Frances, *The Courtesan's Revenge: Harriette Wilson, the Woman who Blackmailed the King*, 2003

Wilson, Harriette, *The Memoirs of Harriette Wilson, Written by Herself*, 2 vols., 1825

Wilson, Jessie Aitken, *Memoir of George Wilson*, Edinburgh, 1860

Wise, Sarah, *The Italian Boy: Murder and Grave-Robbery in 1830s London*, 2004

Wohl, Anthony S., *The Eternal Slum: Housing and Social Policy in Victorian London*, 1977

—*Endangered Lives: Public Health in Victorian Britain*, 1983

Wolff, Sir Henry Drummond, *Rambling Recollections*, 2 vols., 1908

Wood, Henry J., *My Life of Music*, 1938

Wood, Rev. Theodore, *The Rev. J. G. Wood: His Life and Work*, 1890

Worth, George J., *James Hannay: His Life and Works*, Lawrence, Kansas, 1964

Wright, Ned, *Ned Wright: The Story of His Life*, 1873

[Wright, Thomas] A Journeyman Engineer, *Some Habits and Customs of the Working Classes*, 1867

—*The Great Unwashed*, 1868

Wroth, Warwick, *The London Pleasure Gardens of the Eighteenth Century*, 1896

—*Cremorne and the Later London Gardens*, 1907

Wyndham, Henry Saxe, *The Annals of Covent Garden Theatre from 1732 to 1897*, 2 vols., 1906

Wyndham, Horace, *The Nineteen Hundreds*, New York, 1923

—*Victorian Sensations*, 1933

Wynter, Andrew, *Subtle Brains and Lissom Fingers: Being Some of the Chisel-Marks of Our Scientific and Industrial Progress*, 1863 (3rd edn, 1869)

Yates, Edmund, *His Recollections and Experiences*, 2 vols., 1884

Yelling, J. A., *Slums and Slum Clearance in Victorian London*, 1986

Young, G. M. (ed.), *Early Victorian England 1830–1865*, 2 vols., 1934

INDEX